INTERNATIONAL ENVIRONMENTAL GOVERNANCE

Volume 15

Yearbook of International Cooperation on Environment and Development 1999–2000

T0347368

Full list of titles in the set
INTERNATIONAL ENVIRONMENTAL GOVERNANCE

Yearbook of International Cooperation on Environment and Development 1999–2000

Edited by Helge Ole Bergesen, Georg Parmann and Øystein B. Thommessen

from Routledge

First published in 1999

This edition first published in 2009 by Earthscan

Copyright © The Fridtjof Nansen Institute, 1999

ISBN 978-1-84407-995-7 (hbk Volume 15)
ISBN 978-0-415-85220-3 (pbk Volume 15)
ISBN 978-1-84407-984-1 (International Environmental Governance set)
ISBN 978-1-84407-930-8 (Earthscan Library Collection)

For a full list of publications please contact:

First issued in paperback 2013

Earthscan
2 Park Square, Milton Park, Abingdon, Oxon OX14 4RN
Simultaneously published in the USA and Canada by Earthscan
52 Vanderbilt Avenue, New York, NY 10017
Earthscan is an imprint of the Taylor & Francis Group, an informa business

Earthscan publishes in association with the International Institute for Environment and Development

A catalogue record for this book is available from the British Library

Library of Congress Cataloging-in-Publication Data has been applied for

Publisher's note
The publisher has made every effort to ensure the quality of this reprint, but points out that some imperfections in the original copies may be apparent.

At Earthscan we strive to minimize our environmental impacts and carbon footprint through reducing waste, recycling and offsetting our CO_2 emissions, including those created through publication of this book.

**YEARBOOK
OF INTERNATIONAL CO-OPERATION ON
ENVIRONMENT AND DEVELOPMENT
1999/2000**

YEARBOOK
of International Co-operation on Environment and Development
1999/2000

an independent publication from
the Fridtjof Nansen Institute, Norway

Editors
Helge Ole Bergesen, Georg Parmann, and Øystein B. Thommessen

Assistant Editor
Stian Reklev

Earthscan Publications Ltd, London

First published in the UK in 1999 by
Earthscan Publications Ltd

Copyright © The Fridtjof Nansen Institute, 1999

8th edition. Yearbooks before 1998 published as *Green Globe Yearbook*

A catalogue record for this book is available from the British Library

ISBN: 1 85383 630 3
ISSN: 1500-6980
Page design and typesetting by The Fridtjof Nansen Institute
Maps by Torstein Olsen, GRID-Arendal

Cover design, layout, and paste-up by Morten Mathiesen, Scandinavian University Press
Cover illustration: NPS/Images

Yearbook website: http://www.ext.grida.no/ggynet

For a full list of publications, please contact:
Earthscan Publications Ltd
120 Pentonville Road
London N1 9JN
Tel: 0171 278 0433
Fax: 0171 278 1142
email: earthinfo@earthscan.co.uk
http://www.earthscan.co.uk

Earthscan is an editorially independent subsidiary of Kogan Page Ltd
and publishes in association with WWF-UK and the
International Institute for Environment and Development

Acknowledgements

In preparing this eighth edition of the *Yearbook* we have benefited and relied on quite a number of actors. Each has played a part in enabling us to present this edition and several deserve special mention.

We want to express our appreciation of the smooth and effective co-operation we have established with Earthscan Publications, especially our publisher, Jonathan Sinclair Wilson, and managing editor, Frances MacDermott. Caroline Richmond has been essential to ensuring the quality of this volume by suggesting improvements during her dedicated editorial assistance. We also use this opportunity to thank the marketing staff for their continuing support.

Since we began publishing the *Yearbook* in 1992, we have relied on both practical and professional support of staff at the Fridtjof Nansen Institute. We are especially grateful to its Director, Kåre Willoch, for his enthusiasm and moral support, to Regine Andersen, Steinar Andresen, Douglas Brubaker, Kristin Rosendal, and Jørgen Wettestad for their editorial advice in the review process, to Davor Vidas for editorial and legal advice related to several entries in the Agreements section, to Ann Skarstad for her editorial assistance, and to Ivar Liseter, Morten Sandnes, Henning Simonsen, Hans Håkon Skjønsberg, and Ole Asbjørn Winther for their administrative support. We are especially indebted to our consultant in China, Zhu Rong-fa, for his comments and suggestions, based on the production of the Chinese version of the *Yearbook*.

We extend our sincere thanks to the contributors to the Current Issues and Key Themes section in this edition for conscientiously keeping their deadlines, while at the same time following up our suggestions for improvements. Thanks are also due to our network of officials at international organizations and secretariats for their continuous interest, support, and patience; their responses to our yearly drafts and questionnaire give us a myriad of details, rendering them an invaluable source of information for the reference sections in the *Yearbook*.

As previously, we have benefited from professional advice from our Advisory Panel in preparing the Current Issues and Key Themes section, especially editorial advice in the review process from Bruce Davis, Julie Fisher, Farhana Yamin, and Alexey Yablokov. We are especially indebted to the chairman of the Panel, Willy Østreng, for his never-ending encouragement.

Special thanks are due to Morten Mathiesen of the Scandinavian University Press for his highly skilled handling of the design, graphics, and paste-up, and to Torstein Olsen of the Global Resource Information Database (GRID)-Arendal for his equally professional technical support in producing maps and tables—both for the *Yearbook* and its website. They are among our most experienced technical contributors, and their assistance in the final stages of production remains essential. The staff at Konsis Grafisk also deserve mention for technical support in producing film.

Finally, we acknowledge the financial support provided, without ever interfering in our editorial independence, by the Research Council of Norway, the Norwegian Agency for Development Co-operation (NORAD), the Norwegian Ministry of the Environment, and the Norwegian Ministry of Foreign Affairs.

The Editors

Advisory Panel to the Yearbook

Homero Aridjis, President,
Grupo de los Cien Internacional,
Mexico DF, Mexico

Alicia Bárcena, Senior Advisor,
UNEP Regional Office for Latin America,
Mexico DF, Mexico

Leif E. Christoffersen, Senior Fellow,
Noragric, Agricultural University of Norway,
Ås, Norway

Michael Zammit Cutajar, Executive Secretary,
Climate Change Secretariat (UNFCCC),
Bonn, Germany

Bruce W. Davis, Professor and Deputy Director,
Institute of Antarctic and Southern Ocean Studies,
University of Tasmania,
Hobart, Australia

Raimonds Ernšteins, Director,
Centre for Environmental Science and Management
Studies (CESAMS), University of Latvia,
Riga, Latvia

Julie Fisher, Programme Officer,
The Kettering Foundation,
Dayton, Ohio, USA

Susan George, Associate Director,
Transnational Institute,
Amsterdam, The Netherlands

Ernst B. Haas, Professor,
University of California,
Berkeley, California, USA

Calestous Juma, Special Advisor,
Center for International Development,
Harvard University,
Cambridge, Massachusetts, USA

Roger Kohn, Head
Information Office,
International Maritime Organization,
London, United Kingdom

Martin Kohr, Director,
Third World Network (TWN),
Penang, Malaysia

Geoffrey Lean, Environment Correspondent,
Independent on Sunday,
London, United Kingdom

Jeremy Leggett, International Science Director,
Greenpeace International,
London, United Kingdom

Magnar Norderhaug, Director,
Worldwatch Norden,
Tønsberg, Norway

Amulya K. Reddy, Professor and President,
International Energy Initiative (IEI),
Bangalore, India

Bruce M. Rich, Senior Attorney and Director,
International Program, Environmental Defense
Fund (EDF),
Washington, DC, USA

Peter H. Sand, Lecturer,
Institute of International Law, University of Munich,
Munich, Germany

Richard Sandbrook, Executive Director,
International Institute for Environment and
Development (IIED),
London, United Kingdom

Lawrence Susskind, Ford Professor,
Department of Urban Studies and Planning,
Massachusetts Institute of Technology (MIT),
Cambridge, Massachusetts, USA

Alexey V. Yablokov, Professor and Chairman,
Center for Russian Environmental Policy,
Moscow, Russian Federation

Farhana Yamin, Director,
Foundation for International Environmental Law
and Development (FIELD), University of London,
London, United Kingdom

Willy Østreng, Professor and Chairman of the Panel,
Norwegian University of Science and Technology,
Trondheim, Norway

Contents

Intergovernmental Organizations (IGOs)

Non-Governmental Organizations (NGOs)

COUNTRY PROFILES

Contributors to this Yearbook

James Cameron is a practising barrister who specializes in international environmental law and the law of the World Trade Organization (WTO). He is a founder director of Foundation for International Environmental Law and Development (FIELD) and of counsel to Baker and McKenzie, an international law firm in Chicago. He is professor of law at the College of Europe, Bruges, Belgium, and Lecturer at the School of Oriental and African Studies (SOAS), University of London; has been specialist adviser to the House of Commons select committee on the environment; and is currently an adviser to the British Foreign Secretary, Robin Cook MP, on global environmental policy. He is the author of many specialist texts on environmental law and policy, including *Trade and Environment: The Search for Balance* (with Demaret and Gerardin); *Interpreting the Precautionary Principle* (with O'Riordan); and *Improving Compliance with International Environmental Agreements* (with Werksman and Roderick). He is on the board of editors of *RECIEL* (*Review of EC and International Environmental Law*) and the *ITLR* (*International Trade Law Reports*). E-mail: c18@soas.ac.uk

Beatrice Chaytor is currently Staff Lawyer on the Trade and Environment Programme at FIELD. She was Legal Adviser to the Sierra Leone Ministry of Trade, Industry, and State Enterprises and represented Sierra Leone in the WTO Committee on Trade and Environment during the 1995–6 session. She is member of the Task Force on Trade and Environment at the IUCN Centre for Environmental Law. Other work has included acting as Legal Adviser to the Government of St Lucia prior to negotiations on the 2nd phase of Lomé IV; producing guidelines for drafting legislation for the phase-out of PVC in Sweden; writing a review of sectoral and environmental laws in Sierra Leone; work on a consolidated forestry legislation for Ghana; and advising on a new South African forestry legislation. Among her publications are: *Free Trade and Sustainable Development: The European Community's Internal Market in Bananas*; *Taxes for Environmental Purposes: The Scope for Border Tax Adjustment under WTO Rules*; *The Potential for EIA Procedures to Enhance Public Participation in Trade Policy Decision-Making*; and *Developing Countries and GATT/ WTO Dispute Settlement: A Profile of Enforcement in Agriculture and Textiles*. E-mail: bc4@soas.ac.uk

Edgar Gold is a Senior Partner with the law firm Huestis Holm in Halifax, Nova Scotia, where he specializes in maritime, energy, environmental, and international commercial law. He is former President of the Canadian Maritime Law Association and a Titulary Member of the Comité Maritime International. Dr Gold is a Master Mariner (UK and Canada) and served at sea for 16 years, including several years in command. He was Professor of Maritime Law (1975–94) and Professor of Resource and Environmental Studies (1986–94) at Dalhousie University, and continues to hold the position of Adjunct Professor in both departments. He participated in all sessions of the Third UN Conference on the Law of the Sea 1973–82 and also served on the Executive Committee of the Law of the Sea Institute. He is a former Executive Director of the Oceans Institute of Canada and remains a member of the Institute. He is Visiting Professor of Maritime Law and the Canadian Member of the Board of Governors of the World Maritime University, Malmö, Sweden, and the International Maritime Organization (IMO)-International Maritime Law Institute, Malta. Among his special areas of interest and expertise are maritime law, international marine and environmental law and policy, maritime training, and international ocean development. Dr Gold has active experience in most regions of the world and has more than 250 publications in the ocean law and policy field. He was awarded the Commander's Cross of the Order of Merit by the German government and the Order of Canada by the Canadian government in 1997. E-mail: golde@compuserve.com

Joyeeta Gupta is a Senior Researcher at the Institute for Environmental Studies, Vrije Universiteit, Amsterdam. Dr Gupta has Bachelors' degrees in economics (Delhi University) and law (Gujarat University), a Master's degree in law (Harvard Law School), and a PhD in law (Vrije Universiteit, Amsterdam), and has worked for environmental non-governmental organizations (NGOs) in India, the USA, and the Netherlands. Since 1989 she has been working on the climate change issue, first as an in-house consultant to the Dutch Ministry for Housing, Spatial Planning, and Environment, and then as senior researcher at the Institute for Environmental Studies at the Vrije Universiteit in Amsterdam. Her most recent book is *The Climate Change Convention and Developing Countries: From Consensus to Conflict?* (1997). E-mail: joyeeta.gupta@ivm.vu.nl

Abram Ioirysh is LLD and Professor of Law at the Institute of State and Law of the Academy of Sciences of the Russian Federation. He is a leading Russian expert on atomic law and as such is a consultant of the State Duma of Russia (parliament). He participated in the elaboration of national nuclear legislation and international agreements in this field. Dr Ioirysh is the author of 15 books and more than 150 other publications on legal aspects of the peaceful uses of nuclear energy, including *Atom and Law* (1969), *Legal Problems of the Peaceful Uses of Atomic Energy* (1979), *Atomic Energy: Legal Problems* (1979), *Hiroshima* (1979), *Scientific and Technological Progress and New Legal Problems* (1981), *Nuclear Propelled Vessels* (1989), *Nuclear Genie* (1994), and *Lessons of A. D. Sakharov* (1996).

Adil Najam is currently an Assistant Professor of International Relations and Environmental Policy at Boston University, USA. He is associated with the Intergovernmental Panel on Climate Change (IPCC) as a Chapter Lead Author, is a Visiting Fellow at the Sustainable Development Policy Institute (SDPI), and is on the Board of Governors of the Pakistan Institute of Environment-Development Action Research (PIEDAR). He has published widely in leading journals on North–South environmental relations, developing countries in international environmental policy and negotiation, the implementation of environmental treaties, the role of NGOs in national and international policy, and on NGO accountability. His forthcoming book is titled *International Environmental Negotiation in an Unequal World*. E-mail: anajam@bu.edu

G. Kristin Rosendal is programme director and senior research fellow at the Fridtjof Nansen Institute (FNI), Norway. She holds a PhD in political science from the University of Oslo and has worked as a research fellow at FNI since 1989; she is currently directing the Programme on Global Environment and Resource Management. Her main research interest is international environmental negotiations, with special emphasis on the North–South debate on genetic resources, biological diversity, and property rights. She has published extensively in these fields, and her most recent book is *Implementing International Environmental Agreements in Developing Countries: The Creation and Impact of the Convention on Biological Diversity* (1999). She is also co-editor of *Biotechnology Annual Review*. E-mail: kristin.rosendal@fni.no

Roland Timerbaev, PhD, former Professor of International History at the Moscow Institute of International Relations, the Monterey (California) Institute of International Studies, and the Moscow Nuclear Engineering Institute. He was Russian arms control negotiator and participated in the negotiation of, *inter alia*, the Nuclear Non-Proliferation Treaty. In 1988–92 he was Ambassador to the IAEA and other international organizations in Vienna. He is the author of nine books and more than 100 other publications, including *Peaceful Atom on International Arena* (1969), *Verification of Arms Control and Disarmament* (1983), *Problems of Verification* (1984), *Complete Prohibition of Nuclear Tests* (1987), *Russia and Nuclear Non-proliferation, 1945–1968* (1999). E-mail: rtimerbaev@glasnet.ru(1999). E-mail: rtimerbaev@glasnet.ru

Introduction

Helge Ole Bergesen, Georg Parmann, and Øystein B. Thommessen

As demonstrated in earlier editions of this *Yearbook*, the road from declarations to implementation of sustainable development can be long, unpredictable, and frustrating. Sometimes there is reason to suspect that not all governments have been equally happy about the outcome of a conference and that some have quietly entertained hopes that the rhetoric would soon fade away. On many occasions, however, most governments are probably sincere in their wishes to seek international solutions to a given environment and development problem, but they do not foresee the difficulties that arise in the follow-up process.

Our contributors in the Current Issues and Key Themes section to this volume point out some of the most important obstacles that appear on the path leading from words to deeds:

• diverging political interests are, not unexpectedly, a real concern when economic and political stakes are high, as witnessed in the negotiations on climate change and biodiversity. Spillover from the general north–south cleavage can hardly be avoided, as emphasized by both Joyeeta Gupta and Kristin Rosendal in their analyses of these areas;

• national sovereignty remains sensitive to intrusion from intergovernmental organisations, especially when the subject matter touches on security issues, as is the case with the nuclear safety regime (see Timerbaev and Iorysh);

• established institutions do not easily and voluntarily adapt to the new demands of sustainable development. As shown by Chaytor and Cameron (and supported by Rosendal), the World Trade Organization is a case in point. Its established objectives and procedures are clearly in need of reform if new environmental requirements are to be taken seriously. Even if such changes are long overdue, institutional inertia and organizational turf fights, often stimulated by political disagreement, lead to frustrating delays;

• unilateral measures from individual governments acting alone can work against even the best of intentions, as Edgar Gold shows in his analysis of US legislation to prevent ship-source marine pollution. In the absence of wide support from both governmental and non-governmental actors, unilateralism can easily backfire;

• insufficient national capacity whether in the field of nuclear safety or concerning the protection of biodiversity, remains a serious obstacle that cannot be solved through declarations.

Despite these persistent problems, recent developments include reasons for optimism—not as before by way of successfully negotiated treaties or conferences held in the floodlight of world media, but in much subtler ways: one crucial factor underlined by several of our contributors is the enduring competition for the best image and the most attractive ideas. While this used to be the battleground reserved for NGOs, it is now forcefully pursued also by international business, as demonstrated by Adil Najam in his account of the World Business Council for Sustainable Development. The importance of the image competition lies in the expectations created in what is often a war of words. Companies that consistently present themselves as environmental champions have to follow suit in order to avoid future damage to the very reputation they so eagerly promote. Intergovernmental agreements can have a decisive impact on corporate behaviour under these circumstances by providing visible benchmarks—for example the 'Kyoto targets', which international oil companies, among others, frequently refer to in setting objectives for their future performance (see Gupta).

In addition, the bureaucratic nitty-gritty that takes place from meeting to meeting in intergovernmental fora and from paper to paper in diverse secretariats should not be underestimated. Even at times of political stalemate or confusion, these silent processes can gather institutional strength that provides the agenda, the transparency, and the apparatus that governments will need the day they agree to take another step forward.

We introduce two new agreements in the Agreements section in this *Yearbook*, namely the Convention on Access to Information, Public Participation in Decision Making and Access to Justice in Environmental Matters (Århus Convention) and the Convention on the Prior Informed Consent Procedure for Certain Hazardous Chemicals and Pesticides in International Trade (PIC Convention), both adopted in 1998.

This section also includes major revisions of entries covering the Convention on Long-Range Transboundary Air Pollution (LRTAP)—which presents the new protocols on heavy metals and on persistent organic pollutants—the United Nations Framework Convention on Climate Change (UNFCCC), the Vienna Convention for the Protection of the Ozone Layer, including the Montreal Protocol on Substances that Deplete the Ozone Layer—now including the Montreal Amendment— the Convention on the Control of Transboundary Movements of Hazardous Wastes and their Disposal (Basel Convention), the Convention on the Prevention of Marine Pollution by Dumping of Wastes and Other Matter (London Convention 1972), the International Convention on Civil Liability for Oil Pollution Damage 1969 (1969 CLC), the International Convention on the Establishment of an International Fund for Compensation for Oil Pollution Damage 1971 (1971 Fund Convention), the UN Convention on the Law of the Sea (UNCLOS), regional conventions within the UN Environment Programme (UNEP) Regional Seas Programme—with far more details—and the Convention on Biological Diversity (CBD).

Extensive revisions have been made on entries in the Intergovernmental Organizations (IGOs) section as well, for example, the International Atomic Energy Agency (IAEA), the Organization for Economic Co-operation and Development (OECD), the Environment Policy Committee (EPOC)—which has been expanded considerably— the UNEP, the World Food Programme (WFP), the World Health Organization (WHO), and the World Trade Organization (WTO).

In the Non-Governmental Organizations (NGOs) section we have added the new Basel Action Network (BAN). Since the NGO entries are more condensed than the IGO entries, we recommend that readers who are interested in more details and complete descriptions of the NGOs should visit our website at <http://www.ext.grida.no/ggynet>.

The Country Profiles section includes each year approximately one half of the states that are members of the OECD. Accordingly, 15 states that were not covered in the 1998/99 *Yearbook* are incorporated here. In the subsection covering major non-OECD countries, we have introduced five new entries, supplementing the five non-OECD countries that appeared in the previous volume.

In the process of updating information in these sections, completed in July 1999, all organizations and secretariats listed have had an opportunity to review a draft description of their activities. The responsibility for the selection of entries and the organization of information is, however, ours. As previously, we welcome comments from readers who disagree with our presentation or have other suggestions. Please contact us by mail: The Editors, *Yearbook of International Co-operation on Environment and Development*, FNI, PO Box 326, N-1326 Lysaker, Norway; by telefax: +47 67 111 910; or at our Internet address: <green.yearbook@fni.no>.

Polhøgda, Lysaker, Norway
July 1999

Evaluation of the Climate Change Regime and Related Developments

Joyeeta Gupta

The Climate Change Problem

The greenhouse gases surrounding the earth have made the earth habitable. However, since the industrial revolution, anthropogenic greenhouse gas emissions from industrial and agricultural processes have led to high concentrations of these gases in the atmosphere which may cause an enhanced greenhouse effect. This effect may have severe consequences on the coastal regions of the world and on the life-support systems of ecosystems, and may affect agriculture, food, and water supply.[1]

This essay evaluates the international response to the climate change problem, the national implementation process, the impact of such implementation on the problem, and the barriers and opportunities for further progress. In undertaking the analysis, it will focus on the degree of success achieved in the regime. Success depends on the perspective from which the regime is perceived, and a distinction is drawn here between the success embodied in the regime from a political, legal, institutional, scientific, environmental, and economic perspective.

Defining the limits to the climate change problem is a challenging task. Interviews with negotiators and policy makers reveal that while for some the problem is caused merely by the emissions of greenhouse gases, such as carbon dioxide and methane, for others it is caused by production and consumption patterns, the underlying political and economic systems, and current development patterns. This also has implications for the way in which the solution is perceived. For some the solution is to change the system at the margin and reduce emissions incrementally wherever possible; for others it is structurally to change the production and consumption systems and to hold polluters responsible.[2] Since the emissions of greenhouse gases are closely linked with the economic growth of countries, reducing these emission levels, or even their expansion, is expected to have an impact on national economic growth as it is currently defined.[3]

Thus, decisions that are perceived as having a negative impact on national economic growth should be based on credible scientific evidence. The state of the art knowledge is presented in the five-yearly reports of the Intergovernmental Panel on Climate Change (IPCC). IPCC concludes, on the basis of existing science, that 'the balance of evidence suggests a discernible human influence on the global climate.'[4] However, other scientists claim that the IPCC conclusions are faulty, since they do not adequately take into account the data on water vapour, sulphur dioxide, and aerosols, the complicated role of oceans as sinks for carbon dioxide, and the impact of carbon dioxide emissions in stimulating the growth of plants. They also argue that the IPCC conclusions are based on unrealistic models and are political and not scientific assessments.[5] The scientific debate indicates that there is some degree of confidence in the data on emission levels, but there is less confidence about the role of sinks in absorbing these emissions and the impact of the emissions on the global climate. Given the scientific uncertainty, 'we will have to abandon our unrealistic demand for a single certain truth and instead strive for transparency of the various positions and learn to live with pluralism in climate change risk assessment.'[6] While governments and environmental non-governmental organizations (NGOs) accept the validity of IPCC science, the position of industry has become divided over the years. This is reflected in the negotiations, as can be seen in the following sections.

The International Response

More than a decade after the 1979 World Climate Conference, the adoption took place of the United Nations Framework Convention on Climate Change (UNFCCC) (May 1992)[7], and the Kyoto Protocol to the United Nations Framework Convention on Climate Change (KPFCCC) (December 1997).[8] The most recent meeting of the Conference of the Parties took place in November 1998 in Buenos Aires.

The UNFCCC states that the ultimate objective of the Convention and any related legal instrument is to achieve the stabilization of greenhouse gas concentrations in the atmosphere at a level that would enable ecosystems to adapt naturally and would not harm food production.[9] This objective is to be achieved by measures guided by the principles of equity and the common but differentiated responsibilities and respective capabilities of developed and developing countries (vulnerable countries in particular), and the need for precautionary measures, sustainable development, and a supportive, open economic system.[10]

Furthermore, the Convention divides the world into two groups—developed (Western and Eastern countries with economies in transition) and developing countries. The former are expected in vaguely worded text[11] to reduce their emissions of carbon dioxide and other greenhouse gases not controlled by the treaties on the ozone layer (e.g. nitrous oxide and methane) by the year 2000 to about 1990 levels.[12] The Kyoto Protocol includes explicit targets or 'assigned amounts' for developed countries which are expected jointly to reduce their emissions of six greenhouse gases (among them hydrofluorocarbons, perfluorocarbons, and sulphur hexafluoride) by at least 5 per cent below 1990 levels (and in some cases 1995 levels) in the period 2008–12.[13] Individually, these countries have separate commitments. The European Union countries are expected to reduce their emissions by 8 per cent, the USA by 7 per cent and Japan by 6 per cent. Australia, Iceland, and Norway are allowed to increase their emissions. The remaining countries are allowed varying levels of reduction.[14]

Under the Convention and the Protocol, Western developed countries are expected to provide financial assistance to the developing countries and co-operate in the field of science and technology transfer to enable these countries to adopt more climate-friendly technologies and to adapt to the potential impacts of climate change.[15] The Convention mentions that countries may jointly implement their obligations without defining joint implementation.[16] The view of most Western negotiators was that joint implementation would enable a Western investor to invest in greenhouse gas-friendly projects in Eastern and Central Europe and in the developing countries in return for emission reduction credits.[17] Many developing countries opposed joint implementation because they feared that this would reduce the incentive for developed countries to take serious domestic emission reduction measures, and that the developed countries would buy the cheap emission reduction options in the developing countries. At a later stage, when the developing countries would themselves have to reduce their emissions, only the more expensive emission reduction options would be available.[18] In 1995, at the first Conference of the Parties, a pilot phase on Activities Implemented Jointly was launched which would permit countries to participate voluntarily in such projects, but no crediting was allowed during the pilot phase.[19] The 1997 Kyoto Protocol allows joint implementation with crediting among the developed country parties and establishes a Clean Development Mechanism

(CDM), which aims at enabling projects in developing countries that should achieve sustainable development, contribute to the ultimate objective of the Convention, and assist developed countries in complying with their quantified emission reduction and limitation commitments.

Under the Protocol, countries with commitments are also allowed to participate in emission trading schemes.[20] Such schemes call for the division of a budget of permissible emissions among countries. Those countries that do not use their complete share may sell the unused portion to those who need them. Thus, over-users have an incentive to reduce their emissions and under-users may profit financially. In the Kyoto Protocol, the assigned amounts (or quotas) have been allocated to the developed countries and are equivalent to their emission reduction commitments. The underlying rationale of these co-operative mechanisms is to ensure that global emissions of greenhouse gases are reduced in a cost-effective manner in line with the principles in Article 3 of the UNFCCC.

Under the Convention, five bodies have been established. The Secretariat makes arrangements for the annual meetings of the Conference of the Parties. A Subsidiary Body for Scientific and Technological Advice provides timely advice on scientific and technological issues to the Conference of the Parties. The Subsidiary Body for Implementation provides assistance in assessing and reviewing the implementation of the Convention. The Convention also identified the Global Environment Facility as an interim operating entity to provide financial resources on a grant or concessional basis, including for technology transfer, to the developing countries.[21] The Kyoto Protocol will use the Secretariat and the subsidiary bodies established under the Convention, and the Conference of the Parties to the Convention will serve as the meeting of the Parties to the Protocol. Each party to the Convention is expected to prepare a national communication to report on national emissions and the measures being taken to deal with them.[22]

The negotiations are influenced by the presence of environmental NGOs, representatives from industry, and the scientific community. Around 300 environmental NGOs co-operate under the framework of the Climate Action Network.[23] This network provides information through its daily newsletter *ECO* during the negotiations, lobbies national negotiators, observes proceedings, and makes statements during the negotiations (if the chair permits). Arts (1998) argues that if one were to take the counterfactual argument into account, i.e. if there had been a comparable climate change treaty had the NGOs not been present, then it would be quite clear that the NGOs have had a major impact on the negotiations.[24] He claims, however, that NGOs had no direct impact on the text of the Convention, had some limited indirect impact on certain articles, did not have much impact on the review of the national communications, and had some political influence, but generally overrate their own influence on the Convention.[25] My own observations and interviews indicate that they ensure the transparency of the process, they provide huge amounts of information which is avidly read by negotiators from developed and developing countries, and they very much influence the way negotiators think, even if their influence on the negotiation outcome is less traceable.

The influence of the scientific community through the reports of the IPCC is substantial.[26] The negotiations draw heavily from the scientific reports, and the role of the Subsidiary Body on Scientific and Technological Advice (SBSTA) is to present this scientific material in a usable form to the Conference of the Parties. An IPCC/SBSTA Joint Working Group has been established to ensure linkages between the information needs of the Conference of the Parties and the scientific community. There is thus a regular dialogue between the two communities.[27] At the same time, although IPCC can undertake a literature review of the available science in order to generate answers to the specific questions raised by the policy makers, it does not tackle new research. In general there is satisfaction with the IPCC documents. However, there is some concern about the degree to which social science aspects are reflected in the reports and the degree to which it provides support to the kinds of scientific concerns expressed by the developing countries.[28]

Industries are very active in the negotiation process, and they seek to influence this process through lobbying with negotiators and through the politicians in the domestic context. Although, in the early days of the negotiations, industry opposed action on the climate change issue, there is now a small but growing group that supports climate change policies.

The climate change regime thus has set a process in motion to address a politically difficult problem, and the Kyoto Protocol was one of the 'most complex multilateral negotiations of modern times'.[29] Given the enormous complexity and the diverging definitions of the problem as shown in the first section, this section has demonstrated that, from a political point of view, the differences in perceptions have been temporarily addressed through a common global framework of action. The North–North differences refer to the internal problems that the developed countries were themselves experiencing in articulating definitions, targets, measures, and co-operative mechanisms. For example, while the EU pushed for a 15 per cent reduction target,[30] the USA was only willing to go as far as stabilization of emissions in 2008–12.[31] Despite the divergence of starting points and the inflexibility of negotiating positions, an agreement was reached with legally binding targets. The serious North–South conflict in relation to the so-called voluntary commitments of developing countries was partially resolved through the inclusion of the CDM.[32]

From an economic perspective the regime appears to be cost-effective, since it establishes several flexibility mechanisms and allows the private sector to take a more important role in the process.[33] But implementing the Kyoto Protocol is also quite expensive. While the Clinton administration estimates an annual drop in GDP by 0.5 per cent, others estimate that the drop could be as high at 3 per cent.[34] Models indicate that the costs of achieving the Kyoto commitments primarily through domestic implementation will be in the order of 0.2 per cent to 2 per cent of the GDP in the USA, Europe, and Japan, and that with full trading the loss will be between 0.1 per cent to 0.3 per cent.[35] While these numbers may seem quite palatable, there are other economists who argue that the '35 per cent US CO_2 reduction required by 2008–12 entails economic dislocations that are unjustifiable on the basis of, at best, debatable science.'[36]

Although environmentalists do not think that the Convention goes far enough to address the gravity of the problem (see the section on the impact on the problem), the key success of the regime as it currently stands is in the bureaucratic rituals it has established. Parties to the Convention meet annually, preparatory meetings of the subsidiary bodies take place between one and three times a year, the Secretariat produces regular reports, and countries are in the process of preparing their follow-up national communications. The bureaucratic ritual serves three important purposes that are often underestimated. First, it ensures that there is a regular rhythm in the process, and negotiators and policy makers can feel the relentless pressure of the international process which ensures that the issue remains on the domestic agenda. Second, these procedures bring to light the difficulties in implementing the international agreements, and these difficulties can then be scrutinized and solutions suggested in the various meetings. This is an important part of keeping the process moving, of ensuring that the issue remains on the agenda, and of slowly and steadily enabling progression. Third, these reports provide civil society and NGOs information on the basis of which they can assess the progress made by countries from their perspectives, and identify where specific problems lie and how they can be addressed.

While sometimes such meetings can build up the momentum necessary to negotiate and adopt a protocol, at other times tactical errors can lead to disappointing achievements. Thus, for example, the first Conference of the Parties adopted the Berlin Mandate, which stated that, since the existing commitments of the developed countries were inadequate, a process should be initiated to identify policies and measures for reducing emissions in relation to specific time-frames.[37] This led ultimately to the Kyoto Protocol. However, at the same time the USA's ratification of the Kyoto Protocol was linked to voluntary commitments to be adopted by developing countries.[38] The pressure put on developing countries to adopt commitments voluntarily, contrary to the provisions of the Berlin Mandate, ultimately led to protracted discussions, and little progress was made on the rules and modalities for the co-operative mechanisms at the meeting in Buenos Aires.[39]

National Implementation

As of February 1999, only the Climate Change Convention had entered into effect, and all developed country parties had submitted their first national communications, although 18 were late. Most of these communications have been reviewed in depth and country visits have been made in connection with the reviews.[40] Subak (1997) states that these reviews are in general non-confrontational in nature and that, since at least one-third of the countries had submitted inadequate data, it is difficult to verify the results.[41]

The second communications of the Western developed countries were due in April 1997, and most parties were late in submitting. The countries with economies in transition were due to submit their communications in 1998.[42] According to the Subsidiary Body for Implementation, Argentina, Jordan, Mexico, Micronesia, the Republic of Korea, Senegal, Uruguay, and Zimbabwe were among the earliest developing countries to submit their national communications.[43]

As mentioned earlier, the 'aspirational' goals in the climate treaty are not binding commitments. Nevertheless, many developed countries adopted measures domestically. Bert Bolin, chairman emeritus of IPCC, shows that, in the period 1990–95, the total carbon dioxide emissions in the European Union had decreased by 1 per cent of the 1990 level. This, of course, reflected changes in emission levels ranging from a reduction of 9 per cent in Germany to an increase of 49 per cent in Portugal. The rest of the OECD countries recorded an increase of 8 per cent: New Zealand topped the list with an increase of 16 per cent and Switzerland recorded a decrease of 5 per cent. The countries with economies in transition recorded a decrease of 29 per cent. This implies that the total reduction in the developed countries was in the order of 5 per cent. However, although some developing countries did adopt decisions to promote renewable energy and phase out subsidies,[44] their emissions increased by 25 per cent.[45]

The national communications also indicate the expected emission reductions by the year 2000. The emissions of the developed country parties, including the countries with economies in transition, are expected to be 3 per cent below 1990 levels in the year 2000 (if emissions from land-use change and forestry are omitted), and all countries with economies in transition and seven of the 24 Western countries will emit less than 1990 levels in the year 2000.[46] A key reason for the low growth in the overall emissions is the financial collapse in the countries with economies in transition. For countries such as Japan, the USA, Canada, Australia, Norway, and New Zealand, the difficulties in implementation lie in high, unforeseen economic growth and low prices of energy.[47]

The above discussion would suggest that, even prior to the entry into effect of the UNFCCC, significant emission reductions were recorded. By the year 2000 developed countries will have jointly stabilized their emissions of greenhouse gas emissions, and that should be reason enough to be satisfied with the achievements of the developed countries in relation to the aspirational goals in the UNFCCC. However, there is no sense of euphoria in the countries. This is probably because a closer examination of the data reveals that the emission reductions are more a result of economic collapse in the former Eastern bloc countries (including East Germany) and that the decrease does not reflect a structural change towards reduced emission levels. Subak concludes that, although countries have complied with their reporting requirements, most will not be able actually to achieve the goal of stabilization.[48] Furthermore, the emission reductions in the EU are likely to increase sharply after the year 2000 unless additional measures are adopted. Finally, the emissions in the USA and other developed countries are likely to increase steadily over the coming years. Thus, although the impression appears quite positive on the whole, it does not yet indicate that we have reached the peak of annual Western emission levels.

Since there are no real targets on technology transfer and assistance to developing countries, it is difficult to evaluate the extent of assistance being provided to the developing countries by the developed countries.[49] Large sums of money have been disbursed to assist these countries to prepare national emission inventories.[50] But there has been less money forthcoming to finance technology transfer. Developing countries are not entirely satisfied with the assistance being provided by the developed countries and feel that the developed countries have not adequately demonstrated their lead in this field.[51] In 1998 the US Secretary of State acknowledged to a domestic audience, 'We need support for the Global Environment Facility (GEF), which embodies the partnership for sustainable development that was forged in Rio. This partnership is not helped by the fact that, in each of the last three years, we have fallen short of our pledged share to the GEF. We need to do better than that. We need to meet our commitments—

in full—this year and every year.'[52] The Buenos Aires Plan of Action, a decision adopted at the fourth meeting of the Conference of the Parties, focuses on strengthening the financial mechanism and the development and transfer of technologies, and on maintaining the momentum in relation to Activities Implemented Jointly. At the end of 1998 there were 123 projects accepted, approved, and/or endorsed by national governments as Activities Implemented Jointly Projects, of which two are in Africa, 28 in Central and Southern America, ten in Asia, and the remainder in the countries with economies in transition.[53] Most of these projects are still in a planning stage; evaluating them in relation to the issue of credits is not possible, since credits for reducing emissions are not included in the projects.

The implementation of the Kyoto Protocol calls not only for alert governments but also for co-operative industry and society. Thus far, the Kyoto Protocol has been seen as a signal by some industries which have decided to demonstrate their willingness to take action. The European Business Council for a Sustainable Energy Future, E5, has argued in favour of developing a 'renewable portfolio obligation for all energy service companies',[54] and British Petroleum has adopted 'climate change principles' stating that a constructive precautionary approach needs to be taken within a global long-term framework that also gives weight to the developing world's particular interests. They argue that targets and timetables should be set that give clear signals to industry and that there should be flexible market mechanisms.[55] Shell has established Shell Renewables and on 16 October 1998 announced that it aims to cut its greenhouse gas emission from its global operations by 10 per cent in 2002 in relation to 1990 levels.[56] The European Gas Industry (Eurogas) supports a precautionary policy on the climate change issue.[57] Thus, one could argue that the Kyoto Protocol can be seen as a turning point in the process, since it has ensured a level playing field and has sent the signal that governments are serious about this problem.

Impact on the Problem

Let us now examine the extent to which the measures taken by countries have had or are likely to have a serious impact on the environmental problem at hand. According to the Intergovernmental Panel on Climate Change, 'Stabilization at any of the concentration levels studied (350–750ppmv) is only possible if emissions are eventually reduced to well below 1990 levels.'[58] From a scientific perspective, the decision to adopt binding commitments is a key decision in the right direction, but falls short of what is needed. Bert Bolin states: 'The inertia of the climate change system was not appreciated fully by the delegates in Kyoto. It therefore seems likely that another international effort will be required well before 2010 to consider whether further measures are warranted.'[59] Bill Hare of Greenpeace International explained on 6 March 1999 that the target falls far short of what is needed, since it slows down the projected rise in global temperature by only one tenth to two tenths of a degree centigrade by 2050.[60] These reduction trends are consistent with a stabilization of CO_2 emissions concentrations at 550 parts per million volume. At this level, it is expected that there will be significant ecosystem damage, 60 to 350 million more people will be at risk of hunger, there will be a significant loss of human life, and there will be a 50cm increase in the sea level, with all the attendant impacts.[61]

Furthermore, there is a perception that there are several loopholes in the Protocol. These include the exemption of emissions from international air and marine transport, which is a fast growing sector.[62]

The inclusion of the three new gases in the regime makes the scope more comprehensive, since these are also fast growing greenhouse gases. However, the target of 5.2 per cent applies to all these gases and allows parties to use the base year of 1995 in relation to the three new gases if they so wish. The new base year allowed 'Kyoto signatories the political kudos of agreeing larger numbers for exactly the same real effort'.[63]

Article 3.7 of the Kyoto Protocol allows developed country parties to inflate their base year emissions of CO_2 by including the emissions that occurred in 1990 resulting from land use change and forestry. This provision permits countries such as Australia to increase its emission levels in the base year against which its commitments for the year 2008–12 will be measured.[64]

The inclusion of sinks also complicates the verification of the achievement of the national commitments. The Kyoto Protocol refers to 'net changes in greenhouse gas emissions from sources and removals by sinks resulting from direct human induced land use change and forestry activities'[65] The inclusion of sinks is problematic partly because of the indeterminate language used in the Protocol[66] and, depending on the definitions used and the difficulties in estimating sinks, could imply a loophole in the target.[67] In relation to sinks, Professor Bert Bolin states: 'It is, however, not clear how to achieve what is envisaged in the Protocol.'[68]

There is also the problem of 'hot air', which refers to the fact that some countries have been allocated emission allowances that are higher than their probable future emission levels. If these countries are allowed to trade these emissions, then the related trading is unlikely to result in any real reduction in emissions.[69] Finally, there is the issue of verification of effectiveness. Lanchbery (1998) explains that verifying compliance with the Kyoto Protocol calls for an analysis of comparable national inventories of emissions and removals by sinks. However, there is uncertainty regarding emission factors, emissions from biological processes, and in relation to sinks. The uncertainties range from +/–5 per cent for most energy related sources in developed countries to +/–50 per cent for emissions in relation to forestry, land use, and agriculture. These uncertainties are multiplied if the emissions of different gases are put into one figure by using the global warming potential, which itself has an uncertainty range of about 30 per cent for each gas.[70]

The preliminary examination of the potential impacts of the Kyoto Protocol are that the loopholes, although considered necessary to gain the existing consensus on legally binding targets, have the potential of completely undermining the process. These loopholes may add up to a 10 per cent increase of total emissions from the developed country parties in relation to their 1990 emission levels.[71]

Barriers to Further Progress: Horizontal and Vertical Bottlenecks

The following section argues that there are serious barriers to further progress, but that these bottlenecks can also be avoided. On the basis of 150 interviews, I argued in 1997 that the climate change treaty ran the risk of a horizontal negotiation bottleneck if the developed countries decided against taking domestic measures on the grounds that any measures taken by them would be rendered negligible by the lack of action taken by developing countries, and if developing countries refused to take action on the grounds that the developed countries were responsible for the problem and should take action first. I also argued that the Convention ran the risk of a vertical standstill if, for lack of domestic support, governments are unable to implement the compromise negotiated at the international negotiations.[72]

Events, as they have unfolded since 1997, reveal that these are real concerns. Evidence of the horizontal bottleneck can be seen in the ratification politics in relation to the Kyoto Protocol. This will not enter into effect until 90 days after the date on which 55 Parties to the Convention, emitting at least 55 per cent of the total emissions of carbon dioxide emissions in 1990, have ratified it.[73] This implies that the majority of the developed countries need to ratify the Protocol for it to enter into effect. However, there are indications that the ratification process will not be easy. As of 4 May 1999, 84 countries had signed the Kyoto Protocol and only eight countries (Antigua and Barbuda, Bahamas, El Salvador, Fiji, Maldives, Panama, Trinidad and Tobago, and Tuvalu) had ratified the agreement.[74] Thus, for example, many EU member countries are unlikely to adopt unilateral measures and may not implement the Kyoto Protocol until other countries take on serious measures[75] and until Japan and the USA ratify the agreement. The EU as a whole is unwilling to take action until other Western countries also take action.[76] Furthermore, as mentioned earlier, the US senate will not ratify the agreement until key developing countries adopt meaningful action.[77] (The key developing countries refer to Argentina, Brazil, China, India, and some other large countries). This implies that the leadership role of the North has become conditional, especially since the developing countries negotiated on the understanding that the developed countries would take action first.[78] Considerable pressure was put on the developing countries in Kyoto to make them accept the now excluded article on voluntary measures to be adopted by developing countries. Since then the USA has been sending missions to various developing countries—the Summit of the Americas, China, South Korea, the ASEAN, and G-7 summit—to discuss this issue.[79] While Brazil, China, and India continue to argue that the targets of developed countries should not be linked to developing country participation, Argentina and Kazakhstan announced at the fourth meeting of the Conference of the Parties that they would be willing voluntarily to accept commitments. Although the USA subsequently signed the Kyoto Protocol, ratification does not appear likely in the coming year. Ratification politics appears thus to be one major short-term hurdle.

Having said that, one could also argue that ratification politics does not need to be an insurmountable problem. Clinton himself said, 'I want to emphasize that we cannot wait until the treaty is negotiated and ratified to act.'[80] If industry picks up the signals and begins to invest in new technologies, if civil society engages in social discussion on how best to reduce greenhouse gas emissions, if Europe can build up the courage to develop its strategy to reduce its greenhouse gas emissions, then the process of ratification becomes easier a few years down the road. I would also argue that it does not make sense for the northern countries to make their ratifications dependent on the 'meaningful participation' of developing countries. The reason is simple. Past experience reveals that developing countries (and sometimes the countries with economies in transition) tend to be in non-compliance with their international commitments because, in general, they lack suitably equipped national organizations. Research by Jacobson and Weiss (1995), Peter Sand (1992), and Robert Keohane (1993) shows that the incapacity of states is a critical reason for non-compliance.[81] Without a strong domestic enforcement mechanism, governments in the developing countries may have just nominal power and no real effective strength, especially in relation to environmental issues. So even if there is the desire to meet international obligations expressed by the government, if the stitutional basis for executing that desire is inadequate, he treaty will not be implemented. This has been recognized by many governments and several international ocuments, including Agenda 21,[82] which recommends hat assistance should be given to the developing countries nd countries in transition to a market economy to build nstitutional capacity in their countries. The UNFCCC, oo, includes several articles related to scientific co-operaion, technological co-operation, and financial assistance. iven the commitment of Argentina may have some finanial implications for the USA.[83] The point I am trying to nake here is that forcing developing countries to take on oluntary commitments unnecessarily makes breaches in liplomatic relations without achieving the necessary reults. A Brazilian professor is only one of the many develping country representatives who see diplomatic pressure s 'using, once again, an international agreement as a tool f North–South domination'.[84] Instead one could adopt he advice of Michael Marvin of the US Business Council or Sustainable Energy: 'Start early and start small and ead with the expectation of being followed by the develping countries.'[85]

However, it would not be out of place to make another oint here. While it is very understandable that developng countries feel that the developed countries should take ction first and should not burden the already over-burlened developing countries with new responsibilities, and vhile it makes sense for them to negotiate defensively in his context, I would argue that developing countries need o consider the long-term consequences of their defensive trategy. Projections indicate that the emissions from developing countries will continue to grow, and that develpping countries will also be most vulnerable to the impacts of climate change.[86] Against this context, developing counries need to put the issue of how to develop, and at what ost, onto their own domestic agenda, and they need to nobilize domestic civil society to start thinking of the best vays to address these issues.

A second key horizontal challenge is to ensure that the nternational co-operative mechanisms established under he Kyoto Protocol are successful. Unlike the issues of nonitoring and verification, which can probably be creaively addressed by scientists and policy makers, the issue of allocating emission allowances to countries and allowng them to trade will be complicated. While Schelling 1997) claimed that 'one cannot envision national representatives calmly sitting down to divide up rights in perpetuity worth more than a trillion dollars',[87] the Kyoto Protocol made an attempt at allocating rights among the leveloped countries—much to the annoyance of several leveloping countries. Agarwal and Narain (1998) argue hat the Kyoto Protocol is unfair because it has not taken global equity aspects into consideration.[88] They propose the principle of an equitable sharing of assigned amounts of greenhouse gas emissions as the only fair basis for developing the regime further. Others have proposed that northern emissions should contract to allow the emission levels of all countries eventually to converge.[89] Cooper (1998) anticipates this as a long-term problem, stating that, although giving emission budgets to countries is an elegant solution, the commitments under the Kyoto Protocol will be unimplementable because they raise the problem of international allocation of emission rights.[90] This is because, as Bodansky pointed out in 1993: 'On the one hand, if the per capita or per unit GDP target were set at a level that would stabilize global emissions, countries that have higher than average emission rates, like the US, would have to reduce their emissions substantially; such a target would therefore be politically infeasible. On the other hand, if the target were made high enough to make it acceptable to the United States, then global emissions could increase substantially as states with low emission rates increase theirs to US levels.'[91] Apart from these issues, there is the problem of 'hot air' discussed earlier. There are several authors who argue that the high allocations of assigned amounts to some Central European countries whose emissions are unlikely to reach such a level imply that emission trading may in effect not lead to any real reductions.[92] Then there are the concerns about ensuring that the emission reductions generated in all three co-operative mechanisms—i.e. joint implementation, the Clean Development Mechanism, and emissions trading—are compatible and tradable.[93] Furthermore, some researchers argue that the criteria in these co-operative mechanisms will tend to exclude Africa, as over the last few years only two Activities Implemented Jointly projects have been developed there.[94] There is also a key domestic dimension to the emissions trading issue. How are governments going to divide the permissible emission levels among different producers and consumers? While some favour an auction system, others incline towards the 'grandfathering' system, which allocates emission entitlements on the basis of current pollution levels. Interviews with European and American negotiators indicate that the domestic allocation of emission entitlements is likely to be a major challenge. Tom Spencer, a member of the European Parliament, concludes: 'The existing text on emissions trading offers as many opportunities for fraud and dishonesty as the common agricultural policy.'[95] All these issues indicate that the global community has a very challenging task ahead to develop a legitimate and fair system of co-operation, which creates a new legal tender—emission reduction units or certified emission reductions.

Another major hurdle is the risk of vertical standstill. In 1996 I had argued that, if there is limited local concern, national policy tends to be symbolic, and this leads to rhetorical foreign policy; moreover, such rhetorical foreign policy could make the international regime into a farce.[96] Interviews reveal that within Europe there is a serious concern about the domestic acceptance of emission reduction measures. Negotiators from Europe, the USA, and Japan feel that they have very little domestic support for far-reaching emission reduction measures at home.[97] Earlier research had indicated that, in most developing countries, the issue of climate change is barely on the national political agenda, even though it may be on the formal agenda.[98] In the small island states the climate change issue is on the agenda, but they are hardly in a position to reduce their already low domestic emissions.

On the other hand, there are signs that the public is not indifferent to the issue of climate change. A poll conducted by Louis Harris and Associates indicates that 75 per cent of US voters support the climate change treaty.[99] Another survey conducted by Ohio State University indicates that 80 per cent of Americans believe that reducing air pollution will reduce global warming.[100] A Mellman Group poll indicates that 72 per cent of the US respondents would accept a protocol with substantial cuts of greenhouse gases by 2005.[101] The prime minister's office in Japan conducted a poll that indicated that 79.6 per cent of the respondents support legal regulations to reduce emissions of carbon dioxide.[102] While these polls are quite positive, the above-mentioned interviews with European, American, Japanese, and Canadian negotiators last year indicated that these policy makers are not aware of this support, or are afraid that the public will not endorse their policies.[103] This may indicate that there is a communication gap between the general public and government officials, a relatively easy problem to address. Or, and more seriously, it could indicate that the results of these polls are highly ambiguous. Kempton (1997) argues that, although 72 per cent of US voters may see climate change as a serious threat and 83 per cent would support higher fuel efficiency standards, only 23 per cent would support taxes on energy. He argues that, if one analyses the opinion polls seriously, one sees that those polled are misinformed and 'that most of those polled have not thought about the issue at any length and thus cannot give meaningful responses.' He argues, therefore, for good public awareness campaigns aimed at taking away existing misconceptions rather than providing new information as a critical step for generating legitimate public policy decisions.[104]

Further, although there are indications that some industries are willing to adopt new measures, the hard-liners continue to oppose measures. The chairman of the Global Climate Coalition (GCC), which has about 60 corporations and associations on its board, is noted to have said that any decision to include binding commitments in the Kyoto Protocol would be 'tantamount to Russian roulette'.[105] While the GCC has in a recent document presented estimates of job losses on a state-wise basis going up to 278,000 in the state of California as a result of the Kyoto Protocol,[106] Daniel Lashoff of the Natural Resources Defence Council argues that policies leading to a 10 per cent cut in greenhouse gases by 2010 could lead to 700,000 additional jobs.[107] Interviews with European negotiators and policy makers also indicate that there is a great degree of uncertainty as to whether climate change will lead to job losses or not.[108] In developing countries the chief concern is that action to address climate change is likely to curtail economic growth opportunities for these countries.[109]

Despite these concerns, there is a general positive energy emerging from the regime. The issue is on the agenda of the top politicians of the developed countries. GLOBE International, a network of 550 environmentally committed parliamentarians from over 100 countries, particularly Europe, Japan, Russia, and the United States, stated in its press release on 14 November 1998 that 'the obligation is on us parliamentarians to keep the process alive, and ensure that it remains linked to the electorates around the world, rather than cut off in the corridors, couched in the language of economists and bankers . . . we shall work for the rapid ratification of the Kyoto Protocol, which . . . offers opportunities for both industry and the creation of jobs.'[110] Some industries are taking the initiative to reduce their own emissions. General Motors and Toyota are working on a fuel-efficient car, Texaco on a special conversion programme for natural gas. Civil society, churches, and schools are getting involved in the process. Academicians are doing research and writing articles on ways and means to develop the regime further and to implement its provisions. NGOs are building up the pressure. There are thus indications of increasing public support, a partially co-operative industry, an active non-governmental body, and a growing epistemic community.

In the final analysis there is no clear answer to the question whether the climate change regime has the makings of success. The literature is divided; while many lawyers and policy makers hail the international agreements made thus far as successful, in that they send signals to society and industry, they are afraid that lack of political will and the loopholes in the treaties may minimize the total impact.[111] There are environmentalists,[112] academicians,[113] and business NGOs[114] who think that the design of the Kyoto Protocol is faulty in that it focuses on the wrong instruments, although for different reasons or because it is grossly inadequate to meet the goals.[115] Whether it is inadequate or faulty, the Kyoto Protocol and the institutional features in the regime are not irredeemable, and as such they will stimulate a global learning process. This process in itself has the potential of making the regime successful. If the current or future US president can ensure US ratification of the Kyoto Protocol, or if the European Union ratifies and there is strong support from the civil society, there are strong indications that the remainder of the developed and developing world will also do so. A mid-term assessment and the development of new technologies could lead to a renegotiation of targets—after all, this is what happened in relation to the Montreal Protocol on Substances that Deplete the Ozone Layer. However, the future development of the regime is unlikely to be a smooth and unruffled process. The success of the regime will depend on the extent to which its institutions can change the international discussion from one of economic conflict between countries to one on how best to achieve sustainable development paths which are accessible to all countries. 'If we do it right, protecting the climate will yield not costs, but profits; not burdens, but benefits; not sacrifice, but a higher standard of living.'[116]

Notes and References

The research used in this article is based on the post-doctoral research work on 'Climate Change: Regime Development in the Context of Unequal Power Relations' which is being financially supported by the Netherlands Organization for Scientific Research. The author thanks Helge Ole Bergesen, Jørgen Wettestad, and Øystein B. Thommessen for their comments on this paper.

1 See, for instance, the reports of the Intergovernmental Panel on Climate Change such as J. T. Houghton, L. G. Meira Filho, B. A. Callander, N. Harris, A. Kattenberg, and K. Maskell (eds.) (1996), *Climate Change 1995: The Science of Climate Change* (Cambridge: Cambridge University Press). Their report indicates that the projected increase in the global mean temperature by the end of the next century may be in the order of 1 degree to 3.5 degrees Celsius, and that the sea-level may rise by 0.5m by 2100.

2 Joyeeta Gupta (1997), *The Climate Change Convention and Developing Countries: From Conflict to Consensus* (Dordrecht: Kluwer Academic Publishers).

3 See, for example, Chapters 8 and 9 of the IPCC Working Group 3 Report, *Climate Change 1995: Economic and Social Dimensions of Climate Change* (Cambridge: Cambridge University Press), 263–5.

4 Houghton et al. (eds.) (1996), *Climate Change 1995: The Science of Climate Change*, 4.

5 See, for example, the diverse articles on the subject published in J. Emsley (ed.) (1996), *The Global Warming Debate: The Report of the European Science Forum* (Dorset: Bournemouth Press). In contrast to IPCC reports, this book presents a compilation of papers by different authors and does not attempt at developing a consensus view.

6 Jeroen P. Van der Sluijs (1997), *Anchoring Amid Uncertainty: On the Management of Uncertainties in Risk Assessment of Anthropogenic Climate Change* (PhD thesis, University of Utrecht), 242.

7 United Nations Framework Convention on Climate Change (New York), 9 May 1992, in force 24 March 1994; 31 I.L.M. 1992, 822.

8 Kyoto Protocol to the United Nations Framework Convention on Climate Change, 37 I.L.M. 22; (however, the corrected text is available at the website of the Climate Change Secretariat, <http://www.unfccc.de>).

9 See Article 2 of the FCCC.

10 See Article 3 of the FCCC.

11 See the analysis of P. Sands (1992), 'The United Nations Framework Convention on Climate Change', *Review of European Community and International Environmental Law*, 1: 3, 270–77 at 273; and Daniel Bodansky (1993), 'The United Nations Framework Convention on Climate Change: A Commentary', *Yale Journal of International Law*, 18, 451–588, at 515.

12 See Article 4.2a and b of the FCCC.

13 See Article 3.2 of the KPFCCC.

14 See Annex B of the KPFCCC.

15 See Articles 3.2, 4.3, 4.4, 4.5, 11, 21 of the UNFCCC.

16 See Article 4.2(d) of the FCCC and Gupta (1997), *The Climate Change Convention and Developing Countries*, 116–18.

17 See, for example, J. C. Bollen, O. J. Kuik, J. G. van Minnen, A. M. C. Toet, and M. J. Bennis (1995), *Framework for the Assessment of the Global Potential of Joint Implementation* (Bilthoven: RIVM/IVM Report nr. 481507011); J. Burniaux, J. P. Martin, Giuseppe Nicoletti, and Joaquim Oliveira Martins (1992), *The Costs of Reducing CO2 Emission: Evidence from GREEN* (Paris: OECD Economics Department Working Paper 115).

18 See Chapter 6 in Gupta (1997), *The Climate Change Convention and Developing Countries*, 116–131; and S. Maya and J. Gupta (eds.) (1996), *Joint Implementation for Africa: Carbon Colonies or Business Opportunity? Weighing the Odds in an Information Vacuum* (Harare: Southern Centre for Energy and Environment).

19 Report of the Conference of the Parties at its first session, FCCC/CP/1995/7/Add.1; also available at the web site of the UNFCCC.

20 See Articles 6 and 12 of the Kyoto Protocol to the UNFCCC.

21 See Articles 11 and 21 of the FCCC and Article 11 of the KPFCCC.

22 See Article 12 of the FCCC and Article 7 of the KPFCCC.

23 Presentation by Delia Villagrasa of the Climate Network Europe at the Policy Workshop organized by the European Forum on Integrated Environmental Assessment, and hosted by the Fondazione Eni Enrico Mattei, Milan, 6 March 1999.

24 Bas Arts (1998), *The Political Influence of Global NGOs: Case Studies on the Climate and Biodiversity Conventions* (Utrecht: International Books), 111.

25 Ibid., 156.

26 See, for example, Jeroen P. van der Sluijs (1997), *Anchoring Amid Uncertainty*.

27 This is generally true, although sometimes there is a communication gap between the two groups, and this is reflected in the confused wording on sinks in the Kyoto Protocol. See Farhana Yamin (1998), 'The Kyoto Protocol: Origins, Assessment and Future Challenges', *Review of European Community and International Environmental Law*, 7: 2, 113–27, at 119.

28 See, for example, Sonja Boehmer-Christiansen and Jim Skea (1994), *The Operation and Impact of the Intergovernmental Panel on Climate Change* (Sussex: University of Sussex), STEEP Paper 16; Jacob Swager, 'Climate Change: The Interaction Between Science and Society', paper presented at the Symposium on Integrated Environmental Assessment, organized by CIRED, Toulouse, 24–26 October 1996; Simon Shackley (1997), 'The Intergovernmental Panel on Climate Change: Consensual Knowledge and Global Politics', *Global Environmental Change*, 7: 1, 77–9; Jyoti Parikh (1992), 'IPCC Strategies Unfair to the South, *Nature*, 360, 507–8; and Gupta (1997), *The Climate Change Convention and Developing Countries*, 150–65.

29 See Yamin (1998), 'The Kyoto Protocol', 113.

30 Council of Environmental Ministers (1997), Council Conclusions on Climate Change, Council of Ministers, European Union, 3 March 1997.

31 See, for instance, 'Clinton Presents Emission Plan', *International Herald Tribune*, 23 October 1997, 3.

32 See Jacob Werksman (1998), 'The Clean Development Mechanism: Unwrapping the "Kyoto Surprise", *Review of European Community and International Environmental Law*, 7: 2, 147–57.

33 See, for example, Yamin (1998), 'The Kyoto Protocol', 113–27.

34 This was presented in a paper by Jason Shogren on the benefits and costs of Kyoto, reviewed by Frank J. Convery at the Second Policy Workshop organized by the European Forum on Integrated Environmental Assessment, and hosted by the Fondazione Eni Enrico Mattei, Milan, 5 March 1999.

35 Cited in Chapter 5 in Michael Grubb et al. (1999), *The Kyoto Protocol* (London: Earthscan).

36 See the analysis by Donald A. Carr and William L. Thomas (1998), 'The Kyoto Protocol and US Climate Policy: Implications for American Industry', *Review of European Community and International Environmental Law*, 7: 2, 191–201, at 191.

37 See the report of the first Conference of the Parties, document FCCC/CP/1995/7/Add.1, dec1/CP.1, para 4.

38 See William Jefferson Clinton (1997), remarks by the President on Global Climate Change, National Geographic Society, 22 October 1997; also available at <http://www.whitehouse.gov/ Initiatives/Climate/19971022-6127.html>.

39 See, for example, Emilio Lèbre La Rovere (1999), 'Stalemate in Climate Protection', *Tiempo*, 30; available at <http:// www.cru.uea.ac.uk/tiempo/floor0/recent/issue30/t30a1.htm>; anon. (1999), 'Climate Change, Fourth Conference of Parties', *Globe Europe News*, 1.

40 National Communications from Parties Included in Annex I to the Convention: In-depth Reviews of First and Second National Communications and Scheduling for Future Communications, FCCC/SBI/1998/INF.1.

41 Susan Subak (1997), 'Verifying Compliance with an Unmonitorable Climate Convention', *International Environmental Affairs*, 9: 2, 148–58.

42 National Communications from Parties Included in Annex I to the Convention.

43 Annex on Status of Preparation of National Communications from Parties not Included in Annex I to the Convention, FCCC/ SBI/1998/INF.3/Add.1

44 See for example, the national energy plans in India and China; the presentations made at the NGO workshop on a New Initiative for North-South Dialogue on Climate Change: Good Practices, Technology Innovation and New Partnerships for Sustainable Development, Bonn, 22 October 1997; and Gupta (1997), *The Climate Change Convention and Developing Countries*, 58–64.

45 Bert Bolin (1998), 'The Kyoto Negotiations on Climate Change: A Science Perspective', *Science*, 279, 330–31.

46 Review of the Implementation of the Commitments and of other Provisions of the Convention, FCCC/CP/1998/11.

47 Anon. (1997), 'A Warming World', *The Economist*, 28 June, 49– 50; 'Clinton Presents Emissions Plan'.

48 Subak (1997), 'Verifying Compliance with an Unmonitorable Climate Convention', 148–58.

49 '. . . it is difficult to identify trends in the flow of financial resources and the transfer of technology', Para 44 of the Review of the Implementation of the Commitments and of other Provisions of the Convention, FCCC/CP/1998/11; see also Wanna Tanunchaiwatana (1998), 'Climate Change and Technology Transfer', *Linkages Journal*, 3: 4, 7–8, at 8.

50 See, for example, the Netherlands Climate Change Studies Assistance Programme, financed by the Ministry for Development Co-operation.

51 See, for example, Joyeeta Gupta (1998), 'Leadership in the Climate Regime: Inspiring the Commitment of Developing Countries in the Post-Kyoto Phase' *Review of European Community and International Environmental Law*, 7: 2, 178–88. See also Per Mickwitz (1998), *Positive Measures: Panacea or Placebo in International Environmental Agreements* (Copenhagen: Nord Environment, Nordic Council of Ministers) at 68.

52 See M. Albright, speech at Earth Day to combat climate change, held in the Museum of Natural History, 21 April 1998.

53 Anon. (1998), 'Planned and Ongoing AIJ pilot Projects', *Quarterly Magazine on Joint Implementation*, 4: 4 (December), 14.

54 See, for example, E5 (1998), 'Policy priorities for 1998', European Business Council for a Sustainable Energy Future, press release, 25 February 1998; and E5 (1999), Profile, press release, 16 February 1999.

55 See, for example, BP (1998), *Climate Change Principles*, company brochure; Mike Wriglesworth, 'Integrating Climate Policy: Costs and Opportunities—The BP-Amoco Response', paper presented at the Second Policy Workshop organized by the European Forum on Integrated Environmental Assessment, and hosted by the Fondazione Eni Enrico Mattei, Milan, 5 March 1999.

56 Michael Brandt (1998), 'Royal Dutch Shell Takes Action on Climate Change', *Quarterly on Joint Implementation*, 4: 4, 13.

57 Eurogas (1997), *Natural Gas and Climate Change Policy: the European Gas Industry's View*, company brochure.

58 J. T. Houghton, L. G. Meira Filho, J. Bruce, H. Lee, B. A. Callander, E. Haites, N. Harris, and K. Maskell (eds.) (1995), *Climate Change 1994: Radiative Forcing of Climate Change and an Evaluation of the IPCC IS92 Emission Scenarios* (Cambridge: Cambridge University Press), 22.

59 Bolin (1998), 'The Kyoto negotiations on Climate Change', 330– 31.

60 See presentation of Bill Hare, 'Blue-prints for Climate Policy: Some Key Issues', Second Policy Workshop organized by the European Forum on Integrated Environmental Assessment, and hosted by the Fondazione Eni Enrico Mattei, Milan, 6 March, 1999.

61 Ibid.

62 See Gupta (1997), *The Climate Change Convention and Developing Countries*, 155.

63 Yamin (1998), 'The Kyoto Protocol', 118.

64 See, for example, Yamin (1998), 'The Kyoto Protocol', 119, and Hare, 'Blue-prints for Climate Policy'.

65 See Article 3.3 of the KPFCCC.

66 See Yamin (1998), 'The Kyoto Protocol', 119.

67 See John Lanchbery (1997), *Briefing Paper for the Eighth Session of the AGBM: Some Practical Considerations for a Protocol* (London: Vertic), 97/5; Hare, 'Blue-prints for Climate Policy'.

68 Bolin (1998), 'The Kyoto Negotiations on Climate Change'.

69 Michael Grubb (1998), 'International Emissions Trading under the Kyoto Protocol: Core Issues in Implementation', *Review of European Community and International Environmental Law*, 7: 2, 140–46.

70 John Lanchbery (1998), 'Verifying Compliance with the Kyoto Protocol', *Review of European Community and International Environmental Law*, 7: 2, 170–75.

71 Hare, 'Blue-prints for Climate Policy'.

72 See Gupta (1997), *The Climate Change Convention and Developing Countries*, 187–90.

73 Article 24 of the KPFCCC.

74 See the web site of the Climate Change Secretariat at <http:// www.unfccc.de/fccc/conv/signdate.htm>.

75 See, for example, the position of the Netherlands in the document VROM (1998), *Netherlands National Communication 1998 (Update)* (The Hague: Ministry of Housing, Spatial Planning and Environment), 17.

76 See, for example, EU Council Conclusions, March 1997.

77 'Clinton Presents Emissions Plan'.

78 See J. Gupta and N. van der Grijp (1999), 'Leadership in the Climate Change Regime: The European Union in the Looking Glass: Mirror, Mirror on the Wall, Who is the Leader of Us All ?', *International Journal on Environment and Pollution*, 11.

79 See M. Albright, Earth Day speech to combat climate change.

80 Clinton (1997), remarks by the President on Global Climate Change.

81 Peter H. Sand (1992), 'Summary Report on the Survey', in Sand (ed.), *The Effectiveness of International Environmental Agreements: A Survey of Existing Legal Instruments* (Cambridge: Grotius Publications), 8–18; Harold K. Jacobson and Edith B. Weiss (1995), 'Strengthening Compliance with International Environmental Accords: Preliminary Observations from a Collaborative Project', *Global Governance*, 1: 2, 119–48. See also Robert O. Keohane (1993), 'The Effectiveness of International Environmental Institutions', in P. M. Haas, R. O. Keohane, and M. A. Levy (eds.), *Institutions for the Earth* (Cambridge, MA: MIT Press), 3–24.

82 Report on the UN Conference on Environment and Development, Rio de Janeiro, 3–14 June 1992, UN doc. A/CONF.151/26/Rev.1 (Vols. I–III).

83 See Patrick Michaels's comment cited in anon. (1998), 'Hostility and Frustration Surface as Little Progress is Made at Conference of the Parties', *Climate Watch Brief*, 5–21, published by GCC; available at <http://www.globalclimate.org/CWATCH.htm>.

84 La Rovere (1999), 'Stalemate in Climate Protection'.

85 Cited in Peter H. Stone (1997), 'The Heat's On', *National Journal*, 29/30, 1505.

86 IPCC (1998), *The Regional Impacts of Climate Change: An Assessment of Vulnerability* (Cambridge: Cambridge University Press).

87 Thomas C. Shelling (1997), 'The Cost of Combating Global Warming: Facing the Trade-Offs', *Foreign Affairs*, 76: 6, 8–14.

88 Anil Agarwal and Sunita Narain (1998), *The Atmospheric Rights of all People on the Earth* (Delhi: Centre for Science and Environment). See their website at <http://www.cseindia.org>.

89 Tom Spencer (1998), *Climate Change and the G8: A Guide for Parliamentarians* (London: Globe Papers).

90 Richard N. Cooper (1998), 'Toward a Real Global Warming Treaty', *Foreign Affairs*, 77: 2, 66–79.

91 Bodansky (1993), 'The United Nations Framework Convention on Climate Change', 513.

92 See, for example, Hermann E. Ott (1998), 'Emissions Trading in the Kyoto Protocol: Finished and Unfinished Business', *Linkages Journal*, 3: 4, 18–21, and Fanny Missfeldt (1998), 'Flexibility Mechanisms: Which Path to Take After Kyoto?', *Review of European Community and International Environmental Law*, 7: 2, 128–39.

93 See, for example, Catrinus J. Jepma, Wytze P. van der Gaast, and Edwin Woerdman (1998), *The Compatibility of Flexible Instruments under the Kyoto Protocol* (Bilthoven: National Research Programme on Global Air Pollution and Climate Change), Report no. 410 200 026; Missfeldt (1998), 'Flexibility Mechanisms'.

94 See, for instance, S. Humphreys, Y. Sokona, and J.-P. Thomas (1998), 'Equity in the CDM', *Linkages Journal*, 3: 4, 26.

95 See 'Spencer Welcomes a Climate Protocol with Leaks', press release, 11 December 1997, GLOBE EU, Brussels (GLOBE EU is an all-party association of 96 members of the European Parliament); available at <http://globeint.org/html-europe/general/pr-11-12-97.htm>.

96 J. Gupta (1996), 'The Precautionary Principle and Public Participation with Special Reference to the UN Framework Convention on Climate Change', in David Freestone and Ellen Hey (eds.), *Precautionary Principle: Book of Essays* (The Hague: Kluwer Law International), 231–47.

97 Gupta and van der Grijp (1999), 'Leadership in the Climate Change Regime'.

98 Gupta (1997), *The Climate Change Convention and Developing Countries*, 188–90.

99 Cited in the US Climate Action Network Citizen's Update, 16 January 1998 <http://www.geocities.com/RainForest/6783/KyotoUSCANresp.html>.

100 Jon A. Krosnick and Penny S. Visser (1998), *American Public Opinion on Global Warming*, 2nd edition of an Internet publication of the Departments of Psychology and Political Science, Ohio State University.

101 Memorandum dated 17 September 1997 from the Mellman Group to the World Wildlife Fund containing the Summary of Public Opinion Research Findings.

102 Anon. (1997), 'Japan: Positive Leadership from COP 3 Chair Required', *ECO, Tokyo Special Edition*, 8–9 November.

103 See, for example, Gupta and van der Grijp (1999), 'Leadership in the Climate Change Regime'.

104 Willet Kempton (1997), 'How the Public Views Climate Change', *Environment*, 39: 9, 12–21.

105 Stone (1997), 'The Heat's On', 1505.

106 See anon. (1998), Hostility and Frustration Surface as Little Progress is Made at Conference of the Parties'.

107 Cited in Stone (1997), 'The Heat's On', 1505.

108 These interviews have been conducted by Joyeeta Gupta and Nicolien van der Grijp in the context of a European Commission DG-XII project on European Leadership in the climate change issue.

109 See Gupta (1997), *The Climate Change Convention and Developing Countries*.

110 Anon. (1998), 'Buenos Aires Conference Finishes with Clear Steps to the Future', press release, 14 November 1998, Globe International Secretariat, Brussels.

111 See, for example, Yamin (1998), 'The Kyoto Protocol', 113–27; La Rovere (1999), 'Stalemate in Climate Protection'.

112 See, for example, Anil Agarwal and Sunita Narain (1998), *The Atmospheric Rights of All People on Earth* (Delhi: Centre for Science and Environment), Anil Agarwal and Sunita Narain (1998), *The Kyoto Protocol: What it Says?* (Delhi: Centre for Science and Environment), Anil Agarwal and Sunita Narain (1998), *Politics in the Post-Kyoto World* (Delhi: Centre for Science and Environment).

113 Cooper (1998), 'Toward a Real Global Warming Treaty', 66, argues that, 'whatever one thinks of Kyoto in terms of environmental politics, the troubling fact remains that its underlying approach is bound to fail'. He argues instead for policies and measures.

114 See, for example, the documents produced by the Global Climate Coalition.

115 See, for example, Bolin (1998), 'The Kyoto Negotiations on Climate Change', 330–31.

116 Clinton (1997), remarks by the President on Global Climate Change

Liability and Compensation for Ship-Source Marine Pollution: The International System

Edgar Gold

Introduction

In an increasingly environmentally-conscious world, ship-source marine pollution has, for a long time, been singled out for special attention. This attention is hardly commensurate with its actual contribution to marine pollution, which, today, is considered to be about 12 per cent of the total.[1] In other words, it is land-sourced marine pollution that is today the major problem. This was already recognized a decade ago in an important preparatory document for the United Nations Conference on Environment and Development (UNCED), in which the UN Secretary-General stated:

Dramatic improvements have been made in controlling oil pollution in the past decade owing to the regulation of ship discharges under MARPOL 1973/1978 . . . Accidental spills are relatively isolated geographically so that, aside from tar balls, transient effects in the vicinity of accidents and more chronic conditions in localized sites in some parts of the world, **petroleum pollution does not now represent a severe threat to marine habitats and organisms.** However, since accidental spills cannot be totally avoided, contingency planning and effective response action are essential.[2]

This was also recognized in the deliberations of UNCED itself in Rio de Janeiro in 1992.[3] However, nothing focuses policy-makers' and legislators' attention more directly than a marine disaster. When pollution is involved, a 'media-event' is often the result. The media love maritime accidents, which are gripping and exciting and provide great video images—permitting reporters, totally untrained in maritime matters, to wax eloquently at great length on what has happened—and which can often be used to embarrass government officials and politicians. If oil pollution is involved, all the better!

On the other hand, as strange as it may seem, marine pollution accidents also have positive effects! The former Secretary-General of the International Maritime Organization (IMO), C. P. Srivastava, mentioned on more than one occasion that without the *Torrey Canyon* disaster there probably would have been no IMO or any of its important pollution conventions, and that without the *Amoco Cadiz* oil spill there would probably be no Standards of Training (STCW) or new Salvage Conventions.[4] In fact,

national legislative responses to marine pollution accidents are often directly attributable to the repercussions, political and otherwise, from such accidents. For example, many states, Australia, Canada, and the UK among these, revised their marine pollution legislation after the *Torrey Canyon* accident in 1967. Canada's Shipping Act was again extensively revised after the *Arrow* disaster in 1971, and France revised its legislation extensively after the *Amoco Cadiz* grounding in 1978. In the more recent past, the United States reacted strongly after *Exxon Valdez*; Australia after the *Kirki* and *Iron Baron* disasters; the North African states after the *Kharg V* spill; the Malacca Straits states after the *Nagasaki Spirit* and *Maersk Navigator* collisions; and the UK, again, after the *Braer* and *Sea Empress* groundings. Action at the IMO's international level was commensurately speeded up.

In other words, the periodic serious marine pollution accident appears to have indirect positive benefits for the marine environment by tightening up regulations, focusing attention, stimulating pollution control and related scientific research, and generally raising environmental consciousness in an industry that, despite the IMO's guiding principle of 'safer ships and cleaner seas', has concentrated more on the former than the latter. All of this is very good providing that revisions of laws and updating of responses occur at the international level and are then quickly implemented at the national level. It is hardly necessary to stress that shipping is an international industry that can only be regulated with globally accepted rules developed through intergovernmental organizations (IGOs). This approach ensures uniform solutions expressed in terms of international maritime law.

Unilateralism in an International Setting

Problems arise when states do not implement what they have agreed to internationally or, perhaps even worse, if they seek to take a unilateral approach that is often not based on a full appreciation of the repercussions of such action. The reasons for such action may, at times, be perfectly understandable. If a state has been at the receiving end of a serious pollution accident, there is bound to be reaction, and often overreaction. Politicians will be requested 'to do something' and the international system will be regarded, often incorrectly, as inadequate, ponderous, and too complex. This is exacerbated by the fact that ship-owners do not enjoy a very good public image. The shipping industry is perceived by the public and, thus, by many politicians as a polluting industry which reaps huge profits, operates sub-standard ships under dubious flags crewed by down-trodden Third World citizens, 'fixes' freight rates, and is generally careless about the environment. Although there is a minority in the industry which conforms to all or some of these perceptions, in the modern context such a view is both harmful and erroneous. In general, shipping subscribes to the IMO's 'safer ships and cleaner seas' principle and goes about its business as an essential service to international commerce. Nevertheless, when a serious accident occurs, the temptation to achieve some rapid national political points through unilateral action is there.

This is most easily illustrated by an examination of what has occurred in the USA in the past decade. It provides a very important lesson for any state considering unilateral action.[5] The US position is the result of overreaction to the *Exxon Valdez* disaster, one of the more serious and spectacular marine accidents in recent history, which occurred in US waters, causing serious environmental damage.[6] Direct results of this reaction were the wholesale condemnation of US and international shipping operations, especially the tanker industry, the discarding of international agreements, which the USA had been instrumental in establishing, and new draconian legislation in the form of the US Oil Pollution Act of 1990 (OPA '90).[7] This action resulted in international environmental law, especially as it relates to the compensation and liability for oil pollution regimes, being divided into two major groups—the United States v. the Rest! Unfortunately, this split may well result in the USA generally, and the marine environment specifically, both losing. In addition, there is evidence that this position has seriously affected US credibility in international negotiations. This is of obvious concern to the US Administration, the US State Department, the Maritime Law Association of the United States, and the US and international shipping and marine insurance industries, but, apparently, to few others. The US Coast Guard, which fought valiantly against OPA '90,[8] is now in the unenviable position of having to enforce it.

Shipping: An International Industry

The *Exxon Valdez* grounding was, of course, a very serious accident, and there is no intention to suggest that this was not so. Furthermore, there is considerable merit in the US contention that there are too many serious tanker accidents, that there are too many sub-standard, elderly tankers in operation, and that a serious or catastrophic marine pollution accident will place a severe environmental and economic burden on the coastal state which happens to be the victim. Recent accidents, such as those involving the *Aegean Sea, Haven, Nagasaki Spirit-Maersk Navigator, Mega Borg, Braer, Kirki, Kharg V, Iron Baron,* and *Sea Empress,* lend further credence to this view and, at the same time, provide little comfort to the international shipping industry and their liability insurers. On the other hand, it must also be borne in mind that over 1.4 billion tons of oil are moved annually by some 3000 tankers over an average distance of some 4700 nautical miles and that 99.9995 per cent of this cargo is delivered safely.[9] Yet everyone, regardless of interest, would prefer that pollution incidents be prevented in the first place. In fact, there is no question that much more needs to be done to prevent shipping accidents and resulting pollution. On the other hand, there is no doubt that ship-owners are principally interested in delivering the cargoes entrusted to them without incident. They operate business enterprises that seek a reasonable return on very high investments in a very competitive business which has, especially in recent years, experienced a severe slump in earnings. This recession resulted in many shipping companies going out of business. The oil trade was not spared and too many tankers were chasing fewer and fewer cargoes.[10] In such a competitive market those who spill oil cargoes do not remain in business for long, and even minor spills today often involve costly litigation, very high fines, and cancelled charters. Valuable vessels may be out of service for extended periods or, in serious cases, forever.

As already suggested, shipping is an international industry and, as such, has to be regulated internationally. As a result, the IMO has attempted, ever since its founding in 1958, to balance the various interests involved under its guiding principle of 'towards safer ships and cleaner seas', as already indicated above. At the base of this principle is the undeniable fact that shipping is an essential component of international trade and commerce and that, in the carriage of goods by sea, certain risks are involved. This risk is especially present in the carriage of pollutant cargoes, such as oil and oil products and hazardous and noxious substances that are potentially harmful to the marine environment. As a result, on account of increasing global environmental consciousness, the environmental risk factor has become of almost paramount importance for the maritime industry and its principal global agency, the IMO.[11] The IMO's states membership, including the United States, recognized long ago that an international industry, with transnational trading links, required a uniform international, rather than a unilateral national, regulatory system. If any doubt existed about this fact, it was laid to rest with the conclusion of the United Nations Convention on the Law of the Sea 1982 (UNCLOS), which recognized not only the need for 'generally accepted international regulations' for shipping and navigation, but also that the IMO would be the 'competent international organization' to develop these rules.[12] As a result, the IMO has developed some 50 international conventions, protocols, and related agreements concerned with 'safer ships and cleaner seas'. These treaties have been carefully prepared and negotiated, are widely accepted, and form today what can be called the basis of a significant sector of modern 'international maritime law'.[13]

The International Marine Pollution Liability and Compensation System: Phase I

For almost three decades a reasonable international liability and compensation system for oil-pollution damage has been in operation. Protection and indemnity insurers (P & I Clubs) cover their ship-owner/charterer members for about 30 different risks related to ship operation to a theoretically unlimited ceiling. This system is supported through a complex arrangement of reinsurance and through the International Group of P & I Clubs, which has access to reserves in excess of $US 2 billion. An exception to unlimited coverage relates to oil pollution, with a limitation ceiling of $US 500 million, which, under special circumstances, can be raised to $US 700 million.[14] This is part of a mutual liability system that has worked extremely well for over a century. It spreads the risk evenly across the world fleet, and all ship-owners benefit. In addition, the coverage provided appears to be quite sufficient for all but the most catastrophic accidents. However, P & I coverage for oil pollution damage claims has certain limitations as unlimited coverage for catastrophic accidents is not insurable.

Yet it appears that the mutuality of P & I coverage, and the beneficial service it offers to US and international shipping, has been either not sufficiently considered or ignored by those who have created OPA '90. Instead, OPA '90 attempts to provide coverage for the most catastrophic accident projections possible and, as a result, isolates the USA from a very successful, generally adequate, international liability system. As has been observed: 'In its rush to enact responsive legislation, Congress may have unwittingly compromised its original goal—to provide a simple, uniform program to ensure prompt compensation for oil pollution damage.'[15] Although P & I coverage for ship operational liability is technically unlimited—marine pollution claims being the exception as already noted—all marine risks are subject to the unique maritime law principle of limitation of liability which allows a ship-owner

to assess the total risk exposure in relation to the tonnage of the ship.[16] Such limitation would only be disallowed if the accident which gave rise to the claims put forward would be found by a court to have occurred with the 'actual fault and privity' of,[17] or 'intentionally and recklessly and with knowledge that loss would result',[18] by the ship-owner. In other words, limitation is another well-developed example of an international maritime law principle which attempts to balance risk exposure with transportation costs.

Similar principles apply also to ship-source oil pollution, which, however, is subject to different international legal regimes. At this time two widely accepted international liability and compensation schemes are in existence. The first is the International Convention on Civil Liability for Oil Pollution Damage 1969 (CLC '69), in effect since 1975, and accepted by more than 100 states. The CLC governs the liability of ship-owners for oil pollution damage and makes them strictly liable within a limitation ceiling, also linked to the vessel's tonnage. The amounts recoverable under the scheme are calculated as Special Drawing Rights (SDRs) of the World Bank and are approximately $US 200 per ton, up to a ceiling of $US 18 million.

In cases where the CLC coverage is insufficient, another international scheme comes into operation. This is the International Convention on the Establishment of an International Fund for Compensation for Oil Pollution Damage 1971 (FUND), which entered into force in 1978 and has been accepted by more than 80 states. The FUND is financed by a state levy on oil imports in contracting states and is thus based on 'oil at risk at sea'. It is administered by the International Oil Pollution Compensation Fund (IOPCF), an international organization composed of FUND member states. The funds available are also calculated in SDRs, and are approximately $US 50 million, which, in special circumstances, can be increased to about US$ 100 million. As already indicated, it appears that these schemes provide adequate coverage for all but the most catastrophic oil spills. In fact, to date, only three out of 70 major claims handled by the IOPCF have exceeded available limits.[19] The IOPCF has an excellent reputation in settling claims. Its most difficult claim, the Tanio case, took two years for settlement, but most are settled within weeks or months. This must be compared to the lengthy litigious process in the USA. For example, the *Amoco Cadiz* claim took over ten years to settle! It should also be noted that states considering that the FUND upper limits may be insufficient for very serious accidents have the option to develop their own, additional, national schemes.[20]

In 1984 the IMO concluded two important protocols to the CLC and FUND Conventions.[21] The prime mover behind this initiative had been the USA, which had consistently stated that it could not accept the CLC or FUND regimes unless the upper limits were substantially raised. During the IMO Diplomatic Conference, the US delegation negotiated with considerable skill and achieved almost everything it wanted in terms of raised limits. The new CLC limits were raised to approximately $US 80 million and the FUND limits to about $US 250 million. In addition, coverage was extended into the Exclusive Economic Zone area. Although there was considerable resistance to these higher limits, the US delegation argued successfully that the higher limits could be achieved if they were based on the aggregated quantity of oil imported in three major contracting states. It thus became quite clear that the protocols, and therefore the FUND and CLC limits, could not be achieved unless the USA, the world's major oil importer, became a party! In the end the US position prevailed, particularly as the US delegation assured the Conference that the United States was determined to become a party to the protocols and, thus, the CLC and FUND. At the time the USA was congratulated on what was considered to be a remarkable environmental breakthrough! Following this IMO Conference many states prepared to accept the new protocols. There was considerable feeling that pollution liability, in an environmentally more conscious world, must be subject to a uniform global regime which would have upper limits, but which would, nevertheless, provide adequate coverage for all but the most extreme catastrophic pollution damage, and which would also be within the capacity of the international liability insurance market.

The US Unilateral Approach to Oil Pollution Liability and Compensation

Despite the US success at the IMO Conference, there was immediate difficulty at home. Firstly, the environmental movement was categorically opposed to anything but total and unlimited liability. This was consistent with the movement's 'polluter pays' principle, which ignores or disregards the realities of the shipping industry and its insurance market, as well as the fact that the USA is the most 'energy-hungry' nation on earth, importing over 400 million tons of oil per annum. Secondly, there was also opposition from several US states on the basis that a uniform, global agreement, entered into by the US Federal Government, would pre-empt the right of states to take their own action against polluting vessel owners. Perhaps even these difficulties could have been overcome had it not been for the *Exxon Valdez* and two later serious and highly publicized tanker disasters in US waters.[22] Once the Alaska spill occurred, the relatively modest opposition to the protocols strengthened significantly. The realities of

global uniformity, insurance market capacity, and the US dependence on the international tanker industry were quickly swept away, and the undertakings given by the US delegation at the 1984 IMO Conference were disregarded. Yet even at this stage a study, commissioned by the US Coast Guard, summed up the importance and viability of the international system by concluding that: 'The Protocols in concert with domestic legislation, offer unique solutions that cannot be found in domestic law alone, ... key provisions of the Protocols have met the tests set by the United States ... concerns over state pre-emption have been resolved at the state level.'[23]

It is neither necessary nor appropriate to provide much detail here of OPA '90. However, the process that led to it is of greater relevance. Even before OPA '90, the US law regarding oil pollution had never been straightforward and was often considered a veritable 'lawyer's paradise'. Usually US litigation costs in the area form a major part of the overall claim. Before OPA '90, liability for clean-up and removal costs for polluting substances discharged from vessels in US waters, which include the US 200-mile fishery zone and waters over the US Continental Shelf, had been covered principally by the Federal Water Pollution Control Act (FWPCA).[24] Under this act limited strict liability to the US Government for pollution damage and related costs was imposed on the owner or operator of a vessel which discharged polluting substances. The FWPCA required vessels trading to the USA to carry certificates of financial responsibility which indicated that the vessel was able to meet the requirements of the act. These certificates were normally issued by the vessel's P & I Club, as the act's requirements were considered to be generally equivalent to CLC requirements. In other words, for a number of years, although it was not party to the CLC, the USA tacitly, yet expressly, recognized it! However, the FWPCA did not cover questions of civil liability to those damaged by pollution. This was a significant difference from the CLC provisions. Under the FWPCA, if a discharge with resultant damage occurred, the plaintiff was required to establish culpable negligence in order to recover damages. As already indicated, the inherent weakness in the FWPCA was the need to litigate to establish liability under basic tort/delict principles. Under the CLC/ FUND system, as well as under the CLC and FUND protocols, it is generally sufficient to connect spill damage with a covered vessel and quantify the damage claim, which would then be quickly settled.

OPA '90 solves none of these problems and simply lays the groundwork for much lengthier litigation due to the increased stakes, as the act increases the ship-owner's liability from $US 150 to $US 1200 per ton. Even more litigious is the act's provision that, if a spill occurs due to the gross negligence, wilful misconduct, or violation of *any* federal operating or safety regulation, the spiller's liability is *unlimited*. It is suggested that, in most cases, it would be relatively easy to show *some*, even minor, breach of a federal rule. Accordingly, OPA '90 virtually ensures unlimited liability in many cases! Like the FWPCA, OPA '90 specifically does not pre-empt state laws, which may impose additional or other, heavier liabilities. Thus, if the battle is won at the federal level, the war may be lost in a state court! Recoverable damage categories have also been considerably broadened. Included are not only federal government clean-up claims, but state government claims and private claims for property damage, taking into account economic loss. Recovery for loss of profits or impairment of earning capacity is allowed for, even in cases where there is no provable property damage on the part of the private claimant. In order to ensure compliance, OPA '90 requires the filing of evidence of financial responsibility sufficient to meet the *maximum* 'limited' liabilities set out in the act. Furthermore, insurers providing such evidence are subject to direct legal actions not only for pollution removal costs, but for all pollution damages recoverable under the act.

Liability insurers have so far categorically rejected direct action, which is perceived, particularly by P & I Clubs, as exposing their mutual, non-profit systems to potentially unlimited liability. As a result, P & I Clubs have refused to issue certificates of financial responsibility in compliance with OPA '90 and continue to issue such certificates only with CLC limits. At present the International Association of Independent Tanker Owners (INTERTANKO), joined by the US Federal Government, is also involved in litigation against the state of Washington concerning OPA '90 interpretations. At the heart of the problem is the spectre of unlimited liability. It has been suggested that 'absolute liability subject to limitation may be insurable or reinsurable up to a point. Unlimited liability is not even theoretically insurable on the scale implied by the *Exxon Valdez* experience.'[25]

This difficulty is, to a great extent, a result of the US approach of calculating natural resource damage under OPA '90. Under this approach a system of 'contingent valuation methodology' (CVM) would quantify pollution damage in a much more complex and comprehensive way. Resulting damage assessments could reach billions of dollars in serious cases.[26] The assessment and quantification of realistic environmental damages remains a serious problem.[27] At this stage a 'new liability industry' providing vessel owners trading to US ports with 'Certificates of Financial Responsibility' (COFRs), acceptable to US authorities, has emerged.[28] These schemes are purport to provide the type of liability coverage guarantees required

under OPA '90. However, as there has been no serious oil spill in US waters since they went into operation, it remains to be seen how they will operate in practice.

The International Marine Pollution Liability and Compensation Regime: Phase II

At the IMO in 1992 the international maritime community completed a revised version of the failed 1984 CLC and FUND protocols, but without US support. The new 1992 protocols provide an increased level of liability for marine oil-pollution claims, as originally set out in the 1984 protocols and entered into force in 1996.[29] The CLC Protocol provides the following limits—expressed in Units of Account (UOA), i.e., the Special Drawing Rights (SDRs) of the World Bank system:

Vessels up to 5000 GT—3 million UOA
Vessels over 5000 GT—520 UOA/ton up to 59.7 million UOA.

The FUND Protocol can increase the maximum compensation available to 135 million UOA. However, in cases where at least three FUND members have received at least 600 million tons of contributing oil in the previous year, the limit may be increased to 200 million UOA. In other words, the international system now provides a relatively easily accessible oil-pollution compensation regime providing funds with an upper limit in excess of $US 250 million. Barring catastrophic disasters, this regime should be adequate for all marine oil pollution incidents.

Also in 1996 a new International Convention Relating to the Liability for the Carriage of Hazardous and Noxious Substances at Sea (HNS Convention) was concluded at the IMO. There has been concern for some time that the concentration on oil pollution had neglected pollution damage from other substances, which, in some cases, might be even more harmful to the marine environment than hydrocarbons. A first attempt to conclude an HNS Convention in 1984 failed, and after almost 12 years of further work the 1996 HNS Convention was successfully concluded. It is not yet in force. It basically follows the 'two-tier' liability system developed under the CLC and FUND schemes for oil pollution.[30] The regime provides the following coverage:

Tier I: Vessels up to 2000 GT—10 million UOA
         Vessels up to 50,000 GT—1500 UOA/ton in addition
         Vessels over 50,000 GT—360 UOA/ ton in addition, up to
         100 million UOA
Tier II: International HNS Fund providing compensation up to
         250 million UOA if Tier I is insufficient or unavailable.

Conclusions

There is also ample evidence that the combination of high liability limits, more extensive national, regional, and port state enforcement systems, and commensurate high fines and detentions and delays have resulted in much-improved tanker operational standards, better training systems, and, overall, greatly increased environmental consciousness in the shipping industry.[31] This was confirmed by the UN Secretary-General in the report already cited in the introduction, which confirmed that 'dramatic improvements have been made in controlling oil pollution in the past decade owing to the regulation of ship discharges'.[32]

This is not to suggest that there should be a lessening of concern or vigilance in this area. It was indicated at the outset that there are still too many sub-standard vessels in operation and that the tanker accident record does not provide a real sense of achievement. The human-error cause of most of these accidents is of particular concern to the industry, and there is ample evidence that tougher measures have positive results. However, there are some basic economic problems within the shipping industry, especially the bulk oil sector, that continue to contribute to the 'availability' of sub-standard ships in the global transportation markets. There are two very basic economic reasons: firstly, as already indicated, international oil and bulk freight rates are so low that it is simply not good business for an owner to invest in new building; secondly, although some of the international oil companies are now much more careful about the vessels they charter to carry their cargoes, many charterers are not. Most oil receiving, trading, and refining charterers, as well as bulk commodity charterers, are still too 'bottom-line oriented'—i.e., they will charter the cheapest vessel offered. That vessel is often sub-standard. Also that type of business keeps freight rates artificially low and, in turn, keeps good owners from building new vessels.

In other words, the US reaction or overreaction has a very sound basis of concern, which should not be dismissed. Yet it has to be remembered that the *Exxon Valdez* was a modern state-of-the-art 'very large crude carrier' (VLCC), crewed by highly qualified individuals and owned by the largest corporation in the world, which apparently could absorb a $US 5 billion-plus loss without too much effort. Instead it could easily have involved a 'fly-by-night' VLCC, about 23 years old, poorly maintained, with its eleventh owner, which happens to be a filing cabinet in the Bahamas, and which would disappear at the same rate as the ship! Yet the pollution results from an accident involving either vessel could be similar. However, the sub-standard vessel is much more likely to be involved in an accident. It is in this area that much greater effort has to be concentrated, instead of seeking unrealistic compensation coverage for remote catastrophic accidents. There must be much better voluntary efforts by charterers, importers, and exporters to hire better vessels, even at greater cost. Furthermore, if this sector of the industry will not do this then it is inevitable that much stronger government action must result. If charterers, especially oil companies, would take this step, then most sub-standard vessels would disappear from the seas virtually overnight!

Nevertheless, there is no doubt that the US approach is attractive to policy makers in other states when faced with a difficult pollution problem and an environmentally sensitive electorate, and when it does not have much knowledge of the internationally shipping sector, which appears remote and complex and is, often, conveniently foreign. Added to this is the attractive 'polluter pays' principle, which is much more easily imposed on an international shipping industry than a local polluting industry. Australia, Canada, and the UK have all, in the last decade, experienced serious oil pollution accidents that resulted in searching inquiries into the tanker shipping industry.[33] Although all three states have decided to continue to support the international system, the inquiries held all revealed serious shortcomings in maritime safety and marine pollution control and concluded that further serious pollution incidents are simply unacceptable.

It is hoped that the STCW revisions, the entry into force of the International Safety Management Code (ISM Code) in 1998, and the expansion of the port state control inspection systems will further tighten the enforcement net to ensure maximum compliance with international regulations. It is essential that the uniform international marine pollution compensation system, which is best suited to spread liabilities as evenly as possible among all interested parties, should continue. If the upper limits of such compensation are not considered adequate, then negotiations must take place at the international level to increase these. There must also be more concentration on prevention than on compensation. Whether this is achieved by addressing the serious human-error problems, which are the major cause of maritime accidents, or through attempts to drive sub-standard vessels from the seas, or both, it should be done through a uniform system and not through unilateral action driven by considerations harmful to the health of the maritime industry on which global trade and prosperity depend.

Notes and References

This is a revised and expanded version of a paper presented at the 3rd International Conference on Maritime Law, Piraeus, Greece, May 1998. I would also like to acknowledge the very helpful comments on the first draft of this paper received from Professor Bruce Davis of the Institute of Antarctic and Southern Ocean Studies, University of Tasmania, Hobart, Australia, and Dr Douglas Brubaker, Senior Research Fellow at the Fridtjof Nansen Institute, Oslo, Norway.

1. International Chamber of Shipping (1993), *Shipping and the Environment: A Code of Practice* (London: ICS), 5; see also, A. Boyle and P. Birnie (1992), *International Law and the Environment* (Oxford: Clarendon Press), 263, 300.

2. *Law of the Sea—Protection and Preservation of the Marine Environment.* Report of the UN Secretary-General, UN Doc. A/44/461, 18 September 1989. Emphasis added.

3. United Nations (1993), *Agenda 21: Programme of Action for Sustainable Development—The Rio Declaration on Environment and Development* (New York: UN), Ch.17.

4. International Convention on Standards of Training, Certification and Watchkeeping, 1978 (STCW 1978) and International Convention on Salvage, 1989 (SALVAGE 1989).

5. Edgar Gold, 'Marine Pollution Liability after *Exxon Valdez*: The US 'All or Nothing' Lottery!', *Journal of Maritime Law & Commerce*, 91/22, 423.

6. Although recent studies now consider the actual extent of longer-term damage to be far less than predicted. See, for example, Richard Stone, 'Dispute over 'Exxon Valdez' Cleanup Data gets Messy', *Science*, 93/260, 749.

7. Pub.L. 101–380, 104 Stat. 484 (1990).

8. See Report prepared for the US Coast Guard by Temple, Barker, and Sloane, *The International Oil Spill Protocols: Should the United States Ratify?*, 2 October 1988, Pt. II.

9. James Anderson, 'Clean Seas/Oil Pollution: An Independent Tanker Owner's View', 6th National Marine Conference, Vancouver, October 1990.

10. Tanker rates dropped again in the latter part of 1998. In the first half of the year VLCC rates to the Far East were Worldscale 70–80 ($US 35,000–40,000), but these dropped in the second half to Worldscale 50–55 ($US 25,000–28,000). Rajesh Joshi, 'Building on Strong Foundations', *Lloyd's List 'Maritime Asia'*, October 1998, 55.

11. Edgar Gold (1998), *Gard Handbook on Marine Pollution*, 2nd edn. (Arendal: Assuranceforeningen Gard), Ch. 1.

12. United Nations Convention on the Law, 1982, Parts VII and XII.

13. Edgar Gold (ed.) (1991), *Maritime Affairs: A World Handbook*, 2nd edn. (London: Longman), Chs. 4 & 5.

14. See, for example, Simon Poland and Tony Rooth (1996), *Gard Handbook on P & I Insurance*, 3rd edn. (Arendal: Assuranceforeningen Gard).

15. Thomas Wagner, 'The Oil Pollution Act of 1990: An Analysis', *Journal of Maritime Law & Commerce*, 90/21, 587.

16. As codified in the International Convention Relating to the Limitation of Liability of Owners of Sea-Going Ships 1957 and the International Convention on Liability for Maritime Claims 1976. Although the USA has accepted neither of these widely accepted conventions, the USA instead developed its own limitation of liability regime, the Limitation of Liability Act, 46 App. USC. Para.183.

17. Under the 1957 Limitation Convention.

18. Under the 1976 LLMC Convention.

19. The *Tanio* (France, 1980), *Haven* (Italy, 1991), and *Braer* (UK, 1996) incidents.

20. For example, Canada has developed such a scheme. Under the Canadian Ship-Source Oil Pollution Fund an additional amount of approximately $CA175 million is available to 'top up' the claims fund.

21. Protocol of 1984 to Amend the International Convention on Civil Liability for Oil Pollution Damage 1969; and Protocol of 1984 to Amend the International Convention on the Establishment of an International Fund for Compensation for Oil Pollution Damage 1971.

22. The *American Trader* accident off California and the *Mega Borg* explosion in the Gulf of Mexico.

23. See Temple, Barker, and Sloane, *The International Oil Spill Protocols*.

24. USC, Para.1251, as amended.

25. Protocol of 1992 to Amend the International Convention on the Establishment of an International Fund for Compensation for Oil Pollution Damage 1971 (CLC PROT 1992) has been accepted by 34 states; and Protocol of 1992 to Amend the International Convention on Civil Liability for Oil Pollution Damage 1969 (CLC PROT 1992) has been accepted by 32 states. States parties to the revised CLC and FUND regimes include almost all the major maritime states with the exception of the USA.

26. Ran Hettena, President, Maritime Overseas Corporation and Chairman, Gard P & I Club. Cited in Middleton and Lyons (1990), 'An Industry Pressganged?', *Seatrade Business Review*, May/June, 4.

27. National Oceanic and Atmospheric Administration, 'Natural Resource Damage Assessments under Oil Pollution Act of 1990', 15 CFR Chapter IX. Federal Register, vol. 58, no. 10, 15 January 1993, 4601.

28. An attempt to address this problem was made at the CMI's XXXVth International Conference in Sydney, which produced the 'CMI Guidelines on Oil Pollution Damage'.

29. Among these schemes are SIGCo, Shoreline Mutual, ARVAK, ISL, and COFRSURE. Amongst these schemes are SIGCo, Shoreline Mutual, ARVAK, ISL, and COFRSURE.

30. See Gold, *Gard Handbook on Marine Pollution*, 242–3.

31. John R. Dudley, Barry J. Scott, and Edgar Gold (1994), *Towards Safer Ships & Cleaner Seas—A Handbook for Modern Tankship Operations* (Arendal: Assuranceforeningen Gard), 509.

32. Report of the UN Secretary-General, 'Law of the Sea-Protection and Preservation of the Marine Environment' U.N.Doc.A/44/461, 18 September 1989.

33. Canada: Public Review Panel on Tanker Safety and Marine Spills Response Capability, *Protecting our Waters, Final Report* (Ottawa: Government of Canada, 1990); Australia: Parliament of the Commonwealth of Australia, *Ships of Shame: Inquiry into Ship Safety*, Report from the House of Representatives Standing Committee on Transport, Communications, and Infrastructure (Canberra: Government Publishing Service, 1992); United Kingdom: UK Government, *Safer Ships and Cleaner Seas*, Report of Lord Donaldson's Inquiry into the Prevention of Pollution from Merchant Shipping (London: UK Government, 1994).

Biodiversity: Between Diverse International Arenas

G. Kristin Rosendal

Introduction

The large number of international environmental agreements has been negotiated without explicit measures to resolve the frequently overlapping and conflicting goals of economic regimes.[1] The relative strength between environmental and economic regimes, whether in terms of power and interest structure or in terms of normative persuasion, has yet to be put to any ultimate test. This article examines the interrelationship between one environmental and one trade-related regime, dealing with biodiversity and intellectual property rights respectively.

In response to the rapid loss of species and ecosystem decay world-wide, the Convention on Biological Diversity (CBD) was agreed to in Rio in 1992. Two years later the Trade-Related Aspects of Intellectual Property Rights (TRIPs)—a formal agreement under the World Trade Organization (WTO)—was established. How do the functional scopes of these institutions overlap and what are the implications for the implementation of the objectives of the CBD?[2] The following analysis will show that the overlap between the CBD and TRIPs concerns both diverging regulations pertaining to the same issue-area and also that the two regimes build on diverging norms and principles.[3] The CBD as a global environmental treaty is concerned with conservation and equitable sharing of benefits derived from the world's biological resources. The TRIPs, being part of a trade regime, resents policies that obstruct trade liberalization in any sector—including biotechnology, which is based on the utilization of biological resources. These overlaps may have negative implications for implementation of the CBD on account of asymmetrical strength in the relationship between the two institutions.[4] Institutions geared towards issues with significant effects for security or economy are likely to be given precedence—for instance, by being equipped with stronger compliance mechanisms by the negotiating states.

Three aspects of institutional overlap will be discussed: norms, regulations, and relative strength. First, the different normative approaches to property rights to genetic material inherent in the CBD and TRIPs will be examined. This provides a picture of the background for the institutional overlap. The next section presents the explicit regulations of the two regimes pertaining to the issue-area. The remaining sections deal with the subject of relative strength. The first of these examines the role of norms in the formation of the biodiversity regime. I then discuss the outlook for implementing the objectives of the CBD in light of the institutional overlap. Finally, the international efforts to deal with institutional overlap are presented. This includes a judgement of the strengths of the regulatory and compliance mechanisms of the CBD and TRIPs respectively.

Institutional Overlap: The Role of Diverging Norms

The issue of biological diversity constitutes one of today's greatest challenges, for two main reasons:

- First, the concern with biodiversity stems largely from our increasing awareness that, viewed against the natural average rate, the current rate of species extinction is extremely high.[5]
- Second, as the new biotechnologies greatly enhance the potential utility areas of the world's genetic resources, economic incentives to conserve biological diversity increase.[6]

These developments have had a profound impact on the understanding of property rights to genetic resources—a question on which the CBD and TRIPs display basic normative differences. TRIPs seeks to bolster and harmonize intellectual property rights (IPR) systems, such as patent legislation, in all technological fields world-wide—including biotechnology. The CBD advocates national sovereignty to, and equitable sharing of benefits from, utilization of genetic resources. The background for these diverging views is described here.

The main objective of the CBD is threefold:

- 'to ensure conservation of biological diversity[7] and
- sustainable use of its components; and

- to promote a fair and equitable sharing of the benefits arising out of utilization of genetic resources, including by appropriate access to genetic resources and by appropriate transfer of relevant technologies, and by appropriate funding' (Article 1).

The normative orientation towards equitable sharing, which is a central trait of the CBD, builds on the understanding that costs and benefits of biodiversity have long been asymmetrically distributed—and that this situation needs to be remedied if anyone at all will benefit in the end. The CBD stipulates that those who have the ultimate responsibility of carrying the costs of conservation and sustainable use of the resources must also be given a fair and equitable share in the benefits derived from this use. The major bulk of species diversity is found in the tropical countries of the South. The North possesses the technological strength to exploit the resources commercially and the economic strength to ensure private rights and royalties through patents.

The contrast between the normative approach of the CBD and TRIPs can be traced back to the opposing views on the merits of patents within the field of biological material. A patent is a contract between researcher and society—the researcher making their invention public, rather than keeping it a secret, and society offering royalties for using the invention for a limited period of time. The idea is to provide incentives for innovative research by compensating for the time and costs going into research. The basic principle of the TRIPs agreement on intellectual property rights is to enhance trade liberalization by harmonizing national patent legislation systems.

The economic need for patenting, as seen from the northern biotechnology sector, is based on the high costs of research in biotechnology. The biotechnology sector has been arguing strongly for compensation in terms of royalties, along the lines of other fields of technology.

Along with the developments in biotechnology, there have been legal reinterpretations of national patent laws. There has also been strong pressure to harmonize national patent legislation through TRIPs in the Uruguay Round of the General Agreement on Tariffs and Trade (GATT).[8] Legal reinterpretations were necessary to overcome the technical barriers to patentability. Traditionally, the patent system was limited to technologies dealing with non-organic material. Biological products or processes were originally excluded from patentability on the basis that such inventions could not meet the fundamental patent criteria: *novelty* (not published anywhere before), *inventive step* (the invention must display non-obviousness), *industrial utility* (the invention must have a practical application, to distinguish between basic research and applied technology, which is eligible for patenting), and *reproduc-*

ibility (the application must describe the invention in such detail that other experts may repeat the experiment and arrive at the same results). In addition to these criteria, patent legislation commonly excludes from patentability inventions whose utilization would run counter to *public order or morality*.

However, patenting within biotechnology poses several contentious questions. The biological-conservation-equity dimension opposes the patent-legislation dimension on several aspects.

- **Biological aspect:** Is a product patent on naturally occurring organisms fulfilling the criteria of novelty and inventive step? Biological material was traditionally regarded as a natural rather than an industrial product—a discovery rather than an invention.[9] The process of isolating and describing a micro-organism or a gene may, or may not, be defined as 'inventive enough' to meet this criterion.
- **Social contract aspect:** Unlike traditional breeding methods, the new biotechnologies may meet the reproducibility criterion. However, many biotechnology patent applications fail to fulfil the reproducibility criteria—hence the deal with patents as an alternative to secrecy is forfeited and scientific exchange is impeded.
- **Moral aspect:** There are moral concerns regarding exclusive rights to food, medicinals, and living material. This is based on the notion that food and medicinals should be excluded from patentability because of their fundamental importance to basic human needs.
- **Equity aspect:** Patenting is a long and costly business that can be employed only by large companies—hardly by indigenous and local communities.[10] Patenting may thus be incompatible with fair and equitable sharing of the benefits derived from use of genetic resources.
- **Environmental aspect:** A contested question concerns whether intellectual property rights represent a direct threat to genetic diversity in agriculture. Supporters of intellectual property rights argue about the need to introduce high-yielding varieties, and they have linked to this the use of plant breeders' rights and patents, as preconditions for food security. Opponents argue that the precondition for food security lies in the conservation and sustainable use of a variety of (non-systematically bred) farmers' cultivars or land races. They go on to say that the patent and plant breeders' rights criteria of reproducibility and 'uniform, stable and distinct from existing varieties'[11] inevitably lead to monocultures and loss of genetic diversity.

These controversies indicate the fundamental difference between the normative orientations of the two regimes. While social equity and environmental concerns constitute the basis for the norms and principles engendered by the CBD, TRIPs promotes the privatization of genetic resources through individual rights. Regardless of the 'real' rights and wrongs of the debate, the latter three controversies in particular go to the very core of the bioregime. These controversies may thus represent a barrier to the implementation of the objectives of the CBD—conservation, sustainable use, and equitable sharing.

Institutional Overlap: Diverging Regulations

The TRIPs regulations on property rights to genetic resources

Questions concerning the widening scope of industrial patents were brought up in the Uruguay Round (1988–94) of the GATT. The final text of the agreements established the World Trade Organization (WTO), including the TRIPs Agreement, and was adopted in April 1994. The TRIPs discussion soon became one of the fiercest arenas for the North–South patent controversy. The USA, Japan, and (less adamantly) the EU advocated the principle that all countries should provide and respect intellectual property protection in all technical fields—including biotechnology. Disregarding this principle would constitute a contravention of GATT regulations, making the offending country liable to economic sanctions.[12]

Governments in the South strongly opposed the GATT TRIPs proposals, arguing that patents benefit those states that are already technologically and economically strong.[13] This point was hard to refute, as the South holds no more than 1 to 3 per cent of all patents world-wide.[14] In the initial rounds, India argued against patenting of plant and animal varieties as well as food and pharmaceutical products, citing concern for basic human needs. Moreover, many developing countries maintained that the application of IPR systems would hinder the transfer of technology to the developing world. They also claimed that this system would disregard the very real contributions of generations of farmers to the world's plant genetic resources, the basis of global food security.

The opposition has had some success in GATT. This was partly a result of the mitigating effect of the European Patent Convention (Art. 53(b)), which at the time allowed plant varieties to be excluded from patentability. The final agreement on TRIPs contains the following decisions:

- it grants parties the right to exclude from patentability (Art. 27.3(a)) diagnostic, therapeutic, and surgical methods for the treatment of humans and animals, and (Art. 27.3(b)) plants and animals other than microorganisms;[15]
- it obligates parties to introduce some kind of intellectual property rights for *plant varieties*. TRIPs requires members to provide for the protection of *plant varieties*, either by patents or by establishing an effective *sui generis* system (a legal system of its own kind). *Sui generis* could mean joining the Union for the Protection of New Varieties of Plants (UPOV);
- it obligates those WTO member states that choose the *sui generis* laws to establish these by January 2000. The least developed countries have until 2005 to fulfil their TRIPs obligations. Developing countries may hence create systems better suited to their present needs. In 1999 the *sui generis* option within TRIPs will be up for review by the member states.

The CBD Regulations on Property Rights to Genetic Resources

At the start of the biodiversity negotiations the North's interpretation of the principle of common heritage of mankind did constitute the international regime for exchange of and access to plant genetic resources (seeds). International gene banks were stocked with seeds from the most commonly used food plants. These seeds were collected primarily from the extensive variation found in the South, and the gene banks were based on the North's interpretation of the common heritage principle—*open access, free of charge*.[16]

In response to the developments in GATT among others, developing countries claimed national sovereignty over their genetic heritage, demanding that it be regarded as a national asset along the lines of other natural resources, such as oil and minerals.[17] National sovereignty ended up as the only passageway for reaching consensus about property rights between the North and the South in the CBD text.[18] The CBD states that each country has the sovereign authority to determine access to its genetic resources—through *prior informed consent* and on *mutually agreed terms*. Hence the CBD establishes a new type of property rights regime, where national sovereignty is introduced to counterbalance intellectual property rights. The principle of national sovereignty to natural resources has little material basis. This is because of the 'elusive' character of genetic resources—with actual limited control over these resources in the South. The CBD has no retroactive effect in legal terms; hence the North still has free access to large quantities of genetic resources through the international gene banks.[19]

The CBD equity provisions include:

- provision of new and additional financial assistance to developing countries, over and above Official Development Assistance, to cover 'agreed full incremental costs' of implementing the Convention (Art. 20.2)
- transfer of environmentally safe technology, including biotechnology and technologies covered by intellectual property rights, on 'fair and most favourable terms' (Art. 20)
- obligations for developed and developing countries to share equitably benefits arising from utilization of the knowledge, innovations, and practices of indigenous and local communities with the countries concerned (Art. 8, and 12th preambular)
- obligations to advance priority access to developing-country parties and to share equitably the benefits and the results of research and development arising from the commercial or other utilization of genetic resources, particularly with developing-country parties providing access to genetic resources (Art. 15)
- obligations to advance priority access to developing countries and to share equitably the results and benefits arising from biotechnologies, based on genetic resources, particularly with developing-country parties providing access to genetic resources (Art. 19).

In addition, Article 16(5), says that intellectual property rights systems should 'not run counter to the objectives in the CBD'. This is the place where the diverging regulations and norms of trade regimes, aimed at the biodiversity issue-area, are most explicitly referred to.

Whereas the TRIPs regulations are moulded mainly by the interests of transnational corporations and developed countries, the CBD text is largely reflecting the position of the South. The next two sections address the questions of why this was so and whether this is a trend that will continue in the implementation phase.

Norms and Power in the Formation of the CBD

Was the TRIPs a strategic move by the North to counter the objectives in the CBD? One interpretation of the South's breakthrough in the CBD could be that the North stopped worrying about the output in the biodiversity negotiations, being confident that their interests would be secured by the TRIPs regulations in the WTO. In the same vein, it would seem that the issue has been raised to a higher level. It is now subject to potential conflict between international institutions, as well as between states. This interpretation may go some way in explaining the output. On the other hand, it disregards the fact that it was originally the North that started out pushing for the establishment

of the CBD. First, the CBD was initially part of the North's global environmental agenda, and while WTO/TRIPs touches on central aspects of this issue area it is certainly not a tool for conservation of biodiversity. Second, the CBD text explicitly seeks to counter the possible detrimental effects from WTO/TRIPs. It counters intellectual property rights by introducing *national sovereignty*, *prior informed consent*, and *mutually agreed terms* to regulate access to biological resources. Third, this interpretation does not explain why the United States as the sole OECD country still refuses to ratify the CBD: the USA was certainly not satisfied with the output.

What are the respective strengths of the two institutions? On the normative level, the TRIPs principles of liberal trade theory with industrial patents as part of the package have rather wide support. In the face of this agenda, the claim for 'national sovereignty' in the CBD may appear as protectionism—a barrier to effective trade. On the other hand, the principles of shared benefits and equity in the CBD did achieve legitimacy in the international negotiations.

These observations appeal for a further discussion of the particular institutional setting for these negotiation games. Let us first consider the interplay between power and institutions. Industrialized countries generally dominate fora on economy and trade. Trade regimes may obviously have a greater overall impact, as they define the economic and trade-related framework by which a large array of policies in other sectors must abide. The developing world is highly dependent on market access and also vulnerable to economic sanctions. Hence the rules established by the WTO carry much weight. International fora on economy and trade have strong ramifications to principles connected to high salient issue-areas at the national level.

This links up to the interplay between norms and institutions and how this may affect negotiation results. It is easier for the developing countries to win through with their arguments in UN-related fora such as the Food and Agricultural Organization (FAO) and the United Nations Environment Programme (UNEP) compared to international fora on trade and economy—where use of economic sanctions represents a convincing threat.[20] It is likely that the particular arena of the UNEP biodiversity negotiations gave rise to a recognition that these biological resources did indeed belong to the South. While such sentiments would probably have less impact in fora on economy and trade, the goals associated with the biodiversity negotiations in UNEP may have made the parties more receptive to accepting the legitimacy of granting the South their 'rights'. Moreover, the final stages of negotiating the CBD were conducted at the UN Conference on Environment and Development (UNCED). The norms in the UNCED setting were even more clearly geared towards appeasing the South.[21] The timing may also have played a positive part. As the UNCED Earth Summit approached, and global public attention with it, it became necessary for high level politicians to achieve a credible outcome during this meeting. This underscores the importance of institutions in framing international negotiation outputs.

On the other hand, choosing the UN forum to advocate their environmental agenda may be seen as a strategic move on the part of the North. They could hardly expect acceptance for environmental change in developing countries from regulations originating from any other forum.[22] This means that the manner in which related aspects of the issue has been and is being dealt with in overlapping and partly competing fora may still carry overall structural effects. Dominant actors may still have their way, as they may have a stronger impact on choosing the 'right' forum for advocating their interests. UNCED was clearly the best forum in which to achieve some kind of environmental concessions from the South, whereas the WTO could be used by the North to maintain the economic upper hand.

Implementing the CBD: The Impact of Institutional Overlap

The relationship between intellectual property rights (IPR) systems and the CBD objectives represents a basic challenge for future implementation activities. The focus here is on the relationship between IPR and the principle of equitable sharing as a precondition for conservation and sustainable use of biodiversity in the South.

From a legalistic perspective one of the most relevant formulations in the CBD is the *prior informed consent*. This implies in legal terms that the country providing genetic resources (the owner country) must provide national legislation regulating the appropriation of genetic material.[23] A weak point in this regulation is that, in order to turn down a request for genetic material, the providing country may have to refer to such legal provisions. In the absence of such provisions, there is still a substantial risk that the gene flow must continue free of charge.[24] This may represent an impediment to governments, especially in low income countries, which lack administrative capacity both to enact and to enforce a legal framework.[25]

The practical operation of the prior informed consent principle depends on compatible legislation in user countries. User countries may improve the effectiveness of the prior informed consent rule by enacting national legislation on the import side. Along the lines of the rules governing international trade in endangered species of flora and fauna,[26] national legislation could be tailored to prohibit illegal importation of genetic resources (such as collections conflicting with prior informed consent export rules in the providing country). Likewise, companies and other importers could be obliged to keep records of imported genetic material in order to facilitate monitoring by government authorities. Another suggestion is to require patent applications to give information about how genetic material was obtained.[27]

Among user countries, few efforts can be found. What might have been a striking example of implementation activities moving in the right direction relates to the EU directive on biotechnology patents. Nine years after its initiation by the EU Commission, the directive was subject to yet another amendment by the European Parliament. The Parliament voted to demand safeguards against 'genetic piracy' in developing countries, and wanted explicit commitments to honour the EU's obligations under the CBD. The amendments included demands that the EU's international biodiversity commitments be balanced against obligations to legislate on patents in accordance with GATT and TRIPs. The amendments would require that, when inventions involve biological material of animal or plant origin, patent applications would have to specify their geographical origin and evidence that the material was used in accordance with the legal access and export provisions in force in the place of origin.[28] In the end, the Parliament's amendments were greatly watered down by being moved to the preamble.[29]

The CBD mentions explicitly that the contracting parties shall respect, preserve, and maintain knowledge and practices of *indigenous and local communities*, and encourage the equitable sharing of the benefits arising from utilization of such knowledge and practices. The process of enforcement is less clear, as this brings up the tricky question of interference in domestic affairs, as well as how to identify who should be rewarded.[30] One approach to ensuring the interests of local and indigenous people may be to include and elaborate some kind of community rights. This may either be part of national law as a *sui generis* system or within a protocol under the CBD. Community rights apply to collectives and not individuals—and hence are regarded as incompatible to intellectual property rights systems. The revision of TRIPs in 1999 may show whether community rights can be accepted as a *sui generis* system.

There are some examples of the concept of equitable sharing gaining legitimacy among collecting agencies (private sector users). The UK Royal Botanic Gardens at Kew now states that any net profits derived from collaboration will be shared equally between itself and the supplier. Shaman Pharmaceuticals develops new pharmaceuticals from higher plants and is committed to returning a portion of the profits from its products to all communities and countries in which it works. There is also the case of Biotics, a private British for-profit company that acts as a broker between companies and in-country collectors, granting the latter 50 per cent of Biotics' royalties.[31] The International Co-operation Biodiversity Group (ICBG) is a network of bioprospecting projects sponsored by the US National Science Foundation and the National Institutes of Health (NIH). The 34 projects provide financial rewards to local people, investments in research, and strengthened local institutions in developing countries.[32]

A number of adverse activities can, however, easily be found. Two Australian government agencies have recently been patenting chickpea seeds collected from the International Crops Research Institute for the Semi-Arid Tropics (ICRISAT) in India.[33] This is a clear violation of the deal between the FAO and the Consultative Group on International Agricultural Research (CGIAR) making germplasm in international agricultural research centres part of the FAO international network of gene banks. The deal operates on the principle of free access combined with the principle that users will not patent the material. In practice, a number of violations are occurring, with 40 infringements by Australian organizations and corporations alone.[34]

Dealing with Institutional Overlap

The Conference of the Parties (COP) to the CBD has put much emphasis on examining the relationship between the CBD objectives and the strengthened IPR systems. In Buenos Aires 1996, COP3 asked the Executive Secretary to 'liase with the Secretariat of the World Trade Organization to inform it of the goals and the ongoing work of the CBD and to invite the Secretariat of the WTO to assist in the preparation of a paper for the COP that identifies the synergies and relationship between the objectives of the CBD and the TRIPs Agreement.' Moreover, COP3 issued a *declaration on intellectual property rights*, encouraging governments and organizations to submit case-studies to the Convention's Executive Secretary on the impact of intellectual property rights in regard to the Convention's three main objectives. As the Committee on Trade and the Environment of the WTO began discussion of the relationship between environmental protection and TRIPs in June 1995, it centred on the relationship between that and the CBD. The relationship between TRIPs and CBD will also be a central topic to the review of the TRIPs in 1999.

A crucial question is whether these are actually efforts to come to grips with the diverging regulatory rules of the two regimes. Mere co-ordination of the functional scopes of the CBD and the TRIPs is hardly sufficient to deal with the problems emerging from their opposing norms and regulations:

There are some indications that the potential conflict is taken seriously. A document from COP3 points out three areas of possible complementarity as well as areas for conflict.[35]

- First, *mutually agreed-upon terms* for access to genetic resources could allocate intellectual property rights (IPR) as part of the benefits to be shared among parties to an agreement on genetic resources. Such IPR could be defined under TRIPs-compatible IPR systems.
- Second, the CBD and TRIPs could develop procedures for exchanging relevant information. Countries implementing measures that implicate both agreements, such as rules requiring patent applications to disclose the country of origin of biological material, might report them to the TRIPs Council, while at the same time disclosing the same information to the clearing house mechanism for scientific and technical co-operation established under Article 18(3) of the CBD.
- Third, there is a proposal to require or encourage disclosure in patent applications of the country and community of origin for genetic resources and informal knowledge used to develop the invention. As regards the potential conflict area, national measures to promote technology transfer under CBD Article 16 might raise *most favoured nation* issues if Convention parties and non-parties were treated differently. It might also raise TRIPs issues if owners of proprietary technology were compelled to license technologies on grounds other than those prescribed in the TRIPs Agreement.[36]

Several factors indicate the stronger regulatory force of the TRIPs:

- Intellectual property rights and patenting in the biotechnology sector is a contested, but relatively small, part of a larger issue-area concerning patenting and international trade. The driving forces in this much wider issue-area are powerful and gaining in strength as the opposition is declining with the economic developments in newly industrialized countries (NIC).
- NICs are increasingly accepting patenting as beneficial to their own economies, thus splitting up what used to be a strong and concerted opposition from the South. This development is not likely to be significantly restrained by the CBD objectives. Still, the CBD may have had a mitigating effect in providing pressure for a period of grace for the developing countries (that is, WTO members) in accepting patent systems.
- If WTO members refuse to sign up to TRIPs, they become liable to economic *sanctions*.[37] This makes the WTO a more powerful instrument than the CBD, which does not carry any sanction mechanisms.

- The WTO is also a stronger institution in terms of its compliance mechanism, incorporating different sets of *timetables* for countries to harmonize their patent legislation. The CBD does not provide timetables for parties to comply with its objectives.

The WTO/TRIPs is stronger both in terms of institutional mechanisms and in being controlled by the more powerful states. On the other hand, the legitimacy of the CBD principles is increasing, and there is ample evidence that the issue has been accepted as an important one in the WTO and the CBD alike. The issue has been institutionalized by providing for continued discussions between the two, as well as by institutionalizing representation in the respective fora. The final result of these deliberations is still far from certain, and it is likely to remain a contested international issue for a long time.

Future Prospects and Barriers

Implementation of the CBD objectives will depend partly on the capacity of developing country governments to enact and enforce appropriate domestic legislation. A crucial question for the implementation of the CBD is, however, whether northern governments will comply with the new regime regulating access to and exchange of genetic resources and technology. Whether compensation for use of genetic resources will become a viable concept depends on whether the new dual property rights regime of the CBD will take hold. Perhaps paradoxically, it is the private sector that has taken the largest steps in this direction. The private seeds collection agencies may be more open to seeing the potential competitive advantage of building a fair and above-board image in germplasm transactions. This trend is far from all-inclusive, but it is nevertheless ironic that the public sector seems to be intimidated by what they perceive as a demand from the same private sector actors to provide the biotechnology industry with strong patent systems.

As to whether the TRIPs regulations on patenting will have harmful effects, for instance, for farmers in developing countries, the answer is probably no, in the short-term perspective. One of the underlying threats in the expanding patent legislation—that farmers must pay royalties for reusing seeds – is still a long way from being enforceable. A far more harmful long-term effect of the TRIPs patent regulations is that they reinforce a North–South conflict line in an issue-area where common solutions and co-operation are of paramount importance.

Concern for competitiveness in the biotechnology sector may increasingly take precedence over concerns for improved conservation and equitable sharing of benefits in the biodiversity issue-area. If the TRIPs principles prevail this would essentially imply that those who have the ultimate responsibility for carrying the costs of conservation and sustainable use of the resources will not be given a fair and equitable share in the benefits derived from this use. According to the inherent logic of the CBD, this would undermine efforts to reach the objectives of conservation and sustainable use of biological diversity.

Notes and References

I would like to thank Helge Ole Bergesen, Bruce Davis, Regine Andersen, and Steinar Andresen for very helpful comments on this article.

1. For a more general examination of the relationship between trade and environmental regimes, see the article in this edition of the *Yearbook* by Beatrice Chaytor and James Cameron, 'The Treatment of Environmental Considerations in the World Trade Organization'. See also Konrad van Molkte (1997), 'The Structure of Regimes for Trade and the Environment', in Oran Young (ed.), *Global Governance: Drawing Insights from the Environmental Experience* (Cambridge, MA: MIT Press).
2. This is resting on the assumption that principles, norms, rules, and procedures may have an independent role in moulding behaviour and enhancing domestic implementation among the negotiating parties. The term *implementation* is used to indicate a deliberate effort by national authorities to follow up their international commitments in domestic policies within the specific issue-area.
3. *Regimes* are defined as 'implicit or explicit principles, norms, rules, and decision-making procedures around which actors' expectations converge in a given issue-area': S. Krasner (1982), 'Structural Causes and Regime Consequences: Regimes as Intervening Variables', *International Organization*, 36/2, 185–205. *Institutions* are more broadly defined as 'recognized patterns of behaviour or practice around which expectations converge': Oran R. Young (1982), 'Regime Dynamics: The Rise and Fall of International Regimes', *International Organization*, 36/2, 277. 'Regime' and 'institution' are frequently applied interchangeably, as will also be the case here.
4. For a theoretical elaboration of the concept of overlapping institutions, see Oran R. Young (ed.) (1997), *Global Governance*.
5. For example, the average species lifetime of mammals in fossil records is in the order of 1 million years, which would mean roughly 0.5 extinctions per 100 years for the present mammalian fauna of nearly 5000 species. In fact, however, the current rate of extinction of mammals is roughly 100 times higher than this background rate. In other taxa the discrepancy may be even greater (V. H. Heywood (ed.) (1995), *Global Biodiversity Assessment* (Cambridge: Cambridge University Press), 232). Estimates of the number of existing species in the world vary from about 5 million to 100 million, of which only some 1.7 million have been described scientifically (see: E. O. Wilson (ed.) (1988), *Biodiversity* (Washington, DC: National Academy Press) and E. O. Wilson (1992), *The Diversity of Life* (Cambridge, MA: Harvard University Press)).
6. While the 'old' biotechnology includes such traditional activities as brewing beer and baking bread, the concept of 'new biotechnologies' refers to activities such as tissue culture and recombinant-DNA (r-DNA) techniques. By the year 2000, farm-level sales of products of agricultural biotechnology are expected to have reached some $US 100 billion. As of 1986 the value of global trade in plant-based pharmaceuticals was estimated to be $US 20 billion (Report of Panel II, UNEP/Bio.Div/Panels/Inf.2,

Nairobi, 28 April 1993). Three years later, in 1989, the market value in the North of medicinal plants from the South was estimated to be $US 43 billion. See: P. P. Principe (1989), 'Valuing the Biodiversity of Medicinal Plants', in O. Akerele, V. Heywood, and H. Synge (eds.), *The Conservation of Medicinal Plants* (Cambridge: Cambridge University Press).

7. '*Biological diversity*' is a broad concept which has been used to embody the variability among all living organisms, including diversity within species, among species, and among ecosystems.

8. For a more extended exposé of the developments in patent legislation, see G. Kristin Rosendal (1995), 'The Politics of Patent Legislation in Biotechnology: An International View', in M. R. El-Gewely (ed.), *Biotechnology Annual Review* (Amsterdam: Elsevier), 453–76.

9. More about this in R. S. Crespi (1988), *Patents: A Basic Guide to Patenting in Biotechnology* (Cambridge: Cambridge University Press).

10. The trend is for transnational corporations (TNCs) to register patents in developing countries, not in order to operate their technology there, but to prevent others (especially locals) from copying or using their technology. Thus they may protect these markets for the sale of their products produced in northern countries. (Third World Network (1990), *The Uruguay Round and Third World Sovereignty* (Penang: Third World Network), 30).

11. Union for the Protection of New Varieties of Plants, 1978, para. 2.

12. TRIPs also incorporates the GATT's 'national treatment' and 'most favoured nation' principles. These principles prevent countries from giving priority to domestic industries or treating one importing country better than another. See article by Chaytor and Cameron.

13. See GATT (1989), *Communication from India: Standards and Principles Concerning the Availability, Scope and Use of Trade-Related Intellectual Property Rights*, GATT Secretariat, MTN GNG/NG11/W/37, July.

14. World Commission for Environment and Development (1987), *Our Common Future* (Oxford: Oxford University Press).

15. Multilateral Trade Negotiations, the Uruguay Round, the Negotiations Committee, MTN.TNC/W/124, 13 December 1993, MNT/FA II–Annex 1C. Section 5, article 27 in the agreement on Trade-Related Aspects of Intellectual Property Rights.

16. 'Technically', the collection of seed samples was considered by all as a non-rival and non-exclusive activity. Moreover, no one questioned this practice on moral grounds, as the seeds of our most utilized food plants were seen to be of basic significance to all mankind.

17. Genetic resources differ, however, from oil and minerals in being non-rival and largely non-exclusive goods. Nor is species distribution necessarily confined to national borders. These characteristics will obviously hamper state control over genetic resources.

18. For the first time in the operative text of a treaty the CBD incorporates the Stockholm Declaration Principle 21, which provides that 'States have . . . the sovereign right to exploit their own resources pursuant to their own environmental policies . . .' Decided in Stockholm at the United Nations Conference on Human Environment (UNCHE), 1972.

19. This involves the seeds collected before the CBD entered into force, 31 December 1993.

20. For an extended analysis of the debate leading up to the arrangements in FAO, see G. K. Rosendal (1989), *A Sustainable Development for Plant Genetic Resources: The Output of the Debate in FAO; a Sisyphean Victory for an Environmental Organization?*, R: 010-1989 (Lysaker: Fridtjof Nansen Institute). For a corresponding analysis of the UNEP debate, see G. K. Rosendal (1991), *International Conservation of Biological Diversity: The Quest for Effective Solutions*, R: 012-1991 (Lysaker: Fridtjof Nansen Institute).

21. Even though a recurring criticism from the South was that UNCED was concerned with 'the environmental agenda of the North', developmental issues were nevertheless more overt in this forum than in the preceding UN Conference on the Human Environment (Stockholm, 1972).

22. More about this in G. Kristin Rosendal (1999), *Implementing International Environmental Agreements in Developing Countries: The Creation and Impact of the Convention on Biological Diversity* (Oslo: Oslo University Press).

23. This article has been studied in detail by Frederic Hendrickx, Veit Koester, and Christian Prip (1993), 'Convention on Biological Diversity: Access to Genetic Resources: A Legal Analysis', *Environmental Policy and Law*, 23/6. Veit Koester played a central role throughout the biodiversity negotiation process, acting both as Chairman and Vice Chairman during various parts of negotiations, among other things leading Working Group II.

24. See more about this issue in Frederic Hendrickx, Veit Koester, and Christian Prip (1993), 'Convention on Biological Diversity'.

25. *Unilateral* initiatives in *owner* countries include the access to genetic resources of the Andean Pact and the Thai draft bill on a *sui generis* Plant Variety Protection Act, both seeking to protect the native plant varieties as well as the rights of farmers, local communities, and indigenous peoples. Countries which are in the process of developing access legislation and community/farmers' rights legislation include Brazil, Colombia, Ethiopia, India, South Africa, Tanzania, and Thailand. In addition, a number of countries are developing access legislation or community rights only: Argentina, Bolivia, Costa Rica, Ecuador, Indonesia, Mexico, Papua New Guinea, the Philippines, Venezuela, and Vietnam (Genetic Resources Action International (GRAIN) (1997), *Signposts to Sui Generis Rights*. Resource material from the international seminar on *sui generis* rights, Bangkok, 1–6 December 1997 (Bangkok: BIOTHAI & GRAIN). The enhanced consciousness regarding sovereignty over genetic resources is not confined to the South. After the signing of the CBD, Australia banned any plant or micro-organism from being taken out of the country before they themselves have bioprospected it.

26. The Convention on International Trade in Endangered Species of flora and fauna (Washington, DC, 1973).

27. See Hendrickx, Koester, and Prip, 'Convention on Biological Diversity'.

28. *International Environmental Reporter*, 23 July, 1997, 713–14.

29. This setback may, however, be changing if EU member states (such as the Netherlands), and European Economic Area members (such as Norway), succeed in fighting for the amendments to the patent directive proposed by the European Parliament. The Netherlands, later joined by Italy, filed a challenge to the EU 'Life Patents' directive (19 October, 1998), and the Norwegian government has pledged to veto the directive.

30. In view of the problems facing developing country governments in connection with enforcing catch quotas for foreign fisheries under the UN Convention on the Law of the Sea (UNCLOS), the problems regarding regulation of genes are striking. In addition to the general administrative burdens, the non-exclusive character of genetic resources further complicates control of their movements. This is partly negated, however, by the need for a user to obtain information about the genetic material in question. Without this, it may be difficult to screen genetic material for potentially valuable and interesting traits in secrecy.

31. More about conducts in bioprospecting in Sarah A. Laird (1993), 'Contracts for Biodiversity Prospecting', in *Biodiversity Prospecting* (Baltimore: World Resources Institute Publications), 99–130.

32. While the US Senate leadership still refuses to ratify the CBD, the Clinton administration is thus operational in implementing some of the main objectives of the CBD.
33. *New Scientist*, 14 February, 1998, 14.
34. Ibid.
35. UNEP/CBD/COP/3/23.
36. *Most-favoured nation* is a basic principle of the GATT/WTO regime, saying that any trade advantages conferred by one country to another must be given all GATT parties.
37. Membership in the two regimes is rather similar: By 1998 the WTO had 132 members and 34 observers, of which all but three have applied to join (the Vatican, Cape Verde, and Ethiopia), and about 170 states have ratified the CBD.

International Co-operation in Nuclear Safety

Roland Timerbaev and Abram Ioirysh

Introduction

International co-operation in the peaceful uses of atomic energy started in the mid-1950s as soon as industrially developed countries began their efforts to harness nuclear energy for civilian application. At the beginning, however, nuclear safety was not a priority concern of either governments and intergovernmental organizations or private developers. Although bona fide attempts to ensure nuclear safety were made, in particular on the national level, it was only after major accidents at civilian nuclear power plants occurred that the attention of the world community was focused on the need to establish a universally applicable and effective international regime of nuclear safety.

The IAEA Nuclear Safety Regime

The statute of the International Atomic Energy Agency (IAEA), which entered into force on 29 July 1957 authorized the Agency 'to establish or adopt . . . standards of safety for protection of health and minimization of danger to life and property (including such standards for labour conditions), and to provide for the application of these standards.'[1]

Practical development of effective international co-operation in the field of nuclear safety had its beginning in the early 1960s and reached its present wide-ranging scale in the 1980s and 1990s, after the Chernobyl and Three Mile Island accidents.

Today the international regime of safe development of nuclear energy is based on a system of international legal instruments, international mechanisms, and other intergovernmental structures, as well as on organizational and administrative measures which are aimed at ensuring the protection of the health of population and the sustainability of the environment in the process of peaceful nuclear activities. The creation of the regime was made possible through the elaboration of international recommendations, norms, and standards, the implementation of co-ordinated scientific programs, the exchange of scientific and technological information, the establishment of databases, and the conclusion of international conventions and bilateral and multilateral agreements which required allocation by governments of substantial financial and material resources.

The 1996 Moscow Summit

A significant impetus to the further strengthening of international co-operation was given by the meeting of heads of state and government of leading world powers, who held a conference in Moscow on 19–20 April 1996, which adopted the Nuclear Safety and Security Summit Declaration. In the declaration the leaders of the eight powers stated their commitment 'to give an absolute priority to safety in the use of nuclear energy'.

The summit meeting was preceded by the non-governmental organization (NGO) Preparatory Meeting in Advance of the Nuclear Safety Summit, which took place in Moscow on 17–18 April 1996. The NGO meeting was sponsored by the Center for Russian Environmental Policy (Russia), the Natural Resources Defense Council (United States), and the Bellona Foundation (Norway).

A need for further improvements in the international nuclear safety regime is growing as the development of peaceful uses of nuclear energy continues unabated.

Over the last several years world-wide development of the peaceful uses of nuclear energy in its various applications has continued, though at a slower pace than previously. In 1998, according to the International Atomic Energy Agency, 437 reactor units were in operation, with some countries having 40 per cent or more of nuclear share of electricity generation (Lithuania, France, Belgium, Ukraine, Sweden, Bulgaria, Slovakia, and Switzerland— in the order of percentage). In addition, 36 reactor units were under construction, including six in the Republic of Korea and four each in China, India, the Russian Federation, Slovakia, and the Ukraine.[2]

The Present Safety Regime

At present the international regime of nuclear safety is comprised of the following fundamental elements.

International Norms and Standards

The International Atomic Energy Agency's Board of Governors approved as early as 1960 *The Agency's Health and Safety Measures*. In 1962 the board adopted *Basic Safety Standards for Radioactive Protection*. In 1982 the Agency issued on behalf of the International Labour Organization, the Nuclear Energy Agency, and the World Health Organization, as well as the IAEA, the revised *Basic Safety Standards for Radiological Protection*.

In 1974 the Agency launched its major Nuclear Safety Standards (NUSS) programme, which was largely completed in 1986. This comprehensive series of codes and safety guides is intended to ensure the safe design, siting, and operation of nuclear power reactors and enhance their quality assurance and reliability. The NUSS still remain as universally recognized safety recommendations. In 1987 replies to an IAEA questionnaire from 47 member states showed that the basic concepts, purposes, and functions of their regulatory bodies generally conformed to the NUSS recommendations.

The IAEA Board of Governors on a number of occasions considered proposals to make NUSS recommendations legally binding but decided against such suggestions because of concern that it would thus 'petrify' standards that were likely to be subject to changes over time.

The International Atomic Energy Agency has been sending special missions to observe and improve nuclear safety standards and activities in member states—Radiation Protection Advisory Teams (RARATs), Operational Safety Review Teams (OSARTs), and Assessment of Safety Significant Events Teams (ASSETs).

The IAEA International Nuclear Event Scale (INES) classifies incidents and accidents at nuclear reactors on a scale that ranges from the most minor (level 1) to the most severe (level 7). Levels 1–3 are termed 'incidents' while levels 4–7 are 'accidents'. Chernobyl would have been a level 7 accident. About 60 member states of the Agency use INES.[3]

In 1995 a total of 62 events were communicated through the INES information system, of which 56 occurred in nuclear power plants and six in other facilities. None were at level 3 or higher.[4]

According to the latest available data, of 52 incidents reported in 1996, 27 were below the INES scale, one was classified as a 'serious incident', level 3, which involved overexposure of an individual, seven events were reported at level 2, and the 17 remaining reported events were at level 1.[5]

According to the Russian State Corporation 'Rosenergoatom', as reported by Interfax News Agency on 13 December 1998, in January through November 1998 Russian nuclear power plants had one level 2 incident and three level 1 incidents. During a similar period in 1997,

according to the same source, there were three level 1 incidents.

For many years the Agency has been regularly publishing the *IAEA Safety Standards Series* under five categories: General Safety Issues, Nuclear Safety, Radiation Safety, Radioactive Waste Safety, and Safe Transport.[6]

International Agreements

The Convention on Early Notification of a Nuclear Accident (Notification Convention)[7] is aimed at providing relevant information about nuclear accidents with possible transboundary consequences as early as possible in order to minimize environmental, health, and economic effects.

The Convention was negotiated and concluded under the auspices of the IAEA in 1986, in the wake of the Chernobyl accident. It covers any accident involving a release of radioactive material which occurs or is likely to occur and which has resulted or may result in an international transboundary release that could be of radiological safety significance for another state or states.

Under the Convention, its parties undertake to notify other states forthwith, directly or through the IAEA, the nature of the nuclear accident, the time of its occurrence, and its exact location where appropriate, and promptly provide them with such available information that is relevant to minimizing the radiological consequences.

States may voluntarily notify accidents related to military nuclear activities, with a view to minimizing the radiological consequences of the nuclear accident. All five nuclear-weapon states have declared their willingness to make such notifications.

The IAEA is for all practical reasons a central point in the notification process. Under Article 4 the Agency is to inform states of any notification it has received.

The Convention entered into force on 27 October 1986. As of February 1999 the total number of parties reached 111 states.

After the conclusion of the Convention many states have signed bilateral agreements concerning mutual notification of nuclear accidents. Thus Russia signed bilateral intergovernmental agreements with Finland, Denmark, Sweden, Norway, and some other states. Under these agreements, in the event of a nuclear accident involving facilities or activities of a contracting party, or of persons or legal entities under its jurisdiction or control, it shall forthwith notify the other contracting party. Such bilateral arrangements have contributed to enhancing reciprocal trust and co-operation in addressing any hazardous nuclear accidents.

The Convention on Assistance in the Case of a Nuclear Accident or Radiological Emergency (Assistance Convention)[8] establishes an international framework aimed at facilitating the prompt provision of assistance in the event of a nuclear accident or radiological emergency, directly between states parties, through or from the IAEA, and from other international organizations; and at minimizing consequences and protecting life, property, and the environment from effects of radioactive releases.

Under the Convention, if a state needs assistance in the event of a nuclear accident, whether or not such accident originates within its territory, it may call for such assistance. The Convention does not establish a special mechanism for providing assistance but sets up procedures for establishing such a mechanism which could be established and would function if the need arose to provide assistance.

At the basis of the entire system of requesting and providing assistance lies the principle of respect for the sovereignty of states and of the voluntary nature of providing assistance. Procedures for agreeing to the scope and type of assistance required provide for their specification by a requesting state which, where practicable, would furnish the assisting party with such information as may be necessary for that party to determine the extent to which it is able to meet the request.

As in the case of the Notification Convention, the Assistance Convention assigns to the IAEA a leading role in making necessary arrangements in the event of a nuclear accident or radiological emergency (such as collecting and disseminating information concerning experts, equipment, materials, methodologies, techniques, etc.) which fully corresponds to the Agency's statute and would make ample use of its over 40 years of experience in contributing to the safe development of peaceful uses of nuclear energy.[9]

The Assistance Convention entered into force on 26 February 1987. As of January 1999 the total number of parties to the Convention reached 77 states.

The Convention on Nuclear Safety[10] is aimed at achieving and maintaining a high level of nuclear safety worldwide through the enhancement of national measures and international co-operation, including, where appropriate, safety-related technical co-operation; at establishing and maintaining effective defences in nuclear installations against potential radiological hazards in order to protect individuals, society, and the environment from harmful effects of ionizing radiation from such installation; and at preventing accidents with radiological consequences and mitigating such consequences should they occur.

Under the Convention, each contracting party undertakes to establish and maintain a legislative and regulatory framework to govern the safety of nuclear installations; it shall also establish and designate a regulatory body entrusted with the implementation of such a legislative and regulatory framework. The Convention establishes an important review procedure which would in effect constitute some sort of monitoring of the performance of par-

ties in ensuring the safety of their nuclear installations. Under this review procedure, each party is to submit for review a report on the measures it has taken to implement the obligations of the Convention. Such reports are to be reviewed at periodic meetings of parties (called 'review meetings'). The intervals between review meetings shall not exceed three years. An extraordinary meeting of contracting parties may be held if so agreed by a majority of parties.

The Nuclear Safety Convention was opened for signature on 20 September 1994 and entered into force on 24 October 1996. As of October 1998 there were 65 signatories and 47 parties.

A preparatory meeting of contracting parties was held in Vienna in April 1998 and an organizational meeting in September–October 1998. The majority of the parties, including Russia, have submitted reports required by the Convention. The first review meeting of contracting parties took place in Vienna in April 1999.

The Joint Convention on the Safety of Spent Fuel Management and on the Safety of Radioactive Waste Management was adopted in September 1997, but has not yet entered into force. As of February 1999, 38 states had signed the Convention and six had become parties. The Convention shall enter into force after 25 states have ratified, accepted, or approved it.

The Joint Convention has as its objectives: to achieve and maintain a high level of safety world-wide in spent fuel and radioactive waste management, through the enhancement of national measures and international co-operation, including, where appropriate, safety-related technical co-operation; to ensure that, during all stages of spent fuel and radioactive waste management, there are effective defences against potential hazards so that individuals, society, and the environment are protected from harmful effects of ionizing radiation in such a way that the needs and aspirations of the present generation are met without compromising the ability of future generations to meet their needs and aspirations; and to prevent accidents with radioactive consequences should they occur during any stage of spent fuel or radioactive waste management.

The Convention covers existing facilities and past practices, the siting of proposed facilities, the design and construction of facilities, the assessment of safety of facilities, the operation of facilities, the disposal of spent fuel, the decommissioning of nuclear facilities, the transboundary movement of spent fuel, and radioactive waste, and provides for review procedures of states' performance similar to those set forth in the Nuclear Safety Convention.

The Convention on the Physical Protection of Nuclear Material likewise constitutes a significant part of the international nuclear safety and security regime. Provisions of the Convention oblige parties to ensure that, during international transport across their territory or on ships or aircraft under their jurisdiction, nuclear materials for peaceful purposes (plutonium, uranium-235, uranium-233, and irradiated fuel) are protected at the agreed levels, as categorized in the annexes to the Convention.

Under certain conditions, the Convention shall also apply to nuclear material used for peaceful purposes while in domestic use, storage, and transport.

The Convention entered into force on 8 February 1987. As of November 1998 the total number of parties reached 63 states.

Civil liability for nuclear damage is also considered an indispensable element in the international system of ensuring nuclear safety. However, a universal agreement to regulate civil liability has not yet seen the light of day, and such liability is currently administered by a number of international agreements with limited memberships.

The Vienna Convention on Civil Liability for Nuclear Damage[11] is aimed at establishing minimum standards to provide financial protection against damage resulting from the peaceful uses of nuclear energy. The Convention was adopted on 21 May 1963 but entered into force only 14 years later, on 12 November 1977. By November 1998 the total number of parties reached 31 states. The United States and Russia are not parties to the Convention. The Russian Federation signed it but has not yet consummated the process of ratification: the prospects of ratification by the present State Duma (new parliamentary elections will take place in late 1999) are not at all clear.

Since many countries did not consider satisfactory the provisions of the Vienna Convention, in 1997 governments undertook an important step towards strengthening the liability regime. In September 1997, at a diplomatic conference in Vienna, representatives of 80 states adopted the *Protocol to Amend the Vienna Convention on Civil Liability for Nuclear Damage*, as well as the *Convention on Supplementary Compensation for Nuclear Damage*.

The Protocol sets the limit of possible civil liability of the operator at the level of an approximate equivalent of $US400,000. It contains a broader definition of nuclear damage, which covers the costs for reinstatement of impaired environment and the costs of preventive measures. The Protocol broadens the geographic scope of the Vienna Convention and lengthens the period for claiming compensation for nuclear damage. The Protocol, as of December 1998, was signed by 14 states and ratified by one (Romania). It is still to enter into force.

The Convention on Supplementary Compensation is a legal instrument to which any state may accede, irrespective of its participation in any existing regional or other agreements on civil liability, such as the 1960 OECD *Paris Convention on Third Party Liability in the Field of Nuclear Energy*. The new Convention provides for supplementary compensation for nuclear damage beyond the amount set in the Convention if the contracting parties make available additional public funds. As of December 1998 the Convention was signed by 13 states and ratified by none. It has not yet entered into force.

Both new legal instruments, taken together, are aimed at strengthening the global basis for compensation for nuclear damage as provided for by the existing agreements on civil liability.

In recent years, several important international conventions, negotiated under IAEA auspices, have helped to fill gaps in the international nuclear safety regime. It should be noted, however, that the pace of ratification of the various international conventions concluded is uneven. For a comprehensive international safety regime to be established, states must subscribe to the conventions they have sought, negotiated, and adopted.

The above listed international collaborative efforts to promote a high level of nuclear safety world-wide must, certainly, be based and are dependent upon the prime responsibility of national governments in the field of nuclear safety and radiation protection. Sustainable nuclear safety also requires a supportive economic and legal environment where operators, national regulatory bodies, and the public at large can fully assume their respective responsibilities.

General Assessment of the Safety Regime

In assessing the overall efficacy of the nuclear safety mechanism that has been promoted and developed under the auspices of the International Atomic Energy Agency since the establishment of this organization in late 1950s, one can conclude that during the last decade some important progress has been achieved. Since Chernobyl no major accidents in civilian nuclear activities have taken place, which may be attributed in no small measure to the efforts of the IAEA. However, most of the existing safety norms have a recommendatory nature, since many governments still prefer to rely on national legislation and consider that it is primarily their sovereign right and obligation to enforce safety rules. Thus the Agency has a long way to go before it can become a comprehensive international mechanism for ensuring nuclear safety.

The meeting of the contracting parties of the Nuclear Safety Convention held in April 1999 set a landmark in establishing international monitoring of the safety status of participating countries, but the results of this review are still to be evaluated in terms of their impact on the promotion of a reliable safety regime world-wide.

Review and advisory safety services provided by the IAEA can become purely routine, therefore efforts to keep them relevant to a large and mature modern nuclear industry are necessary.

The Need for Better Safety Culture

Nuclear safety can and must be enhanced by greater transparency in nuclear power activities. All these efforts must be oriented towards developing and continuously upgrading the general nuclear safety culture.

Although humankind has been conducting nuclear activities for over fifty years, one is forced to recognize that there is a general reason for the persistent deficiencies in ensuring operational nuclear safety, even in states with long-standing nuclear programmes. While specific problems and their immediate causes may have been different in any particular case, it seems evident, that the basis of almost all existing problems has been the lack of key elements of a general safety culture.

In order to develop and implant such a safety culture in each and every country engaged in nuclear activities, governments and operators must constantly exert systematic efforts to educate all those who are involved with nuclear installations and nuclear activities.

It is to be expected that newly developing areas of IAEA activities, such as involvement of the Agency in the verification of weapon-origin fissile materials under the tripartite (IAEA, Russia, United States) initiative of September 1996 and, in future, nuclear control agreements (e.g. the Fissile Material Cut-off Treaty which is being negoti-ated by the Geneva Conference on Disarmament), would be of substantial benefit to the general nuclear safety regime.

In conclusion, it is important to emphasize that, whatever efforts are undertaken to improve and enhance nuclear safety and security, their full realization can be achieved only in the framework of the overall security both on national and international levels. Nuclear security is inseparable from general security.

Notes and References

1   IAEA Statute, Art. III.A.6.
2   *IAEA Bulletin* (1998), 40/3, 50.
3   For more on the IAEA activities in the area of nuclear safety, see David Fischer (1997), *History of the International Atomic Energy Agency: The First Forty Years* (Vienna: IAEA), 183–242.
4   *The IAEA Annual Report for 1995* (Vienna: IAEA), GC(40)/8, 43.
5   *IAEA Yearbook 1997*, pp. D 20–21.
6   For more on recent activities of the Agency in nuclear safety, see *IAEA Bulletin*, 40: 2 (1998).
7   For description, see Agreements section in this *Yearbook*
8   For description, see ibid.
9   For more on the two conventions, see A. O. Adede (1987), *The IAEA Notification and Assistance Conventions in Case of a Nuclear Accident. Landmarks in the Multilateral Treaty-making Process* (London/Dordrecht/Boston: Graham & Trotman/ Martinus Nijhoff).
10 For description, see Agreements section in this *Yearbook*.
11 For description, see ibid.

The Treatment of Environmental Considerations in the World Trade Organization

Beatrice Chaytor and James Cameron

Introduction

In the early 1990s the world's attention was brought to the clash of ideals presented by the trade and environment regimes. This clash was illustrated by the 1991 dispute in the GATT between Mexico and the United States over the US ban on Mexican tuna whose harvest incidentally killed dolphins. The manner in which the case was decided by the GATT panel alarmed environmental experts and brought the trade and environmental debate to the top of the agenda of many international institutions. The 1992 United Nations Conference on Environment and Development (UNCED) made recommendations on the relationship between international trade and environmental protection, and the new World Trade Organization (WTO) was assigned a Committee on Trade and Environment (CTE) to examine the relationship and make recommendations on appropriate modifications of the trade rules, as necessary. The political rise of environmental protection concerns took the WTO by surprise. At the national level, protection of the environment has become an important public policy concern, and the development of new instruments of environmental policy is touching on matters addressed by international trade rules. At the same time there has been rapid increase in the number and range of international environmental treaties.

These trends, and their subsequent developments, have made a fairly perceptible impact on the WTO and the conduct of its activities. It has faced growing calls for greater transparency and openness in its work, particularly in the CTE process. But while the WTO has taken small steps towards more openness, the secrecy surrounding the organization's predecessor, the GATT, is still prevalent.[1] And the inability of the WTO to adapt trade rules to take fuller account of emerging environmental concerns has led to present and potential conflicts of policy, as well as to legal obligation.[2]

The CTE process, which was closed to participation by non-governmental actors, has singularly failed to fulfil the mandate it was given. And it has drawn criticism from the environmental community for the secret nature of its discussions. Meanwhile, on the judicial front, there is a growing number of trade and environment disputes appearing before the WTO dispute settlement system, which has forced the Dispute Settlement Body (DSB) to find ways of managing the interrelationship.[3] By and large there has been a careful balancing act by the Appellate Body, where a refining of the trade/environment relationship within the multilateral trading system has been crafted.

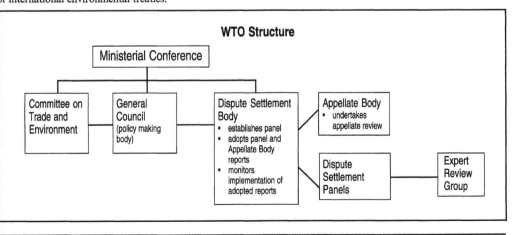

WTO Structure

- Ministerial Conference
  - Committee on Trade and Environment
  - General Council (policy making body)
  - Dispute Settlement Body
    - establishes panel
    - adopts panel and Appellate Body reports
    - monitors implementation of adopted reports
  - Appellate Body
    - undertakes appellate review
  - Dispute Settlement Panels
  - Expert Review Group

Treatment of the Trade/Environment Relationship in the WTO

The Basic Relationship

Environmental problems normally arise where production and consumption activities result in adverse effects on others and those effects are not reflected in market transactions. Because of such externalities, producers and consumers cause excessive amounts of pollution and other forms of environmental degradation. Set in the international context: environmental activities by one state can diminish, through externalities, the welfare of those in other jurisdictions. Externalities can be caused by trade in and regulation of natural resources, products, and wastes. They can also be created by the environmental effects of manufacturing and other processes for producing goods and services. Because of these externalities, trade restrictions, including tariffs and other charges, as well as bans, quotas, and regulatory requirements, may be necessary to promote human welfare.

One solution is to internalize the costs of pollution and environmental degradation within the activities which cause them.[4] But establishing the costs of environmental degradation is a difficult task. The costs are a function of the amount of harm caused or risks of harm posed by the environmental degradation and the economic value that societies place on avoiding such harm. That value is in turn a function of societal preferences for environmental quality versus other goods and services—wealth and risk aversion. There is often uncertainty and disagreement about the extent of harm caused by environmental degradation. As a result there will be wide differences in assessments of the social costs of environmental degradation and corresponding disagreements about the appropriate stringency of the measures needed to internalize them within those activities.

Within the GATT/WTO regime, the Most Favoured Nation (MFN) principle, according to which any trade advantage conferred by one country on another must be extended to all GATT contracting parties, and the National Treatment (NT) provision, under which importing countries must treat imported goods in the same manner as 'like or competing' domestic goods, are considered inviolable. The meaning of 'like product' has become a crucial issue in the trade/environment relationship and is the main stumbling block to any reform of the way in which products are distinguished for environmental protection purposes. Multilateral environmental agreements (MEAs) usually focus on the environmental impact of a product's production, use, and disposal and may not be concerned with, or affect, the actual product at issue. From an environmental standpoint, this makes sense. Environmental regulators want to tackle pollution as early as possible, so they will usually apply the regulation as far upstream in the production process as possible. They also want to control behaviour, and will discriminate between less and more environmentally damaging activities.[5] However, panel reports have ruled that discrimination against a product on the basis of the way in which it was produced and not on the basis of its own characteristics is a violation of the MFN and NT principles.[6] Examples of such measures include import bans on tuna caught with dolphin-unfriendly nets, fur caught in leghold traps, and shrimps fished by methods which kill sea turtles. Furthermore, the trading system discourages efforts to change behaviour outside a particular state's jurisdiction.

The main exceptions from an environmental standpoint to the general WTO principles are contained in GATT Articles XX(b) and XX(g). Article XX(b) provides for an exception for any measures 'necessary to protect human, animal, or plant life or health', while Article XX(g) does so for measures 'relating to the conservation of exhaustible natural resources if such measures are made effective in conjunction with restrictions on domestic production or consumption'. Both exceptions are subject to the requirement that such measures are not applied in a manner which would constitute a means of arbitrary or unjustifiable discrimination between countries where the same conditions prevail or be a disguised restriction on international trade (the headnote). GATT panels have consistently interpreted these exceptions in a narrow way, limiting the scope of environmental protection.

In essence, several questions lie at the heart of the issues in the relationship: should trade restrictive measures be used to further the objectives of multilateral environmental agreements? Should states be able to establish domestic environmental standards which go further than those agreed internationally? Are differing environmental standards a part of comparative advantage? Are less stringent environmental standards a form of trade distortion? Should a state be permitted to impose unilateral trade restrictions to promote its environmental objectives, in its own territory, in foreign states, in areas beyond national jurisdiction?[7]

Differences in Outlook and Values

The current trade/environment debate has been characterized by the highly contentious formulation of the matters at issue. For instance, the relationship has tended to be described as those situations in which environmental arguments are used to support a restriction on free trade. At the heart of the problem is the fact that the WTO rules do not include an express reference to environmental protection, although there is some consensus that this is implied in paragraphs (b) and (g) of the GATT general exception in Article XX.

THE TRADE VIEW

Trade protagonists' viewpoint is that trade promotes economic growth and specialization. In its 1992 report on the relationship, the GATT Secretariat argued that trade was simply a magnifier, enabling countries with adequate sustainable development policies to pursue these better. It said that there was no reason to assume that growth of per capita income, boosted by increased market access and expanding trade, 'necessarily or even on average, damages the environment'.[8] The argument rests on the premise that, by generating wealth, increased trade helps provide the finance necessary for pollution control and remedial cleanup. But this assumes that adequate provision will be made within the revenues generated by trade for protection of a country's environment. Furthermore, the argument ignores the efficiency rationale of preventing rather than mitigating environmental damage.

THE ENVIRONMENTAL VIEW

Environmental experts are concerned about increasing ozone depletion, climate change, species extinction, and the movement of toxic and hazardous wastes which contribute to deterioration in human as well as animal and plant health. It is acknowledged that MEAs, which regulate the environmental behaviour of states and companies, are the most effective means of addressing global environmental problems. Nevertheless, it is still believed that the added ingredient of trade measures is useful to enforce international environmental obligations and raise domestic environmental standards in countries where they are lacking or low. There is concern that trade intensifies the inadequacies of environmental protection policies, with resulting adverse consequences.[9]

DEVELOPING COUNTRY CONCERNS

Because of the manner in which the initial trade and environment debate was framed, a number of developing countries suspected that environmental exceptions to trade rules would be used to inhibit their economic development and would legitimize further northern involvement in matters of national sovereignty. The perception was that current proposals to alter the trade rules were created and structured primarily in OECD countries and express particular northern environmental concerns.[10]

THE POLITICAL PROCESS

On 14 April 1994 a ministerial decision was adopted by WTO members which formally established the CTE.[11] The ten items on the CTE's agenda covered the range of the trade/environment relationship.[12] The broad mandate given to the CTE raised considerable expectations.[13] Its establishment was seen as an important step towards incorporating environmental concerns into the WTO system, especially given the preamble to the agreement establishing the WTO and the expression of environmental considerations in the provisions of other WTO agreements.[14]

Progress in the CTE on analysing and arriving at consensus on the issues has been slow. Advocates of the status quo insisted that a sharp distinction must be made between environmental problems which are intrinsically international because their effects spill over borders, and environmental problems which are essentially domestic. They argued that international trade measures should not be employed in response to purely domestic environmental policies of another country. But the transboundary/domestic distinction is problematic and has not been thoroughly analysed by the CTE. Many of the measures categorized as dealing with transboundary effects can simultaneously have major domestic environmental implications and vice versa. For instance, regulations aimed at domestic producers to encourage recycling of beverage containers may force foreign producers to change their practices in order to serve the domestic market; a ban on the import of products made using chlorofluorocarbons (CFCs), aimed at tackling ozone depletion, may have the effect of putting domestic producers at a competitive advantage in the domestic market. There were also difficult questions of characterization. Should a trade measure be classified according to the intent of the state? If not, what objective criteria should be used and who should decide them?[15] It is suggested that the only type of justified trade intervention is a limited number of multilateral measures to promote participation in and compliance with agreements addressing transboundary environmental issues.[16] An example is the Montreal Protocol provision banning trade in ozone-depleting substances with non-parties.

As part of its terms of reference, the CTE had undertaken to report its findings to the first WTO Ministerial Conference, which took place in Singapore in December 1996. The Ministerial Conference is the highest decision-making body in the structure of the WTO, and is the body responsible for adopting any recommendations on modification of the WTO provisions.[17] However, the CTE's report, which contained no recommendations on modification of GATT rules, was viewed by many as a disappointing product, without substantive analysis and evaluation.[18] The report did not even attempt an honest elaboration of the problems in the trade/environment relationship; it merely summarized the differing views of the CTE's members, reflecting the prejudiced political stances within the Committee. A more benign view is that the report merely illustrated the compromise reached within a forum comprising a range of constituent interests with differences in values and comprehension of the multifaceted relationship between international trade and environmental protection.[19]

From a practical standpoint, the CTE's 1996 report does little to inspire the confidence of the environmental community in its ability to arrive at concrete recommendations for reconciling the trade/environment issues which remain at stake. Some commentators believe that the comprehensive analysis of the relationship can be achieved only if the CTE is open to participation by other actors in the international community, such as non-governmental organizations (NGOs), secretariats of major environmental treaties, and intergovernmental organizations (IGOs) with overlapping responsibilities.[20] In their view, the elements of the solution to the potential trade and environment conflict lie in the content of future MEAs whose design will become more sophisticated. Such policies will have to balance the requirements of economies at different levels of development. Financial, technological, and legal instruments will be required to achieve this balance and, indeed, may take many of the solutions outside the remit of the WTO. For this reason, the argument is made that discussion of the issues in the WTO should involve parties and international bodies with the expertise to respond to developmental or other concerns in the context of the reconciliation of trade and environment. Several intergovernmental organizations already have observer status with the CTE, including the United Nations Environment Programme (UNEP) and the Commission on Sustainable Development (CSD). In the last few years the WTO Secretariat has taken steps to convene public symposia on trade, environment, and sustainable development at which both NGOs and CTE delegates have actively participated. A couple of these symposia have taken place very close to CTE meetings, to encourage interaction between NGOs and delegates.

There is a clear need to provide impetus to the process of the assessment of the trade/environment relationship and to arrive at concrete solutions. It has been suggested that an executive committee would be useful in setting deadlines for the CTE to come up with recommendations.[21] But that still leaves the substantive task of analysis and resolution to the same body. The most that could conceivably be achieved is to establish a process for taking incremental decisions to resolve specific conflicts. In the meantime there is a movement to bring trade and environment back to the top of the political agenda by the convening of a High Level Symposium on Trade and Environment, to take place in Geneva in March 1999. The next WTO Ministerial Conference will take place in late 1999 in the USA, and at that time it is expected that the CTE will continue to keep its mandate but will wind down

its discussions in anticipation of a new round of multilateral trade talks expected in early 2000.

Judicial Activism

The policy and operational failure of the CTE have in effect left to the dispute settlement system the task of reconciling trade and environmental policies to support sustainable development within the multilateral trading system. The WTO's enforcement instrument, the Dispute Settlement Understanding (DSU), creates a binding structure for settling disputes. It contains certain procedural features which could be used positively in order better to reconcile trade and environmental policies. First, the provision of expert opinion to panels could provide a superior understanding of environmental concerns. Secondly, a weightier legal basis for decisions should lead the Dispute Settlement Body (DSB) to interpret environmental provisions within the GATT/WTO with less of a trade-focused political bias. Thirdly, the Appellate Body could place WTO disputes into the broader context of public international law. And lastly, the rule-based context of the dispute settlement system should provide developing countries in particular with greater access and security within the system.

The Appellate Body has carefully crafted a flexible approach to balancing conflicting trade and environmental policy objectives underlying the disputes before it. In the reformulated gasoline case (United States—Standards for Reformulated and Conventional Gasoline),[22] Venezuela and Brazil brought a complaint concerning standards for conventional and reformulated gasoline prescribed under the US Clean Air Act. The substance of the issue was whether the extremely technical specifications issued by the US Environmental Protection Agency for gasoline being sold in the USA, which applied to US refiners, blenders, and importers, were discriminatory. The rules were established in an effort to address the ozone and pollution damage experienced by US cities as a result, principally, of car exhaust fumes. The net effect of the rules was to leave foreign producers at a competitive disadvantage, which the panel held was contrary to GATT Articles I and III. The USA unsuccessfully sought to have the rules brought within the Article XX exceptions, (b), (d), and (g). On appeal, the Appellate Body agreed with the USA that clean air is an exhaustible natural resource. It went on to say that measures to protect clean air were legitimate environmental policy measures which qualified under the Article XX (b) and (g) exceptions. However, the matter was ultimately decided by reference to the headnote of Article XX, and the Appellate Body decided that the measure amounted to unjustifiable discrimination and a disguised restriction on international trade. While the importance of the environmental exceptions appears to have been buttressed and broadened, the Appellate Body's assessment in that case narrowed the application of Article XX through a more rigorous application of the headnote.

The recent shrimp/turtle case produced the same result: the trade-related environmental measure was deemed to be GATT-illegal.[23] The case involved a complaint by Thailand, India, Pakistan, and Malaysia regarding a provision in the US Endangered Species Act (Section 609). Section 609 placed an import ban on shrimp and shrimp products from countries not certified by the USA. Certification under Section 609 required that countries mandate the use of methods which prevent the incidental drowning of turtles from trawlers used to catch shrimp. The law applied within US territorial waters and outside the jurisdiction in the waters of those exporting shrimp to the US market.

At the panel stage the USA admitted that Section 609 violated GATT Article XI: 1 in that it amounted to a restriction on the import of shrimp, but argued that the measure was justified under Article XX (b) and (g) as a means of protecting a species recognized as highly endangered by an international conservation agreement to which all the disputants were parties. The panel decided that the measure was not justified under Article XX (b) or (g), and declared that, to uphold the security of the multilateral trading system, measures such as Section 609 must be prohibited. But the Appellate Body's reasoning appears to have expanded the scope of the environmental exceptions within Article XX. The tone of the report suggests an attempt to accommodate the concerns of both environmental experts and the defenders of the status quo. Significantly, in interpreting the provisions of Article XX (g), the Appellate Body commented that 'the provisions of the GATT must be informed by contemporary concerns of the community of nations about the protection and conservation of the environment.'[24]

Although, progressively, the Appellate Body has adopted an evolutionary approach to interpreting Article XX which contributes substantially to WTO jurisprudence, the same result ensues in each case: environmental concerns appear subordinate to trade policy priorities, and even occasional flexible interpretations cannot compensate for the inherent imbalance the WTO rules cause between trade and environmental policy instruments. The trade objective is ultimately the sieve through which all measures must pass, so that, in effect, there may be an inevitable futility in any trade-related environmental measure being able to withstand the scrutiny of the rigorous headnote test, since of necessity an environmental policy mechanism will usually be discriminatory in its application. This means that reconciliation of the two regimes must therefore come through a modification of Article XX to make express reference to environmental protection.[25]

In this manner, the WTO rules will truly reflect the equal status that trade and environment have in the public policy concerns of WTO members.

Participation by Non-State Actors
Another significant aspect of the shrimp/turtle case was the nominal participation of non-governmental actors in the dispute settlement process by way of the submission of *amicus curiae* briefs to the panel and to the Appellate Body.[26] This was done on the basis of an interest and expertise in the matter of sea turtle conservation. The panel rejected the briefs on the grounds that Article 13 of the DSU did not entitle it to accept non-requested information from non-government sources. The Appellate Body adopted a more flexible stance, accepting those briefs which were annexed to the US submission. Its ruling on the *amicus* briefs appears to leave to the Appellate Body's discretion whether and in what circumstances it will consider such submissions.

The flexibility shown by the Appellate Body offers a long-awaited chance for NGOs to participate in the dispute settlement process. As panels confront more complex factual and legal disputes, the dispute settlement system will obviously need a broader range of fact-finding techniques. NGOs are demonstrating a willingness and capability to provide such scientific and legal expertise. Their input, through *amicus curiae* briefs or otherwise, could present a different perspective from that of governments party to the dispute, and may possibly provide expert information that would ordinarily be unavailable in government submissions.[27]

National and Regional Models
Some regional trade agreements, such as the European Community (EC) and the North American Free Trade Agreement (NAFTA), accord environmental protection policies a higher priority than the GATT/WTO. Of course such regimes have broader political objectives which are independent of and irreducible to trade objectives, and these are enshrined in the respective legislative instruments. But it is helpful to examine the mechanisms which have allowed such regional agreements to achieve the relative success they have.

The European Community
In the EC experience, measures which pursue policy goals independent of the common market must be evaluated for their trade compatibility; the parallels with the jurisprudence of the GATT are therefore patent. Article 36 of the EC Treaty provides less protection for environmental measures than GATT Article XX. It allows member states to adopt measures which are prima facie incompatible with

Articles 30 and 34 for the purposes of protecting a series of non-economic values such as the protection of human health or life, animals, or plants.[28] The European Court of Justice (ECJ) has made clear, in a series of cases, that Article 36 is exhaustive and must be strictly interpreted. Nevertheless, in the Cassis de Dijon case, the ECJ has recognized that, in the absence of Community measures of harmonization, member states may, when adopting measures which apply equally to domestic and imported products, restrict intra-Community trade for motives other than those specifically recognized by Article 36.[29] This would suggest that the ECJ can exempt a broad range of environmental protection regulation. The EC Commission has also underscored the importance of environmental protection as a potential limitation on the prohibition in Article 30.[30] This interpretation was given further acceptance by the ECJ in the waste oils case.[31] The Court was asked to determine if Council Directive 75/439 on the disposal of waste oils conformed, inter alia, to the principles of freedom of trade. The Directive envisaged the assignment of exclusive zones to waste oil collectors, prior approval of undertakings responsible for disposal, and indemnities being granted to undertakings. Significantly, the court made clear that the principle of freedom of trade is not to be viewed in absolute terms, but is subject to certain limits:

... the Directive must be seen in the perspective of environmental protection, which is one of the Community's essential objectives.[32]

This decision clearly signals that, in the absence of Community rules, national measures taken for environmental purposes may constitute 'mandatory requirements' limiting the application of Article 30.[33]

Apart from the flexible use of treaty language, the ECJ has developed clear tests for evaluating environmental measures. The court applies a proportionality test, deciding whether the measure is pertinent, i.e., that there is a causal link between the measure and the attainment of the objective, and secondly whether the measure is the least restrictive means of attaining the objective.[34] This is one of the elements by which the EC has achieved a better balance between free trade and environmental protection.

ECJ jurisprudence has also proved sensitive to local conditions as a factor in determining the necessity of a particular measure. In this respect, the Belgian waste case represents a landmark decision, with important implications for the relationship between trade and environmental protection policies.[35] There, the court accepted the argument put forward by Belgium that its restrictions on the imports of waste were a temporary measure to safeguard the Wallonia region from an influx of waste from neighbouring countries. Thus, the discriminatory effect of the Belgian regulations was overlooked on the basis that local conditions may warrant unique treatment. Applied to the WTO, this type of policy interpretation could enable states with more sophisticated environmental agendas to pursue legitimate preferences where it is justified by local conditions, with less WTO interference.

The analysis of EC law indicates the extent to which the ECJ has developed a flexible approach to balancing trade and environmental priorities. Coupled with the EC Treaty, the jurisprudence of the court has provided more legal justifications for the protection of measures taken for environmental protection, as environmental factors become increasingly evident in decisions of commercial policy.

NAFTA

Under heavy criticism and fear by environmentalists that increased competition due to NAFTA would lower environmental standards and lead to areas designed to exploit the environment as a comparative advantage, Mexico, the United States, and Canada drafted a trade agreement which contains specific provisions designed to balance free trade with environmental protection.

The preamble to the agreement incorporates some of the strongest environmental and conservation language of any trade agreement. It states that states will conduct their trade 'in a manner consistent with environmental protection and conservation' and 'preserve their flexibility to safeguard public welfare to promote sustainable development and strengthen the development and enforcement of environmental laws and regulations.'

Article 104 of the agreement exempts certain (listed) MEAs, including the Montreal Protocol and the Basel Convention, from challenge. In the event that there is inconsistency between NAFTA trade obligations and an MEA, the MEA prevails as long as the party chooses a measure that is least inconsistent with NAFTA. Moreover, Article 1114 states that parties should not attract investment by waiving environmental obligations or lowering standards. Of course it remains to be seen how NAFTA trade and environment disputes will be decided in practice, but, in a sense, the certainty provided by the provisions on potential trade and environment conflicts would suggest that they actually pre-empt and prevent the possibility of dispute between the two regimes.

US Case Law

A look at the US jurisprudence on trade (economic) and environment disputes also serves as a useful model which can provide lessons for the WTO. The Commerce Clause of the US Constitution confers a general grant of power on Congress to regulate trade between the states. In the case of product standards, the Supreme Court's analysis is that, while they may, rarely, discriminate against inter-tate trade, they may nevertheless affect it. It has adopted balance test which weighs the relative importance of the environmental and trade interests at stake. In this respect, the court has allowed a state ban on the sale of milk in plastic containers. It found that the measure passed the Pike test, which held that even a non-discriminatory product will be struck down 'if the burden imposed on [interstate] commerce is clearly excessive in relation to the putative local benefits.'[36] In the case of the import of out-of-state waste, the court has taken a stricter line. It exhibits disapproval of state measures discriminating on their face or in their effects against interstate trade. The court reviewed a Michigan statute barring waste generated in another county, state, or country unless it was explicitly authorized in the receiving county's plan, and found the measure discriminatory.[37] Using the earlier case of Philadelphia v. New Jersey to provide a framework for analysis,[38] the Court held such discrimination against interstate commerce to be unconstitutional unless justified by a valid factor unrelated to economic protectionism. Origin alone was insufficient to validate the discrimination. The balance test adopted by the Supreme Court is widely accepted in the USA, although it is not without controversy.[39]

But where two genuine and legitimate values clash, it is difficult to see how they can be reconciled without using a balancing approach to decide which should be supreme in a given instance. In this sense, trade and environment are placed on an equal footing: if a state measure creates a great burden on trade but generates little environmental benefit, it will be held invalid; conversely, if the environmental benefits flowing from a particular measure are great, with only a small consequent impact on trade, the measure will be found valid.[40] However, the cost-benefit analysis inherent in the balancing approach presents problems about the precision courts are able to bring to bear in this kind of assessment. Indeed, it has been suggested that the balance test is an inherently legislative rather than a judicial choice, and the proper role of courts is not to be 'super-legislatures'.[41] However, in the WTO context, the dearth of substantive rules on environmental protection, coupled with the absence of consensus on the need for modification of the GATT rules in order to support environmental protection measures, has led to the reliance on the Appellate Body as a super legislature.

Challenges and Necessary Reform

Both trade policy and environmental protection policy can be regarded as aiming in different ways at the furtherance of human welfare. Therefore mechanisms must be developed to reconcile these policies in the best way possible rather than to establish any absolute priority between them.

There is some agreement on a few basic issues in the trade/environment relationship: that trade may have positive or negative environmental consequences, that environmental policies may affect trade, that effective means to address and minimize conflicts are necessary, and that complementarities ought to be utilized and developed where possible. Beyond this core of agreement the differences in outlook and values between the trade and environment communities appear intractable.

To start with, certain basic assumptions about the international political and legal system are made within the rules and practice of the GATT/WTO. First, territory is treated as the basis for jurisdiction regardless of the transboundary or extra-jurisdictional dimension of many environmental and economic interests.[42] The unilateral use of trade measures, for instance, is viewed as an exercise of extraterritorial muscle to impose environmental priorities on another nation, undermining that nation's sovereignty.[43] It is feared that this kind of action, if it were to be emulated by several states, would undermine multilateral co-operation and threaten the multilateral trading system. But there are political considerations of how to react either where a government shows no interest in improving its environmental policies or where, theoretically, efficient multilateral instruments for dealing with environmental problems are available but, in practice, simply cannot be adopted or implemented. Secondly, the GATT/WTO regime assumes that political processes within each state will determine the best combination of environmental and other policies for that state.[44] Admittedly, adherence to the GATT/WTO regime would be weakened if sovereign competence was routinely displaced in the environmental arena; on the other hand, national sovereignty sometimes excludes from the decision-making process the victims of transboundary spillovers. Traditional notions of sovereignty, therefore, are not entirely helpful in addressing the 'political failures', which may be just as damaging as 'market failures'. Thirdly, the practice and rhetoric of the GATT/WTO system are based on the general undesirability of using trade restrictions not permitted under existing GATT rules to pursue environmental objectives.[45] Since comparative advantage is at the heart of trade theory, trade restrictions are considered wrong *per se*; they fail to take account of relevant differences in such matters as environmental conditions, absorptive capacities, and social conditions. There is also the political consideration that, if such trade restrictions are allowed, pressure will mount to allow them to be used for differences in labour rights, social policies, and population policy.

Those who advocate the retention of the status quo in the trading system view the potential conflicts between trade rules and environmental protection policies either as trivial or as a problem of modest amendment or interpretation of rules and procedures. On the contrary, some of the conflicts would be more severe if international environmental rules and institutions were not so fragmented compared to the unified and broad WTO structure. Moreover, environmental pressure on trade rules and institutions is likely to be much greater than at first glance and these will have significant legal implications in the future.

In that situation, law, as the effectual embodiment of policy decisions, becomes important in elaborating the trade/environment relationship. But the lack of co-ordination between trade and environmental policy making has prevented the development of a structured legal relationship between the two fields. Legal rules will have to be developed and utilized in a practical way, therefore, so as to contribute to an accommodation between the different normative and institutional systems in order to minimize the disruptive effects of conflicts.

Notwithstanding the pervasive pessimism about its capabilities, the GATT/WTO institutional structure does have the capacity to address these normative conflicts and to take decisions which could serve the interests of sustainable development. International environmental institutions are for the most part not in a position to address trade/environment conflicts in a quasi adjudicative manner, so the principal practical forum for legal conflicts in the area remains the GATT/WTO system.

Conclusions

Reconciling trade and environment in the GATT/WTO has always been problematic, and the trouble lies at the heart of the GATT rules. There is no express reference in the rules to protection of the environment. Because of this problem, the existing substantive and procedural provisions for the integration of the environment of sustainable development with the trade disciplines are fairly limited in their reach.

Progress in the WTO on reconciliation of trade and environment has taken two tracks. The political process in the shape of the CTE has almost ground to a halt, leaving it to the judicial process to make policy through its decisions on trade and environment disputes. Without an express assertion in the rules themselves that commits states to balance environmental considerations with their trade policies, the dispute settlement organs have been rather constrained in their attempts to find an equitable solution to the trade and environmental imperatives of WTO members.

This necessitates some substantive and procedural reforms within the multilateral trading system. There are three principal areas where substantive reform is neces-

sary. The first concerns rectifying the potential conflict between MEAs and WTO obligations. There are two clear ways of formalizing this arrangement to avoid conflict. The first is to amend Article XX to include an exception for 'measures taken pursuant to' an MEA. The second possibility is to negotiate a separate agreement on MEAs and the use of trade related environmental measures. The second area of reform deals with the necessity to establish clear rules regarding trade restrictions based on process and production methods (PPMs). Some production methods which affect the basic characteristic of the final product are clearly recognized in the Agreements on Sanitary and Phytosanitary Measures and Technical Barriers to Trade. Thus the definition and scope of the term 'like product' could easily be broadened under the rules. Reform in this area has clear implications for implementation of the Kyoto Protocol, pursuant to which regulators may wish to distinguish between products on the basis of the volume of greenhouse gas emissions.

The third reform concerns the WTO's interpretation of Article XX and the benefits of adopting the approach taken by regional arrangements in deference to environmental considerations. In the EC example, environmental protection is expressly exempted from the standard prohibitions on restrictions on liberalized trade. And the ECJ has developed a flexible approach in its application of a proportionality test for weighing trade related environmental measures. This has allowed the achievement of a much better balance between free trade and environmental protection. If handled correctly, such regional agreements could have a synergistic relationship with the WTO. They could provide 'pathfinding' solutions which may be applied at the multilateral level.

Reform on the procedural front in the WTO should include mechanisms to provide the public with a forum to voice concerns and allow non-governmental organizations the opportunity to present information to dispute settlement panels by way of an *amicus* brief or through the establishment of the position of an advocate-general, similar to that in the EC legal system.

While it is understandable that the WTO is concerned with potential trade abuses, this should not obstruct environmental policy making and unduly restrict the choices states have to solve environmental problems. If necessary, the WTO can be reformed incrementally, without altering the fundamental rights and obligations of members, until members enter into a fresh round of negotiations to amend those rights. But procedural and substantive reform must take place sooner rather than later.

Notes and References

The authors wish to thank Farhana Yamin for her useful comments on an earlier draft of this chapter.

1. John Jackson (1994), 'Greening the GATT: Trade Rules and Environmental Policy', in James Cameron (ed.), *Trade and Environment: The Search for Balance* (London: Cameron May), 42.

2. Benedict Kingsbury (1994), 'Environment and Trade: The GATT/WTO Regime in the International Legal System', in A. E. Boyle (ed.), *Environmental Regulation and Economic Growth* (Oxford: Clarendon Press), 189.

3. The Dispute Settlement Understanding (DSU) creates a dispute panel and an Appellate Body to adjudicate trade disputes between WTO members. Under the DSU, a WTO member has the right to request the establishment of a panel to settle a dispute; compulsory jurisdiction is thereby passed to the Dispute Settlement Body (DSB). This right also includes an opportunity to appeal the panel's decision before the Appellate Body.

4. See generally in relation to the trade/environment debate: James Cameron, Paul Demaret, and Damien Geradin (eds.), (1994), *Trade and the Environment: The Search for Balance* (London: Cameron May); John Jackson (1992), 'World Trade Rules and Environmental Policies: Congruence or Conflict?', *Washington and Lee Law Review*, 49; Steve Charnovitz (1993), 'Environmentalism Confronts GATT Rules: Recent Developments and New Opportunities', *Journal of World Trade*, 27; Steve Charnovitz (1991), 'Exploring the Environmental Exceptions in GATT Article XX', *Journal of World Trade*, 25; Thomas Schoenbaum (1992), 'Free International Trade and Protection of the Environment: Irreconcilable Conflict?', *American Journal of International Law*, 86.

5. See Beatrice Chaytor and James Cameron (1995), *Taxes for Environmental Purposes: The Scope for Border Tax Adjustment under WTO Rules* (Gland: WWF International).

6. *United States—Restrictions on Imports of Tuna* (1991), GATT Doc. DS21/R, 30 ILM, 1598.

7. Kingsbury (1994), 'Environment and Trade', 192.

8. GATT Secretariat (1992), *Trade and the Environment* (Geneva: GATT), 3, 4.

9. Charles Arden-Clarke (1991), 'The General Agreement on Tariffs and Trade, Environmental Protection and Sustainable Development', *WWF International*, 10.

10. Piritta Sorsa (1992), 'GATT and Environment: Basic Issues and Some Developing Country Concerns', in P. Low (ed.), *International Trade and the Environment*, World Bank Discussion Paper 159, 325–40.

11. Ministerial Decision of 14 April 1994, 33 ILM (1994), 1267.

12. The ten items on the agenda were: multilateral environmental agreements; environmental taxes and the trading system; packaging, labelling, and recycling; information regarding trade related environmental measures; dispute settlement in the WTO and environmental agreements; market access, trade restrictions, and trade distortions; domestically prohibited goods; intellectual property rights; services; and involvement of NGOs in the WTO.

13. The US government declared that the CTE 'will assist efforts to reach international agreements on environmental issues that affect the entire world, such as ozone depletion, global climate change, and biodiversity' (Office of the US Trade Representative (1994), *Uruguay Round—Jobs for the US, Growth for the World*, 19); and GLOBE, an international group of legislators, called for 'the resolution of all outstanding trade and environment matters within two years of the entry into force of the WTO . . .' (Action Agenda: Trade and the Environment, Resolution Adopted Unanimously by 8th GLOBE International General Assembly (2nd March 1994)).

14. The preamble to the agreement establishing the WTO provides that the relations among WTO members in the field of trade and economic endeavour 'should be conducted with a view to raising standards of living and expanding the production of and trade in goods and services, while allowing for the optimal use of resources in accordance with the objectives of sustainable development, seeking both to protect and preserve the environment and to enhance the means for doing so.' Environmental protection provisions are also contained in the Agreements on Technical Barriers to Trade, on Sanitary and Phytosanitary Measures, on Agriculture, on Trade-Related Intellectual Property Rights, and on Subsidies and Countervailing Measures.

15. Daniel C. Esty (1994), 'Unpacking the Trade and Environment Conflict', *Law and Policy in International Business*, 25, 1259.

16. See e.g. Kingsbury (1994), 'Environment and Trade', 195.

17. See Article 10, WTO Charter.

18. See Steve Charnovitz (1997), 'Critical Guide to the WTO's Report on Trade and Environment', in *Arizona Journal of International Comparative Law*, 14, 341; Halina Ward (1996), *Trade Measures and Multilateral Environmental Agreements: Backwards or Forwards in the WTO?* (Gland: WWF International).

19. Beatrice Chaytor and Mathias Wolkewitz (1997), 'Participation and Priorities: An Assessment of Developing Countries Concerns' in the Trade/Environment Interface', *RECIEL*, 6.2. , 157.

20. See NRDC/FIELD (1995), *Environmental Priorities for the World Trading System Recommendations to the WTO Committee on Trade and Environment*, 3.

21. T. J. Shoenbaum (1997), 'International Trade and Protection of the Environment: The Continuing Search for Reconciliation', *American Journal of International Law*, 91, 270. Shoenbaum cites the Consultative Group of 18 which was established by the GATT Council in 1975; a similar group could be revived in this respect.

22. WT/DS2/AB/R, adopted 20 May 1996, reprinted in *International Trade Law Reports*, 1, 68.

23. United States–Imports of Certain Shrimp and Shrimp Products, WT/DS58/AB/R, 12 October 1998.

24. Ibid., para 129.

25. See James Cameron (1996), *The Relationship between the Provisions of the Multilateral Trading System and Trade Measures for Environmental Purposes, Including those Pursuant to Multilateral Environmental Agreements (MEAs)* (Gland: WWF International).

26. *Amicus curiae* means literally 'friend of the court'. A person with strong interest in or views on the subject matter may petition the court for permission to file a brief. Such briefs, which are common in the US legal system, are usually filed in appeals concerning matters of broad public interest.

27. Jackson (1994), 'Greening the GATT', 43.

28. Article 30 of the EC Treaty prohibits all quantitative restrictions on imports and measures having equivalent effect between member states. Article 34 prohibits quantitative restrictions on exports and all measures having equivalent effect between member states.

29. See Case 120/78, Rewe-ZentralAG v. Bundesmonopolverwaltung für Branntwei [1979] ECR, 649.

30. Communication from the Commission concerning the consequences of the judgement given by the Court of Justice on 20 February 1979 in Case 120/78 ('Cassis de Dijon')1980 OJ (C 256), 2.

31. Procureur de la Republique v. Association de Defense des Bruleurs d'Huiles Usagees, Case 240/83 [1984] ECR, 531.

32. Ibid., 548.

33. Damien Geradin (1997), *Trade and the Environment: A Comparative Study of EC and US Law* (Cambridge: Cambridge

University Press), 15.

34. See Case 788/79 [1980] ECR 2,071; Case 104/75 [1976] ECR 613; Case 261/81 [1982] ECR 3,961.
35. Case C-2/90, Commission v. Belgium, [1992] ECR I-4, 43 1.
36. Pike v. Bruce Church, 3 87 US 137, 142 (1970).
37. Fort Gratiot Sanitary Landfill v. Michigan Department of natural Resources, 112 S. Ct 2, 019 (1992).
38. 437 US 617 (1978).
39. Geradin (1997), *Trade and the Environment*, 62–3.
40. Ibid., 63.
41. See e.g. Proctor & Gamble v. Chicago, 509 F. 2d 69, 76 (7th Cir. 1975), cert. denied, 421 US 978 (1975); Stoke-on-Trent City Council v. B&Q [1990] 3 CMLR 41, 49.
42. Kingsbury (1994), 'Environment and Trade', 198–9.
43. GATT Secretariat (1992), *Trade and the Environment*, 8–12; Tuna/Dolphin Panel Report (DS21) (1991), paras 6.2–6.3.
44 Kingsbury (1994), 'Environment and Trade', 199.
45. Ibid.

World Business Council for Sustainable Development: The Greening of Business or a Greenwash?

Adil Najam

Introduction

Writing as the then Chairman on the World Business Council for Sustainable development (WBCSD), Livio DeSimone—Chairman and Chief Executive Officer of the 3M Company—argued that a paradigm shift has taken place since the 1992 Earth Summit in Rio de Janeiro. 'Business . . . used to be depicted as a primary source of the world's environmental problems. Today, it is increasingly viewed as a vital contributor to solving those problems.'[1] Although it is very doubtful that the change took place only—or even primarily—because of the WBCSD, all evidence suggests that this change has indeed happened, and that at some level WBCSD has both contributed to and capitalized upon it.

Evidence of the change is plentiful. Intergovernmental organizations (IGOs), particularly in the United Nations system, have launched major initiatives to woo the private sector. Speaking at the 1999 World Economic Forum at Davos, the UN Secretary General Kofi Annan called for a new 'global compact of shared values and principles' between business leaders and the world body, particularly on environment.[2] A manifestation of this new shift is the so-called Global Sustainable Development Facility— 2B2M: 2 Billion People to Market by 2020 programme, for which the United Nations Development Programme (UNDP) is allegedly gathering corporate sponsorships.[3] At the Rio+5 celebrations in 1997 one of the hottest tickets in town was the high-level round table, co-hosted by WBCSD with the President of the UN General Assembly and attended by a select group of business, government, and non-governmental organization (NGO) leaders.[4] Major research universities are no less enamoured. The most prestigious of institutions, including the Massachusetts Institute of Technology (MIT) in the United States and Cambridge University in the United Kingdom seem to be actively wooing the WBCSD. Even NGOs are no longer immune to the charm of the pin stripes. Over the last few years major environmental groups such as the IUCN – The World Conservation Union, the World Resources Institute (WRI), and the International Institute for Environment and Development (IIED) have all stepped up efforts to seek corporate partnerships—including with WBCSD. Those that are not doing so, such as Greenpeace International, are spending even more effort and time warning the world about the growing influence of big business and its attendant hazards.[5] Ultimately, this may be the biggest testimony to the seriousness of the new clout that big business seems to be acquiring over international environmental discourse.

It is not the purpose of this paper to analyse why this change has happened.[6] Our purpose, instead, is to see how one particular group, the WBCSD, has been able to shape and use the changing landscape to advance its own agendas and influence the international policy discourse on environment and development, and whether the rise of the organization represents a greening of business or simply a 'greenwash'.

Organizational Profile

The World Business Council for Sustainable Development (WBCSD) was formed in January 1995 with the merger of the Business Council for Sustainable Development (BCSD) and the World Industry Council for the Environment (WICE).

The BCSD was a direct outgrowth of the 1992 Earth Summit process. It was formed when Maurice Strong— then Secretary General of the United Nations Conference on Environment and Development (UNCED)—asked the Swiss industrialist Stephan Schmidheiny to act as his special advisor on business and environment. Schmidheiny brought together an impressive international group of top business leaders interested in the environment, and produced the book *Changing Course*.[7] Showcasing an array of case studies of best practice, the book coined the term 'eco-efficiency' and argued that sustainable development was not only good for business, it was 'good business'. The ideas discussed in the book became the basis of a formalized BCSD, and soon afterwards UNCED regional and national chapters began to spring up. To its credit, the BCSD was a major breakthrough because it brought together business leaders at the highest level to express a concern for environmental protection, portray it as a common concern, and break the prevailing mould of expressing the issue only in simplistic and antagonistic 'business *versus* environment' terms.

The genesis of WICE, on the other hand, lies in the International Chamber of Commerce (ICC), which boasts more than 7000 member companies in over 130 countries. In 1990 an ICC Working Party for Sustainable Development, led by Peter Scupholme of British Petroleum and W. Ross Stevens III of Du Pont, produced a Business Charter for Sustainable Development. This Charter was launched in 1991 at the Second World Industry Conference on Environmental Management at Rotterdam, and was followed soon afterwards by the report *From Ideas to Action*, which also outlined cases of positive industry response to environmental issues.[8] In 1993 the ICC reconfigured its Environmental Bureau into an expanded WICE to serve as an industry voice in the follow-up to UNCED. The Charter's 16 principles—ranging from recognizing environmental management as a corporate priority to affirming the precautionary principle—became the guiding foundation for WICE.[9]

Each of the two parents had already established itself as a credible representative of international business on issues of the environment. The BCSD had been a forceful presence at UNCED and had begun to develop links with international NGOs and governments. The ICC, which had long and deep relationships with international business federations and IGOs, ensured an equally prominent position for WICE. The high degree of similarity in goals, overlap in membership, and complementarity in conceptual principles led to their merger into a single entity, the

---

Box 1: The WBCSD Story

1990 UNCED Secretary-General Maurice Strong asks the industrialist Stephan Schmidheiny to be his advisor on business and environment. This leads to the creation of the **Business Council for Sustainable Development (BCSD)**.

1991 The International Chamber of Commerce (ICC) develops a **Business Charter for Sustainable Development,** which is launched in April 1991 at the Second World Industry Conference on Environmental Management in Rotterdam.

1992 BCSD represents business at the **Rio Earth Summit (UNCED)** and releases its report *Changing Course: A Global Business Perspective on Development and the Environment*.

ICC releases its report *From Ideas to Action*.

1993 The **World Industry Council for Environment (WICE)** is founded as an initiative of the International Chamber of Commerce (ICC).

1994 A number of regional and national BCSDs are formed. BCSD sets up a **Sustainable Project Management** in partnership with UNDP.

1995 **The World Business Council for Sustainable Development (WBCSD)** is created through a merger of BCSD and WICE.

1996 WBCSD, UNEP, and the Ceres Initiative launch programme on **financial indicators of sustainable development.** *Financing Change* is published.

WBCSD launches its **International Business Action Plan on Climate Change (IBAPCC).**

The **Foundation for Business and Sustainable Development (FBSD)** is established.

1997 WBCSD co-hosts a **high-level round table of government, NGO, and business leaders on business and environment** as part of the Rio+5 celebrations. WBCSD releases its report on the progress since Rio, *Signals of Change*. It also releases a new book, *Eco-Efficiency*, and a report on *Environmental Performance and Shareholder Value*.

WBCSD launches the **Sustainable Business Challenge,** an Internet-based environmental exam for students preparing for careers in business, finance, and government.

WBCSD signs a **memorandum of understanding with UNDP** to improve environmental performance of companies in developing countries.

1998 The **WBCSD Virtual University** is founded in collaboration with the University of Cambridge and the Norwegian School of Management. *The Sustainable Business Challenge* is published.

WBCSD holds a series of **Stakeholder Dialogues** on Sustainable Consumption, Corporate Social Responsibility, and Sustainable Business.

WBCSD releases its **Survey on Corporate Environmental Reports** and the results of its Global Scenarios project.

WBCSD, which immediately became the most authoritative and pre-eminent business voice on sustainable development. Box 1 lists the key events and milestones in the organization's development.

WBCSD is a pure membership organization in that its 26 member corporations are the principal source of financing and directly participate in agenda setting and governance.[10] However, with the annual membership subcription being US$30,000 and membership offered only by invitation, it is a fairly exclusive club. For all practical purposes it remains a coalition of big businesses, predominantly from the advanced industrialized countries. Although technically there are no barriers—except hefty annual dues—to the inclusion of smaller companies, especially from developing countries, the priorities and focus of the organization is decidedly on issues of greater concern to large corporations.

According to the WBCSD leadership, 'a large membership roster is not our overriding concern.'[11] In fact, the number of total members has not grown substantially since 1995, with most new additions made principally to improve geographic or sectoral coverage. For the most part WBCSD tries to address the geographic imbalance through its global network of 'partner' (but non-member) associations. Efforts have been made to strengthen and activate this network, which now comprises 18 national BCSDs and an assortment of national and international business organizations.

Even in taking over many features of WICE, WBCSD closely mirrors the BCSD design. An important component is that, unlike in WICE, membership is by invitation only 'to companies committed to the concepts of sustainable development and responsible environmental management'.[12] Apart from annual dues, members are also expected to provide in-kind and personnel support, including financial backing for individual working groups, and the active participation, including secondment, of their staff in the WBCSD work programme. In return WBCSD offers them the ability to 'exert greater influence on the framework conditions under which [the member companies] operate by being represented by a credible advocate.'[13] Living up to its claim of speaking 'the language of business', WBCSD makes an appealing case of why major multinational corporations should join its ranks: 'The collective voice of a cross-sectoral and global body like the WBCSD offers companies greater weight in the sustainable development debate than they would otherwise have singly.'[14]

The promise being offered is that 'WBCSD [will provide] companies with an edge on the competition by being aware, ahead of others, and thus able to anticipate the emerging environmental and social trends which might impact their business.'[15] The appeal of the argument is reflected in the WBCSD membership roster, which, although short, includes some very significant corporate players, including such giants as Assurances Générales de France, Rhône-Poulenc (France), Bayer, Hoechst (Germany), Fiat Auto (Italy), Heineken, Philips Electronics, Unilever (Netherlands), Norsk Hydro (Norway), ABB Asea Brown Boveri, Nestlé, Société Générale (Switzerland), British Petroleum, Glaxo Wellcome, ICI, Shell International (United Kingdom), Ontario Hydro (Canada), AT&T, Cargill, CH2M Hill, Dow Chemicals, DuPont, Eastman Kodak, General Motors, International Paper, Johnson & Johnson, Monsanto, Proctor & Gamble, 3M Corporation, Xerox (United States), Hitachi, Mitsubishi, Nissan Motors, Seiko, Sony, Tokyo Electric, Toyota (Japan), and Samsung and LG Group (Korea). A few large corporations from developing countries and transition economies, such as Chemical Works Sokolov (Czech Republic), Aracruz Celulose (Brazil), Grupo Vitro (Mexico), China Petro-Chemical (China), and Inti Karya Persada Tehnik (Indonesia), are also members.

Participation is sought at the very highest level, normally from the chief executive officer (CEO) or equivalent. This ensures an earnestness of commitment from the company and allows WBCSD greater credibility in its advocacy activities. WBCSD is governed by a Council, composed of the CEOs of member companies, which meets once a year to determine organizational priorities and direction. It is also responsible for appointing the Executive Committee, determining membership dues, and approving the budget. Council members co-chair WBCSD working groups and are called upon to speak on its behalf at relevant forums. Each Council Member appoints a 'Liaison Delegate', normally a senior member of their staff, who supports them in their WBCSD responsibilities, participates in working groups on their behalf, and interacts with the Secretariat and other member companies. Liaison delegates meet twice a year in plenary sessions and throughout the year in working group meetings. An Executive Committee of up to 14 CEOs from member companies oversees the management of WBCSD, and normally meets three times a year. It is responsible for appointing the President, approving working groups, WBCSD reports and books, and finalizing the budget. The day-to-day management is handled by a Secretariat in Geneva, headed by a full-time President (Executive Director until 1997). In 1998 the Secretariat had a staff strength of about 30.[16]

Surprisingly, no financial and budgetary data on the organization is publicly available. Not only are the WBCSD annual reports silent on this subject (unlike those that its members are more used to), but repeated requests to obtain this information proved unsuccessful. However, some estimates can be made. The bulk of WBCSD's direct funding comes from the annual membership fee of US$30,000 (for 1998) that each corporate member pays. For 1998, therefore, membership dues would have amounted to US$3.78 million. The total resources made available by the members would, however, be significantly higher, since they would include in-kind and personnel contributions to various working groups as well as experts seconded to the WBCSD Secretariat. For example, in 1998 as many as six staff members working on various projects at the WBCSD Secretariat were on secondment from member companies. In short, it would be fair to say that, unlike even the biggest environmental NGOs, fund-raising and financial concerns have not been major worries for the WBCSD.

The Greening of Big Business . . .

Although sometimes viewed and described by others as an environmental NGO, WBCSD views itself very much as a business organization: a coalition of and advocate for big business on issues pertaining to sustainable development (see Box 2).

While the thrust of the organization's goals pertains to 'participating in policy development in order to secure a regulatory framework for business to operate profitably while preserving the environment and contributing to a sustainable future',[17] it also seeks to 'encourage high standards of environmental management in business itself'.[18] In essence, while much of WBCSD's focus is on projecting the green face of big business, part of its mandate is also to make business greener. This flows directly from the

---

Box 2: WBCSD—Merchant or Citizen?

Is WBCSD an NGO? This question may first seem to be of little more than academic value, but is of significant strategic importance to the organization's ultimate influence. Like many others, this *Yearbook* classifies WBCSD as an Environmental NGO.[1] In fact, one of the biggest measures of the organization's success is that it is seen by many within the environmental community as an environmental NGO focusing on business concerns. This is very different from how the mainstream environmental community tends to view other similarly structured business coalitions—such as, for example, the Chlorine Chemistry Council (CCC)— which is seen as a mere 'lobbyist' and therefore somehow inferior. WBCSD has strategically used this perception of its identity, particularly its image as a 'nonlobby group', to forge closer ties with mainstream environmental groups on the one hand while marketing its ability to do so as a major advantage to its members on the other.[2]

Interestingly, within the bounds of carefully cultivated ambiguity, WBCSD tends to define itself as a business group. The standard line is that it is a 'coalition of international companies united by a shared commitment to the environment and to sustainable development'. In material directed specifically at its corporate members the thrust becomes more direct, and the organization talks with pride of its increasing recognition as 'the leading business advocate on environmental and sustainable development' and how its 'views are being sought by a growing number of stakeholders', such as governments, international organizations, and environmental NGOs.[3]

In the familiar tripartite map of institutional sectors—the prince, the merchant, and the citizen, signifying the institutions of state, business, and civil society respectively—WBCSD would identify itself very much as the voice of the merchant.[4] While it is the merchant speaking, not just to the market but to the citizen, it remains nonetheless a manifestation of the merchant rather than the citizen. Technically, therefore, WBCSD is a lobbying organization for big business no different from the CCC and others. Moreover, it accepts that status without qualms or camouflage. As the WBCSD President, Björn Stigson, put it in a 1998 speech, the world since UNCED has changed in that environmental discussions are no longer bi-polar (governments and NGOs) but are now tri-polar, between 'governments, business and civil society'.[5] Material prepared for its corporate members makes it clear what the organization views itself to be, and not to be: 'Five years ago, it is unlikely that NGOs in particular would have forged links with a business organization like ours.'[6] In short, however else others might choose to classify it, for WBCSD itself, the goal is to make sure that, in all discussions of international environmental policy, big business gets a 'seat at the table' and then to occupy that seat on behalf of big business.[7]

References
1. See section on non-governmental organizations in this *Yearbook*.
2. Ted Button (1998), 'The Work of the World Business Council for Sustainable Development', speech by WBCSD Director External Co-operation, 16 June 1998 (available at: <http://www.wbcsd.ch/Speech/s39.htm>).
3. WBCSD (1997), *The Value of Membership* (Geneva: WBCSD).
4. For the conceptual distinctions between the three, see Adil Najam (1996), 'Understanding the Third Sector: Revisiting the Prince, the Merchant, and the Citizen', *Nonprofit Management and Leadership*, 7: 2, 203–19.
5. Björn Stigson (1998) 'How much can be left to the Private Sector and the Market', speech by WBCSD President, 11 March 1998 (available at: <http://www.wbcsd.ch/Speech/s32.htm>).
6. WBCSD (1997), *The Value of Membership*.
7. WBCSD (undated), *Information and Publications* (Geneva, WBCSD).

second half of its mission statement, which requires it to 'promote the attainment of eco-efficiency through high standards of environmental and resource management in business.'[19]

For WBCSD, like BCSD before it, eco-efficiency is a defining concept and one that the organization spends considerable time and effort in refining and promoting. More specifically, the work of the organization is guided by its four objectives:[20]

- **business leadership:** to be the leading business advocate on issues connected with the environment and sustainable development;
- **policy development:** to participate in policy development in order to create a framework that allows business to contribute effectively to sustainable development;
- **best practice:** to demonstrate progress in environmental and resource management in business and to share leading-edge practices among its members;
- **global outreach:** to contribute through its global network to a sustainable future for developing nations and nations in transition.

The rest of this section will look at the impact WBCSD has had on international environmental policy through its activities in each of these four areas.

Although the goal of **business leadership** and advocacy is intertwined with the remaining three objectives of WBCSD and is often achieved through them, it is here that the organization has demonstrated its greatest influence on international environmental policy. There is an obvious sense of pride in how much clout and influence the organization has come to exert in its advocacy activities that is apparent in WBCSD publications directed at its corporate members:

Our business advocacy activities allow us to anticipate rather than react to the agenda of other stakeholders. By being consulted early in the process, we can influence their priorities and thinking, and so help to shape the end-result. One example of the WBCSD's high profile, government-level involvement is provided by the Rio+5 activities being organized by the UN in 1997 to mark the fifth anniversary of the Rio Earth Summit in 1992. We have been asked to lead the Business and Industry input at the Rio Forum, the UNCSD meetings and the UN General Assembly Special Session—where CEOs from member companies presented the progress achieved by industry since Rio to ministers and heads of state during a High-Level Roundtable co-hosted by the WBCSD. As another example, the OECD has invited two of our Executive Committee members to join its Advisory Board to review its work on environmental issues.[21]

To business executives who, in the past, had been more accustomed to being vilified as environmental villains, the positive attention being showered upon WBCSD by the environmental camp is an obvious source of satisfaction,

even delight. Ever since UNCED, the organization has been spectacularly successful in cultivating a close relationship with key intergovernmental and non-governmental organizations. This strategy of engagement—as opposed to one of defensive retaliation—has paid handsome dividends, and WBCSD has been able to establish partnerships not only with key UN agencies such as UNEP, UNDP, and the CSD, but also with leading environmental groups such as IUCN, WWF, and IIED. Rio+5 may not have been a historic event for most environmental observers, but for WBCSD it was a major watershed. In just five years big business had moved from a position where its views on sustainable development were reluctantly tolerated to one where they are now actively sought. Despite the dismay of some groups, WBCSD, as the most active and representative voice of big business on issues pertaining to sustainable development, is no longer seen as a gate-crasher at international environmental forums, but as an honored guest.

What makes this new-found prominence all the more sweet is the attendant influence over international environmental *policy development* that comes with it. While both BCSD and ICC had a presence at UNCED, their actual participation in policy deliberations was relatively modest.[22] Today, with the ongoing climate change negotiations, for example, this is no longer the case. WBCSD has been an energetic player at every negotiating session and was particularly active at both Kyoto (1997) and Buenos Aires (1998). As the WBCSD President notes, 'business was more in the forefront at Buenos Aires, both in relative numbers and in involvement in the proceedings, and many national delegations now include business representatives.'[23] A strong advocate for 'flexible' arrangements such as emissions trading and Joint Implementation (JI), and opposed to stringent mandatory reductions, WBCSD has been holding a series of workshops around its International Business Action Plan on Climate Change (IBAPCC) to impress its case on government delegations, NGO representatives, and academics. It is safe to say that they have not been devoid of impact—especially since the emergent regime retains many elements that the WBCSD has been advocating.[24]

Ultimately, WBCSD's most important impact on policy is likely to come from the various activities that it has undertaken to put a business stamp on the future global agenda for sustainable development. This includes its policy prescriptions on emergent issues such as trade and environment, financial markets, the paper cycle, fresh water access, and sustainable forests.[25] By far the most potent of such activities is the outreach component targeted at future business and management professionals. The keystone of this programme has been the 'Sustainable Business Challenge', which started as an Internet site that summarizes the main elements of the WBCSD message and offers a multiple-choice test based on this material. Those qualifying can print out a certificate of competence for successfully completing this examination. Originally launched by WBCSD in collaboration with UNEP, it has been a roaring success, estimatedly reaching over a million students. More importantly, it has enabled the WBCSD message to go directly to a whole generation of future business leaders. In 'preparing' for the exam by reading through the site, they have been exposed to WBCSD's version of what sustainable development is and how it is most likely to be achieved; it is this version that they are most likely to accept and absorb.[26]

The success of the initiative was largely instrumental in WBCSD deciding to form, in 1996, the Foundation for Business and Sustainable Development (FBSD), whose goal is to 'promote the business understanding of sustainable development and to encourage education and competence building, research, and demonstration projects in the field of sustainable development.' In 1998 FBSD produced a 180-page book, *The Sustainable Business Challenge: A Briefing for Tomorrow's Business Leaders*, which it hopes will be widely used as a textbook in university-level business courses. Plans are underway to produce a television series on the same theme. Other programmes of the Foundation include an Internet-based 'Eco-Efficiency Kit', a multilingual 'Global Sustainable Development Dictionary', the use of global scenarios as a management learning tool, and support for various research and demonstration projects. Capping all of these is the 'WBCSD Virtual University', which is a joint project with the University of Cambridge and the Norwegian School of Management. Its aim is to 'bring knowledge and appreciation of sustainable development, *the way WBCSD members understand it*, to a global audience through combining the latest distant learning and data technology with proven training traditions' (emphasis added). The outreach potential of such a programme is daunting, and if successful it could ultimately make WBCSD's definition of sustainable development as well known as the Brundtland Commission's.[27]

The practice of consistently focusing on *best practice* within industry on environmental issues has been of strategic as well as substantive importance to WBCSD. Just about every report and book to have come out from WBCSD or its predecessor organizations focuses much of its attention on highlighting case-studies of how specific businesses, mostly member companies, have taken decisions that benefit the environment while maintaining or increasing their long-term profits. This is obviously a heart-warming message, but also has deeper strategic value. For big business in general, which is much more used to being

depicted as an environmental rogue, this provides not just good publicity but vindication. In an era when environmental sensibilities among consumers can cause major dents in corporate profits, this alone can justify the US$30,000 annual membership fee. In effect, WBCSD provides big business with the exact antidote to the many environmental NGOs that have, for years, been highlighting 'worst practice'. In this regard, however, WBCSD is as guilty of focusing on only one side of the coin as those NGOs have been for focusing only on the other.

Having said the above, the reason for focusing on best practice most often cited by the WBCSD relates to the aspiration (and self-perception) of its member companies to 'be among the leaders in good environmental practice'. WBCSD offers them the ability to 'share their experience and expertise with others and keep abreast of best practice in fields to which they might not otherwise have access'. The promise, to the business executive, is of advance information; the attraction, for the environmental policy maker, is of the potential for early dissemination of win–win solutions. The most attractive of these win–win concepts is eco-efficiency, which is 'at the heart of the

---

Box 3: Eco-Efficiency

In introducing the concept in *Changing Course*, BCSD had not provided an exact definition of eco-efficiency beyond stating that 'corporations that achieve ever more efficiency while preventing pollution through good housekeeping, materials substitution, cleaner technologies, and cleaner products and that strive for more efficient use and recovery of resources can be called "eco-efficient".'[1] By 1993 BCSD had a formal definition: 'Eco-efficiency is reached by the delivery of competitively priced goods and services that satisfy human needs and bring quality of life, while progressively reducing ecological impacts and resource intensity throughout the life cycle, to a level at least in line with the earth's estimated carrying capacity.'[2] By 1997 WBCSD was ready to publish a major book on the subject which promoted the concept as a 'marketing philosophy' that has been 'developed by business for business' and highlights the fact that 'the first word of the concept encompasses both *eco*logical and *eco*nomic resources—the second says we have to make optimal use of both.'[3] It went on to specify seven guidelines for operationalizing the concept: a) reduce the material intensity of goods and services; b) reduce the energy intensity of goods and services; c) reduce toxic dispersion; d) enhance material recyclability; e) maximize sustainable use of renewable resources; f) extend product durability; and g) increase the service intensity of products.

It also identified three areas in which more work is required for the full potential of eco-efficiency to be unleashed. This includes better ways to measure eco-efficiency, positive regulatory framework conditions through the provision of incentives and the removal of disincentives, and a deeper understanding of the link between eco-efficiency and long-term shareholder value by capital markets.[4] On each of these fronts, WBCSD is investing significant efforts which have already led to a 'state-of-play' *Report on Eco-Efficiency Metrics and Reporting*, a study on how companies measure and report eco-efficiency, a series of conferences and collaborations designed to interest policy makers in the concept, a study on environmental performance and shareholder value, and a major book on financial markets and sustainable development.[5]

In marketing the concept of eco-efficiency, WBCSD has been careful to relate it to other emerging approaches, particularly the Cleaner Production Programme of the United Nations Environmental Programme (UNEP).[6] However, despite the fact that WBCSD is an institutional affiliate to a journal on the subject, its reports tend not to delve too deep into the link between eco-efficiency as espoused by WBCSD and the emerging scholarly field of industrial ecology. Yet the two are deeply connected.

Both have the goals of reducing material and energy throughput, promoting the reuse and recycling of products, reducing toxic emissions, and emphasizing services. Furthermore, both concepts are proactive, designing out waste and designing in reuse and recycling. However, although the two concepts share the same goals, the systems boundaries to which they apply these goals are different. For eco-efficiency the system boundary is the individual firm, and any unused resource leaving the firm is waste. The industrial ecology approach expands the boundary to include sets of interacting firms so that the unused output from any given firm can potentially be input for other firms in

the system. Industrial ecology is 'the totality or the pattern of relationships between various industrial activities, their products, and the environment',[7] such that 'the consumption of energy and materials is optimized, waste generation is minimized and the effluents of one process . . . serve as the raw material for another process.'[8] At the simplest level, then, eco-efficiency could be seen as a component of industrial ecology at the firm level which could lead to more effective industrial ecology.

Notes and References

1. Stephan Schmidheiny with BCSD (1992), *Changing Course* (Cambridge, MA: MIT Press), xii.
2. This definition was crafted at the First Antwerp Workshop on Eco-Efficiency organized by BCSD in November 1993 and was accepted at subsequent workshops, organized by WBCSD, at Antwerp in March 1995 and at Washington, DC, in October 1995. For more on the progression of the concept's definition, see WBCSD (1996), *Eco-Efficient Leadership* (Geneva: WBCSD).
3. Livio D. DeSimone and Frank Popoff with WBCSD (1997), *Eco-Efficiency: The Business Link to Sustainable Development* (Cambridge, MA: MIT Press), 2–3.
4. Ibid., 21–2.
5. See Markus Lehni (1998), Eco-Efficiency Reporting and Metrics: State-of-Play Report (Geneva: WBCSD); WBCSD (1998), The Application of Sustainable Development Concepts and Eco-Efficiency Metrics in Corporate Environmental Reporting (Geneva: WBCSD); J. Blumberg, G. Blum, and Å. Korsvold (1997), Environmental Performance and Shareholder Value (Geneva: WBCSD); Schmidheiny and Zorraquin with WBCSD (1996), Financing Change.
6. For example, Keith Erlam and Ludolf Plass (1996), Eco-Efficiency and Cleaner Production: Charting the Course to Sustainability (Geneva: WBCSD and UNEP); WBCSD and UNEP (1998), Cleaner Production and Eco-Efficiency: Complementary Approaches to Sustainable Development (Geneva: WBCSD and UNEP).
7. C. K. N. Patel (1992), 'Industrial Ecology', Proceedings of the National Academy of Science, 89, 798–99.
8. Robert A. Frosch and Nicholas E. Gallopoulos (1989), 'Strategies for Manufacturing', *Scientific American*, 261: 3, 144–52.

WBCSD's philosophy'. After having introduced the concept the organization has spent much effort in propagating it, and to its credit it is now, indeed, 'firmly entrenched in the business lexicon'.[28]

Global outreach is an area on which WBCSD has been trying to focus, if only because it remains open to criticism for being an association of predominantly northern (European, North American, and Japanese) corporations. For all practical purposes, and for all the obvious reasons, it remains exactly that. Of the 123 member companies listed in its 1997 *Annual Review*, only one was from Africa, only three from Central and Eastern Europe, and only eight

each from Latin America and Asia (not counting Japan). By way of making up for this imbalance, WBCSD works through a 'global network' of partner organizations with which it has formal and informal links. These range from intergovernmental and non-governmental organizations such as UNDP, the International Institute for Sustainable Development (IISD), and the Stockholm Environment Institute (SEI), to national business groups such as the Confederation of Indian Industry (CII), to a host of national and regional Business Councils for Sustainable Development. Due to its very nature, however, the network remains a loose confederation with only sporadic and opportunistic links to WBCSD's agendas and activities. Althought the WBCSD network has a long way to go to realize its potential, the Council has an obvious interest in strengthening it. Doing so will not only make the WBCSD a more representative global entity but could eventually move it in unintended directions.[29]

... or Greenwash?

For all its success, and partly because of it, WBCSD has also been the target of some scathing criticism, most notably from two NGOs, Greenpeace and Corporate Watch.

Through its various publications and campaigns, Greenpeace has popularized the term 'greenwash', which it defines as 'cynical, superficial, public relations marketing' aimed at projecting a falsely benign environmental corporate image. In fact, it coined the term to describe and expose one of WBCSD's parents, BCSD, and its corporate members. According to *Green or Greenwash? A Greenpeace Detection Kit*, a corporation that fails on any of the CARE criteria—core business, advertising record, research and development funding, and environmental lobbying—is 'probably in the greenwash business'.[30] Like Greenpeace, Corporate Watch, which defines 'greenwashing' as 'the phenomenon of socially and environmentally destructive corporations attempting to preserve and expand their markets by posing as friends of the environment', considers WBCSD to be a 'front' group whose purpose is to greenwash the image of its 'dirty' members.[31] In marking the fifth anniversary of UNCED in 1997, it focused unwanted attention on WBCSD by giving it the so-called Greenwash Award 'for its continuing . . . efforts to portray itself as the savior of the world's environment and the force that will eliminate poverty'.[32]

Environmental fury directed at large corporations is not a particularly new or novel phenomenon. However, the greenwashing charge now being levelled against WBCSD and its cohorts is not just directed at the environmental harm being caused by certain businesses but suggests a conscious cover-up conspiracy to distract public attention and subvert the environmental agenda. To those who have long considered corporate greed as a leading cause of the environmental problematique, the ultimate insult is that big business is now being allowed to 'co-opt' and even 'define' the meaning of sustainable development.[33] What Maria Elena Hurtado of Consumer International describes as 'a new policy by corporations to engage potential critics'[34] is greeted with grave concern by activists. In noting that 'the WBCSD has been tremendously successful in promoting global market liberalization and self-regulation by business instead of government intervention as the recipe for sustainable development',[35] they are outraged that 'the world's governments have allowed corporate greenwash to thwart progress in environmental protection.'[36] Behind what he calls a 'masterful co-optation of ecology', the author Joshua Karliner (1997) sees a 'highly evolved rendition of corporate positioning on issues of environment and development'. His book *The Corporate Planet* elaborates:

The Earth Summit marked the coming of age of corporate environmentalism—the melding of ecological and economic globalization into a coherent ideology that has paved the way for the transnationals to reconcile, in theory and rhetoric, their ubiquitous hunger for profits and growth with the stark realities of poverty and environmental destruction. In the aftermath of Rio, global corporate environmentalism has helped institutionalize ecological concerns as agenda items in the executive suites and boardrooms of some of the world's largest businesses. It has helped build a public image of transnational corporations as the world's responsible global 'citizens'. It has also, to a certain degree, begun to set the terms of the debate along lines favorable to the transnationals . . . Indeed, by focusing a relatively small portion of their vast resources on environmental issues, the global corporations have, in many respects, reframed much of the environmental discussion.[37]

To its critics, WBCSD is guilty of wilful duplicity. According to Greenpeace:

The public message of WBCSD and other groups has been that business now understands and supports the goals of sustainable development and environmental protection, and business will be the leaders achieving both. At the same time, they have been working to avoid regulations of their activities, and working against agreements in the very regimes that UNCED spawned, such as the Climate Convention.[38]

Corporate Watch chimes in with a similar verdict:

The overall tone of recent WBCSD pronouncements is one of reassurance; to governments and NGOs, reassurance that business understands and is voluntarily taking action; and to their members, reassurance that things are changing but not too fast; that some action is needed but not too much. This carefully crafted tone of heartening ambiguity masks the reality that WBCSD members, along with many other large corporations, have pushed hard over the last five years for increased corporate power on the global stage . . . There is simply no evidence that increased corporate rights has led or will lead toward sustainable development or environmental protection, yet this assumption underlies the WBCSD philosophy.[39]

To its credit, the WBCSD has engaged its critics in a dialogue, albeit at a limited level. It has essentially argued that the case laid out by its detractors is oversimplistic, conspiratorial, exaggerated, and based on an unrealistic understanding of how business works.[40] In addressing the critics, the WBCSD Director for External Co-operation, Ted Button, makes the following arguments:

It is inevitable that our proposals on sustainable development will irritate and sometimes annoy pressure groups. Maybe business is not going far enough and fast enough for some participants in the debate, but the Council is genuinely dedicated to making a difference. Also, on some issues we are taking the lead in finding solutions to the

ustainable development challenges . . . This is rather more difficult
han our detractors believe, not least because the international
business community is as varied in its make-up, ideals, approaches
nd needs as the various environmental and social groups who urge us
o move further and faster.[41]

Green or Mean?

So, is the story of the WBCSD a story about the greening
of big business or one about greenwash? The correct answer, as in all such questions, is a little of both.

Indeed, WBCSD has played an important role in mak-
ng major corporations embrace the concept of sustainable development. While not all are equally enthusiastic
about how the concept might change as a result of this
bear-hug, the fact remains that there have been lively dis-
ussions, if not any deep soul-searching, in at least a few
boardrooms. That should be a cause for some satisfaction.
At the same time, it is abundantly clear that at least some
of what WBCSD does can legitimately be called
greenwash. After all, it is part of WBCSD's mandate to
put big business's 'greenest' foot forward. In singing the
virtues of 'best practice' by member companies it has certainly been guilty of overlooking some of the 'worst practice' by the same corporations. Even if WBCSD itself is
not consciously in the business of greenwash, some of its
member companies with less than perfect environmental
records have probably used their association with it as a
means to greenwash their soiled public image.

In the ultimate analysis, the most important thing in this
'Green or Mean?'[42] debate is not to determine which side
is right and which is wrong. What is more important is to
realize that each has been doing what its institutional form
mandates it to do. WBCSD, as the environmental advocate for business that it is, has been highlighting the positive linkages that industry can, and sometimes does, have
with sustainable development. Groups such as Greenpeace
and Corporate Watch, as the environmental watchdogs
that they are, have been focusing public attention on the
negative linkages that industry can, and so often does, have
with sustainable development.[43] Both are doing what they
are supposed, and expected, to do. International efforts
for global sustainable development would probably be that
much weaker if either were to act significantly differently.

Assessing Impact

In assessing the impact that WBCSD has had on the international environment and development, the most important question relates not to perception, but to impact.
In the case of WBCSD, it is important to evaluate its impact separately at two distinct levels: business practice in
the corporations whose interests it claims to represent, and
international policy at the forums that it seeks to influence.

On the first of these, *business practice related to the environment*, it is not clear what the exact impact has been or
is likely to be in the future. This is partly because of self-
selection in membership. Companies have found WBCSD
useful for improving their public image by highlighting the
environmental innovations that they might have undertaken, or simply by associating themselves with other innovative companies. However, the innovations themselves
seem to have happened separately from, and not necessarily because of, WBCSD. To be fair, not enough time
has passed for the organization to trigger significant
changes in business practices. Yet there are some areas
where its work has the clear potential of creating positive
change. One of the most significant of these relates to
metrics for measuring eco-efficiency. This is one area
where the Council is beginning to move from simply highlighting best practice to actually inducing good practice.
An initial survey of environmental reports of member
companies has been completed.[44] However, at this point
their efforts remain focused on the relatively less threatening question of 'how' companies measure eco-efficiency
and shy away from evaluating just how eco-efficient they
really are. The link between sustainable development and
the financial sector is another area where WBCSD has
initiated some interesting discussions.[45] Again, however,
the thrust is on documenting rationale rather than holding companies accountable to some framework of evaluation. While the potential for meaningful impact in both
areas is immense, the real test will be in the earnestness
with which corporations (including WBCSD members)
apply these principles.

At a secondary level, there has been some diffusion of
information about 'best practice' among WBCSD member companies, and beyond that through its publications
programme. More important than that, however, may be
the discussions that WBCSD has facilitated and initiated
within business, and between business and other
stakeholders, on various issues related to operationalizing
sustainable development. While it is obviously difficult to
gauge the direct impact of such activities, it is clear that
this has the potential for eventually triggering change in
corporate practice. In short, although demonstrable evidence of clear change in corporate practice because of
WBCSD actions is hard to come by, the organization
deserves at least a passing grade for initiating activities and
programmes that have the potential for bringing about
positive environmental innovation.

On the second issue, influencing *international policy and
institutions for sustainable development*, the performance
has been clearly impressive. What some in 1992 had considered as being no more than Stephan Schmidheiny's
personal enthusiasm for the subject has, in fact, been institutionalized. In 1999 WBCSD is a bigger and more in-

fluential player than the founders of either BCSD or WICE (or their critics) might have predicted. As an advocacy organization, WBCSD has been an undeniable success. Owing to the critical constituency that it legitimately represents and the human and financial resources at its command, it has been able to attain an impressive presence and prestige in international forums in a very short period of time.

A clear indicator of this influence is its now undisputed position as the most representative and authentic voice for big business on environmental issues and its ability to use this position to reframe discussions on sustainable development around its chosen parameters. By similar token, the potential for WBCSD's most important influence in the long term lies in the planned WBCSD Virtual University being set up under the aegis of FBSD and the inroads that the organization is already making into universities and their business curricula. By its own accounts, as well as those of its critics, WBCSD has managed to gain deep penetration into the corridors of global environmental policy and will be a major player in international environmental policy for the foreseeable future. While some will question the quality of this influence, the influence itself is not in doubt.

What does all of this mean for the larger enterprise for global sustainable development? Can WBCSD ever reconcile the practical and conceptual differences between the goals of sustainable development and corporate profit? Can one wear Birkenstocks with a pin stripe suit? Maybe, but not just yet.

Notes and References

The author would like to thank Jennifer Biringer, Anthony Amato, and Lynette Martyn (all at Boston University) for their research assistance; Addison Holmes and Christine Elleboode at the WBCSD Secretariat in Geneva for responding to various queries; Helge Ole Bergesen, Julie Fisher, Alexey V. Yablokov, G. Kristin Rosendal, and Carlos Martinez-Vela for their comments; and Øystein B. Thommessen for his patience.

1 Livio DeSimone (1996), 'Letter from the Chairman', *Annual Review 1996* (Geneva: WBCSD), 3.
2 Speech by UN Secretary-General Kofi Annan at the World Economic Forum in Davos, Switzerland, 31 January 1999.
3 A recent report alleges that the UNDP is 'selling' its sponsorship to large corporations, including ones with less than perfect environmental records. It claims that 'UNDP is considering creating a special logo to be used by participating corporations' and 'for US$50,000 companies' tarnished images could be brightened by UN partnership.' TRAC (1999), *A Perilous Partnership: The United Nations Development Programme's Flirtation with Corporate Collaboration* (San Francisco: Transnational Resource and Action Center/Institute for Policy Studies/Council on International and Public Affairs); available at <http://www.igc.org/trac/undp/undp.pdf>, 3–4.
4 The exclusive luncheon meeting was attended by 37 invited participants, including 15 high-level representatives of government, among them three heads of state, the Secretary-General of the UN, the Administrator of UNDP, and the UN Under-Secretary-General responsible for the UN Commission on Sustainable Development. For a critical first-hand report of the luncheon round table, see David C. Korten (1997), 'The United Nations and the Corporate Agenda' (available at <http://iisd.ca/pcdf/1997/uncorporate.htm>).
5 See, for example, Jed Greer and Kenny Bruno (1996), *Greenwash: The Reality Behind Corporate Environmentalism* (New York: Apex Press); Greenpeace (1997), *Green or Greenwash?: A Greenpeace Detection Kit* (San Francisco: Greenpeace International); and Josh Karliner (1997), *The Corporate Planet: Ecology and Politics in the Age of Globalization* (San Francisco: Sierra Club Books).
6 For a wide set of interesting but divergent discussions on that subject, see: Paul Hawken (1993), *The Ecology of Commerce* (New York: HarperBusiness); Adil Najam (1993), 'Boardroom Callings: Making Friends with the Earth', *Earth Times*, 35/21; Harris Gleckman (1995), 'Transnational Corporations' Strategic Responses to Sustainable Development', in Helge Ole Bergesen and Georg Parmann (eds.) (1995), *Green Globe Yearbook of International Co-operation and Development 1995* (Oxford: Oxford University Press), 93–106; David C. Korten (1995), *When Corporations Rule the World* (West Hartford, CT: Kumarian Press); Matthias Finger and James Kilcoyne (1997), 'Why Transnational Corporations are Organizing to 'Save the Global Environment'?', *The Ecologist* 27 (July/Aug): 138–42; Karliner (1997), *The Corporate Planet*; Stephan Schmidheiny, Rodney Chase, and Livio DeSimone (1997), *Signals of Change: Business Progress Towards Sustainable Development* (Geneva: WBCSD); Kitty Warnock (1997), 'Green or Mean? Environment and Industry Five Years on from the Earth Summit', *Panos Media Briefing* no. 24 (available at <http://www.oneworld.org/panos/briefing/green.htm>); Michael A. Berry and Dennis A. Rondinelli (1998), 'Proactive Corporate Environment Management: A New Industrial Revolution', *Academy of Management Executive*, 12: 2, 38–50.
7 Stephan Schmidheiny with BCSD (1992), *Changing Course: A Global Perspective on Development and the Environment* (Cambridge, MA: MIT Press).
8 International Chamber of Commerce (1992), *From Ideas to Action* (Paris: ICC).
9 For a discussion on ICC and a critique of its Charter, see Gleckman (1995), 'Transnational Corporations' Strategic Responses to Sustainable Development'.
10 For more on management structures of global associations, see Dennis R. Young, Bonnie L. Koenig, Adil Najam, and Julie Fisher (forthcoming), 'Strategy and Structure in Managing Global Associations', *Voluntas*.
11 WBCSD (1995), *Annual Review 1995* (Geneva: WBCSD), 6.
12 WBCSD (1997), *Annual Review 1997* (Geneva: WBCSD), 18.
13 WBCSD (1997), *The Value of Membership* (Geneva: WBCSD).
14 Ibid.
15 WBCSD (undated), *Information and Publications* (Geneva, WBCSD).
16 Largely based on WBCSD (1997), *The Value of Membership*.
17 WBCSD (undated), *Information and Publications*.
18 WBCSD (1997), *Annual Review 1997*, 2.
19 Ibid., 1.
20 WBCSD (undated), *Information and Publications*, 1.
21 WBCSD (1997), *The Value of Membership*.
22 The distinction is obviously relative. Some , in fact, argue that big business was able significantly to influence Agenda 21, especially in its treatment of transnational corporations. See Karliner (1997), *The Corporate Planet*.

23 Björn Stigson (1998), 'Governments Need to Open Up to Industry to Halt Climate Change', *Earth Times*, 20 December (available at <http://earthtimes.org/dec/business_investinggovernmentsdec20_98.htm>).

24 See WBCSD & ICC (1997), *Business and Climate Change: Case Studies in Greenhouse Gas Reduction* (Kyoto: ICC & WBCSD). Also see David L. Levy (1997), 'Business and International Environmental Treaties: Ozone Depletion and Climate Change', *California Management Review*, 39: 3, 54–71.

25 For example, on sustainability issues related to financial markets and the paper cycle, WBCSD publications are already considered to be among the most authoritative documents to consult. See IIED (1996), *Towards a Sustainable Paper Cycle* (London: IIED & WBCSD); Jerald Blumberg, Georges Blum, and Åge Korsvold (1997), *Environmental Performance and Shareholder Value* (Geneva: WBCSD); Stephan Schmidheiny and Fedrico Zorraquin (1996), *Financing Change: The Financial Community, Eco-effieciency and Sustainable Development* (Cambridge, MA: MIT Press). On other issues, see David Stone, Kristina Ringwood, and Frank Vorhies (1997), *Business and Biodiversity: A Guide for the Private Sector* (Geneva: IUCN and WBCSD); WBCSD (1996), *Trade and Environment: A Business Perspective* (Geneva: WBCSD); Albert Fry (1998), *Industry, Fresh Water, and Sustainable Development* (Geneva: UNEP and WBCSD).

26 Visit <http://www.wbcsd.ch/foundation> to access the Internet sustainability exam.

27 See Jan-Olaf Willums and WBCSD (1998), *The Sustainable Development Challenge: A Briefing for Tomorrow's Business Leaders* (Sheffield: Greenleaf Publishing); FBSD (1998), *Foundation for Business and Sustainable Development: A Status Report* (Oslo: FBSD); FBSD (1998), *The WBCSD Virtual University: Factsheet October 98* (Oslo: FBSD).

28 All quotes from WBCSD (1996), *Annual Review 1996*, 13–14.

29 For the strategies and benefits of institutional networks, see Julie Fisher (1996), *International Networking: The Role of Southern NGOs* (New Haven, CT: Programme on Non-profit Organizations, Yale University), PONPO Working Paper no. 228. For a good description of how expanding international membership, particularly in developing countries, can change the ethos of even long-standing organizations, see Leif E. Christoffersen (1997), 'IUCN: A Bridge-Builder for Nature Conservation', in Helge Ole Bergesen and Georg Parmann (eds.) (1997), *Green Globe Yearbook of International Co-operation and Development 1997* (Oxford: Oxford University Press), 59–69.

30 Greenpeace (1997), *Green or Greenwash?*

31 See <http://www.igc.org/trac/greenwash>.

32 Corporate Watch (1997), 'Greenwash Award for WBCSD' (available at <http://www.igc.org/trac/greenwash/wbcsd.html>).

33 See Greenpeace (1997), 'The Decline of Corporate Accountability' (available at <http://www.greenpeace.org/~comms/97/summit/account.html>).

34 Maria Elena Hurtado (1997), 'Change of Course or Greenwash? Five Years After the Earth Summit, Big Industry Parades its Green Credentials', *World Consumer*, no. 225, June.

35 Corporate Europe Observatory (1998), 'MAIgalomania! Citizens and the Environment Sacrificed to Corporate Investment Agenda', *CEO Briefing Paper* (available at <http://www.xs4all.nl/~ceo/mai>).

36 Kenny Bruno (1997), 'The World of Greenwash' (available at <http://www.igc.org/trac/greenwash/world.html>).

37 Karliner (1997), *The Corporate Planet*.

38 Greenpeace (1997), 'The Decline of Corporate Accountability'.

39 Corporate Watch (1997), 'Greenwash Award for WBCSD'.

40 See *Financial Times* (1997), 'Dialogue Across the Divide', *Financial Times*, 3 September, 24.

41 Ted Button (1997), 'Sincerely Sustainable', *Financial Times*, 5 November, 20.

42 The 'Green or Mean?' terminology is borrowed from Warnock (1997), 'Green or Mean?'.

43 For a detailed analysis of NGOs as 'policy entrepreneurs' and the various roles (monitors, advocates, innovators, service providers) that such groups can play in the policy stream, see Adil Najam (1999), 'Citizen Organizations as Policy Entrepreneurs', in David Lewis (ed.), *International Perspectives on Voluntary Action: Reshaping the Third Sector* (London: Earthscan). For a nuanced view of how NGOs influence governments and policy, see Julie Fisher (1998), *Nongovernments: NGOs and the Political Development of the Third World* (West Hartford, CT: Kumarian Press).

44 See Lehni (1998), *Eco-Efficiency Reporting and Metrics*; WBCSD (1998), *The Application of Sustainable Development Concepts and Eco-Efficiency Metrics in Corporate Environmental Reporting* (Geneva: WBCSD).

45 See Blumberg, Blum, and Korsvold (1997), *Environmental Performance and Shareholder Value*; Schmidheiny and Zorraquin with WBCSD (1996), *Financing Change*.

Note to this section regarding adoption and status of participation of agreements

The terms used in this section, denoting various stages in the status of participation related to international agreements, are legal-technical ones, based on the Law of Treaties as contained in the 1969 Vienna Convention on the Law of Treaties and in the 1986 Vienna Convention on the Law of Treaties between States and International Organizations or between International Organizations, as well as in customary international law. To provide easier reference for readers who are not lawyers, some basic explanations of terms used in the treaty-making process are here provided.

Upon the negotiation of a treaty, there are often several stages required before it enters into force:

- *Adoption* is the formal act by which the form and content of a proposed treaty text are established. As a general rule, the adoption of the text of a treaty takes place through the expression of the consent of the states participating in the treaty-making process. As a rule, however, adoption does not yet mean a consent of a state to be bound by a treaty.

- *Signature* may sometimes be definitive, meaning that it establishes the consent of the state to be bound by the treaty. This is usual in most bilateral treaties. For multilateral treaties, however, the signature is as a rule not definitive, meaning that the treaty is subject to ratification, acceptance, or approval in order to enter into force. Although in those cases the signature does not establish the consent to be bound, it is a means of authentication and expresses the willingness of the signatory state to continue the treaty-making process (i.e. to proceed to ratification, acceptance, or approval). It also creates an obligation to refrain, in good faith, from acts that would defeat the object and the purpose of the treaty.

- *Ratification* defines an international act whereby a state indicates its consent to be bound to a treaty if the parties intended to show their consent by such an act. In the case of multilateral treaties the usual procedure is for the state to notify the depositary of its ratification;

the depositary keeps all parties informed of the situation regarding ratifications. The institution of ratification grants states the necessary time-frame to seek the required approval for the treaty on the domestic level and to enact the necessary legislation to give domestic effect to that treaty.

- *Acceptance* or *approval* have the same legal effect as ratification and consequently express the consent of a state to be bound by a treaty. In the practice of certain states, acceptance and approval have been used instead of ratification when, at a national level, constitutional law does not require the treaty to be ratified by the head of state.

- *Act of formal confirmation* is used as an equivalent for the term 'ratification' when an international organization expresses its consent to be bound to a treaty.

- *Entry into force* of an international treaty does not necessarily coincide with its ratification (acceptance, approval) by individual states. It is common for multilateral treaties to provide for a fixed number of states to express their consent for entry into force. Some treaties provide for additional conditions to be satisfied, e.g. by specifying that a certain category of states must be among the consenters. The treaty may also provide for an additional time period to elapse after the required number of countries have expressed their consent or the conditions have been satisfied. A treaty enters into force for those states which gave the required consent. A treaty may also provide that, upon certain conditions having been met, it shall come into force provisionally.

- *Accession* is the act whereby a state accepts the offer or the opportunity to become a party to a treaty already negotiated and signed by other states. It has the same legal effect as ratification. Accession usually occurs after the treaty has entered into force. The conditions under which accession may occur and the procedure involved depend on the provisions of the treaty; a treaty might provide for the accession of all other states or for a limited and defined number of states.

Convention on Access to Information, Public Participation in Decision Making and Access to Justice in Environmental Matters (Århus Convention)

Objectives

To guarantee the rights of access to information, public participation in decision making, and access to justice in environmental matters in order to contribute to the protection of the right of every person of present and future generations to live in an environment adequate to his or her health and well-being.

Scope

Legal scope
Open to member countries of the UN Economic Commission for Europe (UN/ECE), the European Union (EU), and other states having consultative status with the UN/ECE.

Geographic scope
Regional. UN/ECE region (Europe and North America).

Time and place of adoption

25 June 1998, Århus.

Entry into force

Not yet in force. Enters into force on the ninetieth day after the date of deposit of the sixteenth instrument of ratification, acceptance, approval, or accession.

Status of participation

No ratifications, approvals, acceptances, or accessions by 16 June 1999. 40 Signatories, including the European Union, without ratification, acceptance, or approval.

The Secretary-General of the UN acts as depositary.

Affiliated instruments and organizations

The Convention also contains two *annexes* which form an integral part of the Convention.

The Executive Secretary of the UN/ECE carries out the secretariat functions.

Co-ordination with related instruments
No formal co-ordination yet, but mechanisms for co-ordination are expected to be developed with other UN/ECE environmental conventions having provisions on public participation, in particular the Convention on Environmental Impact Assessment in a Transboundary Context, the Convention on the Protection and Use of Transboundary Watercourses and International Lakes, and the Convention on the Transboundary Effects of Industrial Accidents (see this section).

Secretariat

UN/ECE, 'Environment for Europe' Secretariat,
Environment and Human Settlements Division (ENHS),
Palais des Nations,
CH-1211 Geneva 10,
Switzerland
Telephone: +41-22-9172345
Telefax: +41-22-9070107
E-mail: kaj.barlund@unece.org
or jeremy.wates@unece.org

Director
Mr Kaj Bärlund.

Responsible Officer
Mr Jeremy Wates.

Finance

To be decided by the first Meeting of the Parties.

Budget
Pending the entry into force of the Convention, activities are financed from voluntary contributions.

Rules and standards

Each Party shall:
• take the necessary legislative, regulatory, and other measures, including measures to achieve compatibility between the provisions implementing information, public participa-

tion, and access to justice in the Convention, as well as proper enforcement measures, to establish and maintain a clear, transparent, and consistent framework to implement the provisions of the Convention;
• endeavour to ensure that officials and authorities assist and provide guidance to the public in seeking access to information, in facilitating participation in decision making, and in seeking access to justice in environmental matters;
• promote environmental education and environmental awareness among the public, especially on how to obtain access to information, to participate in decision making, and to obtain access to justice in environmental matters;
• provide for appropriate recognition of and support to associations, organizations, or groups promoting environmental protection and ensure that its national legal system is consistent with this obligation.

The provisions of the Convention shall not affect the right of a Party to maintain or introduce measures providing for broader access to information, more extensive public participation in decision making, and wider access to justice in environmental matters than required by the Convention.

The Convention shall not require any derogation from existing rights of access to information, public participation in decision making, and access to justice in environmental matters.

Each Party shall also:
• promote the application of the principles of the Convention in international environmental decision-making processes and within the framework of international organizations in matters relating to the environment;
• ensure that persons exercising their rights in conformity with the provisions of the Convention shall not be penalized, persecuted, or harassed in any way for their involvement. This provision shall not affect the powers of national courts to award reasonable costs in judicial proceedings.

Within the scope of the relevant provisions of the Convention, the public shall have ac-

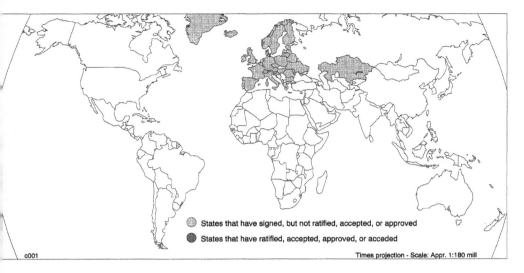

States that have signed, but not ratified, accepted, or approved

States that have ratified, accepted, approved, or acceded

c001
Times projection - Scale: Appr. 1:180 mill

ess to information, have the possibility to participate in decision making, and have access to justice in environmental matters without discrimination as to citizenship, nationality, or domicile and, in the case of a legal person, without discrimination as to where it has its registered seat or an effective centre of its activities.

Monitoring/implementation

Review procedure
The Parties to the Convention shall keep under continuous review the implementation of the Convention and, with this purpose in mind:
• review the policies for and legal and methodological approaches to access to information, public participation in decision making, and access to justice in environmental matters, with a view to further improving them;
• exchange information regarding experience gained in concluding and implementing bilateral and multilateral agreements or other arrangements having relevance to the purposes of the Convention and to which one or more of the Parties are a party;
• seek, where appropriate, the services of competent international bodies and scientific committees in methodological and technical aspects.
The Meeting of the Parties shall establish, on a consensus basis, optional arrangements of a non-confrontational, non-judicial, and consultative nature for reviewing compliance

with the provisions of the Convention. These arrangements shall allow for appropriate public involvement and may include the option of considering communications from members of the public on matters related to the Convention.

Observations or inspections
None by the Convention as such.

Trade measures
No provisions on trade measures to penalize Parties for non-compliance.

Dispute-settlement mechanisms
If a dispute arises between two or more Parties about the interpretation or application of the Convention, they shall seek a solution by negotiation or by any other method of dispute settlement acceptable to the parties to the dispute.
The Parties may submit the dispute to the International Court of Justice or to an arbitration procedure set out in *Annex II*.

Decision-making bodies

Political
After the Convention enters into force, the Meeting of the Parties will become the supreme authority. The first meeting of the COP shall be convened no later than one year after the entry into force of the Convention. Thereafter, ordinary meetings of the Parties shall be held at least once every two years.

The Meeting of the Parties shall by consensus agree upon and adopt at its first meeting rules of procedure. It may consider, as necessary, establishing on a consensus basis financial arrangements.
The Meeting of the Parties shall keep under continuous review the implementation of the Convention (see Monitoring/implementation, above), harmonize policies with other ECE bodies and other competent international bodies, establish subsidiary bodies, prepare protocols and amendments to the Convention, and undertake additional actions.
National and international agencies and qualified NGOs may attend the meetings of the Parties as observers and contribute to its work.

Scientific/technical
Not applicable.

Publications
Up-to-date information is available from UN/ECE. An *Århus Convention Implementation Guide* will be issued as an UN/ECE publication in spring 2000.

Sources on the Internet
<http://www.unece.org/env/europe/ppconven.htm>

Convention on Environmental Impact Assessment in a Transboundary Context

Objectives
- to enhance international co-operation in assessing environmental impacts, in particular in a transboundary context;
- to promote environmentally sound and sustainable development;
- to support the development of anticipatory policies and of measures preventing, mitigating, and monitoring significant adverse environmental impacts in general and more specifically in a transboundary context;
- to promote measures taken at an early planning stage of proposed activities aimed at preventing potentially harmful environmental impacts, in particular those with a transboundary dimension, and to strive towards convergence of relevant national policies and practices;
- to provide for notification and consultation among states concerned on all major projects under consideration that are likely to cause significant adverse environmental impact across boundaries;
- to promote public information and public participation in relevant decision-making processes.

Scope
Legal scope
Open to member countries of the UN Economic Commission for Europe (UN/ECE), the European Union (EU), and other European States having consultative status with the UN/ECE.

Geographic scope
Regional. UN/ECE region (Europe and North America).

Time and place of adoption
25 February 1991, Espoo.

Entry into force
10 September 1997.

Status of participation
25 Parties, including the European Union, by 16 June 1999. 13 Signatories without ratification, acceptance, or approval.

The Secretary-General of the UN acts as depositary.

Affiliated instruments and organizations
The Convention also contains seven *appendices* (see Rules and standards below) which form an integral part of the Convention.

The Executive Secretary of the UN/ECE carries out the secretariat functions.

Secretariat
UN/ECE, Environment and Human Settlements Division (ENHS),
Palais des Nations,
CH-1211 Geneva 10,
Switzerland
Telephone:　　+41-22-9172448
Telefax:　　+41-22-9070107
E-mail: wiecher.schrage@unece.org

Information contact
Mr Wiek Schrage.

Finance
Costs of meetings, documentation, and secretariat services are covered by the regular budget of UN/ECE. Lead countries for activities in the work-plan are responsible for related costs.

The first Meeting of the Parties in May 1998 adopted Decision I/8 on the budget and financial arrangements for the period until the second Meeting of the Parties. According to the Decision the Parties would contribute to the budget of the Convention on a voluntary basis.

Budget
In accordance with Decision I/8, the budget for the Secretariat has been fixed at $US52,150 for the period May 1998 to October 2000.

Rules and standards
The Convention stipulates measures and procedures to prevent, control, or reduce any significant adverse effect on the environment, particularly any transboundary effect on human health and safety, flora, fauna, soil, water, climate, landscape, and historical monuments, which is likely to be caused by a proposed economic activity or any major change to an existing economic activity listed in *Appendix 1*.

Appendix 1 covers 17 groups of activities, such as nuclear and thermal power stations, road and railway construction, chemical installations, waste-disposal facilities, oil refineries, oil and gas pipelines, mining, steel production, pulp and paper manufacturing, and the construction of dams and reservoirs.

Concerned Parties may apply the provisions of the Convention also to other activities (general guidance is included in *Appendix III* for this purpose), and enter into bilateral or multilateral agreements.

Parties will have to establish an environmental impact assessment (EIA) procedure involving public participation and the preparation of EIA documentation described in *Appendix II*. An EIA has to be carried out before the decision is taken to authorize or undertake a proposed activity listed in *Appendix I*.

Parties will also endeavour to ensure that the EIA principles are applied to policies, plans, and programmes. A country under the jurisdiction of which a proposed activity is envisaged will have to notify accordingly any country likely to be affected by it as early as possible and no later than when informing its own public about the proposed activity. The country of origin has to transmit to the affected country or countries the relevant EIA documentation for comments on the proposed activity and its possible transboundary effects.

Arrangements will have to be made in order to ensure that the public, including the public of the affected country or countries, is given the opportunity to submit comments on or objections to the proposed activity.

Consultations may be held between the countries concerned in respect of possible alternatives to the proposed activity, including

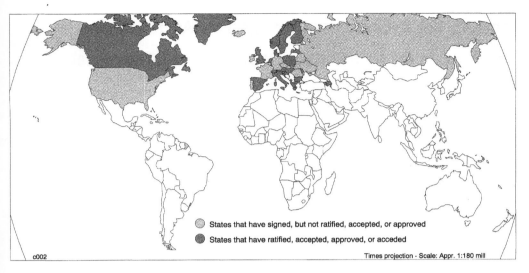

States that have signed, but not ratified, accepted, or approved

States that have ratified, accepted, approved, or acceded

c002   Times projection - Scale: Appr. 1:180 mill

the no-action alternative and possible measures to mitigate adverse effects. Affected countries will be informed about the final decision on the proposed activity and the reasons and considerations on which it is based. Post-project analysis may be undertaken in order to monitor compliance with the conditions set out in the authorization of the activity and the effectiveness of mitigation measures.

Monitoring/implementation

Review procedure
The Parties to the Convention shall keep under continuous review the implementation of the Convention and, with this purpose in mind:
• review the policies and methodological approaches to EIA by the Parties with a view to improving EIA procedures further in a transboundary context;
• exchange information regarding experience gained in concluding and implementing bilateral and multilateral agreements;
• seek, where appropriate, the services of competent international bodies and scientific committees in methodological and technical aspects.

When a country considers that it may be affected by a significant adverse transboundary impact of a proposed activity, and when no notification has taken place, the concerned countries shall, at the request of the affected country, exchange sufficient information to enable discussions to take

place on whether there is likely to be a significant adverse transboundary impact.

If those countries agree that there is likely to be a significant adverse transboundary impact, the provisions of the Convention will apply accordingly. If those countries cannot agree whether there is likely to be a significant adverse transboundary impact, any such country may submit that question to a commission of inquiry in accordance with *Annex IV* to the Convention to advise on its likelihood, unless they agree on another method of settling this question.

Observations or inspections
None by the Convention as such.

Trade measures
No provisions on trade measures to penalize Parties for non-compliance.

Dispute-settlement mechanisms
If a dispute arises between two or more Parties about the interpretation or application of the Convention, they shall seek a solution by negotiation or by any other method of dispute settlement acceptable to the parties to the dispute.

The Parties may submit the dispute to the International Court of Justice or to an arbitration procedure set out in *Appendix VII*.

Decision-making bodies
Political
The Meeting of the Parties will take place once every two years in order to review national

policies and strategies promoting EIA, to consider relevant technical aspects, and to exchange information regarding experience gained in concluding and implementing relevant bilateral and multilateral agreements. The first Meeting of the Parties was held on 18–20 May 1998 in Oslo, Norway, and the second will be held in Sofia, Bulgaria, in October 2000.

Where appropriate, the Meeting will consider and, where necessary, adopt proposals for amendments to the Convention. Agreement on the proposed amendment should be reached by consensus. If no agreement is reached, the amendment shall, as a last resort, be adopted by a three-quarter majority vote of the Parties present and voting at the Meeting.

Scientific/technical
To be decided by the Meeting of the Parties.

Publications
• ECE Environmental Series;
• *Environmental Conventions Elaborated under the Auspices of the UN/ECE*, 1992.
In addition, up-to-date information is available from UN/ECE.

Sources on the Internet
<http://www.unece.org/env/eia_h.htm>
<http://www.mos.gov.pl/enimpas>

Annex 16, vol. II (Environmental Protection: Aircraft Engine Emissions) to the 1944 Chicago Convention on International Civil Aviation

Objectives
• to provide international standardization, through certification procedures, of limitations on aircraft and engine emissions in the vicinity of airports;
• to ensure that replacements with newly designed engines employ the best available emissions-reduction technology.

Scope
Legal scope
Membership is restricted to International Civil Aviation Organization (ICAO) members. A convention providing for the establishment of ICAO was signed at Chicago on 7 December 1944. The organization came into existence on 4 April 1947, after 26 states had ratified the Chicago Convention.

Geographic scope
Global.

Time and place of adoption
30 June 1981, Montreal.

Entry into force
18 February 1982. Entry into force of ICAO annexes is facilitated by a 'tacit consent' procedure, enabling dissenting countries to notify their differences within a specified time-limit, after which the annexes become generally applicable.

Status of participation
185 member States by 30 April 1999. All ICAO member States are potentially involved, although in practice only those ICAO member States manufacturing aircraft and engines are directly involved.

Affiliated instruments and organizations
Annex 16 was originally drafted by a committee of experts nominated by member States plus observers from international organizations. Annexes to the Chicago Convention on International Civil Aviation are adopted and revised by the ICAO Council upon recommendation by the expert committee (see below).

The most recent amendment was adopted by the Council on 26 February 1999 and will enter into force on 4 November 1999. This amendment is a significant change in that it represents a further reduction by an average of about 16 per cent in the stringency of the nitrogen oxide emissions standards for future production engines and will be applicable to new engine designs after 2003.

All member States have the opportunity to comment on the provisions before adoption or to disapprove them and file differences (Article 38 of the Convention).

ICAO places equal emphasis on environmental issues relating to aircraft noise, provisions for which are contained in the related instrument, Annex 16, vol. I (Environmental Protection: Aircraft Noise) (see below). The third edition of this volume entered into force on 11 November 1993.

Administrative functions under the Chicago convention are performed by the ICAO secretariat in Montreal.

Co-ordination with related instruments
ICAO has been liaising with the Conference of the Parties to the UN Framework Convention on Climate Change (UNFCCC) (see this section), the Intergovernmental panel on Climate Change (IPCC), the Montreal Protocol on Substances that deplete the Ozone Layer (see this section), and the UN Economic Commission for Europe (UN/ECE) regarding its Convention on Long-Range Transboundary Air Pollution (LRTAP) (see this section).

Secretariat
International Civil Aviation Organization (ICAO),
999 University Street,
Montreal,
Quebec H3C 5H7,
Canada
Telephone: +1-514-9548219
Telefax: +1-514-9546077
E-mail: icaohq@icao.int

Secretary-General (ICAO)
Mr Renato Cláudio Costa Pereira
(1 August 1997–31 July 2000).

Chief, External Relations and Public Information Office
Mr G. Griffiths.

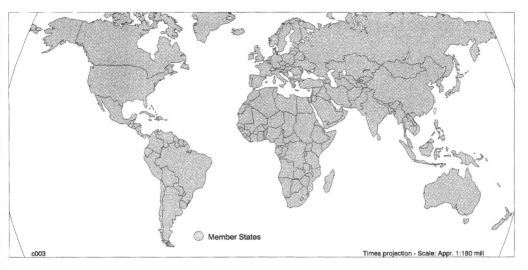

Member States

c003   Times projection - Scale: Appr. 1:180 mill

Number of staff
297 professionals and 458 support staff
(March 1999).

Finance

Budget
The Annex does not provide for regular
meetings and programme activities. Costs
of meetings, documentation, and secretariat
services are covered by the regular ICAO
budget.

Special funds
None.

Rules and standards
Member States are not required to report
compliance, only non-compliance.

Monitoring/implementation

Review procedure
The objectives are considered to have been
met in that all newly designed aircraft engines comply with the requirements of Annex 16, although a number of countries have
filed notifications under Article 38 of the
Convention regarding different national
standards.

Notifications of national differences in
standards are recorded and regularly communicated to all members by way of supplements to Annexes. With regard to Annex
16, vol. II, seven member States had notified national differences and 26 had reported conformity. The remaining members
are presumed to be tacitly conforming. The

following States notified ICAO of differences by 30 March 1999: France, the Netherlands, New Zealand, Qatar, the Russian
Federation, Saudi Arabia, and Vanuatu.

With regard to Annex 16, vol. I, on aircraft noise (see above), nine member States
had notified national differences in standards and 18 had reported conformity. The
remaining members are presumed to be tacitly conforming. The following States had
notified ICAO of differences by 30 March
1999: Canada, Germany, Japan, the Netherlands, New Zealand, the Russian Federation, Switzerland, the United Kingdom, and
the USA.

These notifications are made public.
Potential factors affecting compliance include technical difficulties in meeting the requirements, disagreement with the need for
specific aspects of the requirement, and the
cost of compliance testing. A problem of
major concern to developing countries is the
potential for unilateral or regional operating restrictions on older aircraft not conforming to Annex 16.

Continuous review of Annex 16 by the expert committee and the ICAO Council takes
into account inputs from manufacturers,
operators, airport management, etc. The
flexible ICAO procedure for amendment of
technical annexes allows timely adjustment.

Dispute-settlement mechanisms
Disputes are normally considered by the
ICAO Council, with possible recourse to in-
ternational arbitration or adjudication.

Decision-making bodies

Political
The Assembly, composed of delegates from
all the Contracting States, meets every three
years. The Council, the executive organ, is
composed of 33 representatives of Contracting States elected by the Assembly; it is in
session almost continuously. The Council
elects its own president.

Scientific/technical
ICAO's technical work in the environmental field is undertaken by the Council's
Committee on Aviation Environmental
Protection (CAEP). The Committee was established in 1983 to supersede the Committee on Aircraft Noise (CAN-1972) and the
Committee on Aircraft Engine Emissions
(CAEE-1977). CAEP's main objective is to
discuss and recommend measures to control or minimize the environmental impact
of aviation. It is responsible for proposing
the noise and emissions standards for aircraft certification contained respectively in
Annex 16, vols. I and II. The expert committee reviews, refines, and updates the provisions as necessary. By April 1999 CAEP
had held four meetings.

Publications
The ICAO secretariat publishes current activities in *ICAO Journal* as well as a wide
range of information materials for government and public distribution.

Sources on the Internet
<http://www.icao.int/>

Convention on Long-Range Transboundary Air Pollution (LRTAP)

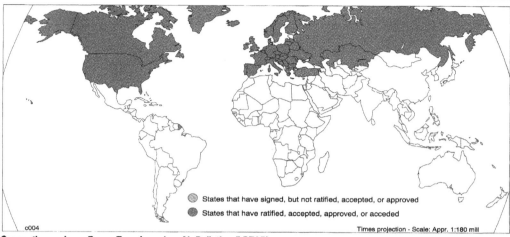

States that have signed, but not ratified, accepted, or approved

States that have ratified, accepted, approved, or acceded

c004   Times projection - Scale: Appr. 1:180 mill

Convention on Long-Range Transboundary Air Pollution (LRTAP)

Objectives
• to protect human beings and their environment against air pollution;
• to limit and, as far as possible, gradually to reduce and prevent air pollution, including long-range transboundary air pollution.

Scope
Legal scope
Open to member States of the UN Economic Commission for Europe (UN/ECE), the European Community, and other European states having consultative status with the UN/ECE.

Geographic scope
Regional. UN/ECE region (Europe and North America).

Time and place of adoption
13 November 1979, Geneva.

Entry into force
16 March 1983.

Status of participation
44 Parties, including the European Community, by 16 June 1999. Two Signatories without ratification, accession, acceptance, or approval.
The Secretary-General of the UN acts as depositary.

Affiliated instruments and organizations
Protocol to the Convention on Long-Range Transboundary Air Pollution on Long-Term Financing of the Co-operative Programme for Monitoring and Evaluation of the Long-Range Transmission of Air Pollutants in Europe (EMEP), Geneva, 28 September 1984. Entered into force on 28 January 1988. 37 Parties, including the European Community, by 16 June 1999. No Signatories without ratification, approval, or acceptance.
The basic objective of the Protocol is:
• to share the costs of a monitoring programme which forms the backbone for review and assessment of relevant air pollution in Europe in the light of agreements on emission reduction. The main objective of EMEP is to provide governments with information on the deposition and concentration of air pollutants as well as on the quantity and significance of long-range transmission of pollutants and of fluxes across boundaries. EMEP has three main components: (*a*) collection of emission data for sulphur dioxide (SO_2), nitrogen dioxide (NO_x), volatile organic compounds (VOCs), ground level ozone, and, more recently, persistent organic pollutants (POPs) and heavy metals and other air pollutants; (*b*) measurement of air and precipitation quality; and (*c*) modelling of the movement of air pollutants.

Protocol to the Convention on Long-Range Transboundary Air Pollution on Further Reduction of Sulphur Emissions (1994 Sulphur Protocol), Oslo, 14 June 1994. Entered into force on 5 August 1998. 22 Parties, including the European Community, by 16 June 1999. Six Signatories without ratification, accession, acceptance, or approval.
The Protocol follows the former Sulphur Protocol adopted in Helsinki on 8 July 1985, which entered into force on 2 September 1987. The basic objective of the first Protocol was to reduce the annual sulphur emissions or the transboundary fluxes by at least 30 per cent as soon as possible and at the latest by 1993, using 1980 levels as the basis for calculation of reductions.
The basic objective of the 1994 Sulphur Protocol is:
• to reduce sulphur emissions to ensure, as far as possible, without entailing excessive cost, that in the long run 'critical loads'—the rates of sulphur deposition which ecosystems and other receptors can tolerate in the long term without suffering damage—are no longer exceeded.

Protocol to the Convention on Long-Range Transboundary Air Pollution concerning the Control of Emissions of Nitrogen Oxides or their Transboundary Fluxes (1988 NO_x Protocol), Sofia, 31 October 1988. Entered into force on 14 February 1991. 26 Parties, including the European Community, by 16 June 1999. Two Signatories without ratifi-

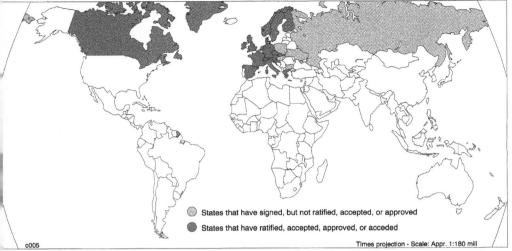

1994 Sulphur Protocol

cation, accession, acceptance, or approval.

The basic objective of the Protocol is:
• to take effective measures to control and/or reduce the Parties' national annual emissions of nitrogen oxides or their transboundary fluxes so that these, at the latest by 31 December 1994, do not exceed their national annual emissions of such substances for 1987 or any previous year to be specified upon signature of, or accession to, the Protocol.

Protocol to the Convention on Long-Range Transboundary Air Pollution concerning the Control of Emissions of Volatile Organic Compounds or their Transboundary Fluxes (1991 VOC Protocol), Geneva, 18 November 1991. Entered into force on 29 September 1997. 17 Parties by 16 June 1999. Seven Signatories, including the European Community, without ratification, accession, acceptance, or approval.

The basic objective of the Protocol is:
• to control and reduce the emissions of VOCs in order to lessen the transboundary fluxes and the fluxes of the resulting secondary photochemical oxidant products so as to protect human health and the environment from adverse effects.

This Protocol offers flexibility to the Parties, which is a completely new feature of this type of international agreement. There are options not only to select the base year, but also to designate particular areas within a country in which the reduction obligation applies, as well as to freeze rather than reduce emissions in countries where the total is very low.

The Executive Body decided in November 1995 to begin negotiations of a protocol on nitrogen compounds, VOCs, and related substances, using a multi-pollutant and multi-effect approach for addressing photochemical pollution, acidification, and eutrophication. For VOCs, it has already been decided that the obligations of the 1991 VOC Protocol should be the starting point for scenario analysis and for negotiations on the reduction of nitrogen compounds and related substances without precluding the possibility of agreement on further or faster emission reduction requirements for VOCs. The protocol is expected to be ready for signing before the end of 1999.

The Executive Body decided in November 1996 to begin negotiations on protocols on heavy metals (HMs) and persistent organic pollutants (POPs) in 1997. Both protocols were finalized in June 1998.

Protocol to the 1979 Convention on Long-Range Transboundary Air Pollution on Heavy Metals (1998 Heavy Metals Protocol), Århus, 24 June 1998. (Not yet in force.) One State had ratified by 16 June 1999. 35 Signatories, including the European Community, without ratification, accession, acceptance, or approval. Enters into force on the ninetieth day after the deposit of the sixteenth instrument of ratification, acceptance, approval or accession.

The Protocol concentrates at first on cad-

mium, mercury, and lead. It includes provisions for adding other metals in future if international action is needed. The basic objectives of the Protocol are:
• to reduce emissions for these three metals below their levels in 1990 (or an alternative year between 1985 and 1995);
• to reduce emissions from industrial sources (iron and steel industry, non-ferrous metal industry), combustion processes (power generation, road transport), and waste incineration. It lays down stringent limit values for emissions from stationary sources and suggests best available techniques (BAT) for these sources, such as special filters or scrubbers for combustion sources or mercury-free processes;
• to phase out leaded petrol;
• to lower heavy metal emissions from other products, such as mercury in batteries, and to propose the introduction of management measures for other mercury-containing products, such as electrical components (thermostats, switches), measuring devices (thermometers, manometers, barometers), fluorescent lamps, dental amalgam, pesticides and paint.

Protocol to the 1979 Convention on Long-Range Transboundary Air Pollution on Persistent Organic Pollutants (1998 POPs Protocol), Århus, 24 June 1998. (Not yet in force.) One State had ratified by 16 June 1999. 35 Signatories, including the European Community, without ratification, accession, acceptance, or approval. Enters into force on the ninetieth day after the de-

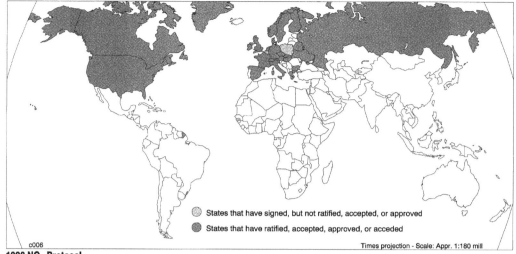

States that have signed, but not ratified, accepted, or approved

States that have ratified, accepted, approved, or acceded

c006

Times projection - Scale: Appr. 1:180 mill

1988 NO$_x$ Protocol

posit of the sixteenth instrument of ratification, acceptance, approval or accession.

The Protocol focuses on a list of 16 substances that have been singled out according to agreed risk criteria. The substances comprise eleven pesticides, two industrial chemicals and three by-products/contaminants. The basic objective of the Protocol is:

• to control, reduce, or eliminate discharges, emissions, and losses of POPs to the environment. The Protocol bans the production and use of some products outright (aldrin, chlordane, chlordecone, dieldrin, endrin, hexabromobiphenyl, mirex, and toxaphene). Others are scheduled for elimination at a later stage (DDT, heptachlor, hexachlorobenzene, PCBs). Finally, the Protocol severely restricts the use of DDT, HCH (including lindane), and PCBs.

The Protocol includes provisions for dealing with the wastes of products that will be banned. It also obliges Parties to reduce their emissions of dioxins, furans, PAHs, and HCB below their levels in 1990 (or an alternative year between 1985 and 1995). For the incineration of municipal, hazardous, and medical waste, it lays down specific limit values.

The UN Economic Commission for Europe (UN/ECE), through the Air Pollution Section of the UN/ECE Environment and Human Settlements Division, plays a central role for the elaboration of the Convention and its protocols and for follow-up action to implement them.

Co-ordination with related instruments
Work on drafting revised or new protocols is co-ordinated through the ECE secretariat, with other competent bodies, especially as regards airborne pollution of adjacent regional sea areas, e.g. the Baltic Sea, through the Helsinki Commission (see this section), and the North Sea, through the OSPAR Commission (see this section).

Secretariat

UN/ECE, Environment and Human Settlements Division (ENHS),
Palais des Nations,
CH-1211 Geneva 10,
Switzerland
Telephone: +41-22-91723-70/54
Telefax: +41-22-9070107
E-mail: air.env@unece.org

Director (ENHS Division)
Mr Kaj Bärlund.

Deputy Directors (ENHS Division)
Mr Lars Nordberg and Ms Christina Von Schweinichen.

Number of staff
Six professionals and two support staff in the Air Pollution Section (June 1999).

Finance

Costs of meetings, documentation, and secretariat services are covered by the regular budget of UN/ECE. International co-ordination costs for the EMEP programme are financed by mandatory contributions from

the Parties to a UN-administered trust fund and were approximately $US1 million for 1990. Costs of other co-operative programmes are covered by voluntary contributions of participating Parties.

Budget
The actual budget for the EMEP programme was $US1,990,415 in 1997 and $1,855,000 in 1998, and is $2,040,500 in 1999.

Rules and standards

Parties are committed to:
• develop by means of exchanges of information, consultation, research, and monitoring, and without undue delay, policies and strategies which shall serve as a means of combating the discharge of air pollutants;
• exchange information on and review their policies, scientific activities, and technical measures aimed at combating, as far as possible, the discharge of air pollutants which may have adverse effects, thereby contributing to the reduction of air pollution, including long-range transboundary air pollution;
• develop the best policies and strategies, including air-quality management systems, and, as part of them, control measures compatible with balanced development, in particular by using the best available technology (BAT) that is economically feasible and low- or non-waste technology.

The sulphur emission reductions in the schedule presented in the following column

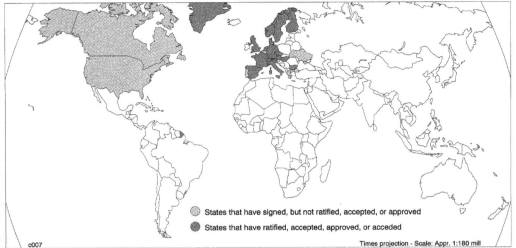

States that have signed, but not ratified, accepted, or approved
States that have ratified, accepted, approved, or acceded

c007   Times projection - Scale: Appr. 1:180 mill

1991 VOC Protocol

give the emission ceilings referred to in the *1994 Sulphur Protocol* (percentage of sulphur emissions reductions, taking 1980 as the base year and the year 2000 for Greece and Portugal).

The *1991 VOC Protocol* specifies three options for emission reduction targets that have to be chosen upon signature:
(*a*) a 30 per cent reduction in emissions of VOCs by 1999, using either 1988 or any other year between 1984 and 1990 as the base year. This option was chosen by Austria, Belgium, Finland, France, Germany, the Netherlands, Portugal, Spain, Sweden, and the United Kingdom with 1988 as the base year, by Denmark with 1985 as the base year, by the Czech Republic, Italy, and Luxembourg with 1990 as the base year, and by Liechtenstein, Switzerland, and the USA with 1984 as the base year;
(*b*) the same reduction as for (*a*) within a Tropospheric Ozone Management Area (TOMA) specified in Annex I to the Protocol and ensuring that by 1999 total national emissions do not exceed 1988 levels. (Annex I specifies TOMAs in Norway (base year 1989) and Canada (base year 1988));
(*c*) finally, where emissions in 1988 did not exceed certain specified levels, Parties may opt for a stabilization at that level of emission by 1999 (this has been chosen by Bulgaria, Greece, and Hungary).

	Year		
	2000	2005	2010
Austria	80		
Belarus	38	46	50
Belgium	70	72	74
Bulgaria	33	40	45
Canada	30		
Croatia	11	17	22
Czech Republic	50	60	72
Denmark	80		
Finland	80		
France	74	77	78
Germany	83	87	
Greece	0	3	4
Hungary	45	50	60
Ireland	30		
Italy	65	73	
Liechtenstein	75		
Luxembourg	58		
Netherlands	77		
Norway	76		
Poland	37	47	66
Portugal	0	3	
Russian Federation	38	40	40
Slovakia	60	65	72
Slovenia	45	60	70
Spain	35		
Sweden	80		
Switzerland	52		
Ukraine	40		
United Kingdom	50	70	80
European Community	62		

Monitoring/implementation

Review procedure
An Implementation Committee was established by the Executive Body in December 1997. The primary functions of the Implementation Committee are to review compliance by the Parties with the reporting requirements of the protocols, and to report on compliance with or implementation of specified obligations in an individual protocol. It is also able to receive submissions from Parties relating to compliance. Two-year reviews are conducted based on detailed questionnaires. At the same time, monitoring data on actual depositions of air pollution are collected and analysed under the EMEP programme and submitted yearly to the Executive Body.

35 Parties (79.5 per cent of the Parties) submitted national reports as requested by the major review in 1998. Parties are requested to update the 1998 major review in 2000. The next major review is scheduled for 2002.

The national emission data and other information required from Parties to the protocols currently in force are further specified in the work plans for implementation of the Convention, adopted annually by the Executive Body. Annual data reporting to the EMEP international centres is generally satisfactory.

Periodic public reviews of national reports and the data collected through EMEP and other co-operative programmes under the Convention have served as a mechanism

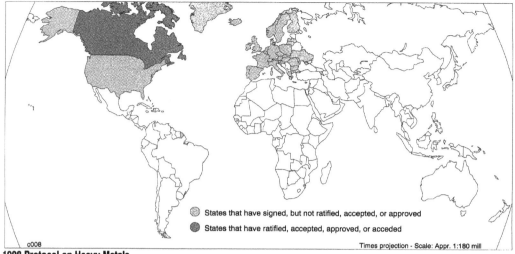

States that have signed, but not ratified, accepted, or approved

States that have ratified, accepted, approved, or acceded

c008   Times projection - Scale: Appr. 1:180 mill

1998 Protocol on Heavy Metals

to induce compliance. The reviews are published after de-restriction by the Executive Body for the Convention. The publicity caused by NGO participation in the annual review meetings may be considered a contributing factor.

Extent of implementation

• *The 1985 Sulphur Protocol*: The first Sulphur Protocol contains two requirements of Parties which remain of particular relevance. The first is to make a 30 per cent cut in sulphur emissions or their transboundary fluxes as soon as possible (the Protocol specified at the latest by 1993, compared to levels in 1980). At the seventh session of the Executive Body in December 1989 the then Parties to the Protocol expressed a common understanding about the interpretation of this provision that it 'means that reductions to that extent should be reached in that time-frame and the levels maintained or further reduced after being reached'. The second requirement is to report emissions of sulphur annually to the Executive Body.

All 21 Parties to the Protocol met the required reductions in 1993. Many Parties significantly exceeded the reductions required, with Austria, Finland, and Sweden reducing emissions by more than 80 per cent. Whilst achieving the required reduction in 1993, Bulgaria narrowly failed to achieve the target in 1994 and 1995, but met it in 1996; future projections indicate the likelihood of its continuing to achieve the target in future years. Reports of emissions for

1996 have been made by 16 of the 21 Parties. Austria, Belarus, Canada, Italy, and Liechtenstein have not submitted sulphur emissions data for the most recent reporting year.

• *The 1988 NO$_x$ Protocol*: Arguably the principal obligation on Parties to the NO$_x$ Protocol is to control and/or reduce their total annual emissions of nitrogen oxides or their transboundary fluxes. it was proposed that these, at the latest by 31 December 1994, should not exceed such emissions for 1987. At its fourteenth session in December 1996, the Executive Body confirmed its understanding that the obligation 'should be taken to mean that emission levels for the years after 1994 should not exceed those specified in that paragraph'. Official submissions suggest that the requirement was met by 19 of the 26 Parties to the Protocol. Bulgaria, the Czech Republic, Germany, and Ukraine went significantly further, with at least one year in the 1994–6 period when emissions were more than 40 per cent lower than in 1987. France narrowly failed to achieve the target for each year in the period 1994–6, and provides no projections to indicate future trends. The USA exercised an option and specified a base year of 1978 when it signed the Protocol, so its target became to control and/or reduce its total annual emissions of nitrogen oxides or their transboundary fluxes so that these, at the latest by 31 December 1994, did not exceed such emissions for 1978, and to ensure that its national average annual transboundary fluxes or national average annual emissions

for the period from 1 January 1987 to 1 January 1996 did not exceed those for the calendar year 1987. The USA failed to achieve the requirement for stabilization in 1994, but the target was achieved in 1995 and 1996; projections for future years indicate attainment of the target for the year 2000 and beyond. Additionally, the average of annual emissions in the period 1 January 1987 to 1 January 1996 was 21,813 kilotons, compared to emissions in 1987 of 20,689 kilotons, so this target was not achieved. Luxembourg submitted no emission data for the base year of 1987, but its emissions were more or less stable throughout the period 1980–96 in the years for which information is available. Four Parties to the Protocol have not reported NO$_x$ emissions for the years 1994–6. Of these four, Italy reported NO$_x$ emissions for the years prior to 1994 which are significantly above the stabilization level. Spain's 1997 response explains that the apparently large rise in its emissions is the result of a methodological change in inventory compilation. When emissions are back-calculated to include off-road vehicles, its emissions rose 1 per cent in the period 1987–93, with a projection for the year 2000 indicating that the target will be met at that time. The remaining two Parties, Greece and the European Community, have not reported NO$_x$ emissions for any year. However, the former ratified the Protocol only during 1998 and the latter claimed in its questionnaire response to

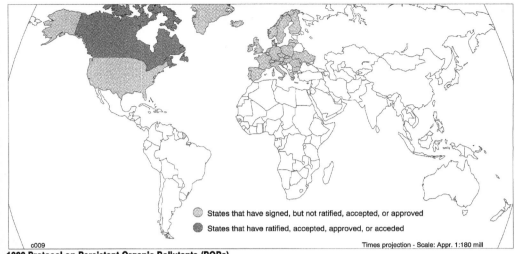

States that have signed, but not ratified, accepted, or approved

States that have ratified, accepted, approved, or acceded

c009   Times projection - Scale: Appr. 1:180 mill

1998 Protocol on Persistent Organic Pollutants (POPs)

have achieved the stabilization target by 1994.

There is a requirement to make unleaded fuel sufficiently available to facilitate the circulation of vehicles fitted with catalytic converters, particularly along main international transit routes. 15 of the 26 Parties have either phased out leaded petrol completely or responded to the questionnaire in specific terms that they had met the terms of the requirement. The Czech Republic, Ireland, Switzerland, and the European Community provided data which would imply that they had also met the requirement.

• *The 1991 VOC Protocol*: The first requirement is for the Parties to control and reduce VOC emissions. Taking the Parties as a whole, the emissions of VOC would appear to have reduced in the face of control measures, although the emissions data set is not complete. The provision in the Protocol which requires concrete reductions in national annual emissions of VOC lays out a number of options, one of which has to be chosen by the Party on signature. In all cases the target has to be achieved by the year 1999.

Environmental monitoring programmes
Monitoring data on actual depositions and concentrations of air pollution are collected and analysed under the EMEP programme (see above). The programme was originally established in 1977 by UN/ECE, the World Meteorological Organization (WMO), and the UN Environment Programme (UNEP).

EMEP collects precipitation gas and aerosol chemistry data from some 100 ground-level monitoring stations in 33 UN/ECE countries. The data are collected daily and are analysed to establish the transportation patterns of essential pollutants. These data are analysed and results published by EMEP's Chemical Co-ordinating Centre (CCC) in Norway. Two meteorological synthesizing centres (MSCs) have been established by EMEP, in Norway and in the Russian Federation, to develop model calculations of long-range transport and deposition of acidifying compounds. (See Sources on the Internet, below.)

Data and information system programmes
The negotiations for the scheme for emission reductions of the 1994 Sulphur Protocol are based on an integrated assessment modelling such as the model known as the Regional Acidification Information and Simulation Model (RAINS), developed by the International Institute for Applied Systems Analysis (IIASA) in Austria.

Decision-making bodies
Political
The Executive Body, formed of the Contracting Parties, meets at least annually. It reviews the implementation of the Convention and has established working groups to prepare appropriate studies, documentation, and recommendations to this end.

Scientific/technical
The Executive Body has established several standing subsidiary bodies to provide the necessary scientific expert advice for policy-making decisions. They are at present:
• Working Group on Effects (composed of government experts and others);
• Working Group on Strategies (composed of government experts and others);
• EMEP Steering Body (composed of government experts and others);
• Working Group on Abatement Techniques (composed of government experts and others).

In December 1997 the Executive Body established an Implementation Committee to review compliance by Parties with their obligations under the protocols to the Convention. The Committee is composed of five legal experts and four technical experts.

Publications
Up-to-date information on the operation of the Convention and its protocols is disseminated through documents for UN/ECE meetings, the UN/ECE Air Pollution Studies series, public-information brochures, etc.

Sources on the Internet
<http://www.unece.org/env/env_eb.htm>
Scientific information on emissions from EMEP:
<http://www.emep.int>

United Nations Framework Convention on Climate Change (UNFCCC)

Objectives
- to stabilize greenhouse-gas concentrations in the atmosphere at a level that would prevent dangerous anthropogenic interference with the climate system, within a time-frame sufficient to allow ecosystems to adapt naturally to climate change;
- to ensure that food production is not threatened;
- to enable economic development to proceed in a sustainable manner.

Scope
Legal scope
Open to all member States of the UN, or of its specialized agencies, or that are Parties to the Statute of the International Court of Justice, and to regional economic integration organizations.

Geographic scope
Global.

Time and place of adoption
Concluded on 9 May 1992 at New York.

Entry into force
21 March 1994.

Status of participation
178 Parties, including the European Economic Community, by 16 June 1999. Six Signatories without ratification, acceptance, or approval.

The Secretary-General of the UN acts as depositary of both the Convention and the Kyoto Protocol.

Affiliated instruments and organizations
Annex I lists developed-country Parties that must adopt measures aimed at returning their greenhouse-gas (GHG) emissions to 1990 levels by the year 2000. It includes the 24 original OECD members, 11 countries with economies in transition, and the European Union.

Annex II lists developed-country Parties

which have a special obligation to help developing countries with financial and technological resources. It includes the 24 original OECD members and the European Union.

The *Berlin Mandate* was adopted at the first Conference of the Parties (COP) on 7 April 1995. It acknowledges that the commitment of developed countries to take measures aimed at reducing their GHG emissions to 1990 levels by the year 2000 is not adequate to achieve the Convention's objective. The main objective of the Mandate was to strengthen the commitments for the developed-country Parties after the year 2000 without introducing any new commitments for developing countries, while reaffirming existing commitments of all Parties contained in Article 4.1 and continuing to advance their implementation. The *ad hoc* Group on the Berlin Mandate met for eight sessions before handing over the results of its work for completion to the third session of the COP in December 1997.

At the second COP, a large number of ministers agreed on the Geneva Ministerial Declaration, which provided political impetus to the Berlin Mandate process. They instructed their representatives to accelerate negotiations on the text of a legally binding protocol or another legal instrument, the outcome of which should encompass quantified legally binding objectives for emission limitations and significant overall reductions within specified time-frames.

By 1 June 1997 a draft text of an instrument was circulated in the six official languages of the UN and served as a basis for the negotiations leading up to the third COP. A number of other proposals on GHG emissions reductions were on the table during this period, including one by the Alliance of Small Island States for a 20 per cent reduction in carbon dioxide (CO_2) by the year 2005; one by the European Union for reductions of 7.5 per cent by 2005 and 15 per cent by 2010 in a 'basket' of gases including CO_2, methane (CH_4) and nitrous oxide (N_2O); one by Japan for a reduction of 5 per cent by 2008–12 (taken as an average over these years), although individual countries could opt for lower targets; one by the USA for returning all GHGs to 1990 levels by 2008–12; and one by the Russian Federation suggesting that each country reduce

its emissions on the basis of its own proposed target, resulting in an overall reduction of some 3 per cent by 2010. The baseline for all proposed reductions would be the year 1990. After ten days of negotiations at the third COP, ministers and other high-level officials from 160 countries reached agreement on a protocol.

Kyoto Protocol to the United Nations Framework Convention on Climate Change (Kyoto Protocol), Kyoto, 11 December 1997. (Not yet in force.) Open for signature from 16 March 1998 to 15 March 1999 and open for accession from the day after the date on which it was closed for signature. Nine ratifications, acceptances, approvals, or accessions by 16 June 1999. 75 Signatories, including the European Economic Community, without ratification, acceptance, or approval. Enters into force on the ninetieth day after the date on which not fewer than 55 Parties to the Convention, incorporating Parties included in Annex I to the Convention which accounted in total for at least 55 per cent of the total CO_2 emissions for 1990 of the Parties included in Annex I, have deposited their instruments of ratification, acceptance, approval, or accession. *Annex A*, listing the GHGs and sectors/source categories lowered by quantified commitments in the Protocol, and *Annex B*, containing quantified emissions limitations or reduction commitments, form an integral part of the Protocol.

The Kyoto Protocol contains individual emission limitations and reductions commitments for Parties included in Annex I to the Convention covering the six main GHGs. These range from an 8 per cent reduction for countries to a 10 per cent increase by the period 2008–12, calculated as an average over these five years. Overall, these individual emission commitments will result in a reduction of 5.2 per cent in emissions of the six GHGs from 1990 levels of Annex I Parties. Reductions in the three most important gases, CO_2, CH_4, and N_2O, will be measured against a base year of 1990. Reductions in three long-lived industrial gases, hydrofluorocarbons (HFCs), perfluorocarbons (PFCs), and sulphur hexafluoride (SF_6), can be measured against either a 1990 or a 1995 baseline.

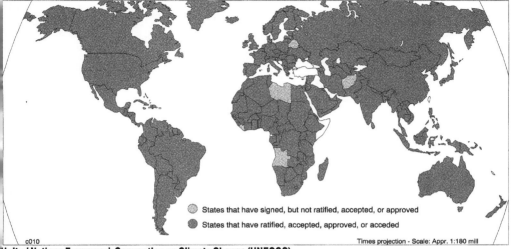

States that have signed, but not ratified, accepted, or approved

States that have ratified, accepted, approved, or acceded

c010   Times projection - Scale: Appr. 1:180 mill

United Nations Framework Convention on Climate Change (UNFCCC)

If compared to expected emissions levels for the year 2000, the total reductions required by the Protocol will actually be about 10 per cent; this is because many industrialized countries have not succeeded in meeting their earlier non-binding aim of returning their emissions to 1990 levels by the year 2000, and their emissions have in fact risen since 1990. Compared to the emissions levels that would be expected by 2010 without emissions-control measures, the Protocol target represents approximately a 30 per cent reduction. (See also Rules and standards, below.)

At the fourth COP during 2–14 November 1998 representatives of 170 governments adopted the two-year *Buenos Aires Plan of Action*. It contains six decisions (see Rules and standards, below) for future work under the Convention and the Kyoto Protocol. To strengthen the implementation of the Convention and prepare for the future entry into force of the Kyoto Protocol, it established deadlines for finalizing the outstanding details of the Kyoto Protocol.

The first COP also made a decision on the launch of a pilot phase for 'activities implemented jointly' (AIJ). The principle of AIJ is that one country (often called host) achieves national development and/or environmental priorities through projects that also provide GHG emission reduction opportunities (e.g. energy-efficiency project improvement) that would not have occurred in the absence of such projects, with another country (often called investor) providing the finance of it. Under the AIJ pilot phase, the investing country,

however, cannot claim credit for the reduced emissions during the pilot phase. The second and fourth COP decided to continue the pilot phase. The fourth COP resolved to begin the process for a review of the AIJ pilot phase with a view to take a conclusive decision on the AIJ pilot phase and the progression beyond no later than the end of the present decade. (See also Rules and standards, *Buenos Aires Plan of Action*, below.)

A decision at the third COP sharpens the Convention's focus on the transfer of technology. It reaffirms the need of information dissemination especially on adaptation technologies. It also aims to establish (an) international technology information centre(s) and identify technology and technology information needs of Parties to the Convention.

Secretariat

Climate Change Secretariat (UNFCCC),
Haus Carstanjen,
Martin-Luther-King-Strasse 8,
D-53175 Bonn, Germany

Mail address:
PO Box 260124,
D-53153 Bonn, Germany

Telephone:	+49-228-8151000
Telefax:	+49-228-8151999
E-mail:	secretariat@unfccc.de

or first initial last name@unfccc.de

Executive Secretary
Mr Michael Zammit Cutajar.

Liaison Officer
Mr Horacio Peluffo.

Number of staff
36 professionals and 32 support staff (July 1999). Augmented by short-term staff and consultants as needed.

Information is also available through:
UNEP Information Unit on the Conventions,
Geneva Executive Center, CP 356,
CH-1219 Châtelaine,
Geneva,
Switzerland.

Telephone:	+41-22-9799242
Telefax:	+41-22-7973464
Contact:	Mr Michael Williams
E-mail:	mwilliams@unep.ch

Finance

The Convention defines a mechanism for providing financial resources for projects which address climate change. This financial mechanism is operated, on an interim basis and under the guidance of the COP, by the Global Environment Facility (GEF) (see IGOs). Projects supported by the GEF are implemented through three implementing agencies: the UN Development Programme (UNDP), the UN Environment Programme (UNEP), and the World Bank (see IGOs). The GEF provides resources for investment projects having global environmental benefits, includ-

States that have signed, but not ratified, accepted, or approved

States that have ratified, accepted, approved, or acceded

c011   Times projection - Scale: Appr. 1:180 mill

Kyoto Protocol

ing projects that reduce emissions of GHGs by increasing energy efficiency and the use of renewable energies. It also supports the building of capacity of developing countries to implement the Convention and prepare national communications to the COP. The GEF promotes bilateral and multilateral co-financing and the leveraging of private sector participation and resources.

The interim arrangements were reviewed by the first COP. It was agreed that the GEF would continue to serve as the interim financial mechanism. (See also Rules and standards, *Buenos Aires Plan of Action*, below.)

Budget
The approved core budget was US8,426,500 in 1997 and $9,645,300 in 1998, and is $11,700,700 in 1999. The proposed programme budget, to be adopted by the fifth COP, is $12,548,000 for 2000 and $12,738,000 for 2001.

Special funds
A Trust Fund for Participation in the UNFCCC Process is designed to receive voluntary contributions to support the participation in the COP and its subsidiary bodies of the representatives of developing-country Parties, in particular those that are least developed countries or small island developing States, and of other Parties with economies in transition. The resources needed for this Fund are estimated to be $4.6 million for the years 1998–9 and $3.7 million for the years 2000–

01. Total income was $2.2 million by 31 March 1999. Total expenditures were $1.5 million in 1998 and are estimated to be $0.6 million in 1999.

A Trust Fund for Supplementary Activities serves as an important resource for the Secretariat in its attempts to respond to the emerging needs and requests of the COP and its subsidiary bodies. It is used to for a variety of activities, including the convening of various workshops and seminars, CD ROMs, the *Who is Who in the UNFCCC Process: Directory of Participants at Meetings of the Convention Bodies*, the Secretariat's website, and website modules devoted to the intergovernmental meetings as well as the UNFCCC Fellowship Programme for professionals from developing countries. The voluntary resources needed for this Fund are estimated to be $4.1 million for the years 1998–9. Total income was $2.9 million by 31 March 1999. Actual expenditures were $1.1 million in 1998 and are estimated to be $1 million in 1999.

Rules and standards
The Parties of the Convention undertake:
• to develop, periodically update, publish, and make available to the COP national inventories of emissions from sources and removals by sinks of all GHGs not controlled by the Montreal Protocol (see this section), using comparable methodologies;
• to formulate, implement, publish, and regularly update national and, where appropriate, regional programmes containing

measures to mitigate climate change by addressing emissions, sinks, and reservoirs of GHGs and to facilitate adequate adaptation to climate change;
• to promote and co-operate in the development, application, and diffusion of technologies, practices, and processes that control, reduce, or prevent GHG emissions;
• to promote sustainable management, and promote and co-operate in the conservation and enhancement, as appropriate, of all sinks and reservoirs of GHGs;
• to promote and co-operate in scientific, technical, socio-economic, and other research, systematic observation, and development of data archives related to the climate system.

The developed-country Parties (including countries with economies in transition) shall adopt national policies and take corresponding measures on the mitigation of climate change, by limiting their anthropogenic emissions of GHGs and protecting and enhancing their GHG sinks and reservoirs. These policies and measures will demonstrate that developed countries are taking the lead in modifying longer-term trends in anthropogenic emissions consistent with the objective of the Convention, recognizing that the return by the end of the present decade to earlier levels of anthropogenic emissions of GHGs not controlled by the Montreal Protocol would contribute to such modification.

These Parties may implement such policies and measures jointly with other Parties, and each of these Parties should communicate, within six months of the entry into force of the Convention and periodically thereafter, detailed information on its policies and measures, as well as on its resulting projected anthropogenic emissions by sources and removals by sinks of GHGs, with the aim of returning these emissions individually or jointly to their 1990 levels.

The developed-country Parties (*not* including countries with economies in transition) shall provide new and additional financial resources to meet full agreed costs incurred by developing-country Parties in complying with their obligations concerning communication of information.

The developed-country Parties shall also provide such resources, including those for transfer of technology, needed by the developing-country Parties to meet the agreed full incremental costs of implementing their commitments.

Each developing-country Party shall make its initial communication within three years of the entry into force of the Convention for that Party or of the availability of financial resources.

The extent to which developing-country Parties will effectively be able to implement their commitments under the Convention will depend on the effective implementation by developed-country Parties of their commitments under the Convention relating to financial resources and their willingness to transfer technology and take fully into account that economic and social development and poverty eradication are the first and overriding priorities of the developing-country Parties.

Parties that are least-developed countries may make their initial communication at their discretion.

The main provisions of the *Kyoto Protocol* imply, e.g.:
• Parties shall, individually or jointly, ensure that their aggregate anthropogenic carbon dioxide equivalent emissions of the GHGs listed in Annex A do not exceed their assigned amounts, calculated pursuant to their quantified emission limitation and reduction commitments inscribed in Annex B and the provisions of Article 3, with a view to reducing their overall emissions of such gases by at least 5 per cent below 1990 levels in the commitment period 2008–12.

The 5.2 per cent reduction in total developed-country emissions will be realized through national reductions as presented in the schedule:

GHG emission targets

Per cent change of GHG emissions by the commitment period 2008–12, taking 1990 as base year

Australia	+8
Austria	–13
Belgium	–7.5
Bulgaria	–8
Canada	–6
Croatia	–5
Czech Republic	–8
Denmark	–21
Estonia	–8
Finland	0
France	0
Germany	–21
Greece	+25
Hungary	–6
Iceland	+10
Ireland	+13
Italy	–6.5
Japan	–6
Latvia	–8
Liechtenstein	–8
Lithuania	–8
Luxembourg	–28
Monaco	–8
Netherlands	–6
New Zealand	0
Norway	+1
Poland	–6
Portugal	+27
Romania	–8
Russian Federation	0
Slovakia	–8
Slovenia	–8
Spain	+15
Sweden	+4
Switzerland	–8
Ukraine	0
United Kingdom	–12.5
USA	–7
European Community	–8

Note: GHG emissions as listed in the Annex A. Some Parties with economies in transition use base years other than 1990: Bulgaria (1988), Hungary (average of 1985–7), Poland (1988), and Romania (1989).

• Each Party included in Annex I shall, by 2005, have made demonstrable progress in achieving its commitments.
• The net changes in GHG emissions by sources and removals by sinks resulting from direct human-induced land-use change and forestry activities, limited to afforestation, reforestation, and deforestation since 1990, measured as verifiable changes in carbon stocks in each commitment period, shall be used to meet the commitments of each Party included in Annex I. The GHG emissions by sources and removals by sinks associated with those activities shall be reported in a transparent and verifiable manner and reviewed in accordance with Articles 7 and 8.

The Protocol encourages governments to pursue emissions reductions by improving energy efficiency, reforming the energy and transportation sectors, protecting forests and other carbon 'sinks', promoting renewable forms of energy, phasing out inappropriate fiscal measures and market imperfections, and limiting methane emissions from waste management and energy systems. It creates new incentives for technological creativity and the adoption of 'no-regrets' solutions that make economic and environmental sense irrespective of climate change.
• Prior to the first session of the COP serving as the meeting of the Parties to the Protocol, each Party included in Annex I shall provide, for consideration by the Subsidiary Body for Scientific and Technological Advice, data to establish its level of carbon stocks in 1990 and to enable an estimate to be made of its changes in carbon stocks in subsequent years;
• Any emission reduction units, or any part of an assigned amount, which a Party acquires from another Party in accordance with the provisions of Article 6 or of Article 17 shall be added to the assigned amount for the acquiring Party. Any emission reduction units, or any part of an assigned amount, which a Party transfers to another Party shall be subtracted from the assigned amount for the transferring Party. Any certified emission reductions which a Party acquires from another Party in accordance with the provisions of Article 12 shall be added to the assigned amount for the acquiring Party. At the third COP, Parties decided that the COP considers issues related to the three mechanisms.
• If the emissions of a Party in a commitment period are less than its assigned amount, this difference shall, on request of that Party, be added to the assigned amount for that Party for subsequent commitment periods.
• Each Party included in Annex I shall strive to implement the commitments mentioned above in such a way as to minimize adverse social, environmental, and economic impacts on developing-country Parties. The Meeting of the Parties (MOP) to the Protocol shall, at its first session, consider what actions are necessary to minimize the adverse effects of climate change and/or the impacts of response measures on Parties. Among the issues to be considered shall be the establishment of fund-

ing, insurance, and transfer of technology.

The six decisions of the *Buenos Aires Plan of Action* are related to:
• the financial mechanism; the Parties agreed that the GEF should be the mechanism to enable developing-country Parties to meet, among other things, the agreed full costs of preparing national communications by maintaining and enhancing national capacity. The fourth COP also decided that the GEF should be an entity entrusted with the operation of the financial mechanism under the Convention and agreed to review its action every four years;
• the development and transfer of technology; this includes a decision on technology transfer under which the Subsidiary Body for Scientific and Technological Advice (SBSTA) (see Decision-making bodies, below) is requested to establish a consultative process to consider a preliminary list of issues and questions about technology transfer. The process is expected to result in recommendations on a 'framework for meaningful and effective actions' to implement Article 4.5 of the Convention. The decision also urges developed-country Parties to provide a list of publicly owned and environmentally sound technologies related to the adaptation and mitigation of climate change. It urges developing-country Parties to submit a list of their prioritized technology needs;
• implementation of Article 4.8 and 4.9 of the Convention (covering also Articles 2.3 and 3.14 of the Kyoto Protocol); this includes, *inter alia*, a decision to consider further issues related to identification of the adverse impacts of climate change and the impacts of implementing response measures under the Convention. The decision also calls for consideration of the actions needed to address these impacts, such as funding, insurance, and transfers of technology;
• activities implemented jointly (AIJ); the Parties agreed to continue the AIJ pilot phase so that developing-country Parties can build capacity and gain further experience;
• the work programme on mechanisms of the Kyoto Protocol; the programme was decided on with a view to taking decisions at the sixth COP in 2000 on the Protocol's flexibility mechanisms, including recommendations to the COP/MOP. Under the mechanisms, Parties can gain credit towards reaching their own reduction targets by helping other countries lower their emissions. An 'emissions trading' regime will allow industrialized-country Parties to buy and sell parts of their assigned amounts among themselves. The Clean Development Mechanism (CDM) and joint implementation (JI) program will pro-vide credits for financing emissions-avoiding projects in developing countries and countries with economies in transition respectively that would not have occurred in the absence of such financing;
• preparations for the first MOP to the Kyoto Protocol; the fourth COP allocated the preparatory work needed for the first MOP. SBSTA will address, *inter alia*, guidelines for national communications, the Subsidiary Body for Implementation (SBI) will address guidelines for review of implementation by expert review teams, and SBI and SBSTA will jointly consider procedures and mechanisms related to compliance. Parties also selected tasks that should be accomplished by the first MOP, including actions related to policies and measures, carbon sinks other than forests, and guide-lines for implementing JI.

Monitoring/implementation

Review procedure
The COP shall keep under regular review the implementation of the Convention and any related instruments that the Conference may adopt and shall make the decisions necessary to promote the effective implementation of the Convention. To this end it shall:
• periodically examine the obligations of the Parties;
• promote and facilitate the exchange of information on, and the co-ordination, as appropriate, of, policies, strategies, and measures adopted by the Parties to address climate change and its effects;
• promote and guide the development and periodic refinements of comparable methodologies;
• assess the implementation of the Convention by the Parties, the overall effects of the measures taken pursuant to the Convention, in particular environmental, economic, and social effects, and the extent to which progress towards the objective of the Convention is being achieved;
• consider and adopt regular reports on the implementation of the Convention and ensure their publication;
• seek to mobilize financial resources.

National communications in accordance with Article 4.2.*b* and 12 of the Convention should describe the Parties' efforts to implement the Convention and quantify present and projected emissions. The Secretariat completed reviews of the first national communications from Annex I Parties in 1997 with the publication of a compilation and synthesis report and reports on individual in-depth reviews. Full text of the in-depth reviews, of reports, and of a compilation and synthesis are made accessible on the Internet (see Sources on the Internet, below).

The second COP requested Annex I Parties to submit their second national communication by 15 April 1997. For those Parties which were due to submit the first communication in 1996, an update of this communication was to be submitted by the same date; second national communications by Parties with economies in transition should in principle have been submitted not later than 15 April 1998. In accordance with a decision at the third COP Croatia, Liechtenstein, Monaco, and Slovenia have been added to Annex I. The first national communications from these Parties were due by 13 February 1999. National inventory data on emissions by sources and removals by sinks are to be submitted on an annual basis by 15 April of each year.

Of the second national communications that were due by 15 April 1997, six (Finland, Germany, the Netherlands, Norway, Switzerland and the United Kingdom) were received on time, 17 were received late, and one (Luxembourg) had not yet submitted by June 1999. Monaco had also submitted its second communication (14 May 1997). Of the second communications that were due by 15 April 1998, four (the Czech Republic, Estonia, Hungary, and Slovakia) were received on time, five were received late, and two (Lithuania and Ukraine) had not yet submitted by June 1999. Of the first national communications that were due by 13 February 1999, one (Monaco, see above) were received on time and three (Croatia, Liechtenstein, and Slovenia) had not yet submitted by June 1999

Information contained in the second national communications was generally of a higher quality than that in the first national communications. The Secretariat co-ordinates in-depth reviews of these second national communications, and a number of the in-depth review reports have been published and posted on the Secretariat's website.

The fourth COP requested Annex I Parties to submit their third communications by 30 November 2001. Subsequent communications will be submitted on a regular basis at intervals of three to five years. Each national communication should be subject to in-depth review and include detailed information on national policies and measures to mitigate climate change.

Of the first communications from developing-country Parties (non-Annex I Parties), six were received in 1997 (Argentina, Jordan, Mexico, Micronesia, Senegal, and Uruguay) and four were received in 1998 (Armenia, Kazakhstan, the Republic of Korea, and Zimbabwe); Mauritius submitted its initial national communication on 18 May 1999.

99 non-Annex I Parties are presently engaged in preparing their national communications. 38 of them expect to finalize the communications during the course of 1999, 35 in 2000, and the rest within years 2001 and 2002. Nine Parties have recently received approval of the GEF for the commencement of their enabling activities projects for the preparation of their initial national communications; eight Parties are currently preparing projects for funding approval by the GEF. Two Parties indicated that they have not yet initiated activities to prepare their national communications and nine Parties have not provided any information relating to the preparation of their communications.

The fourth COP decided that the communications by non-Annex I Parties shall be considered in a facilitative, non-confrontational, and open and transparent manner to ensure that the needs of developing countries identified in their initial communications are brought to the attention of the GEF. A compilation and synthesis report will be produced on the communications and reviewed both by SBSTA and SBI in their next sessions and by the fifth COP.

Of the national GHG inventories for the period 1990–96, four were received by the due date by 15 April 1998 (Ireland, the Netherlands, Switzerland, and the United Kingdom), 22 were received late, and 10 (Bulgaria, Estonia, Iceland, Italy, Lithuania, Luxembourg, Portugal, the Russian Federation, Ukraine, and the European Community) had not submitted by 15 April 1999. 14 Parties reported a full set of data for the entire period 1990–96. Some Parties submitted information in draft or preliminary form, or in parts, or submitted subsequent revisions to their inventories.

The first COP also decided that the pilot phase for activities implemented jointly (see above) should include a system of regular reporting. It will be reviewed no later than the end of 1999 in order to take a conclusive decision on the pilot phase and the progression beyond that.

Environmental monitoring programmes
The *Intergovernmental Panel on Climate Change (IPCC)* was established in 1988 by UNEP and the World Meteorological Organization (WMO) (see IGOs). The IPCC assesses scientific information related to various components of the climate change issue, such as emission of major GHGs, and evaluates the environmental and socio-economic impacts of climate change.

The Parties shall support international and intergovernmental efforts to develop and strengthen the capacities and capabilities of the developing countries in these activities, and promote access to, and exchange of, data and analysis thereof obtained from areas beyond national jurisdiction.

Data and information system programmes
The Secretariat's information unit has developed a number of products aimed at facilitating the task of those participating in the UNFCCC process. This includes all the official documents of the COP and its subsidiary bodies (see Decision-making bodies, below), as well as the full text of national communications received by the Secretariat in electronic format. The contents of this website are made available on CD-ROM for the benefit of users without access to the Internet. To assist Parties who wish to use the Internet in implementing the Convention process, the Secretariat has launched the CC:INFO/Web initiative, resulting in over a dozen national Climate Change websites.

Trade measures
No provisions on trade measures to penalize Parties for non-compliance.

Dispute-settlement mechanisms
In the event of a dispute between Parties concerning the interpretation or application of the Convention, the Parties concerned shall seek a settlement through negotiation or any other peaceful means of their own choice.

Decision-making bodies

Political
The Conference of the Parties (COP), the supreme body of the Convention, which will also serve as the Meeting of the Parties (MOP) to the Kyoto Protocol, consists of representatives of Parties to the Convention. The fifth COP is scheduled to take place between 25 October and 5 November 1999 in Bonn.

Any Party may propose amendments to the Convention. The COP may adopt amendments, annexes, and protocols to the Convention in accordance with the procedure set forth in the Convention. The Parties shall make every effort to reach agreement on any proposed amendment or annex to the Convention by consensus. If all efforts at consensus have been exhausted, the amendment shall, as a last resort, be adopted by a three-quarters majority vote of the Parties present and voting at the meeting. The Kyoto Protocol has similar provisions.

Any body or agency, whether national or international, governmental or non-govern-mental, which is qualified in matters covered by the Convention, or the Kyoto Protocol, and which has informed the Secretariat of its wish to be represented at a session of the COP as an observer, may be so admitted unless at least one-third of the Parties present object.

Scientific/technical
The Subsidiary Body for Scientific and Technological Advice (SBSTA), composed of representatives of the Parties, has been established by the Convention as the link between the policy-oriented needs of the Parties and the scientific, technical, and technological assessments and information provided by international bodies. Under the guidance of the COP, and drawing upon existing competent international bodies, this body shall:
• provide assessments of the state of scientific knowledge relating to climate change and its effects;
• prepare scientific assessments on the effects of measures taken in the implementation of the Convention;
• identify innovative, efficient, and state-of-the-art technologies and know-how and advise on the ways and means of promoting development and/or transferring such technologies;
• provide advice on scientific programmes, on international co-operation in research and development related to climate change, and on ways and means of supporting endogenous capacity building in developing countries;
• respond to scientific, technological, and methodological questions that the COP and its subsidiary bodies may put to the body.

The Subsidiary Body for Implementation (SBI), composed of representatives of the Parties, develops recommendations to assist the COP in the assessment and review of the effective implementation of the Convention.

The first COP established the *ad hoc* Group on Article 13, an open-ended working group of technical and legal experts to elaborate a multilateral consultative process.

Publications
Up-to-date information on the Convention is available through the Secretariat, or through the UNEP Information Unit on the Conventions (see above).

Sources on the Internet
<http://www.unfccc.de>
<http://www.cop3.org>
<http://www.cop4.org>

Vienna Convention for the Protection of the Ozone Layer, including the Montreal Protocol on Substances that Deplete the Ozone Layer

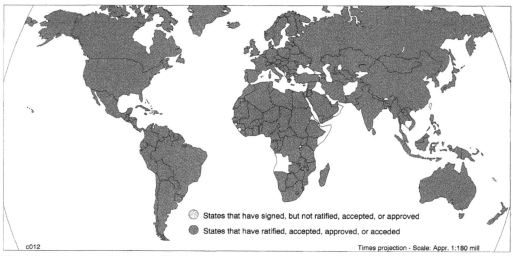

States that have signed, but not ratified, accepted, or approved

States that have ratified, accepted, approved, or acceded

c012   Times projection - Scale: Appr. 1:180 mill

Vienna Convention for the Protection of the Ozone Layer

Objectives
- to protect human health and the environment against adverse effects resulting or likely to result from human activities which modify or are likely to modify the ozone layer;
- to adopt agreed measures to control human activities found to have adverse effects on the ozone layer;
- to co-operate in scientific research and systematic observations;
- to exchange information in the legal, scientific, and technical fields.

Scope
Legal scope
Open to all states and regional economic integration organizations.

Geographic scope
Global.

Time and place of adoption
22 March 1985, Vienna.

Entry into force
22 September 1988.

Status of participation
169 Parties, including the European Economic Community, by 16 June 1999. No Signatories without ratification.

The Secretary-General of the UN acts as depositary.

Affiliated instruments and organizations
Montreal Protocol on Substances that Deplete the Ozone Layer, Montreal, 16 September 1987. Entered into force on 1 January 1989. 168 Parties, including the European Economic Community, by 16 June 1999. No Signatories without ratification.

The basic objective of the Protocol is to protect the ozone layer by taking measures leading to total elimination of global emissions of ozone-depleting substances (ODS) on the basis of developments in scientific knowledge, taking into account technical

and economic considerations and the needs of developing countries.

Amendment to the Montreal Protocol on Substances that Deplete the Ozone Layer (London Amendment), London, 29 June 1990. Entered into force on 10 August 1992. 130 Parties, including the European Community, by 16 June 1999. The London Amendment added 12 new chemicals to the list of controlled substances and 34 new chemicals to the list of transitional substances with reporting requirements. It also added provisions relating to technology transfer and established a financial mechanism which included the establishment of an Interim Multilateral Fund to assist eligible Parties to comply with the control measures. The Fund, which became operational on 1 January 1991, is administered by an Executive Committee of the Parties. Contributions are made by the developed countries. Developing countries with an annual consumption of more than 0.3 kg per capita of chlorofluorocarbons (CFCs) and more than 0.2 kg per capita of halons also make contributions to the Multilateral Fund. By 24 May 1999 125 of the 168 par-

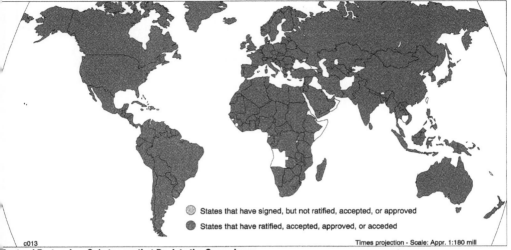

⊛	States that have signed, but not ratified, accepted, or approved
⬤	States that have ratified, accepted, approved, or acceded

c013   Times projection - Scale: Appr. 1:180 mill

Montreal Protocol on Substances that Deplete the Ozone Layer

ies to the Montreal Protocol met this criterion. They are referred to as Article 5 countries.

Adjustments for strengthening the reduction schedules for the original controlled substances came into force automatically in March 1991. The third meeting of the Parties added Annex D, a list of products containing substances from Annex A to the Protocol. From 27 May 1993 Parties cannot import these products from non-Parties.

Amendment to the Montreal Protocol on Substances that Deplete the Ozone Layer (Copenhagen Amendment), Copenhagen, 25 November 1992. Entered into force on 14 June 1994. 92 Parties, including the European Community, by 16 June 1999. The Copenhagen Amendment speeded up the phase-out dates for many ODS, included hydrochlorofluorocarbons (HCFCs) and methyl bromide on the list of controlled substances (see below), and confirmed financial arrangements for supporting the Multilateral Fund (see below).

Amendment to the Montreal Protocol on Substances that Deplete the Ozone Layer (Montreal Amendment), Montreal, 17 September 1997. (Not yet in force.) 15 (Australia, Bolivia, Canada, Chile, Germany, Grenada, Jordan, Republic of Korea, Luxembourg, New Zealand, Norway, Panama, St Kitts and Nevis, Spain, and Trinidad and Tobago) ratifications, acceptances, approvals or accessions by 16 June 1999. Enters into force on the ninetieth day following the

date on which twenty Parties have ratified the Amendment. The Amendment added, *inter alia*, a ban on the import of methyl bromide; an export ban on ODS when a country does not comply with the production controls of the Protocol; and the establishment of a world-wide licensing system, effective in 2000, to track the import and export of ODS and prevent smuggling and illegal traffic of ODS.

Annex I of the Convention sets forth important issues for scientific research on and systematic observation of the ozone layer. *Annex II* of the Convention describes the kinds of information to be collected and shared under its terms.

The World Meteorological Organization (WMO) (see IGOs), together with the UN Environment Programme (UNEP) (see IGOs), plays a central role in harmonizing the policies and strategies on research.

Co-ordination with related instruments
Parties to both the Montreal Protocol and the UN Framework Convention on Climate Change (UNFCCC) (see this section) have noted the interlinkages between implementation of the Montreal Protocol and the Kyoto Protocol to the UNFCCC. The greenhouse gases included in Annex A of the Kyoto Protocol embrace hydrofluorocarbons (HFCs) and perfluorcarbons (PFCs) in view of their high global warming potential, while under the Montreal Protocol these substances are promoted as alternatives to ozone-depleting

substances. The Meeting of the Parties of the two agreements has agreed to co-operate in developing information on these substances that will help the relevant bodies to determine the availability and potential ways and means of limiting emissions of HFCs and PFCs.

Secretariats

UNEP, Ozone Secretariat,
PO Box 30552,
Nairobi,
Kenya

Telephone:	+254-2-621234/623851
Telefax:	+254-2-623913/623601
Telex:	22068 UNEPKE
Cable:	UNITERRA, NAIROBI
E-mail:	ozoneinfo@unep.org
or	madhava.sarma@unep.org

Executive Secretary
Mr K. Madhava Sarma.

Legal Officer
Mr Gilbert M. Bankobeza.

Number of staff
Six professionals and six support staff (June 1999).

Secretariat of the Multilateral Fund for the Implementation of the Montreal Protocol,
Montreal Trust Building,
1800 McGill College Avenue, 27th Floor,
Montreal, Quebec H3A 3J6,
Canada

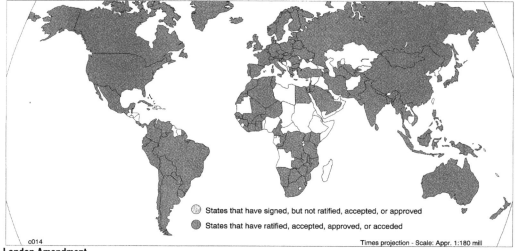

States that have signed, but not ratified, accepted, or approved

States that have ratified, accepted, approved, or acceded

c014

Times projection - Scale: Appr. 1:180 mill

London Amendment

Telephone:	+1-514-2821122
Telefax:	+1-514-2820068
E-mail:	Oelarini@unmfs.org

Chief Officer
Dr Omar E. El-Arini.

Number of staff
Nine professionals and nine support staff (March 1999).

Finance

Budget
The administrative budget for the Convention was $US361,090 in 1997 and $382,342 in 1998, and is $1,207,991 in 1999. The administrative budget for the Protocol was $3,542,263 in 1997 and $3,679,704 in 1998, and is $3,615,740 in 1999. The proposed administrative budget for 2000 is $3,679,704. Budgets are financed through a Trust Fund administered by UNEP to which Parties contribute according to an agreed assessment schedule.

The administrative budget of the Executive Committee and the Secretariat of the Multilateral Fund for the Implementation of the Montreal Protocol was $22.7 million for the period 1991–9.

Main contributors
Main contributors by 25 May 1999 to the Multilateral Fund in the period 1991–8 were the USA, Japan, Germany, Italy, France, Spain, the United Kingdom, and Canada

(accounting for almost 80 per cent of the assessed contributions).

Special funds
The Vienna Convention Trust Fund and Montreal Protocol Trust Fund are intended to ensure adequate finance for the Ozone Secretariat, to service the meetings and to promote the participation of developing countries. The original Protocol, signed in 1987, established a ten-year grace period before developing countries were obligated to follow the agreed reduction schedule for controlled substances.

The Interim Multilateral Fund was established in 1990, with an initial three-year budget of up to $240 million, to meet agreed incremental costs to developing countries of implementing the control measures. The UN Development Programme (UNDP), the World Bank, and UNEP serve as implementing agencies of the Fund. UNEP also serves as the treasurer. After the entry into force of the London Amendment in 1992, the 'interim' Fund formally became the Multilateral Fund, from 1 January 1993.

At the fifth Meeting of the Parties in November 1993, a three-year budget of $510 million for the period from 1994 to 1996 was approved. At the eighth Meeting of the Parties held in November 1996, a replenishment of the Multilateral Fund at a level of $540 million was decided for the period from 1997 to 1999.

The UN Industrial Development Organization (UNIDO) (see IGOs) became the

fourth implementing agency after signing an agreement with the Executive Committee in October 1992.

Rules and standards

Parties of the Montreal Protocol are committed to:
(*a*) control measures to reduce production and consumption of specific substances;
(*b*) control of trade with non-Parties;
(*c*) regularly scheduled assessment and review of control measures;
(*d*) reporting of data;
(*e*) co-operation in research, development, public awareness, and exchange of information;
(*f*) establishment of a financial mechanism and transfer of technology to assist developing countries.

If a developing country considers itself unable to comply with control measures because of inadequate financial or technological assistance provided under the Protocol, it may notify the Ozone Secretariat, and the Parties can consider not invoking non-compliance procedures against the notifying Party. Decisions by the Meeting of the Parties are to be governed by a balanced voting procedure: a two-thirds majority of Parties, comprising separate simple majorities among the developing and industrialized nations.

As amended by the second Meeting of the Parties, in London in 1990, commitments on measures relating to substances that deplete the ozone layer (paragraph (*a*) above)

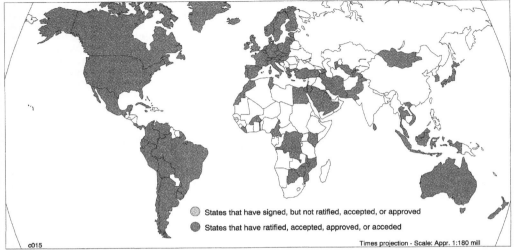

States that have signed, but not ratified, accepted, or approved

States that have ratified, accepted, approved, or acceded

c015

Times projection - Scale: Appr. 1:180 mill

Copenhagen Amendment

involve the phase-out of a specified list of CFCs and halons and of carbon tetrachloride by the year 2000, as well as the phase-out of methyl chloroform by 2005, with scheduled interim reductions for each of the above classes of chemicals.

The London Amendment stipulates the reduction of consumption and production of CFCs by 50 per cent in 1995, by 85 per cent in 1997, and by 100 per cent in 2000.

The 1992 fourth Meeting of the Parties adopted the Copenhagen Amendment to bring forward the phase-out of CFCs and carbon tetrachloride and methyl chloroform by four or more years. For the first time the Parties agreed to bring methyl bromide, a substance used for fumigation of soil, cut flowers, fruits, storage, and structure under the Protocol. The new agreement also stipulates that industrialized countries should phase out:

• halons by January 1994 instead of January 2000;
• hydrochlorofluorocarbons (HCFCs), a less damaging transitional substitute for CFCs, by 2030.

Beginning in 1990, and at least every four years thereafter, the Parties will assess the control measures provided for in the Protocol on the basis of available scientific, environmental, technical, and economic information. Such assessments have so far been completed in 1989, 1991, 1994, and 1998.

In 1997 the Parties to the Montreal Protocol adopted the Montreal Amendment (see above), providing for a ban on the ex-port and import of methyl bromide to and from non-Parties to the Protocol commencing one year after the date of entry into force of the Amendment. A new Article 4A was introduced in the Protocol providing for any Party still producing ozone-depleting substances after the phase-out date to ban the export of used, recycled, and reclaimed substances other than for destruction. Article 4B of the Amendment introduced a licensing system by providing, that effective on 1 January 2000, each Party shall establish and implement a system for licensing the import and export of new, used , recycled, and reclaimed substances.

Monitoring/implementation

Review procedure
Each Party to the Vienna Convention reports every two years to the Secretariat a summary of measures undertaken in the various categories of scientific research and co-operation. These are reviewed and discussed at the Conference of Parties (COP) every three years (every two years until 1993). The reports are public.

The COP to the Convention in 1993 decided that a Party would have fulfilled its reporting obligations under the Convention if it fulfilled its reporting obligations under the Montreal Protocol.

Compliance with obligations under the Montreal Protocol is measured through specific reporting requirements. Compliance in general is monitored through consultations among the Parties and with the Secretariat, and through deliberations of the annual Meeting of the Parties.

Parties to the Protocol provide the Secretariat with annual statistical data on production and on imports and exports of controlled substances, including imports and exports to Parties and non-Parties. The Secretariat prepares a report to the annual Meeting of the Parties by aggregating data in such a way that data declared by Parties at the time of their reporting remains confidential. These reports are public. Review of data in national reports is undertaken by the Secretariat and by the Implementation Committee under the non-compliance procedure of the Montreal Protocol, elected by Meetings of the Parties.

The due date for reporting for each year is 30 September of the succeeding year. Of the 151 Parties due to report for 1995, 107 Parties (71 per cent) had reported by July 1997, of which 91 Parties (60 per cent) reported complete data. Of the 154 Parties due to report for 1996, 111 Parties (72 per cent) had reported by 24 February 1998, of which 101 Parties (66 per cent) reported complete data. Of the 166 Parties due to report for 1997, 134 Parties (60.2 per cent) had reported by 8 June 1999. (Only Kazakhstan and Tajikistan do not yet need to report.)

The reports are prepared in such a way that the information declared as confidential by the Parties at the time of their reporting is not revealed. The reports contain enough information for any reader to verify the compliance of the Parties with the Protocol. The Secretariat distributes publication lists of these reports.

Observations or inspections
None by the Convention as such.

Environmental monitoring programmes
None by the Convention as such. The Global Ozone Observing System, established by the WMO, is the only provider of ozone-related information to UNEP's Global Environmental Monitoring Systems (GEMS) (see IGOs). It has approximately 140 monitoring stations world-wide, which are complemented by remote sensing techniques. It is capable of providing data on both the horizontal and the vertical distribution of ozone and also the total atmospheric concentration.

Trade measures
Trade sanctions are embodied in the Montreal Protocol. The objective of such restrictions is to stimulate as many nations as possible to participate in the Protocol by preventing non-participating countries from gaining competitive advantages and by discouraging the movement of CFC production facilities to such countries.

Each Party shall ban the import of controlled substances from any State not party to the Protocol. As of 1 January 1993 no Party may export any controlled substance to any State not party to the Protocol. As of 27 May 1993 no Party may import products, specified in Annex D of the Protocol, containing substances of Annex A to the Protocol from any non-Party.

At the sixth Meeting of the Parties to the Montreal Protocol, the Parties decided not to elaborate the list of products containing controlled substances in Annex B as specified in Article 4, paragraph 3 *bis*, of the Montreal Protocol. This decision was taken in view of the tightening of the phase-out schedule for Annex B substances from 1 January 2000 to 1 January 1996 and ratification of the Protocol by an overwhelming majority of countries. The elaboration of the list called for in Article 4, paragraph 3, *bis* of the Protocol would be of little practical consequence and the work entailed in drawing up and adopting such a list would be disproportionate to the benefits, if any, to the ozone layer.

Dispute-settlement mechanisms
When approving the Convention, a Party may declare in writing that, for a dispute not resolved by negotiation, or through the good offices or mediation of a third party, it will accept one or both of the following means of dispute settlement as compulsory: arbitration in accordance with procedures adopted by the COP or submission to the International Court of Justice. If Parties have not accepted either procedure, the dispute shall be submitted to a conciliation commission created by the Parties to the dispute, the recommendations of which 'the Parties shall consider in good faith'.

Decision-making bodies

Political
The basic administrative mechanism for the Vienna Convention is the COP held every three years (every two years until 1993). The Bureau of the COP to the Vienna Convention meets intersessionally.

The COP is open to all governments, whether or not they are Parties to the Protocol, as well as observers from international agencies, industry, and non-governmental organizations. States that are not Parties and observers have no voting rights.

The basic administrative mechanism for the Montreal Protocol is the annual Meeting of the Parties. An Implementation Committee has been created, consisting of ten Parties, two each from five geographical groups (Africa, Asia, Eastern Europe, Latin America and the Caribbean, and Western Europe and others (Canada, USA, Australia, and New Zealand)). The Committee is charged with considering and reporting to the Meeting of the Parties any cases of non-compliance coming to its attention. The Meeting is ultimately responsible for deciding upon and calling for steps to bring about full compliance with the Protocol, including measures to assist a Party's compliance.

The Open-Ended Working Group of the Parties and the Bureau of the Montreal Protocol meet intersessionally to develop and negotiate recommendations for the Meeting of the Parties on protocol revisions and implementation issues.

The Meetings of the Parties and the Open-Ended Working Group of the Parties are open to all governments, whether or not they are Parties to the Protocol, as well as to observers from international agencies, industry, and non-governmental organizations.

The Executive Committee of the Multilateral Fund (see above) consists of 14 Parties made up of seven Article 5 and seven non-Article 5 countries. The Committee holds three meetings per year. The term of office of the Committee is one calendar year, and the Chair and Vice-Chair alternate each year between the two groups. The Committee is responsible for developing and monitoring the implementation of specific operational policies, guidelines, and administrative arrangements, including the disbursement of resources for the purpose of achieving the objectives of the Fund. It is assisted by a Secretariat located in Montreal.

The operations of the Executive Committee and the Fund Secretariat are financed by the Multilateral Fund. By May 1999 the Executive Committee had held 27 meetings and taken decisions on policy issues and made disbursements amounting to over $878.3 million, to support more than 2,700 projects and activities in 115 Article 5 countries to be implemented through the four implementing agencies and by bilateral agencies. The implementation of these projects will result in the phase-out of the consumption of more than 119,000 ozone depletion potential (ODP) tonnes and the production of about 42,000 ODP tonnes of ODS. Of this total, about 84,883 ODP tonnes consumption and 10,770 ODP tonnes production of ODS (including 5,970 ODP tonnes of reduced halon production in China in 1998) have been phased out from projects approved in 1998. The Executive Committee approved in November 1997 a plan to phase out the entire halon production and consumption in China, at a cost of $62 million to be disbursed over ten years, and $150 million was approved in March 1999 for the phase out of China's entire production of CFCs, to also be disbursed over ten years. To facilitate the phase out by Article 5 countries, the Committee has approved 102 country programmes (covering an estimated production of 70,000 tonnes and consumption of 155,000 tonnes of ODS) and has funded the establishment and the operating costs of ozone offices in 100 countries. These country programmes account for more than 95 per cent of the consumption and 100 per cent of the production of ODS in Article 5 countries, including all the major consuming countries.

Scientific/technical
The COP to the Vienna Convention has established a Meeting of Ozone Research Managers, composed of government experts on atmospheric research and on research related to health and environmental effects of ozone layer modification, which

meets every three years (every two years until 1993). This group, working closely with the WMO, reviews ongoing national and international research and monitoring programmes to ensure proper co-ordination of these programmes and to identify gaps that need to be addressed. It produces a report to the COP with recommendations for future research and expanded co-operation between researchers in industrialized and developing countries.

At the 1989 Meeting of Parties to the Montreal Protocol, an *ad hoc* Working Group of Legal Experts on Non-Compliance Procedure was established. The Working Group, composed of government experts, is charged with elaborating further procedures on non-compliance.

The Montreal Protocol has established three Panels of Experts, to be convened at least one year before each assessment:
(*a*) the Scientific Assessment Panel, composed of government experts and others, charged with undertaking the review of scientific knowledge in a timely manner as dictated by the needs of the Parties;
(*b*) the Technology and Economics Assessment Panel, which includes many industrial and non-governmental representatives. It analyses and evaluates technical options for limiting the use of ODS, estimates the quantity of controlled substances required by developing countries for their basic domestic needs and the likely availability of such supplies, and assesses the costs of technical solutions, the benefits of reduced use of controlled substances, and issues of technology transfer;
(*c*) the Environmental Effects Assessment Panel surveys the state of knowledge of impacts on health and the environment of altered ozone levels and the resultant increased ultraviolet radiation reaching the Earth's surface.

The Assessment Panels include experts from the non-governmental sector.

Other bodies:
• *ad hoc* Group of Experts on Data Reporting, composed of government experts and others;
• *ad hoc* Technical Advisory Committee on Destruction Technologies, composed of government experts and others.

The project monitoring and evaluation system of the Multilateral Fund has been approved, along with the first work programme of evaluations.

To assist the work of the Executive Committee of the Multilateral Fund, two Subcommittees and one Subgroup have been created from among the members of the Executive Committee. The Subcommittee on Project Review provides advice on project approval and related issues, the Subcommittee on Monitoring, Evaluation, and Finance advises on project implementation and financial matters, and the Subgroup on the Production of ODS Substitutes is finalizing the guidelines for the determination of eligible incremental costs of the phase-out of ODS production in Article 5 countries.

Publications
• *Montreal Protocol Handbook*;
• *Action on Ozone*, newsletter published quarterly;
• assessment reports;
• reports of the meetings of the Executive Committee of the Multilateral Fund;
• Country Programmes Summary Sheets (Multilateral Fund);
• Policies, Procedures, Guidelines and Criteria of the Multilateral Fund.

Sources on the Internet
<http://www.unep.org/ozone>
<http://www.unep.ch/ozone>
<http://www.unmfs.org>

Convention on the Ban of the Import into Africa and the Control

of Transboundary Movements and Management of Hazardous

Wastes within Africa (Bamako Convention)

Objectives
• to protect human health and the environment from dangers posed by hazardous wastes by reducing their generation to a minimum in terms of quantity and/or hazard potential;
• to adopt precautionary measures, ensure proper disposal of hazardous waste;
• to prevent 'dumping' of hazardous wastes in Africa.

Scope
Legal scope
Limited to member States of the Organization of African Unity (OAU).

Geographic scope
Regional.

Time and place of adoption
30 January 1991, Bamako.

Entry into force
22 April 1998.

Status of participation
15 Parties (ten ratifications and five accessions), by 9 March 1999. 12 Signatories without ratification.

Affiliated instruments and organizations
Annex I contains 48 categories of wastes which are subject to control under the Convention. The wastes are classified either as entirely hazardous, such as radionuclides, or as wastes having hazardous substances as part of their constituents, such as metal carbonyls or arsenic.

Annex II specifies the characteristics which identify waste as hazardous. There is, however, a catch-all provision which makes substances subject to regulation under the Convention if they have been declared hazardous and banned or if registration has been refused or cancelled by the country of manufacture. An additional list of regulated substances may arise from the provisions, which requires the Parties to inform the Secretariat of any substances not in Annex I which, under their national laws, are defined as hazardous. Similarly, radioactive wastes which are subject to international controls systems because of their characteristics are covered by the Convention.

Co-ordination with related instruments
Wastes from the operation of ships, the discharge of which is covered by other instruments, are specifically excluded from the applications of the Convention.

Secretariat
Information on the Convention is available from:
Organization of African Unity (OAU),
Environment Division,
Education, Science, Culture, and Social Affairs Department (ESCAS),
PO Box 3243,
Addis Ababa,
Ethiopia

Telephone: +251-1-517700
Telefax: +251-1-517844
Telex: 21046

Director (ESCAS Department)
Professor C. A. L. Johnson.

Head, Press and Information Division
Dr Ibrahim Dagash.

Number of staff
17 professionals and 12 support staff at the ESCAS Department (February 1999).

Finance
The scale of contribution by the Parties to cover administrative expenses is to be decided at the first Conference of the Parties (see below).

Rules and standards
All Parties shall take appropriate legal, administrative, and other measures to prohibit the import of all hazardous wastes, when imported by third parties, from entering the territories of the Contracting Parties.

The Parties agree to ban the dumping of such wastes in the territorial sea, the continental shelf, and the exclusive economic zone.

On wastes generated within Africa, the Parties undertake to submit the details thereof to the Secretariat established by the Convention. Moreover, the Party within whose territory the wastes are generated is urged to ensure availability of disposal facilities; to minimize the output; and to impose strict liability on those generating the wastes. Such Parties are

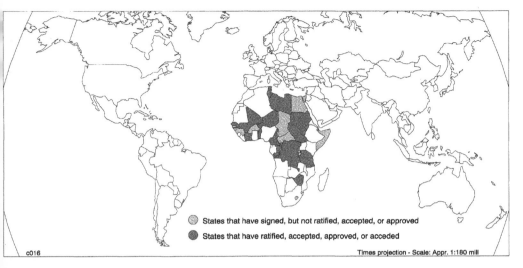

States that have signed, but not ratified, accepted, or approved

States that have ratified, accepted, approved, or acceded

c016   Times projection - Scale: Appr. 1:180 mill

also required to ensure the adoption of pre-cautionary measures to prevent release of such wastes and to enhance clean production methods. Every case of transfer of polluting technologies to Africa is to be kept under systematic review by the Secretariat, which is to make periodic reports to the Conference of the Parties.

Parties shall:
• prevent the export of hazardous wastes to the states which they know have prohibited the same;
• prevent the export of such wastes to a state which does not have the requisite disposal facilities.

In every case, the exported wastes must be handled in an environmentally sound manner.

To protect Antarctica, the Parties agree to prohibit any disposal within any area south of 60°S.

Each Party informs the Secretariat of the wastes banned under the Convention. The Secretariat, in turn, informs all other Parties. It is thereafter the duty of every Party to prohibit the export of such wastes (see above), except for any Party which consents to the importation in writing. In every case, the Parties shall prohibit the export of such wastes to non-Parties which are developing countries.

Monitoring/implementation

Review procedure
Each Party undertakes to adopt national legislation to implement the Convention for the protection of human and environmental

health. To that effect, they agree to adopt standards which are more stringent than those under the Convention or any other provision of international law.

The Conference may adopt amendments and protocols to the Convention in accordance with the procedure set forth in the Convention.

When a Party has reason to believe that another Party is violating the provisions of the Convention, it shall inform the Secretariat and, concomitantly, convey the information to the Party against which the allegation is made. The Secretariat is required to take measures to verify the claim and to report to other Parties on its findings.

Observations or inspections
None by the Convention as such.

Trade measures
No provisions on trade measures to penalize Parties for non-compliance.

Dispute-settlement mechanisms
In the event of a dispute between Contracting Parties concerning interpretation or application of, or compliance with, the provision of the Convention, the Parties involved shall seek solution by negotiations or any other peaceful means of their own choice. Should this fail, the dispute shall be submitted either to an *ad hoc* organ set up by the Conference for this purpose, or to the International Court of Justice.

Decision-making bodies

Political
The Conference of the Parties, the supreme body of the Convention, consists of representatives of all the Contracting Parties. The first meeting of the Conference will be convened by the Executive Director of OAU and is planned to be held in the latter part of 1999. The Conference determines the frequency of meetings.

Any body or agency, whether national or international, governmental or non-governmental, which is qualified in matters relating to hazardous wastes, and which has informed the Secretariat of its wish to be represented at a session of the Conference of the Parties as an observer, may be so admitted according to the rules of procedure of the Convention.

Scientific/technical
The Conference of the Parties establishes such subsidiary bodies as are deemed necessary for the implementation of the Convention.

Publications

Up-to-date information on the Convention is made available through OAU.

Convention on Civil Liability for Damage Caused during Carriage of Dangerous Goods by Road, Rail, and Inland Navigation Vessels (CRTD)

Objectives

To establish uniform rules ensuring adequate and speedy compensation for damage during inland carriage of dangerous goods by road, rail, and inland navigation vessels.

Scope

Legal scope
Open to all states. Regional integration organizations are not specified in the Convention.

Geographic scope
Global.

Time and place of adoption

10 October 1989, Geneva.

Entry into force

Not yet in force. The Convention requires five ratifications, acceptances, approvals, or accessions to enter into force.

Status of participation

No instrument of ratification, acceptance, or approval by 16 June 1999. Two Signatories in 1990 without ratification, acceptance, or approval.
   The Secretary-General of the UN acts as depositary.

Affiliated instruments and organizations

The Inland Transport Committee of the UN Economic Commission for Europe (UN/ECE) fulfils the function of a standing forum for deliberations in matters concerning the Convention.
   The corollary instrument addressing liability for damage from maritime transport of dangerous substances is the International Convention on Liability and Compensation for Damage in Connection with the Carriage of Hazardous and Noxious Substances by Sea (HNS Convention) adopted in 1996 (see this section).

Co-ordination with related instruments
An instrument addressing liability for dangerous activities is under consideration within the Council of Europe.

Secretariat

UN/ECE,
Transport Division,
Palais des Nations,
CH-1211 Geneva 10,
Switzerland
Telephone: +41-22-9172456
Telefax: +41-22-9170039
E-mail: olivier.kervella@unece.org

Director of Transport Division
Mr J. Capel Ferrer.

Chief, Dangerous Goods Section
Mr Olivier Kervella.

Number of staff
Four professionals and two support staff (June 1999) (for the overall work of the division on the transport of dangerous goods and perishable foodstuffs, which is not limited to CRTD matters).

Finance

Budget
The Convention does not provide for regular meetings and programme activities, or a secretariat. Therefore, under the Convention, regular administrative costs do not arise.

Special funds
None.

Rules and standards

The carrier, i.e. the registered owner or other person controlling a road vehicle or an inland navigation vessel or the operator of a railway line, is liable for damage caused during the transport of dangerous goods.
   Damage extends to loss of life or personal injury, loss of or damage to property, loss or damage by contamination to the environment, including reasonable measures for the reinstatement of the environment, and the costs of preventive measures.
   The carrier's liability shall be covered by insurance or financial security, except that States or their constituent parts when acting as carriers do not require insurance cover.
   The carrier may limit his liability per incident, in case of a road or rail carrier, to Spe-

States that have signed, but not ratified, accepted, or approved

States that have ratified, accepted, approved, or acceded

c017

Times projection - Scale: Appr. 1:180 mill

cial Drawing Rights (SDR) 18 million for claims concerning loss of life or personal injury, and to SDR 12 million with respect to other claims; in the case of inland navigation vessels, these figures are SDR 8 million and SDR 7 million respectively.

No claim may be made beyond the regime jurisdiction against the carrier or any person engaged in the transport operation or in related salvage activities.

Action may be brought in the courts of Contracting Parties in which the incident occurred, or damage was sustained, or preventive measures were undertaken, or the carrier has his habitual residence. The carrier may establish a limitation fund in one of the courts where action has been brought. The court where the fund has been established will be responsible for deciding distribution of compensation.

Monitoring/implementation

Review procedure
The Convention does not require Parties to report implementation or supply data regularly and there are no mechanisms for a regular or periodic review of the regime. However, Parties having made reservations to the Convention shall notify to the depositary the contents of their national law.

The Convention also provides for simplified procedures for amendment of compensation figures. Requests for such amendments shall be supported by one-quarter, but at least three, of the Parties. Requests are considered by a Committee of the Parties, which adopts

amendments of limitation figures by a two-thirds majority. An amendment shall be accepted if, within a period of 18 months, not at least one-quarter of the Parties have communicated their non-acceptance. Accepted amendments are binding on all Parties. In deciding, the Committee shall take into account past experience with incidents, changes in monetary value, and the anticipated impact of an amendment on insurance costs.

There are no procedures or mechanisms for the regular taking into account of scientific and technical information, except that dangerous goods are defined as those substances or articles which are either listed in the classes or covered by a collective heading of the classes of the European Agreement concerning the International Carriage of Dangerous Goods by Road (ADR), or subject to the provisions of that Agreement. The regional ADR is regularly updated in the light of scientific and technical information.

Observations or inspections
None by the Convention as such.

Trade measures
No provisions on trade measures to penalize Parties for non-compliance.

Dispute-settlement mechanisms
No mention is made in the Convention of the settlement of disputes.

Decision-making bodies

Political
The Convention does not provide for the establishment of a separate institutional mechanism. The Inland Transport Committee of the ECE fulfils the function of a standing forum for deliberations in matters concerning the Convention. Upon request of one-third, but at least three, of the Parties, the Inland Transport Committee shall convene a Conference of Parties for revising or amending the Convention. Moreover, the Inland Transport Committee shall convene, upon request of one-quarter, but at least three, of the Parties, a Committee constituted of one representative from each Contracting Party for amending compensation amounts according to simplified amendment procedures.

As yet here has been no meeting of the Committee of Contracting Parties or any Conference of Parties.

Scientific/technical
None.

Publications

• annual reports of the ECE;
• *Explanatory Report* (ECE/TRANS/84);
• *Transport Information*, published annually by the ECE.

Sources on the Internet

<http://www.unece.org/unece/trans/danger/danger.htm>

Convention on the Control of Transboundary Movements of Hazardous Wastes and their Disposal (Basel Convention)

Objectives

* to control and reduce transboundary movements of wastes subject to the Convention to a minimum consistent with their environmentally sound management;
* to minimize the hazardous wastes generated, ensuring their environmentally sound management, including disposal and recovery operations, as close as possible to the source of generation;
* to assist developing countries and countries with economies in transition in environmentally sound management of the hazardous and other wastes they generate.

Scope

Legal scope
Open to all states and political and/or economic regional organizations.

Geographic scope
Global.

Time and place of adoption

22 March 1989, Basel.

Entry into force

5 May 1992.

Status of participation

127 Parties, including the European Community, by 16 June 1999. Three Signatories without ratification, acceptance, or approval.

Affiliated instruments and organizations

Amendment to the Convention on the Control of Transboundary Movements of Hazardous Wastes and their Disposal, Geneva, 22 September 1995. (Not yet in force.) 13 states (Denmark, Ecuador, Finland, Luxembourg, Norway, Panama, Paraguay, Slovakia, Spain, Sri Lanka, Sweden, the United Kingdom, and Uruguay) and the European Economic Community had ratified by 16 June 1999. The Amendment enters into force between Parties having accepted it on the ninetieth day after the deposit of instruments of ratification, acceptance, approval, or formal confirmation from 75 per cent of the Parties who accepted it. The decision to establish the Amendment was passed by a consensus of the 82 Parties present at the third Conference of the Parties (COP).

The basic objective is to halt exports of hazardous wastes for final disposal, recovery, or recycling from developed countries (members of the Organization for Economic Co-operation and Development (OECD), European Community (EC), and Liechtenstein) to developing countries. The Amendment bans the export of hazardous wastes destined for final disposal with immediate effect. Export of wastes destined for recovery or recycling operations was phased out by 31 December 1997.

The fourth meeting of the COP (see Decision-making bodies, below) to the Convention took place in Kuching, Malaysia, from 23 to 27 February 1998. To facilitate the implementation of the Amendment, the third COP requested the Technical Working Group (TWG) (see Decision-making bodies, below) to develop lists which, together with definitions existing in the Annex to the Convention, could make the implementation of the Amendment easier and simpler. The incorporation of these lists of wastes prepared by the TWG in the body of the Convention was subject to a major debate at the fourth COP. Parties agreed that there was a need to ensure a firm base and a legal status to both of these lists A and B, and to incorporate them into the body of the Convention as its Annexes VIII and IX. The meeting also agreed on the issue of the establishment and functioning of the mechanism for reviewing these lists in accordance with new technological findings. The list A/Annex VIII to the Convention itemizes the wastes containing, for instance, arsenic, lead, mercury, asbestos, and dozens of other chemicals and substances to be subjected to any transboundary movement from developed to developing countries. List B, the non-hazardous wastes, adopted by the fourth COP as Annex IX to the Convention, exempts from the ban those wastes that can be safely and (profitably) recycled or reused, including scrap iron, steel or copper, certain electronic assemblies, non-hazardous chemical catalysts, and many ceramics, solid plastics and paper, and textile wastes.

The fourth COP also considered the Annex VII, which lists OECD, EC, and Liechtenstein, and decided to leave it unchanged in spite of some countries (Monaco, Israel, and Slovenia) who expressed their wish to be included in between the developed countries in this Annex. The meeting decided to leave Annex VII unchanged in its current structure until the Amendment enters into force. The fourth COP also decided to explore issues relating to Annex VII and requested the TWG in co-operation with the Consultative Subgroup of Legal and Technical Experts to provide parties with a detailed and documented analysis that would highlight issues related to Annex VII. It decided as well to report on the outcome of this work to the fifth COP. It also emphasized that the decisions to be taken are without any prejudice to any future decisions concerning Annex VII.

The fourth COP adopted altogether 25 decisions which developed further and facilitate the implementation of the Convention. It stressed the need for international technical assistance and capacity building and supported the establishment of regional centres for training and technology transfer regarding the environmentally sound management of hazardous wastes and the minimization of their generation. It also appealed to the international community for general support for the above mentioned activities.

The fourth COP recommended faster development of the Protocol on Liability and Compensation for Damage Resulting from the Transboundary Movements of Hazardous Wastes and their Disposal. The further development of this Protocol needs strong political will on the side of the Parties. It is expected that the Protocol will be adopted at the fifth COP.

Replying to the still existing problems of illegal traffic in hazardous wastes, the fourth COP has given higher priority to the work of the prevention of illegal traffic within the process of implementation of the Convention and emphasized the need to build up the capacity of States in preventing illegal traffic and solving the environmental damages caused by existing cases. The COP emphasized the need for further co-operation of the

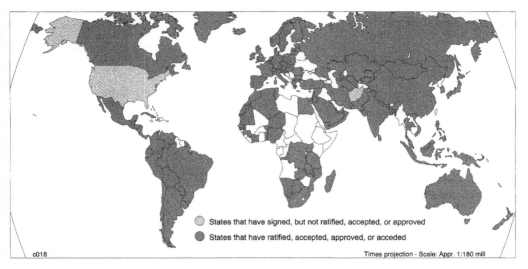

States that have signed, but not ratified, accepted, or approved

States that have ratified, accepted, approved, or acceded

c018   Times projection - Scale: Appr. 1:180 mill

Secretariat on this issue with Interpol as well as with the World Customs Organization. The co-operation should be continued on this issue with the UN regional commissions and secretariats of regional agreements dealing with transboundary movements of hazardous wastes, i.e. the Bamako Convention, the Waigani Convention (see below), the Izmir Protocol for the Mediterranean (see Regional Seas Programme, Barcelona Convention, this section), and others. The COP extended the mandate of the TWG and the Consultative Subgroup of Legal and Technical Experts with the view of further elaborating on the draft guidance elements for conclusion by Parties and states not parties of bilateral, multilateral, and regional agreements and arrangements provided for in Article 11 of the Convention. The COP requested Parties that have entered into these agreements or arrangements to report on it through the Secretariat to the Open-ended *ad hoc* Committee for the Implementation of the Convention (see Decision-making bodies, below).

The meeting established a very ambitious work programme of the TWG going until the millennium and in particular emphasized the need for further development of technical guidelines on waste streams and disposal options which have been very successfully met by the TWG in the past (the TWG developed several sets of technical guidelines which have been adopted by the various COPs).

Co-ordination with related instruments
Co-ordinated activities are taking place with:
• the International Atomic Energy Agency

(IAEA) (see IGOs), regarding *Code of Practice on the International Transboundary Movement of Radioactive Waste*;
• the International Maritime Organization (IMO) (see IGOs), regarding the *London Convention 1972* (see this section) and hazard characterization of wastes;
• the IMO and the IAEA, regarding a draft code for the safe carriage of irradiated nuclear fuel, plutonium, and high-level radioactive wastes on board ships, and dismantling of ships;
• the Co-ordinating Unit for the Mediterranean Action Plan (see Conventions within the UNEP Regional Seas Programme, this section) in the preparation of a protocol on the prevention of pollution of the Mediterranean Sea resulting from the transboundary movements of hazardous wastes and their disposal;
• the Commission on Sustainable Development (CSD) (see IGOs), in a follow-up to Agenda 21 for the development of indicators for sustainable development, including indicators on hazardous wastes;
• the Organization for the Prohibition of Chemical Weapons (OPCW), regarding activities to develop binding instruments on trade in hazardous chemicals, with a view to development of joint training and technical assistance activities;
• the UN Economic Commission for Europe (UN/ECE), on transport of hazardous wastes and hazard classification of wastes;
• the UN Environment Programme (UNEP) (see IGOs) and UN Economic and Social Commission for Asia and the Pacific (ESCAP), regarding a joint project on illegal

traffic in hazardous wastes;
• the Convention on the Ban of the Import into Africa and the Control of Transboundary Movements and Management of Hazardous Wastes within Africa (Bamako Convention) (see this section);
• the Convention to Ban the Importation into Forum Island Countries of Hazardous and Radioactive Wastes and to Control the Transboundary Movement and Management of Hazardous Wastes within the South Pacific Region (Waigani Convention) (see this section);
• the Convention for the Protection of the Natural Resources and Environment of the South Pacific Region (see Conventions within the UNEP Regional Seas Programme, this section);
• the World Customs Organization (WCO), on the separate identification of hazardous wastes in the Harmonized System of the WCO;
• the OECD, on key technical issues regarding hazardous wastes;
• Interpol, on illegal traffic;
• other regional organizations.

Secretariat
Secretariat of the Basel Convention (SBC),
Geneva Executive Centre,
15 chemin des Anémones, Building D,
CH-1219 Châtelaine,
Switzerland
Telephone: +41-22-9799111
Telefax: +41-22-7973454
E-mail: bulskai@unep.ch

Executive Secretary
Dr Iwona Rummel-Bulska.

Number of staff
Eight professionals and six support staff (May 1999).

Finance

Implementation of the Convention and expenditures of the Secretariat are fully financed from contributions by the Parties to the two trust funds established under the Basel Convention. Parties agreed to pay their contributions on the basis of the UN scale of assessment to one of the trust funds, namely the Trust Fund for the Implementation of the Basel Convention. The Basel Convention Technical Co-operation Trust Fund consists of voluntary contributions made by Parties and non-Parties; part of this funding is for assistance to developing countries.

Budget
The approved budget for the Trust Fund for the Implementation of the Basel Convention was $US4,069,700 in 1998, of which $1,129,291 was to be contributed on a purely voluntary basis. The approved budget is $3,764,720 in 1999 and $3,001,854 in 2000.

The approved budget for the Basel Convention Technical Co-operation Trust Fund is $2,647,900 in 1999 and $1,937,900 in 2000.

Special funds
An Emergency Mechanism to assist developing countries in the event of a waste emergency is being considered, as well as a Compensation Fund to be linked to the proposed protocol on liability and compensation for damage resulting from the transboundary movements of hazardous waste and their disposal.

Rules and standards

Parties shall:
• not allow the export of hazardous wastes or other wastes for disposal within the area south of 60°S, whether or not such wastes are subject to transboundary movement;
• prohibit or not permit the export of hazardous wastes and other wastes if the State of import does not consent in writing to the specific import, in the case where that State of import has not prohibited the import of such wastes;
• prohibit all persons under their national jurisdiction from transporting or disposing of hazardous wastes or other type of wastes unless such persons are authorized or allowed to perform such types of operations;
• designate or establish one or more competent authorities and one focal point.

States Parties of export shall not allow the generator of hazardous wastes or other wastes to commence the transboundary movement until it has received written confirmation that the notifier has received the written consent of the State of import.

In case of an accident occurring during transboundary movement of hazardous or other wastes or their disposal likely to present risks to human health and the environment in other States, those States must be immediately informed.

Parties shall adopt technical guidelines for the environmentally sound management of wastes subject to the Convention.

Waste exports are allowed only if the country of export does 'not have the technical capacity' or 'suitable disposal sites', and provided that the country of import has this capacity and facilities, in order to ensure environmentally sound disposal of the waste.

Monitoring/implementation

Review procedure
The COP shall keep under continuous review and evaluation the effective implementation of the Convention and shall undertake an evaluation of its effectiveness three years after the entry into force of the Convention, and at least every six years thereafter.

Before the end of each calendar year, the Parties shall transmit, through the Secretariat, to the COP, a report on the previous calendar year which, *inter alia*, will contain information on the measures adopted by them in implementation of the Convention.

Verification for a breach should be undertaken through the Secretariat, to which the Party which acted in breach of its obligations has the obligation upon the request of any Party to submit all relevant information pertaining to the breach.

Compliance, monitoring, and enforcement of the Convention has begun with the submission of reports to the Open-ended *ad hoc* Committee. Reporting in relation to Articles 13 and 16 of the Convention consists of 49 national reports submitted for the year 1994, 52 national reports submitted for the year 1995 (by 31 May 1999), 27 national reports submitted for the year 1996 (by 31 May 1999), 37 national reports submitted for the year 1997 (by 31 May 1999).

At its third meeting in September 1995, the COP requested that a Consultative Subgroup of Legal and Technical Experts 'study all issues related to the establishment of a mecha-nism for monitoring implementation and compliance' of the Basel Convention. The Group at its first session in June 1996 started to consider the introduction of a non-confrontational and non-judicial procedure to enhance the Basel Convention's implementation and compliance in a non-judicial as well as non-confrontational manner. The COP, when concentrating on enforcement and monitoring of the implementation of and compliance with the Convention, requested the Group to examine further the issues related to the establishment of a mechanism or procedure for monitoring implementation and compliance with the Convention, as well as to look at the existing dispute-settlement mechanism with a view to establishing whether it continues to meet the needs of the Parties.

The fourth COP adopted in 1998 a new instruction manual on the control system for transboundary movements of hazardous waste and other waste and its accompanying notification and movement document. This represent a key document for operating the control system of the Convention. The establishment of regional/subregional centres for training and technology transfer on the environmentally sound management of hazardous wastes facilitates the implementation of the Convention at regional level.

Data and information system programmes
Information Management System on Waste (IMSW) comprises several databases related to reporting requirements of Articles 13 and 16 of the Convention.

Decision-making bodies
Political
The Conference of the Parties (COP), the governing body of the Convention, shall keep under review and evaluate the effective implementation of the Convention, harmonize policies, establish subsidiary bodies, and undertake additional actions. The UN and its specialized agencies, as well as any States not party to the Convention, are also invited to participate as observers at meetings of the COP. The COP can establish subsidiary bodies as deemed necessary for the implementation of the Convention. Any other body or agency, whether international or national, governmental or non-governmental, qualified in the matter of hazardous wastes or other wastes may participate as observers unless one-third of the Parties objects. Meetings are held every other year: COP1 December 1992, COP2 March 1994, COP3 September 1995, and COP4 February 1998. COP5 is scheduled

o be held on 6–10 December 1999 in Basel.

The Extended Bureau, composed of actual Bureau members and previous Bureau members of the COP, is to provide general policy and general operational directions to the Secretariat between meetings of the COP and provide guidance and advice to the Secretariat on the preparation of agendas and other requirements of meetings and in any other matters brought to it by the Secretariat in the exercise of the functions, in particular regarding financial and institutional matters.

Scientific/technical

The COP has established:

an Open-ended *ad hoc* Committee, to facilitate the implementation of the Convention. It meets between the meetings of the Parties. One of its main tasks is to prepare work for consideration of the COP;

• a Technical Working Group (TWG), to prepare technical guidelines for the environmentally sound management of hazardous wastes, to develop criteria on which wastes are suitable for recovery and recycling operations, and to provide guidance on technical matters to the COP. Taking into account development with the Convention, the Group is actively involved in better defining, identifying, and clarifying what hazardous waste is under the Convention;

• an *ad hoc* Working Group of Legal and technical Experts, to consider and develop a draft protocol on liability and compensation for damage resulting from transboundary movements of hazardous wastes and their disposal;

• a Consultative Subgroup of Legal and Technical Experts, to study the issues related to the establishment of a mechanism for monitoring the implementation of and compliance with the Convention and to examine the issues related to the establishment of an emergency fund.

Publications

• annual reports;
• Technical Guidelines (series);
• *Managing Hazardous Wastes* (newsletter).

Sources on the Internet

<http://www.unep.ch/basel>

Convention on the Prior Informed Consent Procedure for Certain Hazardous Chemicals and Pesticides in International Trade (PIC Convention)

Objectives

To promote shared responsibility and co-operative efforts among Parties in the international trade of certain hazardous chemicals in order to protect human health and the environment from potential harm and to contribute to their environmentally sound use, by facilitating information exchange about their characteristics, by providing for a national decision-making process on their import and export and by disseminating these decisions to Parties.

Scope

Legal scope
Open to all states and regional integration organizations.

Geographic scope
Global.

Time and place of adoption

11 September 1998, Rotterdam.

Entry into force

Not yet in force. Enters into force on the ninetieth day after the deposit of the fiftieth instrument of ratification, acceptance, approval, or accession.

Status of participation

No ratifications, acceptances, approvals, or accessions by 16 June 1999. 61 Signatories, including the European Community, without ratification, acceptance, or approval. Open for signature from 12 September 1998 to 10 September 1999 and open for accession from the day after the date on which it is closed for signature.

The Secretary-General of the UN acts as depositary.

Affiliated instruments and organizations

The PIC Convention is also known as the Rotterdam Convention.

According to the Convention, export of a chemical can take place only with the prior informed consent (PIC) of the importing Party.

The PIC procedure is a means for formally obtaining and disseminating the decisions of importing countries as to whether they wish to receive future shipments of a certain chemical and for ensuring compliance with these decisions by exporting countries. The aim is to promote a shared responsibility between exporting and importing countries in protecting human health and the environment from the harmful effects of such chemicals.

The Convention covers pesticides and industrial chemicals that have been banned or severely restricted for health or environmental reasons by participating Parties, and which have been subject to notification by Parties for inclusion in the PIC procedure. Severely hazardous pesticide formulations that present a hazard under the conditions of use in developing-county Parties or Parties with economies in transition may also be nominated. The inclusion of chemicals in the PIC procedure is decided by the Conference of the Parties (COP). The Convention will initially cover at least 27 chemicals carried forward from the present voluntary PIC procedure, and hundreds more are likely to be added as the provisions of the Convention are implemented.

The PIC list includes the following 22 hazardous pesticides: 2,4,5-T, Aldrin, Captafol, Chlordane, Chlordimeform, Chlorobenzilate, DDT, Dieldrin, 1,2-dibromoethane (EDB), Dinoseb, Fluoroacetamide, HCH, Heptachlor, Hexachlorobenzene, Lindane, Mercury compounds, Methamidophos, Methyl-parathion, certain formulations of Monocrotophos, Parathion, Pentachlorophenol, and Phosphamidon. The industrial chemicals are: Crocidolite, Polybrominated Biphenyls (PBB), Polychlorinated Biphenyls (PCB), Polychlorinated Terphenyls (PCT), and Tris (2,3 dibromopropyl) phosphate.

Certain specific groups of chemicals such as narcotic drugs and psychotropic substances, radioactive materials, wastes, chemical weapons, pharmaceuticals, and food and food additives are excluded from the scope of the Convention.

The Convention contains five *annexes* which form an integral part of the Convention:
• *Annex I* comprises information requirements for notifications made pursuant with Article 5 on procedures for banned or severely restricted chemicals.
• *Annex II* consists of criteria for listing banned or severely restricted chemicals in

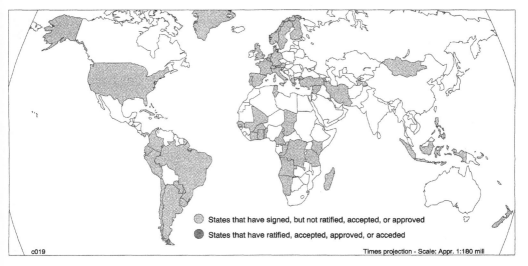

States that have signed, but not ratified, accepted, or approved

States that have ratified, accepted, approved, or acceded

c019

Times projection - Scale: Appr. 1:180 mill

Annex III.
• *Annex III* lists chemicals subject to the PIC procedure (mentioned above).
• *Annex IV* contains information and criteria for listing severely hazardous pesticide formulations in Annex III.
• *Annex V* contains information requirements for export notification.

Co-ordination with related instruments
The current voluntary PIC procedure has been operated jointly by UNEP and FAO since 1989, based on the amended London Guidelines for the Exchange of Information on Chemicals in International Trade and the FAO International Code of Conduct on the Distribution and Use of Pesticides (see this section). The new PIC procedure contained in the Convention is an improvement on the original procedure and is based largely on the experience gained during the implementation of the original.

Governments have agreed to continue to implement the voluntary PIC procedure using the new procedures of the Convention until the Convention formally enters into force. This will avoid a break in the implementation of the PIC procedure.

Secretariat
Establishment of a permanent Convention's secretariat will be approved at the first COP. An Interim Joint FAO/UNEP Secretariat will be operative at the following addresses:
FAO Joint Secretary to PIC,
Plant Protection Service,

Plant Production and Protection Division, Food and Agriculture Organization (FAO), Viale delle Terme di Caracalla, I-00100 Rome, Italy

Telephone:	+39-06-57053441
Telefax:	+39-06-57056347
E-mail:	pic@fao.org

Joint Executive Secretary
Dr Niek A. van der Graaf.

Pesticides Information Officer
Mr Gerold Wyrwal.

UNEP Joint Secretary to PIC,
UNEP Chemicals,
PO Box 356,
15 chemin des Anémones,
CH-1219 Châtelaine, Geneva,
Switzerland

Telephone:	+41-22-9798183
Telefax:	+41-22-7973460
E-mail:	pic@unep.ch

Joint Executive Secretary
Mr Jim Willis.

Programme Officers
Ms Aase Tuxen and Mr Erik Larsson.

Finance
Budget
To be decided by the first COP.

Special funds
FAO and UNEP will maintain the level of contribution under the regular programme.

Rules and standards
The Convention requires that hazardous chemicals and pesticides that have been banned or severely restricted in at least two countries shall not be exported unless explicitly agreed by the importing country. It includes pesticide formulations that are too dangerous to be used by farmers in developing countries. Countries are also obliged to stop national production of those hazardous compounds.

The Convention contains provisions for the exchange of information among Parties about potentially hazardous chemicals that may be exported and imported and caters for a national decision-making process regarding import and compliance by exporters with these decisions.

The provisions regarding information exchange include:
• the requirement for a Party to inform other Parties of each ban or severe restriction on a chemical it implements nationally;
• the possibility for a developing-country Party or a Party with an economy in transition to inform other Parties that it is experiencing problems caused by a severely hazard-

ous pesticide formulation under conditions of use in its territory;
• the requirement for a Party that plans to export a chemical that is banned or severely restricted for use within its territory to inform the importing Party that such export will take place, both before the first shipment and annually thereafter;
• the requirement that an exporting Party, when exporting chemicals that are to be used for occupational purposes, shall ensure that a safety data sheet that follows an internationally recognized format, setting out the most up-to-date information available, is sent to the importer;
• the requirement that exports of chemicals included in the PIC procedure and other chemicals that are banned or severely restricted domestically, when exported, are subject to labelling requirements that ensure adequate availability of information with regard to risks and/or hazards to human health or the environment.

Decisions taken by the importing Party must be trade neutral; that is, if the Party decides it does not consent to accepting imports of a specific chemical, it must also stop domestic production of the chemical for domestic use or imports from any non-party.

The Convention provides for technical assistance between Parties. Parties shall, taking into account in particular the needs of developing countries and countries with economies in transition, co-operate in promoting technical assistance for the development of the infrastructure and the capacity necessary to manage chemicals to enable implementation of the Convention. Parties with more advanced programmes for regulating chemicals should provide technical assistance, including training to other Parties in developing their infrastructure and capacity to manage chemicals throughout their life-cycle.

Each Party must designate one or more national authorities (DNAs) authorized to act on its behalf in the performance of the administrative functions required by the Convention.

Monitoring/implementation
Review procedure
Each Party shall take such measures as may be necessary to establish and strengthen its national infrastructures and institutions for the effective implementation of this Convention. These measures may include, as required, the adoption or amendment of national legislative or administrative measures and may also cover:

• the establishment of national registers and databases including safety information for chemicals;
• the encouragement of initiatives by industry to promote chemical safety;
• the promotion of voluntary agreements, taking into consideration the provisions of Article 16 regarding technical assistance to developing countries and countries with economies in transition.

Each Party shall ensure, to the extent practicable, that the public has appropriate access to information on chemical handling and accident management and on alternatives that are safer for human health or the environment than the chemicals listed in Annex III.

The Parties agree to co-operate, directly or, where appropriate, through competent international organizations, in the implementation of this Convention at the subregional, regional, and global levels.

Nothing in this Convention shall be interpreted as restricting the right of the Parties to take action that is more stringently protective of human health and the environment than that called for in this Convention, provided that such action is consistent with the provisions of this Convention and is in accordance with international law.

The implementation of the Convention will be overseen by the COP. A Chemicals Review Committee (see Decision-making bodies, below) will regularly review notifications and nominations from Parties, and make recommendations to the COP on which chemicals should be included in PIC procedure. The Convention requires that the entire process be conducted in an open and transparent manner.

Observations or inspections
None by the Convention as such.

Trade measures
No provisions on trade measures to penalize Parties for non-compliance.

Dispute-settlement mechanisms
Parties shall settle any dispute between them concerning the interpretation or application of the Convention through negotiation or other peaceful means of their own choice.

On becoming members of the Convention, Parties may, by a written declaration, recognize as compulsory, in relation to any Party accepting the same obligation:
• early arbitration in an annex in accordance with procedures adopted by the COP;
• submission of disputes to the International Court of Justice.

A number of countries expressed the view that dispute settlement and the illicit trafficking of hazardous chemicals should be further discussed before the Convention enters into force.

Decision-making bodies
Political
After the Convention enters into force, the COP will become the supreme authority. The first meeting of the COP shall be convened no later than one year after the entry into force of the Convention. Thereafter, ordinary meetings of the COP shall be held at regular intervals to be determined by the Conference.

The COP shall by consensus agree upon and adopt at its first meeting rules of procedure and financial rules for itself and any subsidiary bodies, as well as financial provisions governing the functioning of the Secretariat.

The COP shall keep under review and evaluate implementation of the Convention, harmonize policies, establish subsidiary bodies, and undertake additional actions.

National and international agencies and qualified NGOs may attend the COP's meetings as observers and contribute to its work.

Scientific/technical
The COP will, at its first meeting, establish a subsidiary body, the Chemical Review Committee, for the purposes of performing the functions assigned to it by the Convention, such as reviewing information from the Parties and making recommendations to the COP. The members of the Committee shall be appointed by the COP and shall consist of a limited number of government-designated experts in chemicals management. The members shall be appointed on the basis of equitable geographical distribution, in particular ensuring a balance between developed and developing Parties. The Committee shall make every effort to make its recommendations by consensus.

Publications
Current information and reports of meetings and workshops are available from FAO.

Sources on the Internet
<http://www.fao.org/ag/agp/agpp/pesticid/pic/pichome.htm>
<http://www.fao.org/pic>

Convention on the Transboundary Effects of Industrial Accidents

Objectives

• to promote prevention of, preparedness for, and response to industrial accidents capable of causing transboundary effects, and international co-operation in these fields by mutual assistance, research, and development, as well as exchange of information and technology regarding industrial accidents in general, and to this end to strive towards convergence of relevant national policies and practices;

• to provide for notification among states concerned (*a*) on any proposed or existing hazardous activity capable of causing transboundary effects in the event of an industrial accident, and (*b*) on any industrial accident, or imminent threat thereof, which causes or is capable of causing transboundary effects;

• to provide for mutual assistance in the event of an industrial accident;

• to promote public information and participation in relevant decision-making processes concerning hazardous activities.

Scope

Legal scope
Open to member countries of the UN Economic Commission for Europe (UN/ECE), the European Community (EC), and other European states having consultative status with the UN/ECE.

Geographic scope
Regional. UN/ECE region (Europe and North America).

Time and place of adoption

17 March 1992, Helsinki.

Entry into force

Not yet in force. Enters into force 90 days after the deposit of 16 instruments of ratification, acceptance, approval, or accession. Expected to enter into force in early 2000.

Status of participation

12 States and the European Community had ratified, accepted, approved, or acceded by 8 July 1999. 16 Signatories without ratification, acceptance, or approval.

The Secretary-General of the UN acts as depositary.

Affiliated instruments and organizations

The Convention contains also 13 *annexes* which form an integral part of the Convention.

The Executive Secretary of the UN/ECE carries out the secretariat functions.

Secretariat

UN/ECE, Environment and Human Settlements Division (ENHS),
Palais des Nations,
CH-1211 Geneva 10,
Switzerland
Telephone: +41-22-9173174
Telefax: +41-22-9170107
E-mail: sergiusz.ludwiczak@unece.org

Information contact
Mr Sergiusz Ludwiczak.

Finance

Not applicable.

Rules and standards

The Convention stipulates measures and procedures:

• to reduce the risk of industrial accidents and improve preventive, preparedness, and response measures, including restoration measures;

• to obtain and transmit identification of hazardous activities that are reasonably causing a transboundary effect;

• to co-operate with other countries to develop off-site and on-site contingency plans, including joint contingency plans regarding industrial accidents, in order to respond properly and mitigate effects, including transboundary effects;

• to ensure that adequate information concerning hazardous activities is given to the public;

• to receive notification in the event of an industrial accident or imminent threat thereof;

• to request assistance from other countries in the event of an industrial accident in order to minimize its consequences, including its transboundary effect;

• to facilitate the exchange of safety technology and the provision of technical assistance;

• to benefit from international co-operation concerning prevention of, preparedness for, and response to industrial accidents, including exchange of information and experience gained from past industrial accidents and research and development in this field.

Monitoring/implementation

Review procedure
The Parties shall report periodically on the implementation of this Convention.

The Conference of the Parties shall, at its first meeting, decide on the method of work, including the use of national centres, co-operation with relevant international organizations, and the establishment of a system with a view to facilitating the implementation of the Convention, in particular for mutual assistance in the event of an industrial accident, and building upon pertinent existing activities within relevant international organizations.

If there is a doubt whether an activity is likely to have a significant adverse transboundary impact and the Parties concerned do not agree on whether the activity is hazardous, in accordance with *Annex I*, the State which could be affected may submit the question to a commission of inquiry in accordance with *Annex II*. The requesting Party or Parties shall notify the secretariat that it is (they are) submitting questions to a commission of inquiry. The notification shall state the subject-matter of the inquiry, in accordance with *Annex III*, and all Parties will immediately be informed of it by the secretariat. The inquiry commission will consist of three members. Both the requesting Party and the other Party to the inquiry procedure shall appoint a scientific or technical expert, and the two experts so appointed shall designate by common agreement a third expert to be the president of the commission. The Parties to the inquiry procedure must facilitate the work of that commission by providing it with all relevant documents, facilities, and information and by enabling it to call witnesses or experts and receive their evidence. If one of the Parties to the inquiry procedure does not appear before the commission or fails to present its case, the other Party may request the commission to continue the proceedings and complete its work. The final opinion of the commission of inquiry shall reflect the view of the majority of its members and shall include any dissenting view.

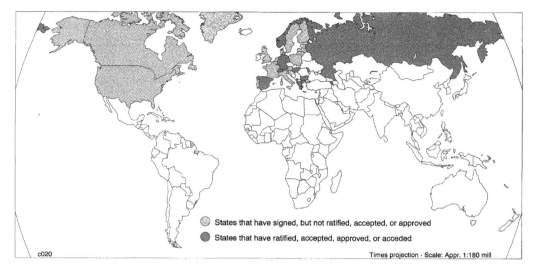

States that have signed, but not ratified, accepted, or approved

States that have ratified, accepted, approved, or acceded

c020

Times projection - Scale: Appr. 1:180 mill

Observations or inspections
None by the Convention as such.

Trade measures
No provisions on trade measures to penalize Parties for non-compliance.

Dispute-settlement mechanisms
If a dispute arises between two or more Parties over the interpretation or application of the Convention, they shall seek a solution by negotiation or by any other method of dispute settlement acceptable to the parties to the dispute.

The Parties may submit the dispute to the International Court of Justice or to an arbitration procedure set out in *Appendix XIII*.

Decision-making bodies

Political
In the decision on the Convention on the Transboundary Effects of Industrial Accidents adopted at their resumed fifth session in Helsinki on 17 March 1992, the Senior Advisers to UN/ECE Governments on Environmental and Water Problems called on the Signatories to strive for the entry into force of the Convention as soon as possible and to seek to implement it to the maximum extent possible pending its entry into force.

In the light of this decision, seven meetings of the Signatories to the Convention, open to all UN/ECE member countries, were held from 1992 to 1998, at which a work plan for its implementation was developed. These meetings reviewed actions taken by Signatories to implement the Convention pending its entry into force, *inter alia*: the development of policies and strategies to reduce the risks of industrial accidents; the strengthening of the ability of future Parties to comply with the provision of the Convention; the development and implementation of training programmes for the staff involved in preparedness for and response to industrial accidents, in particular in countries in transition, through the Regional Co-ordinating Centre for Industrial Training and Exercises in Warsaw; the development and implementation of preventive measures in the ECE countries, especially those in transition, through the Regional Co-ordinating Centre for the Prevention of Industrial Accidents in Budapest; and the improvement of communications by the development and implementation of UN/ECE accident notification systems used in the event of an industrial accident; and experience gained from past industrial accidents.

Once the Convention has entered into force, the Conference of the Parties will meet at least annually in order to review the implementation of the Convention and fulfil such other functions as may be appropriate under the provisions of the Convention.

Where appropriate, the Conference of the Parties will consider and, where necessary, adopt proposals for amendments to the Convention. Agreement on the proposed amendment should be reached by consensus, with the exception of *Annex I*. When all efforts at consensus have been exhausted and no agreement reached, the amendment to *Annex I* shall, as a last resort, be adopted by a nine-tenths majority vote of the Parties present and voting at the meeting.

Scientific/technical
The Conference of the Parties will establish, as appropriate, working groups and other mechanisms to consider matters related to the implementation and development of the Convention and, to this end, to prepare appropriate studies and other documentation and submit recommendations for consideration by the Conference of the Parties.

Publications
• *Environmental Conventions Elaborated under the Auspices of the UN/ECE*, 1992;
• UN Economic Commission for Europe (1994), *Convention on the Transboundary Effects of Industrial Accidents*, ECE/ENHS/NONE/2 (New York and Geneva: UN);
• *Industrial Accidents Manual* [available on the Internet].

Sources on the Internet
<http://www.unece.org/env/teia_h.htm>

Convention to Ban the Importation into Forum Island Countries of Hazardous and Radioactive Wastes and to Control the Transboundary Movement and Management of Hazardous Wastes within the South Pacific Region (Waigani Convention)

Objectives

• to prohibit the importation of hazardous wastes into Pacific Island developing Parties, and to regulate and facilitate the environmentally sound management of such wastes generated within the Convention area;

• to prohibit the importation of all radioactive wastes into Pacific Island developing Parties while at the same time recognizing that the standards, procedures, and authorities responsible for the environmentally sound management of radioactive wastes will differ from those in respect of hazardous wastes;

• to ensure that any transboundary movements of hazardous wastes within the Convention area are completed in a controlled and environmentally sound manner.

Scope

Legal scope

Open to all members of the South Pacific Forum, other states not members of the South Pacific Forum that have territories in the Convention area, and other States that do not have territories in the Convention area pursuant to a decision of the Conference of the Parties (COP). Not open to economic regional organizations.

Geographic scope

Regional. The Convention area comprises:

• the land territory, internal waters, territorial sea, continental shelf, archipelagic waters, and exclusive economic zones established in accordance with the international law of countries and territories located within the South Pacific region;

• those areas of high seas which are enclosed from all sides by the exclusive economic zones referred to above;

• areas of the Pacific Ocean between the Tropic of Cancer and 60°S and between 130°E and 120°W to the Convention area.

Time and place of adoption

16 September 1995, Waigani.

Entry into force

Not yet in force. Enters into force 30 days after the deposit of the tenth instrument of ratification, acceptance, approval, or accession.

Status of participation

Five states had signed and ratified by 4 June 1999. Nine Signatories, without ratification, acceptance, or approval.

The Secretary-General of the South Pacific Forum Secretariat, Suva, Fiji, acts as depositary.

Affiliated instruments and organizations

Annexes contain detailed operational obligations on categories of wastes which are hazardous wastes, a list of hazardous characteristics, disposal operations, notification procedures, and arbitration.

Co-ordination with related instruments

Provisions are established to co-ordinate the Convention with:

• *Convention on the Control of Transboundary Movements of Hazardous Wastes and their Disposal (Basel Convention)* (see this section);

• *Convention on the Prevention of Marine Pollution by Dumping of Wastes and Other Matter (London Convention 1972)* (see this section);

• *Convention for the Protection of the Natural Resources and Environment of the South Pacific Region* (see Conventions within the UNEP Regional Seas Programme, this section);

• *UN Convention on the Law of the Sea (UNCLOS)* (see this section);

• IAEA (see IGOs), regarding *Code of Practice on the International Transboundary Movement of Radioactive Wastes*;

• the South Pacific Nuclear Free Zone Treaty (see IGOs, IAEA).

A memorandum of understanding has been passed with the Secretariat of the Basel Convention.

Secretariat

South Pacific Regional Environment Programme (SPREP),
PO Box 240, Apia,
Western Samoa
Telephone: +685-21929
Telefax: +685-20231
E-mail: sprep@sprep.org.ws

Director
Mr Tamarii Pierre Tutangata.

Legal Officer
Mr Andrea Volentras.

Finance

To be decided by the COP. External assistance is to be sought after.

Budget
Premature.

Special funds
The COP shall consider establishing a revolving fund to assist on an interim basis in case of emergency situations to minimize damage from disasters or accidents arising from transboundary movement or disposal of hazardous wastes within the Convention area.

Rules and standards

Each Pacific Island developing Party shall take appropriate legal, administrative, and other measures within the area under its jurisdiction to ban the import of all hazardous wastes and radioactive wastes from outside the Convention area. Such import shall be deemed an illegal and criminal act.

Each other Party shall take similar measures within the area under its jurisdiction to ban the export of all hazardous wastes and radioactive wastes to all Forum Island countries, or to territories located in the Convention area. Such export shall be deemed an illegal and criminal act.

To facilitate compliance with the above paragraphs, all Parties shall:

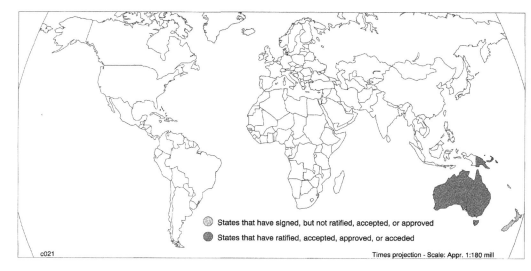

States that have signed, but not ratified, accepted, or approved

States that have ratified, accepted, approved, or acceded

c021

Times projection - Scale: Appr. 1:180 mill

• forward in a timely manner all information relating to illegal hazardous wastes and radioactive import activity within the area under its jurisdiction to the Secretariat, which shall distribute the information as soon as possible to all Parties;

• co-operate to ensure that no illegal import of hazardous wastes and radioactive wastes from a non-Party enters areas under the jurisdiction of a Party to the Convention.

Each Party is recommended to become a Party to the London Convention 1972, the SPREP Convention and its Protocol for the Prevention of Pollution of the South Pacific Region by Dumping, and the Basel Convention.

Each Party shall:

• ensure that, within the area of its jurisdiction, the generation of hazardous wastes is reduced at its sources to a minimum, taking into account social, technological, and economic needs;

• take all appropriate legal, administrative, and other measures to ensure that, within the area under its jurisdiction, all transboundary movements of hazardous wastes generated within the Convention area are carried out in accordance with the provisions of the Convention;

• designate or establish one or more competent authorities and one focal point to facilitate the implementation of the Convention.

The exporting Party shall notify, or shall require the generator or exporter to notify, in writing, through its competent authority, the competent authority of the countries concerned of any proposed transboundary movement of hazardous wastes.

In case of an accident occurring during transboundary movement of hazardous wastes or their disposal likely to present risks to human health and the environment in other States and Parties, those States and Parties must be immediately informed.

Monitoring/implementation

Review procedure
The COP shall keep under continuous review and evaluation the effective implementation of the Convention. The first meeting of the COP shall consider the adoption of any additional measures in accordance with the 'precautionary principle' relating to the implementation of the Convention.

The COP shall establish and/or designate such subsidiary bodies as are deemed necessary for the implementation of the Convention.

Each Party shall submit such reports as the COP requires regarding the hazardous waste generated in the area under its jurisdiction in order to enable the Secretariat to produce a regular hazardous wastes report.

Observations or inspections
None by the Convention as such.

Trade measures
No provisions on trade sanctions to penalize Parties for non-compliance.

Dispute-settlement mechanisms
Parties shall settle any dispute between them concerning the interpretation, application of, or compliance with the Convention, or any protocol thereto, through negotiation or other peaceful means of their own choice.

On becoming a member of the Convention, Parties may, by a written declaration, recognize as compulsory, in relation to any Party accepting the same obligation:

• arbitration in accordance with procedures adopted by the COP in Annex VII;

• submission of disputes to the International Court of Justice.

Decision-making bodies

Political
The COP shall keep under review and evaluate the implementation of the Convention, consider and adopt amendments or protocols, examine and approve the regular budget, harmonize policies, establish subsidiary bodies, and undertake additional actions.

The first meeting of the COP shall be convened not later than one year after the entry into force of the Convention. Thereafter, ordinary meetings shall be held at regular intervals to be determined by the COP at its first meeting. The quorum for meetings shall be two-thirds of the Parties.

Scientific/technical
To be established by the COP.

Publications

None as yet.

Sources on the Internet

<http://www.sprep.org.ws/>

European Agreement Concerning the International Carriage of
Dangerous Goods by Road (ADR)

Objectives
* to increase the safety of international transport by road;
* to lay down provision concerning classification, packaging, labelling, and testing of dangerous goods, including wastes, in harmony with other requirements for other modes of transport, on the basis of the UN Recommendations on the Transport of Dangerous Goods;
* to lay down conditions for the construction, equipping, and operation of vehicles carrying dangerous goods by road.

Scope
Legal scope
Open to all member States of the UN, UN Economic Commission for Europe (UN/ECE), other European States, and other member States of the UN which may be invited to participate in the work of the UN/ECE for questions of specific interest to them, such as the transport of international dangerous goods. Not open to regional integration organizations.

Geographic scope
Regional (Europe, USA, and Canada), but, on account of its legal scope and the international nature of transport, it may extend globally.

Time and place of adoption
30 September 1957, Geneva.

Entry into force
29 January 1968.

Status of participation
34 Parties by 16 June 1999. No Signatories without ratification, acceptance, or approval.

The Secretary-General of the UN acts as depositary.

Affiliated instruments and organizations
Two Annexes are attached to the Agreement, concerning conditions of transport, transport equipment, and transport operations. One Protocol of signature is also attached, and a Protocol amending the Agreement entered into force on 19 April 1985.

The only amendment to the Agreement itself deals with the procedure for amendment of the Annexes. A new Protocol amending the Agreement itself (dealing with the definition of vehicles and again with the procedure for amendment of the Annexes) was adopted on 28 October 1993, but is not yet in force. The Annexes are regularly amended (usually every two years) in parallel with other agreements dealing with the transport of dangerous goods by other modes, such as the Regulations concerning the International Carriage of Dangerous Goods by Rail (RID), the International Maritime Dangerous Goods Code (IMDG Code), and the International Civil Aviation Organization (ICAO)'s Technical Instructions for the Safe Transport of Dangerous Goods by Air, on the basis of the regular updating of the UN Recommendations on the Transport of Dangerous Goods.

The past series of amendments to Annexes A and B of ADR entered into force on 1 January 1999.

Annexes A and B of ADR have now been annexed to Directive 94/55/EC of the Council of the European Union, concerning the approximation of the laws of the member States of the European Union with regard to the transport of dangerous goods by road. This implies that the provisions of Annexes A and B of ADR apply not only to international transport but also to domestic traffic on the territory of member States of the European Union.

The Secretary-General of the UN ensures the administration of the Agreement through the UN Economic Commission for Europe (UN/ECE). The Inland Transport Committee of UN/ECE fulfils the function of a standing forum for deliberations in matters concerning the Agreement.

Co-ordination with related instruments
The UN Economic and Social Council (ECOSOC)'s Committee of Experts on Transport of Dangerous Goods issues recommendations every two years. All international instruments dealing with the transport of dangerous goods, including this Agreement, RID, IMDG Code, and ICAO Technical Instructions, as well as national regulations, are regularly revised and amended on the basis of these recommendations. Annex III of the Basel Convention (see this section) is also based on the UN Recommendation of the Transport of Dangerous Goods. This mechanism ensures co-ordination and harmonization of provisions relating to classification, labelling, marking, packing, documentation, etc.

Secretariat
UN/ECE,
Transport Division,
Palais de Nations,
CH-1211 Geneva 10,
Switzerland
Telephone: +41-22-9172456
Telefax: +41-22-9170039
E-mail: olivier.kervella@unece.org

Director of Transport Division
Mr J. Capel Ferrer.

Chief, Dangerous Goods Section
Mr Olivier Kervella.

Number of staff
Four professionals and two support staff (June 1999) (for the overall work of the division on the transport of dangerous goods and transport of perishable foodstuffs).

Finance
Budget allocated by the UN.

Budget
No information available.

Special funds
None.

Rules and standards
The Parties have agreed to ensure that certain dangerous goods are not accepted for international transport and that other goods be transported under conditions laid down in the Annexes. However, transport operations to which the Agreement applies shall remain subject to national or international regulations applicable in general to road traffic, international road transport, and international trade.

States that have signed, but not ratified, accepted, or approved

States that have ratified, accepted, approved, or acceded

c022

Times projection - Scale: Appr. 1:180 mill

Annex A contains: general provisions; a list of dangerous goods; special provisions for each class (conditions of packing, marking and danger labels, documentation); and classification tests and criteria (packaging standards, and testing and specifications of labels).

Annex B contains: provisions concerning transport equipment and transport operations (mode of carriage, special requirements to be fulfilled by the means of transport and its equipment, general service requirements, special provisions concerning loading and unloading, operation of vehicles); provisions concerning tank-vehicles and tank-containers; electrical equipment; certificates (approval of vehicles, driver training); a list of substances which may be carried in tanks; and danger identification numbers.

Monitoring/implementation

Review procedure
Distribution of documents of the Inland Transport Committee and its subsidiary bodies is limited to governments and specialized agencies, and to intergovernmental and non-governmental organizations which take part in the Committee and its subsidiary bodies.

There are no reporting requirements under the Agreement. Problems relating to the international transport of dangerous goods are regularly discussed by the UN/ECE Working Party on the Transport of Dangerous Goods (see below). Compliance with the ADR is controlled by the police or con-

trol authorities of each Contracting Party. Penalties for non-compliance are imposed in accordance with the national legislation of each Contracting Party.

The Agreement is regularly updated in the light of scientific and technical information.

Observations or inspections
None by the Agreement as such. Inspections are the responsibility of the competent authority of each Contracting Party.

Trade measures
No provisions on trade measures to penalize Parties for non-compliance.

Dispute-settlement mechanisms
The Parties shall as far as possible settle disputes between them by negotiation. Any dispute which is not settled by negotiation shall be submitted to arbitration and the arbitration shall be binding on the parties to the dispute.

Decision-making bodies

Political
The Agreement does not provide for the establishment of a separate institutional mechanism. The Inland Transport Committee of the UN/ECE fulfils the function of a standing forum for deliberations in matters concerning the Agreement. Upon request of any Party, the Secretary-General of the UN shall convene a Conference of Parties for revising or amending the Agreement.

Scientific/technical
The UN/ECE Working Party on the Transport of Dangerous Goods meets twice a year and has 55 members of the UN/ECE, other interested international organizations, and non-governmental organizations. It discusses problems relating to the international transport of dangerous goods. There are joint meetings of the Working Party and of the RID Safety Committee.

Publications

A consolidated edition of ADR and its Annexes incorporating all amendments in force on 1 January 1999 was published under the symbol ECE/TRANS/130, vols. I and II. Diskettes are available.

Other regular publications from UN/ECE are:
• annual reports of the ECE;
• *Transport Information*, published by the ECE;
• *UN Recommendations on the Transport of Dangerous Goods: Model Regulations* (1999) (ST/SG/AC.10/1/Rev.11);
• *UN Recommendations on the Transport of Dangerous Goods: Manual of Tests and Criteria* (1999) (ST/SG/AC.10/11/Rev. 3);
• *European Provisions concerning the International Carriage of Dangerous Goods by Inland Waterway (ADN)* (TRANS/WP.15/148).

Sources on the Internet

<http://www.unece.org/unece/trans/danger/danger.htm>

FAO International Code of Conduct on the Distribution and Use of Pesticides

Objectives

The objectives of this Code are to set forth responsibilities and establish voluntary standards of conduct for all public and private entities engaged in or affecting the distribution and use of pesticides, particularly where there is no national law or only an inadequate law to regulate pesticides.

Specifically, the Code seeks:
- to promote practices which ensure efficient and safe use of pesticides while minimizing health and environmental concern;
- to establish responsible and generally accepted trade practices;
- to assist countries which have not established controls designed to regulate the quality and suitability of pesticide products needed in that country;
- to ensure that pesticides are used effectively for the improvement of agricultural production and of human, animal, and plant health;
- to implement, internationally, an 'information exchange and Prior Informed Consent (PIC) procedure' requiring that no international shipment of a pesticide which has been banned or severely restricted by a country in order to protect human health or the environment should proceed without the agreement of the importing country.

Scope

Legal scope
The Code was adopted unanimously by the Food and Agriculture Organization (FAO) Conference at its 1985 session. Membership of FAO is confined to nations; associate membership to territories or groups of territories. The European Union is given membership as a regional integration organization.

Geographic scope
Global.

Time and place of adoption
19 November 1985, Rome.

Entry into force
Non-mandatory. However, at the request of its member countries and in co-operation with the UN Environment Programme (UNEP),

with which it operates a joint programme on PIC, FAO has been seeking consensus in converting PIC into a legally binding instrument (see Affiliated instruments and organizations, below). After two years of negotiations, the Convention on the Prior Informed Consent Procedure for Certain Hazardous Chemicals and Pesticides in International Trade (PIC Convention) (see this section) was adopted and signed by 61 states. An Interim Resolution calls for changes to be made to the voluntary PIC procedure to bring it in line with the PIC procedure as described in the Convention text.

Status of participation
Not applicable. FAO, which has adopted the Code, had 175 members, including the European Union, by June 1999.

Affiliated instruments and organizations
The Code was amended in 1989 to include the principle of Prior Informed Consent (PIC), which is particularly related to the control of pesticide imports into and exports to developing countries. By June 1999, 166 countries had nominated 232 designated national authorities (DNA) for the implementation of the PIC procedure. The Code is supported by a comprehensive set of technical guidelines on all aspects of pesticide management and control.

FAO, in close collaboration with other UN agencies such as UNEP, the World Health Organization (WHO), and the International Labour Organization (ILO) (see IGOs), assists governments to implement the Code. The PIC Convention will come into force only after deposit of the 50th ratification. Given the need to implement the new procedure immediately, delegates adopted at the Diplomatic Conference in September 1998 an Interim Resolution which asks the Intergovernmental Negotiating Committee (INC) to oversee the implementation of the interim PIC procedure.

Co-ordination with related instruments
The FAO Conference authorized the Director-General to establish a programme jointly

with UNEP for the implementation of PIC procedures.

Secretariat
Plant Protection Service,
Pesticide Management Unit,
Food and Agriculture Organization (FAO),
Viale delle Terme di Caracalla,
I-00100 Rome, Italy
Telephone: +39-06-57053441
Telefax: +39-06-57056347
E-mail: firstname.surname@fao.org

Chief, Plant Protection Service
Dr Niek A. van der Graaff.

Pesticides Information Officer
Mr Gerold Wyrwal.

Finance
Budget
The administrative core budget, covered by FAO's regular budget, is approximately $US500,000 annually.

Special funds
Additional funds are available for technical assistance.

Rules and standards
Although the Code itself is voluntary in nature, it promotes the promulgation and enforcement of legislation governing the import, manufacture, sale, and use of pesticides. The Code takes into account the special circumstances of developing countries.

The supply of data for the registration and approval of pesticides for use in a country is based on harmonized pesticide registration requirements formulated by FAO. Such data, including toxicological information on the pesticide and its environmental effects, are provided by the pesticide industry for officials in the country to decide whether to approve or disapprove the use of the pesticide based on benefit–risk evaluation under conditions of use in the country.

The principle of PIC (see above) concerns the export and import of chemicals and pesticides that are banned or severely restricted for

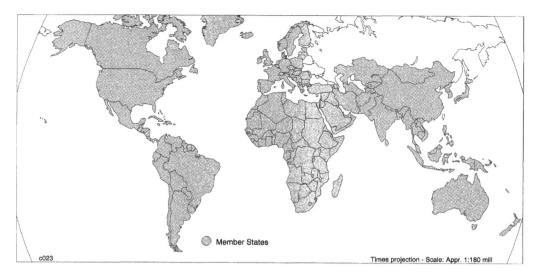

Member States

c023   Times projection - Scale: Appr. 1:180 mill

health or environmental reasons. DNAs in participating countries have been invited to communicate their decisions on 22 pesticides and five industrial chemicals. Control actions taken for health or environmental reasons for the same chemical by two countries from two different PIC regions which is communicated to UNEP or FAO is sufficient to suggest a chemical become subject to the PIC procedure.

The Code describes the shared responsibility of many segments of society, including governments, individually or in regional groupings; industry, including manufacturers, trade associations, formulators, and distributors; users; and public-sector organizations, such as environmental groups, consumer groups, and trade unions.

Monitoring/implementation

Review procedure
The current information on the operation and implementation of the Code is made through reports to the FAO Conference and reports of meetings and workshops which are published and sent to governments. The reports are public.

The provisions of the Code and progress in its implementation are reviewed regularly by panels of experts appointed to deal with specific topics on pesticides. These also include the joint FAO–UNEP panel, which specifically deals with PIC (see below).

In the implementation of PIC, FAO, jointly with UNEP, has published the *Guidance for Governments* document. In addition, FAO has published a decision guidance docu-

ment (DGD) for each pesticide in the PIC procedure, while UNEP has published similar documents on the industrial and consumer chemicals.

Implementation required a preparatory phase, which included the appointment of DNAs by their respective governments and the development of a joint database on banned and severely restricted pesticides and other chemicals. The database now includes notifications of control actions, information sent to DNAs, responses from importing countries, notifications from exporting countries, addresses of DNAs, and the text of DGDs.

Monitoring of the implementation of the Code has made it possible to compile rather detailed 'national profiles' indicating the 'pre-Code' situation in 1986, as well as the status in 1993 concerning pesticide registration, use, management, and control, the enforcement of regulations, and the likely future technical assistance needs of member countries. This work relates directly to recommendations contained in chapter 19 of *Agenda 21* of the UN Conference on Environment and Development (UNCED) (Rio de Janeiro, 1992), and data in 'national profiles' are used routinely by FAO, among other things, in evaluating pertinent requests from developing countries for technical assistance.

Several countries have, consequent to the introduction of the Code, introduced laws in their countries for the effective control of pesticides. Certain countries have, of their own accord, incorporated the Code into their national pesticide legislation. Implementation is also carried out through regional and bi-

lateral projects in individual countries. FAO holds regional workshops on the implementation of the PIC procedure.

Decision-making bodies

Political
The FAO Conference, which meets every two years, reviews the Code and makes recommendations to promote its implementation. The Conference is the major policy-making organ of FAO.

Scientific/technical
FAO and UNEP have established a Joint Expert Group on Prior Informed Consent. The Group is composed of independent experts, representing themselves and not their government, and selected by FAO, based on defined criteria. The function of the Group is to provide advice and guidance for the implementation of PIC, and to prepare and review DGDs and other technical matters. The first meeting of the Group was held in December 1989. Up to December 1996 the Group had met eight times. No further meetings were held.

Publications

The Code has been published as a booklet. Current information on its operation and implementation is available from FAO.

Sources on the Internet

<http://www.fao.org/waicent/faoinfo/
    agricult/agp/agpp/pesticid>
<http://www.fao.org/pic>

Convention on the Prevention of Marine Pollution by Dumping of Wastes and Other Matter (London Convention 1972)

Objectives

To prevent indiscriminate disposal at sea of wastes liable to create hazards to human health, to harm living resources and marine life, to damage amenities, or to interfere with other legitimate uses of the sea. The fundamental principle of the Convention is the prohibition of dumping of certain wastes, the requirement of a specific permit prior to dumping of others, and the demand for a general permit for the rest. The first two categories are determined by Annexes.

Scope

Legal scope

Open for accession by 'any state'. Not open to regional integration organizations. Inter- and non-governmental organizations participate with observer status at the Consultative Meetings of the Contracting Parties of the Convention.

Geographic scope

In addition to the global seas, it includes the exclusive economic zones and territorial waters of the coastal states. The 1996 Protocol (not in force) broadens the scope to include the seabed and the subsoil thereof, but excludes internal waters of States.

Time and place of adoption

13 November 1972, London.

Entry into force

30 August 1975.

Status of participation

77 Parties by 21 April 1999. Five Signatories without ratification, acceptance, or approval.

Affiliated instruments and organizations

• *Annex I* ('black list') includes radioactive wastes, industrial waste, incineration at sea, organohalogenic compounds, mercury and its compounds, and persistent plastics;
• *Annex II* ('grey list') includes products containing significant amounts of, among other things, lead, arsenic, copper, zinc, cyanides, fluorides, pesticides, and their by-products;
• *Annex III* concerns the criteria governing the issuing of permits and specifies the nature of the waste material, the characteristics of the dumping-site, and the method of disposal.

1996 Protocol to the Convention on the Prevention of Marine Pollution by Dumping of Wastes and Other Matter, 1972 (1996 Protocol to the London Convention 1972), London, 7 November 1996. (Not yet in force.) Six states had ratified by 21 April 1999. 14 Signatories subject to ratification or acceptance. Enters into force on the thirtieth day after the deposit of 26 instruments of rati-

fication, acceptance, approval, or accession, of which at least 15 are Contracting Parties to the Convention.

The basic objective of the Protocol adds to the existing provision that Parties shall where practicable eliminate pollution caused by dumping or incineration at sea of wastes or other matter. A fundamental principle of the Protocol is the prohibition of dumping of any wastes or other matter with the exception of these wastes or other matter listed in Annex 1, provided these wastes are assessed in accordance with the provisions set out in Annex 2 to the Protocol, before a permit for sea disposal can be issued.

According to *Annex 1 to the Protocol* the following wastes or other matter are those that may be considered for dumping: dredged material, sewage sludge, fish waste, vessels and platforms, inert, inorganic geological material, organic material of natural origin, and bulky items primarily comprising iron, steel, concrete, and similarly unharmful materials. It replaces the existing 'black' and 'grey' lists in Annex I and II of the Convention. *Annex 2 to the Protocol* replaces the existing Annex III of the Convention and constitutes a functional system for assessing the impact of dumping activities on the marine environment. *Annex 3 to the Protocol* deals with arbitral procedures.

IMO (see IGOs) is responsible for secretariat duties.

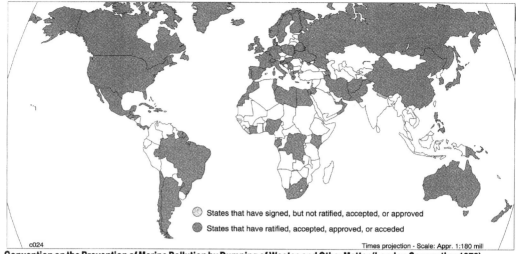

States that have signed, but not ratified, accepted, or approved

States that have ratified, accepted, approved, or acceded

c024   Times projection - Scale: Appr. 1:180 mill

Convention on the Prevention of Marine Pollution by Dumping of Wastes and Other Matter (London Convention 1972)

Co-ordination with related instruments
The requirements of the permitting system for low-level radioactive wastes incorporate the standards of the IAEA (see IGOs).

Secretariat
c/o IMO (see IGOs).

Finance
Contracting Parties contribute on a voluntary basis to projects promoting the implementation of the Convention, and after its entry into force, of the Protocol, to technical co-operation projects. Costs of administration of the Convention are covered by the regular IMO budget.

Rules and standards
The Parties are committed:
• individually and collectively, to promote effective control of all sources of pollution of the marine environment and to take all practicable steps to prevent pollution of the sea caused by the dumping of waste and other matter;
• to take effective measures individually and collectively to prevent marine pollution caused by dumping and to harmonize their policies;
• to prohibit the dumping of waste or other matter except as specified;
• to designate an appropriate authority to issue permits, keep records of dumping,

monitor the condition of the seas, and report on these matters to IMO;
• to apply measures required to implement the Convention for all vessels and aircraft registered in its territory or flying its flag; loading in its territory or territorial sea any matter to be dumped; or believed to be engaged in dumping under its jurisdiction;
• to take measures to prevent and punish contravention of the Convention;
• to develop procedures for effective application on the high seas.

The Convention prohibits the dumping of wastes or other matter including radioactive wastes under Annex I (the 'black list') of the Convention. Grey-listed wastes are categorized under Annex II and may be released only under a special permit based on conditions set by the Convention and its technical advisers. Dumping matter listed in Annex III is allowable only by general permit.

The Amendment of Annexes I and II to extend the prohibition against dumping high-level radioactive waste into prohibition against dumping *all* radioactive wastes entered into force on 20 February 1994, following a moratorium on low-level radioactive wastes which was established in 1983 and extended in 1985. The IAEA (see IGOs) is the adviser to the Convention on radiological matters.

Similar amendments of Annexes I and II were approved to prohibit incineration of industrial waste and sewage sludge and to

prohibit the dumping of industrial waste as from 1 January 1996. These legally binding decisions, which were preceded by earlier policy decisions to that effect, also entered into force on 20 February 1994.

Parties to the *1996 Protocol to the London Convention 1972* shall apply a *precautionary approach* to environmental protection from dumping of wastes or other matter whereby appropriate preventative measures are taken when there is reason to believe that wastes or other matter introduced into the marine environment are likely to cause harm even when there is no conclusive evidence to prove a causal relation between inputs and their effects.

Taking into account the approach that the polluter should, in principle, bear the cost of pollution, each Party shall endeavour to promote practices whereby those it has authorized to engage in dumping or incineration at sea bear the cost of meeting the pollution prevention and control requirements for the authorized activities, having due regard to the public interest.

Monitoring/implementation
Review procedure
Each Contracting Party shall take appropriate measures in its territory to prevent and punish conduct in contravention of the Convention. The Parties also undertake to issue instructions, assist one another, and work together in the development of co-

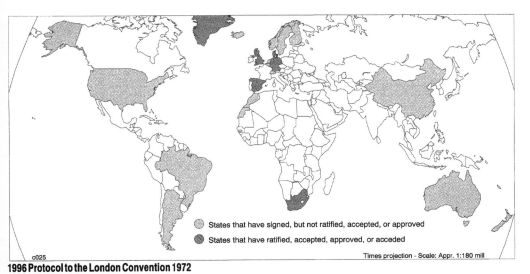

States that have signed, but not ratified, accepted, or approved

States that have ratified, accepted, approved, or acceded

c025

Times projection - Scale: Appr. 1:180 mill

1996 Protocol to the London Convention 1972

operative procedures for the application of the Convention.

The Parties are required to notify IMO directly or through regional secretariats of the nature, quantity, location, time, and method of dumping of all permitted matter, and of their monitoring of the condition of the sea, and of criteria, measures, and requirements adopted in issuing permits in the previous calendar year. By 21 April 1999, 36 national reports (51 per cent of the Parties) were submitted covering activities carried out in 1993. 33 national reports (45 per cent of the Parties) were submitted covering activities carried out in 1994. 39 national reports (52 per cent of the Parties) were submitted covering activities carried out in 1995. 26 national reports (34 per cent of the Parties) were submitted covering activities carried out in 1996. 18 national reports (23 per cent of the Parties) were submitted covering activities carried out in 1997. The latest final report with compilation of such data covers the permits issued in 1995.

Compliance is monitored and measured by the Consultative Meeting of the Contracting Parties. The Consultative Meeting is able to exercise some control over compliance through notification of dumping activities and monitoring reports, but no formal non-compliance procedures, prior notification procedures, or multilateral consultation procedures have been established.

Notification procedures adopted by the Consultative Meeting also call for the Parties to report compliance monitoring and environmental impact assessments. Only 50 per cent of Contracting Parties have fulfilled their obligations under the Convention in this respect, and the Consultative Meeting has sought more effective implementation.

Review of data or information in national reports is made by the Secretariat. These reviews are public and the Secretariat distributes publication lists of such reviews. There is no independent verification of data or information.

The *1996 Protocol* provides that no later than two years after the entry into force of the Protocol, the Meeting of Contracting Parties shall establish those procedures and mechanisms necessary to assess and promote compliance with the Protocol.

Decision-making bodies

Political
The Consultative Meeting of the Contracting Parties to the London Convention is the governing body and meets annually.

Scientific/technical
The Consultative Meeting requests advice on scientific and technical matters from its subsidiary body the Scientific Group and, occasionally, from the Joint Group of Experts on Scientific Aspects of Marine Environmental Protection (GESAMP). The Scientific Group, composed of government experts, responds to scientific requests, reviews the provisions of the Annexes, develops guidelines on monitoring programmes and issues concerning implementation of the Convention. GESAMP is composed of specialized experts nominated by the sponsoring agencies (IMO, FAO, UNESCO/IOC, WMO, WHO, IAEA, UN, and UNEP) (see IGOs). The Consultative Meeting has also established *ad hoc* groups to provide advice on specific issues such as incineration at sea, radioactive waste disposal at sea, legal matters, or the preparation of the review of the London Convention leading to the 1996 Protocol. These are composed of government experts.

Publications

IMO News (quarterly), and reports from IMO.

Sources on the Internet

<http://www.imo.org>

International Convention for the Prevention of Pollution from Ships, 1973, as modified by the Protocol of 1978 relating thereto (MARPOL 73/78)

Objectives

- to eliminate pollution of the sea by oil, chemicals, and other harmful substances which might be discharged in the course of operations;
- to minimize the amount of oil which could be released accidentally in collisions or strandings by ships, including also fixed or floating platforms;
- to improve further the prevention and control of marine pollution from ships, particularly oil-tankers.

The Convention contains special provision for the control of pollution from more than 400 liquid noxious substances, as well as for sewage and garbage disposal, and the control of air pollution from ships' exhausts.

Scope

Legal scope
Open to all states. Not open to regional integration organizations. NGOs and IGOs participate with observer status at meetings of the International Maritime Organization (IMO).

Geographic scope
The global seas.

The Convention designates the Antarctic, Mediterranean, Baltic, Red, and Black Seas, the Gulf of Aden, the Persian Gulf area, and north-west European waters as special areas in which oil discharge is virtually prohibited and the wider Caribbean and the North Sea as special areas subject to more stringent requirements governing the disposal into the sea of ship-generated garbage.

Time and place of adoption

2 November 1973 and 17 February 1978 (protocol), London.

Entry into force

2 October 1983.

Status of participation

106 Parties (94.07 per cent of world tonnage) by 1 June 1999. 33 States have made exceptions for annexes III (17), IV (33), or V (14). No Signatories without ratification, acception, or approval.

Affiliated instruments and organizations

Protocol Relating to the International Convention for the Prevention of Pollution from Ships, London, 1978. The Protocol introduced stricter regulations for ships and stipulates that a ship may be cleared to operate only after surveys and the issuing of an International Oil Pollution Prevention (IOPP) Certificate. The procedure in effect meant that the Protocol had absorbed the parent convention. States which ratify the Protocol must also give effect to the provisions of the Convention; there is no need for a separate instrument of ratification for the latter. The Protocol and the Convention should therefore be read as one instrument.

The governing scheme of the technical *Annexes I–V* is regulation according to type of pollutant: oil, noxious liquid substances (such as chemicals), harmful substances in packaged form, sewage, and garbage. 106 Parties (94.07 per cent of world tonnage) of the Convention had accepted *Annexes I* and *II*, 89 Parties (79.61 per cent of world tonnage) had accepted *Annex III*, 73 Parties (43.11 per cent of world tonnage) had accepted *Annex IV*, and 91 Parties (82.68 per cent of world tonnage) had accepted *Annex V* by 1 June 1999. Of these, the only annex not yet in force is Annex IV. An additional annex, *Annex VI*, on air pollution from ships, was adopted on 26 September 1997. Two Parties (4.83 per cent of world tonnage) had accepted Annex VI by 1 April 1999. It enters into force 12 months after the acceptance by at least 15 Parties of the Convention with not less than 50 per cent of the gross tonnage of the world's merchant shipping fleet.

Several *amendments* have been adopted since 1984 and have come into force. The 1992 amendments, which came into force on 6 July 1995, are generally regarded as the most important changes made to the Convention since the adoption of the 1978 Protocol. In the past, MARPOL, the 1978 Protocol, and many amendments have been concerned mainly with minimizing operational pollution, and they have been concentrated principally on new ships. The 1992 amendments also introduced new regulations which are designed to reduce drastically pollution from accidents; they apply to existing as well as new tankers (see Rules and standards below). A 1996 Amendment concerning reports of incidents involving oil or harmful substances entered into force under the Convention's tacit acceptance procedure on 1 January 1998.

Co-ordination with related instruments
The Convention is a combination of two treaties adopted in 1973 and 1978 respectively.

The Marine Environment Protection Committee (MEPC), one of four main committees of IMO, is responsible for co-ordinating work with other Conventions.

Secretariat

MARPOL
c/o IMO (see IGOs).

Finance

Costs are covered by the regular IMO budget. No core budget available.

Rules and standards

The principal obligations of States Parties are:

- to give effect to the provisions of the Convention and Annexes in order to prevent pollution of the marine environment;
- to prohibit violations, establish sanctions thereto under the law of the administration of the ship concerned, and instigate proceedings if informed of a violation and satisfied that sufficient evidence is available;
- to prohibit violations, and establish sanctions for violations, within the jurisdiction of any Party, and either to cause proceedings to take place or to furnish information to the administration of the ship;
- to apply the provisions of the Convention as may be necessary to ensure that more favourable treatment is not given to ships of non-Parties;
- to co-operate in the detection of violations and in the enforcement of the Convention.

The 1992 MARPOL Amendments include:

- an enhanced programme of inspections

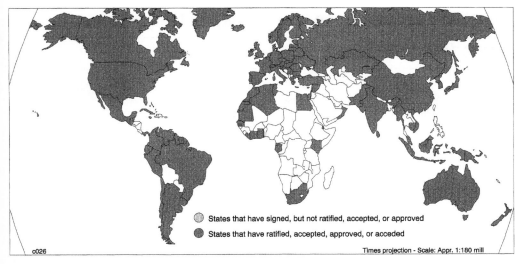

States that have signed, but not ratified, accepted, or approved

States that have ratified, accepted, approved, or acceded

c026   Times projection - Scale: Appr. 1:180 mill

that will apply to all oil-tankers aged five years and more;

• important new changes to the construction requirements for tankers of five years of age and above, including the mandatory fitting of double hulls or an equivalent design.

Other amendments adopted in March 1992 have applied to all new tankers ordered after 6 July 1993. Tankers of 5,000 d.w.t. and above must be fitted with double bottoms and double hulls extending the full length of the ship's side. The 'mid-deck' design is permitted as an alternative, and other designs may be allowed in due course, provided they ensure the same level of protection against pollution.

Monitoring/implementation

Review procedure
Compliance with these commitments is monitored and measured primarily by circulating reports made to IMO by the Parties. Reports made by port States following inspections also enable some monitoring of compliance with their obligations by flag States.

Under the mandatory reporting system of MARPOL, Annex I, annual reports, covering the following matters, have to be submitted to the Convention secretariat for constitution:

(*a*) *Annual enforcement reports* by port and flag States. 18 reports (19 per cent of the Parties) were submitted on activities in 1995. 9 reports (6 per cent of the Parties) were submitted on activities in 1996. 16 re-

ports (15 per cent of the Parties) were submitted on activities in 1997.

(*b*) *Annual summary report* by the Party State's administration of incidents involving spillages of oil of more than 50 tons.

(*c*) *Annual assessment report*, including

• a statistical report by the port State on the effectiveness of port State control (number of inspections and compliance rate);

• reports by the port State on MARPOL violations by ships resulting in detention or denial of entry into port;

• report on penalties imposed by the port State for violations of MARPOL.

18 assessment reports (19 per cent of the Parties) were submitted on activities in 1995. 20 reports (13 per cent of the Parties) were submitted on activities in 1996. 17 reports (16 per cent of the Parties) were submitted on activities in 1997.

However, only a small percentage of Parties have complied with the reporting requirements in the past few years. The reports, which are public, are regarded as useful to promote the effective implementation of the Convention, though some of them are not complete. There is no independent verification of data or information.

The Maritime Safety Committee (MSC) and MEPC have reported a variety of causes which might contribute to the lack of effective implementation by flag States. These include the lack of trained and experienced technical personnel within the flag State administration; the inability to retain skilled personnel: the inappropriate delega-

tion of inspection authority; or the use of insufficiently qualified and experienced surveyors. In addition, the record of port States in supplying reception facilities has been poor in some areas because of financial constraints. Provision of finance and technical assistance is an important factor in enabling some developing States to implement the Convention. The reports of the MSC and MEPC are public (see below).

Decision-making bodies

Political
The MEPC is established as a main forum for activities relating to the Convention. It consists of all member States of IMO, and is empowered to consider any matter within the scope of IMO concerned with prevention and control of pollution from ships. NGOs, which have granted consultative status with IMO, are also represented at MEPC sessions. IGOs which have concluded agreements of co-operation with IMO are also represented.

Scientific/technical
The Sub-Committees on Bulk Liquids and Gases and Flag State Implementation are important subsidiary bodies of the MEPC as far as pollution aspects are concerned.

Publications

IMO News, and reports of the MEPC and MSC of IMO.

Sources on the Internet

<http://www.imo.org>

International Convention on Civil Liability for Oil Pollution Damage 1969 (1969 CLC)

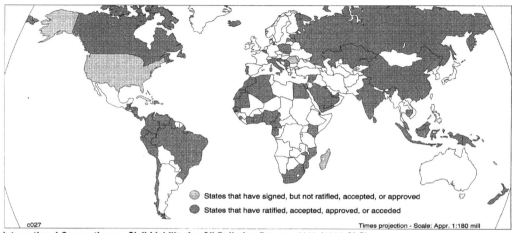

States that have signed, but not ratified, accepted, or approved
States that have ratified, accepted, approved, or acceded

c027   Times projection - Scale: Appr. 1:180 mill

International Convention on Civil Liability for Oil Pollution Damage 1969 (1969 CLC)

Objectives
• to ensure that adequate compensation is available to persons who suffer pollution damage caused by spills of persistent oil from laden tankers;
• to harmonize international rules and procedures for determining questions of liability and for providing adequate compensation in such cases.

Scope
Legal scope
Open to states which are members of the UN, of any of the Specialized Agencies, of the International Atomic Energy Agency (IAEA) (see IGOs), or which are Parties to the Statute of the International Court of Justice. Not open to regional integration organizations.

Geographic scope
Pollution damage caused on the territory, including the territorial sea, of States Parties. The 1992 Protocol (see below) extended the scope to cover the exclusive economic zones (EEZ) of the States Parties.

Time and place of adoption
29 November 1969, Brussels.

Entry into force
19 June 1975.

Status of participation
77 Parties by 1 May 1999. Three Signatories without ratification, approval, or acceptance. From 16 May 1998, Parties to the 1992 Protocol (see below) ceased to be Parties to the 1969 CLC due to a mechanism for compulsory denunciation of the 'old' regime established in the 1992 Protocol. However, for the time being the two regimes are co-existing, since there are a number of states which are Party to the 1969 CLC and have not yet ratified the 1992 regime (which is intended eventually to replace the 1969 CLC).
  The Secretary-General of IMO (see IGOs) performs depositary functions.

Affiliated instruments and organizations
• *Protocol to the International Convention on Civil Liability for Oil Pollution Damage,* London, 1976. Entered into force on 8 April 1981. 54 Parties by 1 May 1999. No Signatories without ratification, acceptance, or approval.
• *Protocol to Amend the International Convention on Civil Liability for Oil Pollution Damage,* London, 1984. (Not in force.) Governments are urged to ratify not the 1984 Protocol but only the 1992 Protocol to avoid a situation in which two conflicting treaty regimes are operational. It is practically certain that this Protocol will never enter into force.
• *Protocol to Amend the International Convention on Civil Liability for Oil Pollution Damage,* London, 1992. Entered into force on 30 May 1996. 45 Parties by 1 May 1999. Two Signatories without ratification, acceptance, or approval. The 1969 CLC as amended by the 1992 Protocol thereto is known as the *International Convention on Civil Liability for Oil Pollution Damage 1992.* (See also Status of participation, above.)

Co-ordination with related instruments
The necessary co-ordination with the operation of the 1971 and 1992 Fund Conventions is ensured by the 1971 and 1992 Funds (see International Oil Pollution Compensation Funds, IGOs).

Secretariat
None. Information is available from the International Oil Pollution Compensation Funds (see IGOs).

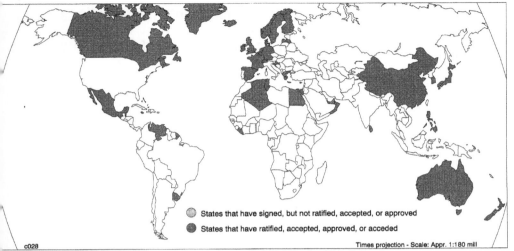

States that have signed, but not ratified, accepted, or approved

States that have ratified, accepted, approved, or acceded

c028
Times projection - Scale: Appr. 1:180 mill

1992 Protocol to Amend the International Convention on Civil Liability for Oil Pollution Damage

Finance

Budget
None.

Rules and standards

System of liability
The 1969 CLC covers pollution damage suffered in the territory (including the territorial sea) of a State Party to the 1969 CLC. The flag of the tanker and the nationality of the shipowner are irrelevant.

The owner of a tanker has strict liability i.e. he is liable also in the absence of fault for pollution damage caused by persistent oil spilled from a laden tanker as a result of an incident. He is exempt from liability only in certain circumstances.

Under certain conditions the shipowner is entitled to limit his liability to 133 special drawing rights (SDR) of the International Monetary Fund (IMF) (see IGOs) per ton of the ship's tonnage or SDR14 million, whichever is the less.

Claims for pollution damage can be made only against the registered owner of the tanker concerned.

The owner of a tanker carrying more than 2,000 tonnes of persistent oil as cargo is obliged to maintain insurance to cover his liability under the 1969 CLC. Tankers must carry a certificate on board attesting the insurance coverage. When entering or leaving a port or terminal installation of a State Party to the 1969 CLC, such a certificate shall also be carried by ships flying the flag of non-CLC States.

The 1969 CLC imposes on States Parties primarily the obligation to incorporate its provisions into domestic law.

The objective of the 1976 Protocol is to replace the original gold-based unit of account by special drawing rights (SDR) of the IMF.

Under the 1992 Protocol, compared with the original version of CLC, the shipowner's liability limit is substantially increased. A special limit of SDR3 million is introduced for small ships below 5,000 units of gross tanker tonnage. The limit increases on a linear scale up to SDR59.7 million for ships over 140,000 units of gross tonnage.

The 1992 Protocol provides a wider scope of application on several points than the Conventions in their original versions. The geographical scope of the 1992 Protocol is extended to include the exclusive economic zone (EEZ) established under the United Nations Convention on the Law of the Sea (UNCLOS) (see this section). Pollution damage caused by spills of persistent oil from unladen tankers is covered under the 1992 Protocol, and expenses incurred for preventive measures are recoverable even when no spill of oil occurs, provided that there was a grave and imminent threat of pollution damage. The Protocol includes a new definition of pollution damage which retains the basic wording of the present definition, but also adds a phrase to clarify that, for environmental damage, only costs incurred for reasonable measures to reinstate the contaminated environment are included in the concept of pollution damage.

Monitoring/implementation

Review procedure
None.

Observations or inspections
None.

Trade measures
None.

Dispute-settlement mechanisms
None.

Decision-making bodies

Political
The 1969 CLC does not have its own institutional apparatus, such as a regular Conference of the Parties. Commitments are not regularly reviewed. However, IMO (see IGOs), as depositary organization, shall convene a conference of States Parties if so requested by at least one-third of the Parties. Such conferences have been convened three times, i.e. for the adoption of the Protocols in 1976, 1984, and 1992.

Scientific/technical bodies
The CLC regime has no system or rules by which scientific and technical knowledge is incorporated into the decision-making process.

Publications

Up-to-date developments are reported in *IMO News*, published quarterly, and in the publications of the International Oil Pollution Compensation Funds (see IGOs).

International Convention on the Establishment of an International Fund for Compensation for Oil Pollution Damage 1971 (1971 Fund Convention)

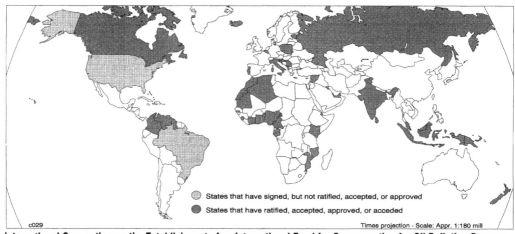

States that have signed, but not ratified, accepted, or approved

States that have ratified, accepted, approved, or acceded

c029   Times projection - Scale: Appr. 1:180 mill

International Convention on the Establishment of an International Fund for Compensation for Oil Pollution Damage 1971 (1971 Fund Convention)

Objectives
• to provide for a compensation system, supplementing that of the International Convention on Civil Liability for Oil Pollution Damage 1969 (1969 CLC) (see this section) in order to ensure full compensation to victims of oil pollution damage caused by persistent oil spilled from laden tankers;
• to distribute the economic burden between the shipping industry and oil cargo interests.

Scope
Legal scope
Open to States Parties to the International Convention on Civil Liability for Oil Pollution Damage 1969 (1969 CLC).

Geographic scope
Pollution damage caused on the territory, including the territorial sea, of States Parties. The 1992 Protocol (see below) extended the scope to cover the exclusive economic zone of States Parties.

Time and place of adoption
18 December 1971, Brussels.

Entry into force
16 October 1978.

Status of participation
51 Parties by 1 May 1999. Two Signatories without ratification, approval, or acceptance. From 16 May 1998, Parties to the 1992 Protocol (see below) ceased to be Parties to the 1971 Fund Convention due to a mechanism for compulsory denunciation of the 'old' regime established in the 1992 Protocol. However, for the time being two Funds (the 1971 Fund and the 1992 Fund) are in operation, since there are some states which have not yet acceded to the 1992 Protocol (which is intended to replace completely the 1971 regimes).

Affiliated instruments and organizations
• *Protocol to the International Convention on the Establishment of an International Fund for Compensation for Oil Pollution Damage*, London, 1976. Entered into force on 22 November 1994. 34 Parties by 1 May 1999. No Signatories without ratification, approval, or acceptance.

• *Protocol to Amend the International Convention on the Establishment of an International Fund for Compensation for Oil Pollution Damage*, London, 1984. (Not in force.) Governments have been urged not to ratify the 1984 Protocol but only the 1992 Protocol to avoid a situation in which two conflicting treaty regimes are operational. It is practically certain that this Protocol will never enter into force.
• *Protocol to Amend the International Convention on the Establishment of an International Fund for Compensation for Oil Pollution Damage*, London 1992. Entered into force on 30 May 1996. 41 Parties by 1 May 1999. Two Signatories without ratification, approval, or acceptance. The 1971 Fund Convention as amended by the 1992 Protocol thereto is known as the *International Convention on the Establishment of an International Fund for Compensation for Oil Pollution Damage 1992 (1992 Fund Convention)*. (See also Status of participation, above.)

Secretariat
International Oil Pollution Compensation Funds (IOPC Funds) (see IGOs).

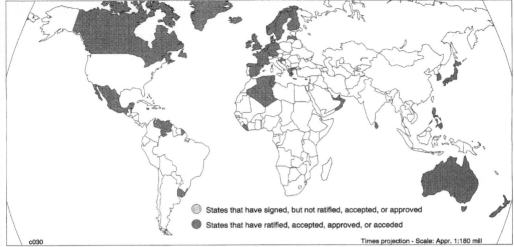

States that have signed, but not ratified, accepted, or approved

States that have ratified, accepted, approved, or acceded

c030   Times projection - Scale: Appr. 1:180 mill

1992 Protocol to Amend the International Convention on the Establishment of an International Fund for Compensation for Oil Pollution Damage

Finance

The system of compensation is financed by contributions of persons who receive more than 150,000 tonnes of crude or heavy oil after sea transport in a State Party during a calendar year. Contributions are determined in proportion to the quantity of oil received.

Budget
Annual secretariat costs amount to approximately £UK2.0 million.

Rules and standards

Compensation system
The 1971 Fund Convention established the 1971 Fund (see IGOs) to administer the system of compensation set up under the Convention.

Under the 1971 Fund Convention compensation is provided up to a flat-rate ceiling if:

(*a*) the shipowner is exonerated from liability;

(*b*) the shipowner and his insurer is financially incapable of paying; or

(*c*) the victims are not fully compensated by the shipowner under the 1969 CLC (see this section).

Compensation for a single incident is limited under the 1971 Fund Convention to 60 million special drawing rights (SDR) of the International Monetary Fund (see IGOs), including the amount actually paid by the

shipowner and his insurer under the CLC.

The objective of the 1976 Protocol is to replace the original gold-based unit of account by special drawing rights (SDR) of the International Monetary Fund.

Under the 1992 Protocol, the maximum amount of compensation payable by the 1992 Fund (the organization established under the 1992 Fund Protocol) is increased to SDR135 million, including the amount actually paid by the shipowner and his insurer under the 1969 CLC as amended by its 1992 Protocol (see this section).

The 1992 Protocol provides a wider scope of application on several points than the Conventions in their original versions. The geographical scope of the 1992 Protocol is extended to include the exclusive economic zone (EEZ) established under the United Nations Convention on the Law of the Sea (UNCLOS) (see this section). Pollution damage caused by spills of persistent oil from unladen tankers is covered under the 1992 Protocol, and expenses incurred for preventive measures are recoverable even when no spill of oil occurs, provided that there was a grave and imminent threat of pollution damage. The Protocol includes a new definition of pollution damage which retains the basic wording of the present definition, but also adds a phrase to clarify that, for environmental damage, only costs incurred for reasonable measures to reinstate the contaminated environment are incorporated in the concept of pollution damage.

Monitoring/implementation

Review procedure
Parties shall communicate annually a list of oil-receiving persons under their jurisdiction and the quantity of oil received by each person. These reports are confidential. The annual submission of lists of contributing persons is closely monitored by the IOPC Funds secretariat.

Decision-making bodies

The IOPC Funds secretariat, led by the Director, is responsible for the conduct of business, including collection of contributions and settlements of claims under the 1971 and 1992 Fund Conventions.

The 1971 Fund Convention has established two decision-making organs, the Assembly of all States Parties, which meets annually, and the Executive Committee, comprising 15 States Parties elected by the Assembly, which meets several times a year. The 1992 Fund Convention has established two decision-making organs, the Assembly of all States Parties, which meets annually, and the Executive Committee, comprising 15 States Parties elected by the Assembly, which meets several times a year.

Publications

Current developments are reported in the Funds' annual report. Also published periodically by the IOPC Funds secretariat are claims manuals.

International Convention on Liability and Compensation for Damage in Connection with the Carriage of Hazardous and Noxious Substances by Sea (HNS Convention)

Objectives

To ensure that adequate, prompt, and effective compensation is available to persons who suffer damage caused by incidents in connection with the carriage by sea of hazardous and noxious substances (HNS).

Scope

Legal scope
Open to all states. Not open to regional economic integration organizations.

Geographic scope
The Convention applies to damage caused on the territory, including the territorial sea, and in exclusive economic zones of States Parties.

Time and place of adoption

3 May 1996, London.

Entry into force

Not yet in force. Enters into force 18 months after the date on which at least 12 states, including four states each with not fewer than 2 million units of gross tonnage, have expressed their consent to be bound by it, provided that persons in these states which will have to make payments into the general account have received at least 40 million tonnes of contributing HNS cargo in the preceding calendar year.

Status of participation

No ratifications or accessions by 1 June 1999. Eight Signatories without ratification, approval, or acceptance.

The Secretary-General of the International Maritime Organization (IMO) (see IGOs) performs depositary functions.

Affiliated instruments and organizations

Annex I consists of a certificate of insurance or other financial security in respect of liability for damage caused by hazardous and noxious substances.

Co-ordination with related instruments
The scope of the treaty is defined by reference to existing international lists of substances, enabling it to be modified as these are amended. The substances include oils and noxious liquid substances carried in bulk as defined in the MARPOL 73/78 (see this section) on marine oil pollution, dangerous, hazardous, or harmful substances, materials, and articles in packaged form covered by the International Maritime Dangerous Goods Code, and various other liquid substances, solid bulk materials, and liquefied gases, together with residues from the previous bulk carriage of substances covered by the above lists. At present, these lists apply to some 6,000 substances.

The Convention shall not apply to pollution damage as defined in the International Convention on Civil Liability for Oil Pollution Damage 1969 (1969 CLC) (see this section).

The Marine Environment Protection Committee (MEPC), one of four main committees of IMO, is responsible for co-ordinating work with other IMO conventions.

Secretariat

A secretariat comprising a Director, and such staff as the administration of the HNS Fund may require, will be established following the entry into force of the Convention. Information is available from IMO (see IGOs).

Finance

Budget
Not yet applicable. The HNS Fund to be established under the Convention will prepare and submit financial statements and budget estimates for each calendar year to the Assembly (see Decision-making bodies, below).

Special funds
See HNS Fund, in Rules and standards, below.

Rules and standards

The Convention defines damage as including loss of life or personal injury; loss of or damage to property outside the ship; loss or damage by contamination of the environment; the costs of preventive measures; and further loss or damage caused by them.

The Convention introduces strict liability for the shipowner, higher limits than the present general limitation regimes, and a system of compulsory insurance and insurance certificates. States which are Parties can decide not to apply it to ships of 200 gross tonnage and below that carry HNS only in packaged form and are engaged on voyages between ports in the same State. Two neighbouring States can further agree to apply similar conditions to ships operating between ports in the two countries.

In order to ensure that shipowners engaged in the transport of HNS are able to meet their liabilities, the Convention makes insurance compulsory for them. A certificate of insurance must be carried on board and a copy retained by the authorities who keep record of the ship's registry.

It has generally been agreed that it would not be possible to provide sufficient cover by the shipowner liability alone for the damage that could be caused in connection with the carriage of HNS cargo. This liability, which creates a first tier of the Convention, is therefore supplemented by a second tier, the HNS Fund, financed by cargo interest.

The Fund will be involved in cases where:
• no liability for the damage arises for the shipowner. This could occur, for example, if the shipowner was not informed that a shipment contained HNS or if the accident resulted from an act of war;
• the owner is financially incapable of meeting the obligations under the Convention in full and any financial security that may be provided under chapter II (on liability) does not cover or is insufficient to satisfy the claims for compensation for damage;
• the damage exceeds the owner's liability under the terms of chapter II.

Contributions to the second tier will be

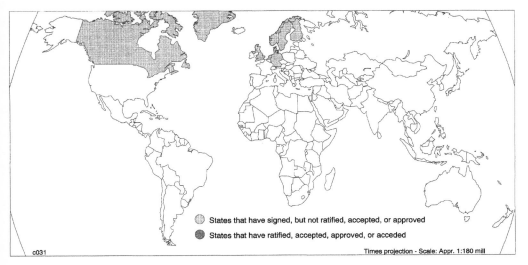

States that have signed, but not ratified, accepted, or approved

States that have ratified, accepted, approved, or acceded

c031

Times projection - Scale: Appr. 1:180 mill

levied on persons in the Contracting Parties who receive a certain minimum quantity of HNS cargo during a calendar year. The tier will consist of one general account and three separate accounts for oil, liquefied natural gas (LNG), and liquefied petroleum gas (LPG). The system with separate accounts has been seen as a way to avoid cross-subsidization between different HNS substances.

The unit of account used in the Convention is the Special Drawing Right (SDR) of the International Monetary Fund (IMF) (see IGOs). At present SDR1 is roughly equivalent to £UK1. The liability limits contained in the first tier are based on the gross tonnage of the ship concerned and are as follows:

- for ships not exceeding 2,000 gt, SDR10 million;
- for ships between 2,001 and 50,000 gt, SDR1,500 per ton, making a maximum of SDR82 million at 50,000gt;
- for ships between 50,001 gt and 100,000 gt, SDR360 per ton, making a maximum of SDR100 million at 100,000 gt;
- for ships exceeding 100,000gt, SDR100 million.

Once these limits are reached, compensation would be paid from the second tier, the HNS Fund, up to a maximum of SDR250 million (including compensation paid under the first tier). The Fund will be made up of contributions paid by the importers of HNS materials (primarily chemical companies).

Monitoring/implementation

Review procedure
Each State Party shall communicate to the Director the name and address of any person who in respect of the State is liable to pay contributions in accordance with the Convention, as well as data on the relevant quantities of contributing cargo for which such a person is liable to contribute in respect of the preceding calendar year.

Where a State Party does not fulfil its obligations to communicate to the Director the information referred to above, and this results in a financial loss for the HNS Fund, that State Party shall be liable to compensate the HNS Fund for such loss. The Assembly shall, on the recommendation of the Director, decide whether such compensation shall be payable by a State Party.

Where a person who is liable to pay contributions does not fulfil the obligations in respect of any such contribution or any part thereof and is in arrears, the Director shall take all appropriate action, including court action, against such a person on behalf of the HNS Fund with a view to the recovery of the amount due. However, where the defaulting contributor is manifestly insolvent or the circumstances otherwise so warrant, the Assembly may, upon recommendation of the Director, decide that no action shall be taken or continued against the contributor.

The Assembly shall review every five years the implementation of the Convention with particular reference to the performance of the system for the calculation of levies and the contribution mechanism for domestic trade; and to perform such other functions as are allocated to it under the Convention or are otherwise necessary for the proper operation of the HNS Fund.

Observations or inspections
None by the Convention as such.

Dispute-settlement mechanisms
Not applicable.

Decision-making bodies
Political
The Fund will have an Assembly consisting of all States which are Parties and a Secretariat headed by a Director. The Assembly will normally meet once a year. The first session shall take place as soon as possible after the entry into force of the Convention.

Scientific/technical
The Assembly shall establish a Committee on Claims for Compensation, with at least seven and not more than 15 members, and any temporary or permanent subsidiary body it may consider to be necessary.

Publications
Up-to-date information on the Convention is available through *IMO News* (quarterly) and other reports from IMO.

Sources on the Internet
<http://www.imo.org>

International Convention on Oil Pollution Preparedness, Response, and Co-operation (OPRC)

Objectives

• to prevent marine pollution incidents by oil, in accordance with the precautionary principle, in particular by strict application of the International Convention for Safety of Life at Sea (SOLAS) and MARPOL 73/78 (see this section);
• to advance the adoption of adequate response measures in the event that an oil pollution incident does occur;
• to provide for mutual assistance and co-operation between States for these aims.

Scope

Legal scope
Open to all states. Not open to regional integration organizations. An international conference comprised of 90 states drafted the final text and adopted the Convention.

Geographic scope
The global seas.

Time and place of adoption

30 November 1990, London.

Entry into force

13 May 1995.

Status of participation

45 Parties (48.74 per cent of world tonnage) by 1 June 1999. Ten Signatories without ratification, approval, acceptance, or accession.

The Secretary-General of IMO performs depositary functions.

Affiliated instruments and organizations

The *Annex* to the Convention provides general principles concerning reimbursements for the costs incurred by nations that assist in responding to spills. In the absence of an existing bilateral or multilateral arrangement, the requesting nation shall reimburse the assisting nation for the costs incurred. However, if an assisting nation acts on its own initiative, it will bear the costs. The costs are to be calculated according to the law and custom of the assisting nation.

Ten affiliated *Resolutions* were adopted by the Conference dealing with, for example, institutional matters, expansion of scope to hazardous substances, and technical co-operation and transfer of technology.

The International Maritime Organization (IMO) (see IGOs) shall act as clearing-house for information submitted to it by the Parties, and facilitate co-operation among the Parties in technical and educational matters. These functions are carried out even before entry into force of the Convention, through implementation of Article 12 dealing with secretariat responsibilities.

Co-ordination with related instruments
As a follow-up to the Convention and, in particular, to the provision requiring all ships to carry oil pollution emergency plans, the Marine Environment Protection Committee (MEPC), one of four main committees of IMO, adopted amendments to Annex 1 of MARPOL 73/78 (see this section). Co-ordination with regional organizations or arrangements are recognized.

Secretariat

c/o IMO (see IGOs).

Finance

Budget
The Convention does not provide for regular meetings and programme activities, or a secretariat. Therefore regular administrative costs do not arise under the Convention.

Special funds
None.

Rules and standards

Parties must require ships, off-shore units, and seaports under their jurisdiction to have oil pollution emergency plans. These are required for:
• oil-tankers of 150 gross tons and above, and other ships of 400 gross tons and above;
• any fixed or floating off-shore installation or structure engaged in gas or oil exploration, exploitation, production activities, or loading or unloading oil;
• any seaport and oil-handling facility that presents a risk of an oil pollution incident.

The Convention has established a reporting procedure on oil pollution incidents.

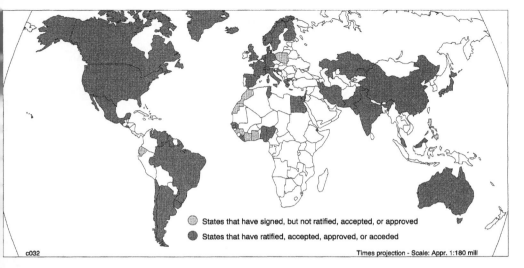

States that have signed, but not ratified, accepted, or approved

States that have ratified, accepted, approved, or acceded

c032   Times projection - Scale: Appr. 1:180 mill

Under this procedure, all persons having charge shall be required to report such incidents to the competent national authority, which must assess the incident and inform other States and/or IMO. Parties shall establish national and, as far as possible, regional systems for preparedness and response. They shall co-operate in pollution response, research, and technical matters.

Monitoring/implementation

Review procedure
Beyond the general obligations to co-operate in research and technical assistance, no provision for disclosure of data is made. Parties are required to ensure that current information is provided to IMO response and preparedness systems. Parties shall evaluate the effectiveness of the Convention together with IMO. No evaluation criteria or time-scales are given.

The MEPC has established the OPRC Working Group which is open to representatives from all IMO members, UN organizations, and intergovernmental organizations in consultative status with IMO. The Working Group reports to the MEPC and meets in conjunction with MEPC meetings. According to the current work plan, the Working Group shall recommend ways and means to improve the involvement of industry (oil, shipping, oil-spill clean-up) in the implementation of the Convention.

Observations or inspections
None by the Convention as such.

Trade measures
No provisions on trade measures to penalize Parties for non-compliance.

Dispute-settlement mechanisms
None.

Decision-making bodies

The Convention does not establish a meeting of the Parties or similar institution. The MEPC is responsible for co-ordinating and administering the activities relating to the Convention. It consists of all member States of IMO. NGOs, which have been granted consultative status with IMO, are also represented at MEPC sessions, as are IGOs which have concluded agreements of co-operation.

Publications

IMO News and reports of the MEPC.

Sources on the Internet

<http://www.imo.org>

International Convention Relating to Intervention on the High Seas in Cases of Oil Pollution Casualties (Intervention Convention)

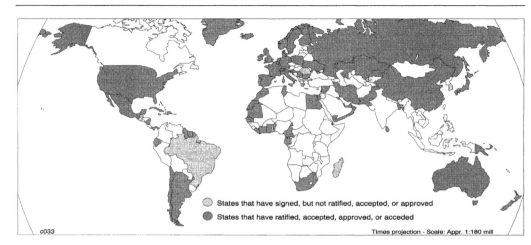

States that have signed, but not ratified, accepted, or approved

States that have ratified, accepted, approved, or acceded

c033

Times projection - Scale: Appr. 1:180 mill

Objectives
• to protect the interest of peoples against the grave consequences of maritime casualties resulting in danger of oil pollution of the sea and coastline;
• to recognize that measures of an exceptional character to protect such interests might be necessary on the high seas, provided these do not affect the principle of freedom of the high seas.

Scope
Legal scope
Membership is open to member States of the UN, any specialized agency, or the International Atomic Energy Agency (IAEA) (see IGOs), or Parties to the Statute of the International Court of Justice.

Geographic scope
The global seas.

Time and place of adoption
29 November 1969, Brussels.

Entry into force
6 May 1975.

Status of participation
73 Parties (68.75 per cent of world tonnage) by 1 June 1999. Six Signatories without ratification or approval.

Affiliated instruments and organizations
Protocol Relating to Intervention on the High Seas in Cases of Marine Pollution by Substances Other than Oil, London, 2 November 1973. Entered into force on 30 March 1983. 42 Parties (44.91 per cent of world tonnage) by 1 June 1999. One Signatory without ratification or approval. The basic objective of the Protocol is to extend the 1969 Convention to apply also to substances other than oil, such as noxious substances, liquefied gases, and radioactive substances.

Secretariat
c/o International Maritime Organization (IMO) (see IGOs).

Finance
Budget
Costs are covered by the regular IMO budget.

Rules and standards
The following are imposed on Parties:
• to consult with other states affected before taking measures;
• to notify proposed measures to any person or company known to have interests which can reasonably be expected to be affected by those measures;
• to use best endeavours to avoid risk to human life and to afford assistance to persons in need;
• to notify without delay states and persons or companies concerned and the Secretary-General of IMO;
• to set up and maintain a list of independent experts;
• to ensure that measures taken are proportionate to the damage, actual or threatened, and necessary to protect the interest of the coastal state;
• to pay compensation for measures taken in excess of those reasonably necessary.

Monitoring/implementation
Review procedure
The Parties are required to report on measures taken under the Convention to IMO and to other states affected.

Decision-making bodies
IMO acts as reporting facility and maintains a list of independent experts.

Publications
Up-to-date information is made available through *IMO News* (quarterly).

Sources on the Internet
<http://www.imo.org>

United Nations Convention on the Law of the Sea (UNCLOS)

Objectives

• to establish a comprehensive legal order to facilitate international communication and promote peaceful uses of the oceans and seas, the equitable and efficient utilization of their resources, the conservation of their living resources, and the study and protection and preservation of the marine environment;

• to integrate and balance the right to exploit natural resources with the duty to manage and conserve such resources and to protect and preserve the marine environment;

• to provide the comprehensive legal framework for the protection and preservation of the marine environment to be complemented and developed by further legal rules at the global or regional level and national measures. This is recognized in the UN Conference on Environment and Development (UNCED)'s Agenda 21, chapter 17 which states that UNCLOS provides the international basis upon which to pursue the protection and sustainable development of the marine and coastal environment and its resources.

No reservations or exceptions may be made to the Convention. States may make exceptions only to certain provisions dealing with compulsory procedures for the settlement of disputes.

Scope

Legal scope
Open to all states, certain self-governing associated states and territories, and international organizations to which their member states have transferred competence over matters governed by the Convention.

Geographic scope
Global.

Time and place of adoption
10 December 1982, Montego Bay, Jamaica.

Entry into force
16 November 1994.

Status of participation

130 Parties, including the European Community, by 15 June 1999. 40 Signatories have not yet ratified or acceded.

The Secretary-General of the UN acts as depositary for the Convention itself and both agreements listed below.

Affiliated instruments and organizations

Agreement relating to the Implementation of Part XI of the United Nations Convention on the Law of the Sea of 10 December 1982. Adopted on 28 July 1994 by the 48th session of the General Assembly of the UN. Entered into force on 28 July 1996. 94 Parties, including the European Community, by 15 June 1999. 19 Signatories have not expressed their consent to be bound.

The Agreement was negotiated to facilitate universal participation in the Convention after a number of countries expressed difficulties with the sea-bed mining provisions contained in Part XI of the Convention. The Agreement addresses a number of those difficulties, particularly the request for a more market-oriented approach, and changes in the institutional arrangements and decision-making processes within the International Sea-Bed Authority (ISBA) (see Secretariats below).

With the entry into force of UNCLOS, the ISBA came into existence and the Agreement started to be provisionally applied pending its entry into force. The provisional application of the Agreement terminated at the date of its entry into force, on 28 July 1996. States and entities which had been applying it provisionally, and for which it was not in force, were able to continue to be members of the Authority on a provisional basis, pending its entry into force for such States and entities. Such provisional membership terminated on 16 November 1998 in accordance with the relevant provisions of the Agreement. Therefore, as of that date, the members of the Authority coincide entirely with the Parties to the Convention. Some of the Parties to the Convention have still to ratify the Agreement.

The Agreement consists of ten articles dealing mainly with procedural aspects such as signature, entry into force, and provisional application. Its Article 2 deals with

the relationship between the Agreement and Part XI of the Convention, and it provides that the two shall be interpreted and applied together as a single instrument. In the event of an inconsistency between the Agreement and Part XI, however, the provisions of the Agreement shall prevail.

The Agreement deals with the various issues that were identified as problems during the informal consultations convened by the Secretary-General of the UN with a view to resolving certain outstanding issues regarding the deep sea-bed mining provisions of the Convention which impeded its universal acceptance. These include: costs to States Parties and institutional arrangements; decision-making mechanisms for the Authority; the Enterprise; transfer of technology; production policy; financial terms of contracts for deep sea-bed mining; and the review Conference.

Agreement for the Implementation of the Provisions of the United Nations Convention on the Law of the Sea of 10 December 1982 relating to the Conservation and Management of Straddling Fish Stocks and Highly Migratory Fish Stocks (1995 Fish Stocks Agreement). (Not yet in force.) Adopted on 4 August 1995. Enters into force 30 days after the deposit of 30 instruments of ratification or accession. 23 states had ratified or acceded by 15 June 1999. 43 Signatories, including the European Community, have not ratified, acceded, or deposited their instrument of formal confirmation.

The Agreement addressed the problems which have prevented the effective implementation of the relevant Convention provisions on the management and conservation of these resources and to facilitate and strengthen co-operation among States. It sets out principles for the conservation and management of straddling fish stocks and highly migratory fish stocks and establishes that such management must be based on the precautionary approach and the best available scientific information. The Agreement elaborates on the fundamental principle, established in the Convention, that States should co-operate to ensure conservation and promote the objective of the optimum utilization of fisheries resources both within and beyond the exclusive economic zone.

The Agreement attempts to achieve this

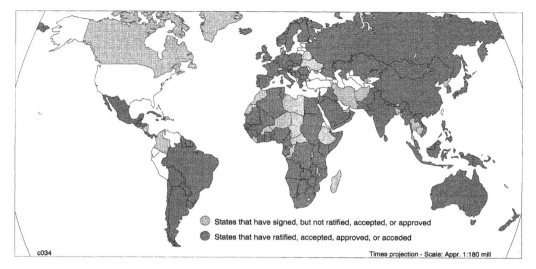

States that have signed, but not ratified, accepted, or approved

States that have ratified, accepted, approved, or acceded

c034

Times projection - Scale: Appr. 1:180 mill

objective by providing a framework for co-operation in the conservation and management of those resources. It promotes good order in the oceans through the effective management and conservation of high-seas resources by establishing, *inter alia*, detailed minimum international standards for the conservation and management of straddling fish stocks and highly migratory fish stocks; ensuring that measures taken for the conservation and management of those stocks in areas under national jurisdiction and in the adjacent high seas are compatible and coherent; ensuring that there are effective mechanisms for compliance and enforcement of those measures on the high seas; ensuring an effective mechanism for settlements of disputes; and recognizing the special requirements of developing states in relation to conservation and management as well as the development, needs, and participation of these countries in the conservation and management of the two types of stocks mentioned above.

The Agreement gives prominence to subregional or regional fisheries management organizations or arrangements as the principal means for implementation of the measures designed to conserve and manage straddling fish stocks and highly migratory fish stocks.

Following the entry into force of the Convention, the *International Sea-Bed Authority* has been established in Kingston, Jamaica, and the *International Tribunal for the Law of the Sea* has been established in Ham-

burg (see Secretariats, below). The members of the Tribunal were elected at the Meeting of the States Parties on 1 August 1996 and were sworn in by the Secretary-General of the UN at a ceremonial inauguration on 18 October 1996 in Hamburg. On 24 May 1999 the States Parties filled the seats of seven of the 21 judges whose terms of office expire on 1 October 1999.

The Convention provides for the establishment of the *Commission on the Limits of the Continental Shelf (CLCS)*, which is entrusted with making recommendations to coastal States on matters related to the establishment of the outer limits of their continental shelf where such limits extend beyond 200 nautical miles from the baselines (see also Decision-making bodies, below). Following the election of the 21 members of the CLCS on 13 March 1997 by the Meeting of States Parties, the CLCS commenced functioning in June 1997; it held its second session in September 1997, its third in May 1998, and its fourth in August–September 1998. At its fifth session in May 1999 the Commission adopted by consensus the Scientific and Technical Guidelines of the Commission on the Limits of the Continental Shelf, which are aimed at assisting coastal states in preparing submissions regarding their claims to extended continental shelves. The Commission will deal with annex II to the Guidelines at its sixth session, scheduled for 30 August–3 September 1999.

Co-ordination with related instruments
The provisions of UNCLOS relating to the protection and preservation of the marine environment are further developed in a large number of global and regional instruments. A comprehensive list of such instruments has been compiled by the Division for Ocean Affairs and the Law of the Sea of the UN Office of Legal Affairs and was published in *Multilateral Treaties: A Reference Guide to Multilateral Treaties and Other International Instruments related to the United Nations Convention on the Law of the Sea* (revised and updated as of 31 December 1996).

Among the most relevant instruments at the global and regional level are:
• *International Convention for the Prevention of Pollution from Ships, 1973, as modified by the Protocol of 1978 relating thereto (MARPOL 73/78)* (see this section), and related International Maritime Organization (IMO) instruments on pollution from ships;
• *Convention on the Prevention of Marine Pollution by Dumping of Wastes and Other Matter (London Convention 1972)* and the *1996 Protocol to the London Convention 1972* (see this section);
• *Global Programme of Action for the Protection of the Marine Environment from Land-Based Activities*, Washington, DC, 1995;
• *Convention on Biological Diversity (CBD)*, 1992 (see this section);
• numerous regional instruments on protection of the marine environment, relating

to different sources of marine pollution, co-operation on combating pollution incidents, and protection of marine areas and species (see this section).

Secretariats

Queries related to the Secretariat of the Convention itself and/or the Secretariat of the CLCS should be directed to:
Division for Ocean Affairs and the Law of the Sea,
Office of Legal Affairs,
DC2-0450,
United Nations,
New York, NY 10017,
USA
Telephone: +1-212-963-3951/3969
Telefax: +1-212-9635847
E-mail: doalos@un.org

Director
Mr Ismat Steiner.

Information Officer
Ms Gabrielle Goettsche-Wanli.

Number of staff
For the years 1998–9, budgetary provisions have been made for 17 professionals and ten general service staff.

International Sea-Bed Authority (ISBA),
14-20 Port Royal Street,
Kingston,
Jamaica
Telephone: +809-9229105
Telefax: +809-9220195
E-mail: postmaster@isa.org.jm

Secretary-General
Mr Satya N. Nandan.

Number of staff
For 1999, budgetary provisions have been made for 19 professionals and 17 general service staff.

International Tribunal for the Law of the Sea (ITLOS),
Wexstrasse 4,
D-20354 Hamburg,
Germany
Telephone: +49-40-356070
Telefax: +49-40-35607245
E-mail: itlos@itlos.hamburg.de

President
Dr Thomas A. Mensah.

Vice-President
Dr Rüdiger Wolfrum.

Registrar of the Tribunal
Mr Gritakumar E. Chitty.

Number of staff
For 2000, budgetary provisions have been made for 13 professionals and 21 support staff.

Finance

Budget
Annual costs at the Division for Ocean Affairs and the Law of the Sea are approximately $US2,800,000, paid from the regular UN budget. Occasionally expert groups are supported from extra-budgetary resources.

The budget for the ISBA was $4,150,500 in 1997 and $4,703,900 in 1998, and is $5,011,700 in 1999, to be paid by the members of ISBA. Members agreed in 1998 to pay their contributions on the basis of the UN scale of assessment

The budget for the Tribunal was $5,767,169 in 1998, and is $6,983,817 in 1999 and $7,657,019 in 2000, paid by the Parties of UNCLOS.

Rules and standards

As regards the protection and preservation of the marine environment, States Parties must, *inter alia:*
• take all measures necessary to prevent, reduce, and control pollution of the marine environment from any source;
• assess the potential effects of planned activities on the marine environment and publish reports thereon;
• monitor the risks or effects of pollution and publish reports thereon;
• co-operate on a global or regional basis in formulating and elaborating international rules, standards, and recommended practices and procedures for the protection and preservation of the marine environment;
• give effect in national law to such adopted international rules, standards, practices, and procedures. For all sea-bed activities, i.e. pollution from sea-bed activities subject to national jurisdiction, pollution from activities in the Area, pollution by dumping, and pollution from vessels, international

rules and standards represent minimum standards. For all land-based activities, i.e. pollution from land-based sources and pollution from or through the atmosphere, national laws need take into account only international rules and standards;
• enforce national laws and regulations which give effect to applicable international rules and standards. While the flag State (State of vessel registry) bears the primary responsibility for enforcement, the Convention also gives the coastal State (in the maritime zones of which the vessel transits) and the port State (State whose ports, including offshore terminals, the vessel visits) enforcement rights;
• adopt measures for the conservation of living resources in maritime areas under their national jurisdiction, and co-operate with each other in taking such measures for high-seas fisheries;
• resort to the compulsory binding procedures provided for in the Convention for the peaceful settlement of their disputes.

The Convention's provisions on the protection and preservation of the marine environment do not apply to a warship, naval auxiliary, or other vessel or aircraft being used, for the time being, only on government non-commercial service. However, flag States are urged to apply these provisions so far as is reasonable and practicable.

Monitoring/implementation

Review procedure
The basic objectives of the Convention in the areas of environment and development have been incorporated into most global and regional instruments. National laws have been extensively amended and further developed, and new laws adopted, mostly in conformity with the Convention. Several international and regional organizations have also taken measures to adjust their mandate and activities to the provisions of the Convention.

It is left to the Parties to devise the ways and means of individually or jointly pursuing systematic and *ad hoc* monitoring programmes, taking into account similar programmes already established by other treaties and organizations.

Particularly in the field of the conservation of living resources and the protection and preservation of the marine environment, implementation of the Convention depends to a great extent on the legislative and other activities of 'competent international organizations' in various degrees. Scientific and technical groups are organized on an *ad hoc* basis to advise on specific issues.

States are regularly informed of national, bilateral, regional, and global legislative and policy developments by means of the *Annual Report of the Secretary-General on Oceans and the Law of the Sea* to the UN General Assembly, the *Law of the Sea Bulletin*, and the *Law of the Sea Information Circular*.

Consequent upon the entry into force of the Convention and in recognition of the principle stated in the Convention that the problems of ocean space are closely interrelated and need to be considered as a whole, the UN General Assembly first explicitly confirmed in resolution 49/28 its role as the global forum competent to review and evaluate annually the implementation of the Convention and other developments relating to ocean affairs and the law of the sea. The General Assembly's consideration of all law of the sea and ocean affairs issues, including the marine environment and fisheries, under a single unified agenda item entitled 'Oceans and the Law of the Sea', as well as the monitoring of the implementation of the two Implementing Agreements, provides the opportunity for a comprehensive and integrated review of all developments and for recommending a coordinated approach to the implementation of the Convention and the Agreements, as well as for promoting compliance and follow-up on non-compliance in general terms.

In order to make the deliberations on oceans and the law of the sea in the General Assembly more effective, the seventh session of the Commission on Sustainable Development (see IGOs), held in New York from 19 to 30 April 1999, recommended the establishment of an open-ended informal consultative process under the aegis of the General Assembly. The consultative process would identify priority areas in ocean affairs, including the necessary actions to be taken. This goal would be achieved through a comprehensive, in-depth, and action-oriented discussion on ocean affairs held annually and open to all stake-holders such as states, UN programmes and agencies, and non-governmental organizations. This recommendation will be considered by the General Assembly during its 54th session and, if adopted, the consultative process is likely to take place for the first time in the year 2000.

Dispute-settlement mechanisms

Compulsory procedures entailing binding decisions: choice of the International Tribunal for the Law of the Sea, the International Court of Justice, Arbitration, or Special Arbitration.

The International Tribunal for the Law of the Sea has jurisdiction over any dispute concerning the interpretation or application of the provisions of the Convention or of an international agreement related to the purposes of the Convention which is submitted to it in accordance with the Convention. Under the *1995 Fish Stocks Agreement* and the *1996 Protocol to the London Convention 1972*, the Parties to a dispute can, if they so agree, submit their dispute to the Tribunal, irrespective of whether they are also Parties to the Convention.

The Tribunal has exclusive jurisdiction, through its Sea-Bed Disputes Chamber, with respect to disputes relating to activities in the international sea-bed area. These matters include disputes between States Parties concerning the interpretation or application of the provisions of the Convention, along with those of the Agreement relating to the Implementation of Part XI of the Convention, concerning the deep sea-bed area; and disputes between States Parties or a contractor and the ISBA. The Tribunal has established the Chamber of Summary Procedure, the Sea-Bed Disputes Chamber, and two standing special chambers: the Chamber on Fisheries Matters and the Chamber on the Marine Environment.

Decision-making bodies

Political

• *The UN General Assembly.* In 1994 the UN General Assembly decided that it was the global institution with the competence to undertake an annual consideration and review and evaluation of the implementation of the Convention and other developments relating to ocean affairs and the law of the sea. To facilitate a comprehensive and integrated review of all developments under the Convention and those taking place under other instruments and processes relating to the implementation and further development of the provisions of the Convention, and in order to promote a coordinated approach to implementation at the global, regional, and national level, the General Assembly has since 1994 consolidated all agenda items dealing with issues relating to oceans affairs and the law of the sea under a single item, 'Oceans and the

Law of the Sea'. The Assembly adopts annually a resolution on oceans and the law of the sea, as well as one resolution on fisheries issues dealing, on alternate years, with the implementation of the 1995 fish stocks Agreement, as well as on other fisheries issues such as large-scale pelagic drift-net fishing, unauthorized fishing in zones of national jurisdiction and on the high seas, and fisheries' by-catch and discards. States are called upon in these resolutions to take certain action. The Assembly reviews biennially the implementation of the *1995 Fish Stocks Agreement*.

• *The Meeting of States Parties.* The Convention provides for the convening of meetings of States Parties by the Secretary-General when he considers it necessary. Such meetings can also be convened when a majority of the States Parties request it, provided that a meeting is not already scheduled to be held within six months of the request. Since the entry into force of the Convention, nine meetings have been convened to deal primarily with organizational matters relating to the establishment of the Tribunal, the election of the members of the Tribunal, the consideration and adoption of the budget of the Tribunal, and the election of the members of the CLCS. The Meeting of States Parties is an independent forum with decision-making powers. Its future role in dealing with questions of implementation of the Convention, as well as its role in reviewing ocean and law of the sea issues, is currently under consideration.

• *The International Sea-Bed Authority (ISBA).* The ISBA is the institution through which Parties to the Convention organize and control activities in an international sea-bed area beyond the limits of national jurisdiction, particularly with a view to administering the resources of that area. The functions, membership, and management of the Authority are affected by the Agreement on the Implementation of Part XI of the Convention (see Affiliated instruments and organizations, above). The Authority functions through three main organs: the Assembly, the supreme organ, which consists of all members of the Authority; the Council, the executive organ, with limited membership comprising 36 members; and the Legal and Technical Commission, comprising 21 members, which assists the Council by making recommendations. The Agreement has also established a Finance Committee of 15 members, to make recommendations to the Assembly and the Council on financial matters, inluding the budget of the Authority. In addition, the Authority has a Secretariat (see Secretariats, above), headed by a Secretary-General, which performs all functions entrusted to him by the organs of the Authority.

The International Tribunal for the Law of the Sea. The Tribunal was established by the Convention for the peaceful settlement of disputes (see above). Through its Sea-Bed Disputes Chamber it also has jurisdiction to provide advisory opinions at the request of the Assembly or the Council of the ISBA on legal questions arising within the scope of their activities. It is composed of 21 judges elected by States Parties to the Convention from among persons with recognized competence in the field of the law of the sea and representing the principal legal systems of the world. The first election was held in August 1996. The members of the Tribunal elect a President and a Vice-President, whose term of office shall be three years. The Tribunal also appoints its Registrar and other officers of the Registry as may be necessary. The President of the Tribunal, as well as the Registrar, reside at the seat of the Tribunal.

Scientific/technical
• *The Secretariat.* With a view to assisting the UN General Assembly in its annual consideration, review, and evaluation of developments pertaining to the implementation of the Convention, as well as other developments relating to ocean affairs and the law of the sea, the Secretary-General is called upon to report on such developments annually to the Assembly. In its resolution 49/28, the Assembly further clarified the nature and scope of the functions of the Secretary-General, including his responsibility of providing information, advice, and assistance to States and international organizations in the better understanding of the Convention, its wider acceptance, uniform and consistent application, and effective implementation.

The Convention also calls on the Secretary-General to perform various duties, among them that of depositary of the Convention and of charts or lists of geographical co-ordinates of baselines and outer limit lines of various maritime zones. The good offices of the Secretary-General were used to resolve the outstanding problems with provisions on the international sea-bed area which impeded universal acceptance of the Convention as a whole. The Division for Ocean Affairs and the Law of the Sea fulfils the responsibilities entrusted to the Secretary-General. It functions as the secretariat of the Convention and also services the meetings of States Parties and those of the CLCS.

• *The Commission on the Limits of the Continental Shelf (CLCS).* The CLCS is composed of 21 members who are experts in the field of geology, geophysics, or hydrography, elected by States Parties to this Convention from among their nationals who serve in their personal capacities, having due regard to the need to ensure equitable geographical representation. The members are elected for five years and may be re-elected in accordance with Annex II, Article 2(4), of the Convention. The Division for Ocean Affairs and the Law of the Sea serves as the Secretariat of the CLCS (see Secretariats, above)

The CLCS shall consider the data and other material submitted by coastal States concerning the outer limits of the continental shelf in areas where those limits extend beyond 200 nautical miles, make recommendations, and provide scientific and technical advice.

Publications

• *Report of the Secretary-General on Oceans and the Law of the Sea*, submitted annually to the General Assembly under the item 'The Law of the Sea';
• *The Law of the Sea Bulletin* contains the texts of relevant national legislation and treaties, as well as other information on the law of the sea, as soon as they are available. Published three or four times a year;
• *Law of the Sea Information Circular.*

Other Law of the Sea publications include collections and analyses of national legislation, legislative histories of Convention provisions, bibliographies, and expert advice on special issues such as baselines, maritime delimitation, exclusive economic zones, high-seas fisheries, continental shelf, and marine scientific research.

Sources on the Internet

Related to the Convention itself, the Tribunal, and CLCS:
<http://www.un.org/Depts/los>
Related to ISBA:
<http://www.isa.org.jm>

Convention for the Protection of the Marine Environment of the

North-East Atlantic (OSPAR Convention)

Objectives
• to safeguard human health and to conserve marine ecosystems and, when practicable, to restore marine areas which have been adversely affected;
• to take all possible steps to prevent and eliminate pollution and enact the measures necessary to protect the sea area against the adverse effects of human activities.

Scope
Legal scope
Open to Parties to the former Oslo Convention or the Paris Convention (see below), any other coastal state bordering the maritime area (see below), any state located upstream on watercourses reaching the maritime area, or any regional economic integration organization having a member state to which the above paragraphs refer.

Geographic scope
Regional. The maritime area covers the north-east Atlantic (westwards to the east coast of Greenland and southwards to the Strait of Gibraltar), including the North Sea, and comprises the internal waters and the territorial sea of the Contracting Parties, the sea beyond and adjacent to the territorial sea under the jurisdiction of the coastal state to the extent recognized by international law, and the high seas, including the bed and subsoil thereof.

Time and place of adoption
22 September 1992, Paris.

Entry into force
25 March 1998. The Convention replaces the Convention for the Prevention of Marine Pollution by Dumping from Ships and Aircraft (Oslo Convention), adopted on 15 February 1972 in Oslo, which entered into force on 6 April 1974, and the Convention for the Prevention of Marine Pollution from Land-based Sources (Paris Convention), adopted on 4 June 1974 in Paris, which entered into force on 6 May 1978.

Status of participation
16 Parties, including the European Union, by 31 May 1999. No Signatories without ratification, acceptance, or approval.

The French Government acts as depositary.

Affiliated instruments and organizations
The different sources of pollution are dealt with in separate annexes:
• *Annex I, On the Prevention and Elimination of Pollution from Land-based Sources*;
• *Annex II, On the Prevention and Elimination of Pollution by Dumping or Incineration.* This Annex includes a moratorium on the dumping of low- and intermediate-level radioactive substances, including wastes, in the north-east Atlantic, which was imposed for 15 years from 1 January 1993. Once the moratorium expires, nations wishing to dump such waste may be allowed to do so only if they prove that a less dangerous disposal method cannot be found. If no request for dumping is made, the moratorium will be extended for a further ten years;
• *Annex III, On the Prevention and Elimination of Pollution from Offshore Sources*;
• *Annex IV, On the Assessment of the Quality of the Marine Environment*;
• *Annex V, On the Protection and Conservation of the Ecosystems and Biological Diversity of the Maritime Area.* Adopted on 24 July 1998. No ratifications by 1 May 1999. Enters into force once it has been ratified by at least seven Contracting Parties.

Co-ordination with related instruments
The OSPAR Commission (see Decision-making bodies, below) works with other regional seas conventions, such as the 1974 Helsinki Convention, the Barcelona Convention, the Convention on Long-Range Transboundary Air Pollution (see this section), and bodies such as IMO and ICES (see IGOs).

The declarations of the ministerial-level North Sea Conferences have laid down principles and targets for the reduction of marine pollution in the North Sea, including dumping. Some of these have been implemented within the framework of the former Oslo and Paris conventions. Recommendations and all other agreements adopted under the former Oslo and Paris conventions will continue to be applicable, unaltered in their legal nature, unless they are terminated by new measures adopted under the OSPAR Convention.

Secretariat
OSPAR Secretariat,
New Court,
48 Carey Street,
London WC2A 2JQ,
United Kingdom
Telephone: +44-171-2429927
Telefax: +44-171-8317427
E-mail: secretariat@ospar.org

Executive Secretary
Mr Ben van de Wetering.

Number of staff
Five executive staff members and seven assistants (May 1999).

Finance
Budget
The total budget was £849,944 in 1998 and is £850,032 in 1999.

Rules and standards
The Contracting Parties shall apply:
• the *precautionary principle*: that is, that preventive measures are taken when there is reason to believe that substances or energy introduced, directly or indirectly, into the marine environment may create hazards to human health, harm living resources and marine ecosystems, damage amenities, or interfere with other legitimate uses of the sea even when there is no conclusive evidence of a causal relationship between inputs and their effects;
• the *polluter pays principle*: by virtue of which costs of pollution prevention, control, and reduction measures shall be borne by the polluter.

In implementing the Convention, Parties shall adopt programmes and measures containing, where appropriate, time-limits for their completion, which take full account of the use of the best available technology

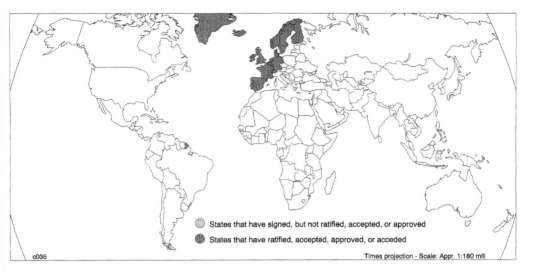

States that have signed, but not ratified, accepted, or approved

States that have ratified, accepted, approved, or acceded

c035   Times projection - Scale: Appr. 1:180 mill

(BAT) and best environmental practice (BEP) designed to prevent and eliminate pollution to the fullest extent.

Contracting Parties shall take, individually and jointly, all possible steps to prevent and eliminate pollution:
• from land-based sources, in particular as provided for in Annex I;
• by dumping or incineration of wastes or other matter, in particular as provided for in Annex II;
• from offshore sources, in particular as provided for in Annex III.
The Parties shall, in particular, as provided for in Annex IV:
• undertake and publish at regular intervals joint assessments of the quality status of the marine environment and of its development, for the marine area, or for regions or subregions thereof;
• include in such assessments both an evaluation of the effectiveness of the measures taken and planned for the protection of the marine environment and the identification of priorities for action.

Monitoring/implementation

Review procedure
The Parties shall report to the Commission at regular intervals on:
• the legal, regulatory, or other measures taken by them for the implementation of the provisions of the Convention and of decisions and recommendations adopted thereunder, including in particular measures

taken to prevent and punish conduct in contravention of those provisions;
• the effectiveness of the measures referred to above;
• problems encountered in the implementation of the provisions referred to above.
The Commission shall:
• on the basis of the reports submitted by the Parties, assess their compliance with the Convention and the decisions and recommendations adopted thereafter;
• when appropriate, decide upon and call for steps to bring about full compliance with the Convention, and decisions adopted thereunder, and promote the implementation of recommendations, including measures to assist a Party to carry out its obligations.

The relevant specialist subsidiary body of the Commission, and subsequently the Commission itself (which includes NGO observers), reviews data or information in the national reports. These reviews are public and the Secretariat of the Commission distributes lists of such reviews.

The Commission is preparing a series of quality status reports to cover the maritime area of the Convention. Five regional quality status reports (rQSRs) will be synthesized into one holistic quality status report, the QSR 2000. The quality status reports will be used as a basis for optimizing ocean management in pursuit of the main aims of the Convention, in reducing contaminant inputs, and for ensuring the sustainable ex-

ploitation of marine resources. The reports are due for publication in 1999 and 2000.

Decision-making bodies

Political
The OSPAR Commission, with representatives of each of the Parties, is the governing body and meets at least annually, sometimes at ministerial level. (The next ministerial meeting will be held in 2003). The quorum for meetings shall be three-quarters of the Parties.

The Commission may unanimously decide to admit any state which is not a Party to the Convention, any international governmental organization, and any non-governmental organizations to be represented by observers at its meetings, or at meetings of its subsidiary bodies.

Scientific/technical
• Assessment and Monitoring Committee (ASMO) and its five working groups;
• Programmes and Measures Committee (PRAM) and its four working groups.

Publications

Annual reports. Lists of OSPAR Commission publications are available through the Internet site (see below) or on demand from the secretariat.

Sources on the Internet

<http://www.ospar.org>

Convention on the Protection of the Marine Environment of the Baltic Sea Area (1974 Helsinki Convention)

Objectives

To take all appropriate measures, individually or by means of regional co-operation, to prevent and abate pollution and to protect and enhance the marine environment of the Baltic Sea area.

Scope

Legal scope
Restricted to the Baltic Sea states which participated in the 1974 Helsinki Conference. Others upon invitation by all the Contracting Parties. Membership open explicitly to the European Community (EC).

Geographic scope
Regional. The Convention covers the Baltic Sea proper, with the Gulf of Bothnia, the Gulf of Finland, and the entrance to the Baltic Sea. Internal waters are not included.

Time and place of adoption

22 March 1974, Helsinki.

Entry into force

3 May 1980.

Status of participation

Ten Parties, including the European Community, by 15 April 1999. No Signatories without ratification, acceptance, or approval.

Affiliated instruments and organizations

Annexes contain detailed operational obligations on substances to be controlled and form an integral part of the Convention.

Co-ordination with related instruments
Upon entry into force of the *Convention on the Protection of the Marine Environment of the Baltic Sea Area (1992 Helsinki Convention)* (see this section), this 1974 Helsinki Convention shall cease to apply.

The provisions concerning the prevention of pollution from ships follow closely the International Convention for the Prevention of Pollution from Ships, 1973, as modified by the Protocol of 1978 relating thereto (MARPOL 73/78) (see this section), where the Baltic Sea area is designated as a 'special area'

whereby far-reaching prohibitions and restrictions on the discharge of ship-generated wastes apply.

Secretariat

Helsinki Commission (HELCOM),
Katajanokanlaituri 6 B,
FIN-00160 Helsinki,
Finland
Telephone: +358-9-6220220
Telefax: +358-9-62202239
E-mail: helcom@helcom.fi

Chairman
Mr Pekka Jalkanen (until end of June 2000).

Executive Secretary
Mr Mieczyslaw Ostojski.

Number of staff
Six professionals and seven support staff (April 1999).

Finance

The income to the budget originates in principle from equal contributions from the Contracting Parties other than the European Community (which contributes 2.5 per cent of the administrative costs), as well as an extra contribution by Finland as the host country. In 1993 a special decision for a transition period of a maximum of three years, and in 1997 for the next five years, was taken concerning the system of sharing the contributions.

Budget
The administrative core budget was approximately FIM10.7 million for 1997/8 and 10.5 million for 1998/9, and is 9.7 million for 1999/2000.

Rules and standards

The Parties are committed:
• to prevent and control pollution from various sources, including pollution from land-based sources, from disposal of wastes at sea by ships or through dumping, and from seabed activities;
• to counteract the introduction of hazardous substances into the Baltic Sea as specified by Annex 1;
• to combat spillages of oil or other harmful substances according to Annex 6 in order to

eliminate or minimize pollution of the Baltic Sea area.

The commitments imposed on the Parties are normally discharge limit values and operational requirements.

Monitoring/implementation

Review procedure
Compliance is controlled by means of obligatory reporting according to a unified procedure, as well as by regular pollution load compilation projects and emission inventories.

Parties also report according to unified reporting formats on the progress and measures in their respective countries regarding implementing HELCOM Recommendations (see below). The reports are private, but a compiled report was available in March 1998. No information is available on the number of national reports submitted.

The appropriate national authorities are obliged to inform the Commission of the quantity, quality, and method of discharge of substances listed in Annex 2, in respect of land-based pollution.

Only dumping of dredged spoils is permitted, and such dumping activities, as well as emergency dumping, are also reported to the Commission.

The Parties are required to develop and apply a system for receiving, channelling, and dispatching reports on significant spillages of oil or other harmful substances.

The Parties must also provide information to the other Parties about their national organizations and regulations on combating pollution at sea by oil.

The work of the Commission and its subsidiary bodies is focused on implementing the relevant provisions of the Convention, as well as on promoting the compliance with their obligations of the Parties under the Convention's regime.

Among the intergovernmental organizations participating in the work of the Commission as observers are the International Atomic Energy Agency (IAEA), International Council for the Exploration of the Sea (ICES), International Maritime Organization (IMO), UN Environment Programme (UNEP), World Health Organization (WHO), World

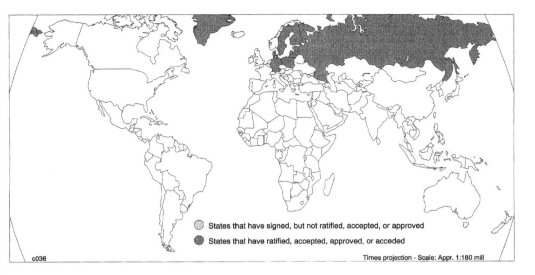

States that have signed, but not ratified, accepted, or approved

States that have ratified, accepted, approved, or acceded

c036

Times projection - Scale: Appr. 1:180 mill

Meteorological Organization (WMO) (see IGOs), Agreement on the Conservation of Small Cetaceans in the Baltic and North Seas (ASCOBANS) (see Convention on the Conservation of Migratory Species of Wild Animals, this section), OSPAR Commission (see this section), Intergovernmental Oceanographic Commission (IOC), International Baltic Sea Fishery Commission (IBSFC), UN Economic Commission for Europe (UN/ECE), and Social Development Fund of the Council of Europe (SDFCE). The governments of Belarus and Ukraine are also participating on these terms.

The following have also been granted observer status with the Commission: Baltic Farmers' Forum on Environment, Baltic Ports Organization (BPO), Baltic and International Maritime Council (BIMCO), Birdlife International, Coalition Clean Baltic (CCB), European Fertilizer Manufacturers' Association (EFMA), European Union for Coastal Conservation (EUCC), European Chlor-Alkali Industry (EURO CHLOR), European Dredging Association (EuDA), European Sea Ports Organization (ESPO), Greenpeace (see NGOs), International Council for Local Environmental Governments (ICLEI), International Network for Environmental Management (INEM), Oil Industry International Exploration & Production Forum (E&P Forum), Union of the Baltic Cities (UBC), Standing Conference of Rectors, Presidents, and Vice-Chancellors of the European Universities (CRE), and World Wide Fund For Nature (WWF) (see NGOs).

Public information on the operation and implementation of the decisions by the Commission is made available to governments through the triennial activities reports as well as the private reports from the annual Helsinki Commission meetings. The Secretariat does not distribute publication lists of such reviews.

Environmental monitoring programmes
The Parties have agreed upon several monitoring programmes by which data on airborne pollution, radioactive substances, and several determinants of the marine environment are collected.

Data and information-system programmes
The *Baltic Marine Environment Bibliography* has been produced by the Commission since the 1970s. An on-line version of this database, *BALTIC*, was established in 1987. It is available through the Technical Research Centre of Finland and is updated once per year.

Decision-making bodies
Political
The Helsinki Commission (HELCOM) is established according to the Convention. The offices of chairman and vice-chairman of the Commission rotate between the Parties in English alphabetical order every two years.

The decisions by the Commission are taken unanimously. Decisions on measures are most often given in the form of Recommendations to be implemented through appropriate national legislation.

Scientific/technical
The Commission has established four permanent Committees, one Task Force, and several permanent and *ad hoc* working groups as subsidiary bodies to the Commission itself or to the Committees. The permanent committees, all of which are composed of government experts and observers, are:
• Environment Committee (EC);
• Technological Committee (TC);
• Maritime Committee (MC);
• Combating Committee (CC);
• the HELCOM Programme Implementation Task Force (HELCOM PITF) was established in 1992 in order to initiate, co-ordinate, and monitor the implementation of the Baltic Sea Joint Comprehensive Environmental Action Programme (JCP). HELCOM PITF consists of members of all the Contracting Parties to the Helsinki Convention and Belarus, Norway, Slovakia, Ukraine, the European Bank for Reconstruction and Development (EBRD), the European Investment Bank (EIB), the Nordic Investment Bank (NIB), the Nordic Environment Finance Corporation (NEFCO), the World Bank (see IGOs), the International Baltic Sea Fishery Commission (IBSFC), and observers, mainly NGOs.

Publications
• *Baltic Sea Environmental Proceedings*;
• *HELCOM NEWS*.

Sources on the Internet
<http://www.helcom.fi>

Convention on the Protection of the Marine Environment of the Baltic Sea Area (1992 Helsinki Convention)

Objectives

To take all appropriate measures, individually or by means of regional co-operation, to prevent and eliminate pollution in order to promote the ecological restoration of the Baltic Sea area and the preservation of its ecological balance.

Scope

Legal scope
Restricted to the states and the European Community which participated in the 1992 Helsinki Conference. Others upon invitation by all the Contracting Parties.

Geographic scope
Regional. The Convention covers the Baltic Sea and the entrance to the Baltic Sea bounded by the parallel of the Skaw in the Skagerrak at 57° 44.43′N. Internal waters are included.

Time and place of adoption

9 April 1992, Helsinki.

Entry into force

Not yet in force. Enters into force two months after the deposit of the last instrument of ratification or approval by all Signatory States bordering the Baltic and by the European Community. Expected to enter into force in 1999.

Status of participation

Seven states and the European Community had ratified by 15 April 1999. Two Signatories without ratification, acceptance, or approval.

The government of Finland acts as depositary.

Affiliated instruments and organizations

The following attached *Annexes* form an integral part of the Convention:
• *Annex I*, on harmful substances to be controlled;
• *Annex II*, on criteria for the use of best environmental practice (BEP) and best available technology (BAT);
• *Annex III*, on criteria and measures concerning the prevention of pollution from land-based sources;
• *Annex IV*, on prevention of pollution from ships;
• *Annex V*, on exemptions from the general prohibition of dumping of waste and other matter;
• *Annex VI*, on prevention of pollution from off-shore activities;
• *Annex VII*, on response to pollution incidents.

The Baltic Marine Environment Protection Commission–Helsinki Commission (HELCOM), established pursuant to the 1974 Helsinki Convention, shall be the Commission for this Convention.

Co-ordination with related instruments
Upon entry into force of this Convention, the *Convention on the Protection of the Marine Environment of the Baltic Sea Area (1974 Helsinki Convention)* (see this section) shall cease to apply.

The provisions concerning the prevention of pollution from ships follow closely the International Convention for the Prevention of Pollution from Ships, 1973, as modified by the Protocol of 1978 relating thereto (MARPOL 73/78) (see this section), where the Baltic Sea area is designated as a 'special area' whereby far-reaching prohibitions and restrictions on the discharge of ship-generated wastes apply.

Secretariat

In accordance with the Resolution by the Diplomatic Conference, the present secretariat of the 1974 Convention will continue with its duties under the 1992 Convention.

Helsinki Commission (HELCOM),
Katajanokanlaituri 6 B,
FIN-00160 Helsinki,
Finland
Telephone: +358-9-6220220
Telefax: +358-9-62202239
E-mail: helcom@helcom.fi

Finance

Budget
The Commission shall adopt an annual or biennial budget when the Convention enters into force. The total amount of the annual or biennial budget, including any supplementary budget adopted by the Commission, shall be contributed by the Parties, other than the European Community (which contributes 2.5 per cent of the administrative costs), in equal parts, unless unanimously decided otherwise by the Commission.

Rules and standards

The Parties shall:
• apply the *precautionary principle*, i.e. take preventive measures when there is reason to assume that substances or energy introduced, directly or indirectly, may create hazards in the marine environment to human health, harm living resources and marine ecosystems, damage amenities, or interfere with other legitimate uses of the sea, even when there is no conclusive evidence of a causal relationship between inputs and their alleged effects;
• promote the use of best environmental practice (BEP) and best available technology (BAT). If the reduction of inputs, resulting from the use of BEP and BAT, as described in Annex II, does not lead to environmentally acceptable results, additional measures shall be applied;
• apply the *polluter-pays principle*;
• ensure that measurements and calculations of emissions from point sources to water and air, and of inputs from diffuse sources to water and air, are carried out in a scientifically appropriate manner in order to assess the state of the marine environment of the Baltic Sea area and ascertain the implementation of the Convention;
• use their best endeavours to ensure that the implementation of the Convention does not cause transboundary pollution in areas outside the Baltic Sea area. Furthermore, the relevant measures shall not lead to unacceptable environmental strains either on air quality and the atmosphere or on waters, soil, and groundwater. Nor shall they lead to unacceptably harmful or increasing waste disposal or to increased risks to human health.

Monitoring/implementation

Review procedure
Each Party shall implement the provisions of

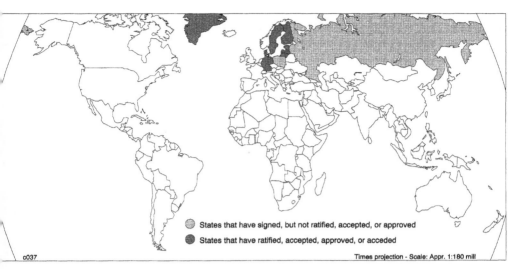

States that have signed, but not ratified, accepted, or approved

States that have ratified, accepted, approved, or acceded

c037

Times projection - Scale: Appr. 1:180 mill

he Convention within its territories, sea, and nternal waters through its national authori-ies.

Parties shall report to the Commission at egular intervals on:

a) the legal, regulatory, or other measures aken for the implementation of the provisions f the Convention, of its Annexes, and of rec-mmendations adopted thereunder;

b) the effectiveness of the measures taken to mplement the provisions referred to in para-raph (a) above;

c) problems encountered in the implemen-ation of the provisions referred to in para-raph (a) above.

On the request of a Party or of the Commis-ion, the Parties shall provide information on ischarge permits, emission data, and data n environmental quality, as far as available.

The Commission shall:

keep the implementation of the Convention nder continuous observation;

make recommendations on measures relat-ng to the purposes of the Convention;

keep under review the contents of the Con-ention, and its Annexes, and recommend mendments as may be required, including he lists of substances and materials as well s the adoption of new Annexes;

define pollution control criteria, objectives or the reduction of pollution, and objectives oncerning measures, particularly those de-cribed in Annex III;

receive, process, summarize, and dissemi-ate relevant scientific, technological, and tatistical information from available ources;

• seek the services of competent regional and other international organizations to collabo-rate in scientific and technological research, as well as other relevant activities pertinent to the objectives of the Convention.

Environmental monitoring programmes
The Parties have agreed upon several moni-toring programmes by which data on air-borne pollution, radioactive substances, and several determinants of the marine environ-ment are collected. The collection of data is performed according to agreed guidelines, and information is stored in database organi-zations which work on a consultancy basis for the Commission.

Data and information-system programmes
The *Baltic Marine Environment Bibliogra-phy* has been produced by the Helsinki Com-mission since the 1970s. An on-line version of this database, *BALTIC*, was established in 1987. It is available through the Technical Research Centre of Finland and is updated once per year. It contains all aspects of the Baltic Sea area, for example, ecology, fauna and flora, fisheries, hydrography, pollution, environmental impact, research planning, and administrative measures.

Decision-making bodies

Political
The Baltic Marine Environment Protection Commission–Helsinki Commission (HELCOM) is established for the purposes of the Convention. The offices of chairman and vice-chairman of the Commission rotate be-

tween the Parties in English alphabetical or-der every two years. Meetings of the Commis-sion shall be held at least once a year upon convocation by the chairman. Extraordinary meetings shall, upon the request of any Party endorsed by another Party, be convened by the chairman and held as soon as possible, and not later than 90 days after the submis-sion of the request.

Unless otherwise provided under the Con-vention, the Commission shall take its deci-sions unanimously. Each Party shall have one vote in the Commission.

The Commission may assume such func-tions as it deems appropriate to further the purposes of the Convention. The Commission appoints an executive secretary and such other personnel as may be necessary, and deter-mines the duties, terms, and conditions of service of the executive secretary.

The executive secretary will be the chief administrative official of the Commission and shall perform the functions that are nec-essary for the administration of the Conven-tion.

Scientific/technical
To be established.

Publications
• *Baltic Sea Environmental Proceedings*;
• *HELCOM NEWS*.

Sources on the Internet
<http://www.helcom.fi>

Conventions within the UNEP Regional Seas Programme

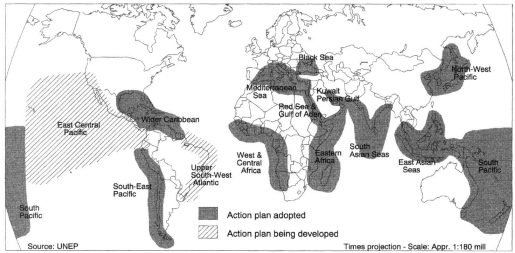

Source: UNEP   Times projection - Scale: Appr. 1:180 mill

Areas covered by the UNEP Regional Seas Programme

Objectives

The Regional Seas Programme of the United Nations Environment Programme (UNEP) was established in 1974 to tie coastal nations together in a common commitment to mitigate and prevent degradation of the world's coastal areas, inshore waters, and open oceans.

Each programme is tailored to the specific needs of its shore-line participants, but is made of similar components:
• an Action Plan for co-operation on the management, protection, rehabilitation, development, monitoring, and research of coastal and marine resources;
• an intergovernmental agreement of a framework convention embodying general principles and obligations (although in some instances there are no legally binding agreements);
• detailed protocols dealing with particular environmental problems, such as oil spills, dumping, emergency co-operation, and protected areas.

Funds for these activities come initially from UNEP and then from trust funds set up by the governments involved.

Scope

Legal scope
Open to coastal states in the respective regions. In some cases, upon invitation, open to other states and intergovernmental integration organizations.

Geographic scope
Regional. The conventions address the needs of particular regions as perceived by the governments concerned. Together with the regional conventions covering the North-East Atlantic (see the OSPAR Convention, this section) and the Baltic Sea area (see the 1974 and 1992 Helsinki conventions, this section), these conventions have a global scope.

There are so far nine regional conventions within the Regional Seas Programme, covering:
• the Black Sea;
• the wider Caribbean;
• the East African seaboard;
• the Persian Gulf;
• the Mediterranean;
• the Red Sea and the Gulf of Aden;
• the South Pacific;
• the South-East Pacific;
• the Atlantic coast of West and Central Africa.

Action Plans have been established for the East Asian Seas, the North-West Pa-cific, and the South Asian Seas. Action Plans are being discussed for the East Central Pacific and the Upper South-West Atlantic.

Programme co-ordination

The programme is under the overall co-ordination of the UNEP Water Branch, but it depends on the work of specialized agencies and co-operating intergovernmental organizations and centres dealing either with specific regions covered by the programme or with specific subjects common to most or all of the regions.

UNEP, Environmental Conventions Division,
PO Box 30552,
Nairobi,
Kenya
Telephone: +254-2-624011
Telefax: +254-2-624300
E-mail: jorge.illueca@unep.org

Director
Mr Jorge Illueca.

Sources on the Internet

<http://www.unep.org/unep/program/
natres/water/regseas/regseas.htm>

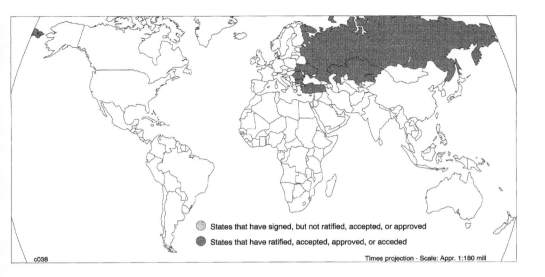

States that have signed, but not ratified, accepted, or approved

States that have ratified, accepted, approved, or acceded

c038   Times projection - Scale: Appr. 1:180 mill

Convention on the Protection of the Black Sea against Pollution

Objectives
To achieve progress in the protection of the marine environment of the Black Sea and in the conservation of its living resources.

Time and place of adoption
21 April 1992, Bucharest.

Entry into force
15 January 1994.

Status of participation
Six Parties by 31 March 1999. No Signatories without ratification, acceptance, or approval.

Affiliated instruments
• *Protocol on Protection of the Black Sea Marine Environment against Pollution from Land-Based Sources*, Bucharest, 21 April 1992. Entered into force on 15 January 1994. Same status of participation as the Convention;
• *Protocol on Co-operation in Combating Pollution of the Black Sea Marine Environment by Oil and Other Harmful Substances in Emergency Situations*, Bucharest, 21 April 1992. Entered into force on 15 January 1994. Same status of participation as the Convention;
• *Protocol on the Protection of the Black Sea Marine Environment against Pollution by Dumping*, Bucharest, 21 April 1992. Entered into force on 15 January 1994. Same status of participation as the Convention.

Secretariat
Black Sea Environmental Programme (BSEP),
Dolmbahce Sarayi II., Harakat Köskü,
80680 Besiktas,
Istanbul,
Turkey
Telephone: +90-212-227992-7/8/9
Telefax: +90-212-2279933
E-mail: blacksea@dominet.in.com.tr

Co-ordinator
Mr Radu Mihnea.

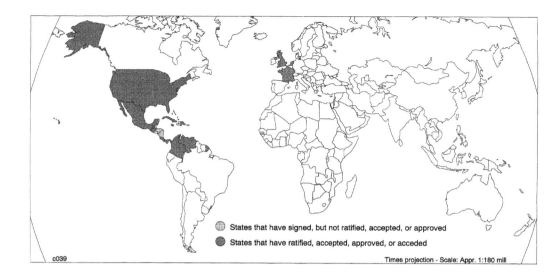

States that have signed, but not ratified, accepted, or approved

States that have ratified, accepted, approved, or acceded

c039

Times projection - Scale: Appr. 1:180 mill

Convention for the Protection and Development of the Marine Environment of the Wider Caribbean Region

Objectives
To achieve sustainable development of marine and coastal resources in the wider Caribbean region through effective integrated management that allows for increased economic growth.

Time and place of adoption
24 March 1983, Cartagena de Indias.

Entry into force
11 October 1986.

Status of participation
20 Parties by 27 May 1999. Three Signatories, including the European Community, without ratification, acceptance, or approval.

Affiliated instruments
• *Protocol Concerning Co-operation in Combating Oil Spills in the Wider Caribbean Region*, Cartagena de Indias, 24 March 1983. Entered into force on 11 October 1986. 20 Parties by 27 May 1999. Two Signatories without ratification, acceptance, or approval;
• *Protocol Concerning Specially Protected Areas and Wildlife to the Convention for the Protection and Development of the Marine Environment of the Wider Caribbean Region*, Kingston, 18 January 1990. (Not yet in force.) Seven states had ratified by 27 May 1999. Nine Signatories without ratification, acceptance, or approval. Nine ratifications or accessions required to enter into force.
• A third *Protocol on Marine Pollution from Land-Based Sources and Activities (LBSMP)* is near completion.

Secretariat
UNEP Regional Co-ordinating Unit for the Caribbean Environment Programme (CAR/RCU),
14–20 Port Royal Street,
Kingston,
Jamaica
Telephone: +1-876-922926-7/8/9
Telefax: +1-876-922-9292/0195
E-mail: uneprcuja@cwjamaica.com

Co-ordinator
Mr Nelson Andrade Colmenares.

Legal Officer
Mr Johan Bäverbrant.

Sources on the Internet
<http://www.cep.unep.org>

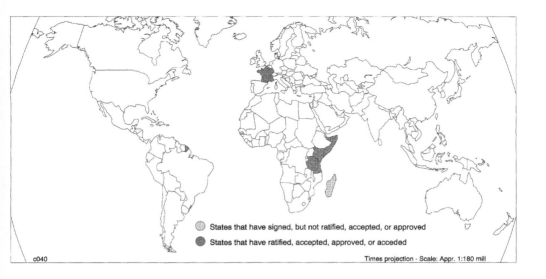

States that have signed, but not ratified, accepted, or approved

States that have ratified, accepted, approved, or acceded

c040   Times projection - Scale: Appr. 1:180 mill

Convention for the Protection, Management, and Development of the Marine and Coastal Environment of the Eastern African Region

Objectives
To protect and manage the marine environment and coastal areas of the Eastern African region.

Time and place of adoption
21 June 1985, Nairobi.

Entry into force
30 May 1996.

Status of participation
Six Parties by 20 June 1999. Two Signatories, including the European Community, without ratification, acceptance, or approval.

Affiliated instruments
• *Protocol Concerning Protected Areas and Wild Fauna and Flora in the Eastern African Region*, Nairobi, 21 June 1985. Entered into force on 30 May 1996. Same status of participation as the Convention;
• *Protocol Concerning Co-operation in Combating Marine Pollution in Cases of Emergency in the Eastern African Region*, Nairobi, 21 June 1985. Entered into force on 30 May 1996. Same status of participation as the Convention.

The first Conference of the Parties (COP) of the Convention in 1997 had established an *Ad Hoc* Committee of Legal and Technical Experts to review the Convention and the Protocol Concerning Protected Areas and Wild Fauna and Flora in the Eastern African Region. The Committee held its first review meeting in Mauritius from 15 to 18 December 1998. Its reports and recommendations will be submitted and discussed at the next COP in August 1999.

Secretariat
UNEP Regional Co-ordinating Unit for the Eastern African Action Plan (EAF/RCU), Sainte-Anne Island, Seychelles, PO Box 487 Victoria, Mahé, Seychelles
Telephone: +248-324525/224688
Telefax: +248-324525/224500/322945
E-mail: uneprcu@seychelles.net

Interim Co-ordinator
Mr Rolph Antoine Payet.

Sources on the Internet
<http://www.unep.org/unep/program/natres/water/regseas/eaf/eaf.htm>

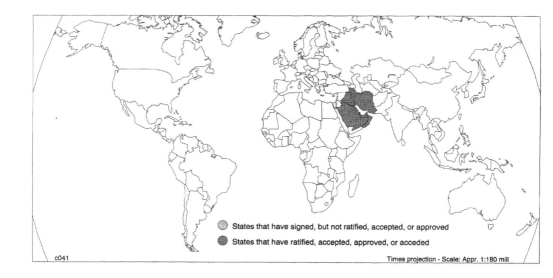

States that have signed, but not ratified, accepted, or approved

States that have ratified, accepted, approved, or acceded

c041

Times projection - Scale: Appr. 1:180 mill

Kuwait Regional Convention for Co-operation on the Protection of the Marine Environment from Pollution

Objectives
To prevent, abate, and combat pollution of the marine environment in the region.

Time and place of adoption
24 April 1978, Kuwait.

Entry into force
1 July 1979.

Status of participation
Eight Parties by 24 June 1999. No Signatories without ratification, acceptance, or approval.

Affiliated instruments
• *Protocol concerning Regional Co-operation in Combating Pollution by Oil and other Harmful Substances in Cases of Emergency*, Kuwait, 24 April 1978. Entered into force on 1 July 1979. Same status of participation as the Convention;
• *Protocol concerning Marine Pollution resulting from Exploration and Exploitation of the Continental Shelf*, Kuwait 1989. Entered into force on 17 February 1990. Same status of participation as the Convention;
• *Protocol for the Protection of the Marine Environment against Pollution from Land-Based Sources*, Kuwait 1990. Entered into force on 2 January 1993. Six Parties by 24 June 1999. One Signatory without ratification, acceptance, or approval;
• *Protocol on the Control of Marine Transboundary Movements and Disposal of Hazardous Wastes and other Wastes*, Tehran, 17 March 1998. Two ratifications by 24 June 1999. Four Signatories without ratification, acceptance, or approval.

Secretariat
Regional Organization for the Protection of the Marine Environment (ROPME), PO Box 26388, 13124 Safat, Kuwait
Telephone: +965-531214-0/3
Telefax: +965-53-35243/24172
E-mail: ropme@kuwait.net or ropme@qualitynet.net

Executive Secretary
Dr Abdul Rahman Al-Awadi.

Acting Co-ordinator
Dr Hassan Mohammadi.

Marine Emergency Mutual Aid Centre (MEMAC), PO Box 10112, Manama, Bahrain
Telephone: +973-274554
Telefax: +973-274551

Director
Captain A. M. Al-Jahani.

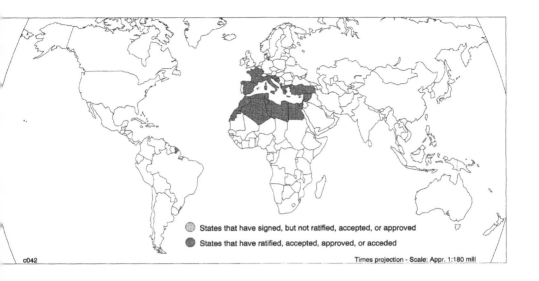

States that have signed, but not ratified, accepted, or approved

States that have ratified, accepted, approved, or acceded

c042

Times projection - Scale: Appr. 1:180 mill

Convention for the Protection of the Marine Environment and the Coastal Region of the Mediterranean (Barcelona Convention)

Objectives

To achieve international co-operation for a co-ordinated and comprehensive approach to the protection and enhancement of the marine environment and the coastal region of the Mediterranean area.

Time and place of adoption

16 February 1976, Barcelona.

Entry into force

12 February 1978.

Status of participation

21 Parties, including the European Community, by 31 March 1999. No Signatories without ratification or approval.

Affiliated instruments

Protocol for the Prevention of Pollution of the Mediterranean Sea by Dumping from Ships and Aircraft or Incineration at Sea (Dumping Protocol), Barcelona, 16 February 1976. Entered into force on 12 February 1978. Same status of participation as the Convention. An amendment was adopted in Barcelona on 10 June 1995. (Not yet in force.) Three acceptances by 31

March 1999. 18 Parties to the Protocol, including the European Community, had not yet accepted the amendment. The new title of the Protocol will be *Protocol for the Prevention and Elimination of Pollution of the Mediterranean Sea by Dumping from Ships and Aircraft or Incineration at Sea*;

• *Protocol Concerning Co-operation in Combating Pollution of the Mediterranean Sea by Oil and Other Harmful Substances in Cases of Emergency (Emergency Protocol)*, Barcelona, 16 February 1976. Entered into force on 12 February 1978. Same status of participation as the Convention;

• *Protocol for the Protection of the Mediterranean Sea against Pollution from Land-Based Sources and Activities (LBS Protocol)*, Athens, 17 May 1980. Entered into force on 17 June 1983. Same status of participation as the Convention. Amendments were adopted in Syracusa on 7 March 1996. (Not yet in force.) Two acceptances by 31 March 1999. 19 Parties to the Protocol, including the European Community, had not yet accepted the amendments;

• *Protocol Concerning Mediterranean Specially Protected Areas (SPA Protocol)*, Geneva, 3 April 1982. Entered into force on 23 March 1986. Same status of participation as the Convention. An amendment was adopted in Barcelona on 10 June 1995. (Not yet in force.) Two ratifications by 31 March 1999. 15 Signatories, including the European Community, without ratification, acceptance, or approval. The new title of the Protocol will be *Protocol Concerning Spe-*

cially Protected Areas and Biological Diversity in the Mediterranean (SPA and Biodiversity Protocol), Barcelona, 1995;

• *Protocol for the Protection of the Mediterranean Sea against Pollution Resulting from Exploration and Exploitation of the Continental Shelf and the Seabed and its Subsoil (Offshore Protocol)*, Madrid, 14 October 1994. (Not yet in force.) One ratification by 31 March 1999. Ten Signatories, including the European Community, without ratification, acceptance, or approval;

• *Protocol on the Prevention of Pollution of the Mediterranean Sea by Transboundary Movements of Hazardous Wastes and their Disposal (Hazardous Wastes Protocol)*, Izmir, 1 October 1996. (Not yet in force.) One ratification by 31 March 1999. Ten Signatories, including the European Community, without ratification, acceptance, or approval.

Secretariat

UNEP Co-ordinating Unit for the Mediterranean Action Plan (MEDU),
48 Vassileos Konstantinou Avenue,
GR-11635 Athens, Greece
Telephone: +30-1-7273100
Telefax: +30-1-725319-6/7
E-mail: unepmedu@unepmap.gr

Co-ordinator
Mr Lucien Chabason.

Sources on the Internet
<http://www.unepmap.org>

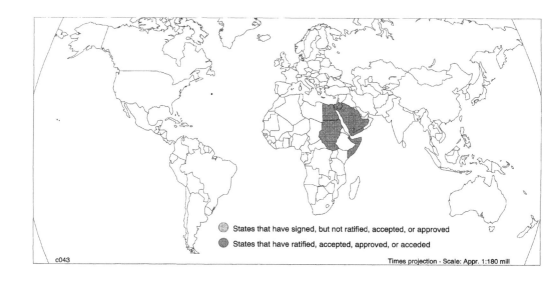

States that have signed, but not ratified, accepted, or approved
States that have ratified, accepted, approved, or acceded

c043   Times projection - Scale: Appr. 1:180 mill

Regional Convention for the Conservation of the Red Sea and Gulf of Aden Environment

Objectives
To ensure conservation of the environment of the Red Sea and Gulf of Aden by the promotion, on a regional basis, of environmental protection and natural resources management in the marine and coastal areas of the region.

Time and place of adoption
14 February 1982, Jeddah.

Entry into force
20 August 1985.

Status of participation
Seven Parties (plus Palestine, represented by the PLO) by 23 June 1999. No Signatories without ratification, acceptance, or approval.

Affiliated instruments
Protocol Concerning Regional Co-operation in Combating Pollution by Oil and Other Harmful Substances in Cases of Emergency, Jeddah, 14 February 1982. Entered into force on 20 August 1985. Same status of participation as the Convention.

Secretariat
Regional Organization for the Conservation of the Environment of the Red Sea and Gulf of Aden (PERSGA),
PO Box 53552,
Jeddah 21583,
Saudi Arabia
Telephone: +966-2-6514472
Telefax: +966-2-6514472
E-mail: persga@computec.com.bh

Secretary-General
Dr Nizar Ibrahim Tawfiq.

States that have signed, but not ratified, accepted, or approved
States that have ratified, accepted, approved, or acceded

c044   Times projection - Scale: Appr. 1:180 mill

Convention for the Protection of the Natural Resources and Environment of the South Pacific Region (SPREP Convention)

Objectives
To protect and manage the natural resources and environment of the South Pacific region.

Time and place of adoption
24 November 1986, Noumea.

Entry into force
22 August 1990.

Status of participation
12 Parties by 16 June 1999. Three Signatories without ratification, acceptance, or approval.

Affiliated instruments
• *Protocol Concerning Co-operation in Combating Pollution Emergencies in the South Pacific Region*, Noumea, 1986. Entered into force on 22 August 1990. Same status of participation as the Convention;
• *Protocol for the Prevention of Pollution of the South Pacific Region by Dumping*, Noumea, 1986. Entered into force on 22 August 1990. 11 Parties by 16 June 1999. Four Signatories without ratification, acceptance, or approval.

Secretariat
South Pacific Regional Environment Programme (SPREP),
PO Box 240,
Apia,
Western Samoa
Telephone: +685-21929
Telefax: +685-20231
E-mail: sprep@sprep.org.ws

Director
Mr Tamarii Peire Tutangata.

Legal Officer
Mr Andrea Volentras.

Sources on the Internet
<http://www.sprep.org.ws/>

States that have signed, but not ratified, accepted, or approved

States that have ratified, accepted, approved, or acceded

c045

Times projection - Scale: Appr. 1:180 mill

Convention for the Protection of the Marine Environment and Coastal Area of the South-East Pacific

Objectives
To protect the marine environment and coastal zones of the South-East Pacific.

Time and place of adoption
12 November 1981, Lima.

Entry into force
19 May 1986.

Status of participation
Five Parties by 31 March 1999. No Signatories without ratification, acceptance, or approval.

Affiliated instruments
• *Agreement on Regional Co-operation in Combating Pollution of the South-East Pacific by Hydrocarbons or Other Harmful Substances in Cases of Emergency*, Lima, 12 November 1981. Entered into force on 14 July 1986. Same status of participation as the Convention;
• *Supplementary Protocol to the Agreement on Regional Co-operation in Combating Pollution of the South-East Pacific by Hydrocarbons or Other Harmful Substances in Cases of Emergency*, Quito, 22 July 1983. Entered into force on 20 May 1987. Same status of participation as the Convention;
• *Protocol for the Protection of the South-East Pacific against Pollution from Land-Based Sources*, Quito, 22 July 1983. Entered into force on 21 September 1986. Same status of participation as the Convention;
• *Protocol for the Conservation and Management of the Protected Marine and Coastal Areas of the South-East Pacific*, Paipa, 22 September 1989. Entered into force on 17 October 1994. Same status of participation as the Convention;

• *Protocol for the Protection of the South-East Pacific against Radioactive Contamination*, Paipa, 21 September 1989. Entered into force on 25 January 1995. Four Parties by 31 March 1999. One Signatory without ratification, acceptance, or approval.

Secretariat
Comisión Permanente del Pacifico Sur (CPPS),
Coruña N3183 y Whymper,
Quito,
Ecuador
Telephone:+593-2-2343-31/35/36/57/58
Telefax: +593-2-234374
E-mail: ulisesmunaylla@porta.net

Secretary-General
Dr Fabian Valdivieso Eguiguren.

Advisor, Plan of Action
Mr Ulises Munaylla.

Sources on the Internet
<http://www.cpps.org>

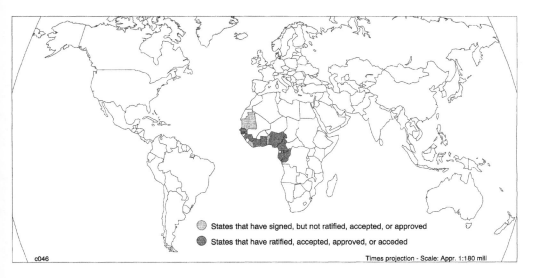

States that have signed, but not ratified, accepted, or approved

States that have ratified, accepted, approved, or acceded

c046

Times projection - Scale: Appr. 1:180 mill

Convention for Co-operation in the Protection and Development of the Marine and Coastal Environment of the West and Central African Region

Objectives
To protect the marine environment, coastal zones, and related internal waters falling within the jurisdiction of the states of the West and Central African region.

Time and place of adoption
23 March 1981, Abidjan.

Entry into force
5 August 1984.

Status of participation
Ten Parties by 31 March 1999. Three Signatories without ratification, acceptance, or approval.

Affiliated instruments
Protocol Concerning Co-operation in Combating Pollution in Cases of Emergency, Abidjan, 23 March 1981. Entered into force on 5 August 1984. Same status of participation as the Convention.

Secretariat
UNEP Regional Co-ordinating Unit for the Western and Central African Action Plan, c/o Department of Environment (WACAF/RCU),
Ministry of Housing, Quality of Life, and Environment,
PO Box 153,
Abidjan,
Côte d'Ivoire
Telephone: +225-210323
Telefax: +225-210495
E-mail: biodiv@africaonline.cu.ci

Acting Co-ordinator
Ms Nasséré Kaba.

Convention on the Conservation of Antarctic Marine Living Resources (CCAMLR)

Objectives

To conserve Antarctic marine living resources (the term 'conservation' includes rational use).

Scope

Legal scope
Open to all states and regional economic integration organizations.

Geographic scope
The Convention applies to the Antarctic marine living resources of the area south of 60°S latitude and to the Antarctic marine living resources of the area between that latitude and the Antarctic Convergence which form part of the Antarctic marine ecosystem.

Time and place of adoption

20 May 1980, Canberra.

Entry into force

7 April 1982.

Status of participation

29 Parties, including the European Community, by 30 April 1999, of which 23 form part of the Commission. No Signatories without ratification, acceptance, or approval.

Instruments of accession to be deposited with the government of Australia.

Affiliated instruments and organizations

Conservation measures (see Rules and standards below).

Co-ordination with related instruments
The Convention is an additional component instrument of the Antarctic Treaty system (see this section).

Secretariat

CCAMLR,
PO Box 213,
North Hobart,
Tasmania, 7002,
Australia
Telephone: +61-3-62310366
Telefax: +61-3-62349965
E-mail: ccamlr@ccamlr.org or

Executive Secretary
Mr Esteban de Salas.

Number of staff
Four professionals and 18 support staff (April 1999).

Finance

The Commission adopts its budget and that of the Scientific Committee at each annual meeting. Each member contributes to the budget. Two criteria form the basis for allocating the budget: the amount harvested and equal sharing. The financial activities are conducted in accordance with financial regulations adopted by the Commission and subject to annual external audit.

Budget
The administrative core budget was $A1.8 million in 1997 and $1.970 million in 1998, and is $2.004 million in 1999.

Special funds
Not applicable.

Rules and standards

The Commission for the CCAMLR is established with the following functions:
• to facilitate research into and comprehensive studies of Antarctic marine living resources and the Antarctic marine ecosystem (e.g. CCAMLR Ecosystem Monitoring Programme (CEMP) (see below));
• to compile data on the status of and changes in populations of Antarctic marine living resources;
• to ensure the acquisition of catch-and-effort statistics on harvested populations;
• to analyse, disseminate, and publish the information referred to above, and the reports of the Scientific Committee;
• to identify conservation needs and analyse the effectiveness of conservation measures;
• to formulate, adopt, and revise conservation measures on the basis of the best scientific evidence available;
• to implement a system of observation and inspection;
• to carry out such other activities as are necessary to fulfil the objective of the Convention;
• to publish and maintain a record of all conservation measures in force and notify them to all members.

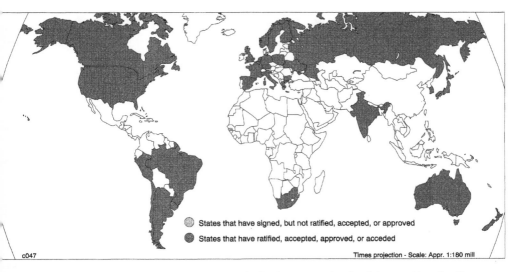

States that have signed, but not ratified, accepted, or approved

States that have ratified, accepted, approved, or acceded

c047

Times projection - Scale: Appr. 1:180 mill

Conservation measures shall become binding upon all members of the Commission 180 days after such notification. If a member, within 90 days, notifies the Commission that it cannot accept the conservation measure, in whole or in part, the measure shall not be binding upon that member.

Parties are required to take any steps necessary for the implementation of the decisions taken.

Monitoring/implementation

Review procedure
Each Party is required to inform the Commission of any activities in violation of the Convention that come to its knowledge. The Commission calls the attention of any State which is not a party to the Convention to activities of its nationals or ships which are felt to be in contravention of the objectives of the Convention.

National reports are submitted in yearly, monthly, or five-day periods, depending on the nature of the report. Some reports are private, others public. There is no independent verification of data or information.

Observations or inspections
A system of inspection to verify compliance with measures adopted by the Commission was established in 1990. Inspection implies the monitoring for compliance with measures in force. Each Party nominates inspectors who are authorized to conduct inspections during the seasons. A scheme of international scientific observation was established in

1992. Observation implies the presence of scientific observers on board fishing and research vessels throughout the voyage.

Environmental monitoring programmes
The CCAMLR Ecosystem Monitoring Programme (CEMP) is intended to detect changes in the condition, abundance, and distribution of species which are not commercially harvested, but which provide some indication of the dynamics and well-being of particular ecosystems. Information obtained from monitoring 'indicator species' can be taken into account in the regulation of human activity to ensure conservation principles of the Convention are met.

Trade measures
An integrated set of political and legal measures was agreed in 1997 and 1998 in order to combat illegal, unregulated, and unreported fishing for Patagonian toothfish (*Dissostichus eleginoides*) in the Convention area. The effectiveness of these measures is being kept under review. Further measures are being considered which relate to Port State control, as well as trade-related measures.

Dispute-settlement mechanisms
The Convention provides for settlement of disputes among Parties concerning the interpretation or application of the Convention to be resolved by peaceful means, including referral of such disputes by mutual agreement to the International Court of Justice or arbitration.

Decision-making bodies
Political
Parties to the Convention give effect to its objectives and principles through the annual Meetings of the Commission. Adoption of measures, by consensus, is the exclusive function of the Commission.

Scientific/technical
The Scientific Committee, composed of experts representing governments, shall: provide a forum for consultation and co-operation concerning the collection, study, and exchange of information; establish criteria and methods; analyse data; and formulate proposals. It provides the essential input into the Commission's deliberations. Decisions in the Committee are reached by consensus.

A Standing Committee on Finance and Administration and a Standing Committee on Observations and Inspection meet each year.

Publications
The secretariat publishes, in addition to different manuals:
• *CCAMLR Newsletter*;
• *Report of the Annual Meeting of the Commission*;
• *Conservation Measures in Force*;
• *Statistical Bulletin*;
• *CCAMLR Science*.

Sources on the Internet
<http://www.ccamlr.org>

International Convention for the Conservation of Atlantic Tunas (ICCAT)

Objectives

To co-operate in maintaining the population of tunas and tuna-like species found in the Atlantic Ocean and the adjacent seas at levels that will permit the maximum sustainable catch for food and other purposes.

Scope

Legal scope
Open to member States of the UN or any of its specialized agencies and to regional integration organizations.

Geographic scope
Regional. Applies to all waters of the Atlantic Ocean and adjacent seas, including the Mediterranean Sea. The longitude of 20°E is used, for scientific purposes, as the border between the Atlantic and the Indian Ocean.

Time and place of adoption

14 May 1966, Rio de Janeiro.

Entry into force

21 March 1969.

Status of participation

27 Parties, including the European Community, by 1 May 1999. Two Signatores without ratification, acceptance, or approval.

The Director-General of FAO (see IGOs) acts as depositary.

Affiliated instruments and organizations

A protocol enabling regional integration organizations to become Parties to the Convention was adopted in Paris on 10 July 1984 and entered into force on 19 January 1997.

A second Protocol was adopted in Madrid on 5 June 1992 to amend paragraph 2 of Article X of the Convention. (Not yet in force.) It enters into force after the deposit of instruments of ratification, acceptance, or approval of 75 per cent of those Contracting Parties which were Parties to the Convention at the time of the adoption of the Protocol, including all those classified as developed market-economy countries. 14 Contracting Parties to the Convention had ratified by 1 May 1999. 15 Contracting Parties to the Convention have not ratified, accepted, or approved. A special procedure was adopted for the entry into force of this Protocol which takes into account that the contributions of the countries with a developed market economy would increase, while those corresponding to developing countries would decrease.

Secretariat

International Commission for the Conservation of Atlantic Tunas (ICCAT),
Calle Corazon de Maria, 8 (6th floor),
E-28002 Madrid,
Spain
Telephone: +34-91-4165600
Telefax: +34-91-4152612
E-mail: peter.miyake@iccat.es
or papa.kebe@iccat.es

Executive Secretary
Dr Adolfo Ribeiro Lima.

Assistant Executive Secretary
Dr Peter M. Miyake.

Number of staff
Four professionals and 11 general service staff (July 1999).

Finance

Funding of the budget is by annual financial contributions made by the members of the Commission. Article X of the Convention defines the current procedures to calculate the country contributions to finance the Commission's budget.

Budget
The administrative core budget was ptas. 165,398,000 in 1997 and 175,797,000 in 1998, and is 198,700,000 in 1999.

Rules and standards

The Commission (see below) shall be responsible for the study of populations of tunas and tuna-like fishes and such other species exploited in tuna fishing in the Convention area as are not under investigation by another international fishery organization.

Studies include:
• research on the abundance, biometry, and ecology of the fishes;
• the oceanography of their environment;
• the effects of natural and human factors upon their abundance.

If, based on scientific findings, the Commission considers it necessary, it recommends to the Parties regulatory measures to ensure maximum utilization of the populations of fish. Such regulatory measures may include a minimum and/or maximum size of fish which may be caught, restrictions on the amount of catch and/or effort, etc.

Monitoring/implementation

Review procedure
The Commission implements the Convention by co-ordinating research, collecting and disseminating statistics and other information on the biology and ecology of tunas, and oceanographic conditions, and by analysing all this information regarding the stock status of fish.

Observations or inspections
Observation and inspection is the responsibility of each Contracting Party government.

Environmental monitoring programmes
The Subcommittee on Environment of the Standing Committee on Research and Statistics reviews environmental conditions in relation to the fisheries. There is also a Subcommittee on By-Catch, which reviews the status of tuna fishery by-catch of non-target species.

Data and information system programmes
The ICCAT Secretariat maintains a database for tunas and related species which in-

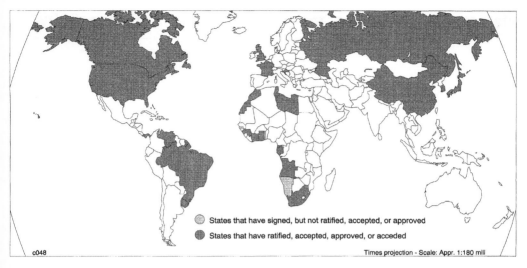

States that have signed, but not ratified, accepted, or approved
States that have ratified, accepted, approved, or acceded

c048

Times projection - Scale: Appr. 1:180 mill

cludes data on catches, fishing power, effort, biological information, and tagging releases and recoveries.

Trade measures

The Bluefin Tuna Statistical Document Programme implemented by the Commission requires all imports of bluefin tunas to Contracting Parties to be accompanied by a validated statistical document. The Commission passed a resolution to ensure the effectiveness of the ICCAT bluefin tunas conservation programmes, allowing the Commission to recommend the Contracting Parties to take non-discriminatory trade restrictive measures, consistent with their international obligations, on bluefin tuna products in any form, from any Party whose vessels have been fishing for Atlantic bluefin tunas in a manner which diminishes the effectiveness of the relevant conservation recommendations of the Commission on Atlantic bluefin tunas. Following this action plan, ICCAT recommended that Contracting Parties prohibit the import of any type of bluefin tuna product from Belize and Honduras (effective from August 1997) and from Panama (effective 1 January 1998).

Dispute-settlement mechanisms

None.

Decision-making bodies

Political

The International Commission for the Conservation of Atlantic Tunas (ICCAT) is established as a governing body and meets annually, usually in November. The Commission, on the basis of scientific evidence, makes recommendations for the maintenance of the populations of tunas and tuna-like fish.

Scientific/technical

The Commission works through four standing committees, comprised of experts representing governments and others:
• Standing Committee on Research and Statistics (SCRS);
• Standing Committee on Finances and Administration (STACFAD);
• Compliance Committee;
• Conservation and Management Measures Committee.

Four panels have also been established to consider and, if necessary, initiate regulatory measures on species covered by the Convention:
• Panel 1: Tropical tunas;
• Panel 2: Temperate tunas (North);
• Panel 3: Temperate tunas (South);
• Panel 4: Other species.

A Permanent Working Group for the Improvement of ICCAT Statistics and Conservation Measures was established in 1992 to review compliance, by non-contracting parties, of the regulatory measures recommended by the Commission.

Publications

The Commission publishes reports of findings, and up-to-date information is available through:
• a newsletter (periodically);
• *Biennial Report* (annually);
• *Statistical Bulletin* (annually);
• *Data Record* (annually);
• *Collective Volume of Scientific Papers* (3–4 volumes per year).

Sources on the Internet

<http://www.iccat.es/>

International Convention for the Regulation of Whaling (ICRW)

Objectives

To establish regulations for purposes of conservation and utilization of whale resources, and to serve as an agency for the collection, analysis, and publication of scientific information related to whales and whaling.

Scope

Legal scope
Open to all States. Not open to regional integration organizations.

Geographic scope
Global.

Time and place of adoption

2 December 1946, Washington.

Entry into force

10 November 1948.

Status of participation

40 Parties by 30 April 1999. No Signatories without ratification, approval, or acceptance.

Instruments of accession and withdrawal are to be deposited with the government of the United States of America.

Affiliated instruments and organizations

The *Schedule to the Convention*, adopted annually since 1949 at meetings of the International Whaling Commission (IWC) (see below), is an integral part of the Convention.

Its purpose is to set the specific conservation regulations applicable.

Co-ordination with related instruments
Although there are no formal mechanisms, Parties will be aware of related treaties and conventions, particularly the UN Convention on the Law of the Sea (UNCLOS) (see this section).

The Commission contributed to the elaboration of the 1984 UNEP–FAO Global Plan of Action for the Conservation, Management, and Utilization of Marine Mammals and has part of the responsibility for its implementation.

Secretariat

International Whaling Commission (IWC),
The Red House,
135 Station Road,
Impington,
Cambridge CB4 9NP,
United Kingdom
Telephone: +44-1223-233971
Telefax: +44-1223-232876
E-mail: iwcoffice@compuserve.com

Secretary
Dr Ray Gambell.

Number of staff
Three professionals and 13 support staff (April 1999).

Finance

The budget is financed mainly by contributions from Parties. There are no special provisions relating to the economic standing of governments, the formula for contributions being based largely on the degree of involvement, and including shares for membership, whaling activity, and size of delegation.

Budget
The annual actual budget was approximately £UK1,146,124 in 1997 and £1,167,560 in 1998, and is £1,323,968 in 1999. The administrative core budget was £833,700 in 1997 and £904,900 in 1998, and is £952,200 in 1999.

Special funds
The Commission allots part of its budget to a research fund for projects related to whales. The most important project has been the Comprehensive Assessment of Whale Stocks.

Rules and standards

The main duty of the Commission is to keep under review and revise as necessary the measures laid down in the Schedule to the Convention governing the conduct of whaling. These include measures:

• to provide for the complete protection of certain species of whales;
• to designate specified ocean areas as whale sanctuaries;
• to set the maximum catches of whales which may be taken in one season;
• to prescribe open and closed seasons and areas for whaling;

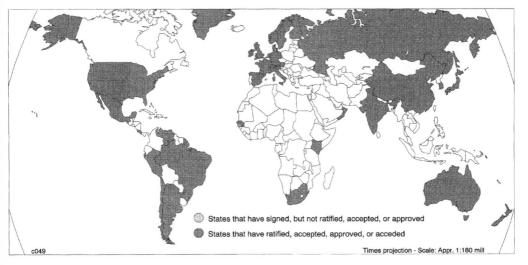

States that have signed, but not ratified, accepted, or approved

States that have ratified, accepted, approved, or acceded

c049   Times projection - Scale: Appr. 1:180 mill

• to fix size limits above and below which certain species of whales may not be killed;
• to prohibit the capture of suckling calves and female whales accompanied by calves;
• to require the compilation of catch reports and other statistical and biological records.

The Convention requires that amendments to the provisions of the Schedule with respect to the conservation and utilization of whale resources be based on scientific findings.

While the Commission generally acts by simple majority, amendment of the Schedule requires a three-quarter majority vote of those casting an affirmative or a negative vote.

The Convention also establishes certain criteria for amendments to the Schedule and provides for a system of notification which allows Parties 90 days after notification of amendments to register an objection. Under an objection, the relevant passages are not enforceable against the country in question.

The Commission agreed in 1982 to set a zero quota on all commercially exploited stocks for the 1986 coastal and 1985–6 pelagic seasons, and thereafter a so-called moratorium, which is still in force, and initiated a comprehensive assessment of whale stocks and the development of a management procedure that should have been finished by 1990. Five possible management procedures were developed by scientists within the Scientific Committee, one of which was recommended as a 'core' procedure and accepted by the Commission in 1991.

At the 1992 annual meeting the Commission adopted the specification developed by the Scientific Committee for the calculation of catch limits in a Revised Management Procedure for baleen whales. In 1994 the Commission accepted and endorsed the Revised Management Procedure for commercial whaling and associated guidelines for surveys and collection of data. However, it noted that work on a number of issues, including specification of an inspection and observer system, remained to be completed before the Commission would consider establishing catch limits other than zero. A comparable management scheme for aboriginal subsistence whaling is now being developed by the Scientific Committee.

In 1979 the Commission established the Indian Ocean north of 55°S as a whale sanctuary where commercial whaling is prohibited. This provision has been supported by the coastal states bordering the Ocean, both members and non-members of the IWC, and will be reviewed by the Commission at its annual meeting in 2002.

After detailed consideration of the legal, political, ecological, management, financial, and environmental issues, the Commission adopted the Southern Ocean sanctuary at the 1994 annual meeting. The purpose of the proposal was stated to be to contribute to the rehabilitation of the Antarctic marine ecosystem and the protection of all southern hemisphere species and populations of baleen and sperm whales on their feeding grounds. This would also link up with the Indian Ocean sanctuary to provide a large area within which whales would be free from commercial catching.

A major new development is the Commission's consideration of whale-watching as a sustainable use of cetacean resources. In 1993 the Commission invited Contracting States to undertake a preliminary assessment of the extent, and economic and scientific value, of whale-watching activities for consideration by a working group at the 1994 meeting. As a result the Commission has reaffirmed its interest in the subject, encouraged some scientific work, and in 1996 adopted objectives and principles for whale-watching, developed by the Scientific Committee.

With increasing awareness that whales should not be considered apart from the marine environment which they inhabit, and that detrimental changes may threaten whale stocks, the Commission decided that the Scientific Committee should give priority to research on the effects of environmental changes on cetaceans. The Scientific Committee examined this issue in the context of the revised management procedure (RMP) and agreed that the RMP adequately addressed such concerns. However, it went on to state that the species most vulnerable to such threats might well be those reduced to levels at which the RMP, even if applied, would result in zero catches. The Committee held two workshops, one on the effects of chemical pollutants in 1995 in Norway, and one on the effects of climate change and ozone depletion in 1996 in the USA, and further activities have followed to take these initiatives forward.

The Commission has endorsed the Scientific Committee's work on these issues and agreed to fund work to carry forward the recommendations specifically to design multidisciplinary and multinational research programmes in co-operation with other relevant organizations.

Aboriginal whaling for subsistence purposes is carried out by native peoples of Greenland, Bequia, Siberia, and Alaska, and the Commission and Scientific Committee are developing a Management Procedure specifically for such non-commercial operation. Catches for scientific purposes are taken by Japan. Norway has resumed commercial whaling under the objection procedure provided by the Convention and is setting its own national catch limits.

Monitoring/implementation

Review procedure
Parties are required to implement the regulations through internal legislation (copies of which are forwarded to the secretariat) and submit reports, as appropriate, on any infraction to the Commission. These reports are made public after submission to the Commission.

An International Observer Scheme was established in 1972 to encourage full and accurate reporting of commercial catches. The Convention requires reports on and penalties imposed for infractions. These reports are reviewed by the Infractions Subcommittee (see below) each year and are also made public after submission to the Commission.

In addition, the Aboriginal Subsistence Whaling Subcommittee and the Scientific Committee monitor and report on relevant matters. Following the 1986 ban on commercial whaling, only 'subsistence' and 'scientific' whaling data are required from six members, all of which have provided their reports. There is no independent verification of the data or information submitted.

Observations or inspections
Compliance with the commercial whaling regulations was monitored by national inspectors and international observers, and their reports and the data submitted were reviewed by the Infractions and Scientific Committee as appropriate (see above).

Trade measures
No provisions on trade measures to penalize Parties for non-compliance.

Dispute-settlement mechanisms
None.

Decision-making bodies

Political
The International Whaling Commission is established as a governing body and meets annually. It is composed of one member (commissioner) from each Contracting Party, who may be accompanied by experts or advisers. The delegates may include industry and other non-governmental representatives as well as scientific advisers. Non-member governments, intergovernmental organizations, and international non-governmental organizations may also attend meetings by invitation in an observer capacity.

Scientific/technical
The Commission works through three standing committees:
• Scientific Committee, composed of government experts and others;
• Technical Committee, composed of experts representing governments;
• Finance and Administration Committee, composed of experts representing governments.

The Scientific Committee reviews scientific information related to whales and whaling, the scientific programmes of the Parties, the scientific permits, and the scientific programmes for which the Parties plan to issue such permits.

In addition, several subcommittees are established, such as the Infractions Subcommittee and Aboriginal Subsistence Whaling Subcommittee.

Publications

The Commission publishes annual reports, a new *Journal of Cetacean Research and Management*, and special issues on whale science. It also holds and publishes catch and related data on whaling operations.

Sources on the Internet

<http://ourworld.compuserve.com/homepages/iwcoffice>

The Antarctic Treaty

Objectives

to ensure that Antarctica is used for peaceful purposes only;

to ensure the continuance of freedom of scientific investigation and international co-peration in scientific investigation in Antarctica;

to set aside disputes over territorial sovereignty.

Scope

Legal scope

The Antarctic Treaty was ratified by 12 Signatory States. In addition it is open for accession by any state which is a member of the UN, or by any other state which may be invited to accede to the Treaty with the consent of all the Contracting Parties whose representatives are entitled to participate in the meetings provided for under Article IX of the Antarctic Treaty (hereinafter: Consultative Parties and Consultative Meetings).

The Consultative Parties are currently made up of the 12 original Signatories, which retain the consultative status unconditionally, and of the 15 acceding states which have been acknowledged to the consultative status conditionally, during such times as they demonstrate their interest in Antarctica by conducting substantial research activity there, such as the establishment of a scientific station or the dispatch of a scientific expedition. There are also 17 non-Consultative Parties, i.e. states which acceded to the Treaty without acquiring consultative status.

Geographic scope

The Antarctic Treaty applies to the area south of 60°S.

Time and place of adoption

1 December 1959, Washington, DC.

Entry into force

23 June 1961.

Status of participation

44 Contracting Parties by 4 June 1999 (consisting of 27 Consultative Parties and 17 non-Consultative Parties).

Affiliated international instruments

The Antarctic Treaty system (ATS) provides the umbrella for a complex system of international instruments of importance for the environment. These include:

- the *Antarctic Treaty* itself (text in United Nations Treaty Series, vol. 402, 71);
- other treaties adopted on the basis of the Antarctic Treaty:

(a) *Convention for the Protection of Antarctic Seals*, adopted at London on 1 June 1972, entered into force on 11 March 1978. 16 Parties by 24 May 1999. One signatory without ratification or acceptance. (Text in United Nations Treaty Series, vol. 1080, 175; reprinted in *International Legal Materials*, 11 (1972), 251.);

(b) *Convention on the Conservation of Antarctic Marine Living Resources (CCAMLR)*, adopted at Canberra on 20 May 1980, entered into force on 7 April 1982. 29 Parties by 30 April 1999. (Text reprinted in *International Legal Materials*, 19 (1980), 837.) (See also this section.);

(c) *Protocol on Environmental Protection to the Antarctic Treaty (Madrid Protocol)*, with four Annexes (Annex I, *Environmental Impact Assessment*; Annex II, *Conservation of Antarctic Fauna and Flora*; Annex III, *Waste Disposal and Waste Management*; and Annex IV, *Prevention of Marine Pollution*), adopted at Madrid on 4 October 1991. (Text reprinted in *International Legal Materials*, 30 (1991), 1461.) The Protocol with Annexes I–IV entered into force on 14 January 1998 after the deposit of instruments of ratification, acceptance, approval, or accession by all 26 States which were Antarctic Treaty Consultative Parties at the date of the adoption of the Protocol. 28 Parties (27 Consultative Parties and 1 non-Consultative Party (Greece)) by 24 May 1999. Ten Signatories without ratification, acceptance, or approval. The Protocol supplements the Antarctic Treaty. The annexes form an integral part of the Protocol. Annexes additional to Annexes I–IV may be adopted; thus Annex V, *Area Protection and Management*, was adopted as an annex to Recommendation XVI–10 at the Sixteenth Consultative Meeting, held in Bonn, 7–18 Octo-

ber 1991. 22 Consultative Parties had accepted or approved Annex V by 24 May 1999. Four additional Consultative Parties must accept or approve it before it can enter into force;

- other international instruments which may be adopted on the basis of the Antarctic Treaty, and under separate treaties associated with the Antarctic Treaty:

(a) 'measures in furtherance of the principles and objectives of the Antarctic Treaty', earlier known as *recommendations* of the Antarctic Treaty Consultative Meetings (ATCMs), of which over 250 have been adopted to date. This category of instruments split into three by a decision of the Nineteenth Consultative Meeting (Seoul, May 1995): measures, decisions, and resolutions;

(b) measures adopted and in effect under separate treaties associated with the Antarctic Treaty (especially measures of the CCAMLR Commission);

(c) various *other instruments*, such as the decisions of Special Consultative Meetings, the results of Meetings of Experts, etc.

Co-ordination with related instruments

ATS has developed through the negotiation of additional component instruments (see above) rather than by a revision of the Antarctic Treaty itself. Part of this process has reference to regulations embodied in other international treaties such as the International Convention for the Prevention of Pollution from Ships, 1973, as modified by the Protocol of 1978 relating thereto (MARPOL 73/78) (see this section), relating to control of marine pollution in the Antarctic Treaty area.

Secretariat

ATS has no permanent secretariat. It operates primarily through annual ATCMs hosted in rotation by Consultative Parties. So far, 23 ATCMs have been held, with the latest in Lima, Peru, from 24 May to 4 June 1999. CCAMLR (see this section) has a permanent secretariat.

Information on ATS is available nationally from the relevant government department of the Contracting Parties. A recent list of national contact points for all Treaty Parties was published in US Department of

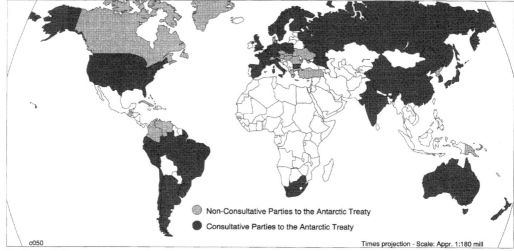

Non-Consultative Parties to the Antarctic Treaty

Consultative Parties to the Antarctic Treaty

c050   Times projection - Scale: Appr. 1:180 mill

The Antarctic Treaty

State, *Handbook of the Antarctic Treaty System*, 8th edn (Washington, DC, April 1994), 291–5. Pursuant to a resolution adopted at the 1998 ATCM, a host country of the Meeting is encouraged to establish a homepage on the Internet and to maintain it three months after the conclusion of a Meeting. Thus far, Norway and Peru, as host countries of the 1998 and 1999 ATCMs respectively, have maintained such home pages, making the official documentation of the Meetings publicly available upon their conclusion. A decision has also been adopted at the 1999 ATCM for the establishment of the Committee for Environmental Protection (CEP) homepage. (See Sources on the Internet, below.) In addition, information is available from the depositary government to the Antarctic Treaty:

Office of Oceans Affairs OES/OA,
Room 5805,
Bureau of Oceans and International Environmental and Scientific Affairs,
United States Department of State,
Washington, DC 20520-7818,
USA
Telephone: +1-202-6473262
Telefax: +1-202-6471106

International Affairs Officer
Harlan K. Cohen.

Up-to-date *scientific* information and bibliographical references are also available from:

Scientific Committee on Antarctic Research (SCAR),
c/o Scott Polar Research Institute,
University of Cambridge,
Lensfield Road,
Cambridge CB2 1ER,
United Kingdom
Telephone: +44-1223-336540
Telefax: +44-1223-336549
E-mail: execsec@scar.demon.co.uk
Internet: http://www.spri.cam.ac.uk/

Executive Secretary
Dr Peter D. Clarkson.

Keeper of Collections and Librarian
Mr William Mills.

Rules and standards

The Treaty imposes a wide range of obligations on Parties. These include prohibition of all military activities, nuclear explosions, and disposal of radioactive waste in Antarctica, as well as requirements to exchange and make freely available information resulting from scientific research activities.

There is an extensive set of binding conservation measures relating to marine living resources, including obligations to collect catch-and-effort statistics. All human activities are subject to detailed rules relating to: environmental impact assessment; conservation of native fauna and flora, including prohibitions on introduction of alien species; waste disposal and waste management; and prevention of marine

pollution. In addition, an extensive system of protected areas has been established.

Related provisions call for environmental monitoring (see Monitoring and implementation, below).

The Madrid Protocol commits the Parties to comprehensive protection of the Antarctic environment and its dependent and associated ecosystems and defines the Antarctic as a natural reserve devoted to peace and science. Building on the existing body of ATS instruments, the Protocol elaborates detailed, mandatory rules to ensure that activities in the Antarctic do not result in adverse environmental effects.

Monitoring and implementation

Review procedure
The various elements of the ATS make provision for the exchange of information of the activity of Parties in the Antarctic Treaty area.

The Protocol calls for annual exchange of information by each Party on what steps have been taken to implement the Protocol. There are also specific requirements under the individual components of the ATS, such as catch data and exploitation effort (see CCAMLR, this section).

Observations or inspections
The Antarctic Treaty accords to Consultative Parties rights of inspection of each other's stations, installations, and equipment in the area, to promote compliance. Observers are appointed by each Consultative

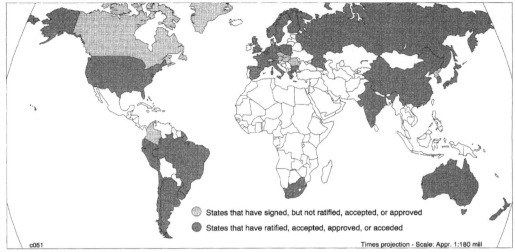

States that have signed, but not ratified, accepted, or approved

States that have ratified, accepted, approved, or acceded

c051

Times projection - Scale: Appr. 1:180 mill

Protocol on Environmental Protection to the Antarctic Treaty (Madrid Protocol)

Party. Both the CCAMLR and the Madrid Protocol build on and extend these provisions.

Dispute-settlement mechanisms
Both the Antarctic Treaty and the CCAMLR provide for a variety of peaceful means of dispute settlement, including a referral of disputes to the International Court of Justice.

The Madrid Protocol introduces compulsory procedures (at the request of any party to a dispute) for its dispute settlement, based on a choice of forum approach (either the International Court of Justice or the special arbitration tribunal, to be instituted in accordance with a schedule to the Protocol).

Decision-making bodies

Political
The Antarctic Treaty Consultative Meeting (ATCM) is the principal decision-making forum of the Antarctic Treaty. Meetings are held annually (every two years up to 1991), hosted in rotation by Consultative Parties. The ATCM adopts measures to regulate the activity in the area. Since 1983 non-Consultative Parties have been invited to attend ATCMs, though only Consultative Parties may take part in decision making.

Meetings are also attended regularly by the representatives of the Commission for the Conservation of Antarctic Marine Living Resources, the Scientific Committee on Antarctic Research (SCAR), and the Coun-

cil of Managers of National Antarctic Programmes (COMNAP), as observers. In addition, by invitation of the Consultative Parties, other inter- and non-governmental organizations, currently including the Antarctic and Southern Ocean Coalition (ASOC), the Intergovernmental Oceanographic Commission (IOC), the International Association of Antarctic Tour Operators (IAATO), the International Hydrographic Organization (IHO), the International Maritime Organization (IMO) (see IGOs), the Pacific Asia Travel Association (PATA), the UN Environment Programme (UNEP) (see IGOs), the World Meteorological Organization (WMO) (see IGOs), the IUCN – The World Conservation Union (see NGOs), and the World Tourism Organization (WTO), may designate experts to attend the ATCMs.

According to Article XII, the Antarctic Treaty opens the possibility for a special conference to review the operation of the Treaty. Such a conference may be convened at the request of any Consultative Party once the Treaty has been in force for 30 years (that is, after 23 June 1991). All Parties, not just Consultative Parties, have the right to participate in this conference.

Scientific/technical
Based on the Madrid Protocol, the Committee for Environmental Protection (CEP) was established at the 1998 ATCM, as an advisory body to the ATCM.

The Treaty and its various component instruments contain requirements that activities in the region be based on scientific advice. The work of SCAR, a committee of the non-governmental International Council of Scientific Unions (ICSU), forms an integral part of the input to decisions taken by the ATCMs. The Madrid Protocol also requires that environmental policies drawn up and adopted by the ATCM shall draw upon 'the best scientific and technical advice available'. The role of SCAR and COMNAP is crucial in this respect.

Publications

Treaty publications are available nationally from the relevant government department of the Parties. Extensive documentation is published by CCAMLR (see this section). In addition, SCAR produces scientific reports related to Antarctic research.

The latest (eighth) edition of the *Handbook of the Antarctic Treaty System* was published by the US Department of State in 1994. *SCAR Bulletin*, a quarterly publication of SCAR within *Polar Record*, the journal of Polar Publications at the Scott Polar Research Institute (see above), also publishes material from ATCMs.

Sources on the Internet

Related to ATCM:
<http://www.antartica-rcta.com.pe>
    Related to CEP:
<http://www.npolar.no/cep>

Convention Concerning the Protection of the World Cultural and Natural Heritage (World Heritage Convention)

Objectives
• to establish an effective system of collective protection of the cultural and natural heritage of outstanding universal value, organized on a permanent basis and in accordance with modern scientific methods;
• to provide both emergency and long-term protection for monuments, monumental sculpture and painting, groups of buildings, archaeological sites, natural features, and habitats of animals and plants of 'outstanding universal value'.

Scope
Legal scope
Open to all states and members of UNESCO (see IGOs), and to other states upon invitation of the UNESCO General Conference. Not open to regional integration organizations.

Geographic scope
Global.

Time and place of adoption
16 November 1972, Paris.

Entry into force
17 December 1975.

Status of participation
156 Parties by 1 June 1999. 31 Signatories without ratification, acceptance, or accession.
    The Director-General of UNESCO acts as depositary.

Affiliated instruments and organizations
World Heritage List, where 582 sites have been inscribed (445 cultural, 117 natural, and 20 with both cultural and natural attributes), in 114 countries which are Parties to the Convention, by 1 June 1999.

Co-ordination with related instruments
The World Heritage Centre meets regularly with the secretariats of other international conventions, such as the Ramsar Convention, the Convention on Biological Diversity (CBD), the Convention on International Trade in Endangered Species of Wild Fauna and Flora (CITES), the Convention to Combat Desertification (CCD), and the Convention on the Conservation of Migratory Species of Wild Animals (CMS) (see this section), to exchange information and to co-ordinate action. A joint website is established at <http://www.biodiv.org/rioconv/websites.html>.

Secretariat
World Heritage Centre,
UNESCO,
7 place de Fontenoy,
F-75352 Paris 07 SP, France
Telephone: +33-1-45681571
Telefax: +33-1-45685570
E-mail: wh-info@unesco.org

Director of the World Heritage Centre
Mr Mounir Bouchenaki.

Number of staff
12 professionals and ten general service staff under its Regular Programme budget (April 1999).

Finance
Costs are covered partly by UNESCO's Regular Programme budget and partly by the World Heritage Fund and other extra-budgetary sources.

Budget
The administrative core budget, provided by UNESCO's Regular Programme, was $US3,825,300 for the years 1996–7 and is $4,646,600 for the years 1998–9. The figure for 1998–9 consists of $3,664,000 for staff and $982,600 for programme activities.

Special funds
Through the World Heritage Fund, established in 1978, any individual, nation, or institution may voluntarily contribute (in accordance with their GNP) to the protection of the heritage in countries where national resources are insufficient. The Fund can be used for preparatory assistance (preparation on World Heritage nominations), technical co-operation (directly for projects at World Heritage properties), training, and emergency assistance. The Fund amounted to approximately $4.4 million in 1998 with contributions from the Parties to the Convention. The main recipients are Parties from the developing countries. In addition there is a World Heritage Emergency Fund, created in 1994, with a total of $600,000 for 1999.

Main contributors
The main contributing Parties to the World Heritage Fund are the USA, Germany, France, Japan, Norway, and the United Kingdom.

Rules and standards
Each Party shall:
• recognize that the duty of identification, protection, conservation, and transmission to future generations of the cultural and natural heritage belongs primarily to that State;
• integrate the protection of their heritage into comprehensive planning programmes, set up services for the protection of their heritage, develop scientific and technical studies, and take necessary legal, scientific, administrative, and financial steps to protect their heritage;
• assist each other in the protection of the cultural and natural heritage.
    Parties are called upon to draw up an inventory of property belonging to their cultural and natural heritage. A World Heritage List of sites of outstanding universal value has been established by the World Heritage Committee, to be updated every year. A second inventory, List of World Heritage in Danger, includes those monuments, buildings, and sites for which major conservation operations are urgently needed.
    Any Party may request assistance for property forming part of its listed heritage, and such assistance may be granted by the World Heritage Fund in the form of studies, provision of experts, training of staff, and supply of equipment, loans, or subsidies.

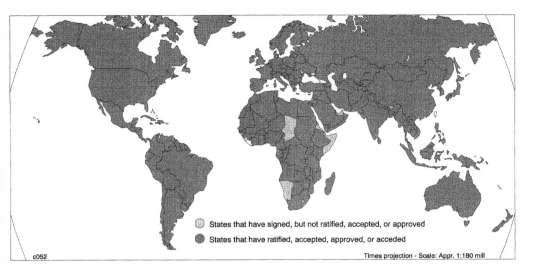

States that have signed, but not ratified, accepted, or approved

States that have ratified, accepted, approved, or acceded

c052

Times projection - Scale: Appr. 1:180 mill

Monitoring/implementation

Review procedure
Parties report to the UNESCO General Conference in their general reports. A complete report from the World Heritage Committee is submitted to the UNESCO General Conference every two years.

Specific requirements for data disclosure are laid out in forms for nominating properties on the World Heritage List and for requesting international co-operation under the Fund, as well as in the formats for periodic reports.

Measurement of the compliance of Parties to commitments are undertaken through the procedures for monitoring of the condition and conservation status of World Heritage properties. This task is undertaken for natural properties by the IUCN – The World Conservation Union (see NGOs), which prepares regular reports for the World Heritage Committee, and for cultural sites by the UNESCO Secretariat, in consultation with the International Council for Monuments and Sites (ICOMOS), the International Centre for the Study of the Preservation and Restoration of Cultural Property (ICCROM), and the countries concerned.

Monitoring is the responsibility of the parties concerned and commitment to provide periodic reports on the state of conservation of the site is consistent with the principles set out in the Convention.

Monitoring, as part of the site management process, remains the responsibility of the Parties where the site is located. Periodic reports may be submitted in accordance with Article 29 of the Convention. Parties are invited to submit periodic reports (every six years) on the legislative and administrative provisions for the application of the Convention, including the state of conservation of the sites located on their territories.

An evaluation of the implementation of the Convention was adopted in 1992. National reports, linked to particular problems of conservation, have been submitted occasionally, but the number of reports requested and submitted is increasing. The reports, which are public, are reviewed by the World Heritage Centre, the advisory bodies to the Convention, the World Heritage Bureau, and the World Heritage Committee. Such reviews are also public. Publication lists of such reviews are not distributed by the Centre.

Observations or inspections
None by the Convention as yet, but the World Heritage Centre has, in co-operation with the advisory bodies, a comprehensive monitoring methodology.

Trade measures
No provisions on trade measures to penalize Parties for non-compliance.

Dispute-settlement mechanisms
No provision is made for the settlement of disputes.

Decision-making bodies

Political
The General Assembly of States Parties meets during the UNESCO General Conference every two years to elect the World Heritage Committee. The Committee, which meets once a year, consists of representatives from 21 of the States Parties to the Convention and makes the decisions relating to the implementation of the Convention, including the allocation of funds. It has established a World Heritage Bureau, which performs a number of functions on behalf of the Committee. This consists of seven members and meets twice a year.

Scientific/technical
Technical and scientific advice is provided by NGOs such as IUCN (see NGOs) for the natural heritage and by ICOMOS and ICCROM for the cultural heritage (see above).

Publications

The World Heritage Centre publishes *World Heritage Newsletter* (three times a year) and *World Heritage Review* (four times a year).

UNESCO publishes regularly an up-to-date *World Heritage List* and *List of States Parties*. The UNESCO *Courier* includes information on World Heritage sites. A map of sites is available from the Secretariat.

Sources on the Internet
<http://www.unesco.org/whc>

Convention on Biological Diversity (CBD)

Objectives

The objectives of this Convention are:
- the conservation of biological diversity;
- the sustainable use of its components;
- the fair and equitable sharing of the benefits arising out of the utilization of genetic resources, including by appropriate access to genetic resources and by appropriate transfer of relevant technologies (taking into account all rights over those resources and to technologies) and by appropriate funding.

Scope

Legal scope
Open to all states and regional economic integration organizations.

Geographic scope
Global.

Time and place of adoption

The agreed text of the Convention was adopted on 22 May 1992 at Nairobi. It was opened for signature in Rio de Janeiro on 5 June 1992.

Entry into force

29 December 1993.

Status of participation

175 Parties, including the European Community, by 26 May 1999. 12 Signatories, without ratification, acceptance, or approval.

The Secretary-General of the UN acts as depositary.

Affiliated instruments and organizations

The Convention has no protocols so far.

The second Conference of the Parties (COP), held in Jakarta in November 1995, decided to establish a negotiation process to develop a protocol on *biosafety* to help minimize the potential risks posed by living modified organisms (LMOs) resulting from modern biotechnology. The draft protocol will cover the transboundary movement and transfer of LMOs and will address both accidental releases and trade. An open-ended working group created to develop a protocol endeavoured to complete its work in 1998. Sessions were held in Århus in July 1996, in Montreal in May 1997, October 1997, February 1998, and August 1998, and finally in Cartagena in February 1999. An extraordinary meeting of the COP, which was to receive the draft protocol for adoption on 22–3 February, was unable to finalize the text. The adoption of the draft protocol, to be named the *Cartagena Protocol on Biosafety to the Convention on Biological Diversity*, had to be postponed. Negotiations will be resumed as soon as practicable and, in any event, no later than the fifth COP in May 2000.

At its third meeting, the COP affirmed its willingness to consider a decision by the FAO Conference (see IGOs) that the revised International Undertaking on Plant Genetic Resources (see this section) should take the form of a protocol to the Convention.

A decision on *intellectual property rights* by the third COP encourages governments and organizations to submit case-studies to the Convention's Executive Secretary on the impact of intellectual property rights in regard to the Convention's objectives: the conservation, sustainable use, and fair and equitable sharing of benefits arising from biological diversity.

Co-ordination with related instruments
The COP has requested the Executive Secretary to collaborate closely with other biodiversity-related conventions (CITES, Ramsar, CMS, and World Heritage conventions (see this section)), the UN Framework Convention on Climate Change (UNFCCC) and the Convention to Combat Desertification (CCD) (see this section), intergovernmental organizations, including the Food and Agriculture Organization (FAO), UNESCO (see IGOs), the Intergovernmental Oceanographic Commission (IOC), and others. In many cases, memoranda of co-operation have been signed between respective secretariats. A joint website, covering CITES, Ramsar, CMS, World Heritage, and CBD Conventions, is established at <http://www.biodiv.org/rioconv/websites.html>.

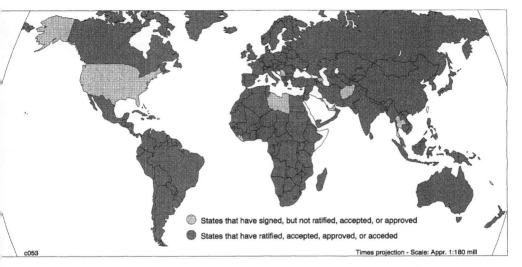

States that have signed, but not ratified, accepted, or approved

States that have ratified, accepted, approved, or acceded

c053

Times projection - Scale: Appr. 1:180 mill

Secretariat

Secretariat of the Convention on Biologi-
cal Diversity,
World Trade Centre,
393 rue St Jacques, office 300,
Montréal, Québec H2Y 1N9,
Canada
Telephone: +1-514-2882220
Telefax: +1-514-2886588
E-mail: secretariat@biodiv.org

Acting Executive Secretary
Mr Hamdallah Zedan.

Information Management Assistant
Ms Fabienne Fon Sing.

Number of staff
27 professionals (including secondments)
and 20 support staff (May 1999).

Finance

The Global Environment Facility (GEF) of
the World Bank, the UN Development Programme (UNDP), and the UN Environment Programme (UNEP) (see IGOs) has
been entrusted on an interim basis with the
operation of the financial mechanism for
the provision of financial resources to developing-country Parties for the purposes
of the Convention. The GEF has offered its
services on a permanent basis to the COP.
Parties agreed at the third meeting in November 1996 that the GEF will continue to
serve on an interim basis as the Convention's funding mechanism.

Budget and trust funds
The administration of the Convention, including the functions of the Secretariat, is
funded by the Trust Fund for the Convention on Biological Diversity, which has been
operative from 1995. The core budget for
the Trust Fund was US$6,561,041 in 1997
and $6,765,208 in 1998, and is $8,303,000
in 1999.

A Special Trust Fund for additional voluntary contributions to the core budget for
approved activities was set at $744,209 for
1997 and $759,384 for 1998, and is
$2,928,200 for 1999.

A Special Voluntary Trust Fund was established for facilitating participation of
developing-country Parties in the Convention process. Its core budget was $1,755,441
for 1997 and $1,725,221 for 1998, and is
2,691,200 for 1999.

*Status of contributions to Trust Fund for the
Convention*
All States Parties are required to contrib-
ute to the Trust Fund.

Of the total pledged contribution of
$5,963,226 for 1998 to the Trust Fund, the
total contributions received amounted to
$4,460,614. Outstanding contributions for
1998 and prior years, core budgets as of 31
December 1998 amounted to $2,317,373.
(Contributions are due on 1 January of the
year in question.)

Additional voluntary contributions were
received between January 1997 and December 1998 from Australia, Austria, Canada,

Denmark, the European Commission, Germany, Ireland, Italy, Japan, Netherlands,
Norway, Slovakia, Spain, Sweden, Switzerland, and the United Kingdom.

Rules and standards

Each Contracting Party shall:
• develop national strategies, plans, or programmes for the conservation and sustainable use of biological diversity or adapt for
this purpose existing strategies, plans, and
programmes which shall reflect, *inter alia*,
the measures set out in the Convention relevant to the Party concerned;
• integrate, as far as possible and as appropriate, the conservation and sustainable use
of biological diversity into the relevant
sectoral and cross-sectoral plans, programmes, and policies;
• identify components of biological diversity important for its conservation and sustainable use;
• monitor the components of biological
diversity through sampling and other techniques;
• identify processes and categories of activities which have or are likely to have significant adverse impacts on the conservation and sustainable use of biological
diversity;
• establish a system of protected areas or
areas where special measures need to be
taken to conserve biological diversity (*in situ*
conservation);
• adopt measures for the *ex situ* conservation of components of biological diversity,

preferably in the country of origin of such components;
- integrate consideration of the conservation and sustainable use of biological resources into national decision making;
- adopt economically and socially sound measures that act as incentives for the conservation and sustainable use of biological diversity;
- establish and maintain programmes for scientific and technical education and training in measures for the identification, conservation, and sustainable use of biological diversity and its components and provide support for such education and training for the specific needs of developing countries;
- introduce appropriate procedures requiring environmental impact assessment of its proposed projects that are likely to have significant adverse effects on biological diversity with a view to avoiding or minimizing such effects.

The authority to determine access to genetic resources rests with the national governments and is subject to national legislation. Access to and transfer of technology to developing countries shall be provided and/or facilitated under fair and favourable terms, including on concessional and preferential terms where mutually agreed, and, where necessary, in accordance with the Financial Mechanism established by the Convention. In the case of technology subject to patents or other intellectual property rights, such access and transfer shall be provided on terms which recognize and are consistent with the adequate and effective protection of intellectual property rights. The Contracting Parties, recognizing that patents and other intellectual property rights may have an influence on the implementation of this Convention, shall co-operate in this regard subject to national legislation and international law in order to ensure that such rights are supportive of and do not run counter to its objectives.

Each Contracting Party shall:
- take legislative, administrative, or policy measures, as appropriate, to provide for the effective participation in biotechnological research activities by those Parties, especially developing countries, which provide the genetic resources for such research, and where feasible in such Parties;
- take all practical measures to promote and advance priority access on a fair and equitable basis by Parties, especially developing countries, to the results and benefits arising from biotechnologies based upon genetic resources provided by those Con-

tracting Parties. Such access shall be on mutually agreed terms.

The developed-country Parties shall provide new and additional financial resources to enable developing-country Parties to meet the agreed full incremental costs to them of implementing measures which fulfil the obligations of the Convention.

Monitoring/implementation

Review procedure
The COP (see below) shall keep under review the implementation of the Convention and establish the form and the intervals for transmitting the information to be submitted in accordance with the Convention and consider such information as well as reports submitted by any subsidiary body.

The Parties shall present reports of measures which they have taken for the implementation of the provisions of the Convention and their effectiveness in meeting the objectives of the Convention. The first reports were due to be submitted by 31 December 1997. 13 annual reports had been submitted within the deadline, and 103 by the time of the fourth COP in Bratislava in May 1998. The fourth COP encouraged Parties that had submitted an interim report to submit full reports by 31 December 1998. It also urged Parties that had not submitted a report to do so by the same date. By that date, 75 full national reports and 37 interim national reports were submitted. 31 Parties had not yet submitted a national report. Based on a revised report on the information contained in these reports from the Executive Secretary, the Subsidiary Body on Scientific, Technical, and Technological Advice (SBSTTA) (see Decision-making bodies, below) will provide advice to the fifth COP on the intervals and form of future national reports, and on ways and means to facilitate further national implementation of the Convention.

Data and information-system programmes
The Clearing-House Mechanism, a database for scientific and technical co-operation, is a needs-driven, decentralized mechanism with information-exchange modalities, including the Internet, and providing access to meta-data for support to national-level decision-making processes for the implementation of the Convention (see also *Co-ordination with related instruments*, above).

Dispute-settlement mechanisms
In the event of a dispute, the Parties involved shall seek solution by negotiation.

Should this fail, they may seek jointly the good offices of, or request mediation by, a third party. Upon becoming members of the Convention, Parties may, by a written declaration to the Depositary, recognize as compulsory, in relation to any Party accepting the same obligation:
- arbitration in accordance with the procedure set out in Part 1 of Annex II; and/or
- submission of the dispute to the International Court of Justice.

If Parties do not accept this procedure, the dispute shall be submitted to a conciliation commission created by the Parties to the dispute, the recommendations of which 'the Parties shall consider in good faith'.

Decision-making bodies

Political
The COP, the governing body of the Convention, consists of representatives of States Parties to the Convention. Ordinary meetings shall be held at regular intervals to be determined by the COP.

The COP considers and undertakes any action required for the achievement of the purpose of the Convention. This includes:
- reviewing scientific, technical, and technological advice;
- considering reports by Parties on their implementation of the Convention;
- considering and adopting protocols, amendments, or annexes;
- establishing such subsidiary bodies as may be necessary for the implementation of the Convention.

The Parties shall make every effort to reach agreement by consensus. If that is not possible, the decision shall, as a last resort, be taken by a two-thirds majority vote of the Parties present and voting. However, in the case of a decision on the Financial Mechanism, no agreement has been reached on the voting procedure.

Observers may participate without the right to vote unless one-third of the Parties present object. Observers may include states not being Parties, or any body or agency, whether governmental or non-governmental, which is qualified in fields relating to conservation or sustainable use of biological diversity and which has informed the Secretariat of its wish to be represented.

The fourth COP decided to hold an open-ended meeting to consider possible arrangements to improve preparations for and conduct of the meeting of the COP. This meeting was held in Montreal on 28–30 June 1999.

The COP met in Nassau (November–December 1994), Jakarta (November 1995), Buenos Aires (November 1996), and Bratislava (May 1998). The fifth meeting will be held in Nairobi (15–26 May 2000).

Scientific/technical
The Subsidiary Body on Scientific, Technical, and Technological Advice (SBSTTA), composed of experts representing governments, has been established to provide the COP and, as appropriate, its other subsidiary bodies with timely advice relating to the implementation of the Convention. This body shall comprise government representatives competent in the relevant field of expertise. It has met four times, in Paris (September 1995) and in Montreal (September 1996, September 1997, and June 1999). The next meeting will be held in Montreal in January/February 2000.

In November 1997 a workshop on traditional knowledge and biodiversity was held in Madrid.

The fourth COP decided to establish an *ad hoc* open-ended inter-sessional working group to address implementation of Article 8(j) and related provisions (traditional knowledge). This working group will meet in Montreal in January 2000.

Publications

Global Biodiversity Outlook, a periodical report on the state of biodiversity worldwide and the implementation of the Convention, is intended to be published in 2000.

Sources on the Internet

<http://www.biodiv.org>

Convention on the Conservation of Migratory Species of Wild Animals (CMS)

Objectives

To conserve those species of wild animals that migrate across or outside national boundaries by developing and implementing co-operative agreements, prohibiting taking of endangered species, conserving habitat, and controlling other adverse factors.

Scope

Legal scope
Open to all states and regional economic integration organizations. Membership of subsidiary 'Agreements' under the Convention is open to all Range States (and the relevant regional integration organizations) for the species covered, including States that are not Parties to the parent Convention.

Geographic scope
Global.

Time and place of adoption

23 June 1979, Bonn.

Entry into force

1 November 1983.

Status of participation

60 Parties, including the European Community, by 1 July 1999. Six Signatories without ratification, acceptance, or approval.

Instruments of accession to be deposited with the government of Germany.

Affiliated instruments and organizations

• *Agreement on the Conservation of Seals in the Wadden Sea.* Entered into force on 1 October 1991. Three Parties by 1 May 1999. No Signatories without ratification, acceptance, or accession;
• *Agreement on the Conservation of Bats in Europe.* Entered into force on 16 January 1994. 14 Parties by 1 May 1999. One Signatory (Belgium) without ratification, acceptance, or accession;
• *Agreement on the Conservation of Small Cetaceans in the Baltic and North Seas (ASCOBANS).* Entered into force on 29 March 1994. Seven Parties by 1 May 1999.

One Signatory (European Community) without ratification, acceptance, or accession;
• *Agreement on the Conservation of African-Eurasian Migratory Waterbirds (AEWA).* Adopted on 16 June 1995. (Not yet in force.) 14 states had ratified by 1 May 1999. 25 Signatories to the Agreement, including the European Community, without ratification, acceptance, or accession. 54 Signatories to the Final Act, including the European Community. Opened for signature on 15 August 1996 until entry into force of the Agreement. Enters into force on the first day of the third month after at least 14 Range States or regional economic integration organizations (comprising at least seven from Africa and seven from Eurasia) have joined. Expected to enter into force during 1999;
• *Agreement on the Conservation of Cetaceans of the Black Sea, Mediterranean Sea and Contiguous Atlantic Area (ACCOBAMS).* Adopted on 24 November 1996. (Not yet in force.) Two states had ratified by 1 May 1999. Ten Signatories to the Agreement without ratification, acceptance, or accession. 16 Signatories to the Final Act, including the European Community.

Memoranda of understanding have also been concluded with a view to promoting the conservation of the western and central Asian populations of the Siberian crane (1 July 1993) and the slender-billed curlew (10 September 1994).

Appendix I covers endangered migratory species, which benefit from strict protection.

Appendix II covers migratory species which have an unfavourable conservation status and which require international agreements for their conservation and management.

UNEP (see IGOs) provides the Secretariat and administers the trust fund for the Convention. Institutional arrangements for Agreements vary, being undertaken by various international organizations or governments.

Co-ordination with related instruments
Agreements between Range States should take account of related instruments such as

the Ramsar Convention (see this section). A joint website, covering CITES, Ramsar, World Heritage, CBD (see this section), and CMS Conventions, is established at <http://www.biodiv.org/rioconv/websites.html>.

Secretariat

UNEP/CMS Secretariat,
United Nations Premises in Bonn,
Martin-Luther-King-Straße 8,
D-53175 Bonn, Germany
Telephone: +49-228-815240-1/2
Telefax: +49-228-8152449
E-mail: cms@unep.de

Executive Secretary
Mr Arnulf Müller-Helmbrecht.

Deputy Executive Secretary
Mr Douglas Hykle.

Number of staff
Seven professionals, including two on secondment, and six support staff (May 1999).

Finance

The Convention is financed entirely by the Parties, on the basis of the UN scale, with a maximum of 25 per cent by any one Party. The Agreements are also to be financed by the Parties to them, but the basis varies.

Budget
The Conference of the Parties (COP), at its fifth meeting in April 1997, adopted a core budget of US$1,437,925 for 1998, $1,741,895 for 1999, and $1,407,980 for 2000. It also agreed to withdraw an additional $630,000 from the Trust Fund in order to finance consultancies during the triennium.

Special funds
The core budget includes funds to assist developing-country participants to attend meetings of experts and of the Standing Committee (see below). Further, some funding support for representatives of developing-country Parties for attendance at meetings of the COP and of the Scientific Council has been made available by a few European governments.

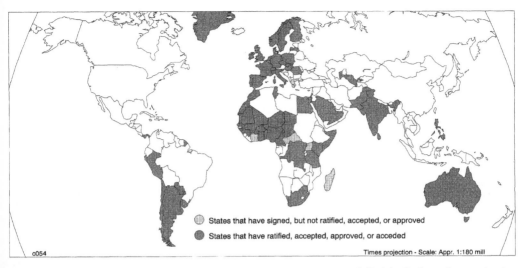

States that have signed, but not ratified, accepted, or approved

States that have ratified, accepted, approved, or acceded

c054

Times projection - Scale: Appr. 1:180 mill

Rules and standards

With respect to endangered migratory species listed in Appendix I, Parties that are Range States are to prohibit the taking of animals belonging to such species, with a few exceptions. Range States are to endeavour to conserve and, where possible, restore the habitats of these species; eliminate, prevent, or minimize impediments to their migration; and prevent, reduce, or control factors endangering them.

'Agreements' to benefit species listed in Appendix II are generally regional, sometimes on a north–south gradient, but taken together should have a global effect. These Agreements, within the framework of the 'umbrella' Convention, can stipulate precise conservation measures and implementation mechanisms.

The Convention provides for reservations on joining and with regard to species listed in the Appendices when they are amended. The Agreement on the Conservation of Seals in the Wadden Sea allows no reservations, whereas the Agreements on Bats in Europe, Small Cetaceans in the Baltic and North Seas, and African-Eurasian Migratory Waterbirds allow for reservations on species covered.

Monitoring/implementation

Review procedure

Parties to the Convention should inform the COP every three years of measures they are taking to implement the Convention for species listed in the Appendices. Initially, provision of information was very poor, but

it has improved gradually. Over half the Parties submitted reports of varying comprehensiveness to the 1997 meeting. The reports, which are made public, are reviewed by the Secretariat and by the COP. No reviews are made by independent bodies.

Parties must also inform the Secretariat of exceptions made to the prohibition on taking of Appendix I species, but, although the Secretariat is aware informally of some cases of such taking, it has never been informed by Parties officially.

Parties are required to inform the Secretariat of those species in the Appendices of which they consider themselves to be Range States. The Secretariat circulates Range State lists to Parties and experts for comments.

Dispute-settlement mechanisms

The Convention provides dispute-settlement procedures, that is, bilateral negotiation, followed by referral to the permanent Court of Arbitration. So far such disputes are not known to have arisen.

Decision-making bodies

Political

The COP is the decision-making organ and can amend the instruments under the Convention and adopt resolutions to improve its implementation. It meets every three years. The Standing Committee, consisting of regional representatives and the depositary government, provides general policy direction and carries out activities on be-

half of the Conference between the triennial meetings.

Amendments to the Convention may be adopted by the COP by a two-thirds majority of members present and voting. They enter into force in regard to all Parties 90 days after the meeting, except for those Parties which file a written reservation within the 90-day period.

Scientific/technical

A Scientific Council is established to provide advice on scientific matters to the COP, to the Secretariat, and, when instructed, to any Party. It can recommend research, provide advice on migratory species listed in Appendices I and II, and advocate specific conservation and management measures to be included in agreements. The Council consists of experts (presently 55) appointed by individual Parties and by the Conference, and may include experts from non-governmental organizations in its working groups.

Agreements may provide for advisory bodies or advice from the Convention's Scientific Council.

Publications

The Secretariat publishes a list of Range States of all migratory species included in the two Appendices, a regular *CMS Bulletin*, and a brochure explaining the aims and operation of the Convention.

Sources on the Internet

<http://www.wcmc.org.uk/cms/>

Convention on International Trade in Endangered Species of Wild Fauna and Flora (CITES)

Objectives
• to ensure, through international co-operation, that the international trade in species of wild fauna and flora does not threaten survival in the wild of the species concerned;
• to protect endangered species from over-exploitation by means of a system of import–export permits issued by a management authority under the control of a scientific authority.

Scope
Legal scope
Open to all states recognized by the UN. Not yet open to regional integration organizations.

Geographic scope
Global.

Time and place of adoption
3 March 1973, Washington, DC.

Entry into force
1 July 1975.

Status of participation
145 Parties by 25 May 1999. Three Signatories without ratification or approval.

Affiliated instruments and organizations
• *Amendment Protocol*, Bonn 1979. Entered into force on 13 April 1987. Related to financial provisions;
• *Amendment Protocol*, Gaborone 1983. (Not yet in force.) 35 of the States that were Parties on 30 April 1983 had accepted this Amendment by 11 February 1999. 54 instruments of ratification, acceptance, approval, or accession are required to enter into force. Related to accession to the Convention by regional economic integration organizations;
• *Appendix I* offers the highest protection, and prohibits (with limited exemptions) the commercial international trade in wild-caught specimens of species threatened with extinction;

• *Appendix II* assigns the responsibility to exporting States to control, through a permit system, such trade in species which could become threatened with extinction if there were no such restriction;
• *Appendix III* requires Parties to control trade in specimens of species which have been protected in certain States and listed by those States;
• *Appendix IV* contains a model export permit. No longer used. A new permit model is included in Resolution Conf. 10.1.
A principal decision of the Conference of the Parties (COP) in November 1994 approved new criteria to determine the classification of a species as protected or endangered.

Co-ordination with related instruments
The International Criminal Police Organization (ICPO), Interpol, the World Customs Organization (WCO), and the Convention on Biological Diversity (CBD).

Secretariat
UNEP/CITES Secretariat,
15 chemin des Anémones,
CH-1219 Châtelaine, Geneva,
Switzerland
Telephone: +41-22-91781-39/40
Telefax: +41-22-7973417
E-mail: cites@unep.ch

Secretary-General
Mr Willem Wynstekers.

Number of staff
25 in total, of which more than one half are professionals (April 1999).

Finance
The budget is covered entirely by contributions of the Parties to a Trust Fund (established in 1984) administered by the UN Environment Programme (UNEP). Contributions from Parties are assessed in accordance with the UN scale of contributions.

Budget
The administrative core budget was SFr.6,505,410 in 1997 and Fr.6,145,964 in 1998, and is estimated to be Fr.7,326,835 in 1999.

Counterpart contributions
The purpose of these contributions is to provide for specific projects not necessarily covered by the budget approved by the Parties. Generally, these projects involve surveys of species or improving enforcement of the Convention.

Rules and standards
Permits are required for species listed in Appendices I and II stating that export-import will not be detrimental to the survival of the species. Trade in species listed in Appendix III is regulated through the issuing of export permits where trade is from the State that listed the species, or otherwise through the issuance of certificates of origin (see below).
If a country does not accept the placing of a species in a certain Appendix, it may enter a reservation (within a specified period of time).
Each Party is required to maintain records of trade in species covering:
• names and addresses of exporters and importers;
• numbers and types of permits and certificates granted;
• states with which trade has occurred;
• numbers or quantities and types of specimens and names of species traded.

Monitoring/implementation
Review procedure
The Parties have an obligation to provide an annual report on all trade in species of flora and fauna listed in the Appendices to the Convention and to provide a biennial report on legislative, regulatory, and administrative measures taken.
Not all Parties meet the reporting requirements; and even those which do submit annual reports often submit them long after the agreed deadlines. Moreover, many of the reports submitted are incomplete.
The annual statistical reports are a vital tool for monitoring both the levels of trade in the listed species and the implementation of the Convention. A comparison of the reports of each Party with those of the other Parties often reveals information on trade of which it was unaware, and can help to

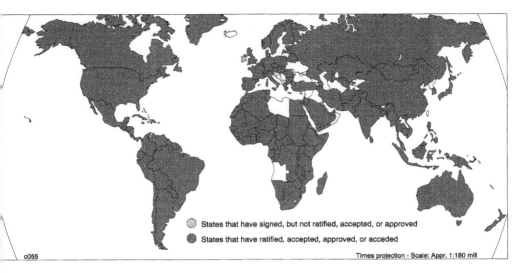

⊙	States that have signed, but not ratified, accepted, or approved
●	States that have ratified, accepted, approved, or acceded

c055   Times projection - Scale: Appr. 1:180 mill

identify violations. 57 national reports (44 per cent of the Parties) for 1995 were submitted within the deadline on 31 October 1996. 48 national reports (36 per cent of the Parties) for 1996 were submitted within the deadline on 31 October 1997. The annual reports are public.

The trade data or other information in national reports are reviewed by the Secretariat and the COP, as well as by independent non-governmental organizations such as WWF and IUCN – The World Conservation Union (see NGOs). The reviews are public after they have been distributed to the Parties.

Each Party is required to establish one or more *Management Authority* to certify that the species has been obtained within the State's protection laws and that shipment will not be harmful to the living specimen concerned. In addition, each Party is required to designate one or more *Scientific Authority* which provides, for example in matters related to the issuance of permits or certificates, advice to its Management Authority on whether the import or export will be detrimental to the survival of the species involved.

If the Secretariat considers that the provisions are not being correctly implemented, it is obliged to inform the Management Authority of the Party concerned, which should reply with the necessary information within one month.

Data and information-system programmes
The Wildlife Trade Monitoring Unit is a data management unit of the World Conservation Monitoring Centre (WCMC), a joint venture between IUCN, WWF (see NGOs), and UNEP. It maintains and updates a database containing all the information from the annual reports.

Trade measures
Although the Convention does not include any provisions to penalize Parties for non-compliance, the Parties have preferred to avoid being cited in the alleged infractions report. Moreover, in the most serious cases of non-compliance, the COP and/or the Standing Committee, advised by the Secretariat, has gone so far as to recommend to the Parties not to accept or issue permits for trade from or to a particular country, pending the correction of the implementation problems that have been identified.

Decision-making bodies
Political
The COP to CITES meets about every two years to examine progress in the restoration and conservation of protected species and to revise the Appendices as appropriate. Amendments to Appendices enter into force automatically in accordance with a procedure not requiring ratification. The majority of decisions (including changes in the Appendices) require a two-thirds majority, with each Party having one vote.

The CITES Standing Committee (SC) is elected at the COP and is composed of representatives from the major geographic regions of CITES (the number of representatives from each region depends on the number of Parties in that region); one representative from the Depositary Government; one from the past host Party; and one from the next host Party. By April 1999 it had 16 members.

The SC provides policy guidelines to the Secretariat; proposes meetings and agendas; oversees the Secretariats' budget and fund-raising activities; appoints working groups; co-ordinates working groups and committees as required; drafts resolutions; acts as the Bureau of the meetings of the COP, and reports to the COP on SC activities.

Scientific/technical
The Animals Committee, Plants Committee, Identification Manual Committee, and Nomenclature Committee, composed of persons chosen by the Parties.

Publications
CITES World (newsletter) (bi-annually).

CITES publications are available through:
IUCN Publications Services Unit,
219c Huntington Road,
Cambridge CB3 0DL,
United Kingdom
Telephone: +44-1223-277894
Telefax: +44-1223-277175
E-mail: info@books.iucn.org
<http://www.iucn.org/bookstore>

Sources on the Internet
<http://www.cites.org>

Convention on Wetlands of International Importance especially as Waterfowl Habitat (Ramsar Convention)

Objectives

The Convention's mission is the conservation and wise use of wetlands by national action and international co-operation as a means to achieving sustainable development throughout the world.

Scope

Legal scope
Membership open to all member States of the UN or members of the specialized agencies and the International Atomic Energy Agency (IAEA) (see IGOs). Not open to regional integration organizations.

Geographic scope
Global.

Time and place of adoption

2 February 1971, Ramsar.

Entry into force

21 December 1975.

Status of participation

114 Parties by 29 April 1999. Two Signatories without ratification, acceptance, or approval.

The Director-General of UNESCO (see IGOs) acts as depositary.

Affiliated instruments and organizations

• *Protocol to Amend the Convention on Wetlands of International Importance especially as Waterfowl Habitat, Paris, 1982.* Entered into force on 1 October 1986. The main objective of the Protocol is to establish a procedure for amending the Convention;
• *Amendments to Arts. 6 and 7 of the Convention, Regina, 1987.* Entered into force on 1 May 1994;
• *List of Wetlands of International Importance (Ramsar List).* The Ramsar List included 977 wetland sites, totalling more than 71 million hectares, by 29 April 1999. The Ramsar Bureau collaborates closely with the IUCN, WWF International (see NGOs), Wetlands International, and Birdlife International.

Co-ordination with related instruments
The Ramsar Convention Bureau meets regularly with the secretariats of other international conventions on nature conservation, such as the Convention on Biological Diversity (CBD), the Convention on International Trade in Endangered Species of Wild Fauna and Flora (CITES), the World Heritage Convention, the Convention to Combat Desertification (CCD), and the Convention on the Conservation of Migratory Species of Wild Animals (CMS) (see this section), to exchange information and to co-ordinate action. A joint website is established at <http://www.biodiv.org/rioconv/websites.html>.

Secretariat

Ramsar Convention Bureau,
Rue Mauverney 28,
CH-1196 Gland,
Switzerland
Telephone: +41-22-9990170
Telefax: +41-22-9990169
E-mail: ramsar@ramsar.org

Secretary-General
Mr Delmar Blasco.

Information officer
Dr Dwight Peck.

Number of staff
Six professionals, seven support staff, and four interns (April 1999).

Finance

Income derives from the Contracting Parties according to the UN scale of assessments for the core funding. Specific projects of at least a similar magnitude are also undertaken outside the core budget.

Budget
The core budget was SFr. 2,857,839 in 1997 and Fr.2,900,000 in 1998, and is Fr.3,237,000 in 1999.

Special funds
The Wetland Conservation Fund, later renamed the Ramsar Convention's Small Grants Fund (SGF), was launched by the Convention in 1990 to assist developing countries by offering financial benefits as well as expert services in the implementation of the Convention. During its first year of existence (1991) contributions amounting to SFr.271,246 were received, and by April 1999 the contributions totalled Fr.4,106,653. Disbursements in 1996 were Fr.502,150 and accumulated disbursements were Fr.2,170,012. Disbursements in 1997 were Fr.1,104,840 and accumulated disbursements were Fr.3,274,852. Disbursements in 1998 were Fr.679,470 and accumulated disbursements were Fr.3,815,821. The strongest contributors over the period 1991–8 have been: Austria, Denmark, France, Germany, Iceland, Japan, the Netherlands, Norway, Sweden, Switzerland, the United Kingdom, and the USA.

15 projects were approved in 1996, 29 in 1997, and 18 in 1998. Others were partially funded or referred to other agencies for further study or funding. Recipients in 1996 were Algeria, Argentina, Bangladesh, Ecuador, Guatemala, Honduras, Iran, Kenya, Mali, Pakistan, the Philippines, Suriname, Togo, Trinidad and Tobago, and Uzbekistan. Recipients in 1997 were Algeria, Armenia, Brazil, Bulgaria, Burkina Faso, Chile, China, Comoros, Costa Rica, Ecuador, Egypt, Estonia, Hungary-Romania-Slovakia-Ukraine (one project), Israel, Malaysia, Mauritania, Mongolia, Namibia, Panama, Papua New Guinea, Peru, Romania, the Russian Federation, Slovakia, Slovenia, Sri Lanka, Suriname, Tunisia, and Zambia. Recipients in 1998 were Bolivia, Chad, Chile, China, Georgia, Ghana, India, Jamaica, Jordan, Namibia, Nicaragua, Panama, the Philippines, Romania, the Russian Federation, Slovakia, South Africa, and Trinidad and Tobago.

A Wetlands for Future Fund, a capacity-building programme for Latin America, is administered by the Bureau jointly with the US State Department and the US Fish and Wildlife Service, which are contributing to the Fund. Disbursements were $US750,000 in its first three-year phase, and the Fund is beginning its second three-year phase in 1999 with the same contribution promised.

Rules and standards

Parties shall:
• designate at least one national wetland for

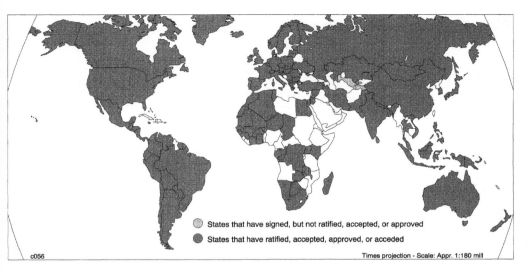

States that have signed, but not ratified, accepted, or approved

States that have ratified, accepted, approved, or acceded

c056

Times projection - Scale: Appr. 1:180 mill

inclusion in a *List of Wetlands of International Importance*;

• formulate and implement their planning so as to promote the conservation of the wetlands included in the List, and as far as possible the wise use of wetlands in their territory;

• establish wetland nature reserves, co-operate in the exchange of information, and train personnel for wetlands management;

• co-operate with other countries concerning shared wetlands and shared wetland species.

Monitoring/implementation

Review procedure

Parties report to each Conference of the Contracting Parties (COP) according to an agreed format. Reports are also required when the ecological character of a listed site is changing or is likely to change so that international consultations may be held on the problem. The reports are due before each triennial meeting of the COP. In 1992, 51 national reports (67 per cent of the Parties) on implementation were submitted by the Parties as required under the Convention for the 1993 meeting. 90 national reports were received from the 92 Parties in advance of the COP in March 1996. 110 national reports were received from the 113 Parties which are due to report in advance of the COP in May 1999. The reports are available on the website (see below). Reviews of data or information in national reports by the secretariat and the Conference are not public, but the Bureau's analyses and the Conference's discussions of national reports are published in proceedings.

A Monitoring Procedure was instituted in 1988 to assist countries in addressing management problems in Ramsar sites. The name was changed in 1996 to Management-Guidance Procedure (MGP). This has been used selectively due to funding restrictions.

In 1990, at Montreux, the COP called for the maintenance of a Record of Ramsar sites where changes in ecological character have occurred, are occurring, or are likely to occur.

During 1995 the MGP was applied to two Ramsar sites in Trinidad and Tobago, during 1996 to one Ramsar site in Denmark, during 1997 to two Ramsar sites in Iran and Guatemala, and during 1998 to four Ramsar sites in Costa Rica (1) and Italy (3).

Environmental monitoring programmes

A Ramsar database has been elaborated with an agreed classification and data system for all wetland sites.

Trade measures

No provisions on trade sanctions to penalize Parties for non-compliance.

Dispute-settlement mechanisms

No provisions on dispute settlement. Disputes are resolved by discussions at the Conference of the Contracting Parties, followed by Conference recommendations.

Decision-making bodies

Political

The Conference of the Contracting Parties (COP) is the governing body and meets every

three years. The implementation of the Convention is reviewed at these meetings. Secretariat functions are performed by the Ramsar Convention Bureau, responsible to a Standing Committee of the Contracting Parties.

Scientific/technical

An expert group, the Scientific and Technical Review Panel, composed of independent scientific experts chosen to represent each of the seven Ramsar regions of the world, has been established to guide policy decisions by the COP. It normally meets twice a year.

Participation by non-governmental observers is encouraged both in meetings of the Contracting Parties and in the Panel.

Publications

In addition to annual reports and conference proceedings, the Ramsar Bureau publishes:

• *Ramsar Newsletter* (four times a year);

• *Directory of Wetlands of International Importance* (triennial);

• *Ramsar Manual*;

• *Towards the Wise Use of Wetlands*, a collection of guidelines and case-studies;

• *The Legal Development of the Ramsar Convention*;

• *The Economic Valuation of Wetlands 1997*;

• *Wetlands, Biodiversity, and the Ramsar Convention* (1997).

Sources on the Internet

<http://www.ramsar.org>

Convention to Combat Desertification (CCD)

Objectives

To combat desertification and mitigate the effects of drought in countries experiencing serious drought and/or desertification, particularly in Africa, through effective actions at all levels, supported by international co-operation and partnership arrangements, in the framework of an integrated approach which is consistent with Agenda 21, with a view to contributing to the achievements of sustainable development in affected areas.

Scope

Legal scope
Open to all member States of the UN or any of its specialized agencies, Parties to the Statute of the International Court of Justice, and regional economic integration organizations.

Geographic scope
Global.

Time and place of adoption

17 June 1994, Paris.

Entry into force

26 December 1996.

Status of participation

151 Parties, including the European Community, by 26 May 1999. Nine Signatories without ratification, accession, acceptance, or approval.

Affiliated instruments and organizations

The full title of the Convention is *The United Nations Convention to Combat Desertification in those Countries Experiencing Serious Drought and/or Desertification, Particularly in Africa.*

The Convention contains four regional implementation *Annexes*, for Africa, Asia, Latin America and the Caribbean, and the northern Mediterranean. The *African Annex* is the most elaborate, both in form and content, of all the annexes. It comprises 19 articles and addresses a broad range of issues, including commitments and obligations of both African and developed-country Parties. Explicit reference is made with regard to technical assistance and co-opera-

tion to ensure that preference is given to the utilization of less costly local experts. Emphasis is placed on the need for increased co-ordination among the key players involved in desertification activities, including donors, national governments, NGOs, and local populations. The annex also contains provisions for financial mechanisms and resources, and co-ordination, partnership, and follow-up arrangements.

The other annexes are shorter, and reflect the different priorities of the regions. The *Asian Annex* is relatively general in scope, particularly concerning finances. The *Latin American and Caribbean Annex* mentions the important links between desertification and loss of biological diversity, as well as debt issues, unfavourable international economic trade practices, and other socio-economic factors. It also emphasizes traditional knowledge, know-how, and practices. The *Northern Mediterranean Annex* is more scientifically oriented. It stresses urbanization and agricultural practices as economic causes of desertification, and provides for collaboration with other regions in the preparation and implementation of action programmes. It is also unique in that it clearly disqualifies the region from eligibility for funds raised through the main Convention.

A *Global Mechanism*, located at the International Fund for Agricultural Development (IFAD) (see IGOs) in Rome, undertakes actions to mobilize and maximize adequate and substantial financial resources to finance activities under action programmes. The Conference of the Parties (COP) endorsed collaborative institutional arrangements between IFAD, the UN Development Programme (UNDP), and the World Bank (see IGOs) in support of the Mechanism.

Co-ordination with related instruments
Co-ordinated activities will take place with other relevant international agreements, particularly the UN Framework Convention on Climate Change (UNFCCC) and the Convention on Biological Diversity

Secretariat

Secretariat of the Convention to Combat Desertification,
PO Box 260129,

Haus Carstanjen,
D-53153 Bonn, Germany
Telephone: +49-228-8152800
Telefax: +49-228-8152899
E-mail: secretariat@unccd.de

UNCCD Executive Secretary
Mr Hama Arba Diallo.

External Relations Officer
Mr Rajeb Boulharouf.

Number of staff
40 in total (professionals, support staff, and temporary) (April 1998).

Global Mechanism to the CCD,
c/o International Fund for Agricultural Development (IFAD) (see IGOs).

Managing Director
Mr Per Ryden.

Finance

Budget
The secretariat's operating budget was $US6 million in 1998 and is $6.1 million in 1999.

Rules and standards

Affected-country Parties undertake:
• to give due priority to combating desertification and mitigating the effects of drought, and allocating adequate resources in accordance with their conditions and capabilities;
• to establish strategies and priorities, within the framework of sustainable development plans and/or policies, to combat desertification and mitigate the effects of drought;
• to address the underlying causes of desertification;
• to promote awareness and facilitate participation of local populations;
• to provide an enabling environment by strengthening relevant existing legislation or by enacting new laws and establishing long-term policies.

Developed-country Parties undertake:
• actively to support, as agreed, individually or jointly, the efforts of affected developing-country Parties, particularly those in Africa and the least-developed countries, to combat desertification and mitigate the effects of drought;
• to provide substantial financial resources

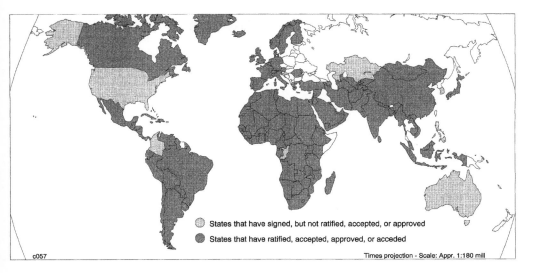

States that have signed, but not ratified, accepted, or approved
States that have ratified, accepted, approved, or acceded

c057   Times projection - Scale: Appr. 1:180 mill

and other forms of support to assist developing-country Parties, particularly those in Africa, effectively to develop and implement their own long-term plans and strategies to combat desertification and mitigate the effects of drought;
• to promote the mobilization of new and additional funding through the Global Environment Facility (GEF) (see IGOs);
• to encourage the mobilization of funding from the private sector and other non-governmental sources;
• to promote and facilitate access by affected-country Parties, particularly affected developing-country Parties, to appropriate technology, knowledge, and know-how.
National Action Programmes shall:
• incorporate long-term strategies to combat desertification and mitigate the effects of drought;
• give particular attention to the implementation of preventive measures;
• enhance national climatological and hydrological capabilities;
• promote policies and strengthen institutional frameworks;
• provide for effective popular participation;
• require regular review of implementation.
Elements of the National Action Programmes may include provisions relating to:
• improvements of national economic environments with a view to strengthening programmes aimed at the eradication of poverty and at ensuring food security;
• sustainable management of natural resources;

• sustainable agriculture practices;
• development and efficient use of various energy sources;
• strengthening of capabilities for assessment and monitoring;
• capacity building, education, and public awareness.

Monitoring/implementation
Review procedure
Each Party shall communicate to the COP, for consideration at its ordinary sessions, reports on the measures which it has taken for the implementation of the Convention. The COP shall determine the timetable for submission and the format of such reports, and regularly review the implementation of the Convention and the functioning of its institutional arrangements in the light of the experience gained at the national, subregional, regional, and international levels and on the basis of the evolution of scientific and technological knowledge.

Beginning at its third session, and at every other session thereafter, the COP will focus on national reports from the African region. Beginning at its fourth session, and continuing at every other session thereafter, the COP will focus on reports from countries of other regions. The third COP will consider the establishment of a mechanism to assist in the regular review of implementation.

Decision-making bodies
Political
The COP, the supreme body of the Conven-

tion, comprises representatives of all Parties to the Convention. It meets once a year for its first five sessions and shall keep under review and evaluate implementation of the Convention, harmonize policies, establish subsidiary bodies, and undertake additional actions.

National and international agencies and qualified NGOs may attend the COP's meetings and contribute to its work.

Scientific/technical
The Committee on Science and Technology provides the COP with information and advice on scientific and technological matters relating to combating desertification and the effects of drought. The COP may, as necessary, appoint *ad hoc* panels to provide information and advice through the Committee on specific issues regarding science and technology. The first COP established an *ad hoc* group on benchmarks and indicators, the second COP established an *ad hoc* group on traditional knowledge. Furthermore the third COP will focus on early-warning systems in its broadest sense.

Publications
• CCD Convention kit comprising Convention booklet, explanatory leaflet, ten fact sheets, and a folder;
• *CCD Newsletter* (bi-annually);
• comics catalogue.

Sources on the Internet
<http://www.unccd.de>

FAO International Undertaking on Plant Genetic Resources

Objectives

To ensure that plant genetic resources (PGR) of economic and/or social interest, particularly for agriculture, will be explored, preserved, evaluated, and made available for plant breeding and scientific purposes.

Scope

Legal scope
Open to all member States of the UN Food and Agriculture Organization (FAO) (see IGOs), non-member States which are members of the UN, and regional integration organizations.

Geographic scope
Global.

Time and place of adoption

23 November 1983, Rome.

Entry into force

1 January 1984.

Status of participation

113 countries had adhered to the Undertaking by April 1999.

Affiliated instruments and organizations

The Undertaking is overseen by the FAO Commission on Genetic Resources for Food and Agriculture (CGRFA), where governments are currently negotiating its revision in harmony with the Convention on Biological Diversity (CBD) (see this section). This process, launched by the 1993 FAO Conference, covers, *inter alia*, the issues of access on mutually agreed terms to PGR, including *ex situ* collections not addressed by the Convention, and the realization of 'Farmers' Rights'. The second session of the Conference of the Parties (COP) to the CBD recognized the special nature of agricultural biodiversity and its distinctive features and problems needing distinctive solutions, and declared its support for this process. The third session of the COP to the CBD affirmed its willingness to consider a decision by the FAO Conference that the revised International Undertaking should take the form of a protocol to the CBD. The CGRFA, during negotiations in April 1999, set a target date of completing the revision by November 2000.

The Commission covers all components of biodiversity of relevance to food and agriculture. In the field of PGR, the Commission has developed a number of negotiated elements which form the *FAO Global System on Plant Genetic Resources*. These include:

• *International Code of Conduct for Plant Germplasm Collecting and Transfer*, an important tool in regulating the collection and transfer of PGR, with the aim of facilitating equitable access to these resources and promoting their utilization and development. It was adopted by the FAO Conference in November 1993 and became operative in January 1994;

• *Draft Code of Conduct for Biotechnology*, as it affects the conservation and use of genetic resources for food and agriculture;

• *International Network of* ex situ *Collections, under the Auspices and/or Jurisdiction of FAO* and with the technical assistance of the International Plant Genetic Resources Institute (IPGRI). On 26 October 1994, 12 International Agricultural Research Centres of the Consultative Group on International Agricultural Research (CGIAR) signed agreements with FAO to bring their *ex situ* collections into the Network under its auspices. By September 1996, 40 countries had offered to put national *ex situ* collections under the auspices of FAO and/or to store international collections in their gene bank. During 1998 and 1999, agreements were signed with the governments of India, Papua New Guinea, Indonesia, and IPGRI, bringing regional collections of the International Coconut Genetic Resources Network (COGENT) held by the last named on behalf of COGENT under FAO auspices;

• *Network of* in situ *Conservation Areas*, with special emphasis on wild relatives of cultivated plants, as well as on the promotion of 'on-farm' conservation and utilization of land races;

• *Crop related Networks*, a co-ordinated approach to identifying, evaluating, and conserving the genetic variability of selected crop species, with the aim of improving cultivars and their adaption to farmers'

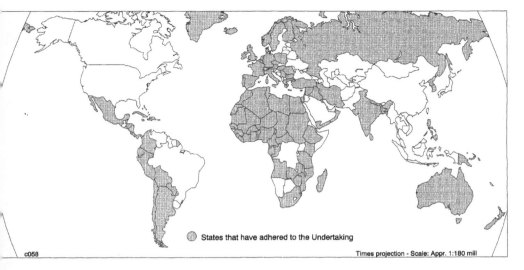

States that have adhered to the Undertaking

c058   Times projection - Scale: Appr. 1:180 mill

.eeds;

World Information and Early Warning System on Plant Genetic Resources (WIEWS), which collects and disseminates data and facilitates the exchange of information on PGR and related technologies and draws rapid attention to hazards threatening the operation of gene banks and the loss of genetic diversity throughout the world;

- *Report on the State of the World's Plant Genetic Resources*, periodically reports on the conservation and utilization of PGR, to assist the Commission in its monitoring function;
- *Global Plan of Action on Plant Genetic Resources*, a rolling plan aimed at rationalizing and co-ordinating efforts in this area to assist the Commission in its co-ordination function.

The first Report on the State of the World's PGR and Global Plan of Action were developed for the Fourth International Technical Conference on PGR (Leipzig, 17–23 June 1996). The Global Plan of Action was formally adopted by 150 countries at Leipzig. In adopting the World Food Summit Plan of Action in November 1996, countries committed themselves to implementing the Plan. The third COP to the CBD in Buenos Aires (4–15 November 1996) endorsed the Plan's policies and priorities and encouraged Parties actively to implement the Plan. The CGRFA monitors and oversees the implementation of the GPA;

- *International Fund for Plant Genetic Resources* (see Special funds, below).

Co-ordination with related instruments
The Commission facilitates co-operation with other conventions and IGOs, such as the Convention on Biological Diversity (CBD) (see this section) and the Commission on Sustainable Development (CSD) (see IGOs).

Secretariat

The Secretariat of the FAO Intergovernmental Commission on Genetic Resources for Food and Agriculture acts as secretariat of the Undertaking.

c/o Food and Agricultural Organization (FAO),
Viale delle Terme di Caracalla,
I-00100 Rome,
Italy
Telephone: +39-06-57054986
Telefax: +39-06-5705-3152/6347
E-mail: jose.esquinas@fao.org

Secretary
Dr José T. Esquinas-Alcázar.

Number of staff
Two professionals and three support staff supported by a number of professional staff from the FAO divisions concerned (April 1999).

Finance

International administration costs of the CGRFA are covered by the regular budget of FAO.

Budget
The administrative core budget was $US900,000 in 1997 and $900,000 in 1998, and is $900,000 in 1999.

Special funds
In November 1991 the FAO Conference approved an annex to the Undertaking which established that 'Farmers' Rights' should be implemented through an international fund on PGR to support plant genetic conservation and utilization programmes, particularly in the developing countries. It also established that the priorities of the fund will be overseen by the Commission on PGR (see below). The fund is yet to be established.

The fund, possible institutional mechanisms, and policy issues are being considered by the Commission in the context of the negotiations for the revision of the Undertaking.

Rules and standards

In its current form, the Undertaking covers both *ex situ* and *in situ* conservation as well as sustainable utilization of PGR.

The Parties shall:
- provide access to the materials which have been collected or conserved in pursuance of its terms, and the export of such

material for scientific or plant-breeding purposes is to take place unrestrictedly on the basis of mutual exchange or on mutually agreed terms;

• give early warning when there is reason to believe that the effective conservation of material held in a collection centre might be prejudiced, with a view to prompt international action to safeguard it;

• mount exploration missions to identify PGR which are in danger of extinction, as well as those that may be useful for development. They agree to put in place legislation to protect plants and their habitats and to take steps to collect genetic material;

• pledge themselves to build up institutional and technical capabilities in developing countries, intensifying plant-breeding and germplasm maintenance activities on the international level, establishing gene banks, setting up an internationally coordinated network of collections, putting in place an international data system, and providing an early warning system to alert the international community of threats to the continued security of any centre at which plant genetic material is collected.

The Undertaking is currently voluntary and, as such, does not impose legally binding obligations on the Parties.

Monitoring/implementation

Review procedure
States are required to provide the Director-General of FAO with annual reports of the steps which have been taken by them in pursuance of the terms of the Undertaking.

Observations or inspections
None by the Agreement as such.

Data and information-system programmes
See World Information and Early Warning System on PGR (WIEWS) under Affiliated instruments and organizations, above.

In preparation for the Fourth International Technical Conference on PGR (see above), more than 150 countries prepared detailed national reports. This information was captured in the WIEWS and formed the basis of the Report on the State of the World's PGR. This Report will be periodically updated under the guidance of the Commission. It underpins the rolling Global Plan of Action, which will also be periodically updated. The Commission oversees and monitors the implementation of the Plan.

For a full list of WIEWS databases, see the website at:
<http:// http://apps2.fao.org/wiews>

The operation of the Undertaking is reviewed at regular meetings of the Commission.

Trade measures
No provisions on trade measures to penalize Parties for non-compliance.

Dispute-settlement mechanisms
The Undertaking makes no reference to dispute settlement. Matters of controversy between the Parties are usually resolved by negotiation and the agreed result endorsed, in appropriate cases, by the Commission or the FAO Conference.

Decision-making bodies

Political
The Commission on Genetic Resources for Food and Agriculture (CGRFA) (previously the Commission on Plant Genetic Resources (CPGR)), with 160 member countries and the European Community by May 1999, including donors and users of germplasm, funds, and technologies, monitors the implementation of the Undertaking and discusses, on an equal footing, matters related to PGR. It meets in regular sessions every two years. The Commission can establish subsidiary intergovernmental working groups to assist it. Currently, there are working groups on animal and on plant genetic resources for food and agriculture.

Scientific/technical
None, but draws on the resources of FAO, as well as IPGRI (see above), which is part of the Consultative Group on International Agricultural Research (CGIAR).

Publications

• *Plant Genetic Resources Newsletter*, by FAO/IPGRI (three times a year);
• *State of the World's PGR*;
• *Global Plan of Action on Plant Genetic Resources*;
• *The Appropriation of the Benefits of Plant Genetic Resources for Agriculture: An Economic Analysis of the Alternative Mechanisms for Biodiversity Conservation*;
• *Sovereign and Property Rights over Plant Genetic Resources*;
• *Providing Farmers' Rights through* in situ *Conservation of Crop Genetic Resources*;
• *Identifying Genetic Resources and their Origin: The Capabilities and Limitations of Modern Biochemical and Legal Systems*;
• *Information on* ex situ *Collections Maintained in Botanic Gardens*;
• *Contribution to the Estimation of Countries' Interdependence in the Area of Plant Genetic Resources*;
• *Access to Plant Genetic Resources and Intellectual Property Rights*;
• *Recent Developments in Biotechnology as they Relate to Plant Genetic Resources for Food and Agriculture*;
• *Recent Developments in Biotechnology as they Relate to Animal Genetic Resources for Food and Agriculture*;
• *Possible Formulas for the Sharing of Benefits Based on Different Benefit-indicators* (CGRFA-8/99/8);
• *The State of the World's Plant Genetic Resources for Food and Agriculture* (CD-Rom).

Sources on the Internet
<http://www.fao.org/ag/cgrfa>

International Tropical Timber Agreement, 1994 (ITTA, 1994)

Objectives

• to provide an effective framework for consultation, international co-operation, and policy development among all members with regard to all relevant aspects of the world timber economy;

• to provide a forum for consultation to promote non-discriminatory timber trade practices;

• to contribute to the process of sustainable development;

• to enhance the capacity of members to implement a strategy for achieving exports of tropical timber and timber products from sustainable managed sources by the year 2000;

• to promote the expansion and diversification of international trade in tropical timber from sustainable sources by improving the structural conditions in international markets;

• to promote and support research and development with a view to improving forest management and efficiency of wood utilization as well as increasing the capacity to conserve and enhance other forest values in timber-producing tropical forests;

• to develop and contribute towards mechanisms for the provision of new and additional financial resources and expertise needed to enhance the capacity of producing members to attain the objectives of this Agreement;

• to improve market intelligence with a view to ensuring greater transparency in the international tropical timber market;

• to promote increased and further processing of tropical timber from sustainable sources in producing member countries with a view to promoting their industrialization and thereby increasing their employment opportunities and export earnings;

• to encourage members to support and develop industrial tropical timber reforestation and forest management activities as well as rehabilitation of degraded forest land, with due regard for the interest of local communities dependent on forest resources;

• to improve marketing and distribution of tropical timber exports from sustainable managed sources;

• to encourage members to develop national policies aimed at sustainable utilization and conservation of timber-producing forests and their genetic resources and at maintaining the ecological balance in the regions concerned, in the context of tropical timber trade;

• to promote the access to, and transfer of, technologies and technical co-operation to implement the objectives of this Agreement;

• to encourage information sharing on the international timber market.

Scope

Legal scope
Open to any state that produces or consumes tropical timber, and to intergovernmental organizations having responsibilities in respect of the negotiation, conclusion, and application of international agreements.

Geographic scope
Global.

Time and place of adoption

26 January 1994, Geneva. The 1994 Agreement is the successor agreement to the ITTA, 1983, which was adopted on 18 November 1983, Geneva.

Entry into force

1 January 1997 for an initial period of four years. (The ITTA, 1983, entered into force on 1 April 1985.)

Status of participation

53 members (Belgium and Luxembourg occupying a joint membership), comprising 29 producing and 24 consuming members, including the European Union, by 16 June 1999. Two Signatories, comprising two consuming members, without ratification, acceptance, approval, definitive signature, or provisional application.

The Secretary-General of the UN acts as depositary.

Affiliated instruments and organizations

The International Tropical Timber Organization (ITTO), established by the ITTA, 1983, is administering the provisions and supervising the operation of this Agreement.

Co-ordination with related instruments
ITTO is active in post-UNCED initiatives and has filled one post on the secretariat of the *ad hoc* Intergovernmental Panel on Forests (IPF) by secondment and funded another, besides serving on the High-Level Inter-Agency Task Force (HLIATF) which supports the IPF. It serves on the Forestry Advisors' Group (FAG) of FAO (see IGOs) and attends sessions of the Committee on Forestry (COFO). In commodities and trade, ITTO is recognized as an International Commodity Body (ICB) by the Common Fund for Commodities, which has co-financed four ITTO projects. Liaison with UNCTAD and attendance at the Trade and Environment Committee of the World Trade Organization (WTO) (see IGOs) is complemented by private-sector links for promotion of its interests in sustainable forest management through the UCBD (Union de Commerce des Bois Durs/Hardwood Traders Union) in Europe, the IHPA (International Hardwood Products Association) in North America, and the JLIA (Japan Lumber Importers' Association) in Japan. ITTO serves on the Timber Working Group of the Convention on International Trade in Endangered Species (CITES) (see this section), and is linked to the Center for International Forestry Research (CIFOR), part of the the Consultative Group for International Agricultural Research (CGIAR) network. Its work on guidelines, criteria, and indicators for sustainable forest management was the first in the field, and the Organization actively participates in recent multilateral and bilateral initiatives along these lines, such as Helsinki, Montreal, and Tarapoto. ITTO's Executive Director is a council member of the World Commission on Forests and Sustainable Development (WCFSD).

Secretariat

International Tropical Timber Organization (ITTO),
International Organizations Center, 5th Floor,
Pacifico-Yokohama,
1-1-1, Minato-Mirai,
Nishi-ku,
Yokohama,
220-0012 Japan
Telephone: +81-45-2231110
Telefax: +81-45-2231111
E-mail: itto@mail.itto-unet.ocn.ne.jp

Executive Director
Dr B. C. Y. Freezailah.

Information Officer
Mr Takeichi Ishikawa.

Number of staff
15 professionals and 14 support staff (December 1998).

Finance

The administrative budget is financed by annually assessed contributions from all member countries in proportion to their votes in the International Tropical Timber Council (ITTC) (see below). In hosting ITTO, the government of Japan and the City of Yokohama provide office accommodation, cover the administrative costs of the biannual Council sessions, and contribute three support staff.

Budget
The administrative budget was $US4.1 million in 1997 and $3.9 million in 1998.

Main contributors
Contributors in 1999 are all the members, except the European Union *per se*, whose constituent states contribute.

64 per cent of the members fulfilled their financial obligations as required by the Agreement in 1994 (77 per cent of expected financial contributions), 73 per cent fulfilled their obligations in 1995 (85 per cent of expected financial contributions), and 80 per cent fulfilled their obligations in 1996 (82 per cent of expected financial contributions).

Special funds
Funding of project activities is from voluntary contributions of members, trade associations, service groups, the private sector, and the *Common Fund for Commodities*.

Generally, contributions earmarked for specific projects are pledged by donors at each Council session, i.e. twice a year. Project proposals originate from members and are technically appraised by an independent Panel of Experts before being examined by the relevant committee. ITTO funding is a grant, not a loan. $US148 million had been donated for the implementation of projects and pre-project and other activities by December 1997; accumulated disbursements at this date were $112 million.

Main contributors are Japan, Switzerland, the USA, the Netherlands, Denmark, Australia, Norway, the United Kingdom, Finland, Austria, France, and Sweden, as well as the Common Fund for Commodities and other donors including NGOs and the private sector.

Recipients are producer member countries, consumer countries with developing economies, and some executing agencies in consumer member countries.

The idea is to encourage consumer countries and their importing industries to contribute towards achieving sustainable use and conservation of tropical forests. The private sector and conservation organizations also make financial contributions to ITTO's project activities.

The *Bali Partnership Fund* is a new fund established under the ITTA, 1994, to assist members to make the necessary investments to achieve the Year 2000 Objective (see below).

Rules and standards

Members are required:
• to pay their annual assessed contributions to the administrative account;
• to provide data to create transparency of the tropical timber economy and enable the secretariat to prepare an *Annual Review and Assessment of the World Tropical Timber Situation*;
• to adhere to decisions made by the Council.

Members are committed to the Year 2000 Objective. It is ITTO's goal that, by the year 2000, all tropical timber entering international trade will be produced from forests under sustainable management. Members are invited to submit reports to the Council annually on their progress towards achieving the Year 2000 Objective, initiated in 1990. A mid-term review was conducted in 1995.

Members have adopted guidelines for the sustainable management of natural tropi-

cal forests, for the establishment and sustainable management of planted tropical forests, and for the conservation of biological diversity in tropical production forests, as well as criteria for the measurement of sustainable rropical forest management. The Organization is also currently preparing guidelines for the sustainable development of forest industries and for the protection of tropical forests against fire. The ITTO Manual for Project Formulation also contains guidelines for ensuring local community participation in the project cycle and to take account of the environmental impacts of projects.

All these commitments and guidelines have been adopted by the ITTC (see below), after due consultation in the ITTO forum, where, apart from members, non-governmental conservation organizations and timber trade associations also take part. Legal implementation and enforcement of practical measures are left to member countries themselves.

The operational activities of the Council and the Committees are:
• recommendations to the Council on project and pre-project proposals and on the policy work programme, including the ITTO Action Plan;
• effective appraisal, monitoring, evaluation, and follow-up of projects and pre-projects and the development of policy ideas;
• specific technical tasks allotted to each committee under the ITTA, 1994.

Monitoring/implementation

Review procedure
Members are expected to submit data annually on their national production, trade, supply, stocks, consumption, and prices of tropical timber for the *Annual Review and Assessment of the World Tropical Timber Situation*. Members are required to supply other statistical data and specific indicators as requested by the Council.

Members are also required to report annually on activities aimed at achieving sustainable forest management and on progress towards ITTO's Year 2000 Objective. Ten members submitted such reports during 1993–4. Six members submitted such reports during 1996. (No data covering 1995.) 33 statistical reports (63 per cent of members) were submitted in 1993–4, 46 reports (88.5 per cent of members) in 1995, and 44 reports (88 per cent of members) in 1996. A summary of these reports is public.

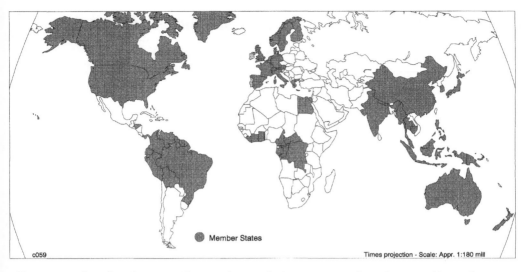

Member States
c059   Times projection - Scale: Appr. 1:180 mill

The assessment of compliance by members to ITTA principles is the responsibility of the Council and the Permanent Committees (see Decision-making bodies below). Emphasis is placed on monitoring and review of ITTO projects and the programme set up by the Action Plan. An expert panel has been established for the technical assessment of project proposals. There is no independent verification of data or information, but non-governmental organizations (NGOs) may address report issues in the Council (see below). They are accorded observer status and are given the chance to speak. These reviews are public and the secretariat distributes a publications list and Council reports.

Observations or inspections
None by the Agreement as such.

Environmental monitoring programmes
ITTO supports several projects, pre-projects, and activities that include various environmental monitoring components.

Trade measures
Nothing in the ITTA, 1994, authorizes the use of measures to restrict or ban international trade in timber and timber imports, particularly measures concerning imports and utilization.

Dispute-settlement mechanisms
Any complaint that a member has failed to fulfil its obligations under the Agreement and any dispute concerning the interpretation or application of the Agreement shall be referred to the Council for decision. Decisions of the Council shall be final and binding.

Decision-making bodies
Political
The ITTA, 1994, has established the International Tropical Timber Organization (ITTO), which functions through its supreme governing body, the International Tropical Timber Council (ITTC). The Council meets twice a year and consists of all members of the Organization.

Voting, very rarely used, is based on simple majorities in each of the producer and consumer caucuses. Only financial members may vote, and the 1,000 votes allotted to each caucus are shared out among these members according to the rules set out in the ITTA, 1994.

The Council's work consists in formulating overall policies, approving the programme of work for the Organization, allocating funds for its implementation, recommending amendments to the Agreement, and undertaking an annual review and assessment of the tropical timber mar-

ket and economy. Non-member governments and organizations may attend upon invitation from the Council as observers of the meetings of the Council.

Scientific/technical
The Permanent Committees, which are open to all members, are:
• Committee on Economic Information and Market Intelligence;
• Committee on Reforestation and Forest Management;
• Committee on Forest Industry;
• Committee on Finance and Administration.

All committees are composed of government experts and experts from trade organizations and conservation NGOs.

Publications
Annual reports, *Annual Review of the World Tropical Timber Situation*, Council reports, technical series, policy development series, information papers, pre-project and project reports, and reports of seminars and workshops are published regularly. ITTO has also two serial publications: *Forest Management Update* and *Market Information Service* (newsletter).

Sources on the Internet
<http://www.itto.or.jp>

Convention on Assistance in the Case of a Nuclear Accident or Radiological Emergency (Assistance Convention)

Objectives
• to set out an international framework aimed at facilitating the prompt provision of assistance in the event of a nuclear accident or radiological emergency, directly between States Parties, through or from the International Atomic Energy Agency (IAEA) (see IGOs), and from other international organizations;
• to minimize consequences and to protect life, property, and the environment from effects of radioactive releases.

Scope
Legal scope
Open to all states, international organizations, and regional integration organizations.

Geographic scope
Global.

Time and place of adoption
26 September 1986, Vienna.

Entry into force
26 February 1987.

Status of participation
76 states and three intergovernmental organizations (the Food and Agriculture Organization (FAO), the World Health Organization (WHO), and the World

Meteorological Organization (WMO) (see IGOs) were Parties by 1 May 1999. 21 Signatories without ratification, acceptance, or approval.
The IAEA acts as depositary.

Affiliated instruments and organizations
No amendments have been proposed.
The IAEA is in charge of administering the Convention.

Co-ordination with related instruments
The IAEA Board of Governors has established an Expert Working Group to consider additional measures to improve co-operation in the field of nuclear safety.

Secretariat
IAEA (see IGOs).

Finance
Budget
Costs are covered by the regular IAEA budget.

Special funds
Not applicable.

Rules and standards
Parties shall co-operate between themselves and with the IAEA to facilitate prompt assistance in the event of a nuclear accident or radiological emergency.

Parties shall request the Agency to use its best endeavours in accordance with the provisions of this Convention to promote, facilitate, and support the co-operation between the Parties provided for in this Convention.
If a Party needs assistance in the event of a nuclear accident or radiological emergency, whether or not such an accident or emergency originates within its territory, jurisdiction, or control, it may call for such assistance from any other Party, from the Agency, or from other IGOs.
A Party to which a request for such assistance is directed shall promptly decide and notify the requesting Party, directly or through the Agency, whether it is in a position to render the assistance requested, and the scope and terms of the assistance.
A Party may request assistance relating to medical or temporary relocation into the territory of another Party of people involved in a nuclear accident or radiological emergency.
A Party requesting assistance shall provide the assisting State with such information as may be necessary for that Party to determine the extent to which it is able to meet the request.
Parties shall notify the IAEA of experts, equipment, and materials which could be made available in case of a nuclear accident or radiological emergency.

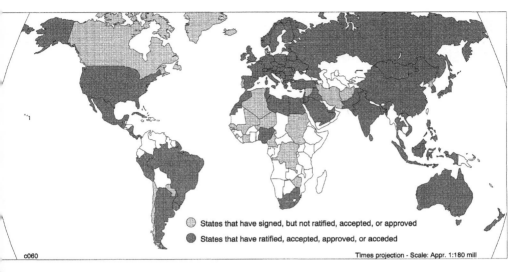

States that have signed, but not ratified, accepted, or approved

States that have ratified, accepted, approved, or acceded

c060   Times projection - Scale: Appr. 1:180 mill

Monitoring/implementation

Review procedure
There are no reporting obligations under the Convention unless a nuclear accident or radiological emergency occurs, which has not been the case since 1986. The IAEA has, however, been asked for assistance 19 times in the framework of this Convention: in the case of the radiological accidents or incidents at Goiânia, Brazil, in September 1987, in Nicaragua in August 1987, in Uganda in November 1988, in El Salvador in February 1989, in Tunisia in December 1990, in Viet Nam in January 1993, in Costa Rica in May 1993, in Estonia in November 1994, in Chile and Peru in August 1996, in Russia and Venezuela in June 1997, in Bangladesh in July 1997, in Georgia in October 1997, in Russia (Chechenia) in January 1998, in Georgia in August 1998 and in October 1998, in Turkey in January 1999, and in Peru in March 1999.

No compliance controls are provided.

All information on implementation of the Convention is made available directly to governments and the competent authorities designated. In addition, the IAEA issues a wide range of public information materials relating to the Convention. There is no independent verification of data or information.

At national level, designated national authorities are responsible for issuing and receiving notifications and information.

Observations or inspections
None by the Convention as such.

Trade measures
No provisions on trade measures to penalize Parties for non-compliance.

Dispute-settlement mechanisms
In the event of a dispute between the Parties, or between a Party and the IAEA, concerning the interpretation and application of the Convention, the Parties shall consult with a view to settling the dispute by negotiation or by any other peaceful means.

However, if the dispute cannot be settled within one year from the request for consultation, the dispute shall be submitted to arbitration or referred to the International Court of Justice for decision.

A Party may declare that it does not consider itself bound by either or both of these dispute-settlement procedures when signing, ratifying, approving, or acceding to the Convention.

Decision-making bodies

Political
The only organ referred to in the Convention is the IAEA. No meeting of Parties has taken place so far.

Scientific/technical
Technical assistance is provided by the IAEA. No long-term scientific advisory functions or participation from NGOs and industry are foreseen.

Publications

Up-to-date information is available through *IAEA Bulletin* (quarterly) and the IAEA's annual reports.

Sources on the Internet

<http://www.iaea.or.at/worldatom/glance/legal>

Convention on Early Notification of a Nuclear Accident (Notification Convention)

Objectives

To provide relevant information about nuclear accidents with possible international transboundary consequences as early as possible in order to minimize environmental, health, and economic consequences.

Scope

Legal scope
Open to all states, international organizations, and regional integration organizations.

Geographic scope
Global.

Time and place of adoption

26 September 1986, Vienna.

Entry into force

27 October 1986.

Status of participation

81 states and three intergovernmental organizations (the Food and Agriculture Organization (FAO), the World Health Organization (WHO), and the World Meteorological Organization (WMO) (see IGOs) were Parties by 1 May 1999. 18 Signatories without ratification, acceptance, or approval.

The International Atomic Energy Agency (IAEA) (see IGOs) acts as depositary.

Affiliated instruments and organizations

No amendments have been proposed.

The IAEA Secretariat is in charge of administering the Convention.

Co-ordination with related instruments
The IAEA Board of Governors has established an Expert Working Group to consider additional measures to improve co-operation in the field of nuclear safety.

Secretariat

IAEA (see IGOs).

Finance

Budget
Costs are covered by the regular IAEA budget.

Special funds
Not applicable.

Rules and standards

In the event of any nuclear accident with actual or potential transboundary effects involving its facilities or activities from which a release of radioactive material occurs or is likely to occur, the Party shall notify other states which may be physically affected, directly or through the IAEA, and the IAEA itself, of the nature of the accident, its location, and the time of its occurrence.

The State Party is also required to provide other states and the IAEA promptly with specified information relevant to minimizing the radiological consequences in those states.

Parties are further required to respond to a request by an affected State for additional information or consultation.

In addition, each Party shall make known its competent authorities or point of contact responsible for issuing and receiving the notification and information referred to above.

States may voluntarily notify accidents related to military nuclear activities, with a view to minimizing the radiological consequences of the nuclear accident. All five nuclear-weapon states have declared their intention to make such notifications.

The information to be provided in case of a nuclear accident shall comprise the following data:
(*a*) the time, the exact location where appropriate, and the nature of the accident;
(*b*) the facility or activity involved;
(*c*) the assumed or established cause and the foreseen development of the nuclear accident relevant to the transboundary release of the radioactive material;
(*d*) the general characteristics of the radioactive release, including, as far as practicable and appropriate, the nature, probable physical and chemical form, quantity, composition, and effective height of the radioactive release;

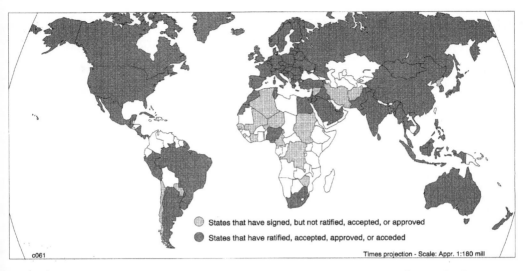

States that have signed, but not ratified, accepted, or approved

States that have ratified, accepted, approved, or acceded

c061   Times projection - Scale: Appr. 1:180 mill

(*e*) information on current and predicted meteorological and hydrological conditions necessary to forecasting the transboundary release of the radioactive materials;

(*f*) the results of environmental monitoring relevant to the transboundary release of the radioactive materials;

(*g*) the off-site protective measures taken or planned;

(*h*) the predicted behaviour over time of the radioactive release.

Monitoring/implementation

Review procedure
The information above shall be supplemented by further relevant information on the development of the emergency situation with the inclusion of its foreseeable and actual termination. Information may be used without restriction except when such information is provided in confidence by the notifying Party.

All information on implementation of the Convention is made available directly to governments and the competent authorities designated. In addition, the IAEA issues a wide range of public information materials relating to the Convention. There is no independent verification of data or information.

At national level, designated national authorities are responsible for issuing and receiving notifications and information.

Observations or inspections
None by the Convention as such.

Trade measures
No provisions on trade measures to penalize Parties for non-compliance.

Dispute-settlement mechanisms
In the event of a dispute between the Parties, or between a Party and the IAEA, concerning the interpretation and application of the Convention, the Parties shall consult with a view to settling the dispute by negotiation or by any other peaceful means.

However, if the dispute cannot be settled within one year from the request for consultation, the dispute shall be submitted to arbitration or referred to the International Court of Justice for decision.

A Party may declare that it does not consider itself bound by either or both of these dispute-settlement procedures when signing, ratifying, approving, or acceding to the Convention.

Decision-making bodies
Political
The only organ referred to in the Convention is the IAEA. No meetings of Parties have taken place so far.

Scientific/technical
Technical assistance is provided by the IAEA. No long-term scientific advisory functions or participation from NGOs and industry are foreseen.

Publications
Up-to-date information is available through *IAEA Bulletin* (quarterly) and the IAEA's annual reports.

Sources on the Internet
<http://www.iaea.or.at/worldatom/glance/legal>

Convention on Nuclear Safety

Objectives
- to achieve and maintain a high level of nuclear safety world-wide through the enhancement of national measures and international co-operation, including, where appropriate, safety-related technical co-operation;
- to establish and maintain effective defences in nuclear installations against potential radiological hazards in order to protect individuals, society, and the environment from harmful effects of ionizing radiation from such installations;
- to prevent accidents with radiological consequences and to mitigate such consequences should they occur.

Scope
Legal scope
Open to all states and regional organizations of an integration or other nature.

Geographic scope
Global.

Time and place of adoption
17 June 1994, Vienna. Open for signature on 20 September 1994.

Entry into force
24 October 1996.

Status of participation
51 Parties by 26 May 1999. 19 Signatories without ratification, acceptance, or approval.

The International Atomic Energy Agency (IAEA) (see IGOs) acts as depositary.

Affiliated instruments and organizations
No amendments have yet been proposed. Any Contracting Party may propose amendments. Proposed amendments shall be considered at a meeting of the Contracting Parties (see Decision-making bodies, below).

The IAEA Secretariat is in charge of administering the Convention.

Co-ordination with related instruments
None.

Secretariat
IAEA (see IGOs).

Finance
Budget
Costs are covered by the regular IAEA budget.

Special funds
Not applicable.

Rules and standards
The specific safety obligations in the Convention are based on what are termed fundamental safety provisions rather than on very detailed standards; guidance on the more detailed internationally agreed safety standards are already available and these are also continually updated.

The fundamental safety obligations of the Convention begin with a requirement for each State to maintain a legislative and regulatory framework; that is, to have:
- specific national safety requirements;
- a licensing procedure;
- inspection, assessment, and enforcement policies.

There is also a requirement that the body which implements the regulatory function be separate from other bodies concerned with the promotion and utilization of nuclear energy. The Convention underscores that the prime responsibility for safety rests with the State where a nuclear installation is located, and more specifically the holder of the operating licence, that is, the utility or operating organization.

There is a series of general safety obligations which emphasizes the need:
- to take steps to assure that all organizations involved with nuclear installations give priority to safety;
- to provide adequate financial and human resources;
- to give attention to human factor and quality assurance.

There is also a series of more detailed obligations related to siting, design, construction, and operation requirements. These speak to the need:
- to evaluate all site-related factors such as seismology and flooding factors;
- to use proven technologies;
- to have approved operating procedures;
- to report promptly on accidents;
- to collect and analyse operating experience;
- to minimize nuclear waste;
- to prepare and test emergency plans.

In addition, the obligations contain some requirements for interactions with neighbouring countries:
- States should, upon request, provide information to a neighbouring state in the vicinity of a proposed nuclear installation, (if they are likely to be affected) to enable them to assess the probable safety impact on their territory;
- States should also ensure that their own population and the competent authorities of states in the vicinity of a nuclear installation are provided with appropriate information for emergency planning and response;
- States which do not have a nuclear installation but could be affected by a neighbouring country's installation should have emergency plans which are tested.

The Convention has 16 specific articles defining obligations of the Convention, and it provides for a forum to discuss nuclear safety conditions in each State. The forum will be the mechanism to identify problems, concerns, and uncertainties or omissions. The Convention also provides a mechanism to make the public aware of the issues.

Monitoring/implementation
Review procedure
Each Contracting Party shall, prior to meetings of the Contracting Parties, submit a report on the measures it has taken to implement each of the obligations of the Convention—as these meetings are held for the purpose of reviewing the reports submitted. Subgroups comprised of representatives of the Parties may be established and may function during the review meetings as deemed necessary for the purpose of reviewing subjects contained in the reports. Each Party shall have a reasonable opportunity to discuss the reports submitted by other Parties and to seek clarification of such reports.

The first Review Meeting pursuant to Article 20 of the Convention was held at the Headquarters of IAEA, being the Secretariat under the Convention, in Vienna between 12 and 23 April 1999.

45 Contracting Parties participated,

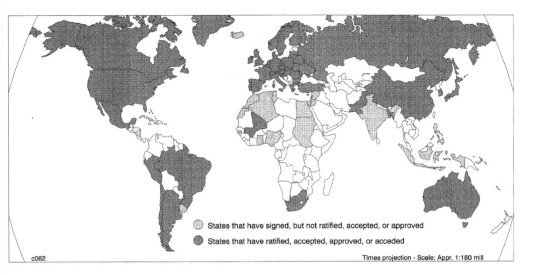

States that have signed, but not ratified, accepted, or approved

States that have ratified, accepted, approved, or acceded

c062   Times projection - Scale: Appr. 1:180 mill

namely: Argentina, Armenia, Australia, Austria, Belarus, Belgium, Brazil, Bulgaria, Canada, Chile, China, China, Croatia, the Czech Republic, Denmark, Finland, France, Germany, Greece, Hungary, Ireland, Italy, Japan, the Republic of Korea, Latvia, Lebanon, Lithuania, Luxembourg, Mexico, the Netherlands, Norway, Pakistan, Peru, Poland, Portugal, Romania, the Russian Federation, Slovakia, Slovenia, South Africa, Spain, Sweden, Switzerland, Turkey, Ukraine, and the United Kingdom.

Six months before the Review Meeting, Contracting Parties submitted national reports on steps and measures taken to implement Convention obligations. In the following months the Parties reviewed each other's reports and exchanged written questions and comments. At the Review Meeting, Parties organized themselves into six country groups.

Pursuant to Article 25 of the Convention, the Parties adopted, by consensus, a document addressing issues discussed and conclusions reached, entitled *Summary Report of the Review Meeting of Contracting Parties to the Convention on Nuclear Safety*. It is available on the IAEA's website under the following address: <http://www.iaea.or.at/worldatom/glance/legal/revmtg0199.html>.

Observations or inspections
None by the Convention as such.

Trade measures
No provisions on trade measures to penalize Parties for non-compliance.

Dispute-settlement mechanisms
In the event of a disagreement between two or more Parties concerning the interpretation and application of the Convention, the Parties shall consult within the framework of the meeting of the Parties with a view to resolving the disagreement.

Decision-making bodies
Political
The meeting of the Contracting Parties is the governing body of the Convention. Each Party shall be represented at such meetings by one delegate and by such alternates, experts, and advisers as it deems necessary. The meeting shall keep under review and evaluate implementation of the Convention. It shall also consider and adopt, by consensus, amendments to the Convention. In the absence of consensus, the meeting shall decide whether to submit proposed amendments to a diplomatic conference. A decision to submit a proposed amendment to a diplomatic conference shall require a two-thirds majority vote of the Contracting Parties present and voting at the meeting, providing that at least one-half of the Parties are present at the tie of voting. The diplomatic conference shall make every effort to

ensure amendments are adopted by consensus. Should this not be possible, amendments shall be adopted with a two-thirds majority of all Parties.

The Parties may invite, by consensus, any IGO which is competent in respect of matters governed by the Convention to attend, as an observer, any meeting, or specific sessions thereof. Observers shall be required to accept in writing, and in advance, confidentiality according with the provisions in the Convention.

The first meeting of the Parties was held at the IAEA from 22 to 25 April 1997.

Scientific/technical bodies
To be decided. Technical assistance may be provided by the IAEA if such services can be undertaken within its programmes and regular budget or from voluntary funding provided from another source. No long-term scientific advisory functions or participation from NGOs and industry are foreseen.

Publications
Up-to-date information is available through *IAEA Bulletin* (quarterly) and the IAEA's annual reports.

Sources on the Internet
<http://www.iaea.or.at/worldatom/glance/legal>

Vienna Convention on Civil Liability for Nuclear Damage

Objectives

To establish minimum standards to provide financial protection against damage resulting from peaceful uses of nuclear energy.

Scope

Legal scope
Open to all member States of the UN, or members of the UN specialized agencies or the International Atomic Energy Agency (IAEA) (see IGOs). Not open to regional integration organizations.

Geographic scope
Global.

Time and place of adoption

21 May 1963, Vienna.

Entry into force

12 November 1977.

Status of participation

32 Parties by 26 May 1999. Six Signatories without ratification, acceptance, or approval.

The IAEA acts as depositary.

Affiliated instruments and organizations

• *Optional Protocol Concerning the Compulsory Settlement of Disputes*, Vienna, 1963 (see below). Entered into force on 13 May 1999 upon the second ratification. Two Parties by 26 May 1999.

• *Joint Protocol Relating to the Application of the Vienna Convention and the Paris Convention*, Vienna, 21 September 1988. Entered into force on 27 April 1992. 20 Parties by 26 May 1999. 12 Signatories without ratification, acceptance, or approval. The Paris Convention on Third Party Liability in the Field of Nuclear Energy is regional in scope and administered by the OECD Nuclear Energy Agency (NEA). The address of the Agency is Le Seine-St Germain, 12 boulevard des Îles, F-92130 Issy-les-Moulineaux, France. Telephone: +33-1-45241010. Telefax: +33-1-45241110. Internet: <http://www.nea.fr/>
• *Protocol to Amend the Vienna Convention on Civil Liability for Nuclear Damage*, Vienna, 12 September 1997. (Not yet in force.) One ratification by 26 May 1999. 13 Signatories without ratification, acceptance, or approval. Open for signature by all states until its entry into force. It enters into force three months after the date of deposit of the fifth instruments of ratification, acceptance, or approval. The main objective of the Protocol is to set the possible limit of the operator's liability at not less than 300 million Special Drawing Rights (SDRs).

The IAEA Secretariat is in charge of administering the Convention.

Co-ordination with related instruments
Since 1987 a review of all aspects of international law on liability for nuclear damage has been instituted by the Standing Committee on Liability for Nuclear Damage, within the framework of the IAEA. The

first stage of this work led to the adoption of the Joint Protocol (see above). With respect to the revision of the Vienna Convention, the next stage led to the adoption of both the Protocol to Amend the Vienna Convention on Civil Liability for Nuclear Damage (see above) and a new convention in 1997.
• *Convention on Supplementary Compensation for Nuclear Damage*. Adopted in Vienna on 12 September 1997. (Not yet in force.) One ratification by 26 May 1999. 12 Signatories without ratification, acceptance, or approval. Enters into force on the ninetieth day following the date on which at least five states with a minimum of 400,000 units of installed nuclear capacity have deposited an instrument. The main objective of the Convention is to define additional amounts to be provided through contributions by States Parties on the basis of installed nuclear capacity and UN rate of assessment. It is an instrument to which all states may adhere regardless of whether they are parties to any existing nuclear liability conventions or have nuclear installations on their territories.

Secretariat

IAEA (see IGOs).

Finance

Budget
No costs of administration.

Special funds
None.

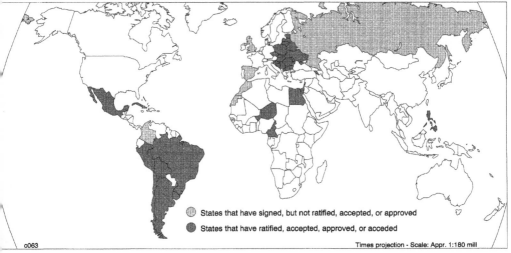

States that have signed, but not ratified, accepted, or approved

States that have ratified, accepted, approved, or acceded

c063   Times projection - Scale: Appr. 1:180 mill

Rules and standards

The operator of a nuclear installation shall be liable for nuclear damage on provision of proof that such damage was caused by an incident within the installation, or involving nuclear material originating therefrom or being sent thereto.

The liability of the operator in such a case shall be absolute, but the courts may make a finding of contributory negligence on the part of the person suffering such damage; in any case the operator will not be liable if the nuclear incident was due directly to act of armed conflict, civil war, insurrection, or a grave natural disaster of an exceptional character.

The Convention has established limits of liability and limitation of action.

The operator is required to maintain insurance or financial security to cover liability.

Parties shall:

ensure the payment of compensation in cases where they do not provide for insurance of the operator or beyond the yield of such insurance and up to the operator's liability;

provide for necessary jurisdictional competences, and recognize final judgements entered by foreign courts in accordance with the Convention.

They shall not invoke immunities in legal proceedings under the Convention.

The principal benefit for all countries participating in the Convention is the right of their nationals to claim compensation in case of nuclear damage caused by installations situated in the territory of a Contracting Party. Currently, the minimum amount of compensation is subject to review and subsequent adoption; the benefit may be expected to increase substantially in the near future.

Monitoring/implementation

Review procedure
There is no mechanism for the promotion of implementation and follow-up on non-compliance. Parties do not regularly report about implementation and do not have to disclose or supply data.

Observations or inspections
None by the Convention as such.

Trade measures
No provisions on trade measures to penalize Parties for non-compliance.

Dispute-settlement mechanisms
The Convention has no rules concerning the settlement of disputes. But, the International Conference on Civil Liability for Nuclear Damage of 1963 adopted an Optional Protocol Concerning Compulsory Settlement of Disputes (see above).

Decision-making bodies

Political
The Convention does not provide for institutional or administrative arrangements. No regular meetings or programme activities are envisaged. A Standing Committee on Civil Liability for Nuclear Damage was established within the framework of the IAEA. This Committee has met occasionally to discuss issues relevant to the Convention. The Committee was composed of 15 States. Limitations concerning participation were removed as the Committee was transformed into an open-ended negotiation forum and renamed a Standing Committee on Liability for Nuclear Damage. Currently, about 60 delegations from both developing and industrialized countries as well as NGOs attend its sessions and the mandate of the Committee has been extended to include international liability matters.

Scientific/technical
There are no elaborated mechanisms for regular review of provisions or consideration of scientific and technical information. However, the Board of Governors of the IAEA may take decisions on minor technical issues. The Board may also provide legal assistance if requested in case of countries without nuclear programmes. Participation does not imply any financial obligations.

Publications

Up-to-date information is available through *IAEA Bulletin* (quarterly) and the IAEA's annual reports.

Sources on the Internet

<http://www.iaea.or.at/worldatom/glance/legal>

Convention on the Protection and Use of Transboundary Watercourses and International Lakes (ECE Water Convention)

Objectives

• to strengthen national and international actions aimed at the protection and ecologically sound management of transboundary waters, both surface waters and groundwaters, and related ecosystems, including the marine environment;
• to prevent, control, and reduce the releases of hazardous, acidifying, and eutrophying substances into the aquatic environment;
• to promote public information and public participation in relevant decision-making processes.

Scope

Legal scope
Open to member countries of the UN Economic Commission for Europe (UN/ECE), the European Union (EU), and other European states having consultative status with the UN/ECE.

Geographic scope
Regional. UN/ECE region (Europe and North America).

Time and place of adoption
17 March 1992, Helsinki.

Entry into force
6 October 1996.

Status of participation
24 Parties, including the European Union, by 16 June 1999. Six Signatories without ratification, acceptance, or approval.

The Secretary-General of the UN acts as depositary.

Affiliated instruments and organizations

Protocol on Water and Health to the Convention on the Protection and Use of Transboudary Watercourses and International Lakes, London, 17 June 1999. 35 Signatories by 17 July 1999. The Protocol was adopted at the third Ministerial Conference on Environmental and Health in London (16–18 June 1999).

The Convention contains also four *annexes* which form an integral part of the Convention.

Co-ordination with related instruments
The Parties shall exchange information regarding experience gained in concluding and implementing bilateral and multilateral agreements or other arrangements regarding the protection and use of transboundary waters to which one or more Parties are part.

Secretariat
UN/ECE, Environment and Human Settlements Division (ENHS),
Palais des Nations,
CH-1211 Geneva 10,
Switzerland
Telephone: +41-22-917-2373/3158
Telefax: +41-22-9070107
E-mail: rainer.enderlein@unece.org

Secretary to the Meeting of the Parties
Mr Rainer E. Enderlein.

Rules and standards
The Parties shall take all appropriate measures:
• to prevent, control, and reduce pollution of waters causing or likely to cause transboundary impact;
• to ensure that transboundary waters are used with the aim of ecologically sound and rational water management, conservation of water resources, and environmental protection;
• to ensure that transboundary waters are used in a reasonable and equitable way, taking into particular account their transboundary character, in the case of activities which cause or are likely to cause transboundary impact;
• to ensure conservation and, where necessary, restoration of ecosystems.
In taking these measures, the Parties shall be guided by the following principles:
• the *precautionary principle*, by virtue of which action to avoid the potential transboundary impact of the release of hazardous substances shall not be postponed on the ground that scientific research has not fully proved a causal link between those substances, on the one hand, and the potential transboundary impact, on the other hand;
• the *polluter-pays principle*, by virtue of which the costs of pollution prevention, control, and reduction measures shall be borne by the polluter;
• water resources shall be managed so that the needs of the present generation are met without compromising the ability of future generations to meet their own needs.

Measures for the prevention, control, and reduction of water pollution shall be taken, where possible, at source. These measures shall not directly or indirectly result in a transfer of pollution to other parts of the environment.

The Parties will have to set emission limits for discharges from point sources based on the best available technology; issue authorizations for the discharge of waste water and monitor compliance therewith; adopt water-quality criteria and define water-quality objectives; apply at least biological treatment or equivalent processes to municipal waste water; develop contingency plans; apply environmental impact assessment and the ecosystem approach in water management; and develop and implement appropriate measures and best environmental practices to reduce the input of nutrients and hazardous substances from diffuse sources, in particular from agriculture.

The riparian Parties shall co-operate on the basis of equality and reciprocity, in particular through bilateral and multilateral agreements, in order to develop harmonized policies, programmes, and strategies covering the relevant catchment areas, or parts thereof, aimed at the prevention, control, and reduction of transboundary impact, and at the protection of the environment of transboundary waters or the environment influenced by such waters, including the marine environment.

The Convention establishes the minimum requirements for the agreements or other arrangements between Parties bordering the same transboundary waters.

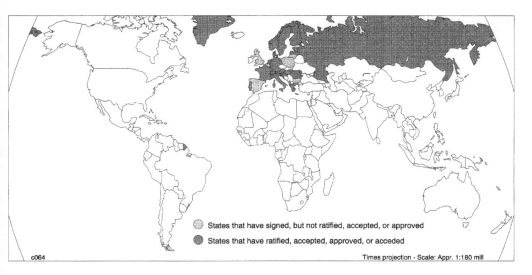

○ States that have signed, but not ratified, accepted, or approved

● States that have ratified, accepted, approved, or acceded

c064   Times projection - Scale: Appr. 1:180 mill

Monitoring/implementation

Review procedure
The Parties shall report periodically on the implementation of this Convention.

The Meeting of the Parties (see below) shall keep the Convention under continuous review and, with this purpose in mind:
• review the policies for and methodological approaches to the protection and use of transboundary waters of the Parties with a view to further improving the protection and use of transboundary waters;
• exchange information regarding experience gained in concluding and implementing bilateral and multilateral agreements or other arrangements regarding the protection and use of transboundary waters to which one or more of the Parties are party.

Under the auspices of the UN/ECE Committee on Environmental Policy, the Working Party on Water Problems at its annual sessions reviewed action taken to implement the Convention pending its entry into force and took steps to bring closer together policies and strategies on transboundary waters.

After the entry into force, Finland, the host country for the first Meeting of the Parties, agreed to lead the preparatory process until that meeting, which was held in Finland on 2–4 July 1997.

The programme of work (1997–2000) covers five priority areas: joint bodies (e.g. river and lake commissions), assistance to countries in transition, integrated management of water and related ecosystems, land-based pollution control, and water supply and human health.

Environmental monitoring programmes
Parties bordering the same transboundary water shall establish and implement joint programmes for monitoring the conditions of transboundary waters, including floods and ice drifts, as well as transboundary impact; agree upon pollution parameters and pollutants whose concentrations in transboundary waters shall be regularly monitored; carry out joint or co-ordinated assessments of the condition of transboundary waters and the effectiveness of measures taken to prevent, control, and reduce transboundary impact; exchange reasonably available data on environmental conditions of transboundary waters, including monitoring data; inform each other about critical situations that may have transboundary impact; and make available to the public results of water and effluent sampling, together with the results of checking compliance with the water-quality objectives and the permit conditions.

The Convention obliges the riparian Parties furthermore to harmonize rules for the setting-up and operation of monitoring programmes, measurement systems, devices, analytical techniques, data processing, and evaluation procedures.

Trade measures
No provisions on trade measures to penalize Parties for non-compliance.

Decision-making bodies

Political
The Meeting of the Parties is the supreme decision-making body. The first meeting was held in Finland on 2–4 July 1997 and the second meeting is tentatively scheduled to be held in The Hague, the Netherlands, in March 2000.

At their meetings, which shall be held at least every three years, the Parties shall keep under continuous review the implementation of the Convention and consider and adopt proposals for further development or amendments to the Convention.

Scientific/technical
The implementation of the programme of work is supported by the Working Group on Water Management as well as by task forces on monitoring and assessment of transboundary waters; laboratory quality management and accreditation; water and health; flood prevention; prevention of industrial accidents; and legal issues.

Publications
• UN/ECE Water Series;
• *Environmental Conventions Elaborated under the Auspices of the UN/ECE*, 1992;
• *Bilateral and Multilateral Agreements and Other Arrangements in Europe and North America on the Protection and Use of Transboundary Waters*, ECE/ENVWA/32, 1993 (and the 1994 and 1995 updates published as Adds. 1 and 2 to this publication).

Sources on the Internet
<http://www.unece.org/env/water_h.htm>
<http://www.waterland.net/riza/imac-water>

Tables of Agreements and Degrees of Participation, by Country

Abbreviations

GENERAL ENVIRONMENTAL CONCERNS
Convention on Access to Information, Public Participation in Decision-Making and Access to Justice in Environmental Matters (Århus Convention): *Information, Particip., and Justice*
Convention on Environmental Impact Assessment in a Transboundary Context: *Environm. Impact Assessment*

ATMOSPHERE
Annex 16, vol. II (Environmental Protection: Aircraft Engine Emissions) to the 1944 Chicago Convention on International Civil Aviation: *Aircraft Engine Emissions (ICAO)*
Convention on Long-Range Transboundary Air Pollution: *Transb. Air Pollution (LRTAP)*
- *1994 Sulphur Protocol*
- *1998 NO$_x$ Protocol*
- *1991 VOC Protocol*
- *1998 Heavy Metals Protocol*
- *1998 POPs Protocol*

United Nations Framework Convention on Climate Change: *Climate Change (UNFCCC)*
- *Kyoto Protocol*

Vienna Convention for the Protection of the Ozone Layer: *Ozone Layer Convention*
- Montreal Protocol on Substances that Deplete the Ozone Layer: *Montreal Protocol*
- *London Amendment*
- *Copenhagen Amendment*

HAZARDOUS SUBSTANCES
Convention on the Ban of the Import into Africa and the Control of Transboundary Movements and Management of Hazardous Wastes within Africa: *Bamako Convention*
Convention on Civil Liability for Damage Caused during Carriage of Dangerous Goods by Road, Rail, and Inland Navigation Vessels: *CRTD*
Convention on the Control of Transboundary Movements of Hazardous Wastes and their Disposal: *Basel Convention*
Convention on the Prior Informed Consent Procedure for Certain Hazardous Chemicals and Pesticides in International Trade: *PIC Convention*
Convention to Ban the Importation into Forum Island Countries of Hazardous and Radioactive Wastes and to Control the Transboundary Movement and Management of Hazardous Wastes within the South Pacific Region: *Waigani Convention*
Convention on the Transboundary Effects of Industrial Accidents: *Transb. Effects of Indust. Accidents*
European Agreement Concerning the International Carriage of Dangerous Goods by Road: *Dangerous Goods by Road (ADR)*
FAO International Code of Conduct on the Distribution and Use of Pesticides: *Distrib. and Use of Pesticides*

MARINE ENVIRONMENT
Global Conventions
Convention on the Prevention of Marine Pollution by Dumping of Wastes and Other Matter: *London Convention 1972*
- *1996 Protocol to LC 1972*

International Convention for the Prevention of Pollution from Ships, 1973, as modified by the Protocol of 1978 relating thereto: *MARPOL 73/78*
International Convention on Civil Liability for Oil Pollution Damage 1969: *1969 CLC*
- *1992 CLC Protocol*

International Convention on the Establishment of an International Fund for Compensation for Oil Pollution Damage 1971: *1971 Fund Convention*
- *1992 Fund Protocol*

International Convention on Liability and Compensation for Damage in Connection with the Carriage of Hazardous and Noxious Substances by Sea: *HNS Convention*
International Convention on Oil Pollution Preparedness, Response, and Co-operation: *OPRC*
International Convention Relating to Intervention on the High Seas in Cases of Oil Pollution Casualties: *Intervention Convention*
United Nations Convention on the Law of the Sea: *UNCLOS*

Regional Conventions
Convention for the Protection of the Marine Environment of the North-East Atlantic: *OSPAR Convention*
Convention on the Protection of the Marine Environment of the Baltic Sea Area: *1974 Helsinki Convention*
Convention on the Protection of the Marine Environment of the Baltic Sea Area: *1992 Helsinki Convention*

Conventions within the UNEP Regional Seas Programme:
- Convention on the Protection of the Black Sea against Pollution: *Black Sea*
- Convention for the Protection and Development of the Marine Environment of the Wider Caribbean Region: *Wider Caribbean Region*
- Convention for the Protection, Management, and Development of the Marine and Coastal Environment of the Eastern African Region: *Eastern African Region*
- Kuwait Regional Convention for Co-operation on the Protection of the Marine Environment from Pollution: *Kuwait Region*
- Convention for the Protection of the Marine Environment and the Coastal Region of the Mediterranean (Barcelona Convention): *Mediterranean Sea*
- Regional Convention for the Conservation of the Red Sea and Gulf of Aden Environment: *Red Sea and Gulf of Aden*
- Convention for the Protection of the Natural Resources and Environment of the South Pacific Region (SPREP Convention): *South Pacific Region*
- Convention for the Protection of the Marine Environment and Coastal Area of the South-East Pacific: *South-East Pacific*
- Convention for Co-operation in the Protection and Development of the Marine and Coastal Environment of the West and Central African Region: *West and Centr. African Region*

MARINE LIVING RESOURCES
Convention on the Conservation of Antarctic Marine Living Resources: *Antarc. Marine Living Res. (CCAMLR)*
International Convention for the Conservation of Atlantic Tunas: *Atlantic Tunas (ICCAT)*
International Convention for the Regulation of Whaling: *Regulation of Whaling (ICRW)*

NATURE CONSERVATION AND TERRESTRIAL LIVING RESOURCES
Antarctic Treaty
- Protocol on Environmental Protection to the Antarctic Treaty: *Madrid Protocol*
Convention Concerning the Protection of the World Cultural and Natural Heritage: *World Heritage Convention*
Convention on Biological Diversity: *Biological Diversity (CBD)*
Convention on the Conservation of Migratory Species of Wild Animals: *Migr. Species of Wild Animals (CMS)*
Convention on International Trade in Endangered Species of Wild Fauna and Flora: *CITES*
Convention on Wetlands of International Importance especially as Waterfowl Habitat: *Ramsar Convention*
Convention to Combat Desertification: *Conv. to Combat Desertification (CCD)*
FAO International Undertaking on Plant Genetic Resources: *Plant Genetic Resources*
International Tropical Timber Agreement, 1994: *Tropical Timber (ITTA, 1994)*

NUCLEAR SAFETY
Convention on Assistance in the Case of a Nuclear Accident or Radiological Emergency: *Assistance Convention*
Convention on Early Notification of a Nuclear Accident: *Notification Convention*
Convention on Nuclear Safety: *Nuclear Safety*
Vienna Convention on Civil Liability for Nuclear Damage: *Civil Liability for Nuclear Damage*

FRESHWATER RESOURCES
Convention on the Protection and Use of Transboundary Watercourses and International Lakes: *ECE Water Convention*

Key

General
States that have signed, but not ratified, accepted, or approved

States that have ratified, accepted, approved, or acceded

Antarctic Treaty
Non-Consultative Parties to the Antarctic Treaty

Consultative Parties to the Antarctic Treaty

Aircraft Engine Emissions (ICAO) and
Distrib. and Use of Pesticides
Member States

Plant Genetic Resources
States that have adhered to the Undertaking

Tropical Timber (ITTA, 1994)
Member States

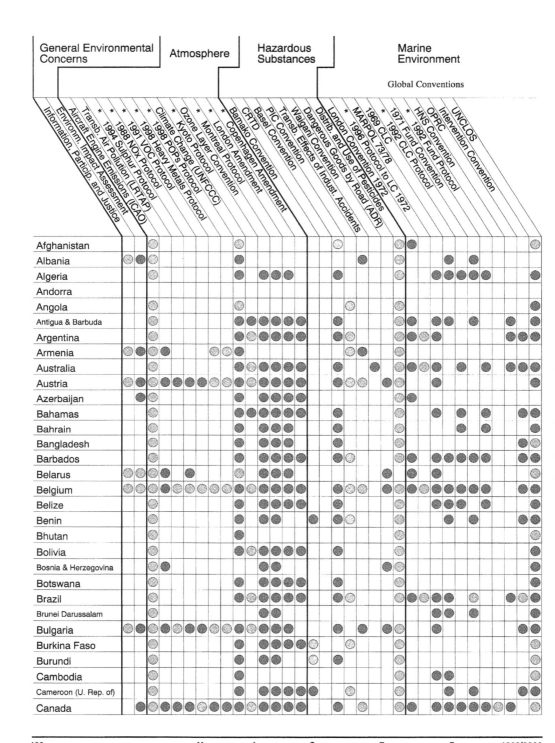

	Information, Particip. and Justice	Environm. Impact Assessment	Aircraft Engine Emissions (ICAO)	Transb. Air Pollution (LRTAP)	1994 Sulphur Protocol	1988 NOx Protocol	1991 VOC Protocol	1998 Heavy Metals Protocol	1998 POPs Protocol	Climate Change (UNFCCC)	Kyoto Protocol	Ozone Layer Convention	Montreal Protocol	London Amendment	Copenhagen Amendment	Bamako Convention	CRTD	Basel Convention	PIC Convention	Transb. Effects of Indust. Accidents	Walgani Convention	Dangerous Goods by Road (ADR)	Distrib. and Use of Pesticides	London Convention 1972	1996 Protocol to LC 1972	MARPOL 73/78	1969 CLC	1992 CLC	1971 Fund Convention	1992 Fund Protocol	HNS Convention	OPRC Convention	Intervention Convention	UNCLOS
Afghanistan		◐								◐								◐				◐				◐ ●								◐
Albania	◐ ◐ ●									◐													●			◐				◐ ◐ ◐				
Algeria		◐								◐			● ● ●					◐								◐			◐ ◐ ◐ ◐ ●					●
Andorra																																		
Angola		◐								◐											◐					◐								●
Antigua & Barbuda		◐								● ● ● ● ●							◐						◐ ●		● ◐	●			◐ ●			◐ ●
Argentina		◐								● ● ◐ ● ●							◐ ◐					◐ ● ◐ ●			●						● ● ●
Armenia	◐ ●	◐ ●				◐ ◐							◐ ◐					◐																	
Australia		◐								● ◐ ● ● ●			●			●					● ◐ ● ◐		●		●		● ● ●
Austria	◐ ●	◐ ● ● ● ● ● ● ●									● ◐ ◐			●		◐													
Azerbaijan	◐ ●									● ● ●												◐										
Bahamas		◐								● ● ● ●			◐					◐			●		● ●		● ●
Bahrain		◐								● ● ●			◐					◐				● ●			●
Bangladesh		◐								● ● ●			◐					◐							● ●
Barbados		◐								● ● ● ●			◐ ◐				◐	●			● ● ● ●			● ●
Belarus	◐ ◐ ◐	●	◐						◐			◐					◐								●
Belgium	◐ ● ◐ ● ◐ ◐ ● ● ●									● ◐ ●			◐ ◐ ◐		●		● ● ● ● ● ● ◐		● ●
Belize		◐								● ● ● ●			◐					◐			● ● ●			●
Benin		◐								◐		● ●			●	◐ ◐					◐			●		●		●
Bhutan		◐								◐								◐											●
Bolivia		◐								● ● ● ● ●			◐					◐							●
Bosnia & Herzegovina	◐ ●								◐ ●			◐ ◐					◐										●
Botswana		◐								● ● ● ●			◐					◐						●
Brazil		◐								● ● ● ◐ ●		● ◐					● ◐ ● ●	●		● ● ●
Brunei Darussalam		◐								◐													● ● ◐			●
Bulgaria	◐ ◐ ● ◐ ● ● ◐ ● ◐ ●	◐ ● ●							● ◐	●	●					◐					● ●
Burkina Faso		◐								● ● ● ● ● ◐		◐					◐					●
Burundi		◐								● ● ◐		◐		●						◐				●
Cambodia		◐								●			◐					◐			● ●			●
Cameroon (U. Rep. of)		◐							● ● ● ●			◐			◐		◐			●		●		● ●
Canada	◐ ◐ ● ● ● ◐ ● ◐ ● ● ● ◐ ●						◐		◐		◐			● ◐ ● ● ● ● ● ◐ ●		●

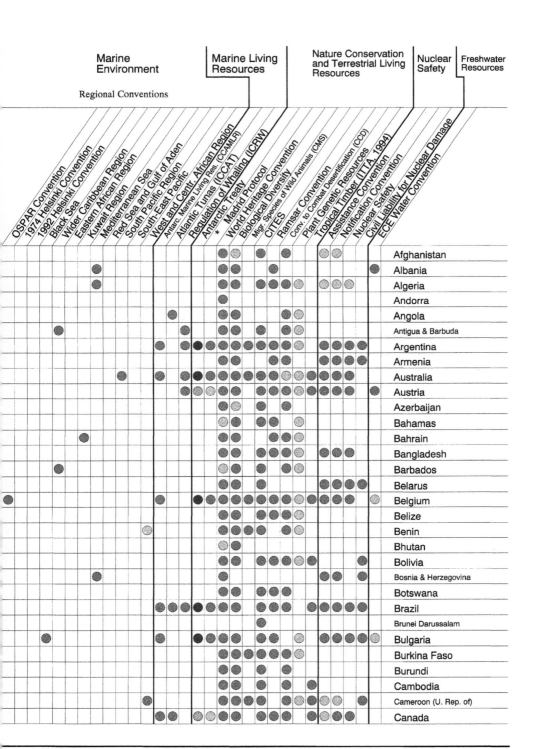

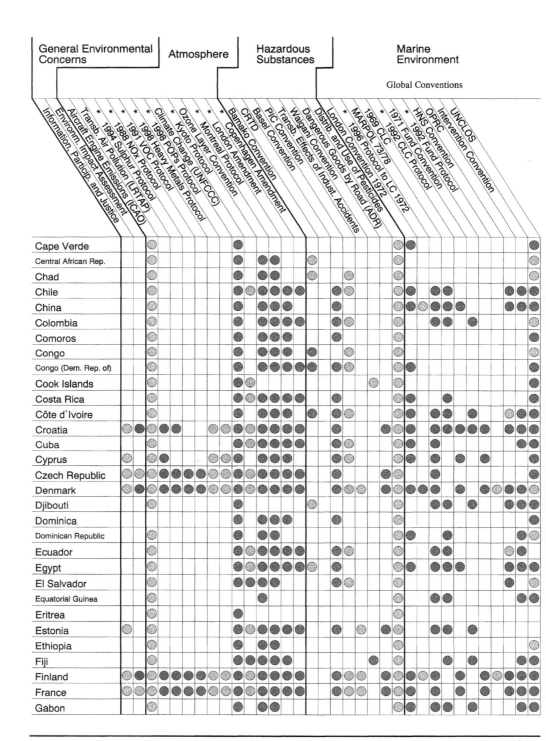

General Environmental Concerns — **Atmosphere** — **Hazardous Substances** — **Marine Environment**

Global Conventions

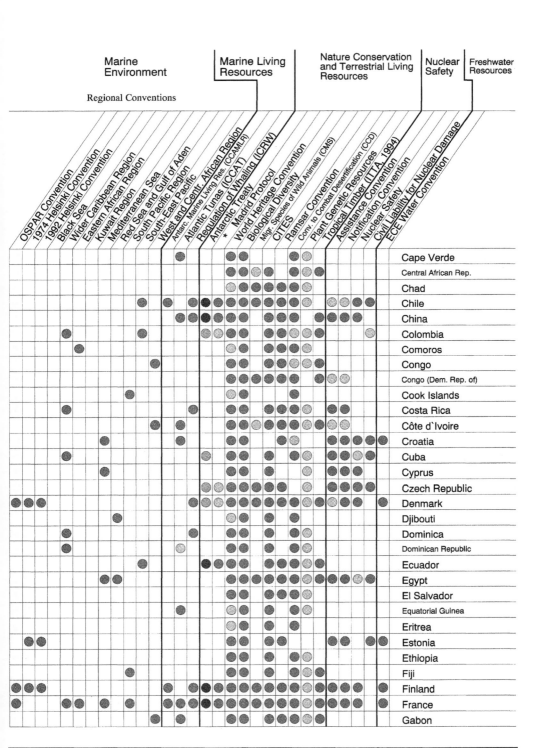

Marine Environment | Marine Living Resources | Nature Conservation and Terrestrial Living Resources | Nuclear Safety | Freshwater Resources

Regional Conventions

	Cape Verde
	Central African Rep.
	Chad
	Chile
	China
	Colombia
	Comoros
	Congo
	Congo (Dem. Rep. of)
	Cook Islands
	Costa Rica
	Côte d'Ivoire
	Croatia
	Cuba
	Cyprus
	Czech Republic
	Denmark
	Djibouti
	Dominica
	Dominican Republic
	Ecuador
	Egypt
	El Salvador
	Equatorial Guinea
	Eritrea
	Estonia
	Ethiopia
	Fiji
	Finland
	France
	Gabon

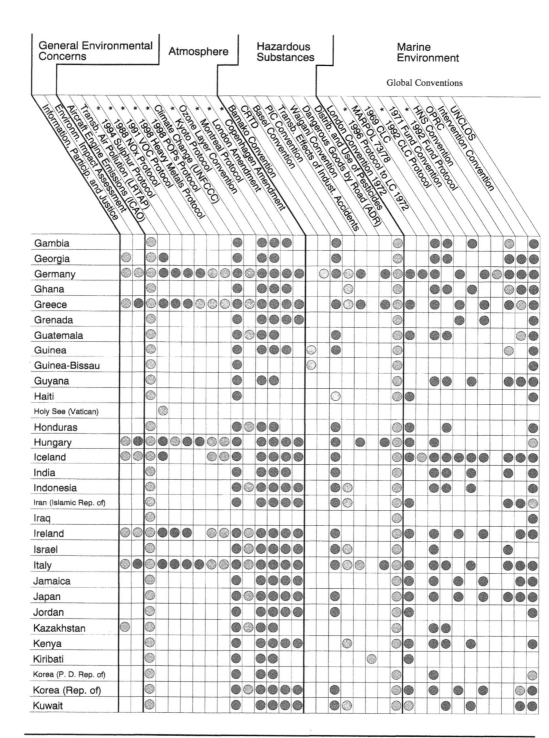

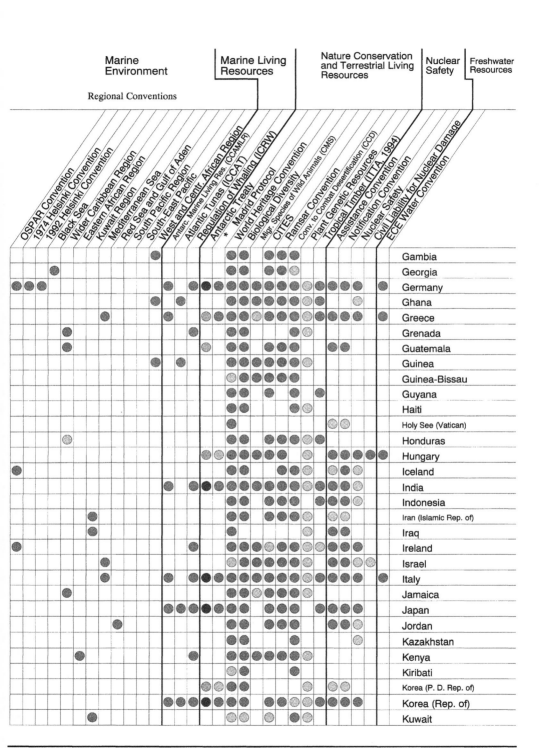

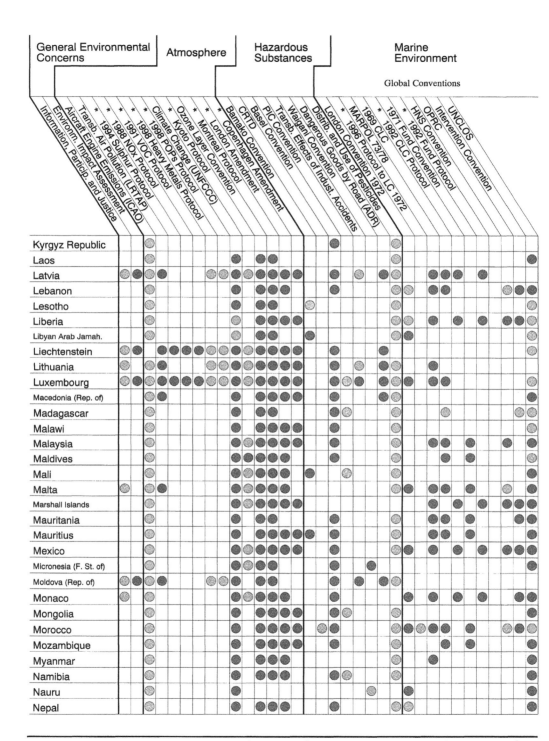

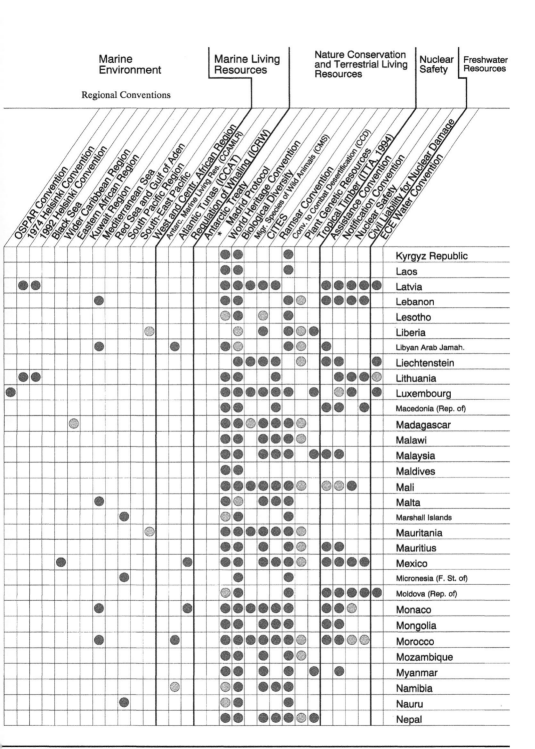

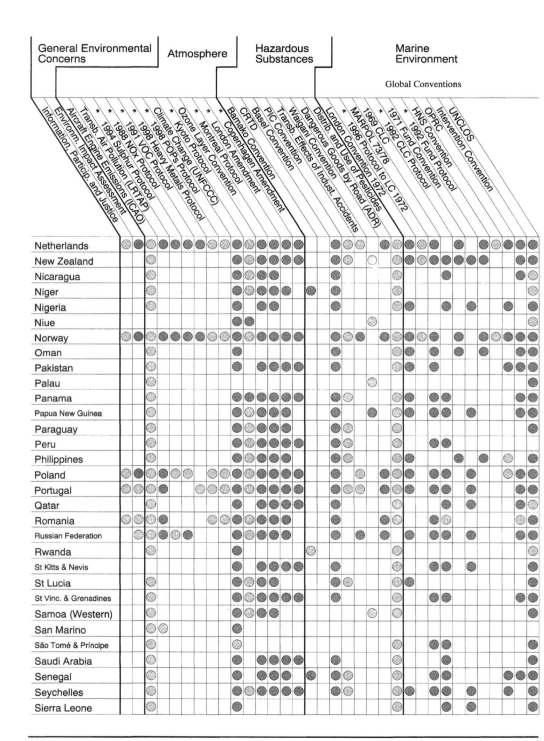

General Environmental Concerns | Atmosphere | Hazardous Substances | Marine Environment

Column headers:
- Information. Particip. and Justice
- Environm. Impact Assessment
- Aircraft Engine Emissions (ICAO)
- Transb. Air Pollution (LRTAP) *
- 1994 Sulphur Protocol *
- 1988 NOX Protocol *
- 1991 VOC Protocol *
- 1998 Heavy Metals Protocol
- 1998 POPs Protocol
- Climate Change (UNFCCC) *
- Kyoto Protocol
- Ozone Layer Convention *
- Montreal Protocol *
- London Amendment
- Copenhagen Amendment
- Barnako Convention
- CRTD
- Basel Convention
- PIC Convention
- Transb. Effects of Indust. Accidents
- Waigani Convention
- Dangerous Goods by Road (ADR)
- Distrib. and Use of Pesticides
- London Convention 1972
- 1996 Protocol to LC 1972
- MARPOL 73/78
- 1969 CLC
- 1992 CLC
- 1971 Fund Convention
- 1992 Fund Protocol
- HNS Convention
- OPRC Convention
- Intervention Convention
- UNCLOS

Country rows:
- Netherlands
- New Zealand
- Nicaragua
- Niger
- Nigeria
- Niue
- Norway
- Oman
- Pakistan
- Palau
- Panama
- Papua New Guinea
- Paraguay
- Peru
- Philippines
- Poland
- Portugal
- Qatar
- Romania
- Russian Federation
- Rwanda
- St Kitts & Nevis
- St Lucia
- St Vinc. & Grenadines
- Samoa (Western)
- San Marino
- São Tomé & Príncipe
- Saudi Arabia
- Senegal
- Seychelles
- Sierra Leone

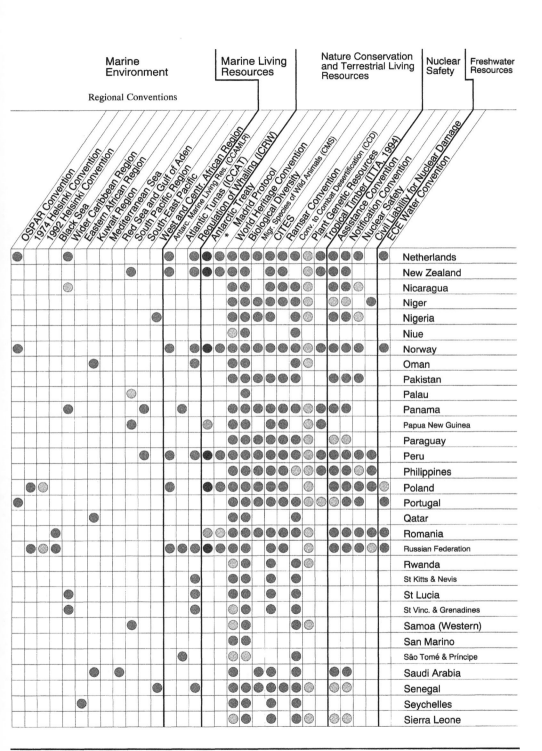

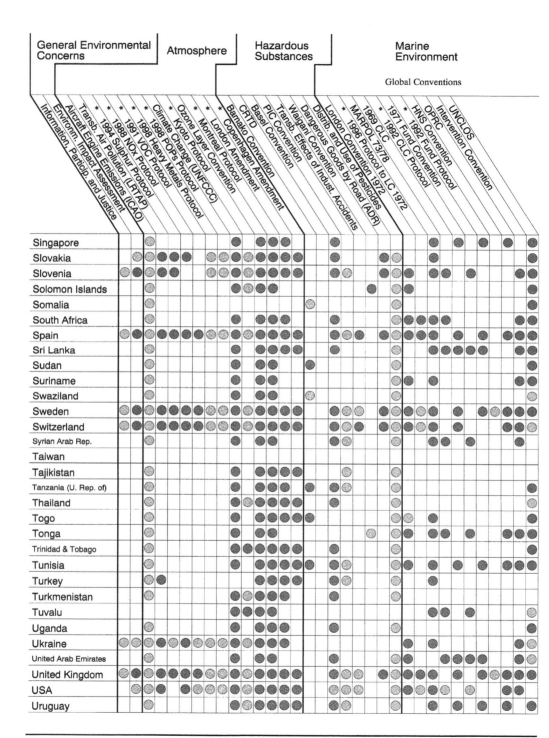

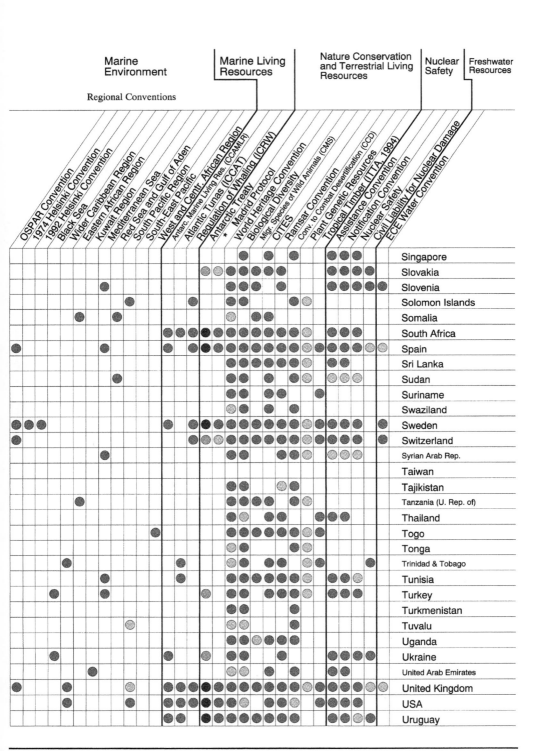

Marine Environment

Marine Living Resources

Nature Conservation and Terrestrial Living Resources

Nuclear Safety

Freshwater Resources

Regional Conventions

Singapore
Slovakia
Slovenia
Solomon Islands
Somalia
South Africa
Spain
Sri Lanka
Sudan
Suriname
Swaziland
Sweden
Switzerland
Syrian Arab Rep.
Taiwan
Tajikistan
Tanzania (U. Rep. of)
Thailand
Togo
Tonga
Trinidad & Tobago
Tunisia
Turkey
Turkmenistan
Tuvalu
Uganda
Ukraine
United Arab Emirates
United Kingdom
USA
Uruguay

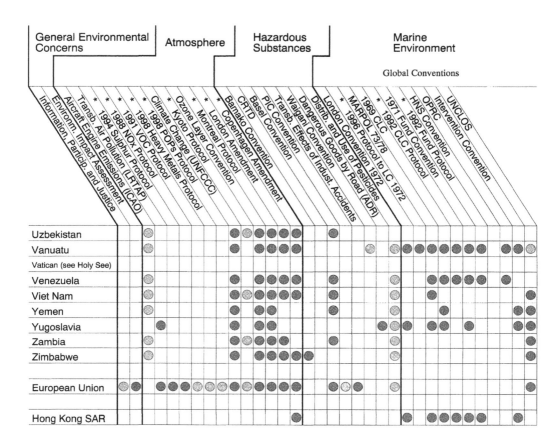

Column group headers: **General Environmental Concerns** · **Atmosphere** · **Hazardous Substances** · **Marine Environment** (Global Conventions)

Column labels (left to right):
- Information, Particip. and Justice
- Environm. Impact Assessment
- Aircraft Engine Emissions (ICAO)
- Transb. Air Pollution (LRTAP)
- 1988 NOx Protocol
- 1991 VOC Protocol
- 1994 Sulphur Protocol
- 1998 Heavy Metals Protocol
- 1998 POPs Protocol
- Climate Change (UNFCCC)
- Kyoto Protocol
- Ozone Layer Convention
- Montreal Protocol
- London Amendment
- Copenhagen Amendment
- Bamako Convention
- Basel Convention
- CRTD
- PIC Convention
- Transb. Effects of Indust. Accidents
- Walgani Convention
- Dangerous Goods by Road (ADR)
- Distrib. and Use of Pesticides
- London Convention 1972
- 1996 Protocol to LC 1972
- MARPOL 73/78
- 1969 CLC
- 1992 CLC
- 1971 Fund Convention
- 1992 Fund Protocol
- HNS Convention
- OPRC Convention
- Intervention Convention
- UNCLOS

Country rows:
- Uzbekistan
- Vanuatu
- Vatican (see Holy See)
- Venezuela
- Viet Nam
- Yemen
- Yugoslavia
- Zambia
- Zimbabwe
- European Union
- Hong Kong SAR

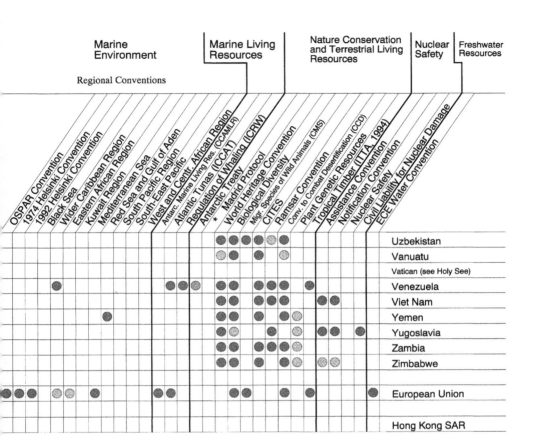

	Marine Environment — Regional Conventions												Marine Living Resources			Nature Conservation and Terrestrial Living Resources											Nuclear Safety			Freshwater Resources
	OSPAR Convention	1974 Helsinki Convention	1992 Helsinki Convention	Black Sea	Wider Caribbean Region	Eastern African Region	Kuwait Region	Mediterranean Sea	Red Sea and Gulf of Aden	South Pacific Region	South East Pacific	West and Centr. African Region	Antarc. Marine Living Res. (CCAMLR)	Atlantic Tunas (ICCAT)	Regulation of Whaling (ICRW)	Antarctic Treaty	Madrid Protocol	World Heritage Convention	Biological Diversity	Migr. Species of Wild Animals (CMS)	CITES	Ramsar Convention	Conv. to Combat Desertification (CCD)	Plant Genetic Resources	Tropical Timber (ITTA, 1994)	Assistance Convention	Notification Convention	Nuclear Safety	Civil Liability for Nuclear Damage	ECE Water Convention

Country rows:

- Uzbekistan
- Vanuatu
- Vatican (see Holy See)
- Venezuela
- Viet Nam
- Yemen
- Yugoslavia
- Zambia
- Zimbabwe
- European Union
- Hong Kong SAR

Intergovernmental Organizations (IGOs)

including United Nations specialized agencies

Commission on Sustainable Development (CSD)

Objectives

- to monitor progress in the implementation of Agenda 21 and activities related to the integration of environmental and developmental goals throughout the UN system;
- to consider information provided by governments regarding the activities they undertake to implement Agenda 21;
- to review the progress in the implementation of the commitments set out in Agenda 21, including those related to the provision of financial resources and transfer of technology;
- to receive and analyse relevant input from competent non-governmental organizations (NGOs), including the scientific and the private sector;
- to enhance the dialogue, within the framework of the UN, with NGOs, and with the independent sector, as well as with other entities outside the UN system.

Organization

Type
Intergovernmental organ of the UN. Functional Commission of the UN Economic and Social Council (ECOSOC). Reports to the UN General Assembly through ECOSOC. Established as an institutional arrangement to the follow-up to the UN Conference on Environment and Development (UNCED) in Rio de Janeiro, June 1992.

Membership
The CSD is composed of representatives of 53 states, elected for a three-year period by ECOSOC. Other member States of the UN, non-member States, intergovernmental organizations (IGOs), including regional integration organizations, and accredited NGOs participate in the work of the CSD as observers.

Founded
16 February 1993.

Secretariat
CSD Secretariat,
Division for Sustainable Development,
UN Department of Economic and Social Affairs (DESA),
United Nations,
2 UN Plaza, Room DC2-2220,
New York, NY 10017,
USA
Telephone: +1-212-9633170
Telefax: +1-212-9634260
E-mail: dsd@un.org

Director
Ms JoAnne DiSano.

Information Officer
Ms Pragati Pascale (UN Department for Public Information).

Number of staff
87.

Activities
The first Multi-Year Thematic Programme of Work was agreed for 1994–6 with the following cross-sectoral clusters to be reviewed and monitored on a yearly basis:
- critical elements of sustainability (chs. 2–5 of Agenda 21);
- financial resources and mechanisms (ch. 33);
- education, science, transfer of environmentally sound technologies, co-operation, and capacity building (chs. 16 and 34–7);
- decision-making structures (chs. 8 and 38–40);
- roles of major groups (non-governmental sectors) (chs. 23–32).

The Programme also specified the sectoral clusters that would receive special attention between 1994 and 1996:
- 1994: health, human settlements, and fresh water (chs. 6, 7, 18, and 21); and toxic chemicals and hazardous wastes (chs. 19, 20, and 22);
- 1995: land, desertification, forests, and biodiversity (chs. 10–15);
- 1996: atmosphere, oceans, and all kinds of seas (chs. 9 and 17).

All cross-sectoral clusters were under review annually, with particular emphasis on selected chapters within a cluster. The purpose in combining sectoral themes with cross-sectoral chapters is to enable a more integrated view of how the cross-sectoral elements interact and contribute to the sectoral issues in the Agenda 21 implementation process.

According to a decision adopted at the Commission's first substantive meeting in June 1993, governments are encouraged to submit their national reports on the implementation of Agenda 21 not less than six months before the Commission's session. It is up to individual governments to decide on the degree of detail and regularity of their reporting to the CSD.

Reports are also requested from organizations of the UN system, including international financial institutions and the Global Environment Facility (GEF) (see this section), as well as international, regional, and subregional IGOs outside the UN system.

In carrying out its programme of work, the CSD took into account the results of major intergovernmental events and negotiating processes, with a view to integrating these activities in the review of the implementation of Agenda 21.

The 1997 session had an overall review and appraisal of Agenda 21 in preparation for that year's special session of the UN General Assembly (UNGA). The special session of the UNGA took place in New York on 23–7 June 1997.

The second Multi-Year Thematic Programme of Work for 1998–2002 was adopted by the UN General Assembly at its special session in June 1997. It follows the previous format but reduces the numbers of agenda items considered annually. The Programme specifies the following clusters that will receive special attention in the period:

- 1998: (a) freshwater management, (b) transfer of technology, capacity building, education, and science, and (c) industry;
- 1999: (a) oceans and seas, (b) consumption and production patterns, (c) tourism, and (d) review of Programme for Sustainable Development of Small Island Developing States (SIDS);
- 2000: (a) land resources, (b) financial resources, trade and investment, and economic growth, and (c) agriculture;
- 2001: (a) atmosphere and energy, (b) information for decision making and participation (c) international co-operation for an enabling environment, and (d) energy and transport as economic factors;
- 2002: comprehensive review of Agenda 21 implementation.

Poverty and consumption and production patterns are overriding issues for the sessions in this period. The elimination of annual examination of all cross-sectoral issues reduces the frequency of national reports dealing with these elements. The sixth CSD session took place 20 April–1 May 1998 and the seventh session took place 19–30 April 1999.

Decision-making bodies

The 53 members of the CSD are elected by the UN ECOSOC. The members serve for a three-year period and are encouraged to be represented at the ministerial level. Membership will rotate among governments of the UN, drawn on the following geographical basis: Africa (13), Asia (11), Latin America and the Caribbean (10), and North America, Europe, and other (19). The CSD has its sessions annually for two or three weeks.

The members of the CSD elect the Chair and four Vice-Chairs for each session. These five members constitute the Bureau of the CSD.

The CSD establishes intersessional *ad hoc* expert groups to assist the Commission on issues related to the implementation of Agenda 21. In 1997 it created an Intergovernmental Forum on Forests.

The CSD receives substantive services from the Division for Sustainable Development (DSD) of the UN Department of Economic and Social Affairs (DESA).

Finance

CSD activities are financed through the regular UN budget and through voluntary extra-budgetary contribution.

Budget
Not applicable.

Publications

CSD Update (bi-monthly newsletter).

Sources on the Internet

<http://www.un.org/esa/sustdev/csd.htm>
<gopher://gopher.un.org:70/11/esc/cn17>
National implementations of the Agenda 21 commitments at:
<http://www.un.org/esa/agenda21/natlinfo>

European Union (EU): Environment

Objectives

Environment policy was built into the Treaty by the Single European Act of 1987 and its scope was extended by the Treaty on European union of 1992. This allowed the use of majority voting on environmental legislation and introduced as a principle of Treaty law the concept of sustainable growth which respects the environment. While leaving plenty of scope for national action and allowing member States to take even tougher measures than those agreed at union level, the Treaty says that Union policy should contribute to the pursuit of:
* preserving, protecting, and improving the quality of the environment;
* protecting human health;
* ensuring a prudent and rational utilization of natural resources;
* promoting measures at the international level to deal with regional or world-wide environmental problems.
* The Treaty requires Union policy to aim 'at a high level of protection', and at rectifying environmental damage at source, and to be based on taking preventive action and making the polluter pay.

The new Treaty of Amsterdam, when ratified, will further strengthen environmental objectives, particularly in terms of sustainable development and integration of environment into other policy areas.

Organization

Type

Intergovernmental organization (IGO). The institutions of the EU have a definite legal status and extensive powers of their own. The European Union, which incorporates the European Community (EC), comprises three juridically distinct entities: European Economic Community (EEC); Euratom; and European Coal and Steel Community (ECSC).

The EU consists of four main institutions, which all play an important role in EU environmental policy:
* the Council of Ministers;
* the European Commission;
* the European Court of Justice;
* the European Parliament.

Due to the central role of the European Commission in preparing, proposing, and verifying environmental legislation, in the following we shall focus on this organization.

Membership

Any European state can apply for membership. The terms of its admission will be agreed between the original member States and the applicant state. 15 member States (Austria, Belgium, Denmark, Finland, France, Germany, Greece, Ireland, Italy, Luxembourg, the Netherlands, Portugal, Spain, Sweden, and the United Kingdom) by June 1999.

Founded

The Treaty establishing the EEC was signed in Rome on 25 March 1957. (The European Community was founded on 8 April 1965. The European Union came into being on 1 November 1994.)

Secretariat

European Commission,
Rue de la Loi 200,
B-1049 Brussels,
Belgium
Telephone: +32-2-2991111
Telefax: Information is available from the switchboard operator.

President

Mr Romano Prodi.

Commissioner for Environment

Ms Margot Wallström.

Directorate-General (DG) XI: Environment, Nuclear Safety and Civil Protection
Postal address and telephone: as above
Location: blvd. du Triomphe 174 and avenue de Bealieu 5.

Information officer (DGXI)

Mr Saturnino Muñoz Gómez.

European Environment Agency (EEA),
Kongens Nytorv 6,
DK-1050 Copenhagen K,
Denmark
Telephone: +45-33-367100
Telefax: +45-33-367199

-mail: eea@eea.eu.int

xecutive Director
Ir Domingo Jiménez-Beltrán.

ommunications Officer
Ir Ernst R. Klatte.

umber of staff
7,000 at the Commission, 500 at DGXI,
nd 71 at EEA (December 1998).

Activities

he major environmental activities of the
uropean Commission consist of:

policy activities, through developing EC
nvironmental Action Programmes (1973,
977, 1983, 1987, and 1992). The fifth Pro-
ramme lays out the EC's environmental
oals for sustainable development and in-
erim targets and objectives for the year
000. It identifies the most pressing envi-
onmental concerns; lists priorities; selects
arget sectors, including energy, industry,
ransport, agriculture, and tourism; broad-
ns the range of instruments (political and
nancial) needed to achieve goals; and sets
p three *ad hoc* dialogue groups—a con-
ultative forum, an implementation net-
ork, and an environment policy review
roup—to promote a greater sense of re-
ponsibility among the principal actors tar-
eted by the Programme, and to ensure ef-
ective and transparent application of
neasures.

A review of the programme was set for
995, which marked the midway point be-
ween the priming and full-steam phases of
ne Programme. The review, which was
ompleted in December 1995, examined to
hat extent the Programme has been im-
lemented and in the light of this analysed
ritically the Programme's priorities.

On 10 January 1996 the Commission ap-
roved a progress report on the implemen-
ation of the fifth Programme. The report
dentifies progress made as well as the ar-
as where the process of moving forward
owards sustainability should be given much
reater impetus. Based on the conclusions
f the progress report, and on the updated
tate of the Environment Report published
y the EEA in November 1995, the Com-
nission adopted, on 24 January 1996, a
raft Decision of the European Parliament
nd the Council on the Review of the Pro-
ramme aimed at speeding the process of
nproving the environment of the Union
nd of moving towards sustainable economic and social development in the EU.
The Decision is still under debate by Parliament and Council;

• *legal activities*, through providing environmental legislation in the form of regulations, directives, or decisions. Approximately 300 legal texts related to the
environment currently exist;

• *research and technological development
(RTD) activities*, through developing research and development programmes
within the area of the environment. The
*Science and Technology for Environment
Protection (STEP)* Programme was
adopted in June 1991. It replaced the previous STEP and the European Programme on
Climatology and Natural Hazards). The
STEP programme aimed to develop the scientific knowledge and technical know-how
which the Union needs in order to carry out
its role concerning the environment. The
programme ran until 31 December 1994.
The *Fourth Framework Programme*, which
is the Community's principal medium-term
plan for research activities at Community
level, runs for four years, from 1994 to 1998.
There are four main activities, and the environment features in the first, which deals
with research, technological development,
and demonstration programmes. The Environment and Climate Programme will establish networks of excellence and RTD in
three areas:
(*a*) research into the natural environmental quality and global change;
(*b*) environmental technologies;
(*c*) space technology applied to earth observation and environmental research;

• *monitoring and implementation activities*.
According to the Treaty of Rome, the Commission is responsible for ensuring that the
EC environmental legislation is properly
implemented and for reporting cases of infraction to the European Court of Justice.

The *Co-ordination of Information on the
Environment (CORINE) Programme*
(1985–90) had as its principal aim to gather,
co-ordinate, and ensure consistency of information on the state of the environment
in the EU. The CORINE Programme was
wound up in 1990, and the Commission
proposed the setting-up of an agency,
known as the *European Environment Agency
(EEA)*, the same year. EEA was set up by
Council Regulation (EEC) No. 1210/90 of
7 May 1990 on the establishment of the
European Environment Agency and the
European Environment Information and
Observation Network (EIONET). The EEA
was fully operational as of 1 January 1996.

EEA's objective is to provide the Community and the member States with objective, reliable, and comparable information
at European level, enabling them to take the
requisite measures to protect the environment, to assess the results of such measures,
and to ensure that the public is informed
about the state of the environment. The
Agency is an independent legal entity with
all the rights and responsibilities that attend
such status in the countries where it operates. It seeks to establish a position at the
hub of a decentralized, distributive network
designed to make maximum use of resources already existing throughout Europe.

The Agency's achievements so far include: the development of monitoring and
databases on the state of the environment
and media and source-oriented monitoring;
the establishment of eight European Topic
Centres (ETCs), institutions, or organiza-
tions contracted by EEA to execute particu-
lar tasks identified in a multi-annual work
programme, many of which are already
operational. By December 1997 these ETCs
consisted of:
• Inland Waters (Medmenham, United
Kingdom);
• Marine and Coastal Environment (La
Spezia, Italy);
• Air Quality (Bilthoven, the Netherlands);
• Air Emissions (Berlin, Germany);
• Nature Conservation (Paris, France);
• Land Cover (Sweden);
• Catalogue of Data Sources (Germany);
• Soil (Valencia, Spain);
• Waste (Copenhagen, Denmark).

Decision-making bodies

The Council of Ministers is the main decision-making body concerning environment-
related legislation. According to the Single
European Act, there are two main procedures:
(1) decisions in accordance with Article 130
require unanimity and restrict the role of
the European Parliament to non-binding
consultation;
(2) decisions in accordance with Article
100(*a*) require a qualified majority and increase the influence of the European Parliament, if a proposal relates to the establishment and functioning of the internal
market.

In cases of majority voting, 87 votes are
distributed among the member States in the
Council, broadly reflecting the size of their
populations.

The EEA directs its work along the lines of a medium-term multi-annual work programme agreed by a Management Board, consisting of one representative of each EEA member State, two representatives of the European Commission, and two scientific personalities nominated by the European Parliament. They are assisted by a Scientific Committee, whose members are appointed for a four-year term.

Finance

The budget is based on financial contributions of member States.

Budget

The total budget for the European Community was approximately ECU89 billion in 1997 and ECU89 billion in 1998, and is ECU97 billion in 1999.

The budget of DGXI was approximately ECU133 million in 1997 and ECU158 million in 1998, and is ECU196 million in 1999.

EEA's budget was ECU16.7 million in 1997 and ECU16.7 million in 1998, and is ECU18.1 million in 1999.

Main contributors

Main contributors to the total budget for the European Community in 1997 were Germany (27 per cent), France (17 per cent), United Kingdom (14 per cent), and Italy (13 per cent).

Special funds

The Financial Instrument for the Environment (LIFE) is established to assist the development and implementation of the EU's environmental policy. LIFE may also provide technical environmental assistance for non-EU countries bordering the Mediterranean and the Baltic, and for implementing international agreements relating to regional and global environmental problems. The finance required for the first operational phase, from 1992 until 1994, was an estimated ECU400 million.

For the second operational phase, 1996–9, ECU450 million is required. Of this, ECU13.5 million (3 per cent) is made available for measures, demonstration schemes, awareness campaigns, incentives, and technical assistance.

Publications

DGXI produces a range of publications on environmental themes as well as six newsletters. Details can be found in the on-line publications catalogue on the Internet at: <http://europa.eu.int/comm/dg11/pubs/home.htm>

The EEA publishes a quarterly newsletter. It also publishes:
• annual reports;
• Environmental Issues series;
• Environmental Monographs series;
• Topic Report series;
• Expert's Corner series.
Other relevant publications are:
• *Europe's Environment: The Dobris Assessment* (1995);
• *Europe's Environment: The Second Assessment* (1998);
• *Environment in the European Union* (November 1995);
• *Environment in the European Union at the Turn of the Century* (1999);
• The joint EEA/Co-operative Programme for Monitoring and Evaluation of the Long Range Transmission of Air Pollutants in Europe (EMEP) (see Agreements, Convention on Long-Range Transboundary Air Pollution) *Atmospheric Emission Inventory Guidebook* (February 1996).

Sources on the Internet

<http://europa.eu.int>
<http://europa.eu.int/comm/dg11>
<http://www.eea.eu.int>
<http://www.eionet.eu.int>

Food and Agriculture Organization (FAO)

Objectives
* to raise the levels of nutrition and standards of living of the populations of member countries;
* to secure improvements in the efficiency of production and distribution of all food and agricultural products;
* to improve the conditions of rural populations;
* to contribute towards an expanding world economy and towards ensuring freedom from hunger for humanity.

Organization

Type
Intergovernmental organization (IGO). A specialized agency of the UN. Linked to UN Economic and Social Council (ECOSOC).

Membership
Membership is confined to nations; associate membership to territories or groups of territories. The European Union (EU) is given membership as a regional integration organization and can vote on behalf of its member countries in certain matters. The total membership of FAO by 1 July 1999 was 175 countries and the EU.

Founded
16 October 1945.

Secretariat
FAO, Viale delle Terme di Caracalla, I-00100 Rome, Italy
Telephone: +39-06-57051
Telefax: +39-06-57053152
E-mail: firstname.surname@fao.org

Director-General
Dr Jacques Diouf.

Media Support
Mr Peter Lowrey.

Number of staff
939 professionals and 1,349 support staff at headquarters, in addition to 671 professionals and 1,271 support staff at field, regional, and country offices (February 1999).

Activities
In fulfilling its aims to combat poverty and malnutrition, FAO carries out four major functions: it collects, analyses, and disseminates information; advises governments on policies and programmes; provides technical assistance; and offers governments and experts a neutral forum in which to meet to discuss issues related to food and agriculture. The major areas of FAO activity are: crop production, livestock, natural resources, research and technology, rural development, nutrition, food and agricultural policy, fisheries, and forestry.

Main conventions on environment under the auspices of FAO
* *International Convention for the Conservation of Atlantic Tunas (ICCAT)*, Rio de Janeiro, 1966 (see Agreements);
* *FAO International Code of Conduct on the Distribution and Use of Pesticides*, Rome, 1985 (see Agreements);
* *FAO International Undertaking on Plant Genetic Resources*, Rome, 1983 (see Agreements);
* *Code of Conduct for Responsible Fisheries*, Rome, 1995;
* *Global Plan of Action on Plant Genetic Resources*, Rome, 1996 (see Agreements, FAO International Undertaking on Plant Genetic Resources);
* *Convention on the Prior Informed Consent Procedure for Certain Hazardous Chemicals and Pesticides in International Trade (PIC Convention)*, Rotterdam, 1998 (see Agreements). Operated jointly with the UN Environment Programme (UNEP);
* *International Plan of Action for the Management of Fishing Capacity*, Rome, 1999;
* *International Plan of Acton for the Conservation and Management of Sharks*, Rome, 1999;
* *International Plan of Action for Reducing Incidental Catch of Seabirds in Longline Fisheries*, Rome, 1999.

Environmental activities
The Organization has intensified its interdisciplinary work to ensure the integration of environmental considerations in all FAO activities, giving high priority to the prevention of environmental degradation and emphasizing sustainable development in agriculture, fisheries, and forestry.
FAO advises governments on policy planning and environmental protection in a wide range of sectors, including the management of soil and water resources, farming systems, genetic resources, irrigation systems, integrated pest management, integrated plant nutrition, and watershed management.

Decision-making bodies
The Conference, which meets every two years, is the major policy-making organ of FAO. All members are represented and each has one vote. The Conference is responsible for approving the FAO budget and Programme of Work, adopting procedural rules and financial regulations, admitting new members, formulating recommendations on food and agricultural questions, and reviewing the decisions of the FAO Council and subsidiary bodies. The FAO Council is composed of 49 members elected by the Conference for three-year terms. The Council is the executive organ of the Conference and exercises powers delegated to it by the Conference. The FAO Council is assisted by eight major committees covering agriculture; commodity problems; constitutional and legal matters; forestry; fisheries; world food security; finance; and FAO programmes.

Finance
Contributions from member countries for implementation of the Regular Programme of Work are based on per capita income. The Field Programme is financed by three major sources: government trust funds, the UNDP, and FAO's own Technical Co-operation Programme.

Budget
The budget is $650 million for the years 1998–9.

Special funds
The *Technical Co-operation Programme (TCP)* allows the Organization to respond to special needs of member countries. The total budget is $78.9 million for 1998–9, financed by member countries through the regular budget.

Publications
* *FAO Plant Protection Bulletin* (quarterly);
* *Food Outlook* (monthly).

Sources on the Internet
<http://www.fao.org>

Global Environment Facility (GEF)

Objectives
To serve as a mechanism for international co-operation for the purpose of providing new and additional grant and concessional funding to meet the agreed global environmental benefits in the following focal areas:
- biological diversity;
- climate change;
- international waters;
- ozone layer depletion.

Projects addressing land degradation, primarily desertification and deforestation, as they relate to the focal areas, are also eligible for funding.

The GEF shall ensure the cost-effectiveness of its activities in addressing the targeted global environmental issues, and shall fund programmes and projects which are country-driven and based on national priorities designed to support sustainable development.

Organization
Type
Intergovernmental organization (IGO). The GEF is implemented by the UN Development Programme (UNDP), the UN Environment Programme (UNEP), and the World Bank (see this section).

Membership
Any member State of the UN or any of its specialized agencies may become a Participant in the GEF. There were 165 Participants by 1 July 1999.

Founded
28 November 1991. The instrument establishing the new GEF entered into force on 1 July 1994.

Secretariat
GEF Secretariat,
1818 H Street NW,
Washington, DC 20433,
USA
Telephone: +1-202-4730508
Telefax: +1-202-522-3240/3245
E-mail: harcher@worldbank.org or
[first initial last name]@worldbank.org

Chairman and Chief Executive Officer
Dr Mohamed T. El-Ashry.

External Relations Co-ordinator
Mr Hutton Archer.

Number of staff
30 professionals and ten administrative staff (July 1999).

Activities
The GEF was initially set up in 1991 as a three-year pilot programme, jointly implemented by UNDP, UNEP, and the World Bank. The aim was to provide grants and low-interest loans to developing countries to help them carry out programmes to relieve pressures on global ecosystems.

The restructured GEF is based on a set of principles agreed to by the Participants. The GEF operates the financial mechanism of both the Framework Convention on Climate Change (see Agreements) and the Convention on Biological Diversity (see Agreements). The Council approved an operational strategy for the GEF in October 1995.

There is agreement that the GEF should work with the regional development banks, the UN agencies, and bilateral agencies to involve them in GEF technical assistance and investment projects. The implementing agencies are working with the regional development banks and UN agencies on the modalities for such co-operation.

Decision-making bodies
The GEF has an Assembly, which consists of representatives of all participating countries. The Assembly meets every three years and had its first meeting in New Delhi in April 1998. The Assembly reviews the general policies and in addition evaluates the operation of the Facility on the basis of reports submitted by the Council. The Council is the main governing body responsible for developing, adopting, and evaluating the operational policies and programmes for GEF-financed activities. It consists of 32 members, with 16 members from developing countries (six each from Africa and Asia, and four seats for Latin America), 14 from developed countries, and two from the countries of Central and Eastern Europe and the former Soviet Union. The Council meets twice a year, or as frequently as necessary.

When consensus is not possible, a double-majority voting system will be used, requiring a majority of participating countries and 60 per cent donor support. It is intended that the system will protect the interests of both donor and recipient countries.

The GEF Secretariat services and reports to the Assembly and the Council and ensures that any project proposed for GEF funding is consistent with GEF policies, operational strategies, and work programmes. It is supported administratively by the World Bank, but operates in a functionally independent manner.

The Scientific and Technical Advisory Panel (STAP) is an advisory body. UNEP serves as the secretariat for STAP.

Finance
Funding comes from the donors, which include both developing and developed countries. Contributions from developed countries are roughly in line with a formula based on their shares in the World Bank's International Development Association (see this section). 28 countries have announced pledges to the GEF, including ten developing countries. Total multilateral pledges and contributions to the Trust Fund was $US2 billion for 1994–7 and is estimated to be $2.75 billion for 1998–2001. GEF funding will be available for projects and other activities that address the Facility's objectives.

Budget
The total GEF corporate budget was $36.8 million for the financial year 1997/98 and $39.2 million for 1998/99, and is $22.2 million for 1999/2000. The core budget for the GEF Secretariat was 6.9 million for 1997/98 and $7.4 million for 1998/99, and is $6.6 million for 1999/2000.

Main contributors
The main contributors are the USA, Japan, Germany, France, and the United Kingdom. These countries provided 57.58 per cent of the Facility's funding for the 1994–7 period.

Publications
GEF publishes annual reports, working-paper series, policy publications, and the *Operational Report*. Its book, *Valuing the Global Environment*, includes essays from more than 30 world leaders.

Sources on the Internet
<http://www.gefweb.org>

International Atomic Energy Agency (IAEA)

Objectives
- to encourage and assist research on and development and practical application of atomic energy for peaceful purposes throughout the world;
- to act as an intermediary in the supply of materials, services, equipment, and facilities;
- to foster the exchange of scientific and technical information;
- to encourage the exchange and training of scientists and experts;
- to establish standards and administer safeguards against the misuse of aid provided by or through the Agency;
- to carry out safeguards to verify compliance of non-nuclear weapon States party to the Non-Proliferation Treaty (NPT) and other treaties that they use fissionable material for peaceful purposes only.

Organization
Type
Intergovernmental organization (IGO). An independent IGO within the UN system.

Membership
Open to all states, whether UN members or not. 128 member States by May 1999. Not open to regional integration organizations.

Founded
29 July 1957.

Secretariat
International Atomic Energy Agency (IAEA),
Vienna International Centre,
Wagramerstrasse 5,
PO Box 100,
A-1400 Vienna,
Austria
Telephone: +43-1-26000
Telefax: +43-1-26007
E-mail: official.mail@iaea.org

Director-General
Dr Mohamed ElBaradei
(December 1997–December 2001).

Director, Division of Public Information
Mr David Kyd.

Number of staff
847 professionals and 1,286 support staff (December 1998).

Activities
222 safeguard agreements were in force with 138 member States (and with Taiwan) by end of 1998. During 1998, 2,507 safeguard inspections were performed in 68 member States (including Taiwan). There were 897 nuclear installations under IAEA safeguards by end of 1998. This represents approximately 95 per cent of the world's nuclear facilities and materials outside the five nuclear-weapon states. IAEA safeguards inspections in these facilities to verify that the fissionable material is used for peaceful purposes only.

Main conventions on environment under the auspices of IAEA
- *Vienna Convention on Civil Liability for Nuclear Damage*, Vienna, 21 May 1963 (see Agreements);
- *Joint Protocol Relating to the Application of the Vienna Convention and the Paris Convention on Third Party Liability in the Field of Nuclear Energy*, Vienna, 21 September 1988 (see Agreements, Vienna Convention on Civil Liability for Nuclear Damage);
- *Convention on the Physical Protection of Nuclear Material*, Vienna, 26 October 1979. Entered into force on 8 February 1987. 64 Parties (including EURATOM) by 1 April 1999. Six Signatories without ratification, acceptance, or approval;
- *Convention on Assistance in the Case of a Nuclear Accident or Radiological Emergency (Assistance Convention)*, Vienna, 26 September 1986 (see Agreements);
- *Convention on Early Notification of a Nuclear Accident (Notification Convention)*, Vienna, 26 September 1986 (see Agreements);
- *Convention on Nuclear Safety*, Vienna, 17 June 1994 (see Agreements);
- *Joint Convention on the Safety of Spent Fuel Management and on the Safety of Radioactive Waste Management*, Vienna, 5 September 1997. (Not yet in force.) Nine ratifications by 12 May 1999. 30 Signatories without ratification, acceptance, or ap-

proval. It enters into force on the ninetieth day after the deposit of the twenty-fifth instrument of ratification, acceptance, or approval, including the instruments of 15 states each having an operational nuclear power plant;
• *Convention on Supplementary Compensation for Nuclear Damage*, Vienna, 12 September 1997.(Not yet in force.) (See Agreements, Vienna Convention on Civil Liability for Nuclear Damage.)

International conventions which request member States to conclude agreements with the IAEA
• *Treaty for the Prohibition of Nuclear Weapons in Latin America (Tlatelolco Treaty)*. Signed at Mexico, Distrito Federal, on 14 February 1967. Entered into force on 22 April 1968. 32 Parties by 1 January 1999. One Signatory without ratification, acceptance, or approval;
• *Treaty on the Non-Proliferation of Nuclear Weapons (NPT)*. Signed at London, Moscow, and Washington on 1 July 1968. Entered into force on 5 March 1970. 187 Parties by 14 April 1999. No Signatories without ratification, acceptance, or approval;
• *South Pacific Nuclear Free Zone Treaty (Rarotonga Treaty)*. Signed at Rarotonga on 6 August 1985. Entered into force on 11 December 1986. 12 Parties by 26 May 1999. One Signatory without ratification, acceptance, or approval;
• *African Nuclear-Weapon-Free Zone Treaty (Treaty of Pelindaba)*. Opened for signature in Cairo on 11 April 1996. (Not yet in force.) Eight ratifications by 26 May 1999. 42 Signatories without ratification, acceptance, or approval;
• *Treaty of the Southeast Asia Nuclear-Weapon-Free Zone (Treaty of Bangkok)*. Opened for signature in Bangkok on 15 December 1995. Entered into force on 27 March 1997. Nine Parties by 26 April 1999. One Signatory without ratification, acceptance, or approval.

Environmental activities
Many of the IAEA programmes contribute directly or indirectly to the goals of sustainable development and protection of the environment as set out in *Agenda 21*, the outcome of the 1992 UN Conference on Environment and Development (UNCED). Of particular relevance in this context are the programmes on food and agriculture, isotope hydrology (work on both climate change and water resources), and waste

management. The IAEA also takes an active role in inter-agency co-ordination of the implementation of Agenda 21.
Chapter 17 of the Agenda 21 agreement calls for 'new approaches to marine and coastal area management and development at the national, sub-regional, regional, and global levels' and the strengthening of inter-agency co-operation in this regard. Emphasis was also placed on building the capacities of national and regional institutions (especially in developing countries) for making environmental assessments and controlling marine pollution.
The IAEA Marine Environment Laboratory (MEL) in Monaco responds regularly to requests for technical assistance from many other UN agencies, international organizations, and governments. Within the UN, co-operative activities are formally established with the UN Environment Programme (UNEP) (see this section) and the Intergovernmental Oceanographic Commission (IOC) of UNESCO. There is also extensive collaboration with the World Meteorological Organization (WMO), the World Health Organization (WHO), and the Food and Agriculture Organization (FAO) (see this section), as well as IUCN – World Conservation Union (see NGOs), in programmes of assistance for developing countries.
Over the past decade, MEL's expertise has been applied to many pressing international environmental challenges, such as:
• tracking the effects of ocean disposal of nuclear wastes;
• assessing and mitigating the marine impacts of the Gulf War;
• investigating the radiological consequences of nuclear weapons testing in the Pacific;
• analysing the greenhouse effect and the potential for global warming;
• studying the impacts of industrial and agro-chemical pollution on marine ecosystems.
MEL has been engaged in deepening scientific understanding of marine radioactivity since its beginnings. Over the decades, moreover, research has broadened to include analysis of a wide range of non-radioactive pollutants in the marine environment, using nuclear and isotopic techniques.
MEL examines the consequences of radioactive discharges and disposals by monitoring and assessing radionuclide levels and modelling their dispersion in the marine environment. The results then assist states in radiological assessments related to nu-

clear weapons test sites and nuclear waste disposal areas, and in emergency responses to accidents at sea. To facilitate this work, MEL has created a Global Marine Radioactivity Database (GLOMARD) to provide states with radioactivity baseline data on seawater, sediment, and biota for undertaking assessments.
In co-operation with the IAEA's Departments of Research and Isotopes and Technical Co-operation, MEL provides support to developing states in obtaining high quality data on marine radioactivity and radioecology, while the non-nuclear contaminants are covered through close co-operation with other specialized agencies, including UNEP, the IOC of UNESCO, UNESCO (see this section) and the UN Development Programme (UNDP). The Laboratory also supports marine pollution monitoring and research in developing countries by conducting joint exercises and training courses as part of an integrated programme of quality assurance for states.
Radiotracer methods are used to study agrochemical compounds, such as pesticides, and their accumulation and effects in marine systems. They are also applied in establishing the pathways and accumulations of heavy metals and other toxic elements in the marine environment and their effects on people and the ecosystem.
MEL conducts regional exercises for quality assurance in the Mediterranean, the Persian Gulf area, the western and southeast Pacific, west and central Africa, east Africa, South-East Asia, the Caribbean, the south-west Atlantic, the Arctic, the Baltic, and the Black Sea.
Together with experts from the Russian Federation, Norway, and the USA, MEL has been undertaking five expeditions to and laboratory analysis of samples collected in the Kara and Barents Seas to determine potential hazards to humans and the marine environment from dumped wastes, including reactors. Computer models have also been developed to predict the dispersion of any future leakage, and laboratory studies of concentration factors and distribution coefficients in Arctic conditions have been carried out.
Nuclear weapons test in the south Pacific. At the request of the French government, MEL has participated in an in-depth analysis of the radiological consequences of several decades of weapons testing on the Mururoa and Fangataufa atolls in French Polynesia. The study was directed by a special international advisory committee con-

ened by IAEA's Director-General, and its findings were discussed at an international conference in Vienna from 30 June to 3 July 1998. The study found that the terrestrial and aquatic environments of the atolls that are accessible to people contain residual radioactive material attributable to the nuclear tests, but at generally very low concentrations which the study concluded were of no radiological significance.

Rising waters of the Caspian Sea. In collaboration with the Isotope Hydrology Section in IAEA headquarters, UNEP, and governments from affected zones, MEL is conducting studies to understand better the causes of the dramatically rising levels of the Caspian Sea. By employing isotopic techniques to study the water cycle, the investigation will provide a new platform for the affected countries to co-operate in solving this environmental crisis.

Pollution of the Black Sea. In collaboration with the IAEA's Technical Co-operation Department and UNDP, MEL is at the centre of a combined research and capacity-building initiative that addresses the rapidly deteriorating condition of Black Sea waters. Isotope tracers are being used to investigate water circulation and pollutant behaviour, while equipping and training activities ensure an improved regional ability to monitor and control the quality of the marine environment.

The IAEA provides extensive support to member States in their endeavour to understand better the origin and replenishment of their groundwater resources by integrating isotope techniques into water resource assessment approaches. In 1998 environmental ministers signed the *Black Sea Declaration*, which stresses the important role played by the IAEA in upgrading the capabilities of member States in the region to assess the marine environment. In this connection, a cruise was also organized to sample sea water, sediments, and biota in the Black Sea with the participation of member State laboratories in the region.

Shortage of water is a key development issue in much of Africa. In 1998 technical co-operation activities aimed at promoting the use of isotope hydrology in combination with other techniques to improve the development and management of water resources were under implementation in 16 countries. Activities of a regional model project were completed with tangible achievements in the four countries concerned (Egypt, Ethiopia, Morocco, and Senegal). In Egypt, for example, the IAEA's

support was connected to national efforts for reclamation of new lands on the fringes of the Nile flood plain. The project enabled the preparation of a comprehensive hydrogeological map to be used in the future management of water resources of the areas investigated at Wadi Qena and Esna.

Building upon the management experience and promising results of this project, a new regional programme was formulated for countries in eastern and southern Africa (Kenya, Madagascar, Namibia, South Africa, United Republic of Tanzania, Uganda, and Zimbabwe). The aim of the programme is to foster regional co-operation in water resource assessment and management, and to enable national water sector authorities and end-users to devise appropriate policies and strategies for optimum management of existing resources. In South Africa, for example, the IAEA's assistance will help in the assessment of the recharge and storage capacity of fractured-rock aquifer systems in the Northern Province which constitute the main water supply for the 3.6 million inhabitants of the region.

Today it is generally accepted that global budgeting of atmospheric carbon is a prerequisite for projections of future atmospheric levels and their impact on the climate. For more than 35 years the IAEA/WMO Global Network for Isotopes in Precipitation (GNIP) has provided the basic isotopic data necessary for the use of hydrogen and oxygen isotopes in hydrological investigations relating to water resources assessment. In recent years the GNIP database, which at present comprises more than 250,000 isotopic and meteorological data from more than 500 locations, has also proved essential in palaeoclimatology and in the verification and further improvement of atmospheric circulation models to be used for the prediction of the global climate change and its impact on the water cycle. The scientific achievements made by the IAEA during the last decade include a review of the GNIP database through which the relationship between surface air temperature and the stable isotopic composition of precipitation has been refined.

Considerable efforts have been directed towards improving predictions of climate changes induced by human activities and their impact on the global environment. One promising approach is the study of past climate changes through isotope investigations of climate archives. Isotope techniques have proved to be indispensable as proxy

indicators of the climate and a dating tool for past climatic events. Substantial progress has been made in this field through the Co-ordinated Research Programme (CRP) of IAEA on the use of isotope techniques in palaeoclimatology, with special reference to continental isotope indicators of palaeoclimate.

A significant part of the Agency's overall programme in the field of environmental protection is played by the joint FAO/IAEA Division of Nuclear Techniques in Food and Agriculture, almost entirely devoted to increasing food production while reducing the environmental impact of fertilizer and pesticide use.

The IAEA's laboratory at Seibersdorf acts as a sample collection, data acquisition, and distribution centre in the Background Air Pollution Monitoring Network (BAPMON) of the WMO (see this section).

Under the IAEA's Radioactive Waste Management Advisory Programme (WAMAP), advisory services are available to member States needing advice on establishing national waste-management programmes and technical assistance on specific waste-management issues or problems.

The IAEA provides various services to member States in the field of safe operation of nuclear power plants and nuclear facilities to protect the environment from contamination.

Decision-making bodies

The policy-making organs of the IAEA are the Board of Governors and the General Conference. The General Conference is composed of representatives of all the IAEA member States. The Board of Governors, IAEA's executive body, is composed of representatives of 35 governments, of which 13 are designated by the Board itself for a period of one year and 22 are elected by the General Conference for a period of two years. The Secretariat is headed by a Director-General appointed by the Board with the approval of the General Conference.

Finance

IAEA financial resources fall into two categories—the regular budget and the voluntary contributions. The regular budget provides for the normal administrative expenses of the IAEA (safeguard inspections, safety services, environmental activities, publications, research conferences, and information services). It is funded by contributions based on annual assessments of member States and by miscellaneous income. The Technical Assistance and Co-operation Fund consists of voluntary contributions used for financing the IAEA's technical co-operation programme. It is funded by contributions from member States and the UN.

Budget
The regular budget was US$221.3 million in 1998 and $224.3 million in 1999, and is estimated at $229.4 million in 2000.

Main contributors
Main contributors in 1999 are the USA (25.772 per cent), Japan (18.328 per cent), Germany (9.816 per cent), France (6.619 per cent), Italy (5.498 per cent), the United Kingdom (5.174 per cent), and the Russian Federation (2.929 per cent).

Special funds
The target for voluntary contributions for the IAEA Technical Assistance and Co-operation Fund (TACF), established in 1959, was set at $68 million in 1997 and $71.5 million in 1998, and is set at $73 million in 1999. IAEA Technical Co-operation Model Projects will have been introduced in about two-thirds of all recipient member States by 1999. 59 new Model Projects began operation on 1 January 1999, bringing the total number to 122. The number of countries with operational Model Projects now stands at 59.

In line with world-wide trends in technical assistance, environmental issues were emphasized in the IAEA's 1999 Technical Co-operation Programme. The IAEA was represented at several UN follow-up meetings to the UN Conference on Environment and Development (UNCED), and IAEA proposals have been submitted to the Global Environment Facility (GEF) (see this section) and to Capacity 21 (launched by UNDP).

Total new resources equalled $63 million in 1998. $53.4 million was pledged in voluntary contributions to the Technical Co-operation Fund (TCF), which was 74.7 per cent of the target. The adjusted programme, which includes assistance brought forward, amounted in 1998 to $79,115,000. The actual delivery of the programme to recipient member States rose a significant 6.4 per cent in 1998 to a record of $64,521,000. The highest amounts went to Europe (with 24.3 per cent), followed closely by Africa (23.6 per cent). Latin America (19 per cent), East Asia and the Pacific (14.1 per cent) and West Asia (12.3 per cent). The remaining 6.7 per cent went to the interregional programme.

A thematic breakdown of the disbursements shows shifts in the IAEA's Technical Co-operation Programme delivery. *Safety* has now taken first place with almost 22 per cent, which is a significant increase over the 18 per cent recorded in 1997. *Human Health*, with 21 per cent, was in second place. For the first time since 1992 *Food*

and Agriculture is not in the top spot, and now represents 16 per cent delivery. The two categories *Physical and Chemical Sciences* and *Marine Environment, Water Resources and Industry* each came in with 11 per cent. *Nuclear Fuel Cycle and Waste Technology* received 7 per cent and *Nuclear Power* 6 per cent. *Human Resource Development and Capacity Building* made up 5 per cent and five other minor themes totalled 1 per cent.

A total of 14 interregional and 146 regional training courses were held in 1998 in 58 countries. Of these, 160 courses took place in developing countries. 99 countries benefited through participating in training courses in 1998. A total of 2,012 scientists were trained.

Publications and databases
The IAEA publishes books, reports, proceedings, safety manuals, statistics, etc. Regular publications are:
- *IAEA Bulletin* (quarterly);
- *IAEA Newsbriefs* (bi-monthly);
- *International Nuclear Information System (INIS) Atomindex*;
- *Nuclear Fusion* (monthly);
- *Meetings on Atomic Energy* (quarterly).

Regular IAEA on-line databases are:
- *International Nuclear Information System (INIS)*;
- *Power Reactor Information System (PRIS)*;
- *International Information System for the Agricultural Sciences and Technology (AGRIS)*.

Sources on the Internet
<http://www.iaea.or.at/worldatom>

International Council for the Exploration of the Sea (ICES)

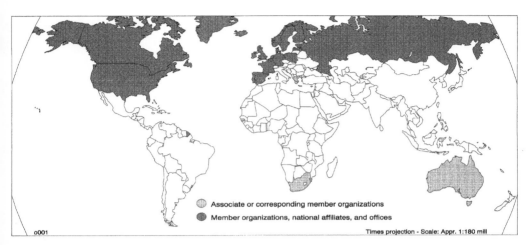

Associate or corresponding member organizations
Member organizations, national affiliates, and offices

0001   Times projection - Scale: Appr. 1:180 mill

Objectives

• to promote and encourage research and investigation for the study of the marine environment and its living resources in the North Atlantic and adjacent seas;
• to publish or disseminate the results of this research, including the provision of scientific information and advice, to national governments, regional fishery management, and pollution control commissions.

Organization

Type
Intergovernmental organization (IGO).

Membership
Open to any State upon approval by three-quarters of its member States. 19 member States by 16 June 1999. Three states, the European Commission, 28 IGOs, and one NGO have observer status.

Founded
22 July 1902.

Secretariat

ICES, Palægade 2–4,
DK-1261 Copenhagen K, Denmark
Telephone: +45-33-154225
Telefax: +45-33-934215
E-mail: ices.info@ices.dk

General Secretary
Professor Christopher C. E. Hopkins.

Number of staff
Ten professionals and 23 support staff (June 1999).

Activities

ICES co-ordinates work on scientific issues in relation to living marine resources, oceanography, and the marine environment, including contaminants and their effects. Much of the work of ICES is conducted under approximately 90 working groups or study groups, approximately one-third of which cover assessment of the stocks of various species of commercial fish and shellfish. Other groups are concerned with physical, chemical, and biological oceanography, issues related to the study of marine contaminants and their effects, mariculture issues, and methods of measurement and assessment. This work is co-ordinated by seven Science Committees (Oceanography, Marine Habitat, Fisheries Technology, Living Resources, Resource Management, Mariculture, and Baltic) and two Advisory Committees, the Advisory Committee on Fishery Management (ACFM) and the Advisory Committee on the Marine Environment (ACME). The overall scientific work is co-ordinated by the Consultative Committee.

In support of these activities, ICES maintains databases on oceanographic conditions in the North Atlantic, and for the Northeast Atlantic (including the Baltic Sea and Arctic waters) on contaminants in marine media (biota, sea water, and sediments, including

some data on biological effects of contaminants), fish diseases, and fisheries statistics.

In mid-1996 ICES established a project office to co-ordinate the North Atlantic Regional Programme of GLOBEC (Global Ocean Ecosystem Dynamics). GLOBEC will provide an enhanced understanding of oceanic mesoscale physical and biological interactions, contributing to the international global change research effort.

Decision-making bodies

The ICES Council, composed of two delegates appointed by each member government, elects the Bureau. The Council holds statutory meetings, termed the Annual Science Conference.

Finance

Budget
The administrative budget is Dkr.22.7 million for 1999/2000.

Publications

• *ICES Annual Report*;
• *ICES/CIEM Information* (bi-annual);
• *ICES Techniques in Marine Environmental Sciences* (approx. four issues a year).

Sources on the Internet

<http://www.ices.dk>
<ftp://server.ices.dk>

International Fund for Agricultural Development (IFAD)

Objectives

• to mobilize additional resources to be made available on concessional terms for agricultural development in developing countries;
• to focus attention on the needs of the poorest rural communities, in particular small farmers, the landless, fishermen, livestock herders, and impoverished rural women;
• to pay special attention to grassroots development and innovative approaches which build on local participation and the preservation of the natural resource base;
• to provide financing primarily for projects and programmes specifically designed to introduce, expand, or improve food production systems and to strengthen related policies and institutions within the framework of national priorities and strategies, taking into consideration: the need to increase food production in the poorest food-deficient countries, the potential for increasing food production in other developing countries, and the importance of improving the nutritional level and living conditions of the poorest populations in developing countries.

Organization

Type
Intergovernmental organization (IGO). International financing institution which is a specialized agency of the UN.

Membership
States. The Fund was established as a part-nership of industrialized countries, oil-producing and -exporting countries, and other developing countries which joined together to raise funds and share in the governance arrangements. The Agreement establishing IFAD organized membership into three categories in order to reflect this special character of the institution. Before February 1997, member States were divided into three categories: Category I, 22 developed nations (OECD members); Category II, 12 petroleum-exporting states (OPEC members); and Category III, 126 developing countries. Now Category I has been reclassified as List A; Category II as List B, and Category III as List C (see also Decision-making bodies, below).

Countries not original members of IFAD may join after approval of their membership by the Governing Council and accession to the IFAD agreement. Not open to regional integration organizations. Total of 161 member States by 15 July 1999.

Founded
11 December 1977.

Secretariat

International Fund for Agricultural Development (IFAD),
107 via del Serafico,
I-00142 Rome,
Italy
Telephone: +39-06-54592215
Telefax: +39-06-54592143
E-mail: communications@ifad.org

President and Chairman of the Executive Board
Mr Fawzi Hamad Al-Sultan (1997–2001).

Communications and Public Affairs Coordinator
Ms Farhana Haque-Rahman.

Number of staff
126 professionals and 164 general service staff (December 1998). The Fund has no field, regional, or country offices.

Activities

IFAD projects range from provision of farming inputs and services (seed, fertilizer, tools, and agricultural research and extension) to irrigation, storage facilities, access roads, and credit to poor farmers and workers who would have no other source of loans.

IFAD lends money, most of which is on highly concessional or low-interest terms, and is concerned not only with raising agricultural production but also with improving local prospects for employment, nutrition, and income distribution.

Between 1978 and 1998, IFAD had committed a total of $US6.4 billion in loans and grants for financing 520 projects in 113 developing countries. The total cost of these projects amounts to about $18.5 billion, which includes contributions from external co-financiers ($5.7 billion) and from government of recipient countries ($6.7 billion).

Environmental activities

As the first international financial institution to respond to the socio-economic crisis in sub-Saharan Africa, IFAD launched the Special Programme for Sub-Saharan Africa (SPA) in January 1986, with a target for resource mobilization of $US300 million for the first phase (SPA I) of the Programme. The resources contributed exceeded the Programme's original target and amounted to $322.8 million.

The objectives of SPA I were to help restore the productive capacity of small farmers, promote traditional food crops grown mainly by smallholders, and initiate small-scale water control schemes as well as measures for environmental protection and policy assistance for governments. By the end of 1992 IFAD had fully exhausted all resources of SPA I in supporting 32 projects in 22 sub-Saharan African countries.

The second phase of the Programme (SPA II), which became effective in January 1993, preserves the focus of the first phase while extending its conceptual frame and operational scope. Specifically it carries environmental and soil conservation objectives from on-farm to off-farm (particularly in the common property resource domain) and addresses overall coping strategies for households and communities through economic diversification. The list of countries eligible for assistance grew from 22 under SPA I to 27 under SPA II, including Benin, Burundi, Central African Republic, Comoros, Equatorial Guinea, Madagascar, Malawi, Rwanda, and Sierra Leone.

The resources received for Phase II amounted to $65 million, which were also committed in support of 13 projects. In September 1995 the Executive Board decided to merge the SPA with IFAD's Regular Programme.

In 1997 IFAD was given the responsibility of hosting the Global Mechanism of the Convention to Combat Desertification (CCD) (see Agreements). Following an agreement in April 1997, the Fund and the World Bank (see this section) initiated a joint Global Environment Facility (GEF) 'accelerated learning programme' to assist dryland countries in controlling land degradation, alleviating poverty, and addressing global environmental objectives. It is intended that the development of a demonstration pipeline of GEF land-degradation projects will allow the GEF to play a useful role in countering land degradation in the context of the CCD.

Decision-making bodies

The highest directing body of IFAD is the Governing Council, where all the member States are represented by a Governor and an Alternate Governor. The Council meets annually and elects the President of the Fund by a two-thirds majority for a four-year term.

Under the new voting system approved in February 1997, member States have two types of vote: an original membership vote (equal votes for all members) and votes based on the size of contributions to the Fund's resources. Under the old system all three categories had equal voting powers.

Current operations are supervised by an Executive Board composed of 18 Members and 18 Alternate Members. The Board is elected by the Council for a three-year period. In addition to the conduct and general operation of IFAD, it approves loans and grants for projects and holds three regular sessions a year.

The secretariat is headed by the President of IFAD and is responsible for the management of the Fund. It has three main administrative departments:
• Economic Policy and Resource Strategy Department;
• Programme Management Department, with five regional divisions, as well as a Technical Advisory Division;
• Management and Personnel Services Department, including Office of the Secretary, Personnel Division, Management of Information Services, and Administrative Services Unit.

Other units are: offices of Evaluation and Studies, Internal Audit, Legal Services, and Controller and Treasury.

Finance

The Fund is financed by contributions from its member States. Its initial resources, in 1977, amounted to $US900 million. The First Replenishment (effective on 18 June 1982) amounted to $1,012 million. The Second Replenishment (effective on 27 November 1986) amounted to $474 million. The Third Replenishment (effective on 24 December 1990) amounted to $558 million. The Fourth Replenishment (effective on 29 August 1997) amounted to $435 million. Additional complimentary contributions to the Fourth Replenishment brought the total to about $460 million.

Budget

The administrative budget was US$51.03 million in 1997, including a contingency of $300,000; and $52.2 million in 1998, including a contingency of $400,000. The administrative costs represent 12 per cent of resources committed.

Publications

• annual reports;
• *Reports of the Sessions of Governing Council* (annual);
• *IFAD Update Bulletin* (quarterly);
• IFAD Operations by country (IFAD in India, Indonesia, the Philippines, Uganda, Argentina, Chile, Venezuela, Tanzania, Zimbabwe, and Kenya);
• The State of World Rural Poverty (series);
• *Meeting the Challenge of Hunger and Poverty*;
• *Providing Food Security for All.*

Sources on the Internet

<http://www.ifad.org>

International Labour Organization (ILO)

Objectives

To establish social justice as the foundation for universal and lasting peace, by unifying governments, employers, and workers in common action to promote human rights, generate employment, and improve living and working conditions.

Organization

Type
Intergovernmental organization (IGO). A specialized agency within the UN system. The tripartite structure of the ILO, whose organs involve organizations representing employers and workers along with governments, is unique in the UN system.

Membership
Open to members of the UN. Non-members of the UN must be approved by the General Conference by a two-thirds majority. 174 members by 30 June 1999.

Founded
11 April 1919.

Secretariat

International Labour Office,
4 route des Morillons,
CH-1211 Geneva,
Switzerland
Telephone: +41-22-7996111
Telefax: +41-22-7988685
E-mail: doscom@hq1.ilo.ch

Director General
Mr Juan Somavia.

Director of Public Information
Mr Michel Barton.

Number of staff
The staff of the Office, at headquarters, and at field, regional, and country offices totals about 2,225 (June 1999).

Activities

One of the oldest and most important functions of the ILO is the adoption, by the tripartite International Labour Conference, of conventions and recommendations which set international labour standards. The ILO has adopted 182 conventions and 190 recommendations, forming an international labour code as a guideline for national law and practice in all spheres of labour activities. Through ratification by member States, conventions create binding obligations to put their provisions into effect. More than 6,600 ratifications have been registered. Recommendations provide guidance on policy, legislation, and practice.

International technical co-operation is carried out in the major fields of standards, employment, training, working conditions, labour administration and labour relations, enterprise development, and social security.

Main conventions on environment under the auspices of ILO
• Convention No. 115 Concerning the Protection of Workers against Ionizing Radiations, 1960;
• Convention No. 136 Concerning Protection against Hazards of Poisoning Arising from Benzene, 1971;
• Convention No. 139 Concerning Prevention and Control of Occupational Hazards Caused by Carcinogenic Substances and Agents, 1974;
• Convention No. 148 Concerning the Protection of Workers against Occupational Hazards in the Working Environment Due to Air Pollution, Noise, and Vibration, 1977;
• Convention No. 155 Concerning Occupational Safety and Health and the Working Environment, 1981;
• Convention No. 162 Concerning Safety in the Use of Asbestos, Geneva, 1986;
• Convention No. 170 on Safety in the Use of Chemicals at Work, 1990;
• Convention No. 174 Concerning the Prevention of Major Industrial Accidents, 1993.

Environmental activities

In the area of the environment, the ILO's actions have been extended beyond the traditional emphasis on occupational safety and health and the working environment to include: strengthening the role of trade unions and employers' organizations in securing sustainable development; environment and development training; employment, poverty, and development issues; and environmental concerns related to women and indigenous and tribal peoples.

Decision-making bodies

The International Labour Conference, which meets annually, is composed of national delegations comprising two government delegates, one delegate representing employers and one representing workers. The Governing Body, composed of 56 members (28 governments, 14 employers and 14 workers), meets three times a year and supervises the work of the ILO. It takes decisions on ILO policy, decides the agenda of the International Labour Conference, adopts the draft programme and budget of ILO for submission to the Conference, and elects the Director-General. The International Labour Office acts as secretariat to the Organization.

Finance

Apportioned among member governments according to a scale of contributions approved by the Conference.

Budget

The administrative budget was $US500 million for 1996–7 and is $481 million for 1998–9.

Publications

- *World of Work Magazine* (five times a year);
- *International Labour Review* (quarterly);
- *Yearbook of Labour Statistics*;
- *World Labour Report*;
- *World Employment*.

Sources on the Internet

<http://www.ilo.org>

International Maritime Organization (IMO)

Objectives
* to provide machinery for co-operation among governments on technical matters affecting international merchant shipping, with special responsibility for safety at sea;
* to ensure that the highest possible standards of safety at sea and of efficient navigation are achieved;
* to prevent pollution of the sea caused by ships and other craft operating in the marine environment;
* to be responsible for convening international maritime conferences and drafting international maritime conventions.

Organization
Type
Intergovernmental organization (IGO), specialized agency of the UN within the UN system, linked to the UN Economic and Social Council (ECOSOC).

Membership
Governments of 157 states by 1 April 1999. Not open to regional integration organizations.
Consultative status with 35 intergovernmental organizations (December 1998). 53 non-governmental organizations (NGOs) enjoy consultative status with IMO (December 1998).

Founded
6 March 1948, Geneva. The original name was Inter-Governmental Maritime Consultative Organization (IMCO). This was changed to International Maritime Organization (IMO) on 22 May 1982.

Secretariat
International Maritime Organization (IMO),
4 Albert Embankment,
London SE1 7SR,
United Kingdom
Telephone: +44-171-7357611
Telefax: +44-171-5873210
E-mail: info@imo.org

Secretary-General
Mr William A. O'Neil (Canada).

Head, Information Office
Mr Roger Kohn.

Number of staff
124 professionals and 168 support staff (April 1999).

Activities
IMO has drawn up and promoted the adoption of 35 conventions and protocols, nearly all of which are now in force. Conventions and protocols are binding legal instruments and, upon entry into force, their requirements must be implemented by all States Parties.

Main conventions on the environment under the auspices of IMO (see Agreements)
* *International Convention on Civil Liability for Oil Pollution Damage 1969 (1969 CLC)*, Brussels, 1969, 1976, and 1984;
* *International Convention Relating to Intervention on the High Seas in Cases of Oil Pollution Casualties (Intervention Convention)*, Brussels, 1969.
* *International Convention on the Establishment of an International Fund for Compensation for Oil Pollution Damage 1971 (1971 Fund Convention)*, Brussels, 1971;
* *Convention on the Prevention of Marine Pollution by Dumping of Wastes and Other Matter (London Convention 1972)*, London, 1972;
* *International Convention for the Prevention of Pollution from Ships, 1973, as modified by the Protocol of 1978 relating thereto (MARPOL 73/78)*, London, 1973 and 1978;
* *International Convention on Oil Pollution Preparedness, Response, and Co-operation (OPRC)*, London, 1990;
* *International Convention on Liability and Compensation for Damage in Connection with the Carriage of Hazardous and Noxious Substances by Sea (HNS Convention)*, London, 3 May 1996.

In addition IMO adopts numerous non-treaty instruments, such as codes of practice and recommendations, which, although not mandatory, provide a basis for legislation in member States. This helps prevent unilateral, unco-ordinated, and possibly conflicting standards.

An important function of IMO is to facilitate technical co-operation within the scope of the Organization. For this purpose, it provides advice and assistance to developing countries in the technical, legal, and administrative fields. Its Technical Co-operation Programme assigns very high priority to maritime training at all levels. It provides opportunities for training in national and regional maritime training institutions and for specialized training for senior maritime personnel at the World Maritime University, established by IMO in Malmö, Sweden. Branches of the World Maritime University have been established in countries throughout the world, and these also provide training in specialized areas.

Decision-making bodies
Political
The IMO Assembly is the supreme governing body and meets biennially. It is open to all member States as well as representatives of the intergovernmental and non-governmental organizations in consultative status with IMO. One of the Assembly's most important tasks is to adopt the numerous resolutions and recommendations that have been prepared during the previous two years by subsidiary bodies.

It also elects the members of the IMO Council for the next two years. The Council is IMO's only elective body and consists of 32 member States. In electing the members of the Council the Assembly shall observe the following criteria:
(a) eight shall be states with the largest interest in providing international shipping services;
(b) eight shall be other states with the largest interest in international seaborne trade;
(c) 16 shall be states not elected under (a) or (b) above which have special interests in maritime transport or navigation, and whose election to the Council will ensure the representation of all major geographic areas of the world.

In November 1993 the Assembly adopted an amendment to the IMO Convention which, upon entry into force, will increase the size of the Council to 40. Groups (a) and (b) will be increased to ten members and group (c) to 20. The amendment will enter into force 12 months after being accepted by two-thirds of IMO member States. 78 member States had accepted the Amendment by 1 April 1999.

The Council normally meets twice a year and acts as the governing body of IMO between sessions of the Assembly. It is also responsible for preparing for the Assembly's consideration the budget and work programme that it is to handle.

Scientific/technical
There are five main committees consisting of all member States:
• The Maritime Safety Committee (MSC), the highest technical body for the Organization, was set up in 1973. It is composed of government experts and experts from organizations which have been granted consultative status with IMO. The MSC has nine subcommittees dealing with different aspects of safety, such as the carriage of dangerous goods, fire protection, training, etc. All members of IMO are entitled to take part, together with representatives of non-IMO states which are parties to treaties in respect of which the Committee exercises functions;
• The Legal Committee, composed of government experts and experts from organizations which have been granted consultative status with IMO, was set up after the Torrey Canyon disaster in 1967. Its functions are to consider any legal matters falling within the scope of IMO;
• The Marine Environment Protection Committee (MEPC), composed of government experts and experts from organizations which have been granted consultative status with IMO, and set up in 1973, is responsible for co-ordinating and administering the activities of the organization concerning the prevention and control of pollution;
• The Technical Co-operation Committee, composed of government experts and experts from organizations which have been granted consultative status with IMO, and first set up in 1972, has the main functions of establishing directives and guidelines for the execution of IMO's comprehensive programme of assistance to developing countries in maritime transport, of monitoring the programme's progressive development, and of reviewing its results. It acts to help governments implement IMO conventions and other instruments through various forms of assistance;
• The Facilitation Committee, a subsidiary body of the IMO Council and composed of government experts and experts from organizations which have been granted consultative status with IMO, has the main function of directing IMO efforts to reduce unnecessary formalities and obstructions to allied trade.

Most of the draft resolutions submitted to the Assembly for consideration have been prepared by the MSC and the MEPC.

Finance

Contributions to the IMO budget are based on a formula which is different from that used in other United Nations agencies. The amount paid by each member State depends primarily on the gross tonnage of its merchant fleet.

Budget
The total approved budget by appropriation for the years 1996-7 was UK£36,612,200 (£17,975,100 for 1996 and £18,637,100 for 1997) and the budget for the years 1998-9 amounts to £36,612,200 (£17,946,100 for 1998 and £18,666,100 for 1999).

Assessments on member States amounted to £17,685,100 in 1996, £18,347,100 in 1997, and £17,606,100 in 1998.

The actual administrative costs at headquarters were £17,040,143 in 1996, £17,546,138 in 1997, and £17,943,353 in 1998.

Main contributors
The top ten contributors for 1997 were Panama, Liberia, Japan, Greece, Cyprus, Bahamas, the USA, Norway, Malta, and the Russian Federation. The top ten contributors for 1998 were Panama, Liberia, Japan, Greece, Bahamas, Cyprus, the USA, Norway, Malta, and Singapore.

Special funds
Financial support for IMO projects is provided in various ways. IMO's Technical Co-operation Programme, with a total delivery of $US5.4 million in 1994, $7.7 million in 1995, and $5.9 million in 1996, was until 1997 funded not from IMO's own resources, but mainly from the UN Development Programme (UNDP) (see this section). However, since UNDP funding dropped from some $8 million in 1988 to some $0.5 million in 1996, with no new major projects in the pipeline, IMO secured extra budgetary resources amounting to some $6,530,000 for project activities during 1997 and $5,474,100 for project activities during 1998. In addition, the Technical Co-operation Fund, built up by donations, provided UK£2,475,000 for the period 1996-7 and is contributing UK£2,850,000 for 1998-9 project activities.

The Programme was introduced more than 25 years ago with the main goal of bridging the gap between the developed and the developing maritime nations in matters concerning sea transport and related activities. Prominent among the aims of the Programme are improving safety at sea, reducing marine pollution, and mitigating effects of pollution. Various agencies, such as UNDP, the UN Environment Programme (UNEP) (see this section), and governments, make funds available on an *ad hoc* basis, contributing directly to environment- and development-motivated projects within the framework provided by the MEPC.

Publications

IMO has about 250 titles (books, reports, proceedings, conventions, pamphlets, codes, etc). A catalogue is available from the secretariat.

IMO News, the magazine of IMO, is published quarterly.

Sources on the Internet
<http://www.imo.org>

International Monetary Fund (IMF)

Objectives

- to promote international monetary co-operation through a permanent institution which provides the machinery for consultation and collaboration on international monetary problems;
- to facilitate the expansion and balanced growth of international trade;
- to promote exchange stability and maintain orderly exchange agreements among members and avoid competitive exchange depreciation.

Organization

Type
Intergovernmental organization (IGO). An agreement of relationship concluded with the UN outlines a programme of mutual assistance between the UN and the Fund as an independent international organization and a UN specialized agency. The IMF co-operates particularly with the UN Conference on Trade and Development (UNCTAD), the World Trade Organization (WTO), and the International Bank for Reconstruction and Development of the World Bank (IBRD) (see this section).

Membership
Open to all countries. Not open to regional integration organizations. Ratification of the articles and acceptance of conditions laid down by the Fund are conditions of membership. Total of 182 members by 1 August 1999.

Founded
27 December 1945.

Secretariat

International Monetary Fund (IMF),
700 19th Street,
Washington, DC 20431 NW,
USA
Telephone: +1-202-6237000
Telefax: +1-202-6234661
E-mail: publicaffairs@imf.org

Managing Director
Mr Michel Camdessus (1997–2000).

Director of External Relations
Mr Thomas Dawson II.

Number of staff
1,525 professionals, 671 support staff, and 428 other authorized staff at headquarters and in field, regional, and country offices (June 1999).

Activities

The Fund operates a range of financial facilities to help member countries in balance of payments difficulty resolve their problems through sound policy changes. The facilities include a Compensatory and Contingency Financing Facility, which makes additional resources available to compensate for unexpected temporary shortfalls in export earn-ings for commodities, and for certain contingencies, such as sudden increases in interest-rates; and an Enhanced Structural Adjustment Facility (ESAF), which provides highly concessional loans to low-income developing members facing protracted balance-of-payments problems.

The IMF, together with the IBRD, has developed an Initiative to resolve the debt problems of the Heavily Indebted Poor Countries (HIPCs). It was designed to care the debt-servicing burden of the HIPCs that follow sound policies but for which traditional debt-relief mechanisms would be inadequate to secure a sustainable external debt position over the medium term. The IMF has in the last two years began releasing a substantial amount of information in hard copy and on its website (see Sources on the Internet, below). In April 1997, for example in the wake of discussions as to the value of transparency in enhancing the effectiveness of surveillance, the Board agreed to the voluntary issuance of press information notices following the conclusion of Article IV consultation discussions for those members seeking to make known to the public the IMF's views about their economies.

Environmental activities
The Fund's mandate is to promote international monetary co-operation and stability. Fund staff seek to develop greater understanding of the interplay between economic policies, economic activity, and environmental change, drawing upon the expertise of other

institutions with environmental competence and responsibilities. This work enables Fund staff to conduct better-informed discussions with national authorities who face macro-economic policy choices entailing major environmental implications.

Decision-making bodies

The IMF operates through a Board of Governors, a Board of Executive Directors, an Interim Committee on the International Monetary System, and a Managing Director and staff. The Board of Governors consists of one Governor and one Alternate Governor appointed by each member country—typically the minister of finance or governor of a central bank. An annual meeting of the Board in conjunction with that of the World Bank Group is held each autumn. All powers of the Fund are vested in the Board. The Executive Board is responsible for the daily business of the Fund. It consists of the Managing Director as Chair and 24 Executive Directors, who are appointed or elected by individual member countries or by groups of countries. Each member has an assessed quota, which is subscribed and determines voting power. As of June 1999 the United States, as the largest contributor, had 17.4 per cent of the voting power,

while the smallest contributors held considerably less than 1 per cent each. Access to use of the Fund's resources is also determined in relation to quota, taking account of the balance-of-payments needs of the member and the strength of the policies it agrees to implement to restore balance-of-payments viability. The USA, Japan, Germany, France, and the United Kingdom, in that order, have the largest quotas (with the quotas of France and the United Kingdom equal). The total of members' quotas, as of June 1999, was, in Special Drawing Rights (SDR), about SDR209.6 billion.

Finance

The general resources of the Fund have been supplemented by borrowing from member countries in strong payments positions. These borrowed resources are made available to member countries under a variety of facilities and policies.

Administrative budget
IMF's administrative budget was $US503.7 million for the financial year 1997/98 and $519.5 million for 1998/99, and is $575.8 million for 1999/2000.

Use of Fund resources
The total of stand-by and extended arrangements in effect as of 31 May 1999 was SDR48.6 billion, of which SDR18.2 billion was undrawn. The total of SAF and ESAF arrangements was SDR4.1 billion, of which SDR2.2 billion was undrawn.

Publications

• annual reports (include the IMF Annual Report and the Annual Report on Exchange Arrangement and Exchange Restrictions);
• *IMF Survey* (23 times a year);
• *Finance and Development* (quarterly);
• *World Economic Outlook* (bi-annual in World Economic and Financial Surveys (WEFS) series);
• *International Capital Markets* (annual in WEFS series);
• *IMF Staff Papers* (quarterly scholarly journal);
• Economic Issues series;
• Occasional Papers series;
• working papers;
• policy discussion papers;
• staff country reports;
• books and manuals.

Sources on the Internet
<http://www.imf.org>

International Oil Pollution Compensation Funds (IOPC Funds)

Objectives

International Oil Pollution Compensation Fund 1971 (1971 Fund)
To administer the system of additional compensation created under the International Convention on the Establishment of an International Fund for Compensation for Oil Pollution Damage 1971 (1971 Fund Convention) (see Agreements), i.e. to provide supplementary compensation to victims of oil pollution damage in states which are Parties to the 1971 Fund Convention who, if the total amount of the proven damage exceeds the limit of the shipowner's liability, cannot obtain full compensation for the damage under the International Convention on Civil Liability for Oil Pollution Damage 1969 (1969 CLC) (see Agreements).

International Oil Pollution Compensation Fund 1992 (1992 Fund)
To administer the regime of compensation created under the 1971 Fund Convention as amended by the 1992 Protocol thereto, known as the International Convention on the Establishment of an International Fund for Compensation for Oil Pollution Damage 1992 (1992 Fund Convention), i.e. to provide supplementary compensation to victims of oil pollution damage in states which are Parties to the 1992 Fund Convention who, if the total amount of the proven damage exceeds the limit of the shipowner's liability, cannot obtain full compensation for the damage under the 1969 CLC as amended by the 1992 Protocol thereto, known as the International Convention on Civil Liability for oil Pollution Damage 1992 (1992 CLC).

Organization

Type
Intergovernmental organizations (IGOs).

Membership
Members of the 1971 Fund are states which have ratified, acceded to, approved, or accepted the 1971 Fund Convention (51 member States by 1 May 1999) (see 1971 Fund Convention, Agreements). Observer status is granted to States which have notified the Secretariat that they are considering ratification of the 1971 Fund Convention, and to seven IGOs and 13 NGOs.

Members of the 1992 Fund are states which have ratified, acceded to, approved, or accepted the 1992 Fund Convention (42 member States by 1 May 1999). Observer status is granted to States which are members of the 1971 Fund but not of the 1992 Fund and to States which have notified the Secretariat that they are considering ratification of the 1992 Fund Convention and to seven IGOs and 14 NGOs.

Founded
The 1971 Fund was established in London on 17 October 1978. The 1992 Fund was established in London on 30 May 1996.

Secretariat

International Oil Pollution Compensation Funds (IOPC Funds),
4 Albert Embankment,
London SE1 7SR,
United Kingdom
Telephone: +44-171-5822606
Telefax: +44-171-7350326
E-mail: info@iopcfund.org

Director
Mr Måns Jacobsson
(1 January 1985–31 December 1999).

Number of staff
Nine professionals and 13 support staff (July 1999).

Activities

The major activities at the 1971 and 1992 Funds are:
• to administer the system of compensation established under the 1971 Fund Convention and 1992 Fund Convention;
• to handle claims for compensation arising out of oil pollution incidents and pay compensation to victims;
• to levy contributions to finance the activities of the 1971 and 1992 Funds;
• to promote ratification of the 1971 and 1992 Fund Conventions.

Decision-making bodies

The 1971 Fund and the 1992 Fund each have an Assembly which meets annually as the supreme governing body. Sessions of each Assembly are open to the governments of all respective member States. States and organizations which have observer status with the respective Fund are invited as observers.

Decisions of the Assembly and of its subsidiary bodies shall be made, elections shall be determined, and reports, resolutions, and recommendations shall be adopted by a majority of the members present and voting. Each member has one vote.

The 1971 Fund and the 1992 Fund each have an Executive Committee, comprising 15 member States elected by the Assembly, which meets several times a year. The main function of the Executive Committees is to approve settlements of claims, to the extent that the Director is not authorized to do so. Voting rules are similar to the rules of the Assembly.

Finance

Each Fund is financed by contributions of persons who receive more than 150,000 tonnes of crude or heavy fuel oil after sea transport in a member State of the respective organization during a calendar year. Contributions are determined in proportion to the quantity of oil received.

Budget
Annual secretariat costs amount to approximately £UK2.0 million.

Publications
• annual reports;
• claims manuals;
• texts of conventions on liability and compensation for oil pollution damage.

Organization for Economic Co-operation and Development (OECD), Environment Policy Committee (EPOC)

Objectives

to contribute to sustainable development at the global, regional, and national level;

to contribute to the advancement of integrated policies for the management of the environment of OECD member countries and selected non-member countries, individually or in an international context;

to provide and disseminate high-quality and reliable environmental information and data;

to provide a platform for discussion on environmental issues for governments, NGOs, business, trade unions, and scientific institutions.

Organization

Type
Intergovernmental organization (IGO).

Membership
Open to states and regional integration organizations. 29 member States and the Commission of the European Communities with full membership by July 1999. The Slovak Republic, the UN Environment Programme (UNEP) (see this section), the Council of Europe, the UN Economic Commission for Europe (UN/ECE), and the UN Commission on Sustainable Development (CSD) (see this section) hold observer status.

Founded
OEEC: 1948, OECD: 1960.
OECD Environment Committee: 1970, replaced by Environment Policy Committee (EPOC): 1992.

Secretariat

OECD, Environment Policy Committee (EPOC),
2 rue André Pascal,
F-75775 Paris Cedex 16,
France
Telephone: +33-1-45248200
Telefax: +33-1-45247876
E-mail: env.contact@oecd.org

Secretary-General (OECD)
Mr Donald Johnston.

Director for the Environment
Ms Joke Waller-Hunter.

Executive Secretary, EPOC
Ms Amy Plantin.

Number of staff
105, including professional and support staff (July 1999), all located at headquarters.

Activities

EPOC has a work programme composed of 12 activities:
• *Environmental Outlook and Strategy.* An OECD 'Environmental Outlook' is being developed to generate an economy-based vision of environmental conditions in 2020. It will be made up of quantitative projections and qualitative assessments of environmental change in OECD member countries. A new Environmental Strategy to be developed from the base of the Outlook will help member countries create the right conditions for environmental sustainability, using economic, regulatory, voluntary, or social policy instruments;
• *Integrating Economic and Environmental Policies.* The successful integration of economic and environmental policies can bring multiple benefits. An important first step towards integration is to identify the impacts on the environment of economic support measures, such as subsidies. At the same time OECD is looking at a range of other policies which can be used to help foster policy integration, such as taxes, charges, and tradable permits. Agriculture is one of the sectors of the economy where failure to integrate environmental and economic policies is most evident. Through a Joint Working Party with the OECD Committee for Agriculture, EPOC will continue its work on such issues as sustainable agriculture, the development of agri-environmental indicators, climate change and agriculture, eco-labelling of agricultural produce, and the environmental implications of structural and technological change;
• *Globalisation and the Environment.* The opening-up of the world's trade and investment regimes, an important element of globalization, is likely to have a substantial effect on the environment—nationally, regionally, and globally. The OECD has examined the interaction between trade and the environment for most of the past decade. The focus is currently on issues such as the environmental effects of trade liberalisation, the trade dimensions of sustainable product policies, the assessment of the environmental effects of trade agreements (and vice versa), and the extent to which trade and environment policies in OECD countries have been transparent to the general public. A second significant feature of globalization has been the phenomenal growth in flows of private capital, including foreign direct investment (FDI). The impacts of both FDI and portfolio flows of investment are being examined by the OECD;
• *Increasing Resource Efficiency.* The sustainable management of natural resources is becoming ever more important, both for OECD and non-OECD countries, as the focus of environmental concern shifts away from pollution-related problems towards resource-based ones. To improve understanding of how resource efficiency can contribute to sustainable development the Environment Programme has a major new cross-cutting project. This inter-disciplinary work is examining sectoral trends in eco-efficiency, case-studies of progress and specific policy instruments, including extended producer responsibility, integrated product policies, and the reform of prices, market structures, and regulation;
• *Sustainable Consumption.* The OECD countries are the world's largest consumers of natural resources. A major cross-cutting activity in the Programme is looking at how products and services can be consumed with less of a strain on natural resources and lower levels of pollution. New indicators of sustainable consumption patterns—with an initial report being published in the first half of 1999—an overview of policy instruments for influencing consumer demand, a detailed analysis of four 'domains' where an influence on consumer demand will be critical—food, transport, tourism, and housing—and a study of how globalization affects consumption patterns will all help OECD governments to select the best mix of policies;
• *Climate Change and Environmentally Sustainable Transport.* The OECD helps to

Associate or corresponding member organizations

Member organizations, national affiliates, and offices

o002

Times projection - Scale: Appr. 1:180 mill

advance the ongoing international discussions on global climate change with its annual Forum on Climate Change. The Forum involves both non-member countries and important stakeholders. An Annex I Expert Group of specialists from member countries and countries in transition provides a platform for the development of analysis and an exchange of ideas among this gathering of nations. The Programme is also working towards an economic and environmental assessment of the wide range of domestic policies used to address climate change. Domestic policies are likely to be successful if they target multiple policy objectives at the same time, so it is important to take into account the ancillary benefits of measures to reduce greenhouse gases. Analysis is also focusing on the Kyoto mechanisms, including emissions trading, the Clean Development Mechanism (FDM), and Joint Implementation (JI). The OECD has been studying the relationship between transport and the environment since the earliest days of its environmental work, initially with a focus on air pollution, noise, and fuel used from motor vehicles. Transport is a major contribution to environmental problems at the local, regional, and global levels. It is now the fastest-growing source of greenhouse gas emissions, so analysis of how better to manage these and other environmental effects is closely integrated with work on climate change, as well as with that on sustainable consumption and on sectoral policy integration. The OECD's project Environmentally Sustainable Transport is examining what kind of policy framework will be

necessary to ensure that transport systems are environmentally sustainable in the year 2030 and beyond. By developing a set of essential criteria to be met, and then by using alternative projections to explore different paths forward, this work is helping to show the policies that will be required in the years to come;
• *The Environmental Health and Safety Programme.* The OECD Chemicals Programme, now the Environmental Health and Safety (EHS) Programme, was established in 1971 to increase the OECD's capacity to foster international co-operation in order to help ensure the safety of the products of this massive industry. The work on chemicals and other topics in the field of environmental health and safety is intended to assist member countries by developing high-quality instruments for use in the protection of health and the environment, avoiding the duplication of effort among countries, and minimising non-tariff barriers to trade. The OECD has developed a set of Test Guidelines and laid down agreed Principles of Good Laboratory Practice so that safety tests undertaken in one member country do not have to be needlessly repeated elsewhere. The OECD is also assisting its member countries in developing risk-management approaches such as analysis of socio-economic factors and risk communication. The OECD has developed harmonised criteria for classifying hazardous chemicals which will be applied globally through the United Nations. In parallel with the OECD work to help member countries and industry with the registration of new chemicals, the EHS Programme allows member countries to share the

burden of testing existing chemicals that are produced in high volumes (defined as more than 1,000 tons in any one country). This massive workload is divided up among the participating countries, which share the data they generate and then make a co-operative hazard assessment. The registration by public authorities of potentially harmful releases of pollutants into air, water, and soil, as well as of wastes transferred elsewhere for treatment and disposal, allows a database to be built up. This is a Pollutant Release and Transfer Register, or PRTR. The OECD provides countries with guidance on how to develop a PRTR system.

The EHS Programme is also developing harmonised methodologies for assessing the safety of the products of modern biotechnology, such as genetically modified crops and micro-organisms. There is intense public interest in these, and the OECD data are made widely available through the 'Bio-Track On-Line' system on the Internet. The Pesticide Programme is helping OECD countries share the work of pesticide registration by harmonizing both the way in which the industry submits data (electronically) to the regulatory authorities, and the way in which regulators produce review reports. The Pesticide Programme also helps member countries to find ways of reducing the risks associated with pesticide use and enables them to stay informed about other countries' activities;
• *Waste Management.* A series of OECD Council Acts establish a broad framework for the control of transfrontier movements of hazardous wastes, such as the toxic residues

from chemical and manufacturing industries. The OECD framework also includes a control system for wastes which can be reused or recycled and are moved between OECD countries. Procedures for the management of the transfrontier movement of wastes exist additionally under the Basel Convention (see Agreements) and within the European Union (see this section), and steps are now underway to harmonize the procedures and requirements of the different systems;

• *Co-operation with Non-Member Countries.* Sharing analysis and knowledge and engaging non-member countries in a constructive dialogue is essential for OECD countries in an era of global interdependence. The OECD Environment Directorate housed the secretariat for a Task Force for the Implementation of the Environmental Action Programme in Central and Eastern Europe (EAP). The Task Force provides a forum for dialogue and co-operation between countries in transition and the members of the OECD, as well as international organizations active in the region and partners from business, labour, and non-governmental organizations. The main objective of the Task Force is to facilitate implementation of the policy and institutional aspects of the EAP: by promoting the integration of environmental considerations into the processes of economic and political reform; by upgrading institutional and human capacities for environmental management; by broadening political support for environmental improvement; and, by promoting the mobilization and cost-effective use of financial resources. There is growing co-operation with the Russian Federation and China. An Environmental Performance Review of the Russian Federation is being published in 1999. Several OECD workshops on the use of economic and other policy instruments have been held with China, and others are planned on environmental monitoring, environmental indicators, and environmental financing, particularly in the water sector;

• *Environmental Performance Reviews.* The OECD's Environmental Performance Reviews scrutinize the efforts of its member countries to reach their environmental goals, both domestic objectives and international commitments, and recommend changes that could lead to better performance. The process is one of 'peer review' in which experts from the governments of several OECD countries and the OECD secretariat spend two weeks in a given country reviewing its performance. Their report is discussed in depth in EPOC's Working Party on Environmental Perform-

ance before it is finalised. Four or five OECD countries are examined in this way each year, with the first cycle of performance reviews now almost complete. A second cycle beginning in 2000 will place more emphasis on the use of indicators to measure performance and the integration of environmental, economic, and social policies to achieve sustainable development;

• *Environmental Data and Information.* The OECD has long been the authoritative source of environmental data on its member countries—on pollution, natural resources such as forest cover and richness of fauna and flora, and on energy, transport, industry, and agriculture. These data are essential, since they provide a strong factual and quantitative basis for much of the rest of the work of the Environment Programme. Ensuring that the public has easy access to environmental information is also a high priority, and to this end work is continuing in support of OECD countries' efforts, which are spurred on in part by the 1998 *OECD Council Recommendation on Environmental Information.* Linked to this Recommendation, an overall review of environmental information in OECD countries is being undertaken as part of the Environment Programme. The review will also contribute to the discussion on environmental information to be held in 2001 under the auspices of the UN Commission on Sustainable Development (CSD) (see this section);

• *Environmental Indicators.* Environmental progress across the OECD is monitored with the help of the environmental indicators developed under the Programme. The widely used 'Pressure-State-Response' framework helps decisionmakers and the public to see how environmental, economic, and social indicators are interconnected. The OECD regularly publishes a core set of such indicators, covering both environmental and socio-economic issues. New studies are under way on indicators of sustainable consumption and on indicators of the interface between three major economic sectors and the environment: transport, agriculture, and energy. An allied activity is the development of 'environmental accounting', which assesses the natural-resources base of a given country to complement the information provided by conventional national accounting systems.

Decision-making bodies

The supreme body of the OECD is its Council, composed of one representative from each member State. The Council meets either at permanent representative level (about once a

fortnight) under the chairmanship of the Secretary-General, or at ministerial level (usually once a year) under the chairmanship of a minister elected annually. Decisions and recommendations are adopted by mutual agreement of all members of the Council. The Council is assisted by an Executive Committee, composed of 14 members of the Council designated annually by the latter. The major part of the OECD's work is, however, prepared and carried out by numerous specialized committees and working parties.

The Environmental Policy Committee, which is composed of high-level government officials, is serviced by the Environment Directorate. The Environment Directorate works closely with many other bodies, particularly those of the UN and the European Community—as well as other sectoral directorates in OECD.

Finance

The OECD is funded by contributions from its member States on the basis of an agreed scale of contributions. The scale is calculated essentially in terms of the capacity of the member, States to contribute as determined by reference to their 'taxable' income. Each country's contribution represents between 0.1 per cent and 25 per cent of the total budget.

Budget
The OECD budget amounted to about FFr 1.3 billion in 1998, of which approximately 80 per cent finances the cost of staff.

Publications

• *Improving the Environment Through Reducing Subsidies*
   Part I: Summary and Policy Conclusions
   Part II: Analysis and Overview of Studies;
• *Eco-Efficiency*;
• *Water Management: Performance and Challenges in OECD Countries*;
• *Towards Sustainable Development: Environmental Indicators*;
• *Agriculture and the Environment: Issues and Policies*;
• Environmental Performance Reviews;
• *Climate Change: Mobilising Global Effort*;
• *Globalisation and the Environment: Perspectives from OECD and Dynamic Non-Member Countries.*

Sources on the Internet
<http://www.oecd.org>

United Nations Children's Fund (UNICEF)

Objectives

Guided by the Convention on the Rights of the Child and the Convention on the Elimination of All Forms of Discrimination against Women, adopted by the UN General Assembly respectively, the objectives of UNICEF are:

- to work for the well-being of children and women and advocates for the protection of their rights world-wide;
- to strive to establish children's rights as enduring ethical principles and international standards of behaviour towards children;
- to mobilize political will and material resources to help countries, particularly developing countries, ensure a 'first call for children' and to build their capacity to form appropriate policies and deliver services for children and their families.

Organization

Type
An integral part of the UN system. UNICEF is a subsidiary body of the UN General Assembly, to which it reports through the UN Economic and Social Council (ECOSOC).

Membership
UNICEF has no membership. It works with and/or receives financial support from almost all countries. The UNICEF Executive Board consists of 36 States elected by ECOSOC. They serve three-year terms, with approximately one-third of the terms expiring annually.

Founded
11 December 1946.

Secretariat

UNICEF House,
3 United Nations Plaza,
New York, NY 10017,
USA
Telephone: +1-212-3267000
Telefax: +1-212-888-7465/7454
E-mail: netmaster@unicef.org

Executive Director
Ms Carol Bellamy.

Director of Division of Communication
Vacant.

Number of staff
1,202 international professionals, 1,090 national professionals, and 3,302 general service staff serving world-wide (December 1998). Of these, 272 professionals and 296 general service staff were employed at New York headquarters.

Activities

UNICEF was originally created to meet the emergency needs of children in war-ravaged countries in the aftermath of the Second World War. Since 1953 the organization has stressed long-term programmes to benefit children in developing countries. Through its extensive field network and in partnership with governments, local communities, non-governmental organizations, and other UN agencies, UNICEF supports community-based programmes in primary health care and immunization, nutrition, education, water supply, environmental sanitation and gender and development. UNICEF also seeks to improve the lives of children in especially difficult circumstances, including working children, street children, abused children, children with disabilities, and children affected by war and HIV/AIDS, and works increasingly to promote equality for girls and the empowerment of women. UNICEF country programmes are based on the Convention on the Rights of the Child and other international human rights standards.

Priorities are set according to need. Almost all resources are therefore invested in the least-developed countries, especially in sub-Saharan Africa, with the greatest share going to children in the high-risk early years, up to the age of five.

Emergency relief and rehabilitation remain an important part of the agency's work. In 1998 UNICEF provided about $US115.3 million worth of emergency assistance (18 per cent of its total programme expenditure) to over 55 countries in Africa, Asia, Latin America, the Middle East, and Central and Eastern Europe.

Environmental activities
UNICEF participated actively in the UN Conference on Environment and Development (UNCED). It made successful efforts to include children's needs and interests in Agenda 21 and is helping countries to implement it.

At the Special Session of the UN General Assembly to Review and Appraise Implementation of Agenda 21, held in New York in June 1997, UNICEF promoted children's environmental health issues, highlighted the urgent need for access to safe water and environmental sanitation. It also actively participated in the major NGO event known as Rio+5 Forum held prior to the UNGASS. Earlier at the International Conference on Population and Development (ICPD), held in Cairo in September 1994, UNICEF emphasized the linkage between poverty, population growth, and environmental deterioration, and the need to resolve these problems to improve the situation of children.

Besides advocacy on sustainable development for children at national and international levels, UNICEF has long supported community-based programmes in safe water supply and environmental sanitation, including hygiene education. After the Earth Summit, UNICEF adopted an approach called Primary Environmental Care which emphasises integration of interventions for meeting people's basic needs, empowering communities, and protecting local environmental resources. Attention was drawn to the special vulnerability of children living in a fragile environment. Many UNICEF-supported country programmes contain activities that result in improved environments for children and women, such as promoting fuel-efficient, smokeless cook stoves, solar cookers, social forestry, home gardening, and environmental education.

Recently, more emphasis is placed on programming for child rights which include, albeit indirectly, the right of a child to live and grow in a safe environment. UNICEF recognises that there are important environmental issues that need to be addressed at three stages of a child's life cycle: early childhood, the period for obtaining basic education, and adolescence. But UNICEF support mainly focuses on environmental sanitation and hygiene since microbiological contaminants remain the biggest environmental threat to child survival, growth, and development, and a direct cause of malnutrition leading to stunting and wasting of young children.

Household food security poses a challenge, especially in arid developing countries. Environment-friendly food production methods to ease pressure on scarce land resources are supported. Home vegetable gardening, fruit tree nurseries, fish-ponds, and the raising of small livestock, undertaken with regard for fragile rural ecosystems, are promoted to improve family diets and combat malnutrition as well as to produce a surplus for sale to improve family income.

In the cities UNICEF addresses the needs of poor mothers and children through the Child Friendly Cities (CFC) initiative. It involves the provision of maternal and child health, water, and sanitation, and education services to ill-served marginal urban areas, squatter settlements, and slums. Increasingly its attention is directed to the environmental health problems in poor urban areas, issues that closely relate to poor sanitation and industrial pollution.

UNICEF collaborates closely with the UN Environment Programme (UNEP) in developing information material on environmental problems affecting children, including lead and pesticide poisoning. It also worked with the World Wide Fund For Nature (WWF) (see NGOs) on freshwater studies and environmental impact in India. Recently UNICEF is co-operating closely with WHO on water quality issues, especially the arsenic and fluoride contamination in groundwater.

Decision-making bodies

The Executive Board, the UNICEF governing body comprising 36 members states, meets in one annual session to discuss major policy issues and introduce new initiatives. Three additional sessions yearly deal with programme, budget, organizational, and other issues.

The secretariat is headed by an Executive Director, appointed by the Secretary-General of the UN in consultation with the Board. The Executive Director is responsible for the administration of UNICEF as well as for the appointment and direction of UNICEF staff. Regional offices in Abidjan, Amman, Bangkok, Bogotá, Geneva, Kathmandu, and Nairobi provide and co-ordinate specialized support for the 125 country offices which are the key operational units for advocacy, advisory services, programming, and logistics.

Headquarters in New York develops and directs policy, manages resources, and deals with donor governments and NGOs. UNICEF also has offices in Tokyo and Brussels, a supply centre in Copenhagen, and a research centre in Florence. 37 National Committees for UNICEF, mostly in industrialized countries, help in fund-raising and advocacy.

Finance

UNICEF is unique among UN organizations in that it relies entirely upon voluntary contributions to finance its activities. Total income was $US944 million in 1996, $902 million in 1997, and $966 million in 1998; 33 per cent of the 1998 income came from non-governmental/private sector sources. More than 100 governments, including those that benefit from UNICEF co-operation, provided 69 per cent.

UNICEF supports programmes for children in 161 developing countries and territories. Total expenditure was $936 million in

1996, $913 million in 1997, and $882 million in 1998.

Budget
The approved support budget is $266 million for the years 2000–01 for headquarters (New York, Geneva, Copenhagen, Florence, and Tokyo), $55 million for regional offices, and $223 million for field offices.

Main contributors
The top ten contributors for 1998 were USA ($161.5 million/0.6 per capita), Sweden ($75.1 million/8.48 per capita), Norway ($71.4 million/16.21 per capita), the Netherlands ($44.7 million/2.86 per capita), Japan ($38.7 million/0.31 per capita), the United Kingdom ($38.6 million/0.65 per capita), Denmark ($37.7 million/7.13 per capita), Canada ($23.7 million/0.78 per capita), Switzerland ($14.3 million/2.02 per capita), and Finland ($14.3 million/2.78 per capita).

Publications

• *The Progress of Nations* (annual);
• *The State of the World's Children* (annual);
• *UNICEF Facts and Figures* (annual);
• *UNICEF Annual Report*;
• sectoral studies and newsletters;
• *UNICEF at a Glance*.

Sources on the Internet

<http://www.unicef.org>

United Nations Development Programme (UNDP)

Objectives

• to help the UN become a powerful and cohesive force for sustainable human development;

• to focus its own resources on a series of objectives central to sustainable human development: poverty eradication, environmental regeneration, job creation, and advancement of women;

• to strengthen international co-operation for sustainable human development and serve as a major substantive resource on how to achieve it.

Organization

Type
Intergovernmental organization (IGO). An organ of the UN. Linked to the UN General Assembly through UN Economic and Social Council (ECOSOC).

Membership
Open to all members and observers of the UN, of its specialized agencies, and of the International Atomic Energy Agency (IAEA) (see this section). 195 member States by March 1998. In addition, many territories around the world are beneficiaries of UNDP assistance.

Founded
November 1965, through a merger of two predecessor programmes for UN technical co-operation.

Secretariat

UN Development Programme (UNDP),
1 United Nations Plaza,
New York, NY 10017,
USA
Telephone: +1-212-906-5000/5315
Telefax: +1-212-9065364
E-mail: upd050
or hq@undp.org

Administrator
Mr Mark Malloch Brown.

Director, Division of Public Affairs
Mr Djibril Diallo.

Number of staff
Approximately 4,700 world-wide, over 85 per cent of whom serve in UNDP's programme country offices (March 1998).

Activities

Through a network of 137 offices world-wide, UNDP works with 174 countries and territories to build capacities for sustainable human development. To execute the programmes and projects it supports, it draws upon the national technical capacities of programme-countries, as well as the expertise of more than 30 international and regional agencies and non-governmental organizations (NGOs).

People are at the centre of all UNDP activities, which focus on four priority themes: poverty eradication; creation of jobs and sustainable livelihoods; advancement of women; and protection and regeneration of the environment. Within this context, UNDP is frequently asked to assist in promoting sound governance and market development, and to support the rebuilding of societies in the aftermath of war and humanitarian emergencies. Global and interregional programmes address world-wide problems, including food security and HIV–AIDS.

A *Human Development Report*, published yearly for UNDP since 1990 and drafted by a team of independent consultants, assists the international community in developing new, practical, and pragmatic concepts, measures, and policy instruments for promoting more people-oriented development.

UNDP normally also plays the chief co-ordinating role for operational development activities undertaken by the whole UN system. This includes administering special-purpose funds and programmes such as the Office to Combat Desertification and Drought (UNSO); the UN Capital Development Fund (UNCDF); the UN Volunteers (UNV); and the UN Development Fund for Women (UNIFEM).

Environmental activities
Environment was one of the main themes for UNDP's 1992–6 programming cycle. Environmental objectives were therefore included in 87 per cent of the country programmes approved for this period and virtually all activities are screened for their environmental impact. Programmes to build capacities for sustainable development and natural resource management are supported in such sectors as food security, forestry, water and sanitation, energy, and urban development.

UNDP assisted developing-country governments, local NGOs, and grass-roots organizations in preparing for the 1992 UN Conference on Environment and Development (UNCED). As a follow-up to UNCED, it is (1) assisting the developing countries in integrating environmental concerns into development plans, and (2) providing support in strengthening capacity for management of environment and sustainable development programmes as called for in Agenda 21, UNCED's blueprint for action. For this purpose UNDP launched Capacity 21, which became fully operational in June 1993. At the time of launching, the Capacity 21 Trust Fund held $US11 million ($10 million contributed by Japan and $1 million by Austria). Other donors added their contributions, and by May 1996 the total contributions to Capacity 21 (both through its trust fund and other mechanisms) stood at approximately $57 million. By the end of 1998, about 50 countries had Capacity 21 programmes and 20 others were being assisted.   UNDP promotes and supports environmental programmes in co-operation with a wide variety of partners in government, NGOs, community-based groups, UN organizations, and academic and research institutions. Global environmental programmes in which it participates include:

• The *Global Environment Facility (GEF)* (see this section) is a financial mechanism that provides grant and concessional funds to recipient countries for projects and activities that aim to protect the global environment. The GEF is jointly managed by UNDP, the UN Environment Programme (UNEP), and the World Bank. GEF resources are available for projects and other activities that address biological diversity, climate change, international waters, and depletion of the ozone layer. Activities addressing land degradation, primarily desertification and deforestation, as they relate to the four focal areas, are also eligible for funding. The GEF was restructured in 1994 with pledges of over $2 billion for a three-year period. In its GEF activities, UNDP has concentrated on capacity-building programmes, technical assistance, and training. UNDP's portfolio to date is over $756 million and contains approximately 260 rojects, encompassing enabling activities, ull projects, the project development facility nd pre-investment feasibility studies. JNDP also manages the GEF Small Grants 'rogramme, which was replenished at $24 nillion. The Small Grants Programme sup- orts community-based projects in the GEF nematic areas. By the end of 1998 it had unded more than 1,000 local community rojects;

The *Multilateral Fund of the Montreal 'rotocol* (see Agreements). Currently UNDP s assisting 65 developing countries in the lanning, preparation, and implementation f country programmes, projects, and ectoral activities to replace and phase out hlorofluorocarbons (CFCs), halons, and ther ozone-depleting substances. UNDP is ne of four implementing agencies for this und (along with the UNEP, the UN Indus- rial Development Programme, and the Vorld Bank (see this section)). Between 1991 nd December 1997 UNDP received $190 nillion for 730 projects. Upon completion hese projects will eliminate 24,226 tonnes per ear of ozone-depleting substances from the vorld's atmosphere;

The *Office to Combat Desertification and 'rought (UNSO)* is the central entity within JNDP for spearheading work on esertification control and drought prepar- dness in all affected UNDP programme ountries world-wide. UNSO concentrates its vork on the root causes of dryland degrada- ion in supporting the implementation of the JN Convention to Combat Desertification CCD) (see Agreements). Current activities ocus on working with/through UNDP's ountry offices in providing conceptual, tech- ical, and financial support to national and ubregional Action Programme processes to ombat desertification, with emphasis on ef- ective participatory planning processes and artnership building among all stakeholders. 1oreover, UNSO is involved in cross-cutting upport activities critical for the implemen- ation of the CCD at national, subregional, nd regional levels, such as national esertification funds, drought preparedness nd mitigation, assessment, and monitoring f desertification/environmental information ystems, promotion of exchange of experi- nces and know-how in dryland management,

building on indigenous knowledge and liveli- hood systems. UNSO also develops advocacy materials and collaborates with other UN agencies and NGOs to generate improved knowledge of linkages between desertification and other development challenges, such as food security, poverty, rural–urban migra- tion, biodiversity, and climate change;

• UNDP's *Sustainable Development Net- working Programme* makes relevant country-specific information on sustainable development readily available to a wide range of development partners, including decision makers responsible for planning and imple- menting sustainable-development strategies and community-based organizations. It is currently implemented in 30 developing coun- tries;

• *Environmental management guidelines* and a companion *training programme* devel- oped by UNDP facilitate a consistent ap- proach to the environmental aspects of all projects and programmes which receive sup- port. Training in the application of these guidelines is progressively being extended to staff in UNDP country offices through work- shops that include representatives of govern- ments, UN agencies, NGOs, the private sec- tor, the media, and academia;

• 41 new national UNDP *posts for sustain- able development officers* were established in early 1994. The national staff members serve as advisers to UNDP resident representatives and other development professionals in their respective countries of service, advocate the integration of environmental considerations into UNDP-supported activities, and pro- mote and support specific initiatives such as Capacity 21 and the GEF.

Decision-making bodies

The UNDP is headed by an Administrator, who is responsible to a 36-nation Executive Board, representing all major regions and both donor and recipient countries. The Board, in turn, reports to the UN General Assembly through the Economic and Social Council (ECOSOC). In addition to setting policy guidelines, the Board approves the volume of assistance allocated to each coun- try, as well as all country programmes.

Finance

The UNDP is financed by yearly voluntary contributions from member States of the UN or its related agencies. Country contributions to UNDP totalled $US848 million in 1996, $761 million in 1997, and $746 million in 1998 (core resources). In 1998, UNDP re- ceived additional non-core financial re- sources, raising the total amount to $2.2 bil- lion.

Budget
Annual expenditures are approximately $1.5 billion.

Main contributors
For 1998 the USA was the largest donor to UNDP (12.12 per cent); followed by Den- mark (11.34 per cent); the Netherlands (11.04 per cent); Japan (10.71 per cent); Norway (10 per cent); Sweden (8.04 per cent); Germany (7.62 per cent); the United Kingdom (6.7 per cent); Switzerland (5.6 per cent); and Canada (3.93 per cent).

Main recipients
58 per cent of UNDP's total resources in 1997 were allocated for the countries designated as 'least-developed' by the UN General Assem- bly. 87 per cent of UNDP's country-pro- gramme funds went to countries with annual per capita GNPs of $US750 or less.

Associated funds
The UNDP manages several associated funds, which received an estimated $75.4 million in voluntary contributions in 1996. Among them are the UN Capital Develop- ment Fund (UNCDF), the UN Volunteers (UNV), and the UN Development Fund for Women (UNIFEM). UNDP also provides management support services for bilateral projects and programmes financed through multilateral financing institutions.

Publications

• annual reports;
• *Human Development Report* (annual);
• *UNDP Flash* (weekly news bulletin);
• *Choices* (quarterly magazine covering de- velopment issues).

Sources on the Internet

<http://www.undp.org>
<gopher://gopher.undp.org>

United Nations Educational, Scientific, and Cultural Organization (UNESCO)

Objectives

To contribute to peace and security in the world by promoting collaboration among nations through education, science, culture, and communication in order to further universal respect for justice, for the rule of law, and for the human rights and fundamental freedoms which are affirmed by the Charter of the UN for the peoples of the world, without distinction of race, sex, language, or religion.

Organization

Type
Intergovernmental organization (IGO). A specialized agency of the UN.

Membership
Member States of the UN. Non-members of the UN may be admitted as members by a two-thirds vote in the General Conference. Not open for regional integration organizations. 186 member States and four associate members by July 1999.

Founded
4 November 1946.

Secretariat

UNESCO,
7 place de Fontenoy,
F-75352 Paris 07 SP,
France
Telephone: +33-1-45681000
Telefax: +33-1-45671690
E-mail: initial letter of the first name.name@unesco.org

Director-General
Dr Federico Mayor Zaragoza (1993–9).

The 30th session of the General Conference, which will be held from 26 October to 17 November 1999, will have the task of electing the Director-General.

Director, Office of Public Information
Ms H.-M. Gosselin.

Number of staff
747 professionals and 970 support staff at headquarters; 329 professionals and 285 support staff at field offices or in field projects (July 1999).

Activities

UNESCO's five main functions are:
• to conduct prospective studies in order fully to understand the origins and consequences of the profound changes taking place today, along with the place occupied by education, science, culture, and communication;
• to contribute to the advancement, transfer, and universal sharing of knowledge. To this end, UNESCO initiates and co-ordinates regional or world-wide networks which have a triple vocation: research, exchange of research results, and training;
• to participate in the efforts of member States in order to set international standards;
• to respond to requests for technical assistance from member States;
• to collect and distribute world-wide specialized information.

Environmental activities
UNESCO's role in the environmental field is: to improve understanding of the natural and human environment and of complex environmental and development issues; to contribute to problem solving by providing policy-relevant information to decision makers; to increase scientific and technical expertise; to foster institutional development and change; to provide the public with the knowledge and skills needed for sustainable development through both formal education programmes and public awareness activities; and to promote international co-operation and exchange, with emphasis on addressing the needs of developing countries.

UNESCO is actively involved in the implementation of Agenda 21, the Convention on Biological Diversity, and the UN Framework Convention on Climate Change (see Agreements). UNESCO's activities to follow up the UN Conference on Environment and Development (UNCED) cut across all its areas of competence, and include the following: Man and the Biosphere Programme; Intergovernmental Oceanographic Commission and programmes on marine-science-related issues; International Hydrological Programme, Earth Sciences and Natural Hazards programmes, including the International Geological Correlation Programme; Network of Microbial Resources Centres;

UNESCO–UNEP International Environmental Education Programme; Management of Social Transformations Programme.

Decision-making bodies

The General Conference, composed of representatives from member States, meets biennially to decide the policy, programme, and budget of UNESCO. The Executive Board consists of representatives of 58 member States elected for a single four-year term; elections are held every two years on a rotation basis. The General Conference elects board members on the basis of balanced geographical distribution, allocating one seat for every three member States in each of UNESCO's five electoral groups. The Board meets twice a year and is responsible for the execution of the programme adopted by the Conference.

Finance

Each member State contributes according to the scale of assessments adopted by the UN General Assembly.

Budget
The budget was $US518,455,000 for the years 1996–7 and is $544,367,250 for 1998–9. The proposed budget for 2000-2001 is $544,367,250.

Main contributors
Extra-budgetary resources, which amounted to $203.2 million for the years 1996–7 and are expected to amount to $250 million for 1998–9 and $250 million for 2000-2001, are used mostly to implement operational projects. A major part of these resources comes from governments and institutions under funds-in-trust arrangements by the World Bank and regional development banks and funds, institutions and individuals. Operational activities are also financed by UN agencies, particularly the UN Development Programme (UNDP) and the UN Population Fund (UNFPA) (see this section).

Publications

Nature and Resources (quarterly).

Sources on the Internet

<http://www.unesco.org>
<http://mirror-us.unesco.org>

United Nations Environment Programme (UNEP)

Objectives

To provide leadership and encourage partnership in caring for the environment by inspiring, informing, and enabling nations and peoples to improve their quality of life without compromising that of future generations.

Organization

Type
Intergovernmental organization (IGO). Subsidiary to the UN General Assembly and the Economic and Social Council (ECOSOC).

Membership
Member States of the UN and its specialized agencies. Non-member states, IGOs, and international non-governmental organizations (NGOs) with an interest in the environment participate as observers. There are 185 member States by 29 June 1999.

Founded
15 December 1972 by the UN General Assembly. Established as a result of the UN Conference on the Human Environment in Stockholm, June 1972.

Secretariat

UN Environment Programme (UNEP),
PO Box 30552,
United Nations Avenue, Gigiri,
Nairobi,
Kenya
Telephone: +254-2-621234
Telefax: +254-2-62-3927/3692
E-mail: cpiinfo@unep.org

Executive Director
Mr Klaus Töpfer
(February 1998–January 2002).

Chief, Communications and Public Information
Mr Tore J. Brevik.

Number of staff
116 professionals and 157 support staff at headquarters (June 1999). 158 professionals and 143 support staff at regional and other offices (June 1998).

Activities

The 1998–9 UNEP Programme is built on:
• developing and promoting state of the art scientific assessments;
• formulating policy options for enhancing environmental management;
• leveraging knowledge for building consensus on critical environmental problems and issues;
• assisting governments at the global, regional, subregional, and national levels in formulating environmental management strategies;
• promoting more effective co-operation and co-ordination in the field of the environment with partners within and outside the UN system.

In line with the Nairobi Declaration adopted at the nineteenth Session of the Governing Council in February 1997, priority is being given to the following core elements of the Programme:
• to analyse the state of the global environment and assess global and regional environmental trends, to provide policy advice and early warning information on environmental threats, and to catalyse and promote international co-operation and action, based on the best scientific and technical capabilities available;
• to further the advance of international environmental law aiming at sustainable development, including the growth of coherent interlinkages among existing international environmental conventions;
• to advance the implementation of agreed international norms and policies, to monitor and foster compliance with environmental principles and international agreements, and to stimulate co-operative action to respond to emerging environmental challenges;
• to strengthen its role in the co-ordination of environmental activities in the UN system in the field of environment, as well as its role as an implementing agency of the Global Environment Facility (GEF), based on its comparative advantage and scientific and technical expertise;
• to promote greater awareness of and facilities for effective co-operation among all sectors of society and actors involved in the implementation of the international agenda, and to serve as an active link between the scientific community and policy makers at the national and international levels;

• to provide policy and advisory services in key areas of institutional building to governments and other relevant institutions.

UNEP's most important function is to serve as a forum for addressing existing and emerging environmental issues at the global and regional levels. Since it was established, it has served as the primary means of bringing environmental experts together to share experiences and address global environmental issues collectively.

UNEP works to win the co-operation and participation of governments, the international scientific and professional communities, and NGOs. The first UN agency to be based in a developing country (Nairobi, Kenya), UNEP also has regional or liaison offices in Bangkok, Geneva, New York, Mexico City, and Manama (Bahrain). During the years 1996–7 UNEP's programme was implemented through three divisions:
• The *Division of Environmental Information and Assessment (DEIA)*, which is responsible for: (*a*) analysing the state of the global environment, assessing global and regional environmental trends, and providing policy advice and early warning information on environmental threats, in order to catalyse and promote international co-operation and action; (*b*) improving access to, and dissemination of, information for environmental decision making and policy setting; and (*c*) enhancing country capabilities to generate, exchange, manage, and use such information for environmental actions. DEIA provides support in harmonizing the sectoral assessment and monitoring aspects of UNEP's Programme to ensure co-ordination and overall coherence of these activities. Through the co-ordination of UN System-Wide Earthwatch and participation in other international collaborative programmes on environmental information and assessment, DEIA fulfils UNEP's fundamental co-ordinating and promotive mandate. It further assists co-ordination and promotion of policy-relevant research.

In co-operation with the rest of UNEP, other UN agencies, IGOs, network partners, private scientific institutes, and NGOs, DEIA focuses on (*a*) preparing state of the environment reports such as the Global Environment Outlook (GEO), as well as other integrated environmental assessment reports and sectoral assessments; (*b*) developing har-

monized methodologies and tools for policy-relevant environmental assessments, including distributed data systems, bibliographic environmental information exchange, indicators, models, and scenarios; (c) promoting the Global Environmental Monitoring System (GEMS), Global Resource Information Database (GRID), UNEP's global environmental information exchange network INFOTERRA, the Environment and Natural Resource Information Networking (ENRIN), and the GEO Collaborating Centres network; (d) supporting and promoting advisory services and technical assistance to developing countries and countries with economies in transition for environmental assessments, reporting and data generation, exchange, management, and use of environmental data and information; (e) co-ordinating and improving access to telecommunications services (including the Internet) so as to improve exchange of the environmental data and information products of UNEP and its partners with and among scientific community and policy makers, and their dissemination through environmental information and assessment networks of UNEP; (f) developing and co-ordinating inter-agency policies, strategies, and action plans to implement UN General Assembly, Commission on Sustainable development (CSD), and UNEP Governing Council decisions on the UN System-Wide Earthwatch, and providing links to the Inter-Agency Environment Co-ordination Group (IAEG), Committee of International Development Institutions on the Environment (CIDIE), and other areas of UNEP's interest in observing, assessment, and reporting activities across the UN system; and (g) promoting and co-ordinating targeted scientific research in critical environmental areas in co-operation with partners and in collaboration with other substantive units of UNEP;
• The *Division of Programme*, which is responsible for the development of an integrated environmental programme designed to address environmental processes and changes taking place in the biosphere. This Division addresses environmental issues in co-operation with partner agencies and centres of environmental studies at the global, regional, and national levels. It is designed and structured to address issues in the areas of freshwater, ocean, and coastal areas, dryland ecosystems and desertification control, atmosphere, biodiversity including biotechnology and biosafety, human health and welfare, and international law;
• The *Division of Policy, Inter-Agency and*

External Affairs, which supports the Executive Director in maintaining a close working relationship with governments, with the UNEP Governing Council and its subsidiary bodies, with the rest of the UN system, and generally with all UNEP's partners. This is achieved through the development and co-ordination of environmental and institutional policy, the effective maintenance of external relations, the management of inter-agency affairs, and the organizations of meetings of the Governing Council, the High Level Committee of Ministers and Officials, and the Committee of Permanent Representatives. The Gender Focal Point also discharges her/his functions from this division.

The Division is responsible, in collaboration with the relevant substantive units, for UNEP's co-ordination with other UN agencies in order to carry out the Nairobi Declaration mandate to promote the coherent implementation of the environmental dimension of sustainable development within the UN system, and to strengthen UNEP's role in the co-ordination of environmental activities in the UN system.

In 1996–7 UNEP collaborated on 20 projects with co-operating agencies and 120 projects with supporting organizations. 87 projects were internally implemented.

The *Global Environment Facility (GEF)* (see this section) promotes international co-operation and fosters action to protect the global environment. It was established in 1991, as a pilot phase, and stemmed from the world-wide momentum generated by the UN Conference on Environment and Development (UNCED) for concerted actions to protect the environment for present and future generations. It was restructured in 1994 with a capital of $US2 billion. The GEF was established on the basis of collaboration and partnership between UNEP, the UN Development Programme (UNDP) (see this section), and the World Bank (see this section). It has been designated as a financial mechanism providing new and additional financial resources to eligible countries, to meet the agreed incremental costs of measures aimed at achieving global environmental benefits in the areas of biological diversity, climate change, international waters, and the protection of the ozone layer. In addition, activities related to land degradation, in particular desertification and deforestation, are eligible as they relate to one of the four focal areas. UNEP has a key role in the GEF. It catalyses the development of scientific and technical analysis, advances environmental management in GEF-financed activities, and provides guidance on environ-

mental assessments and policy frameworks and plans, and to international environmental agreements.

UNEP provides also the secretariat of the Scientific and Technical Advisory Panel (STAP) of the GEF, comprising 12 world-renowned experts in the fields relevant to the GEF activities and designated by the Executive Director of UNEP.

Main conventions on the environment under the auspices of UNEP (see Agreements)
• *Convention on International Trade in Endangered Species of Wild Fauna and Flora (CITES)*, Washington, DC, 1973;
• *Convention on the Conservation of Migratory Species of Wild Animals (CMS)*, Bonn, 1979;
• *Vienna Convention for the Protection of the Ozone Layer*, Vienna, 1985, including the *Montreal Protocol on Substances that Deplete the Ozone Layer*, Montreal, 1987;
• *Convention on the Control of Transboundary Movements of Hazardous Wastes and their Disposal (Basel Convention)*, Basel, 1989;
• *Convention on Biological Diversity (CBD)*, adopted in Nairobi and opened for signature in Rio de Janeiro, 1992;
• Conventions within the *UNEP Regional Seas Programme*;
• *Lusaka Agreement on Co-operative Enforcement Operations Directed at Illegal Trade in Wild Fauna and Flora*, Lusaka, 1994;
• *Convention on the Prior Informed Consent Procedure for Certain Hazardous Chemicals and Pesticides in International Trade (PIC Convention)*, Rotterdam, 1998 (see Agreements). Operated jointly with the Food and Agriculture Organization (FAO).

Decision-making bodies

UNEP has the following main components: the Governing Council, composed of 58 member States elected for four years, which reports to the UN General Assembly through ECOSOC. The Council assesses the state of the world environment, establishes UNEP's programme priorities, and approves the budget. The membership of the Governing Council is made up on the following geographical basis: Africa (16), Asia (13), Latin America and the Caribbean (10), Eastern Europe (6), Western Europe, North America, and other (13).

A High-Level Committee of Ministers and Officials (HLCOMO) was established by a decision of the Governing Council in April

1997 as a subsidiary body of the Council. It has the mandate to consider the international environmental agenda and to make reform and policy recommendations to the Governing Council. It also provides guidance and advice to UNEP's Executive Director on emerging environmental issues; enhances the collaboration and co-operation of UNEP with other relevant multilateral bodies as well as with the environmental conventions and their secretariats; and supports the Executive Director in mobilizing adequate and predictable financial resources for UNEP's implementation of the global environmental agenda approved by the Council. The Committee consists of 36 members elected from among members of the UN and its specialized agencies. Members serve for two years, taking into account the principle of equitable regional representation as reflected in the composition of the Council.

The Committee of Permanent Representatives, the other subsidiary organ of the Governing Council, whose membership is open to Permanent Representatives accredited to UNEP from among members of the UN and its specialized agencies, has the mandate to: review, monitor, and assess the implementation of decisions of the Council; review reports on the effectiveness, efficiency, and transparency of the functions and work of the secretariat and make recommendations thereon to the Council; and prepare draft decisions for consideration by the Council.

The Secretariat, headed by the Executive Director, supports the Governing Council, co-ordinates environmental programmes within the UN system, and administers the Environment Fund.

Finance

UNEP is financed through the regular budget of the UN, the Environment Fund, Trust Funds, and counterpart contributions.

Budget
The budget for the Environment Fund for financing UNEP's programme activities was $US102.36 million for 1996–7, and is $107.5 million for 1998–9 and $119.4 million for 2000–01.

Main contributors
Main contributors in 1998 were the USA ($8.2 million), the United Kingdom ($7.2 million), Germany ($5.3 million), Japan ($5 million), Finland ($3 million), Sweden ($2.6 million), Switzerland ($2.5 million), Denmark ($2.3 million), the Netherlands ($2 million), and Norway ($1.9 million).

Special funds
The Environment Fund is a voluntary fund used to finance the costs of the implementation of UNEP's programme of work. Some programmes are financed totally by the Environment Fund, but most are funded from more than one source, including the Trust Funds and Counterpart Contributions.

Publications

In addition to studies, reports, legal texts, technical guidelines, etc.:
- *Environment in Print 2000* (UNEP's publications catalogue);
- *Annual Report of the Executive Director*;
- *Our Planet* (bi-monthly);
- *UNEP News* (monthly);
- *Industry and Environment Review* (quarterly);
- Technical Reports (series);
- Environment and Trade (series) (25 publications);
- *Environmental Law Bulletin* (bi-annually);
- *Global Environment Outlook Report* (every two years) (GEO 2000 due in September 1999);
- *Desertification Control Bulletin* (bi-annually);
- *Earth Views* (quarterly newsletter of the Environment Assessment Division);
- *OzonAction*;
- *APELL* (newsletter);
- *UNEP Chemicals*;
- *IETC's Insight*.

Sources on the Internet

<http://www.unep.org>
<gopher://gopher.unep.org>
<ftp://ftp.unep.org>

United Nations Industrial Development Organization (UNIDO)

Objectives

Within the UN system, UNIDO has the lead role in industrial development. It is mandated by its Constitution to promote and accelerate industrial development in developing countries and promote industrial co-operation. The ultimate aim is to create a better life for people by laying the industrial foundations for long-term prosperity and economic strength. Acting as a global forum for industrial development, UNIDO brings together representatives of government, industry, and the public and private sector from developed and developing countries as well as countries with economies in transition. UNIDO is also a service organization, putting into practice through its technical co-operation programmes the principles developed at the global forum level.

Organization

Type
Intergovernmental organization (IGO). A specialized agency of the UN. Linked to UN Economic and Social Council (ECOSOC) on matters of inter-agency concern.

Membership
Open to members of the UN. 168 member States by 15 July 1999.

Founded
1 January 1967. Status as a fully specialized agency since 17 December 1985.

Secretariat

UNIDO,
Vienna International Centre,
Wagramerstrasse 5,
PO Box 300,
A-1400 Vienna,
Austria
Telephone: +43-1-260260
Telefax: +43-1-2692669
E-mail: unido-pinfo@unido.org

Director-General
Mr Carlos Alfredo Magariños
(December 1997–December 2001).

Head, UNIDO Press Office
Mr Robert Cox.

Number of staff
222 professionals and 367 support staff at headquarters (July 1999).

Activities

The *Business Plan on the Future Role and Functions of UNIDO* approved by the seventh session of the General Conference, Vienna, 1–5 December 1997, sets the basis for UNIDO's programme and structure. It regroups activities into two main areas:
• strengthening of industrial capacities, comprising: promotion of investment and related technologies, and programmes in support of the global forum function and policy advice, including those relating to: industrial policy

advice based on action-oriented research; institutional capacity building at the country and sectoral levels; quality, standardization, and metrology; industrial information through networking, including information on the transfer of technology; industrial statistics.
• cleaner and sustainable industrial development, comprising: support programmes on environmentally sustainable industrial development strategies and technologies, including transfer of environmental technologies within industrial subsectors assigned a high priority; and development of specific norms and standards relating to environmentally sustainable industrial development strategies and technologies, and implementation of international protocols, agreements, and conventions.

While maintaining its universal character and vocation, UNIDO pursues a geographical, sectoral, and thematic concentration of its activities as follows: services to least developed countries (LDCs), in particular in Africa, with special attention to the regional and subregional level; services in support of agro-based industries and their integration through subsectoral linkages into national industrial structures; services in support of small- and medium-scale enterprises (SMEs) and their integration into national industrial structures.

Environmental activities
Within the UN, UNIDO has the responsibil-

y to ensure that cleaner industrialization is t the centre of the development agenda. It elps governments integrate environmentally ustainable industrial development (ESID) oncepts at the policy level and build up national capacity to acquire cleaner technologies, and deals with environmental concerns elated to health and safety in the workplace. UNIDO integrates environmental considerations into its technical assistance projects, which include cleaner industrial production nd pollution control measures for air and vater emissions. In co-operation with the UN Environment Programme (UNEP) (see this ection), UNIDO promotes national cleaner roduction centres (NCPs) and supports their oles in providing technical information and dvice on cleaner production, demonstrating leaner production techniques and technologies, and training industry and government rofessionals. UNIDO participates in several conventions, such as the Multilateral und for the Implementation of the Montreal Protocol (see Agreements): UNIDO as one of he four implementing agencies provides technical assistance and support services at the lant level for phasing out ozone-depleting ubstances in the refrigerants, solvents, oams, halons, and fumigants sectors, as well s the UN Framework Convention on Climate Change (UNFCCC) (see Agreements).

Decision-making bodies

The General Conference, comprising all member States, reviews UNIDO strategies and policy concepts on industrial development. The Industrial Development Board, consisting of 53 member States, reviews implementation of the approved work programme, the corresponding regular and operational budgets, and the implementation of the General Conference decisions. The Programme and Budget Committee, comprising 27 member States, assists the Board in preparing its work programmes and budget.

Finance

Contributions from member States, UN system funds, government funds, development finance institutions, trust funds, and voluntary contributions through the Industrial Development Fund (IDF) (see below).

Budget
The regular budget, consisting of assessed contributions by member States, is US$129.5 million for the years 1998–9 and is $132.9 million for 2000–01.

Main contributors
The five largest donors to the regular budget in 1998-99 are Japan (21.8 per cent), Germany (12.6 per cent), France (8.9 per cent), United Kingdom (7.3 per cent), and Italy (7.3 per cent).

Special funds
UNIDO administers the UN Industrial Development Fund (IDF), a voluntary fund aimed at enhancing UNIDO's ability to meet the needs of developing countries. Net approvals, including the Montreal Protocol, were $61.3 million in 1997 and 39.6 million in 1998. Main contributors in 1998 were Switzerland, Japan, the Netherlands, Italy, and Austria.

Publications

• annual reports;
• *International Yearbook of Industrial Statistics*;
• Emerging Technology Series;
• *Industrial Africa* (newsletter);
• *UNIDOScope* (electronic newsletter on the homepage).

Sources on the Internet

<http://www.unido.org>

United Nations Population Fund (UNFPA)

Objectives

- to assist countries: in providing reproductive health and family-planning services on the basis of individual choice; in formulating population strategies in support of sustainable development; and in advocacy for issues related to population, reproductive health, and the empowerment of women;
- to advance the strategy endorsed by the 1994 International Conference on Population and Development (ICPD), which emphasized the inseparability of population and development and focused on meeting individuals' needs rather than demographic targets;
- to promote co-operation and co-ordination among UN system organizations, bilateral agencies, governments, non-governmental organizations, and the private sector in addressing issues of population and development, reproductive health and family planning, and gender equality and women's empowerment.

Organization

Type
Intergovernmental organization (IGO). Co-ordination with other UN agencies and organizations is maintained through the mechanism of the Administrative Committee on Co-ordination and through meetings of a Joint Consultative Group on Policy composed of the following five funding agencies: the UN Development Programme (UNDP), UNFPA, UNICEF, the World Food Programme (WFP), and the International Fund for Agricultural Development (IFAD) (see this section).

Membership
Not applicable.

Founded
1969.

Secretariat

UN Population Fund (UNFPA),
220 East 42nd Street,
New York, NY 10017,
USA
Telephone: +1-212-2975020
Telefax: +1-212-5576416
E-mail: ryanw@unfpa.org

Executive Director
Dr Nafis Sadik.

Director, Information and External Relations
Mr Stirling D. Scruggs.

Number of staff
94 professionals and 117 support staff at headquarters and Geneva. 79 professional staff, 404 support staff, and 130 national professional officers in the field (June 1999).

Activities

UNFPA has three main programme areas: reproductive health, including family planning and sexual health; population and development strategy; and advocacy.

In reproductive health, UNFPA supports the provision of a wide range of family-planning methods and related information within a constellation of integrated services, which also includes, among others: safe motherhood; counselling; and prevention of infertility, abortion, reproductive tract infections, and sexually transmitted diseases, including HIV–AIDS. It also helps to meet the reproductive health needs of adolescents and of women in emergency situations such as natural disasters and armed conflicts. UNFPA supports technical assistance, training, and research in these areas.

The Fund assists national efforts to formulate and implement comprehensive population policies as an integral part of sustainable development strategies. This includes support for data collection and analysis, and research.

UNFPA is an advocate for the goals of the International Conference on People and Development (ICPD), including better reproductive health, longer life expectancy, lower infant and maternal mortality, closing the gender gap in education, and strengthening national capacity to formulate and implement population and development strategies.

Environmental activities
UNFPA adopted policy guidelines on population and environment in 1989 to promote the integration of environmental concerns into population activities. In line with these guidelines and Agenda 21, UNFPA supports a range of projects dealing with the impact on the environment and vice versa of population factors such as growth, distribution, age structure, and migration in particular. The Programme of Action of the

ICPD emphasized the close links between population issues, sustainable development, and environmental protection. As an integral part of the implementation of the Programme of Action, UNFPA will take new initiatives in many fields, including the field of population and environment.

Decision-making bodies

The Executive Board of the UNDP (see this section) and UNFPA act as the governing body, under the policy supervision of the UN Economic and Social Council (ECOSOC).

Finance

Voluntary contributions from governments and private donors, the majority of which pledge on a yearly basis.

Budget
Expenditure was $US300.3 million in 1996, $306.8 million in 1997, and $305.1 million in 1998 (provisional), of which $216.6 million was project expenditure and $98.5 million was expenditure on administrative and programme support services.

Total income was $319.9 million in 1997, of which $290.1 million was from regular income and $29.8 million was provided through multi- and bilateral co-financing, and $309 million in 1998, of which $277 million (provisional) was from regular income and 32.3 million was provided through multi- and bilateral co-financing. Estimated total income as of 31 May 1999 is $288 million for 1999.

Main contributors
The five largest donors in 1998 were Japan, the Netherlands, Denmark, Norway, and the USA. The total number of donors in 1998 consisted of 95 governments.

Publications

- *Populi*, the UNFPA magazine (four issues a year);
- *State of World Population Report* (annual);
- *Population in the 21st Century: UNFPA and Agenda 21*.

Sources on the Internet

<http://www.unfpa.org>

World Bank

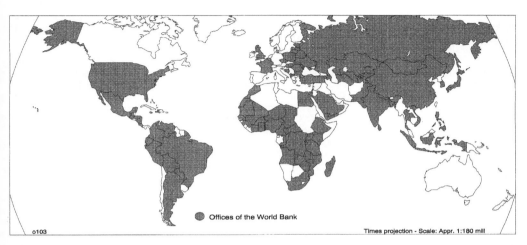

Offices of the World Bank

o103   Times projection - Scale: Appr. 1:180 mill

Objectives

- to help raise standards of living in developing countries by channelling financial resources to them from industrialized countries;
- to provide capital for productive purposes, particularly the development of productive facilities and resources in developing countries;
- to promote private foreign investment for productive purposes and, where necessary, supplement private investment by providing finance;
- to identify the more useful and urgent projects required to support economic and social development;
- to ensure that such projects are given appropriate priority by arranging or guaranteeing finance.

Organization

The World Bank includes the International Bank for Reconstruction and Development (IBRD) and the International Development Association (IDA). IBRD was established on 27 December 1945 when representatives of 28 countries signed the Articles of Agreement which had been drawn up at the Bretton Woods Conference in July 1944. IDA was established on 24 September 1960 in Washington, DC. The name 'World Bank' is generally taken to mean the IBRD and IDA together.

Type
Intergovernmental organization (IGO).

IBRD and IDA are both UN specialized agencies. Besides IBRD and IDA, the World Bank Group includes the International Finance Corporation (IFC) and the Multilateral Investment Guarantee Agency (MIGA).

Membership
Membership is open to all members of the International Monetary Fund (IMF) (see this section). Not open to regional integration organizations. IBRD had 182 member States and IDA had 160 member States by 30 June 1999. A country must be a member of the IBRD before it can join the IDA.

Founded
27 December 1945 (IBRD); 24 September 1960 (IDA).

Secretariat

The World Bank,
1818 H Street NW,
Washington, DC 20433,
USA
Telephone: +1-202-4771234
Telefax: +1-202-4776391
E-mail: pic@worldbank.org

The World Bank had offices in 90 countries (see illustration) by June 1999.

President
Mr James D. Wolfensohn.

Director, Environment Department
Mr Robert Watson.

Vice-President, External Affairs
Vacant.

Number of staff
Total of 6,017 professionals and 2283 support staff at headquarters (May 1999).

Activities

The World Bank finances infrastructure facilities such as roads, railways, and power facilities as well as small-scale projects such as providing credits to micro-entrepreneurs and farmers. It has increased emphasis on investments which can directly affect the well-being of the masses of poor people, e.g. in developing countries, by making them more productive and by including them as active participants in the development process.

Environmental activities
Policy and research work on the environment is conducted in all the Bank's sectors, but especially in energy, industry, urban infrastructure, and agriculture.

Incorporating environmental considerations into decision making has been a prime focus of activity, and several activities are concerned with the effects of rapidly growing energy use on pollution.

Central to integrating environmental concerns into the Bank's activities is the Operational Directive on Environmental Assessment, approved in October 1989. The Directive mandates an environmental assessment for all projects that may have a significant impact on the environment. In the fiscal year 1992 the Directive was revised to require that people affected by Bank-supported projects have access to the information contained in the assessment.

The Bank works closely with the UN Development Programme (UNDP) (see this section) and often serves as executing agency for UNDP projects.

The Bank co-operated with UNDP and the UN Environment Programme (UNEP) in the three-year pilot programme Global Environment Facility (GEF) (see this section), which provided grants and low-interest loans to developing countries to help them carry out programmes to relieve pressures on global ecosystems. The pilot programme was adopted in 1991. The restructured GEF was established by the same implementing agencies in 1994.

In the fiscal year 1997 the World Bank was involved with 166 environmental projects to assist developing countries in three broad areas: pollution control and protection of the urban environment; natural resource management and protection of the rural environment; and institution building. These projects involved $US11.6 billion in loans. Each loan is disbursed usually over a five- to ten-year period.

The Bank's environmental strategy has four basic objectives:
• to assist developing countries set priorities, build up institutions, and implement programmes for sound environmental stewardship;
• to ensure that potentially adverse environmental effects from World Bank-financed projects are addressed;
• to assist member States build up the links between poverty reduction and environmental protection;
• to address global environmental challenges through participation in the GEF.

Decision-making bodies

All powers of the Bank are vested in a Board of Governors, which consists of one Governor appointed by each member State. The Governors have delegated most of their powers to the Executive Directors responsible for matters of policy and approval of all the loans

made by the Bank. The Bank's operation is the responsibility of a President selected by the Executive Directors, who is, *ex officio*, their Chairman.

IDA is a separate legal entity with its own financial resources. It has the same Board of Governors and the same Executive Directors representing countries that are members of both IBRD and IDA. The President of the Bank is *ex officio* President of IDA and the officers and staff of the Bank also serve IDA. Each member has an assessed quota, which is subscribed and determines voting-power in IDA and IBRD. By June 1998 the USA, as the largest contributor, had 14.93 per cent of the voting power in IDA. Japan (10.58 per cent), Germany (6.98 per cent), the United Kingdom (5 per cent), and France (4.21 per cent) have, together with the USA, the largest share of voting-power. By June 1998 the voting-power in IBRD of the five largest shareholders was as follows: USA (16.68 per cent), Japan (8 per cent), Germany (4.57 per cent), the UK (4.38 per cent), and France (4.38 per cent).

Finance

The IBRD, which accounts for about three-quarters of all World Bank lending, raises most of its money on the world's financial markets. It sells bonds and other debt securities to pension funds, insurance companies, corporations, other banks, and individuals around the world. In 1997 the IBRD borrowed $US7,682 million after swaps. Other sources of funds are shareholders' capital and retained earnings.

IDA, however, depends almost entirely on the wealthier member governments for its financial resources. Donors are asked every three years to replenish IDA funds. 34 countries committed $18 billion for IDA operations during the Tenth Replenishment, from 1993 to 1996. The Eleventh Replenishment (IDA11) financed projects over the three years which began on 1 July 1996. Funding for the IDA11 allowed IDA to lend about $22 billion, of which donors' contributions provided about $11 billion. Additional funds come from IBRD's profits and from borrowers' repayments of earlier IDA credits.

Budget
The approved administrative budget for the World Bank was $1,374.7 million in 1997 and $1,423.9 million in 1998, and is $1,461.5 million in 1999.

Main contributors
The largest pledges to IDA11 were made by the USA, Japan, Germany, France, the United Kingdom, and Italy. IDA11 donors also included developing countries such as Botswana, Brazil, South Africa, and Turkey.

Lending
Developing countries borrow from the Bank because they need capital, technical assistance, and policy advice. There are two types of Bank lending. The first type is for developing countries that are able to pay near-market interest rates. The money for these loans comes from investors around the world. These investors buy bonds issued by the World Bank.

The second type of loan goes to the poorest countries, which are usually not creditworthy in the international financial markets and are unable to pay near-market interest rates on the money they borrow. IDA loans (known as credits) have maturities of 35 or 40 years with a ten-year grace period on repayment of principal. There is no interest charge, but credits do carry a small service charge, currently 0.75 per cent.

IDA funds are allocated to the borrowing countries in relation to their size, income level, and track record of success in managing their economies and their ongoing IDA projects. During the IDA11 period, between 45 and 50 per cent of IDA funds went to countries in Sub-Saharan Africa. Most of the rest went to Asian countries such as Bangladesh, India, Vietnam, Pakistan, and Nepal, with smaller amounts allocated to China and the poorer nations of Latin America and the Caribbean, the Middle East, Europe, and Central Asia.

Publications

• numerous research studies, country reports, etc.;
• annual reports;
• *Annual Report on the Environment*;
• *World Development Report* (annual);
• *Environment Matters* (newsletter of the World Bank Environment Community);
• *Global Development Finance*;
• *Trends in Developing Countries*;
• *World Bank Atlas*.

Sources on the Internet
<http://www.worldbank.org>

World Food Programme (WFP)

Objectives

WFP provides food aid to developing countries both to promote economic and social development and to help meet emergency needs. To this end, WFP's assistance, targeted at the neediest and most vulnerable groups of people, is provided in support of a variety of government-aided projects and emergency operations. WFP also gives priority to disaster prevention, emergency preparedness and mitigation, and post-disaster rehabilitation activities.

Organization

Type
Intergovernmental organization (IGO).

Membership
No general members (see Decision-making bodies, below).

Founded
24 November 1961.

Secretariat

World Food Programme (WFP),
68/70 via Cesare Giulio Viola,
Parco dei Medici,
I-00148 Rome,
Italy
Telephone: +39-06-65131
Telefax: +39-06-659063-2/7
E-mail: wfpinfo@wfp.org

Executive Director
Ms Catherine Bertini.

Head of Information
Mr Trevor Rowe.

Number of staff
268 professionals and 318 general service staff at headquarters; 765 professionals and 765 general service staff are in the field (December 1998). 2,905 temporary staff are engaged in emergency operations.

Activities

WFP operational activities in 1998 were: 19 countries with country programmes, representing an approved resource level of $US1.4 billion; 125 development projects (including activities within approved country programmes) with operational expenditure of $254.3 million: 60 emergency operations with an operational expenditure of $697.0 million; 23 protracted relief operations and protracted relief and recovery operations with an operational expenditure of $218.5 million.

WFP's development portfolio has been declining continually since the late 1980s, when it had reached more than $3.5 billion. At $254.3 million, operational expenditure for development in 1998 was the lowest for more than 20 years.

WFP-assisted development projects have traditionally fallen almost exclusively within two broad categories: (1) agricultural and rural development and (2) human resource

development. WFP's expenditures for projects aimed at assisting agricultural and rural development totalled $134 million in 1998. Expenditures for human resource development projects, mainly for mothers and pre-school and primary-school children, in 1998 were valued at $120.5 million. Well over 50 per cent of WFP development assistance directly supports women's advancement.

Environmental activities
WFP spends US$230 million a year on forestation, soil conservation and other activities to promote environmentally sustainable agricultural production.

WFP's ongoing projects that have natural resource and environmental components totalled 84 in 1998. They include forestry activities, land and water development activities, rangeland development, and forestry and agricultural training.

WFP has taken a number of initiatives to address environmental concerns in both its relief and development interventions, including collaboration with UN High Commissioner for Refugees (UNHCR) in 1998 to identify sustainable environmental management practices in areas hosting large numbers of refugees.

Based on these experiences, WFP has adopted a policy to ensure that environmental issues are systematically considered in the design and implementation of all interventions and programmes.

WFP's environmental policy identifies the main elements required for formulating

an environmentally sound programming response. These include:
• ensuring that the energy and environmental implications of the WFP-provided food basket are taken into account. For example, assessing the fuel requirements to cook different types of foods when determining the composition of the food basket and identifying mitigation measures (such as providing cooking fuel or training in fuel-saving techniques) to help reduce the rate of deforestation;
• undertaking environmental reviews in selected types of interventions. Environmental reviews will be required for development activities implemented in the areas of natural resources or creation of assets, such as road improvements, irrigation, and water works. Technical assistance will be sought from government counterparts, NGOs, and staff of specialised agencies;
• ensuring sound procurement, storage, use and disposal of hazardous chemicals required for WFP operations. WFP will minimise or, where possible, phase out the use of the most hazardous chemicals, including certain pesticides and fumigants. Work has been undertaken in collaboration with the Food and Agriculture Organization (FAO) and the World Health Organization (WHO) (see this section) to identify best practices for the use of hazardous chemicals;

• developing partnerships to effectively strengthen WFP's capacities to address environmental issues.

Decision-making bodies

The Executive Board, comprising 36 members, is WFP's governing body. It consists of members elected by the FAO Council (see this section) and the UN Economic and Social Council (ECOSOC) who serve three-year terms and are eligible for re-election. The Board provides a forum for inter-governmental consultation on national food aid programmes and policies; reviews trends in food aid requirements and availability, and formulates proposals for effective co-ordination of multilateral, bilateral, and non-governmental food aid programmes, including emergency aid.

Finance

WFP is funded by voluntary contributions from donor countries and intergovernmental bodies made in commodities, cash, and services.

Budget
WFP's annual expenditure amounted to $US1.2 billion in 1996, $1.2 billion in 1997, and $1.2 billion in 1998. Nine per cent of the budget has been devoted to administration.

Main contributors
In 1998: the USA, the EU, Japan, the United Kingdom, Canada, Germany, Australia, the Netherlands, Denmark, and Norway.

Special funds
WFP has special funds for dealing with emergency situations such as the International Emergency Food Reserve (IEFR) and the Intermediate Response Account (IRA). In 1995 the IRA was redesigned to be both a revolving and a replenishment fund.

Contributions for 1998 to the IEFR totalled $991 million. Contributions to the IRA totalled $15 million, well below the $35 million annual target.

Publications
• annual reports;
• *Tackling Hunger in a World of Plenty: Tasks for Food Aid*;
• *Ending the Inheritance of Hunger: Food Aid for Human Growth*;
• *Enabling Development*.

Sources on the Internet
<http://www.wfp.org>

World Health Organization (WHO)

Following the reorganization of the WHO in 1998–99, the outcome at headquarters in Geneva is a new organizational structure around nine clusters. The cluster mainly concerned with international co-operation in environment and development is the Sustainable Development and Healthy Environments (SDE) cluster. SDE consists of four departments and one special advisory unit (Health and Human Rights). The departments are: (1) Emergency and Humanitarian Action (EHA); (2) Health in Sustainable Development (HSD); (3) Nutrition for Health and Development (NHD); and (4) Protection of the Human Environment (PHE). For the purpose of this *Yearbook*, we limit our attention to the latter, which embodies four departments: (a) Water, Sanitation, and Health; (b) Occupational and Environmental Health; (c) Food Safety; and (d) Chemical Safety.

Objectives

The role of PHE is to advocate, promote, and carry out international work in health and environment, including the development and promotion of evidence-based guidelines; the monitoring and assessment of environmental quality; environmental and health impact assessment; support for national capacity building in environmental health; and the provision of advice, guidance, and technical assistance to WHO member States.

PHE's mandate encompasses global, regional, and country level environmental management, as well as health protection from environmental hazards including water and sanitation; health aspects of water resources management; control of air and water quality; pollution control; occupational health, radiation protection, electromagnetic fields, ultraviolet radiation, and hazardous wastes management; chemical hazards; poisonings and food safety; and environmental settings supportive of health.

Organization

Type
Intergovernmental organization (IGO). A specialized agency of the UN, linked to the UN Economic and Social Council (ECOSOC).

Membership
All member States of the UN may become members of WHO by accepting its Constitution. Other countries may be admitted as members on approval of their application by a simple majority vote of the World Health Assembly. Territories not responsible for the conduct of their own international relations may become associate members. There were 191 member States by 30 June 1999.

Founded
7 April 1948.

Secretariat

World Health Organization (WHO),
20 avenue Appia,
CH-1211 Geneva,
Switzerland
Telephone: +41-22-7912111
Telefax: +41-22-7910746
E-mail: info@who.ch
or pfistera@who.int

Director-General
Dr Gro Harlem Brundtland
(21 July 1998–20 July 2003).

Head of Information of WHO
Ms Vaijayanti Naravane.

Executive Director, SDE
Ms Poonam Khetrapal Singh.

SDE Documentation Centre
Ms Anne-Marie Pfister.

Head, PHE
Dr Richard Helmer.

Number of staff
Approximately 3,800 health and other experts in both professional and service categories, working at WHO headquarters (30 per cent), in the six regional offices (40 per cent), and in countries (30 per cent) (July 1999).

Activities

PHE's programmes focus on:
• building evidence base and normative function (assessment of physical, chemical,

and biological health risks) for the environment and health;
• assessing relevant global and regional status and trends;
• identifying and promoting good practices in health risk management (including evidence for the effectiveness of technical, strategic, and policy interventions);
• providing support to WHO member States in national and local capacity development and implementation in specific settings, including support to international legal and regulatory initiatives and agreements.

PHE has a good 'track record' for settings-specific activities (e.g. 'Healthy Cities'), extensive co-operation with WHO regional offices and environment centres; and network building through WHO collaborating centres, facilitating their substantive inputs to all major programme areas.

Due to the pervasive nature of both environmental health problems and solutions, PHE takes an intersectoral approach to its work, integrating concerns such as global climate change, public participation, freedom of information, and environmental equity into its overall programmes structure.

Decision-making bodies

The World Health Assembly is the policy-making body of WHO and meets in annual session. The Executive Board, which meets at least twice a year, acts as the executive organ of the Assembly. The Board is composed of 32 persons technically qualified in the field of health, each one designated by a member State elected to do so by the Assembly. Member States are elected for three-year terms.

Six regional offices have been established as integral parts of the Organization, each consisting of a regional committee and a regional office. Regional committees meet in annual sessions. The Secretariat is headed by the Director-General, who is appointed by the Assembly on the nomination of the Board.

Finance

The budget is made up of assessed contributions from member States and associate members. This is known as the regular budget. WHO also receives voluntary contributions from member States and from other sources, often referred to as extra-budgetary contributions.

Budget
The regular WHO administrative budget is US$842.6 million for the years 1998–9 and is $842.6 million for 2000–01. Estimated extra-budgetary contributions are $958.2 million for 2000–01.

The regular SDE budget is $48.7 million for 2000–01. Estimated extra-budgetary contributions are $110 million.

Publications

• *World Health* (monthly);
• *Bulletin of the World Health Organization* (monthly);
• *Health and Environment in Sustainable Development—Five Years after the Earth Summmit* (WHO/EHG/97.8).

Sources on the Internet

WHO:
<http://www.who.int>
SDE/EHA:
<http://www.who.int/eha>
SDE/HSD:
<http://www.who.int/ico>
SDE/NHD:
<http://www.who.int/nut>
SDE/PHE:
<http://www.who.int/peh>

World Meteorological Organization (WMO)

Objectives

• to facilitate international co-operation in the establishment of networks of stations for the making of meteorological observations as well as hydrological and other geophysical observations related to meteorology and to promote the establishment and maintenance of centres charged with the provision of meteorological and related services;

• to promote the establishment and maintenance of systems for rapid exchange of meteorological and related information;

• to promote standardization of meteorological and related observations and ensure the uniform publication of observations and statistics;

• to further the application of meteorology to aviation, shipping, water problems, agriculture, and other human activities;

• to promote activities in operational hydrology and further close co-operation between Meteorological and Hydrometeorological Services;

• to encourage research and training in meteorology, and, as appropriate, in related fields, and to assist in co-ordinating the international aspects of such research and training.

Organization

Type
Intergovernmental organization (IGO). A specialized agency of the UN. Agreements and working arrangements with governmental and non-governmental organizations (NGOs), other national, regional, and international scientific organizations, and UN agencies.

Membership
States and territories. 179 member States and six Territories by 9 July 1999.

Founded
23 March 1950.

Secretariat

World Meterological Organization (WMO),
41 avenue Giuseppe Motta,
PO Box 2300,
CH-1211 Geneva 2,
Switzerland
Telephone: +41-22-7308111
Telefax: +41-22-7342326
E-mail: al-ghanem_t@gateway.wmo.ch

Secretary-General
Mr Godwin O. P. Obasi.

Chief Information and Public Affairs Officer
Mr Taysir M. Al-Ghanem.

Number of staff
117 professionals and 130 support staff at headquarters (December 1998). Six professionals and 7 support staff at field, regional, or country offices.

Activities

WMO carries out its work through eight major scientific and technical programmes which have strong components in each region: the World Weather Watch Programme, World Climate Programme, Atmospheric Research and Environment Programme, Applications of Meteorology Programme, Hydrology and Water Resource Programme, Education and Training Programme, Regional Programme, and Technical Co-operation Programme.

Environmental activities
The WMO works through its members to provide authoritative scientific measurements, as well as assessments and predictions of the state and the composition of the global atmosphere and of the Earth's freshwater resources.

The WMO promotes increasingly effective application of meteorological and hydrological information in seeking environmentally sound and sustainable development.

With climate change as an issue of growing concern, the World Climate Programme provides an inter-agency interdisciplinary framework to address the full range of climate and climate change issues.

It calls attention to the need for global action for the reduction of ozone-depleting chemicals and to reduce pollution of the atmosphere, on the basis of available scientific information.

It has several programmes and activities operated jointly with other IGOs and NGOs.

These include the Intergovernmental Panel on Climate Change (IPCC) to provide assessments of available scientific information on climate change and the resulting environmental and socio-economic impacts, the Global Climate Observing System (GCOS) to provide observations for monitoring climate and detecting climate change and to support climatological applications for national economic development and research, and the World Climate Research Programme (WCRP), which aims to develop an improved understanding of climate and predictions of global and regional climate changes on all time-frames.

WMO is also actively involved in the work of the Conference of the Parties to the UN Framework Convention on Climate Change (UNFCCC), Convention to Combat Desertification (CCD), the Montreal Protocol on Substances that Deplete the Ozone Layer (see Agreements), and several aspects of Agenda 21 of the UN Conference on Environment and Development (UNCED).

The Atmospheric Research and Environment Programme (AREP) co-ordinates and fosters research on the structure and composition of the atmosphere and its related physical characteristics; the physics of weather processes; and weather forecasting on various time- and space-scales in particular for meteorological events with high socio-economic impact. The Programme consists of four major components: the Global Atmospheric Watch, the World Weather Research programme (WWRP), Tropical Meteorology Research and Physics and Chemistry of Clouds, and Weather Modification Research.

A majority of natural disasters are weather- or climate-related, such as tropical cyclone, tornado, storm surge, flood, and drought. WMO, through its members and their national Meteorological and Hydrological Services, and in co-operation with other UN agencies and international organizations, is contributing to disaster preparedness and mitigation by means of prediction and warnings.

Decision-making bodies

The main bodies of WMO are the World Meteorological Congress, which meets every four years and in which all member States and Territories are represented, and the Executive Council, composed of 36 directors of national Meteorological and Hydrological Services, which meets at least once a year to review the activities of the Organization and to implement the programmes approved by the Congress. The six regional associations (Africa, Asia, South America, North and Central America and the Caribbean, South-West Pacific, and Europe) are composed of member governments, and work to co-ordinate meteorological and related activities within their respective regions. The eight technical commissions, composed of experts designated by member States, study matters within their specific areas of competence. These are the commissions for:

- aeronautical meteorology;
- agricultural meteorology;
- atmospheric sciences;
- basic systems;
- climatology;
- hydrology;
- instruments and methods of observations;
- marine meteorology.

The Secretariat, headed by a Secretary-General, serves as the administrative, documentation, and information centre of the Organization.

Finance

Contributions of members according to a proportional scale adopted by percentage assessment of total contribution.

Budget
The approved budget is SFr.255 million for the years 1996–9 and SFr.252.3 million for 2000–03.

Special funds
In addition to the extra-budgetary funds for activities in respect of technical co-operation projects, WMO administers several trust funds and special accounts financed by various member States and international organizations.

Publications

- *WMO Bulletin* (quarterly);
- *World Climate News* (quarterly);
- *El Niño Update* (monhtly since November 1997);
- mandatory publications;
- programme-supporting publications;
- special environmental reports.

Sources on the Internet

<http://www.wmo.ch>

World Trade Organization (WTO)

Objectives

The main objectives of World Trade Organization (WTO) are:
- to supervise and liberalize international trade;
- to supervise the settlements of commercial conflicts.

The WTO shall facilitate the implementation, administration, and operation, and further the objectives of the General Agreement on Tariffs and Trade (GATT) 1994 and the Multilateral Trade Agreements (which are binding on all members), including the General Agreement on Trade in Services and the Agreement on Trade-Related Aspects of Intellectual Property Rights (TRIPS), and shall also provide the framework for the implementation, administration, and operation of the Plurilateral Trade Agreements (which are binding on the members that have accepted them, but which do not create either obligations or rights for members that have not accepted them).

The main objectives of GATT 1994 are:
- to enter into reciprocal and mutually advantageous arrangements directed to the substantial reduction of tariffs and other barriers to trade;
- to eliminate discriminatory treatment in international trade relations.

WTO members recognize that their relations in the field of trade and economic endeavour should be conducted with a view to contributing to the following objectives:
- to raise standards of living, ensuring full employment and a large and steadily growing volume of real income and effective demand;
- to expand the production of and trade in goods and services, while allowing for the optimal use of the world's resources in accordance with the objective of sustainable development, seeking both to protect and to preserve the environment and to enhance the means for doing so in a manner consistent with the member's respective needs and concerns at different levels of economic development;
- to ensure that developing countries, and especially the least developed among them, secure a share in the growth in international trade commensurate with the needs of their economic development.

Organization

Type
Intergovernmental organization (IGO). An independent IGO within the UN system.

Membership
Any state or separate customs territory possessing full autonomy in the conduct of external trade may apply for WTO membership. Membership entails accepting all the results of the Uruguay Round of Multilateral Trade Negotiations (1986–94) without exception and the submission of national tariff schedules on goods and initial commitments on services. WTO had 134 members, including the European Union, and 36 observer countries, by July 1999.

Founded
1 January 1995.

Secretariat

World Trade Organization,
Centre William Rappard,
154 rue de Lausanne,
CH-1211 Geneva 21,
Switzerland
Telephone: +41-22-7395111
Telefax: +41-22-7395458
E-mail: enquiries@wto.org

Director-General
Vacant.

Director of Information
Mr Keith Rockwell.

Number of staff
500 at the WTO Secretariat (December 1998).

Activities

Environmental activities
When trade ministers approved the results of the Uruguay Round negotiations in Marrakesh in April 1994, they took a decision to begin a comprehensive work programme on trade and environment in the WTO. Since 1994 this work programme has provided the focus of discussions in the Committee on Trade and the Environment (CTE) (see below).

The CTE has a twofold mandate:
- to identify the relationship between trade measures and environmental measures, in order to promote sustainable development;
- to make appropriate recommendations on whether any modifications of the provisions of the multilateral trading system are required, compatible with the open, equitable, and non-discriminatory nature of the system.

This broad-based mandate covers goods, services, and intellectual property rights and builds on progress already achieved in the previous GATT Group on Environmental Measures and International Trade. Since 1997 the CTE has adopted a thematic approach to broaden and deepen its discussions and to allow all items of the work programme to be addressed in a systematic manner.

After the 1996 Ministerial Conference in Singapore, the CTE decided to follow a 'cluster' or thematic approach to broaden and deepen its discussions of the items in its work programme. Thus, in 1997, under the chairmanship of Ambassador Björn Ekblom (Finland), members discussed in May items related to market access and in September items relevant to the linkages between the multilateral environment and trade agendas.

With respect to the second 'cluster' of items, the CTE organized, in September 1997, an information session with representatives from the secretariats of the Convention on International Trade in Endangered Species of Wild Flora and Fauna (CITES); the Convention on the Control of Transboundary Movements of Hazardous Wastes and their Disposal (Basel Convention); the Montreal Protocol on Substances that Deplete the Ozone Layer; the UN Convention on the Law of the Sea (UNCLOS); the Convention on Biological Diversity (CBD) (see Agreements for these conventions); the UNEP International Register of Potentially Toxic Chemicals (IRPTC) Programme; the Multilateral Fund for the Implementation of the Montreal Protocol; and the Global Environment Facility (GEF) (see this section). The Secretariat of the UN Framework Convention on Climate Change (UNFCCC) (see Agreements) was unable to participate in the meeting, but submitted a statement.

At its meeting in March 1998, the CTE elected Ambassador Chak Mun See (Singapore) as Chairman and adopted its work programme and schedule of meeting for 1998. It addressed items relevant to the theme of market access and held substantive discussions on the following sectors: agriculture, energy fisheries, forestry, non-ferrous metals, textiles and clothing, leather, and environmental services.

At the March meeting the CTE also established a WTO environmental database which can be accessed electronically by members. The WTO Secretariat is to maintain the database and conduct comprehensive reviews on an annual basis of all the environment-related notifications made by members. The environmental database is seen as an important step towards increasing the transparency of trade-related environmental measures notified by WTO members.

At its meeting from 23 to 24 July 1998, the CTE invited secretariats of several multilateral environmental agreements (MEAs) and UNEP to an information session to increase members' awareness of trade-related developments in environmental forums. Members welcomed the MEA presentations and background papers prepared for this session, which had contributed to an understanding of the core environment principles and approaches underlying the development of MEAs. The MEA information sessions were valuable in enhancing domestic policy co-ordination on trade and environment issues.

In relation to the linkages between the multilateral environment and trade agendas, members focused on four items of the work programme. There was discussion of the relationship between MEAs and the WTO, including with respect to dispute settlement; the export of domestically prohibited goods (DPGs); and aspects of the WTO Agreement on Trade-Related Aspects of Intellectual Property Rights (TRIPS), including its relationship to the CBD. New papers were presented on issues relevant to the TRIPS Agreement. Discussion was also held on eco-labelling, the environmental effects of removing trade distortions and environmental services.

At the CTE's meeting held from 26 to 27 October 1998, members addressed trade in services and the environment; relations with NGOs; and items on the work programme related to the themes of the linkages between the multilateral environment and trade agendas, and market access.

Under the theme of market access, members discussed eco-labelling, and continued the sectoral analysis of the environmental benefits of trade liberalization. Statements were made by members on the agriculture, energy, fisheries, and forestry sectors. Three papers were presented: Argentina's on non-trade concerns in the next agricultural negotiations; Japan's addressing the environmen-

tal effects of agricultural trade liberalization; and Brazil's on the trade and environmental benefits of removing trade restrictions to trade in ethanol. Brazil and Canada announced initiatives to further discussions on the sustainable management of all types of forests to contribute to the ongoing work of the Intergovernmental Forum on Forests.

In relation to the linkages between the multilateral environment and trade agendas, members commented briefly on the recent Appellate Body Report on US Import Prohibition of Certain Shrimp and Shrimp Products and the Secretariat's revised paper on GATT/WTO dispute settlement practice relating to Article XX. The relationship between the TRIPS Agreement and the CBD was also addressed.

Observer status in the CTE was extended to the International Plant Genetic Resources Institute.

The CTE, on 18–19 February 1999, addressed items on its work programme related to the theme of market access. Members made statements on environmental assessments of trade agreements, eco-labelling and certification, and the environmental benefits of removing trade restrictions and distortions.

With respect to eco-labelling, Brazil contributed a new paper on its certification programmes for leather and forestry products. For discussion at this meeting, the Secretariat also prepared a new paper on technical barriers to the market access of developing countries.

Under the item dealing with market access and the environmental benefits of trade liberalization, Members continued the sectoral discussions of agriculture, energy, fisheries, forestry, and leather. New Zealand and Zimbabwe presented new papers on this item in general. Concerning the agricultural sector, Norway, Japan, and Brazil contributed national experience papers. A new paper on agricultural export subsidies, cosponsored by 14 countries, was also discussed. With respect to the fisheries sector, Iceland contributed a new paper on its fisheries management system.

Observer status in the CTE was extended to the South Pacific Forum.

A highlight of WTO activities in trade and environment in 1999 was the holding of the WTO High Level Symposium on Trade and Environment held at the WTO headquarters in Geneva from 15 to 16 March. Some 87 environment-related NGOs and academia, and 40 industry federations and consumer groups participated in the symposium.

The Environment Symposium was followed by the WTO High Level Symposium on Trade and Development.

Decision-making bodies

The Ministerial Conference, comprising all members, is the main governing body of the WTO, and meets at least every two years. A General Council, composed of all members, oversees operation of the WTO between meetings of the Ministerial Conference, including acting as a dispute-settlement body and administering the trade policy review mechanism.

The Council has established subsidiary bodies such as the Council for Trade in Goods, the Council for Trade in Services, the Trade-Related Aspects of Intellectual Property Rights (TRIPs) Council, and the Committee on Trade and the Environment (CTE).

Decision making is by consensus. If a decision cannot be arrived at by consensus, the matter at issue shall be decided by voting at meetings of the Ministerial Conference and the General Council. Each member of WTO has one vote.

Finance

Each member contributes its share in the expenses of the WTO in accordance with the financial regulations adopted by the General Council. Contributions by members reflect shares in international trade in goods, services, and intellectual property.

Budget
The administrative budget of WTO was SFr.115.9 million in 1998 and is Fr.122 million in 1999.

Main contributors
Main contributors in 1998 were the USA, Japan, France, the United Kingdom, Italy, Canada, the Netherlands, Hong Kong, Belgium, the Republic of Korea, Spain, Singapore, and Switzerland.

Publications

- annual reports;
- *WTO Focus* (10 times a year);
- *Trade and Environment Bulletin* (following each meetings of the CTE);
- *International Trade* (annual).

Sources on the Internet

<http://www.wto.org>

The NGOs are selected on the following criteria:
- that they are multinational, with member organizations, national affiliates, or offices;
- that they are active over a period, i.e. *ad hoc* organizations are not included. A few networks which seem to have influence beyond a particular event are included;
- that a substantial part of their activities are within the environment and development. For organizations with a main focus on development, an environmental component is also required;
- that they are reasonably independent of governments (an exception has been made for IUCN);
- that they are not a foundation or research organization.

The Editors

Basel Action Network (BAN)

Objectives
• to prevent the globalization of the toxic crisis from the trade in toxic products, toxic technologies, and toxic wastes;
• the ratification and implementation of the Basel Convention and the Basel Ban Amendment.

Organization
Non-governmental organization (NGO). Founded in 1997.

Membership
Membership open to non-profit NGOs only. 23 member organizations in 15 countries by May 1999.

Secretariat
c/o Asia Pacific Environmental Exchange, 1827 39th Avenue E., Seattle, Washington 98112, USA
Telephone: +1-206-7206426
Telefax: +1-206-7206426
E-mail: info@ban.org
<http://www.ban.org/>

Number of staff
Two professionals.

Budget
No budget information available.

Activities
In order to reach its objectives, BAN works on several levels:
• it operates a website on the transboundary movements of hazardous waste;
• it maintains a clearing-house function for academics, journalists, and others regarding the transboundary movements of hazardous waste;
• it attends key Basel meetings, including all Conferences of Parties, and works as an advocacy observer to end toxic trade of all kinds;
• it participates in bilateral and multilateral campaigns against key waste trade activities, such as the Formosa Plastics dumping in Cambodia, Shipbreaking etc.
• it co-operates with and co-ordinates member groups and others to ensure ratification of the Basel Convention (see Agreements) and the Basel Ban Amendment;
• it works to prevent the trade organizations from impeding or eroding the mandates of the Basel Convention, or countries' rights to ban the import or export of hazardous wastes, products, or technologies.

Climate Action Network (CAN)

Objectives
• to promote government and individual action to limit human-induced climate change to ecologically sustainable levels;
• to co-ordinate information exchange on international, regional, and national climate policies and issues;
• to formulate policy options and position papers on climate-related issues;
• to undertake further collaborative action to promote effective non-governmental organizations' (NGOs) involvement in efforts to avert the threat of global warming.

Organization
Non-governmental organization (NGO). Observer status at UN negotiations under the Framework Convention on Climate Change (FCCC) (see Agreements). Accredited to the Climate Change Secretariat. Founded in March 1989.

Membership
Non-governmental, citizen-based organizations with a special interest in climate-related issues. Eight regional offices covering 265 member organizations in 75 countries by January 1999.

Secretariat
CAN has established the following regional focal points:

Climate Network Africa (CNA),
PO Box 76479,
Nairobi,
Kenya
Telephone: +254-2-545241
Telefax: +254-2-559122
E-mail: cna@meteo.go.ke

Climate Action Network South Asia (CANSA),
Bangladesh Centre for Advanced Studies, House 23 Road 10a (New) Dhanmondi, Dhaka,
Bangladesh
Telephone: +880-2-815829
Telefax: +880-2-863379
E-mail: atiq.r@bdcom.com

Climate Action Network South-East Asia (CANSEA),
Jln. Solong Raya no. 17,
Jakarta 13240,
Indonesia

Telephone: +62-21-4712363
Telefax: +62-21-4712363
E-mail: gugus@jakarta.wasantra.net.id

Climate Action Network Central and Eastern Europe (CANCEE),
Terra Mileniul III,
str Brasov no. 19,
B1 OD5, Sc. A,
Apartment 22, S6
BG-773691 Bucharest,
Romania
Telephone: +40-1-7452487
Telefax: +40-1-7452487
E-mail: iandrei@pcnet.pcnet.ro
<http://www.climatenetwork.org>

Climate Network Europe (CNE),
44 rue du Taciturne,
B-1000 Brussels,
Belgium
Telephone: +32-2-2310180
Telefax: +32-2-2305713
E-mail: canron@gn.apc.org

Climate Action Network UK (CAN UK),
49 Wellington Street,
London WC2 2E 7BN,
United Kingdom
Telephone: +44-171-8361110
Telefax: +44-171-4970447
E-mail: canuk@gn.apc.org

Climate Action Network Latin America (CANLA),
Casilla 16749 Correo 9,
Santiago,
Chile
Telephone: +56-2-2777104
Telefax: +56-2-2777104
E-mail: relac@huelen.reuna.cl

US Climate Action Network (US CAN),
1200 New York Avenue, NW,
Suite 400,
Washington, DC 20005,
USA
Telephone: +1-202-2892401
Telefax: +1-202-2891060
E-mail: cielne@igc.apc.org

Number of staff (all regional offices)
Ten professionals and 15 support staff (January 1999).

Budget
No information available.

Activities

Activities are organized through the regional focal points:

• *Climate Network Africa (CNA)* is an African NGO focal point on climate change activities. It acts as a resource centre for climate change, desertification, and ozone depletion issues. Networking is an important part of CNA's activities, as is information dissemination through *IMPACT Newsletter*;

• *CAN South Asia (CANSA)* research activities include climate change and poverty; climate, environment, and population; and climate change and natural disasters;

• *CAN South-East Asia (CANSEA)* has established core groups in the Philippines, Indonesia, and Malaysia, and others are being sought in Thailand and other Indo-Chinese countries;

• *Climate Action Network Central and Eastern Europe (CANCEE)* has 21 NGOs affiliated in 14 countries;

• *Climate Network Europe (CNE)* was the first Climate Network node. It was created as an NGO service on climate change issues managed by the Stockholm Environment Institute (SEI). It has regularly co-ordinated activities between 74 European NGOs and also acts as a resource centre for climate change information;

• *CAN UK* co-ordinates regular meetings of the Greenhouse Round-Table for information exchange and strategy building among 16 key NGOs in the United Kingdom, focusing on a range of issues such as transport, energy efficiency, water resources, development, and nature conservation;

• *CAN Latin America (CANLA)* consists of organizations in most countries of the region;

• *US CAN* is the focal point of global warming research and advocacy by American NGOs. It has contributed to the scientific capacity of the NGOs within the UN climate convention negotiations and has benefited from interaction with southern NGOs on the complexities of development issues in the South. US CAN is expanding its domestic efforts at the state and local level by pursuing several legislative and administrative initiatives designed to reduce emissions of CO_2 and other greenhouse gases. It publishes the newsletter *Hotline* on a regular basis.

Consumers International (CI)

Objectives

• to promote and protect consumers' rights and interests world-wide through research, information, and education;
• to help build the organizations that make up the global consumer movement;
• to assist and promote genuine efforts throughout the world in consumer self-organization as well as governmental efforts to further the interests of the consumer;
• to support and strengthen member organizations;
• to influence the institutions which formulate global and regional policy affecting consumers.

Organization

Non-governmental organization (NGO). Consultative status with IAEA, UN Economic and Social Council (ECOSOC), UNESCO, FAO, WHO, UNICEF, and UNIDO (see IGOs), International Standards Organization (ISO), and International Civil Aviation Organization (ICAO). Founded as International Organization of Consumers Unions (IOCU) on 1 April, 1960.

Membership

Consumer associations, government-financed consumer councils, consumer bodies supported by family organizations, labour unions, and similar groups. Total of 76 full member organizations in 50 countries and three territories. 130 affiliate member organizations in 76 countries and two territories, of which 46 countries and two territories have affiliate member organizations only (see table attached to this section). 40 government affiliate member organizations in 33 countries and one territory (five countries and one territory where the government associate member organizations are the only member organizations) by January 1999.

Secretariat

Consumers International (CI),
Head Office,
24 Highbury Crescent,
London N5 1RX,
United Kingdom
Telephone: +44-171-2266663
Telefax: +44-171-3540607
E-mail: consint@consint.org
<http://www.consumersinternational.org>

Number of staff

74 (April 1999).

Budget

The total core budget was £UK1.17 million in 1997 and £1.19 million in 1998, and is £1.21 million in 1999.

Activities

Three specific consumer rights and one consumer responsibility are directly related to sustainable development: the right to the satisfaction of basic needs, to safety, and to a healthy environment; and the ecological responsibility to be sensitive to what consumption of goods does to the environment.

Through its regional offices and programmes, CI promotes an exchange of skills and experiences between consumer groups throughout the world. It has developed expertise in a number of key areas that support the work of its member organizations. These include: model consumer-protection legislation, consumer magazine development, product-testing support, media and communications support, consumer education, and national and international advocacy guidelines.

CI links the work of its member organizations through information networks, regular publications, seminars, workshops, and a triennial world congress. It initiates research and action and publishes briefings on many international issues.

Earth Council

Objectives

The mission of the Earth Council is to support and empower people in building a more secure, equitable, and sustainable future. It has three fundamental objectives for its work:

• to promote awareness and support for the needed transition to more sustainable and equitable patterns of development;
• to encourage public participation in decision making;
• to build bridges of understanding and co-operation between important actors of civil society and governments world-wide.

Organization

Non-governmental organization (NGO). Accredited to UN Economic and Social Council (ECOSOC). Founded September 1992.

Membership

In addition to the governing body of 18 members, drawn from the world's political, business, scientific, and non-governmental communities, there are 16 people who are honorary members. The Earth Council has 92 partner organizations working with sustainable development.

Secretariat

Earth Council,
APDO 2323-1002,
San José,
Costa Rica
Telephone: +506-2561611
Telefax: +506-2552197
E-mail: eci@terra.ecouncil.ac.cr
<http://www.ecouncil.ac.cr>

Number of staff

13 professionals and 14 support staff at headquarters (October 1997).

Budget

No information available.

Activities

The Earth Council, in collaboration with its partner organizations, is now in Phase II of the Making Sustainability Work Programme, a campaign called 'Towards a Millennium Earth Initiative'.

The campaign, running from 1997 to 2000, focuses on the following strategic programmes:
• strengthening multi-stakeholder participatory mechanisms for operationalizing sustainable development, through Local Agenda 21 and National Councils on Sustainable Development (NCSDs) as key entry points to integrate economic, social, and ecological interests into national and local development plans, and harmonize these within regional and global alliances and accords;
• building and exchanging knowledge capital for effective and informed participation for operationalizing management systems at local and national levels;
• facilitating the mobilization and deployment of various investment capitals (social, knowledge, and financial) to finance sustainable development programmes and projects;
• working to adopt and integrate ethical and democratic principles and values into the policy frameworks of key actors through the Earth Charter and developing a regional sustainability mediation function;
• providing technical and knowledge support, information services, and communication linkages for informed participation of local and national councils, groups, and networks.

At the Earth Council meeting in November 1998, Earth Council decided to focus on convening the voices and groupings of the 'sustainable development constituency'. This will be carried out through a Global Earth Forum, held every two years.

Earthwatch Institute

Objectives

• to improve human understanding of the planet, the diversity of its inhabitants, and the processes that affect the quality of life on Earth;
• to act as a bridge between science and the community by enabling members of the public to join scientists in the field and act as their assistants;
• to sustain the world's environment, to monitor global change, to conserve endangered species and habitats, to explore the vast heritage of the people, and to foster world health and international co-operation.

Organization

Non-governmental organization (NGO). Consultative status with IUCN (see this section). Founded in 1972.

Membership

Individuals, organizations, corporations, and schools. About 50,000 individual members and four Earthwatch Institute offices in four countries by February 1999.

Secretariat

Earthwatch Institute,
57 Woodstock Road,
Oxford OX2 6HJ,
United Kingdom
Telephone: +44-1865-311600
Telefax: +44-1865-311383
E-mail: info@uk.earthwatch.org
<http://www.earthwatch.org>

Number of staff

19 professionals (February 1999).

Budget

The world-wide budget was $US10.5 million in 1997 and $10.5 million in 1998, and is $10 million in 1999. The administrative budget of the Secretariat was $US4 million in 1997 and $1.6 million in 1998, and is $1.6 million in 1999.

Activities

Earthwatch Institute sponsors more than 140 projects in 50 countries. Projects are year-round and each volunteer pays a share of the cost to cover field-work, food, and lodging. The volunteers must be 16 years or older and no special skills are needed. Projects are 2–3 weeks in length.

Volunteer tasks can range from tracking endangered rhinos in Zimbabwe, to excavating Mayan ruins in Mexico, to surveying one of the last remaining freshwater lakes in Kenya. Volunteers are an invaluable resource to scientists in collecting data pertaining to critical environmental issues.

Since 1972 more than 50,000 volunteers have contributed over $US35 million to search for solutions to important environmental problems world-wide.

The Centre for Field Research receives more than 400 proposals each year from scholars who need the help of volunteers. The Centre, with its academic advisory board, is responsible for peer review, screening, and selection of projects for Earthwatch Institute support.

Earthwatch Institute arranges human resource capacity training through hands-on field-work, especially for nationals from non-industrialized countries.

Environment Liaison Centre International (ELCI)

Objectives

To strengthen the collective action of non-governmental organizations (NGOs) and community-based organizations (CBOs) world-wide towards a healthy, productive, and sustainable environment for all life, through:
• supporting NGOs and CBOs to build on each other's strengths;
• reflecting their needs, aspirations, and knowledge in governance at all levels;
• using the output of global processes at local levels.

Organization

Non-governmental organization (NGO). ELCI is a networking instrument for NGOs. Consultative status with UNEP and the Food and Agriculture Organization (FAO) (see IGOs) and UN Economic and Social Council (ECOSOC). Accredited to, among others, the Intergovernmental Negotiating Committee on Desertification (see

Agreements, Convention to Combat Desertification (CCD)), the Meetings of the Conference of the Parties to the Convention on Biological Diversity (see Agreements), the Montreal Protocol (see Agreements, Vienna Convention), the UN Commission on Human Settlements (UNCHS)/Habitat II, and UNESCO (see IGOs). Founded in 1974.

Membership
Non-governmental organizations worldwide. Total of 880 full member organizations in 112 countries and three territories by April 1999.

Secretariat
Environment Liaison Centre International (ELCI),
PO Box 72461,
Nairobi,
Kenya
Telephone: +254-2-576114/25/54
Telefax: +254-2-562175
E-mail: ealitsi@iconnect.co.ke
<http://riod.utando.com>
<ftp://riod.utando.com>

Number of staff
Eight professionals and 12 support staff (April 1999).

Budget
The administrative budget was $2.0 million in 1997 and $2.6 million in 1998, and is $495,000 in 1999.

Activities
ELCI engages its member organizations in programme activities by focusing on the following three strategies:
• organizing programme activities through member working groups which will mobilize organizations to join together to address specific sectoral or cross-cutting issues simultaneously at the local and global levels;
• strengthening communication and information systems to facilitate the efficient functioning of this world-wide action network;
• moving to a decentralized, regionally focused organizational structure.

Programmes being implemented by member working groups are concentrated in three thematic areas:
• natural resource management, including indigenous knowledge, medicinal plants and biodiversity, and sustainable agriculture and food security;
• technology and environment, including

human settlements and alternative energy;
• certification of forest products.

The working group programmes are implemented in three phases: I) organizing members around sectoral issues, collectively defining terms of reference and developing an action plan for the working group; II) developing protocols for communication and decision making and operating structures and codes of practice for the functioning of the working groups, developing models and guidelines for mainstreaming cross-cutting issues, including gender, youth, and governance; and III) implementation of the action plan, including:
• a local support subgroup based on the eco-volunteer model (supporting existing initiatives developed by local groups to solve environmental problems in their communities);
• documenting community action experiences as a basis for advocacy and campaigning;
• building consensus on key issues on which to focus during relevant intergovernmental meetings;
• co-ordinating training workshops;
• facilitating participation in policy meetings;
• analysing implications of policy decisions for stakeholders at regional, national, and local levels;
• monitoring implementation of international agreements.

European Environmental Bureau (EEB)

Objectives
• to bring together environmental non-governmental organizations in the member States in order to strengthen their effect and impact on the environmental policy and projects of the European Union (EU);
• to promote an equitable and sustainable life-style;
• to promote the protection and conservation of the environment, and the restoration and better use of human resources;
• to use educational and other means to increase public awareness of these problems;
• to make all necessary information available to members and other organizations likely to assist in the realization of these aims;
• to promote and strengthen environmental policy at the global level, e.g. in the

framework of the follow-up on the UN Conference of Environment and Development (UNCED).

Organization
Non-governmental organization (NGO). Consultative status with the Council of Europe, and relations with the Commission of the European Union, the European Parliament, the Economic and Social Committee of the European Union, the OECD (see IGOs), and national sustainable development councils in Belgium and Ireland. Founded 13 December 1974.

Membership
NGOs, dealing with environmental conservation and protection, as full, associate, or affiliate members from the European Economic Area (EEA). Corresponding NGO members from non-EEA member States. 73 full member organizations in 16 countries by April 1999. 23 associate, 21 affiliate, and 11 corresponding member organizations.

Secretariat
European Environmental Bureau (EEB),
34 boulevard de Waterloo,
B-1060 Brussels,
Belgium
Telephone: +32-2-2891090
Telefax: +32-2-2891099
E-mail: info@eeb.org
<http://www.eeb.org>

Number of staff
Four full-time professionals, four part-time professionals, and two support staff in Brussels (April 1999).

Budget
The budget was ECU1,050,000 in 1997 and ECU900,000 in 1998, and is ECU1,288,000 in 1999.

Activities
The activities of the EEB focus on the EU's role in the field of environment, both within and beyond the EU's borders.

The EEB lobbies the European institutions to push them in their decision making towards a sustainable Europe in order to make a high level of environmental protection the basis for all programmes, plans, and policies. It achieves its objectives through a mixture of lobbying and generalized and specific publications, in addition to five to seven seminars or conferences, workshops, or round tables, which are open to the public.

During the period 1998–2000, the EEB will continue and increase pressure on the EU for effective, transparent, decisive, and sufficient environmental legislation; work for enlargement of the EU as a means for an improved environment and sustainable development; push for a sustainable development strategy for the EU; and promote green leadership of the EU in the global arena.

On top of the EEB's priority list for 1998–2000 are agriculture, industry, a sustainable development action plan for the EU, and greening the structural funds.

Forest Stewardship Council (FSC)

Objectives
To support environmentally appropriate, socially beneficial, and economically viable management of the world's forests.

Organization
Non-governmental organization (NGO). Liaison status with TC207, an International Standardization Organization (ISO) technical committee. Founded October 1933.

Membership
Representatives from environmental institutions, the timber trade, the forestry profession, indigenous peoples' organizations, community forestry groups, and forest product certification organizations. The FSC had 308 members in 50 countries by April 1999.

Secretariat
Forest Stewardship Council,
Avenida Hidalgo 502,
68000 Oaxaca,
Oaxaca,
Mexico
Telephone: +52-951-46905/63244
Telefax: +52-951-62110
E-mail: fscoax@fscoax.org
<http://www.fscoax.org>

Number of staff
Five professionals and five support staff at the Secretariat (April 1999).

Budget
The total budget was $780,500 in 1997 and $1,570,000 in 1998, and is $2,000,000 in 1999.

Activities
The mission of FSC is to support environmentally appropriate, socially beneficial, and economically viable stewardship of the world's forests. The organization hopes to accomplish this goal by evaluating, accrediting, and monitoring certification bodies, and by strengthening national certification and forest management capacity through training, education, and the development of national certification initiatives.

The FSC does not certify products itself; rather it ensures consumers that certification organizations have the highest level of credibility and integrity. The FSC provides this assurance by evaluating, accrediting, and monitoring certifiers of forest and forest products based on their adherence to the FSC principles, criteria, and guidelines for certifiers.

The FSC principles and criteria are intended to apply to all types of forests. They are designated to allow flexibility in their application through the development of national and regional standards, which fit ecological, social, and economic circumstances. The principles and criteria provide consistency among certifiers and their standards by supplying an overall framework for developing and evaluating local and national forest management standards.

The FSC also promotes forest stewardship by encouraging the development of local forest management standards worldwide. It encourages the formation of national and regional working groups to develop forest management standards. FSC provides guidelines and technical assistance to working groups and interested stakeholders for developing national and regional standards. To ensure that certification is based on realistic and locally defined forest management practices and to secure the consistency and integrity of standards in different countries around the world, FSC formally endorses those standards which clearly meet all FSC requirements, including the process leading to their development.

Friends of the Earth International (FoEI)

Objectives
- to protect the Earth against deterioration and restore damage inflicted upon the environment as a result of human activity and negligence;
- to preserve the Earth's ecological, cultural, and ethnic diversity;
- to increase public participation and democratic decision making in the protection of the environment and the management of natural resources, first and foremost by the people most directly affected;
- to achieve social, economic, and political justice and equal access to resources and opportunities on a local, national, and international level;
- to promote environmentally sustainable development on a local, national, and global level.

Organization
Non-governmental organization (NGO). Observer status at FAO, IMO, London Convention 1972, International Oil Pollution Compensation Fund, Barcelona Convention (see UNEP Regional Seas Programme, Agreements), International Whaling Commission (IWC) (see ICRW, Agreements), Ramsar Convention, International Tropical Timber Agreement (ITTA). Consultative status at UNESCO, UN Economic and Social Council (ECOSOC), and UN Economic Commission for Europe (UN/ECE). Participates in the meetings of International Atomic Energy Agency (IAEA), Intergovernmental Panel on Climate Change (IPCC) (see Framework Convention on Climate Change, Agreements), Montreal Protocol on Substances that Deplete the Ozone Layer, and others. Member of ELCI and IUCN (see this section). Founded in 1971.

Membership
National member groups and NGOs. Each national member group is an autonomous body with its own funding and strategy. Total of 59 national member groups in 58 countries and one territory, with about one million individual members by January 1999. Eight affiliated NGOs and one collaborating organization.

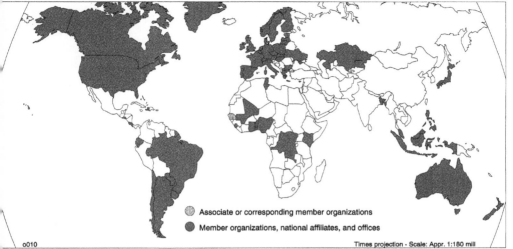

Associate or corresponding member organizations

Member organizations, national affiliates, and offices

o010   Times projection - Scale: Appr. 1:180 mill

Friends of Earth International (FoEI)

Secretariat
Friends of the Earth International (FoEI),
PO Box 19199, 1000 GD Amsterdam,
The Netherlands
Telephone: +31-20-6221369
Telefax: +31-20-6392181
E-mail: foeint@antenna.nl
<http://www.xs4all.nl/~foeint>

Number of staff
Three professionals, three support staff,
and four volunteers at the International Secretariat (January 1999).

Decision-making bodies
An Annual General Meeting of the national
organizations elects the FoEI Executive
Committee. The International Secretariat
in Amsterdam is crucial in the co-ordination of information exchange, joint campaigns, the development of the network, and
fundraising.

Finance and budget
Each national group is responsible for its
own budget and makes annual contributions
to the FoEI Secretariat. Main sources are
fees, donations, and subsidies.
  FoEI's total budget was $US675,000 in
1997 and $700,000 in 1998, and is $680,000
in 1999. The administrative budget of the
Secretariat was $US288,000 in 1997 and
$306,000 in 1998, and is $310,000 in 1999.

Activities
FoEI works to create networks of environmental, consumer, and human-rights organizations world-wide.
  It co-ordinates their activities at the international level through campaigns led by
national member groups. Main international co-ordinating areas are political
lobbying, flow of information through the
FoEI network, and citizen action with the
following principal areas: climate change,
tropical rainforests, ozone pollution, and
marine conservation. In 1999/2000 FoEI
has campaigns and projects running on
energy/climate change, mining, wetlands,
international finance institutions, sustainable societies, Amazonia, and environmentally sustainable trade. In addition it
lobbies on subjects such as Antarctica,
biosafety, G-8, and maritime issues.
  The organization keeps an eye especially
on sustainability, and looks at ways in
which the North can reduce its consumption of natural resources and the environmental space of the South can be increased.

Greenpeace International

Objectives
• to stop the chemicalization of the planet
and the trade in toxic waste and dirty technology;
• to protect the Earth's biological diversity of species in the ocean and on land;
• to end the threat of nuclear weapons, nu-

clear weapons testing, nuclear power, and
nuclear waste;
• to protect the Earth's atmosphere from
ozone depletion and build-up of greenhouse
gases and push for clean and alternative
energy and refrigeration technologies.

Organization
Non-governmental organization (NGO),
with offices world-wide. Consultative status with UN Economic and Social Council
(ECOSOC). Accredited to more than 30 international and regional organizations
dealing with environmental issues.
Founded in 1971.

Membership
World-wide individual membership of 2.5
million supporters in 158 countries by January 1999. Presences in 40 countries.

Secretariat
Greenpeace International,
Keizersgracht 176,
1016 DW Amsterdam,
The Netherlands
Telephone: +31-20-5236222
Telefax: +31-20-5236200
E-mail: webmaster@xs2.greenpeace.org
<http://www.greenpeace.org/>

Number of staff
About 1,000 world-wide (December 1998).
There are about 75 professionals at the In-
ternational Secretariat.

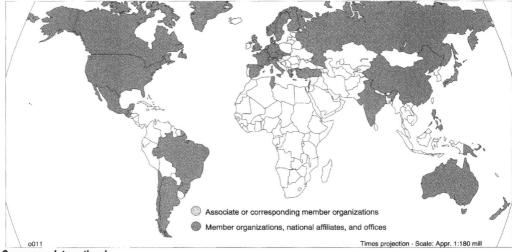

Associate or corresponding member organizations

Member organizations, national affiliates, and offices

o011   Times projection - Scale: Appr. 1:180 mill

Greenpeace International

Finance and budget

Financed by voluntary contributions from the public and from the sale of merchandise. The budget was $US28 million in 1997 and $24.4 million in 1998, and is $26.7 million in 1999.

Activities

In 1999 Greenpeace will focus campaign resources in a number of areas. These will include special efforts:
• to protect the planet's climate and ozone layer by ensuring that governments of industrialized countries radically cut emissions of polluting greenhouse and ozone-depleting gases;
• to protect the marine environment from over-fishing, pollution, and dumping of waste and other hazardous substances;
• to transform refrigeration, air-conditioning, and other industries in order to eliminate the use of ozone-depleting chemicals;
• to monitor and ensure enforcement of global controls on the international waste trade;
• to stop clearcutting and protect ancient rainforests, and to promote economic alternatives to intensive logging;
• to eliminate the use of hazardous chemicals, in particular chlorine, which is still used widely for paper bleaching, PVC, and other industrial applications, in spite of mounting evidence of their devastating impacts on human and animal health;
• to stop commercial whaling;

• to eliminate the use of drift-nets;
• to halt the nuclear threat.

International Chamber of Commerce (ICC)

Objectives
• to serve world business by promoting trade and investment and the market economy system;
• to represent business and defend the interests of the private sector in developed and developing countries and in the economies in transition;
• to facilitate commercial transactions among nations through the provision of practical services and training for business people.

Organization
Non-governmental organization (NGO). The ICC has first-class consultative status with the UN and its specialized agencies. The ICC was founded in June 1919, the Commission on Environment in 1978.

Membership
National committees or groups in 60 countries and two territories by May 1999.

Secretariat
ICC,
38 cours Albert 1er,
F-75008 Paris, France

Telephone:	+33-1-49532828
Telefax:	+33-1-49532924
E-mail:	icc@iccwbo.org
<http://www.iccwbo.org>	

Number of staff
90 professionals (May 1999).

Budget
No information available.

Activities
The ICC Commission on Environment, with members drawn from a wide cross-section of global industry, develops policy positions on four core areas of interest:
• *trade and environment*;
• *sustainable development*;
• *climate change*;
• *biosociety*.
The Commission also has standing advisory groups on environmental management systems (EMS) and waste management. The Commission works to formulate policy positions which are presented to all key UN agencies and conventions, as well as the World Trade Organization (WTO) (see IGOs).

The ICC also promotes its 1991 ICC Business Charter for Sustainable Development to industries world-wide.

International Confederation of Free Trade Unions (ICFTU)

Objectives
• to maintain and develop a powerful and effective international organization at world-wide and regional levels composed of free and democratic trade unions independent of any external domination and pledged to the task of promoting the interests of working people throughout the world and of enhancing the dignity of labour;
• to promote fair and just economic development on the basis that this development can ultimately be fair and socially just only if it is at the same time sustainable;
• to defend the right of individuals to mutual protection of their interests through forming and joining trade unions;
• to promote equality of opportunity for all people.

Organization
Non-governmental organization (NGO). Consultative status with the UN system. Accredited to UN Economic and Social Council (ECOSOC), ILO, IMF, UNESCO, FAO, UNIDO, IAEA, the World Bank, WTO, and WHO (see IGOs). Founded in December 1949.

Membership
Trade unions world-wide. 213 affiliated organizations in 134 countries and ten territories representing 123 million working people by January 1999.

Secretariat
International Confederation of Free Trade Unions (ICFTU),
Blvd. Émile Jacqmain 155 B1,
B-1210 Brussels,
Belgium
Telephone: +32-2-2240211
Telefax: +32-2-2015815/
                 2030756/2240297
E-mail: internetpo@icftu.org
<http://www.icftu.org>

Number of staff
70 at Head Office (January 1998).

Budget
The total budget was $US14.7 million in 1997 and $13.1 million in 1998, and is expected to be $13.1 million in 1999.

Activities
ICFTU made environment and development one of the main themes at its World Congress in 1996 and focused particularly on the international aspects of sustainable development.

It stressed the importance of involving workers in the decision-making process as the only means of ensuring that the necessary changes are carried out fairly, efficiently, and with the minimum amount of social disruption commensurate with achieving the goal of sustainable development.

It further stressed the need for resources to be made available in and to developing countries in order to ensure that they have the wherewithal to be able to undertake the sometimes costly activities that will be necessary to protect the environment.

The ICFTU sends a large delegation each year to the UN Commission for Sustainable Development (CSD) (see IGOs) in New York, with a particular focus on the Agenda 21 follow-up to the Rio Summit. The ICFTU has further been represented and taken an active role in the 1997 Kyoto and 1998 Buenos Aires conferences on Climate Change.

International Solar Energy Society (ISES)

Objectives
• to provide a common meeting-ground for all those concerned with the nature and utilization of solar energy;
• to foster science and technology relating to the applications of solar energy;
• to promote education and encourage research and development;
• to gather, compile, and disseminate information in these fields.

Organization
Non-governmental organization (NGO). Consultative status (category C) with UNESCO (see IGOs). Member of the UN Economic and Social Council (ECOSOC). Founded 24 December 1954.

Membership
Organizations, corporations, individuals, scientists, engineers, and others with a special interest in solar energy. Members in 128 countries or territories. National and regional sections in 48 countries by January 1999, representing 4,000 individual members.

Secretariat
International Solar Energy Society (ISES),
Villa Tannheim,
Wiesentalstrasse 50,
D-79115 Freiburg,
Germany
Telephone: +49-761-4590650
Telefax: +49-761-4590699
E-mail: hq@ises.org
<http://www.ises.org>
<http://wire.ises.org:8888/wire/wire.nsf>

Budget
No budget information is available.

Activities
The Society's interests embrace all aspects of solar energy, including characteristics, effects, and methods of use.

It organizes major international congresses on solar energy at which numerous scientific and technical papers are presented and discussed. These congresses are held every two years in different countries. The 1997 congress was held in Taejon, South Korea, where emphasis was placed on the rapid procurement of economic viability for solar energy technologies, and the increased global use of new and renewable sources of energy. The 1999 congress will be held in Jerusalem, Israel, in early July.

ISES publishes the proceedings of each international congress, usually in four volumes.

IUCN – The World Conservation Union

Objectives
The mission of IUCN is to influence, encourage, and assist societies throughout the world to conserve the integrity and diversity of nature. The objectives are:
• to secure the conservation of nature, and especially of biological diversity, as an essential foundation for the future;
• to ensure that, where the Earth's natural resources are used, this is done in a wise, equitable way;
• to guide the development of human communities towards ways of life that are both of good quality and in enduring harmony with other components of the biosphere.

Organization
Non-governmental organization (NGO). Consultative status with UN Economic and Social Council (ECOSOC), FAO, IMO, and

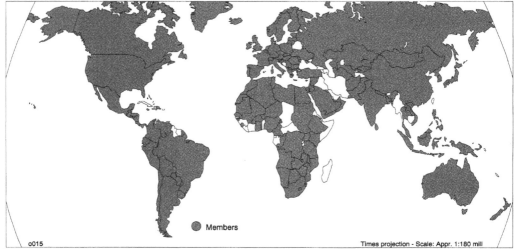

o015 Times projection - Scale: Appr. 1:180 mill

IUCN – The World Conservation Union

UNESCO (see IGOs). Founded 5 October 1948.

Membership
States (74), government agencies (106), national NGOs (650), international NGOs (61). Total of 928 members in 140 countries and territories by March 1999. 37 non-voting affiliates.

Secretariat
IUCN – The World Conservation Union, 28 rue Mauverney, CH-1196 Gland, Switzerland
Telephone: +41-22-9990001
Telefax: +41-22-9990002
E-mail: mail@hq.iucn.org

Director-General
Dr Maritta R. von Bieberstein Koch-Weser.

Director of Communications
Mr Javed Ahmad.

Publications Officer
Ms Deborah Murith.

IUCN Environmental Law Centre, Godesbergerallee 108–112, D-Bonn 53175, Germany

Telephone: +49-228-2692231
Telefax: +49-228-2692246
E-mail: iucn-elc@wunsch.com
<http://iucn.org>

Number of staff
820, of which 120 are based at headquarters and 700 are outposted staff, including consultants (March 1999).

Decision-making bodies
Political
A World Conservation Congress (previously General Assembly), which meets every three years, consists of delegates from the member bodies. The Congress elects the President, the Regional Councillors, and the Commission Chairs. The Council, which meets at least annually, consists of the President, up to four Vice-Presidents, 24 Regional Councillors, five appointed Councillors, and six Chairs of Commissions.

Scientific/technical
The six IUCN Commissions are:
• Ecosystem Management;
• Education and Communication;
• Environmental Law;
• Environmental, Economic, and Social Policy;
• Species Survival;
• World Commission on Protected Areas.

Finance and budget
IUCN membership dues constitute a basic source of discretionary funds. Specific financing of programmes and projects is also provided by individual governments and aid agencies, multilateral organizations (including UN agencies such as UNESCO and UNEP (see IGOs) and the Commission of the European Union), international NGOs (such as the World Wide Fund For Nature (WWF) (see this section)), foundations, the corporate sector, and individual donors. IUCN receives its income from government sources, foundations, corporations, membership, and others. The largest government supporters have been the Netherlands, Sweden, and Switzerland.

The total expenditure was SFr.63 million in 1996, Fr.76.1 million in 1997, and Fr.84.6 million in 1998.

Activities
IUCN carries out a single integrated programme. Approved by the triennial World Conservation Congress (previously General Assembly) (see below), the programme is co-ordinated by the central Secretariat (both at headquarters and in the regional and country offices) and implemented with assistance from the network of volunteer experts in the IUCN Commissions, consultants, and a wide range of IUCN members and collaborating agencies. The Union's activities include:
• harnessing the strengths of its members, Commissions, and other constituents to

build global partnerships for conservation;
• catalysing action by the Union's members, Secretariat, and Commissions in order to achieve more effective conservation of nature and natural resources in keeping with the principles set out in *Caring for the Earth*, the 1991 follow-up to the World Conservation Strategy (1980);
• providing a forum for government and NGO members to discuss global and regional conservation issues, including their scientific, educational, legal, economic, social, cultural, and political dimensions;
• contributing to an increased global awareness of the interrelationships between conservation, long-term survival, and human well-being, through publications, information dissemination, and education;
• communicating authoritative statements on conservation, drawing on the expertise of its members, Commissions, and Secretariat;
• developing national and regional strategies for sustainability, capacity building, and institutional support, a process often led by IUCN regional and country offices, in collaboration with governments and NGOs;
• influencing national and international legal and administrative instruments to safeguard the environmental rights of future generations;
• participating actively in the preparation of international conventions relevant to the conservation of nature and natural resources and equitable and sustainable resource use.

The IUCN Commissions (see below) constitute a global network of more than 8000 scientists and professionals.

The Environmental Law Centre (ELC) and the Commission on Environmental Law implement the legal aspects of the IUCN Law Programme. The main goals of the Environmental Law Programme are to promote the creation of sound international and national environmental legal instruments, to monitor developments in the field of environmental law, and to provide assistance and service in this field, especially to developing countries. It has been instrumental in the development of several conservation conventions, and, in addition to practice-oriented legal analysis and studies, carries out specific projects in over 20 countries. Its Environmental Law Information System (ELIS) comprises a comprehensive collection of material on international and national environmental law with more than 115,000 citations.

Pesticide Action Network (PAN)

Objectives
• to advocate adoption of ecologically sound practices in place of pesticide use;
• to encourage citizen action to challenge global proliferation of pesticides;
• to defend basic rights to health and environmental quality;
• to ensure transition to a just and viable society.

Organization
International coalition of non-governmental organizations (NGOs). Founded in 1984.

Membership
PAN had a total of five regional centres in five countries by May 1999. It is a coalition of over 400 citizens' groups in more than 60 countries.

Secretariat
The Pesticide Action Network has five regional centres:

Pesticide Action Network North America,
49 Powell Street, Suite 500,
San Francisco, CA 94102,
USA
Telephone: +1-415-9811771
Telefax: +1-415-9811991
E-mail: panna@panna.org
<http://www.panna.org/panna/>

Pesticide Action Network Asia–Pacific,
PO Box 1170,
10850 Penang,
Malaysia
Telefax: +60-4-6577445
E-mail: panap@panap.po.my

Pesticide Action Network Latin America,
Red de Acción en Alternativas al Uso de Agroquímicos,
Apartado Postal 11-0581,
Av. Mariscal Miller 2622-Lince,
Lima,
Peru
Telephone: +51-14-404359
Telefax: +51-14-404359
E-mail:rapalpe@mail.cosapidata.com.pe

Pesticide Action Network Europe,
c/o The Pesticides Trust,
Eurolink Business Centre,
49 Effra Road,
London SW2 1BZ,
United Kingdom
Telephone: +44-171-2748895

Telefax: +44-171-2748895
E-mail: pesttrust@gn.apc.org

Pesticide Action Network Africa,
Abou Thiam,
BP 15938,
Dakar-Fann,
Senegal
Telephone: +221-25-2914
Telefax: +221-25-2914
E-mail: panafric@sonatel.senet.net

Budget
The PAN centres each have their own budget. No information available.

Activities
PAN's activities combine information services, networking, and direct action. Although PAN's work is directed mainly towards pesticides and agriculture, its activities overlap many areas, including development policy, the environment, biotechnology, trade, health, wildlife, consumer protection, and community organizing. Each PAN centre works towards the same goals, but there may be differences in the ways in which issues are given priority.

Since its inception, PAN has published broadly on the uses of, consequences of, and alternatives to pesticides. As a result it has gathered a wealth of knowledge which is used through networking, education programmes, and bridge building between consumers, farmers, activist groups, business, and decision makers.

Campaigning for legislation to reduce the use of pesticides, lobbying, development monitoring, and promoting alternatives to pesticides are also important areas of PAN's activities. In 1999 PANNA ran, amongst others:
• a *methyl bromide* campaign, working to ensure that phase-out targets are met;
• a *fight hunger without pesticides* campaign, to prevent intensive use of chemicals and genetically engineered crops by lobbying development aid institutions, advising them to eliminate subsidies and support farmer to farmer education in management techniques;
• a *sustainable cotton production* campaign, promoting ecological pest control alternatives;
• a campaign to prevent the export of banned pesticides;
• a campaign to reform the World Bank's policies on pest control to support sustainable agriculture and farmer participation.

Sierra Club

Objectives
* to protect uninhabited places;
* to promote responsible use of the Earth's ecosystems and resources;
* to protect and restore the quality of the natural and human environment.

Organization
Non-governmental organization (NGO). Consultative status with UN Economic and Social Council (ECOSOC) and observer status with the International Whaling Commission (IWC) (see Agreements). Member of IUCN (see this section) and the Forest Stewardship Council (FSC) (see this section). The Sierra Club was founded in 1892, the International Program, as the international arm of the Sierra Club, in 1972.

Membership
Individuals and groups, primarily in North America. 600,000 members in 27 countries and offices in two countries (75 in USA and two in Canada) by January 1999.

The Club is also assisted by the Sierra Club Foundation (which has its own budget and staff).

Secretariat
The Washington Legislative Office is located at:
Sierra Club, International Program,
408 C Street, NE,
Washington, DC 20002,
USA
Telephone: +1-202-5471141
Telefax: +1-202-5476009
E-mail: information@sierraclub.org
<http://www.sierraclub.org>

Number of staff
250 professionals and 100 support staff (January 1999).

Budget
The total budget was $US52 million in 1996 and $50 million in 1997, and $50 million in 1998.

Activities
The Sierra Club is currently working for legislation that guarantees clean air and water; to regulate the use and disposal of poisonous toxic chemicals; to set aside the most special places for parks and wilderness; to protect tropical forests; to ensure that environmental trade agreements do not override US environmental laws; and to increase support for stabilizing population growth.

The Club pursues its aims through programmes to influence public policy, education, and litigation, and to provide assistance to environmentally minded candidates for public office. One programme aims to strengthen the safety of environmental activists in developing countries. The Club also runs campaigns on human rights and the environment and on global warming.

Society for International Development (SID)

Objectives
SID is a network of individuals and institutions concerned with participative, pluralistic, and sustainable development. It seeks to:
* bridge the gap between development theory and practice, between development policy makers and grassroot organizations, and between development experts and the general public;
* identify, gather, and disseminate information on innovative development initiatives to all relevant actors;
* mobilize and strengthen civil society groups by actively building partnerships among them and with other sectors.

Organization
Non-governmental organization (NGO). Consultative status (category I) with UN Economic and Social Council (ECOSOC). Consultative status with UNESCO, FAO, ILO, IFAD, UNCTAD, UNEP, UNFPA, and UNICEF (see IGOs), and with the Council of Europe. Founded 19 October 1957.

Membership
Individual and corporate members; associated institutional and international sponsors. Over 6,000 members in 115 countries and 62 local chapters by January 1999. Institutional presence through chapters and/or institutional members in 52 countries. It works with more than 200 associations, networks, and institutions, involving academia, parliamentarians, students, political leaders, and development experts, both at local and international levels.

Secretariat
Society for International Development,
207 via Panisperna,
I-00184 Rome,
Italy
Telephone: +39-06-4872172
Telefax: +39-06-4872170
E-mail: info@sidint.org
<http://www.sidint.org>

Budget
The budget was $US1,600,000 in 1997 and $1,800,000 in 1998, and is $2,000,000 in 1999.

Activities
SID's portfolio in the period 1998–2000 springs from a combination of two areas of activity and five thematic themes of interest. Most projects have elements from the two activity areas and from three or four of the interest areas.

The two areas of activity are:
* strengthening local innovations through local development initiatives. SID aims to draw public attention to innovative approaches to local development problems and to analyse the relationship between these experiments and the institutional framework;
* opening dialogues between the local and the global: activities in this area seek to enlarge political debates in order to address the contest between the local and the global. In addition, these projects intend to draw attention to the social and economic consequences of institutions and to the diversity of possible institutional arrangements. Finally, through the projects in this category, SID attempts to act as a catalyst between different constituencies.

The five areas of interest are:
* sustainable livelihoods;
* democratic approaches to governance;
* women's empowerment for economic and social justice;
* international relations, global values, and global governance;
* strengthening civil society in post-conflict situations.

Towards the end of 1998 the following SID projects were in the implementation phase or the advanced planning stage:
* the *Sustainable Livelihoods* project, a pilot project on addressing conflicts over natural resources, and *Innovative Institutions as a Basis for Democratization in the South* to strengthen local innovations;
* the *Democratization for Africa* project to examine possible future scenarios for

Third World societies and to broaden people's participation in the democratic proc-
ss;

the *Reproductive Health, Women's Empowerment, and Population Policies*
project, and a pilot project on *Adolescent
Reproductive Health*, to bring together
women's groups to promote the reproductive rights health agenda at local and in-
ernational levels;

the *Women and Cyberculture* project to
engage women from the technical, research,
and activist community to help transform
the new information communication technology into tools for advocacy and empowerment at the local and international levels;

the *People's Peace Process* initiative to
contribute to catalysing the process of partnership building between Israeli and Pal-
stinian civil society groups;

the *European Policies and Democratic
Governance Programme*;

*Responses to Globalization: Rethinking
Equity in Health.*

Third World Network (TWN)

Objectives

to promote a greater articulation of the
needs and rights of people of the Third
World;

to encourage a fair distribution of world
resources and forms of development which
fulfil people's needs and are ecologically
and humanely harmonious;

to exchange information and present
Third World perspectives to the industri-
lized countries as well as within the Third
World itself.

Organization

Non-governmental organization (NGO).
Consultative status with UN Conference
on Trade and Development (UNCTAD) and
UN Economic and Social Council
(ECOSOC). Accredited to the CSD (see
IGOs). Founded 14 November 1984.

Membership

NGOs and individuals. Nine full member
organizations in nine countries. Offices in
five countries by January 1999.

Secretariat

Third World Network (TWN),
228 Macalister Road,
10400 Penang,
Malaysia

Telephone: +60-4-2266 159/728
Telefax: +60-4-2264505
E-mail: twn@igc.apc.org
twnet@po.jaring.my
<http://twnside.org.sg>

Budget

No budget information is available.

Activities

The activities of TWN include:
• participation and involvement in global
and regional processes such as the CSD (see
IGOs), the Biological Diversity Convention (see Agreements), the General Agreement on Tariffs and Trade (GATT), the
World Bank (see IGOs), etc.;
• networking with NGOs on development
and the environment;
• research activities and publication of
books, magazines, and a news features service in the area of economics, the environment, health, and other development issues;
• organizing seminars, conferences, and
workshops.

Water Environment Federation (WEF)

Objectives

• to preserve and enhance the global water environment;
• to guide technological developments in
water quality and provide technical information to a world-wide audience;
• to review and comment on environmental regulations and legislation;
• to build alliances with other organizations;
• to export quality services to its members.

Organization

Non-governmental organization (NGO).
Consultative status with UNESCO (see
IGOs). Founded in 1928.

Membership

WEF is a federation of 73 member associations in 26 countries (representing 42,000
individual members) (May 1999). It has
five corresponding associations in five
countries, and members in 85 countries.

Secretariat

Water Environment Federation,
601 Wythe Street,
Alexandria, VA 22314-1994,
USA

Telephone: +1-703-6842400
Telefax: +1-703-6842492
E-mail: beisenberg@wef.org
<http://www.wef.org>

Number of staff
110 professionals (May 1999).

Budget

The total budget was $US17.5 million in
1996, $17.5 million in 1997, and $18 million in 1998.

Activities

For nearly 70 years WEF has guided technological developments in water quality
and provided its members and the public
with the latest information on waste-water treatment and water quality protection.
Federation representatives testify before
government bodies, and they review and
comment on environmental regulations and
legislation. The federation also provides
expertise on issues ranging from non-point
source pollution and hazardous waste to
biosolids reuse and groundwater contamination.

Through a co-operative agreement with
the Global Bureau of the US Agency for
International Development (AID), WEF
participates in the Environmental Pollution Prevention Project (EP3), which focuses on creating and supporting locally
sustainable pollution prevention programmes in developing countries.

Under a co-operative agreement with the
US Environmental Protection Agency's
Office of Water, WEF works together with
counterparts in Central and Eastern Europe
to solve environmental management and
waste-water treatment problems. The Federation is also working to create or expand
environmental professional associations in
Asia.

WEF sponsors technical meetings of representatives from Pacific Rim countries to
discuss environmental problems in the Pacific area. The Federation is active in efforts such as the Stockholm Water Prize and
Symposium, and the Global Water Network. In addition, it also arranges several
conferences and training programmes on
water quality and pollution control technology and issues. As a result, the Federation has published widely on these subjects.

Women's Environment and Development Organization (WEDO)

Objectives

WEDO is an international advocacy network actively working to transform society to achieve social, political, and environmental justice for all through the empowerment of women, and their equal participation with men, in decision making from grassroots to global arenas.

Organization

Non-governmental organization (NGO). Consultative status with UN Economic and Social Council (ECOSOC), the Global Water Partnership (GWP), the Earth Charter, the World Civil Society Conference, and the Millennium NGO Forum. Accredited to the Commission on Sustainable Development (CSD) (see IGOs) the International Conference on Population and Development (ICPD), the World Summit on Social Development (WSSD), the Fourth World Conference on Women (FWCW), Habitat II, the Commission on Status of Women (CSW), and the World Food Summit. Founded in 1990.

Membership

Network of 23,000 individuals and groups in more than 100 countries.

Secretariat

Women's Environment and Development Organization,
355 Lexington Avenue, 3rd Floor,
New York, NY 10017-6603,
USA
Telephone: +1-212-9730325
Telefax: +1-212-9730335
E-mail: wedo@igc.apc.org
<http://www.wedo.org>

Number of staff

13 professional full-time staff and three support staff (January 1999).

Budget

The annual operating budget was $US1.2 million in 1997 and $1.3 million in 1998, and is $1.5 million in 1999.

Activities

WEDO works to expand the development of a strong international women's monitoring and advocacy network for the integrated follow-up of all the major UN conferences. It provides and receives information and facilitates mutual flow of information among networks. Its work includes promoting new resource development for monitors in the global South. Among its activities are periodic training, exchanges and workshops, and the development of monitoring indicators, as well as continued strategic planning for advocacy initiatives towards the year 2000 review of the World Conference on Women, the Social Summit, and the Millennium People's Assembly.

WEDO supports the women's caucus project at the national level and development of new advocacy primers and manuals to serve this constituency. It seeks to provide a base for informed public education and action campaigns on the accountability of governments, the UN, the World Bank, the International Monetary Fund, the World Trade Organization, and transnational corporations.

Other campaigns will be carried out on concrete strategies from the UN Conference agendas such as Diverse Women for Biodiversity, overcoming poverty, structural debt relief, and gender exclusion. WEDO has a major focus on environment-linked cancers and policy changes at the government and private sector levels. It is committed to the completion and adoption of the Earth Charter, the full participation and leadership of women in country national councils for sustainable development, and global water policy.

World Business Council for Sustainable Development (WBCSD)

Objectives

- to be a leading business advocate for issues regarding the environment and sustainable development;
- to participate in policy development to create the right framework conditions for business to make an effective contribution towards sustainable development;
- to demonstrate progress in environmental and resource management in business and share leading-edge practices among members;
- to contribute to a sustainable future for developing nations and nations in transition.

Organization

Non-governmental organization (NGO). The Council was formed through a merger between the Business Council for Sustainable Development (BCSD) in Geneva and the World Industry Council for the Environment (WICE) in Paris. It maintains close links with the International Chamber of Commerce (ICC) (see this section). Founded in January 1995.

Membership

Membership of the WBCSD is by invitation to companies from around the world. As of 1 January 1999, 125 international companies in 30 countries were members.

In addition, the organization's Regional Network Program consists of 18 regional and national business councils and five BCSD partner organizations, in India, the Philippines, South Africa, Zimbabwe, and Russia.

Secretariat

World Business Council for Sustainable Development,
160 route de Florissant,
CH-1231 Conches-Geneva,
Switzerland
Telephone: +41-22-8393100
Telefax: +41-22-8393131
E-mail: info@wbcsd.ch
<http://www.wbcsd.ch>

Number of staff

30 professionals (January 1999).

Budget

No information available.

Activities

The WBCSD concentrates on five focus areas: eco-efficiency, sustainability through the market, corporate social responsibility, climate and energy, and natural resources. Further, in 1998 the organization embarked on two cross-cutting themes: technology and Innovation, and member sharing experience.

The WBCSD also has a Scenario Unit which provides services to WBCSD members. In 1996 the Foundation for Business and Sustainable Development was created with a specific educational remit to encourage major research initiatives. The Sustainable Business Challenge on the Internet, <http://challenge.bi.no>, is the first project initiated by the Foundation. In association with the University of Cambridge in the

United Kingdom, the Foundation has also developed a virtual university on the Internet.

The WBCSD continues to promote and disseminate eco-efficiency both at the practical level (through the encouragement of hands-on involvement with member companies and by publishing case-studies), and at the communications level. The WBCSD translated eco-efficiency publications into new languages in 1998 (Japanese), and published new publications on the subject of eco-efficiency.

An Eco-Efficiency Case Study Guide and Collection was launched on the WBCSD web site. The case-studies, chosen to show the real benefits—economic and environmental—achievable through eco-efficiency, are arranged under three key headings: cost savings, risk management, and market expansion.

A two-year long European Eco-efficiency Initiative, co-organized by the WBCSD in partnership with European Partners for the Environment (EPE), was launched in October 1998. This initiative aims to promote eco-efficiency across Europe.

In 1998 the WBCSD sought to bring a practical voice to the climate change debate, and focused its work on realistic, serious, and viable solutions to the climate change problem, including the flexibility mechanisms. The WBCSD participated in the Fourth Conference of the Parties in Buenos Aires in 1998, and was represented by Council Members at the Plenary Session.

The WBCSD has also been on the leading edge of opening up the dialogue between business leaders and environmental organizations. In September 1998 the WBCSD organized a two-day multi-level stakeholder dialogue on the topic of corporate social responsibility (CSR), which involved 60 high-level participants drawn from a diverse range of interest extending from business and academia to church groups, indigenous peoples, and human rights organizations.

On the topic of sustainability through market, the WBCSD held two stakeholder dialogues. The first one, on rights, roles, and responsibilities, helped to clarify the roles to be played by the various stakeholders and to outline ways to work together. The second, on innovation, was intended to help companies understand and anticipate the potential social consequences of innovation.

World Federalist Movement (WFM)

Objectives
• to promote the application of democratic federalist philosophy to matters of international democracy, such as promoting the democratization of the UN, and to seek to invest legal and political authority in global institutions to deal with problems which can be treated only at the global level, while affirming the sovereignty and diversity of peoples, local authorities, and the nation-state in matters which are essentially internal;
• to advocate measures to abolish war, by supporting efforts of the UN and its specialized agencies to preserve peace and protect life, and create and sustain environmental mechanisms and institutions.

Organization
Non-governmental organization (NGO). Consultative status with UN Economic and Social Council (ECOSOC). Accredited to UNESCO (see IGOs). Founded in 1947.

Membership
NGOs, parliamentary organizations, youth organizations, and individuals. 23 full member organizations in 20 countries by June 1999.

Secretariat
World Federalist Movement (WFM), 777 UN Plaza, New York, NY 10017, USA
Telephone: +1-212-5991320
Telefax: +1-212-5991332
E-mail: wfm@igc.org
<http://www.worldfederalist.org/>

Number of staff
Nine professionals and two support staff (January 1998).

Budget
The budget for the national and international movements was approximately $US2.5 million in 1996, $2.5 million in 1997, and $3 million in 1998. The international secretariat budget was $US400,000 in 1996, $500,000 in 1997, and $650,000 in 1998.

Activities
WFM focuses most of its activities on lobbying for supranational solutions to international environmental and developmental problems, with particular attention to the increasing economic globalization.

WFM is involved in campaigns to assure that governments implement the 1992 Earth Summit's Agenda 21 action plan. In order to achieve this, WFM calls for major institutional reforms, such as expanding UNEP (see IGOs) and enabling the UNCSD (see IGOs) to monitor the environmental records of the World Bank and the WTO (see IGOs).

WFM also works with several governments and other NGOs to achieve stronger binding enforcement mechanisms for the treaties covered by the UN Law of the Sea regime.

World Wide Fund For Nature (WWF)

Objectives
To conserve nature and ecological processes by:
• preserving genetic, species, and ecosystem diversity;
• ensuring that the use of renewable resources is sustainable both now and in the longer term;
• promoting actions to reduce pollution and the wasteful exploitation and consumption of resources and energy.

Organization
Non-governmental organization (NGO). Works in conjunction with governments, other NGOs, scientists, business and industry, the world's major religions, and people at the local level. Consultative status (category i) with UN Economic and Social Council (ECOSOC). *Founded* 11 September 1961. Formerly known as World Wildlife Fund, and continues to be known under its former name in Canada and the United States.

Membership
More than 4.7 million regular supporters world-wide. National organizations in 26 countries and one territory by January 1999. 22 programme offices. Associate organizations in five countries.

Secretariat
WWF International, Avenue du Mont-Blanc, CH-1196 Gland, Switzerland

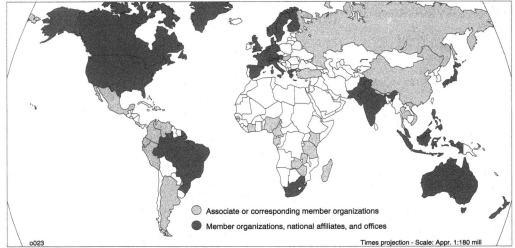

Associate or corresponding member organizations

Member organizations, national affiliates, and offices

o023   Times projection - Scale: Appr. 1:180 mill

World Wide Found For Nature (WWF)

Telephone: +41-22-3649111
Telefax: +41-22-3645358
E-mail: infobox@wwfnet.org
<http://www.panda.org>

Decision-making bodies
Board of Trustees (meets twice a year), Executive Committee, Programme Committee (twice a year).

Finance and budget
Sources of income in 1998 were individuals (48 per cent), governments and aid agencies (20 per cent), earned income (11 per cent), trusts and foundations (7 per cent), legacies (6 per cent), licensing (3 per cent), corporations (3 per cent), and others (2 per cent). WWF International benefits from substantial endowments, such as The 1001: A Nature Trust, to meet its basic running costs. This ensures that all contributions go directly to WWF's conservation programmes.

The overall income of WWF International, including all national organizations, was SFr.350 million in 1995/6,

Fr.430 million in 1996/7, and Fr.470 million in 1997/8.

WWF International's income was SFr.54.5 million in 1995/6, Fr.72 million in 1996/7, and Fr.74 million in 1997/8.

Activities
WWF actively supports and operates biodiversity conservation programmes on the ground in Africa, Asia, Europe, and Latin America. Since 1985 the WWF network has invested in more than 13,100 projects in 157 countries. World-wide, WWF undertakes more than 1,200 projects every year.

WWF's international campaigns have sought to spotlight crucial environmental issues and influence national and international policy decisions. Current WWF efforts range from eliminating destructive fishing methods and promoting sustainable forestry practices to advocating a reduction in greenhouse-gas emissions and lobbying for more equitable trade between industrial and developing countries. The organization also sponsors educational and training programmes for park and wildlife managers, ecologists, and teachers;

works with industry associations to improve environmental practices; and reinforces the effectiveness of wildlife trade monitoring through the TRAFFIC Network (the wildlife trade monitoring programme of WWF) and IUCN – The World Conservation Union.

WWF is emphasizing capacity building through such grant schemes as 'Across the Waters' and the WWF Prince Bernhard Scholarships for Nature Conservation.

In October 1996 WWF launched WWF2000—The Living Planet Campaign, based on WWF's three initiatives—Forests for Life, Endangered Seas, and Climate Change—and on the WWF Global Conservation Programme. The Living Planet Campaign focuses on three goals: to conserve spaces, to protect species, and to change consumption patterns. The campaign is a conservation action campaign, linking people, government, and organizations around the world through the Gifts to the Earth Initiative and by the conserving the Global 200 eco-regions, a representative selection of the world's most outstanding and distinctive biological regions.

Other Networking Instruments

Arab Network for Environment and Development (RAED)

Objectives
• to gather, disseminate, and exchange regional and international data on different environmental and developmental problems;
• to co-ordinate between regional community organizations in the exchange of skills and information;
• to mobilize already existing grass-roots organizations to have a share in this information and to partake in the problem-solving process;
• to create new grass-roots activities to be implemented by RAED's member organizations;
• to encourage the inclusion of community participation projects in government programmes.

Secretariat
c/o The Arab Office for Youth and Environment (AOYE),
PO Box 2,
Magles El Shaab,
Cairo,
Egypt
Telephone: +20-2-3041634
Telefax: +20-2-3041635
E-mail: aoye@ritsec1.com.eg

Main publications
Montada Al-Biah (monthly newsletter).

Sources on the Internet
<http://www.ecouncil.ac.cr/ngoexch/aoye.htm>

Both ENDS

Objectives
Both ENDS' founding mission is to support and strengthen southern NGOs in the field of environment and development. For the years 1998–2000 its specific objectives are:
• to identify innovative initiatives which combine ecological sustainability and social justice;
• to strengthen these initiatives through strategic co-operation, lobby and campaign activities, and support in capacity building;
• to present these initiatives in an interactive 'Encyclopedia of Sustainability' on the Internet, through media packs, and in various international forums.

Secretariat
Both ENDS,
Damrak 28–30,
1012 LJ Amsterdam,
The Netherlands
Telephone: +31-20-6230823
Telefax: +31-20-6208049
E-mail: info@bothends.org

Main publications
• general access guides;
• fund-raising guides;
• information sheets and packages.

Sources on the Internet
<http://www.bothends.org>

Global Legislators Organization for a Balanced Environment (GLOBE)

Objectives
• to enhance international co-operation between parliamentarians on global environmental issues;
• to highlight environmental problems and urge effective action by governments and private sector leaders, and to suggest alternative approaches;
• to create pressure to develop common environmental policy for sustainability across the planet.

Secretariat
GLOBE International,
50 rue du Taciturne,
B-1000 Brussels,
Belgium
Telephone: +32-2-2306589
Telefax: +32-2-2300104
E-mail: globeinter@village.uunet.be

Sources on the Internet
<http://globeint.org>

Regional Environmental Center for Central and Eastern Europe (REC)

Objectives
• to assist in solving the environmental problems in Central and Eastern Europe through the promotion of co-operation among NGOs, governments, business, and other environmental stakeholders;
• to promote free exchange of information and public participation in environmental decision making.

Secretariat
The Regional Environmental Center for Central and Eastern Europe,
Head Office,
Ady Endre ut 9–11,
H-2000 Szentendre,
Hungary
Telephone: +36-26-311199
Telefax: +36-26-311294
E-mail: info@rec.org

The REC has local offices in 15 Central and East European countries.

Main publications
• directories of environmental NGOs, businesses, and governments in Central and Eastern Europe;
• handbooks and manuals on public participation in environmental decision making in Central and Eastern Europe;
• regional reports on the approximation of European Union environmental legislation; the use of Economic Instruments; the status of Local, Regional and National Environmental Action Plans in Central and Eastern Europe;
• market surveys on the CEE environmental technology markets;
• regular quarterly newsletter (*The Bulletin*) in English and 15 local languages.

Sources on the Internet
<http://www.rec.org>

United Nations Non-Governmental Liaison Service (UN-NGLS)

Objectives
• to promote increased UN–NGO dialogue, understanding, and co-operation on international sustainable development issues;
• to bring important development and environment activities and issues of the UN system to the attention of NGOs;
• to work with southern and northern NGOs seeking access to UN system events, processes, and resources.

Organization
NGLS is an inter-agency programme of the UN system established in 1975.

Secretariat
UN-NGLS,
Palais des Nations,
CH-1211 Geneva 10,
Switzerland
Telephone: +41-22-9172076
Telefax: +41-22-9170049
E-mail: ngls@unctad.org

UN-NGLS,
Room FF-346,
United Nations,
New York, NY 10017,
USA
Telephone: +1-212-9633125
Telefax: +1-212-9638712
E-mail: ngls@undp.org

Main publications
• *Go Between* (bi-monthly newsletter);
• *The NGLS Handbook: UN Agencies Programmes, and Funds Working for Economic and Social Development*;
• *United Nations System: A Guide for NGOs*;
• *Voices from Africa* (series);
• *Roundup* (bi-monthly);
• *E+D File* (bi-monthly);
• *Development Dossiers* (series).

Sources on the Internet
<http://ngls.tad.ch>
E-conference: <ngls.news>

Tables of International Organizations and Degrees of Participation, by Country and Territory

Intergovernmental Organizations (IGOs)
International Council for the Exploration of the Sea (ICES)
OECD, Environment Policy Committee (EPOC)

Key

 States with observer status

 Member States

Non-Governmental Organizations (NGOs)
Basel Action Network (BAN)
Climate Action Network (CAN)
Consumers International (CI)
Earthwatch Institute
Environmental Liaison Centre International (ELCI)
European Environmental Bureau (EEB)
Forest Stewardship Council (FSC)
Friends of the Earth International (FoEI)
Greenpeace International
International Chamber of Commerce (ICC)
International Confederation of Free Trade Unions (ICFTU)
International Solar Energy Society (ISES)
IUCN - The World Conservation Union
Pesticide Action Network (PAN)
Sierra Club
Society for International Development (SID)
Third World Network (TWN)
Water Environment Federation (WEF)
World Business Council for Sustainable Development (WBCSD)
World Federalist Movement (WFM)
World Wide Fund For Nature (WWF)

Key

 General
Associate or corresponding member organizations

 Member organizations, national affiliates, and offices

 IUCN - The World Conservation Union
Members

Note: Most of the IGOs are not included, as the degree of participation is almost universal. For the degree of participation regarding the European Union (EU) and the Commission on Sustainable Development (CSD), see entries in the IGO subsection.

	Intern. Council for the Exploration of the Sea (ICES)	OECD, Environment Policy Committee (EPOC)	Basel Action Network (BAN)	Climate Action Network (CAN)	Consumers International (CI)	Earthwatch Institute	Environm. Liaison Centre International (ELCI)	European Environmental Bureau (EEB)	Forest Stewardship Council (FSC)	Friends of the Earth International (FoEI)	Greenpeace International	Intern. Chamber of Commerce (ICC)	Intern. Confederation of Free Trade Unions (ICFTU)	Intern. Solar Energy Society (ISES)	IUCN - The World Conservation Union	Pesticide Action Network (PAN)	Sierra Club	Society for International Development (SID)	Third World Network (TWN)	Water Environment Federation (WEF)	World Business Council for Sust. Devel. (WBCSD)	World Federalist Movement (WFM)	World Wide Fund for Nature (WWF)
Afghanistan															●								
Albania				●	●										●								
Algeria				●			●							●	●								
Andorra															●								
Angola				●										●	●								
Antigua & Barbuda															●								
Argentina				●	●		●			●	●	●	●	●	●			●			●	●	●
Armenia																							
Australia	●	●		●	●	●	●		●	●	●	●	●	●	●			●		●	●	●	●
Austria		●		●	●		●	●	●	●	●	●	●	●	●			●					●
Azerbaijan																							
Bahamas												●			●								
Bahrain													●										
Bangladesh				●	●		●				●		●	●	●			●	●		●		
Barbados							●							●	●								
Belarus				●	●																		
Belgium	●	●		●	●		●	●	●	●	●	●	●	●	●			●				●	●
Belize							●							●	●								
Benin					●		●				●				●								
Bhutan																							●
Bolivia				●	●		●			●				●	●								
Bosnia & Herzegovina																							
Botswana					●		●							●	●			●					
Brazil			●	●	●		●		●	●	●	●	●		●			●			●	●	●
Brunei Darussalam															●								
Bulgaria				●	●	●					●		●	●	●						●		
Burkina Faso				●	●		●					●		●	●								
Burundi							●																
Cambodia																							
Cameroon (U. Rep. of)				●			●	●						●	●			●				●	●
Canada	●	●	●	●	●		●		●	●	●	●	●	●	●		●	●			●	●	●
Cape Verde				●											●								

	ICES	EPOC	BAN	CAN	CI	Earthwatch	ELCI	EEB	FSC	FoEI	Greenpeace	ICC	ICFTU	ISES	IUCN	PAN	Sierra Club	SID	TWN	WEF	WBCSD	WFM	WWF
Central African Rep.							●						●										
Chad							●						●										
Chile			●	○			●	●	●	●	●	●		●							●		
China				●			●				●	●		●	●							●	○
Colombia							●		●			●		●	●					●		●	○
Comoros																							
Congo							●					●		●									
Congo (Dem. Rep. of)							●			●		●		●									
Cook Islands												●											
Costa Rica							●		●	●		●		●	●							○	○
Côte d'Ivoire			●				●					●											○
Croatia				●	○							●		●	●							●	
Cuba							●																
Cyprus					●			●	○		●	●	●	●	●							●	
Czech Republic		●		●				○			●	●		●	●							●	
Denmark	●	●		●	●		●	●	●	●	●	●	●	●	●			●			●	●	●
Djibouti												●											
Dominica												●											
Dominican Republic					○		●					●		●								●	
Ecuador				●	●		●		●	●		●		●									○
Egypt					○		●					●		●	●					●			
El Salvador					●		●			●		●						●			○		
Equatorial Guinea																							
Eritrea												●											
Estonia	●		●					●	●						●								
Ethiopia							●								●				○				
Fiji				●			●				●	●						●					○
Finland	●	●		●	●		●	●	●	●	●	●		●	●			●			○	●	●
France	●	●	●	●	●		●	●		●	●	●		●	●			●				●	●
Gabon					○		●					●											○
Gambia							●					●											
Georgia					○			○		●				●	●								

	Intern. Council for the Exploration of the Sea (ICES)	OECD, Environment Policy Committee (EPOC)	Basel Action Network (BAN)	Climate Action Network (CAN)	Consumers International (CI)	Earthwatch Institute	Environm. Liaison Centre International (ELCI)	European Environmental Bureau (EEB)	Forest Stewardship Council (FSC)	Friends of the Earth International (FoEI)	Greenpeace International	Intern. Chamber of Commerce (ICC)	Intern. Confederation of Free Trade Unions (ICFTU)	Intern. Solar Energy Society (ISES)	IUCN - The World Conservation Union	Pesticide Action Network (PAN)	Sierra Club	Society for International Development (SID)	Third World Network (TWN)	Water Environment Federation (WEF)	World Business Council for Sust. Devel. (WBCSD)	World Federalist Movement (WFM)	World Wide Fund for Nature (WWF)
Germany	●	●		●	●		●	●	●	●	●	●	●	●	●		●	●		●	●	●	●
Ghana				●	●		●		●	●				●	●			●	●				
Greece	●	●		●	●		●	●		●	●	●	●	●	●								●
Grenada										●					●								
Guatemala				●			●		●		●				●								
Guinea				●			●								●								
Guinea-Bissau							●								●	●							
Guyana				●			●			●					●								
Haiti		●								●								●					
Holy See (Vatican)															●								
Honduras				●			●		●				●		●						●		
Hungary		●		●	●		●	●		●		●	●	●	●			●		●			●
Iceland	●	●		●	●							●	●		●								
India		●	●	●			●		●		●	●	●	●	●			●	●		●	●	●
Indonesia		●	●	●			●		●	●		●	●		●				●		●		●
Iran (Islamic Rep. of)											●												
Iraq																							
Ireland	●	●		●	●			●		●	●		●	●	●								
Israel				●			●			●	●	●	●	●	●			●			●	●	
Italy		●		●	●		●	●	●	●	●	●	●	●	●			●			●	●	●
Jamaica				●			●							●	●								
Japan		●		●	●	●		●		●	●	●	●	●	●			●			●	●	●
Jordan							●					●	●		●								
Kazakhstan															●								
Kenya				●	●		●		●	●			●		●			●					●
Kiribati															●								
Korea (P. D. Rep. of)															●								
Korea (Rep. of)		●			●		●					●	●	●	●						●	●	●
Kuwait							●						●		●								
Kyrgyz Republic															●								
Laos															●								
Latvia	●			●						●			●		●								

Country / Territory	ICES	EPOC	BAN	CAN	CI	Earthwatch	ELCI	EEB	FSC	FoEI	Greenpeace	ICC	ICFTU	ISES	IUCN	PAN	Sierra Club	SID	TWN	WEF	WBCSD	WFM	WWF
Lebanon							●				●	●	●		●								
Lesotho					◐		●								●								
Liberia					◐		●						●				●						
Libyan Arab Jamah.							●								●								
Liechtenstein															●								
Lithuania				●	◐					●		●	●		●								
Luxembourg	●			●	●			●		●	●	●	●		●								
Macedonia (Rep. of)					◐						●				●								
Madagascar															●								◐
Malawi					◐		●						●		●								
Malaysia			●	●	●		●			●	●		●	●	●	●			●	●	●	◐	●
Maldives																							
Mali				●	●		●			●			●		●								
Malta				●	●		●	●	◐		●	●	●		●								
Marshall Islands				●																			
Mauritania							●						●		●								
Mauritius					●		●						●		●			●					
Mexico	●			●	●		●			●		●	●	●	●			●		●	●		◐
Micronesia (F. St. of)																							
Moldova (Rep. of)				●					◐				●		●								
Monaco															●								
Mongolia					◐								●		●								
Morocco				●	◐		●					●	●		●								
Mozambique					◐				●				●		●								
Myanmar																							
Namibia							●						●		●		●						
Nauru																							
Nepal				●	◐		●			●			●	●	●							●	◐
Netherlands	●	●	●	●	●		●	●	●	●	●	●	●		●			●		●	●	●	●
New Zealand	●			●	●		●		●	●	●		●		●						●	●	●
Nicaragua					◐		●		●				●		●								
Niger				●			●						●		●								

	ICES	EPOC	BAN	CAN	CI	EWI	ELCI	EEB	FSC	FoEI	GP	ICC	ICFTU	ISES	IUCN	PAN	SC	SID	TWN	WEF	WBCSD	WFM	WWF
Nigeria				●			●	●	●						●			●				●	●
Niue																							
Norway	●	●	●	●	●		●	●	●	●	●	●	●	●	●			●			●	●	●
Oman															●								
Pakistan				●	●		●					●	●		●			●					●
Palau																							
Panama				●			●	●				●			●								
Papua New Guinea				●			●	●	●			●			●								
Paraguay							●		●			●			●			●					
Peru				●	●		●		●			●	●		●	●							●
Philippines				●	●		●			●	●	●	●	●	●			●	●	●	●		●
Poland	●	●	●	●			●	●				●	●		●							●	
Portugal	●	●	●	●			●	●	●	●		●			●							●	
Qatar																							
Romania				●	●							●	●		●								
Russian Federation	●			●	●			●		●			●		●			●			●	●	●
Rwanda							●								●								
St Kitts & Nevis															●								
St Lucia															●								
St Vinc. & Grenadines															●								
Samoa (Western)				●			●	●							●	●							
San Marino															●								
São Tomé & Príncipe																							
Saudi Arabia							●					●			●								
Senegal			●	●			●			●			●		●	●	●	●					
Seychelles				●											●								
Sierra Leone							●		●			●			●								
Singapore							●				●	●			●					●			
Slovakia		●	●	●					●	●		●	●		●								
Slovenia		●		●									●	●									
Solomon Islands								●		●													
Somalia																							

	Intern. Council for the Exploration of the Sea (ICES)	OECD, Environment Policy Committee (EPOC)	Basel Action Network (BAN)	Climate Action Network (CAN)	Consumers International (CI)	Earthwatch Institute	Environm. Liaison Centre International (ELCI)	European Environmental Bureau (EEB)	Forest Stewardship Council (FSC)	Friends of the Earth International (FoEI)	Greenpeace International	Intern. Chamber of Commerce (ICC)	Intern. Confederation of Free Trade Unions (ICFTU)	Intern. Solar Energy Society (ISES)	IUCN - The World Conservation Union	Pesticide Action Network (PAN)	Sierra Club	Society for International Development (SID)	Third World Network (TWN)	Water Environment Federation (WEF)	World Business Council for Sust. Devel. (WBCSD)	World Federalist Movement (WFM)	World Wide Fund for Nature (WWF)
South Africa	●	●		●	●		●		●			●	●	●	●			●			●	●	●
Spain	●	●		●	●		●	●	●	●	●	●	●	●	●			●			●	●	●
Sri Lanka				●	●		●					●	●		●			●					
Sudan							●								●								
Suriname							●							●									
Swaziland												●		●									
Sweden	●	●		●	●		●	●	●	●	●	●	●	●	●					●	●	●	●
Switzerland		●		●	●			●	●	●	●	●	●	●	●			●		●	●	●	●
Syrian Arab Rep.												●			●								
Taiwan		●		●	●							●								●	●		
Tajikistan																							
Tanzania (U. Rep. of)			●	●			●					●			●			●					●
Thailand				●	●		●		●			●			●			●			●	●	●
Togo			●	●			●			●		●	●		●								
Tonga															●								
Trinidad & Tobago				●			●								●								
Tunisia				●	●		●			●	●	●	●		●			●					
Turkey		●		●			●	●			●	●	●	●	●			●			●		●
Turkmenistan				●											●								
Tuvalu																							
Uganda				●			●							●									
Ukraine			●	●					●		●		●	●									
United Arab Emirates				●											●								
United Kingdom	●	●	●	●	●	●	●	●	●	●	●	●	●	●	●	●		●		●	●	●	●
USA	●	●	●	●	●	●	●		●	●	●	●	●	●	●	●	●	●		●	●	●	●
Uruguay				●	●				●		●				●					●	●		
Uzbekistan															●								
Vanuatu														●									
Vatican (see Holy See)																							
Venezuela				●	●		●		●			●	●		●			●				●	●
Viet Nam				●	●										●								●
Yemen															●								

	Intern. Council for the Exploration of the Sea (ICES)	OECD, Environment Policy Committee (EPOC)	Basel Action Network (BAN)	Climate Action Network (CAN)	Consumers International (CI)	Earthwatch Institute	Environm. Liaison Centre International (ELCI)	European Environmental Bureau (EEB)	Forest Stewardship Council (FSC)	Friends of the Earth International (FoEI)	Greenpeace International	Intern. Chamber of Commerce (ICC)	Intern. Confederation of Free Trade Unions (ICFTU)	Intern. Solar Energy Society (ISES)	IUCN - The World Conservation Union	Pesticide Action Network (PAN)	Sierra Club	Society for International Development (SID)	Third World Network (TWN)	Water Environment Federation (WEF)	World Business Council for Sust. Devel. (WBCSD)	World Federalist Movement (WFM)	World Wide Fund for Nature (WWF)
Yugoslavia								●				●	●		●								
Zambia			●	●			●					●			●			●					●
Zimbabwe			●	●			●		●			●	●	●				●			●		●
European Union	●	●																					
Bermuda												●											
French Polynesia												●											
Hong Kong SAR				●						●		●											●
Macau				●																			
Montserrat												●											
Neth. Antilles				●				●															
New Caledonia					●							●											
Puerto Rico				●	●							●											

COUNTRY PROFILES

OECD countries

Selected non-OECD countries

Key

..	data not available
–	nil or negligible figure
n.a.	not applicable
n.p.	not party to the attached convention

Abbreviations

CFC	chlorofluorocarbons
CO_2	carbon dioxide
GDP	gross domestic product
GNP	gross national product
ha	hectares
HFC	hydrofluorocarbons
HM	heavy metals
inh	inhabitants
N_2O	nitrous oxide
NMVOC	non-methane volatile organic compunds
NO_2	nitrogen dioxide
NO_x	nitrogen oxides (or oxides of nitrogen)
PFC	perfluorocarbons
SDR	Special Drawing Rights, IMF unit of account
SF_6	sulphur hexafluoride
SO_2	sulphur dioxide
SO_x	sulphur oxide
toe	metric tonnes of oil equivalent

Australia

Area and population
Total area (km²): 7,713,000
Population (million): 18.6
Population density (inh/km²): 2.4
Life expectancy at birth (years): 80 (1998)
  (world average: 63)
Total fertility rate (children): 1.8 (1998)
  (world average: 2.9)

Economy
GNP per capita ($US000): 20.5 (1997)
  (world average: 5.1)

Growth rate
Average annual growth rate (%):
GNP per capita 1996–97: 1.8 (world average: 1.8)
GDP 1990–97: 3.7 (world average: 2.3)

Relations to Main International Agreements and Intergovernmental Organizations
Debt to the United Nations
Prior years: –
1998: $US1,015
Total: $US1,015

Compliance with reporting requirements

	Latest report submitted (latest year due to report)	Proportion of national reports submitted by all Parties (%)	Quality of data submitted
Transb. Air Pollution (LRTAP)	n.a.	..	n.a.
Climate Change (UNFCCC)	Late (1997)	100	..
Montreal Protocol	Late (1997)	60	Complete
Basel Convention	No report (1999)	31	n.a.
London Convention 1972	On time (1998)	..	..
MARPOL 73/78	On time (1998)	15	..
CITES	No report (1998)	49	n.a.
Ramsar Convention	Late (1998)	97	Complete

Contributions to funds related to agreements and main IGOs with environmental activities

	Amount	Share of total budget (%)
Transb. Air Pollution (LRTAP): Programme for Monitoring and Evaluation of the Long-Range Transmission of Air Pollutants in Europe (EMEP) (1999)	n.a.	n.a.
Ozone Layer Convention: Multilateral Fund for the Implementation of the Montreal Protocol (1997)	$US2,719,451	1.73
Global Environment Facility (GEF) (1994–7)	SDR20,840,000	1.44
International Maritime Organization (IMO) (1998)	$US182,115	0.61
United Nations Development Programme (UNDP) (1998)	$US8,260,000	1.11
United Nations Environment Programme (UNEP): Environment Fund (1998)	$US311,400	0.67
United Nations Population Fund (UNFPA) (1997)	$US1,593,750	0.55

General Environment and Development Performance Indicators

Official development aid (ODA)
Average annual ODA ($US million/% of GNP):
1993–95: 1,080/–

Per capita ($US):
1995: 67
(OECD average 1995: 65)

Energy consumption

	1973	1990	1996	(OECD average 1996)
Total (million toe)	40.0	58.1	66.1	(120.0)
Per capita (toe)	2.96	3.40	3.61	(3.19)
Per GDP (toe/$US000)	0.22	0.20	0.19	(0.17)

Central government expenditure on education, defence, and health

	Percentage of total central government expenditure		Percentage of GDP	
	1987	1996	1987	1996
Education	7.2	7.6	2.0	2.0
Military/defence	8.7	7.0	2.4	1.8
Health	12.0	14.3	3.3	3.8

Specific Environment Indicators

Atmosphere

SO$_x$ EMISSIONS
Total emissions (000 tonnes):
1980: ..
1985: ..
1995: 2,150

Per unit of GDP (kg/$US000):
1995: 6.7
(OECD average: 2.4)

Per capita (kg/capita):
1995: 119.1
(OECD average: 40.1)

Change from 1980 (%): ..

National emissions reduction target:
(*a*) according to official statement:
Stabilization of greenhouse gases not controlled by the Montreal Protocol at 1988 levels by 2000, and a 20% reduction by 2005. Whether this is a gas-by-gas target or a general target is not specified.

(*b*) according to the 1985 Sulphur Protocol:
n.a.

(*c*) according to the 1994 Sulphur Protocol:
n.a.

NO$_x$ EMISSIONS

Total emissions (000 tonnes):
1980: ..
1987: 2,198
1995: 2,129

Per unit of GDP (kg/$US000):
1995: 6.8
(OECD average: 2.4)

Per capita (kg/capita):
1995: 119.4
(OECD average: 39.7)

Change from 1987 (%): –3.1

National emissions reduction target:
(a) according to official statement:
Stabilization of greenhouse gases not controlled by the Montreal Protocol at 1988 levels by 2000, and a 20% reduction by 2005. Whether this is a gas-by-gas target or a general target is not specified.

(b) according to the NO$_x$ Protocol:
n.a.

CO$_2$ EMISSIONS

Energy-related emissions (million tonnes):
1973: 175.6
1990: 263.0
1996: 303.3

Per unit of GDP (tonnes/$US000):
1996: 0.87
(OECD average: 0.63)

Per capita (tonnes/capita):
1996: 16.6
(OECD average: 11.1)

Change from 1990 (%): +15.3

National emissions reduction target:
(a) according to official statement:
To stabilize emissions of greenhouse gases (not controlled by the Montreal Protocol on Ozone Depleting Substances), based on 1998 levels, by the year 2000, and to reduce those emissions by 20% by 2005. Whether this is a gas-by-gas target or a general target is not specified.

(b) emissions reduction target, covering CO$_2$ and five other greenhouse gases, according to the Kyoto Protocol:
+8% by the period 2008–12, taking 1990 as base year. Not ratified.

CH$_4$ EMISSIONS (METHANE)

Total emissions (000 tonnes):
1985: ..
1990: 5,590
1995: 5,302

Per unit of GDP (kg/$US000):
1995: 15.8

Per capita (kg/capita):
1995: 293.8

Change from 1990 (%): –5

National emissions reduction target:
(a) according to official statement:
To stabilize emissions of greenhouse gases (not controlled by the Montreal Protocol on Ozone Depleting Substances), based on 1998 levels, by the year 2000, and to reduce those emissions by 20% by 2005. Whether this is a gas-by-gas target or a general target is not specified.

(b) emissions reduction target, covering CH$_4$ and five other greenhouse gases, according to the Kyoto Protocol:
+8% by the period 2008–12, taking 1990 as base year. Not ratified.

CFC CONSUMPTION

Total consumption (tonnes):
1986: 14,290
1996: 234

Per capita (kg/capita):
1996: 0.01

Change from 1986 (%): –98.4

National reduction target according to the Montreal Protocol, Copenhagen Amendment:
–75% by 1994, taking 1986 as base year. Complete elimination by 1996. Target not achieved.

Hazardous substances

Consumption of pesticides per km² of arable land
(kg active ingredients per km²):
1980: ..
1985: ..
1995: ..
(OECD average 1995: 337)

Change from 1985 (%): ..
(OECD average: –15.8)

Hazardous waste
Production:
Total (000 tonnes): 426 (1992)

Per unit of GDP (kg/$US000): 1.5
(OECD average mid-1990s: 6.6)

Imports:
Total (000 tonnes): –
% production: –

Exports:
Total (000 tonnes): 3
% production: 0.7

Amounts to be managed (000 tonnes): 423

Nuclear waste
Total (tonnes HM): – (1996)
Per unit of total primary energy supply (tonnes/Mtoe): –

Marine living resources
Fish catches in marine and inland waters
Total catch (000 tonnes):
1980: 132
1990: 208
1995: 194

% of world catches:
1995: 0.2

Per capita (kg/person):
1995: 10.6

Nature conservation and terrestrial living resources
Wooded area
Area (000 km²):
1995: 1,491,750

Change in wooded area
Area (000 km²):
1990–95: –

As percentage of total area:
1990–95: –

Forest damage
Trees with greater than 25% defoliation (%):
1990: ..
1997: ..

Recycling of paper and cardboard
Recycling rate (%):
1985: 36
1990: 51
1995: 50
(OECD average 1995: 42)

Change from 1985 (%): +38.9

Protection (totally and partially) of natural areas
Area (000 ha): 53,708 (1997)
Percentage of land area: 7.0

World Heritage sites
Number: 11 (1997)
Area (000 ha): 42,479

Threatened species
Percentage of species known, mid-1990s:
Mammals: 13.8
Birds: 5.9
Fish: 0.4
Reptiles: 3.0
Amphibians: 5.0
Vascular plants: 4.0

Wetlands of international importance
Number: 49 (1997)
Area (000 ha): 5,067

Freshwater resources
Safe water
Percentage of the population having access: 95 (1995)

Annual internal renewable water resources
Total (km³): 343.0
Per capita (m³): 18,963 (1995)

Annual withdrawals
1970–98:
Total (km³): 14.60
Percentage of total water resources: 4
Per capita (m³): 933

Waste-water treatment
Percentage of population served by waste-water treatment plants:
All treatments:
1985: ..
1995: ..

Austria

Area and population
Total area (km²): 84,000
Population (million): 8.1
Population density (inh/km²): 97.0
Life expectancy at birth (years): 77 (1998)
  (world average: 63)
Total fertility rate (children): 1.4 (1998)
  (world average: 2.9)

Economy
GNP per capita ($US000): 28.0 (1997)
  (world average: 5.1)

Growth rate
Average annual growth rate (%):
GNP per capita 1996–97: 1.9 (world average: 1.8)
GDP 1990–97: 1.6 (world average: 2.3)

Relations to Main International Agreements and Intergovernmental Organizations
Debt to the United Nations
Prior years: –
1998: $US773,879
Total: $US773,879

Compliance with reporting requirements

	Latest report submitted (latest year due to report)	Proportion of national reports submitted by all Parties (%)	Quality of data submitted
Transb. Air Pollution (LRTAP)	1996 data reported	..	Complete
Climate Change (UNFCCC)	Late (1997)	100	..
Montreal Protocol	Late (1997)	60	Complete
Basel Convention	On time (1999)	31	..
London Convention 1972	n.a.	..	n.a.
MARPOL 73/78	No report (1998)	15	n.a.
CITES	On time (1998)	49	Complete
Ramsar Convention	Late (1998)	97	Complete

Contributions to funds related to agreements and main IGOs with environmental activities

	Amount	Share of total budget (%)
Transb. Air Pollution (LRTAP): Programme for Monitoring and Evaluation of the Long-Range Transmission of Air Pollutants in Europe (EMEP) (1999)	$US44,865	2.20
Ozone Layer Convention: Multilateral Fund for the Implementation of the Montreal Protocol (1997)	$US1,589,409	1.01
Global Environment Facility (GEF) (1994–7)	SDR14,280,000	0.99
International Maritime Organization (IMO) (1998)	$US30,850	0.10
United Nations Development Programme (UNDP) (1998)	$US10,050,000	1.35
United Nations Environment Programme (UNEP): Environment Fund (1998)	$US463,679	0.99
United Nations Population Fund (UNFPA) (1997)	$US545,956	0.19

General Environment and Development Performance Indicators

Official development aid (ODA)
Average annual ODA ($US million/% of GNP):
1993–95: 655/–

Per capita ($US):
1995: 95
(OECD average 1995: 65)

Energy consumption

	1973	1990	1996	(OECD average 1996)
Total (million toe)	17.0	21.1	22.2	(120.0)
Per capita (toe)	2.24	2.73	2.76	(3.19)
Per GDP (toe/$US000)	0.16	0.13	0.12	(0.17)

Central government expenditure on education, defence, and health

	Percentage of total central government expenditure		Percentage of GDP	
	1987	1996	1987	1996
Education	9.7	9.2	3.9	3.8
Military/defence	2.8	2.0	1.1	0.8
Health	12.2	13.0	4.9	5.4

Specific Environment Indicators

Atmosphere

SO$_x$ EMISSIONS
Total emissions (000 tonnes):
1980: 397
1985: 195
1995: 64

Per unit of GDP (kg/$US000):
1995: 0.4
(OECD average: 2.4)

Per capita (kg/capita):
1995: 8.0
(OECD average: 40.1)

Change from 1980 (%): –83.9

National emissions reduction target:
(*a*) according to official statement:
No specified target beyond the Sulphur Protocol.

(*b*) according to the 1985 Sulphur Protocol:
–30% by 1993, taking 1980 as base year. Target achieved.

(*c*) according to the 1994 Sulphur Protocol:
–80% by 2000, taking 1980 as base year.

NO_x EMISSIONS
Total emissions (000 tonnes):
1980: 246
1987: 234
1995: 175

Per unit of GDP (kg/$US000):
1995: 1.2
(OECD average: 2.4)

Per capita (kg/capita):
1995: 21.7
(OECD average: 39.7)

Change from 1987 (%): −25.2

National emissions reduction target:
(a) according to official statement:
−40% by 1996, −60% by 2001, and −70% by 2006, taking 1985 as base year.

(b) according to the NO_x Protocol:
Stabilization by 1995, taking 1987 as base year.

CO_2 EMISSIONS
Energy-related emissions (million tonnes):
1973: 58.6
1990: 58.5
1996: 62.7

Per unit of GDP (tonnes/$US000):
1996: 0.36
(OECD average: 0.63)

Per capita (tonnes/capita):
1996: 7.8
(OECD average: 11.1)

Change from 1990 (%): +5.6

National emissions reduction target:
(a) according to official statement:
20% reduction of 1988 levels by 2005. Applies to all anthropogenic CO_2 emissions, but energy-related emissions get particular emphasis.

(b) emissions reduction target, covering CO_2 and five other greenhouse gases, according to the Kyoto Protocol:
−8% for EU as a whole; and

−13% for Austria according to the EU burden-sharing plan of 17 June 1998, by the period 2008–12, compared to 1990 levels.
Not ratified.

CH_4 EMISSIONS (METHANE)
Total emissions (000 tonnes):
1985: ..
1990: 587
1995: 580

Per unit of GDP (kg/$US000):
1995: 3.9

Per capita (kg/capita):
1995: 72.1

Change from 1990 (%): −1

Emissions reduction target, covering CH_4 and five other greenhouse gases, according to the Kyoto Protocol:
−8% for EU as a whole; and
−13% for Austria according to the EU burden-sharing plan of 17 June 1998, by the period 2008–12, compared to 1990 levels.
Not ratified.

CFC CONSUMPTION
Total consumption (tonnes):
1986: 7,760
1996: n.a.

Per capita (kg/capita):
1996: n.a.

Change from 1986 (%): n.a.

National reduction target according to the Montreal Protocol, Copenhagen Amendment:
n.a.

Hazardous substances
Consumption of pesticides per km² of arable land
(kg active ingredients per km²):
1980: 264
1985: 346
1995: 225
(OECD average 1995: 337)

Change from 1985 (%): −34.9
(OECD average: −15.8)

Hazardous waste
Production:
Total (000 tonnes): 513 (1994)

Per unit of GDP (kg/$US000): 3.2
(OECD average mid-1990s: 6.6)

Imports:
Total (000 tonnes): 16
% production: 3.1

Exports:
Total (000 tonnes): 27
% production: 5.3

Amounts to be managed (000 tonnes): 502

Nuclear waste
Total (tonnes HM): – (1996)
Per unit of total primary energy supply (tonnes/Mtoe): –

Marine living resources
Fish catches in marine and inland waters
Total catch (000 tonnes):
1980: 4
1990: 1
1995: –

% of world catches:
1995: –

Per capita (kg/person):
1995: –

Nature conservation and terrestrial living resources
Wooded area
Area (000 km²):
1995: 38,780

Change in wooded area
Area (000 km²):
1990–95: –

As percentage of total area:
1990–95: –

Forest damage
Trees with greater than 25% defoliation (%):
1990: 9.1
1997: 7.1

Recycling of paper and cardboard
Recycling rate (%):
1985: 37
1990: 37
1995: 65
(OECD average 1995: 42)

Change from 1985 (%): +75.7

Protection (totally and partially) of natural areas
Area (000 ha): 2,344 (1997)
Percentage of land area: 28.3

World Heritage sites
Number: 0 (1997)
Area (000 ha): –

Threatened species
Percentage of species known, mid-1990s:
Mammals: 37.5
Birds: 28.1
Fish: 42.5
Reptiles: 100
Amphibians: 94.7
Vascular plants: 7.2

Wetlands of international importance
Number: 9 (1997)
Area (000 ha): 103

Freshwater resources
Safe water
Percentage of the population having access: .. (1995)

Annual internal renewable water resources
Total (km³): 56.30
Per capita (m³): 6,857 (1998)

Annual withdrawals
1970–98:
Total (km³): 2.36
Percentage of total water resources: 4
Per capita (m³): 304

Waste-water treatment
Percentage of population served by waste-water treatment plants:
All treatments:
1985: 65.0
1995: 74.7

Czech Republic

Area and population
Total area (km²): 79,000
Population (million): 10.3
Population density (inh/km²): 130.7
Life expectancy at birth (years): 74 (1998)
  (world average: 63)
Total fertility rate (children): 1.2 (1998)
  (world average: 2.9)

Economy
GNP per capita ($US000): 5.2 (1997)
  (world average: 5.1)

Growth rate
Average annual growth rate (%):
GNP per capita 1996–97: 0.8 (world average: 1.8)
GDP 1990–97: 1.0 (world average: 2.3)

Relations to Main International Agreements and Intergovernmental Organizations
Debt to the United Nations
Prior years: –
1998: $US262,724
Total: $US262,724

Compliance with reporting requirements

	Latest report submitted (latest year due to report)	Proportion of national reports submitted by all Parties (%)	Quality of data submitted
Transb. Air Pollution (LRTAP)	1996 data reported	..	Complete
Climate Change (UNFCCC)	On time (1998)	100	..
Montreal Protocol	Late (1997)	60	Complete
Basel Convention	On time (1999)	31	..
London Convention 1972	n.a.	..	n.a.
MARPOL 73/78	No report (1998)	15	n.a.
CITES	On time (1998)	49	Complete
Ramsar Convention	On time (1998)	97	Complete

Contributions to funds related to agreements and main IGOs with environmental activities

	Amount	Share of total budget (%)
Transb. Air Pollution (LRTAP): Programme for Monitoring and Evaluation of the Long-Range Transmission of Air Pollutants in Europe (EMEP) (1999)	$US5,769	0.28
Ozone Layer Convention: Multilateral Fund for the Implementation of the Montreal Protocol (1997)	$US376,958	0.24
Global Environment Facility (GEF) (1994–7)	SDR4,000,000	0.28
International Maritime Organization (IMO) (1998)	$US14,858	0.05
United Nations Development Programme (UNDP) (1998)	–	–
United Nations Environment Programme (UNEP): Environment Fund (1998)	$US91,185	0.20
United Nations Population Fund (UNFPA) (1997)	$US59,880	0.02

General Environment and Development Performance Indicators

Official development aid (ODA)
Average annual ODA ($US million/% of GNP):
1993–95: 129/–

Per capita ($US):
1995: –14
(OECD average 1995: 65)

Energy consumption

	1973	1990	1996	(OECD average 1996)
Total (million toe)	..	..	27.7	(120.0)
Per capita (toe)	..	..	..	(3.19)
Per GDP (toe/$US000)	..	..	..	(0.17)

Central government expenditure on education, defence, and health

	Percentage of total central government expenditure		Percentage of GDP	
	1987	1996	1987	1996
Education	..	11.6	..	4.3
Military/defence	..	5.5	..	2.0
Health	..	17.1	..	6.3

Specific Environment Indicators

Atmosphere

SO$_x$ EMISSIONS
Total emissions (000 tonnes):
1980: 2,257
1985: 2,277
1995: 1,091

Per unit of GDP (kg/$US000):
1995: 12.2
(OECD average: 2.4)

Per capita (kg/capita):
1995: 105.6
(OECD average: 40.1)

Change from 1980 (%): –51.7

National emissions reduction target:
(*a*) according to official statement:
No specified target beyond the Sulphur Protocol.

(*b*) according to the 1985 Sulphur Protocol:
–30% by 1993, taking 1980 as base year. Target not achieved.

(*c*) according to the 1994 Sulphur Protocol:
–50% by 2000, –60% by 2005, and –72% by 2010, taking 1980 as base year.

Total emissions (000 tonnes):
1980: 937
1987: 816
1995: 412

Per unit of GDP (kg/$US000):
1995: 4.6
(OECD average: 2.4)

Per capita (kg/capita):
1995: 39.9
(OECD average: 39.7)

Change from 1987 (%): −49.5

National emissions reduction target:
(a) according to official statement:
No specified target beyond the NO$_x$ Protocol.

(b) according to the NO$_x$ Protocol:
Stabilization by 1995, taking 1987 as base year.

CO$_2$ EMISSIONS
Energy-related emissions (million tonnes):
1973: ..
1990: 163.8
1996: 119.6

Per unit of GDP (tonnes/$US000):
1996: 4.48
(OECD average: 0.63)

Per capita (tonnes/capita):
1996: 11.6
(OECD average: 11.1)

Change from 1990 (%): −27.0

Emissions reduction target, covering CO$_2$ and five other greenhouse gases, according to the Kyoto Protocol: −8% by the period 2008–12, taking 1990 as base year. Not ratified.

CH$_4$ EMISSIONS (METHANE)
Total emissions (000 tonnes):
1985: ..
1990: 888
1995: 733

Per unit of GDP (kg/$US000):
1995: 7.9

Per capita (kg/capita):
1995: 71.0

Change from 1990 (%): −17

Emissions reduction target, covering CH$_4$ and five other greenhouse gases, according to the Kyoto Protocol: −8% by the period 2008–12, taking 1990 as base year. Not ratified.

CFC CONSUMPTION
Total consumption (tonnes):
1986: 5,460
1996: 50

Per capita (kg/capita):
1996: −

Change from 1986 (%): −99.1

National reduction target according to the Montreal Protocol, Copenhagen Amendment:
A freeze of 1995–7 average level by 1999, −50% by 2005, −85% by 2007, and complete elimination by 2010.

Hazardous substances
Consumption of pesticides per km^2 of arable land
(kg active ingredients per km^2):
1980: ..
1985: 287
1995: 106
(OECD average 1995: 337)

Change from 1985 (%): −63.0
(OECD average: −15.8)

Hazardous waste
Production:
Total (000 tonnes): 1,867 (1994)

Per unit of GDP (kg/$US000): 21.9
(OECD average mid-1990s: 6.6)

Imports:
Total (000 tonnes): 6
% production: 0.3

Exports:
Total (000 tonnes): 1
% production: –

Amounts to be managed (000 tonnes): 1,872

Nuclear waste
Total (tonnes HM): 45 (1996)
Per unit of total primary energy supply (tonnes/Mtoe):
1.1

Marine living resources
Fish catches in marine and inland waters
Total catch (000 tonnes):
1980: ..
1990: ..
1995: 1

% of world catches:
1995: –

Per capita (kg/person):
1995: 0.1

Nature conservation and terrestrial living resources
Wooded area
Area (000 km²):
1995: 26,300

Change in wooded area
Area (000 km²):
1990–95: +10

As percentage of total area:
1990–95: –

Forest damage
Trees with greater than 25% defoliation (%):
1990: 45.3
1997: 68.6

Recycling of paper and cardboard
Recycling rate (%):
1985: ..
1990: 10
1995: ..
(OECD average 1995: 42)

Change from 1985 (%): ..

Protection (totally and partially) of natural areas
Area (000 ha): 1,223 (1997)
Percentage of land area: 15.8

World Heritage sites
Number: 0 (1997)
Area (000 ha): –

Threatened species
Percentage of species known, mid-1990s:
Mammals: 29.9
Birds: 28.2
Fish: 6.2
Reptiles: 61.5
Amphibians: 65.0
Vascular plants: 20.3

Wetlands of international importance
Number: 9 (1997)
Area (000 ha): 39

Freshwater resources
Safe water
Percentage of the population having access: .. (1995)

Annual internal renewable water resources
Total (km³): 58.21
Per capita (m³): 5,964 (1998)

Annual withdrawals
1970–98:
Total (km³): 2.74
Percentage of total water resources: 5
Per capita (m³): 266

Waste-water treatment
Percentage of population served by waste-water treatment
plants:
All treatments:
1985: 47.5
1995: 56.0

Denmark

Area and population
Total area (km²): 43,000
Population (million): 5.3
Population density (inh/km²): 123.8
Life expectancy at birth (years): 76 (1998)
   (world average: 63)
Total fertility rate (children): 1.7 (1998)
   (world average: 2.9)

Economy
GNP per capita ($US000): 32.5 (1997)
   (world average: 5.1)

Growth rate
Average annual growth rate (%):
GNP per capita 1996–97: 3.1 (world average: 1.8)
GDP 1990–97: 2.3 (world average: 2.3)

Relations to Main International Agreements and Intergovernmental Organizations
Debt to the United Nations
Prior years: –
1998: –
Total: –

Compliance with reporting requirements

	Latest report submitted (latest year due to report)	Proportion of national reports submitted by all Parties (%)	Quality of data submitted
Transb. Air Pollution (LRTAP)	1996 data reported	..	Complete
Climate Change (UNFCCC)	Late (1997)	100	..
Montreal Protocol	On time (1997)	60	Complete
Basel Convention	No report (1999)	31	n.a.
London Convention 1972	No report (1998)	..	n.a.
MARPOL 73/78	No report (1998)	15	n.a.
CITES	On time (1998)	49	Complete
Ramsar Convention	On time (1998)	97	Complete

Contributions to funds related to agreements and main IGOs with environmental activities

	Amount	Share of total budget (%)
Transb. Air Pollution (LRTAP): Programme for Monitoring and Evaluation of the Long-Range Transmission of Air Pollutants in Europe (EMEP) (1999)	$US32,946	1.61
Ozone Layer Convention: Multilateral Fund for the Implementation of the Montreal Protocol (1997)	$US1,318,383	0.84
Global Environment Facility (GEF) (1994–7)	SDR25,080,000	1.73
International Maritime Organization (IMO) (1998)	$US306,874	1.02
United Nations Development Programme (UNDP) (1998)	$US84,550,000	11.34
United Nations Environment Programme (UNEP): Environment Fund (1998)	$US2,392,573	5.12
United Nations Population Fund (UNFPA) (1997)	$US33,824,416	11.78

General Environment and Development Performance Indicators
Official development aid (ODA)
Average annual ODA ($US million/% of GNP):
1993–95: 1,470/1.0

Per capita ($US):
1995: 311
(OECD average 1995: 65)

Energy consumption

	1973	1990	1996	(OECD average 1996)
Total (million toe)	16.1	14.1	16.4	(120.0)
Per capita (toe)	3.21	2.74	3.11	(3.19)
Per GDP (toe/$US000)	0.17	0.11	0.11	(0.17)

Central government expenditure on education, defence, and health

	Percentage of total central government expenditure		Percentage of GDP	
	1987	1996	1987	1996
Education	9.0	9.4	3.4	3.9
Military/defence	5.3	4.0	2.0	1.7
Health	1.2	0.8	0.4	0.3

Specific Environment Indicators
Atmosphere

SO_x EMISSIONS
Total emissions (000 tonnes):
1980: 449
1985: 339
1995: 148

Per unit of GDP (kg/$US000):
1995: 1.5
(OECD average: 2.4)

Per capita (kg/capita):
1995: 28.3
(OECD average: 40.1)

Change from 1980 (%): –67.0

National emissions reduction target:
(a) according to official statement:
No specified target beyond the Sulphur Protocol.

(b) according to the 1985 Sulphur Protocol:
–30% by 1993, taking 1980 as base year. Target achieved.

(c) according to the 1994 Sulphur Protocol:
–80% by 2000, taking 1980 as base year.

NO$_x$ EMISSIONS
Total emissions (000 tonnes):
1980: 281
1987: 309
1995: 251

Per unit of GDP (kg/$US000):
1995: 2.6
(OECD average: 2.4)

Per capita (kg/capita):
1995: 48.0
(OECD average: 39.7)

Change from 1987 (%): −18.8

National emissions reduction target:
(a) according to official statement:
−50% from the agricultural sector into the aquatic environment and to the air by 2000, taking 1985 as base year. −40% by 2000 and −60% by 2010 in the transport sector, taking 1988 as base year. Total reduction of 35% by 2000, taking 1988 as base year.

(b) according to the NO$_x$ Protocol:
Stabilization by 1995, taking 1987 as base year.

CO$_2$ EMISSIONS
Energy-related emissions (million tonnes):
1973: 59.4
1990: 52.8
1996: 72.3

Per unit of GDP (tonnes/$US000):
1996: 0.49
(OECD average: 0.63)

Per capita (tonnes/capita):
1996: 13.7
(OECD average: 11.1)

Change from 1990 (%): +36.7

National emissions reduction target:
(a) according to official statement:
20% reduction of 1988 levels by 2005. Applies to national emissions adjusted for climate and electricity imports and exports.

(b) according to the Kyoto Protocol:
Emissions reduction target, covering CO$_2$ and five other greenhouse gases, according to the Kyoto Protocol:
−8% for EU as a whole; and
−21% for Denmark according to the EU burden-sharing plan of 17 June 1998, by the period 2008–12, compared to 1990 levels.
Not ratified.

CH$_4$ EMISSIONS (METHANE)
Total emissions (000 tonnes):
1985: 452
1990: 407
1995: 401

Per unit of GDP (kg/$US000):
1995: 4.0

Per capita (kg/capita):
1995: 76.7

Change from 1990 (%): −1

Emissions reduction target, covering CH$_4$ and five other greenhouse gases, according to the Kyoto Protocol:
−8% for EU as a whole; and
−21% for Denmark according to the EU burden-sharing plan of 17 June 1998, by the period 2008–12, compared to 1990 levels.
Not ratified.

CFC CONSUMPTION
Total consumption (tonnes):
1986: n.a.
1996: n.a.

Per capita (kg/capita):
1996: n.a.

Change from 1986 (%): n.a.

National reduction target according to the Montreal Protocol, Copenhagen Amendment:
−75% by 1994, taking 1986 as base year. Complete elimination by 1996.

Hazardous substances
Consumption of pesticides per km^2 of arable land
(kg active ingredients per km^2):
1980: 186
1985: 263
1995: 212
(OECD average 1995: 337)

Change from 1985 (%): −19.3
(OECD average: −15.8)

Hazardous waste
Production:
Total (000 tonnes): 250 (1995)

Per unit of GDP (kg/$US000): 2.2
(OECD average mid-1990s: 6.6)

Imports:
Total (000 tonnes): 64
% production: 25.6

Exports:
Total (000 tonnes): 30
% production: 12.0

Amounts to be managed (000 tonnes): 284

Nuclear waste
Total (tonnes HM): – (1996)
Per unit of total primary energy supply (tonnes/Mtoe): –

Marine living resources
Fish catches in marine and inland waters
Total catch (000 tonnes):
1980: 2,032
1990: 1,476
1995: 1,999

% of world catches:
1995: 2.2

Per capita (kg/person):
1995: 379.9

Nature conservation and terrestrial living resources
Wooded area
Area (000 km²):
1995: 4,450

Change in wooded area
Area (000 km²):
1990–95: –

As percentage of total area:
1990–95: –

Forest damage
Trees with greater than 25% defoliation (%):
1990: 21.2
1997: 20.7

Recycling of paper and cardboard
Recycling rate (%):
1985: 31
1990: 35
1995: 44
(OECD average 1995: 42)

Change from 1985 (%): +41.9

Protection (totally and partially) of natural areas
Area (000 ha): 1,368 (1997)
Percentage of land area: 32.2

World Heritage sites
Number: 0 (1997)
Area (000 ha): –

Threatened species
Percentage of species known, mid-1990s:
Mammals: 24.0
Birds: 12.9
Fish: 18.2
Reptiles: –
Amphibians: 28.6
Vascular plants: 9.8

Wetlands of international importance
Number: 38 (1997)
Area (000 ha): 1,833

Freshwater resources
Safe water
Percentage of the population having access: 100 (1995)

Annual internal renewable water resources
Total (km³): 11.00
Per capita (m³): 1,092 (1998)

Annual withdrawals
1970–98:
Total (km³): 1.20
Percentage of total water resources: 11
Per capita (m³): 233

Waste-water treatment
Percentage of population served by waste-water treatment plants:
All treatments:
1985: 91.0
1995: 99.0

Finland

Area and population
Total area (km²): 338,000
Population (million): 5.1
Population density (inh/km²): 15.3
Life expectancy at birth (years): 77 (1998)
  (world average: 63)
Total fertility rate (children): 1.7 (1998)
  (world average: 2.9)

Economy
GNP per capita ($US000): 24.1 (1997)
  (world average: 5.1)

Growth rate
Average annual growth rate (%):
GNP per capita 1996–97: 4.3 (world average: 1.8)
GDP 1990–97: 1.1 (world average: 2.3)

Relations to Main International Agreements and Intergovernmental Organizations
Debt to the United Nations
Prior years: –
1998: –
Total: –

Compliance with reporting requirements

	Latest report submitted (latest year due to report)	Proportion of national reports submitted by all Parties (%)	Quality of data submitted
Transb. Air Pollution (LRTAP)	1996 data reported	..	Complete
Climate Change (UNFCCC)	On time (1997)	100	..
Montreal Protocol	Late (1997)	60	Complete
Basel Convention	On time (1999)	31	..
London Convention 1972	No report (1998)	..	n.a.
MARPOL 73/78	On time (1998)	15	..
CITES	On time (1998)	49	Complete
Ramsar Convention	Late (1998)	97	Complete

Contributions to funds related to agreements and main IGOs with environmental activities

	Amount	Share of total budget (%)
Transb. Air Pollution (LRTAP): Programme for Monitoring and Evaluation of the Long-Range Transmission of Air Pollutants in Europe (EMEP) (1999)	$US25,842	1.27
Ozone Layer Convention: Multilateral Fund for the Implementation of the Montreal Protocol (1997)	$US1,134,636	0.72
Global Environment Facility (GEF) (1994–7)	SDR15,450,000	1.07
International Maritime Organization (IMO) (1998)	$US103,968	0.35
United Nations Development Programme (UNDP) (1998)	$US11,450,000	1.54
United Nations Environment Programme (UNEP): Environment Fund (1998)	$US3,073,307	6.58
United Nations Population Fund (UNFPA) (1997)	$US14,538,564	5.06

General Environment and Development Performance Indicators

Official development aid (ODA)
Average annual ODA ($US million/% of GNP):
1993–95: 345/–

Per capita ($US):
1995: 76
(OECD average 1995: 65)

Energy consumption

	1973	1990	1996	(OECD average 1996)
Total (million toe)	19.4	22.6	23.2	(120.0)
Per capita (toe)	4.16	4.53	4.54	(3.19)
Per GDP (toe/$US000)	0.23	0.17	0.17	(0.17)

Central government expenditure on education, defence, and health

	Percentage of total central government expenditure		Percentage of GDP	
	1987	1996	1987	1996
Education	13.9	10.1	4.3	4.1
Military/defence	5.3	3.9	1.7	1.5
Health	10.6	3.0	3.3	1.2

Specific Environment Indicators

Atmosphere

SO$_x$ EMISSIONS
Total emissions (000 tonnes):
1980: 584
1985: 382
1995: 96

Per unit of GDP (kg/$US000):
1995: 1.2
(OECD average: 2.4)

Per capita (kg/capita):
1995: 18.8
(OECD average: 40.1)

Change from 1980 (%): –83.6

National emissions reduction target:
(*a*) according to official statement:
No specified target beyond the Sulphur Protocol.

(*b*) according to the 1985 Sulphur Protocol:
–30% by 1993, taking 1980 as base year. Target achieved.

(*c*) according to the 1994 Sulphur Protocol:
–80% by 2000, taking 1980 as base year.

NO$_X$ EMISSIONS
Total emissions (000 tonnes):
1980: 295
1987: 288
1995: 263

Per unit of GDP (kg/$US000):
1995: 3.3
(OECD average: 2.4)

Per capita (kg/capita):
1995: 51.5
(OECD average: 39.7)

Change from 1987 (%): –8.7

National emissions reduction target:
(a) according to official statement:
No specified target beyond the NO$_X$ Protocol.

(b) according to the NO$_X$ Protocol:
Stabilization by 1995, taking 1987 as base year.

CO$_2$ EMISSIONS
Energy-related emissions (million tonnes):
1973: 49.3
1990: 54.4
1996: 64.2

Per unit of GDP (tonnes/$US000):
1996: 0.47
(OECD average: 0.63)

Per capita (tonnes/capita):
1996: 12.5
(OECD average: 11.1)

Change from 1990 (%): +18.0

Emissions reduction target, covering CO$_2$ and five other greenhouse gases, according to the Kyoto Protocol:
–8% for EU as a whole; and
0 for Finland according to the EU burden-sharing plan of 17 June 1998, by the period 2008–12, compared to 1990 levels.
Not ratified.

CH$_4$ EMISSIONS (METHANE)
Total emissions (000 tonnes):
1985: ..
1990: 246
1995: 241

Per unit of GDP (kg/$US000):
1995: 2.9

Per capita (kg/capita):
1995: 47.2

Change from 1990 (%): –2

Emissions reduction target, covering CH$_4$ and five other greenhouse gases, according to the Kyoto Protocol:
–8% for EU as a whole; and
0 for Finland according to the EU burden-sharing plan of 17 June 1998, by the period 2008–12, compared to 1990 levels.
Not ratified.

CFC CONSUMPTION
Total consumption (tonnes):
1986: 3,301
1996: n.a.

Per capita (kg/capita):
1996: n.a.

Change from 1986 (%): n.a.

National reduction target according to the Montreal Protocol, Copenhagen Amendment:
–75% by 1994, taking 1986 as base year. Complete elimination by 1996.

Hazardous substances
Consumption of pesticides per km^2 of arable land
(kg active ingredients per km^2):
1980: 90
1985: 82
1995: 43
(OECD average 1995: 337)

Change from 1985 (%): –48.1
(OECD average: –15.8)

Hazardous waste
Production:
Total (000 tonnes): 559 (1992)

Per unit of GDP (kg/$US000): 7.5
(OECD average mid-1990s: 6.6)

Imports:
Total (000 tonnes): 5
% production: 0.9

Exports:
Total (000 tonnes): 22
% production: 3.9

Amounts to be managed (000 tonnes): 542

Nuclear waste
Total (tonnes HM): 68 (1996)
Per unit of total primary energy supply (tonnes/Mtoe): 2.2

Marine living resources
Fish catches in marine and inland waters
Total catch (000 tonnes):
1980: 173
1990: 142
1995: 167

% of world catches:
1995: 0.2

Per capita (kg/person):
1995: 32.6

Nature conservation and terrestrial living resources
Wooded area
Area (000 km²):
1995: 231,860

Change in wooded area
Area (000 km²):
1990–95: –1,810

As percentage of total area:
1990–95: –0.8

Forest damage
Trees with greater than 25% defoliation (%):
1990: 17.3
1997: 12.2

Recycling of paper and cardboard
Recycling rate (%):
1985: 39
1990: 41
1995: 57
(OECD average 1995: 42)

Change from 1985 (%): +46.2

Protection (totally and partially) of natural areas
Area (000 ha): 1,823 (1997)
Percentage of land area: 6.0

World Heritage sites
Number: 0 (1997)
Area (000 ha): –

Threatened species
Percentage of species known, mid-1990s:
Mammals: 11.9
Birds: 6.8
Fish: 11.7
Reptiles: 20.0
Amphibians: 20.0
Vascular plants: 6.7

Wetlands of international importance
Number: 11 (1997)
Area (000 ha): 101

Freshwater resources
Safe water
Percentage of the population having access: 100 (1995)

Annual internal renewable water resources
Total (km³): 110.00
Per capita (m³): 21,344 (1998)

Annual withdrawals
1970–98:
Total (km³): 2.20
Percentage of total water resources: 2
Per capita (m³): 440

Waste-water treatment
Percentage of population served by waste-water treatment plants:
All treatments:
1985: 72.1
1995: 77.0

Greece

Area and population
Total area (km²): 132,000
Population (million): 10.7
Population density (inh/km²): 80.8
Life expectancy at birth (years): 78 (1998)
  (world average: 63)
Total fertility rate (children): 1.3 (1998)
  (world average: 2.9)

Economy
GNP per capita ($US000): 12.0 (1997)
  (world average: 5.1)

Growth rate
Average annual growth rate (%):
GNP per capita 1996–97: 3.1 (world average: 1.8)
GDP 1990–97: 1.8 (world average: 2.3)

Relations to Main International Agreements and Intergovernmental Organizations
Debt to the United Nations
Prior years: $US382,852
1998: $US942,628
Total: $US1,325,480

Compliance with reporting requirements

	Latest report submitted (latest year due to report)	Proportion of national reports submitted by all Parties (%)	Quality of data submitted
Transb. Air Pollution (LRTAP)	1996 data reported	..	Complete
Climate Change (UNFCCC)	Late (1997)	100	..
Montreal Protocol	No report (1997)	60	n.a.
Basel Convention	On time (1999)	31	..
London Convention 1972	No report (1998)	..	n.a.
MARPOL 73/78	On time (1998)	15	..
CITES	Late (1998)	49	Complete
Ramsar Convention	Late (1998)	97	Complete

Contributions to funds related to agreements and main IGOs with environmental activities

	Amount	Share of total budget (%)
Transb. Air Pollution (LRTAP): Programme for Monitoring and Evaluation of the Long-Range Transmission of Air Pollutants in Europe (EMEP) (1999)	$US16,735	0.82
Ozone Layer Convention: Multilateral Fund for the Implementation of the Montreal Protocol (1997)	$US698,237	0.44
Global Environment Facility (GEF) (1994–7)	SDR3,570,000	0.25
International Maritime Organization (IMO) (1998)	$US1,374,136	4.59
United Nations Development Programme (UNDP) (1998)	–	–
United Nations Environment Programme (UNEP): Environment Fund (1998)	$US25,000	0.05
United Nations Population Fund (UNFPA) (1997)	–	–

General Environment and Development Performance Indicators
Official development aid (ODA)
Average annual ODA ($US million/% of GNP):
1993–95: –22/–

Per capita ($US):
1995: –
(OECD average 1995: 65)

Energy consumption

	1973	1990	1996	(OECD average 1996)
Total (million toe)	9.2	15.1	17.2	(120.0)
Per capita (toe)	1.03	1.48	1.64	(3.19)
Per GDP (toe/$US000)	0.16	0.18	0.19	(0.17)

Central government expenditure on education, defence, and health

	Percentage of total central government expenditure		Percentage of GDP	
	1987	1996	1987	1996
Education	7.8	9.6	2.8	3.1
Military/defence	8.4	7.3	3.0	2.4
Health	7.9	6.7	2.8	2.2

Specific Environment Indicators
Atmosphere

SO$_x$ EMISSIONS
Total emissions (000 tonnes):
1980: 400
1985: 500
1995: 510

Per unit of GDP (kg/$US000):
1995: 5.2
(OECD average: 2.4)

Per capita (kg/capita):
1995: 50.6
(OECD average: 40.1)

Change from 1980 (%): +27.5

National emissions reduction target:
(a) according to official statement:
No specified target beyond the Sulphur Protocol.

(b) according to the 1985 Sulphur Protocol:
n.a.

(c) according to the 1994 Sulphur Protocol:
–3% by 2005 and –4% by 2010, taking 2000 as base year.

NO$_X$ EMISSIONS
Total emissions (000 tonnes):
1980: 217
1987: 308
1995: 338

Per unit of GDP (kg/$US000):
1995: 3.5
(OECD average: 2.4)

Per capita (kg/capita):
1995: 33.5
(OECD average: 39.7)

Change from 1987 (%): +9.7

National emissions reduction target:
(a) according to official statement:
No specified target beyond the NO$_X$ Protocol.

(b) according to the NO$_X$ Protocol:
Stabilization by 1995, taking 1987 as base year.

CO$_2$ EMISSIONS
Energy-related emissions (million tonnes):
1973: 36.3
1990: 72.3
1996: 77.6

Per unit of GDP (tonnes/$US000):
1996: 0.84
(OECD average: 0.63)

Per capita (tonnes/capita):
1996: 7.4
(OECD average: 11.1)

Change from 1990 (%): +7.3

Emissions reduction target, covering CO$_2$ and five other greenhouse gases, according to the Kyoto Protocol:
–8% for EU as a whole; and
+25% for Greece according to the EU burden-sharing plan of 17 June 1998, by the period 2008–12, compared to 1990 levels.
Not ratified.

CH$_4$ EMISSIONS (METHANE)
Total emissions (000 tonnes):
1985: ..
1990: 343
1995: ..

Per unit of GDP (kg/$US000):
1995: ..

Per capita (kg/capita):
1995: ..

Change from 1990 (%): ..

Emissions reduction target, covering CH$_4$ and five other greenhouse gases, according to the Kyoto Protocol:
–8% for EU as a whole; and
+25% for Greece according to the EU burden-sharing plan of 17 June 1998, by the period 2008–12, compared to 1990 levels.
Not ratified.

CFC CONSUMPTION
Total consumption (tonnes):
1986: n.a.
1996: n.a.

Per capita (kg/capita):
1996: n.a.

Change from 1986 (%): n.a.

National reduction target according to the Montreal Protocol, Copenhagen Amendment:
–75% by 1994, taking 1986 as base year. Complete elimination by 1996.

Hazardous substances
Consumption of pesticides per km² of arable land
(kg active ingredients per km²):
1980: ..
1985: 186
1995: 243
(OECD average 1995: 337)

Change from 1985 (%): +30.6
(OECD average: –15.8)

Hazardous waste
Production:
Total (000 tonnes): 450 (1992)

Per unit of GDP (kg/$US000): 4.1
(OECD average mid-1990s: 6.6)

Imports:
Total (000 tonnes): –
% production: –

Exports:
Total (000 tonnes): –
% production: –

Amounts to be managed (000 tonnes): 450

Nuclear waste
Total (tonnes HM): – (1996)
Per unit of total primary energy supply (tonnes/Mtoe): –

Marine living resources
Fish catches in marine and inland waters
Total catch (000 tonnes):
1980: 105
1990: 137
1995: 166

% of world catches:
1995: 0.2

Per capita (kg/person):
1995: 15.9

Nature conservation and terrestrial living resources
Wooded area
Area (000 km²):
1995: 26,200

Change in wooded area
Area (000 km²):
1990–95: –

As percentage of total area:
1990–95: –

Forest damage
Trees with greater than 25% defoliation (%):
1990: 17.5
1997: 23.7

Recycling of paper and cardboard
Recycling rate (%):
1985: 25
1990: 28
1995: 19
(OECD average 1995: 42)

Change from 1985 (%): –24.0

Protection (totally and partially) of natural areas
Area (000 ha): 288 (1997)
Percentage of land area: 2.2

World Heritage sites
Number: 2 (1997)
Area (000 ha): –

Threatened species
Percentage of species known, mid-1990s:
Mammals: 37.1
Birds: 11.8
Fish: 36.9
Reptiles: 5.2
Amphibians: –
Vascular plants: 1.9

Wetlands of international importance
Number: 10 (1997)
Area (000 ha): 164

Freshwater resources
Safe water
Percentage of the population having access: .. (1995)

Annual internal renewable water resources
Total (km³): 45.15
Per capita (m³): 4,279 (1998)

Annual withdrawals
1970–98:
Total (km³): 5.04
Percentage of total water resources: 11
Per capita (m³): 523

Waste-water treatment
Percentage of population served by waste-water treatment plants:
All treatments:
1985: 10.0
1995: ..

Hungary

Area and population
Total area (km²): 93,000
Population (million): 10.1
Population density (inh/km²): 109.7
Life expectancy at birth (years): 71 (1998)
  (world average: 63)
Total fertility rate (children): 1.5 (1998)
  (world average: 2.9)

Economy
GNP per capita ($US000): 4.4 (1997)
  (world average: 5.1)

Growth rate
Average annual growth rate (%):
GNP per capita 1996–97: 4.3 (world average: 1.8)
GDP 1990–97: –0.4 (world average: 2.3)

Relations to Main International Agreements and Intergovernmental Organizations
Debt to the United Nations
Prior years: –
1998: –
Total: –

Compliance with reporting requirements

	Latest report submitted (latest year due to report)	Proportion of national reports submitted by all Parties (%)	Quality of data submitted
Transb. Air Pollution (LRTAP)	1996 data reported	..	Complete
Climate Change (UNFCCC)	On time (1998)	100	..
Montreal Protocol	On time (1997)	60	Complete
Basel Convention	No report (1999)	31	n.a.
London Convention 1972	No report (1998)	..	n.a.
MARPOL 73/78	No report (1998)	15	n.a.
CITES	On time (1998)	49	Complete
Ramsar Convention	Late (1998)	97	Complete

Contributions to funds related to agreements and main IGOs with environmental activities

	Amount	Share of total budget (%)
Transb. Air Pollution (LRTAP): Programme for Monitoring and Evaluation of the Long-Range Transmission of Air Pollutants in Europe (EMEP) (1999)	$US5,721	0.28
Ozone Layer Convention: Multilateral Fund for the Implementation of the Montreal Protocol (1997)	$US257,245	0.16
Global Environment Facility (GEF) (1994–7)	–	–
International Maritime Organization (IMO) (1998)	$US14,858	0.05
United Nations Development Programme (UNDP) (1998)	–	–
United Nations Environment Programme (UNEP): Environment Fund (1998)	$US115,648	0.25
United Nations Population Fund (UNFPA) (1997)	–	–

General Environment and Development Performance Indicators

Official development aid (ODA)
Average annual ODA ($US million/% of GNP):
1993–95: –36/–

Per capita ($US):
1995: 26
(OECD average 1995: 65)

Energy consumption

	1973	1990	1996	(OECD average 1996)
Total (million toe)	18.1	22.0	18.1	(120.0)
Per capita (toe)	1.74	2.12	1.77	(3.19)
Per GDP (toe/$US000)	0.75	0.61	0.56	(0.17)

Central government expenditure on education, defence, and health

	Percentage of total central government expenditure		Percentage of GDP	
	1987	1996	1987	1996
Education	3.3	2.5	1.6	1.1
Military/defence	3.6	1.8	1.7	0.8
Health	7.9	5.7	3.8	2.5

Specific Environment Indicators

Atmosphere

SO$_x$ EMISSIONS
Total emissions (000 tonnes):
1980: 1,633
1985: 1,403
1995: 705

Per unit of GDP (kg/$US000):
1995: 11.4
(OECD average: 2.4)

Per capita (kg/capita):
1995: 68.9
(OECD average: 40.1)

Change from 1980 (%): –56.8

National emissions reduction target:
(*a*) according to official statement:
No specified target beyond the Sulphur Protocol.

(*b*) according to the 1985 Sulphur Protocol:
–30% by 1993, taking 1980 as base year. Target achieved.

(*c*) according to the 1994 Sulphur Protocol:
–45% by 2000, –50% by 2005, and –60% by 2010, taking 1980 as base year. Not ratified.

NO$_x$ EMISSIONS
Total emissions (000 tonnes):
1980: 273
1987: 265
1995: 182

Per unit of GDP (kg/$US000):
1995: 3.0
(OECD average: 2.4)

Per capita (kg/capita):
1995: 17.8
(OECD average: 39.7)

Change from 1987 (%): –31.3

National emissions reduction target:
(a) according to official statement:
No specified target beyond the NO$_x$ Protocol.

(b) according to the NO$_x$ Protocol:
Stabilization by 1995, taking 1987 as base year.

CO$_2$ EMISSIONS
Energy-related emissions (million tonnes):
1973: 66.4
1990: 67.7
1996: 59.1

Per unit of GDP (tonnes/$US000):
1996: 1.84
(OECD average: 0.63)

Per capita (tonnes/capita):
1996: 5.8
(OECD average: 11.1)

Change from 1990 (%): –12.7

Emissions reduction target, covering CO$_2$ and five other greenhouse gases, according to the Kyoto Protocol: –6% by the period 2008–12, taking 1990 as base year. Not ratified.

CH$_4$ EMISSIONS (METHANE)
Total emissions (000 tonnes):
1985: 664
1990: 776
1995: ..

Per unit of GDP (kg/$US000):
1995: ..

Per capita (kg/capita):
1995: ..

Change from 1990 (%): ..

Emissions reduction target, covering CH$_4$ and five other greenhouse gases, according to the Kyoto Protocol: –6% by the period 2008–12, taking 1990 as base year. Not ratified.

CFC CONSUMPTION
Total consumption (tonnes):
1986: 5,468
1996: –

Per capita (kg/capita):
1996: –

Change from 1986 (%): –100

National reduction target according to the Montreal Protocol, Copenhagen Amendment: –75% by 1994, taking 1986 as base year. Complete elimination by 1996. Target achieved.

Hazardous substances
Consumption of pesticides per km^2 of arable land
(kg active ingredients per km^2):
1980: 627
1985: 499
1995: 153
(OECD average 1995: 337)

Change from 1985 (%): –69.3
(OECD average: –15.8)

Hazardous waste
Production:
Total (000 tonnes): 3,537 (1994)

Per unit of GDP (kg/$US000): 58.3
(OECD average mid-1990s: 6.6)

Imports:
Total (000 tonnes): –
% production: –

Exports:
Total (000 tonnes): 10
% production: 0.3

Amounts to be managed (000 tonnes): 3,527

Nuclear waste
Total (tonnes HM): 55 (1996)
Per unit of total primary energy supply (tonnes/Mtoe):
2.2

Marine living resources
Fish catches in marine and inland waters
Total catch (000 tonnes):
1980: 34
1990: 16
1995: 13

% of world catches:
1995: –

Per capita (kg/person):
1995: 1.3

Nature conservation and terrestrial living resources
Wooded area
Area (000 km²):
1995: 17,630

Change in wooded area
Area (000 km²):
1990–95: +680

As percentage of total area:
1990–95: +4.0

Forest damage
Trees with greater than 25% defoliation (%):
1990: 21.7
1997: 19.4

Recycling of paper and cardboard
Recycling rate (%):
1985: ..
1990: ..
1995: ..
(OECD average 1995: 42)

Change from 1985 (%): ..

Protection (totally and partially) of natural areas
Area (000 ha): 629 (1997)
Percentage of land area: 6.8

World Heritage sites
Number: 1 (1997)
Area (000 ha): –

Threatened species
Percentage of species known, mid-1990s:
Mammals: 69.9
Birds: 27.1
Fish: 19.5
Reptiles: 100
Amphibians: 100
Vascular plants: 6.7

Wetlands of international importance
Number: 19 (1997)
Area (000 ha): 150

Freshwater resources
Safe water
Percentage of the population having access: .. (1995)

Annual internal renewable water resources
Total (km³): 6.00
Per capita (m³): 604 (1998)

Annual withdrawals
1970–98:
Total (km³): 6.81
Percentage of total water resources: 114
Per capita (m³): 660

Waste-water treatment
Percentage of population served by waste-water treatment plants:
All treatments:
1985: 25.0
1995: 32.0

Iceland

Area and population
Total area (km²): 102,819
Population (million): 0.3
Population density (inh/km²): 2.6
Life expectancy at birth (years): 79 (1998)
  (world average: 63)
Total fertility rate (children): 2.0 (1998)
  (world average: 2.9)

Economy
GNP per capita ($US000): 25.0 (1997)
  (world average: 5.1)

Growth rate
Average annual growth rate (%):
GNP per capita 1996–97: .. (world average: 1.8)
GDP 1990–97: 2.0 (world average: 2.3)

Relations to Main International Agreements and Intergovernmental Organizations
Debt to the United Nations
Prior years: –
1998: –
Total: –

Compliance with reporting requirements

	Latest report submitted (latest year due to report)	Proportion of national reports submitted by all Parties (%)	Quality of data submitted
Transb. Air Pollution (LRTAP)	1996 data not reported	..	n.a.
Climate Change (UNFCCC)	Late (1997)	100	..
Montreal Protocol	On time (1998)	60	Complete
Basel Convention	On time (1999)	31	..
London Convention 1972	No report (1998)	..	n.a.
MARPOL 73/78	No report (1998)	15	n.a.
CITES	n.a.	49	n.a.
Ramsar Convention	On time (1998)	97	Complete

Contributions to funds related to agreements and main IGOs with environmental activities

	Amount	Share of total budget (%)
Transb. Air Pollution (LRTAP): Programme for Monitoring and Evaluation of the Long-Range Transmission of Air Pollutants in Europe (EMEP) (1999)	–	–
Ozone Layer Convention: Multilateral Fund for the Implementation of the Montreal Protocol (1997)	$US55,124	0.04
Global Environment Facility (GEF) (1994–7)	–	–
International Maritime Organization (IMO) (1998)	$US14,749	0.05
United Nations Development Programme (UNDP) (1998)	–	–
United Nations Environment Programme (UNEP): Environment Fund (1998)	$US50,000	0.11
United Nations Population Fund (UNFPA) (1997)	$US6,993	–

General Environment and Development Performance Indicators

Official development aid (ODA)
Average annual ODA ($US million/% of GNP):
1993–95: ../..

Per capita ($US):
1995: –
(OECD average 1995: 65)

Energy consumption

	1973	1990	1996	(OECD average 1996)
Total (million toe)	0.8	..	1.9	(120.0)
Per capita (toe)	..	..	8.44	(3.19)
Per GDP (toe/$US000)	..	..	0.33	(0.17)

Central government expenditure on education, defence, and health

	Percentage of total central government expenditure		Percentage of GDP	
	1987	1996	1987	1996
Education	14.0	12.8	4.0	4.1
Military/defence	–	–	–	–
Health	24.5	23.2	7.1	7.5

Specific Environment Indicators

Atmosphere

SO$_x$ EMISSIONS
Total emissions (000 tonnes):
1980: 9
1985: 7
1995: 8

Per unit of GDP (kg/$US000):
1995: 1.7
(OECD average: 2.4)

Per capita (kg/capita):
1995: 30.3
(OECD average: 40.1)

Change from 1980 (%): –5.8

National emissions reduction target:
(a) according to official statement:
Stabilizing net anthropogenic emissions of all greenhouse gases at 1990 levels by 2000.

(b) according to the 1985 Sulphur Protocol:
n.a.

(c) according to the 1994 Sulphur Protocol:
n.a.

NO$_x$ EMISSIONS
Total emissions (000 tonnes):
1980: 14
1987: 19
1995: 23

Per unit of GDP (kg/$US000):
1995: 4.8
(OECD average: 2.4)

Per capita (kg/capita):
1995: 85.4
(OECD average: 39.7)

Change from 1987 (%): +21.1

National emissions reduction target:
(a) according to official statement:
Stabilizing net anthropogenic emissions of all greenhouse gases at 1990 levels by 2000.

(b) according to the NO$_x$ Protocol:
n.a.

CO$_2$ EMISSIONS
Energy-related emissions (million tonnes):
1973: ..
1990: 2.5
1996: 2.5

Per unit of GDP (tonnes/$US000):
1996: 0.37
(OECD average: 0.63)

Per capita (tonnes/capita):
1996: 9.3
(OECD average: 11.1)

Change from 1990 (%): –

National emissions reduction target:
(a) according to official statement:
To stabilize anthropogenic emissions of all greenhouse gases at 1990 levels by 2000. This applies to net emissions.

(b) emissions reduction target, covering CO$_2$ and five other greenhouse gases, according to the Kyoto Protocol:
+10% by the period 2008–12, taking 1990 as base year. Not ratified.

CH$_4$ EMISSIONS (METHANE)
Total emissions (000 tonnes):
1985: ..
1990: 14
1995: 14

Per unit of GDP (kg/$US000):
1995: 2.8

Per capita (kg/capita):
1995: 52.4

Change from 1990 (%):–

National emissions reduction target:
(a) according to official statement:
Stabilizing net anthropogenic emissions of all greenhouse gases at 1990 levels by 2000.

(b) emissions reduction target, covering CH$_4$ and five other greenhouse gases, according to the Kyoto Protocol:
+10% by the period 2008–12, taking 1990 as base year. Not ratified.

CFC CONSUMPTION
Total consumption (tonnes):
1986: 195
1996: –

Per capita (kg/capita):
1996: –

Change from 1986 (%): –100

National reduction target according to the Montreal Protocol, Copenhagen Amendment:
–75% by 1994, taking 1986 as base year. Complete elimination by 1996. Target achieved.

Hazardous substances
Consumption of pesticides per km² of arable land (kg active ingredients per km²):
1980: ..
1985: ..
1995: ..
(OECD average 1995: 337)

Change from 1985 (%): ..
(OECD average: –15.8)

Hazardous waste
Production:
Total (000 tonnes): 6 (1994)

Per unit of GDP (kg/$US000): 1.2
(OECD average mid-1990s: 6.6)

Imports:
Total (000 tonnes): –
% production: –

Exports:
Total (000 tonnes): 1
% production: 16.7

Amounts to be managed (000 tonnes): 5

Nuclear waste
Total (tonnes HM): – (1996)
Per unit of total primary energy supply (tonnes/Mtoe): –

Marine living resources
Fish catches in marine and inland waters
Total catch (000 tonnes):
1980: 1,515
1990: 1,505
1995: 1,613

% of world catches:
1995: 1.8

Per capita (kg/person):
1995: 5,974.1

Nature conservation and terrestrial living resources
Wooded area
Area (000 km²):
1995: 1,450

Change in wooded area
Area (000 km²):
1990–95: +50

As percentage of total area:
1990–95: +3.6

Forest damage
Trees with greater than 25% defoliation (%):
1990: ..
1997: ..

Recycling of paper and cardboard
Recycling rate (%):
1985: ..
1990: 10
1995: 30
(OECD average 1995: 42)

Change from 1985 (%): ..

Protection (totally and partially) of natural areas
Area (000 ha): 972 (1997)
Percentage of land area: 9.7

World Heritage sites
Number: 0 (1997)
Area (000 ha): –

Threatened species
Percentage of species known, mid-1990s:
Mammals: –
Birds: 13.3
Fish: –
Reptiles: ..
Amphibians: ..
Vascular plants: 7.6

Wetlands of international importance
Number: 3 (1997)
Area (000 ha): 59

Freshwater resources
Safe water
Percentage of the population having access: .. (1995)

Annual internal renewable water resources
Total (km³): 168.00
Per capita (m³): 606,498 (1998)

Annual withdrawals
1970–98:
Total (km³): 0.16
Percentage of total water resources: –
Per capita (m³): 636

Waste-water treatment
Percentage of population served by waste-water treatment plants:
All treatments:
1985: ..
1995: 4.0

Ireland

Area and population
Total area (km²): 70,000
Population (million): 3.6
Population density (inh/km²): 51.5
Life expectancy at birth (years): 76 (1998)
  (world average: 63)
Total fertility rate (children): 1.8 (1998)
  (world average: 2.9)

Economy
GNP per capita ($US000): 18.3 (1997)
  (world average: 5.1)

Growth rate
Average annual growth rate (%):
GNP per capita 1996–97: 7.3 (world average: 1.8)
GDP 1990–97: 6.5 (world average: 2.3)

Relations to Main International Agreements and Intergovernmental Organizations
Debt to the United Nations
Prior years: –
1998: –
Total: –

Compliance with reporting requirements

	Latest report submitted (latest year due to report)	Proportion of national reports submitted by all Parties (%)	Quality of data submitted
Transb. Air Pollution (LRTAP)	1996 data reported	..	Complete
Climate Change (UNFCCC)	Late (1997)	100	..
Montreal Protocol	On time (1997)	60	Complete
Basel Convention	No report (1999)	31	n.a.
London Convention 1972	On time (1998)	..	..
MARPOL 73/78	No report (1998)	15	n.a.
CITES	n.a.	49	n.a.
Ramsar Convention	Late (1998)	97	Complete

Contributions to funds related to agreements and main IGOs with environmental activities

	Amount	Share of total budget (%)
Transb. Air Pollution (LRTAP): Programme for Monitoring and Evaluation of the Long-Range Transmission of Air Pollutants in Europe (EMEP) (1999)	$US10,680	0.52
Ozone Layer Convention: Multilateral Fund for the Implementation of the Montreal Protocol (1997)	$US358,868	0.25
Global Environment Facility (GEF) (1994–7)	SDR1,710,000	0.12
International Maritime Organization (IMO) (1998)	$US25,254	0.08
United Nations Development Programme (UNDP) (1998)	$US3,080,000	0.41
United Nations Environment Programme (UNEP): Environment Fund (1998)	$US136,750	0.29
United Nations Population Fund (UNFPA) (1997)	$US429,935	0.15

General Environment and Development Performance Indicators

Official development aid (ODA)
Average annual ODA ($US million/% of GNP):
1993–95: 114/–

Per capita ($US):
1995: 43
(OECD average 1995: 65)

Energy consumption

	1973	1990	1996	(OECD average 1996)
Total (million toe)	5.4	7.7	8.7	(120.0)
Per capita (toe)	1.77	2.21	2.40	(3.19)
Per GDP (toe/$US000)	0.23	0.17	0.13	(0.17)

Central government expenditure on education, defence, and health

	Percentage of total central government expenditure		Percentage of GDP	
	1987	1996	1987	1996
Education	11.8	13.2	5.9	5.0
Military/defence	2.8	2.8	1.4	1.1
Health	12.4	15.2	6.2	5.8

Specific Environment Indicators

Atmosphere

SO$_x$ EMISSIONS
Total emissions (000 tonnes):
1980: 222
1985: 141
1995: 166

Per unit of GDP (kg/$US000):
1995: 3.1
(OECD average: 2.4)

Per capita (kg/capita):
1995: 46.1
(OECD average: 40.1)

Change from 1980 (%): –25.2

National emissions reduction target:
(*a*) according to official statement:
No specified target beyond the Sulphur Protocol.

(*b*) according to the 1985 Sulphur Protocol:
n.a.

(*c*) according to the 1994 Sulphur Protocol:
–30% by 2000, taking 1980 as base year.

NO$_X$ EMISSIONS
Total emissions (000 tonnes):
1980: 83
1987: 115
1995: 116

Per unit of GDP (kg/$US000):
1995: 2.2
(OECD average: 2.4)

Per capita (kg/capita):
1995: 32.2
(OECD average: 39.7)

Change from 1987 (%): +0.9

National emissions reduction target:
(a) according to official statement:
No specified target beyond the NO$_X$ Protocol.

(b) according to the NO$_X$ Protocol:
Stabilization by 1995, taking 1987 as base year.

CO$_2$ EMISSIONS
Energy-related emissions (million tonnes):
1973: 23.2
1990: 33.2
1996: 36.5

Per unit of GDP (tonnes/$US000):
1996: 0.56
(OECD average: 0.63)

Per capita (tonnes/capita):
1996: 10.1
(OECD average: 11.1)

Change from 1990 (%): +9.9

Emissions reduction target, covering CO$_2$ and five other greenhouse gases, according to the Kyoto Protocol:
–8% for EU as a whole; and
+13% for Ireland according to the EU burden-sharing plan of 17 June 1998, by the period 2008–12, compared to 1990 levels.
Not ratified.

CH$_4$ EMISSIONS (METHANE)
Total emissions (000 tonnes):
1985: ..
1990: 811
1995: 812

Per unit of GDP (kg/$US000):
1995: 14.2

Per capita (kg/capita):
1995: 225.7

Change from 1990 (%): –

Emissions reduction target, covering CH$_4$ and five other greenhouse gases, according to the Kyoto Protocol:
–8% for EU as a whole; and
+13% for Ireland according to the EU burden-sharing plan of 17 June 1998, by the period 2008–12, compared to 1990 levels.
Not ratified.

CFC CONSUMPTION
Total consumption (tonnes):
1986: n.a.
1996: n.a.

Per capita (kg/capita):
1996: n.a.

Change from 1986 (%): n.a.

National reduction target according to the Montreal Protocol, Copenhagen Amendment:
–75% by 1994, taking 1986 as base year. Complete elimination by 1996.

Hazardous substances
Consumption of pesticides per km^2 of arable land
(kg active ingredients per km^2):
1980: 132
1985: 188
1995: 210
(OECD average 1995: 337)

Change from 1985 (%): +12.1
(OECD average: –15.8)

Hazardous waste
Production:
Total (000 tonnes): 248 (1995)

Per unit of GDP (kg/$US000): 4.0
(OECD average mid-1990s: 6.6)

Imports:
Total (000 tonnes): –
% production: –

Exports:
Total (000 tonnes): 16
% production: 6.5

Amounts to be managed (000 tonnes): 231

Nuclear waste
Total (tonnes HM): – (1996)
Per unit of total primary energy supply (tonnes/Mtoe): –

Marine living resources
Fish catches in marine and inland waters
Total catch (000 tonnes):
1980: 149
1990: 216
1995: 381

% of world catches:
1995: 0.4

Per capita (kg/person):
1995: 105.2

Nature conservation and terrestrial living resources
Wooded area
Area (000 km²):
1995: 5,700

Change in wooded area
Area (000 km²):
1990–95: +700

As percentage of total area:
1990–95: +14.0

Forest damage
Trees with greater than 25% defoliation (%):
1990: ..
1997: ..

Recycling of paper and cardboard
Recycling rate (%):
1985: 10
1990: 11
1995: 12
(OECD average 1995: 42)

Change from 1985 (%): +20.0

Protection (totally and partially) of natural areas
Area (000 ha): 59 (1997)
Percentage of land area: 0.9

World Heritage sites
Number: 0 (1997)
Area (000 ha): –

Threatened species
Percentage of species known, mid-1990s:
Mammals: 16.1
Birds: 24.7
Fish: ..
Reptiles: –
Amphibians: 33.3
Vascular plants: ..

Wetlands of international importance
Number: 45 (1997)
Area (000 ha): 67

Freshwater resources
Safe water
Percentage of the population having access: .. (1995)

Annual internal renewable water resources
Total (km³): 47.00
Per capita (m³): 13,187 (1998)

Annual withdrawals
1970–98:
Total (km³): 0.79
Percentage of total water resources: 2
Per capita (m³): 233

Waste-water treatment
Percentage of population served by waste-water treatment plants:
All treatments:
1985: ..
1995: ..

Republic of Korea

Area and population
Total area (km²): 98,460
Population (million): 46.4
Population density (inh/km²): 471.3
Life expectancy at birth (years): 74 (1998)
  (world average: 63)
Total fertility rate (children): 2.5 (1998)
  (world average: 2.9)

Economy
GNP per capita ($US000): 10.6 (1997)
  (world average: 5.1)

Growth rate
Average annual growth rate (%):
GNP per capita 1996–97: 3.8 (world average: 1.8)
GDP 1990–97: 7.2 (world average: 2.3)

Relations to Main International Agreements and Intergovernmental Organizations
Debt to the United Nations
Prior years: –
1998: –
Total: –

Compliance with reporting requirements

	Latest report submitted (latest year due to report)	Proportion of national reports submitted by all Parties (%)	Quality of data submitted
Transb. Air Pollution (LRTAP)	n.a.	..	n.a.
Climate Change (UNFCCC)	Data reported 1998	100	..
Montreal Protocol	Late (1997)	60	..
Basel Convention	On time (1999)	31	..
London Convention 1972	No report (1998)	..	n.a.
MARPOL 73/78	No report (1998)	15	n.a.
CITES	On time (1998)	49	Complete
Ramsar Convention	Late (1998)	97	Complete

Contributions to funds related to agreements and main IGOs with environmental activities

	Amount	Share of total budget (%)
Transb. Air Pollution (LRTAP): Programme for Monitoring and Evaluation of the Long-Range Transmission of Air Pollutants in Europe (EMEP) (1999)	n.a.	n.a.
Ozone Layer Convention: Multilateral Fund for the Implementation of the Montreal Protocol (1997)		
Global Environment Facility (GEF) (1994–7)	SDR4,000,000	0.28
International Maritime Organization (IMO) (1998)	$US421,321	1.41
United Nations Development Programme (UNDP) (1998)	$US1,830,000	0.25
United Nations Environment Programme (UNEP): Environment Fund (1998)	$US160,000	0.34
United Nations Population Fund (UNFPA) (1997)	–	–

General Environment and Development Performance Indicators

Official development aid (ODA)
Average annual ODA ($US million/% of GNP):
1993–95: 32/–

Per capita ($US):
1995: –1
(OECD average 1995: 65)

Energy consumption

	1973	1990	1996	(OECD average 1996)
Total (million toe)	..	..	119.8	(120.0)
Per capita (toe)	..	..	..	(3.19)
Per GDP (toe/$US000)	..	..	..	(0.17)

Central government expenditure on education, defence, and health

	Percentage of total central government expenditure		Percentage of GDP	
	1987	1996	1987	1996
Education	19.0	19.9	2.8	3.7
Military/defence	27.1	17.3	4.0	3.2
Health	2.2	0.7	0.3	0.1

Specific Environment Indicators

Atmosphere

SO$_x$ EMISSIONS
Total emissions (000 tonnes):
1980: ..
1985: 1,352
1995: 1,532

Per unit of GDP (kg/$US000):
1995: 3.0
(OECD average: 2.4)

Per capita (kg/capita):
1995: 34.0
(OECD average: 40.1)

Change from 1980 (%): ..

National emissions reduction target:
(*a*) according to official statement:
..

(*b*) according to the 1985 Sulphur Protocol:
n.a.

(*c*) according to the 1994 Sulphur Protocol:
n.a.

NO$_x$ EMISSIONS
Total emissions (000 tonnes):
1980: ..
1987: 837
1995: 1,152

Per unit of GDP (kg/$US000):
1995: 2.2
(OECD average: 2.4)

Per capita (kg/capita):
1995: 25.5
(OECD average: 39.7)

Change from 1987 (%): +37.6

National emissions reduction target:
(a) according to official statement:
..

(b) according to the NO$_x$ Protocol:
n.a.

CO$_2$ EMISSIONS
Energy-related emissions (million tonnes):
1973: ..
1990: 246.0
1996: 408.9

Per unit of GDP (tonnes/$US000):
1996: 1.05
(OECD average: 0.63)

Per capita (tonnes/capita):
1996: 9.0
(OECD average: 11.1)

Change from 1990 (%): +66.2

National emissions reduction target according to the
Kyoto Protocol:
n.a.

CH$_4$ EMISSIONS (METHANE)
Total emissions (000 tonnes):
1985: ..
1990: ..
1995: ..

Per unit of GDP (kg/$US000):
1995: ..

Per capita (kg/capita):
1995: ..

Change from 1990 (%): ..

National emissions reduction target according to the
Kyoto Protocol:
n.a.

CFC CONSUMPTION
Total consumption (tonnes):
1986: 8,529
1996: 8,220

Per capita (kg/capita):
1996: 0.18

Change from 1986 (%): –4

National reduction target according to the Montreal
Protocol, Copenhagen Amendment:
A freeze of 1995–7 average level by 1999, –50% by 2005,
–85% by 2007, and complete elimination by 2010.

Hazardous substances
Consumption of pesticides per km² of arable land
(kg active ingredients per km²):
1980: ..
1985: 997
1995: 1,257
(OECD average 1995: 337)

Change from 1985 (%): +26.1
(OECD average: –15.8)

Hazardous waste
Production:
Total (000 tonnes): 1,622 (1995)

Per unit of GDP (kg/$US000): 2.9
(OECD average mid-1990s: 6.6)

Imports:
Total (000 tonnes): –
% production: –

Exports:
Total (000 tonnes): –
% production: –

Amounts to be managed (000 tonnes): 1,622

Nuclear waste
Total (tonnes HM): 254 (1996)
Per unit of total primary energy supply (tonnes/Mtoe): 1.6

Marine living resources
Fish catches in marine and inland waters
Total catch (000 tonnes):
1980: 2,091
1990: 2,467
1995: 2,320

% of world catches:
1995: 2.5

Per capita (kg/person):
1995: 50.9

Nature conservation and terrestrial living resources
Wooded area
Area (000 km²):
1995: 64,600

Change in wooded area
Area (000 km²):
1990–95: –160

As percentage of total area:
1990–95: –0.2

Forest damage
Trees with greater than 25% defoliation (%):
1990: ..
1997: ..

Recycling of paper and cardboard
Recycling rate (%):
1985: ..
1990: 44
1995: 53
(OECD average 1995: 42)

Change from 1985 (%): ..

Protection (totally and partially) of natural areas
Area (000 ha): 682 (1997)
Percentage of land area: 6.9

World Heritage sites
Number: 0 (1997)
Area (000 ha): –

Threatened species
Percentage of species known, mid-1990s:
Mammals: 12.1
Birds: 7.4
Fish: 7.5
Reptiles: 38.5
Amphibians: 40.0
Vascular plants: 0.9

Wetlands of international importance
Number: 1 (1997)
Area (000 ha): –

Freshwater resources
Safe water
Percentage of the population having access: 89 (1995)

Annual internal renewable water resources
Total (km³): 66.10
Per capita (m³): 1,469 (1995)

Annual withdrawals
1970–98:
Total (km³): 27.60
Percentage of total water resources: 42
Per capita (m³): 632

Waste-water treatment
Percentage of population served by waste-water treatment plants:
All treatments:
1985: 6.3
1995: 42.0

Luxembourg

Area and population
Total area (km²): 2,568
Population (million): 0.4
Population density (inh/km²): 164.4
Life expectancy at birth (years): 77 (1998)
  (world average: 63)
Total fertility rate (children): 1.6 (1998)
  (world average: 2.9)

Economy
GNP per capita ($US000): .. (1997)
  (world average: 5.1)

Growth rate
Average annual growth rate (%):
GNP per capita 1996–97: .. (world average: 1.8)
GDP 1990–97: .. (world average: 2.3)

Relations to Main International Agreements and Intergovernmental Organizations
Debt to the United Nations
Prior years: –
1998: $US155,711
Total: $US155,711

Compliance with reporting requirements

	Latest report submitted (latest year due to report)	Proportion of national reports submitted by all Parties (%)	Quality of data submitted
Transb. Air Pollution (LRTAP)	1996 data reported	..	Complete
Climate Change (UNFCCC)	Late (1997)	100	n.a.
Montreal Protocol	On time (1997)	60	Complete
Basel Convention	No report (1999)	31	n.a.
London Convention 1972	No report (1998)	..	n.a.
MARPOL 73/78	No report (1998)	15	n.a.
CITES	Late (1998)	49	Complete
Ramsar Convention	No report (1998)	97	n.a.

Contributions to funds related to agreements and main IGOs with environmental activities

	Amount	Share of total budget (%)
Transb. Air Pollution (LRTAP): Programme for Monitoring and Evaluation of the Long-Range Transmission of Air Pollutants in Europe (EMEP) (1999)	$US3,242	0.16
Ozone Layer Convention: Multilateral Fund for the Implementation of the Montreal Protocol (1997)	$US128,623	0.08
Global Environment Facility (GEF) (1994–7)	SDR4,000,000	0.28
International Maritime Organization (IMO) (1998)	$US57,448	0.19
United Nations Development Programme (UNDP) (1998)	–	–
United Nations Environment Programme (UNEP): Environment Fund (1998)	$US26,283	0.06
United Nations Population Fund (UNFPA) (1997)	$US279,939	0.10

General Environment and Development Performance Indicators

Official development aid (ODA)
Average annual ODA ($US million/% of GNP):
1993–95: ../..

Per capita ($US):
1995: ..
(OECD average 1995: 65)

Energy consumption

	1973	1990	1996	(OECD average 1996)
Total (million toe)	2.9	3.0	3.2	(120.0)
Per capita (toe)	8.39	7.74	7.74	(3.19)
Per GDP (toe/$US000)	0.48	0.29	0.29	(0.17)

Central government expenditure on education, defence, and health

	Percentage of total central government expenditure		Percentage of GDP	
	1987	1996	1987	1996
Education	16.6	14.7	1.2	1.2
Military/defence	2.1	1.5	0.9	0.8
Health	1.4	0.2	0.1	–

Specific Environment Indicators

Atmosphere

SO$_x$ EMISSIONS
Total emissions (000 tonnes):
1980: 24
1985: 17
1995: 8

Per unit of GDP (kg/$US000):
1995: 0.7
(OECD average: 2.4)

Per capita (kg/capita):
1995: 19.4
(OECD average: 40.1)

Change from 1980 (%): –66.7

National emissions reduction target:
(a) according to official statement:
No specified target beyond the Sulphur Protocol.

(b) according to the 1985 Sulphur Protocol:
–30% by 1993, taking 1980 as base year. Target achieved.

(c) according to the 1994 Sulphur Protocol:
–58% by 2000, taking 1980 as base year.

NO$_x$ EMISSIONS
Total emissions (000 tonnes):
1980: 23
1987: 22
1995: 20

Per unit of GDP (kg/$US000):
1995: 1.7
(OECD average: 2.4)

Per capita (kg/capita):
1995: 48.4
(OECD average: 39.7)

Change from 1987 (%): –9.1

National emissions reduction target:
(*a*) according to official statement:
No specified target beyond the NO$_x$ Protocol.

(*b*) according to the NO$_x$ Protocol:
Stabilization by 1995, taking 1987 as base year.

CO$_2$ EMISSIONS
Energy-related emissions (million tonnes):
1973: 16.3
1990: 10.9
1996: 9.1

Per unit of GDP (tonnes/$US000):
1996: 0.66
(OECD average: 0.63)

Per capita (tonnes/capita):
1996: 21.9
(OECD average: 11.1)

Change from 1990 (%): –16.5

Emissions reduction target, covering CO$_2$ and five other greenhouse gases, according to the Kyoto Protocol:
–8% for EU as a whole; and
–28% for Luxembourg according to the EU burden-sharing plan of 17 June 1998, by the period 2008–12, compared to 1990 levels.
Not ratified.

CH$_4$ EMISSIONS (METHANE)
Total emissions (000 tonnes):
1985: ..
1990: 25
1995: 23

Per unit of GDP (kg/$US000):
1995: 1.9

Per capita (kg/capita):
1995: 55.7

Change from 1990 (%): –8

Emissions reduction target, covering CH$_4$ and five other greenhouse gases, according to the Kyoto Protocol:
–8% for EU as a whole; and
–28% for Luxembourg according to the EU burden-sharing plan of 17 June 1998, by the period 2008–12, compared to 1990 levels.
Not ratified.

CFC CONSUMPTION
Total consumption (tonnes):
1986: n.a.
1996: n.a.

Per capita (kg/capita):
1996: n.a.

Change from 1986 (%): n.a.

National reduction target according to the Montreal Protocol, Copenhagen Amendment:
–75% by 1994, taking 1986 as base year. Complete elimination by 1996.

Hazardous substances
Consumption of pesticides per km^2 of arable land
(kg active ingredients per km^2):
1980: ..
1985: ..
1995: 444
(OECD average 1995: 337)

Change from 1985 (%): ..
(OECD average: –15.8)

Hazardous waste
Production:
Total (000 tonnes): 180 (1995)

Per unit of GDP (kg/$US000): 140.6
(OECD average mid-1990s: 6.6)

Imports:
Total (000 tonnes): –
% production: –

Exports:
Total (000 tonnes): 180
% production: 100

Amounts to be managed (000 tonnes): –

Nuclear waste
Total (tonnes HM): – (1996)
Per unit of total primary energy supply (tonnes/Mtoe): –

Marine living resources
Fish catches in marine and inland waters
Total catch (000 tonnes):
1980: –
1990: –
1995: –

% of world catches:
1995: –

Per capita (kg/person):
1995: –

Nature conservation and terrestrial living resources
Wooded area
Area (000 km²):
1995: 880

Change in wooded area
Area (000 km²):
1990–95: –

As percentage of total area:
1990–95: –

Forest damage
Trees with greater than 25% defoliation (%):
1990: 20.8
1997: 29.9

Recycling of paper and cardboard
Recycling rate (%):
1985: ..
1995: ..
1995: ..
(OECD average 1995: 42)

Change from 1985 (%): ..

Protection (totally and partially) of natural areas
Area (000 ha): .. (1997)
Percentage of land area: ..

World Heritage sites
Number: .. (1997)
Area (000 ha): ..

Threatened species
Percentage of species known, mid-1990s:
Mammals: 54.1
Birds: 20.0
Fish: 38.2
Reptiles: 100
Amphibians: 100
Vascular plants: 14.5

Wetlands of international importance
Number: .. (1997)
Area (000 ha): ..

Freshwater resources
Safe water
Percentage of the population having access: .. (1995)

Annual internal renewable water resources
Total (km³): ..
Per capita (m³): .. (1998)

Annual withdrawals
1970–98:
Total (km³): ..
Percentage of total water resources: ..
Per capita (m³): ..

Waste-water treatment
Percentage of population served by waste-water treatment plants:
All treatments:
1985: 83.0
1995: 87.5

Mexico

Area and population
Total area (km²): 1,958,000
Population (million): 98.5
Population density (inh/km²):50.0
Life expectancy at birth (years): 72 (1998)
  (world average: 63)
Total fertility rate (children): 2.9 (1998)
  (world average: 2.9)

Economy
GNP per capita ($US000): 3.7 (1997)
  (world average: 5.1)

Growth rate
Average annual growth rate (%):
GNP per capita 1996–97: 6.2 (world average: 1.8)
GDP 1990–97: 1.8 (world average: 2.3)

Relations to Main International Agreements and Intergovernmental Organizations

Debt to the United Nations
Prior years: –
1998: $US89,776
Total: $US89,776

Compliance with reporting requirements

	Latest report submitted (latest year due to report)	Proportion of national reports submitted by all Parties (%)	Quality of data submitted
Transb. Air Pollution (LRTAP)	n.a.	..	n.a.
Climate Change (UNFCCC)	Data reported 1997	100	..
Montreal Protocol	On time (1997)	60	Complete
Basel Convention	No report (1999)	31	n.a.
London Convention 1972	No report (1998)	..	n.a.
MARPOL 73/78	No report (1998)	15	n.a.
CITES	On time (1998)	49	Complete
Ramsar Convention	On time (1998)	97	Complete

Contributions to funds related to agreements and main IGOs with environmental activities

	Amount	Share of total budget (%)
Transb. Air Pollution (LRTAP): Programme for Monitoring and Evaluation of the Long-Range Transmission of Air Pollutants in Europe (EMEP) (1999)	n.a.	n.a.
Ozone Layer Convention: Multilateral Fund for the Implementation of the Montreal Protocol (1997)		
Global Environment Facility (GEF) (1994–7)	SDR4,000,000	0.28
International Maritime Organization (IMO) (1998)	$US83,582	0.28
United Nations Development Programme (UNDP) (1998)	$US320,000	0.04
United Nations Environment Programme (UNEP): Environment Fund (1998)	$US78,326	0.17
United Nations Population Fund (UNFPA) (1997)	$US44,687	0.02

General Environment and Development Performance Indicators

Official development aid (ODA)
Average annual ODA ($US million/% of GNP):
1993–95: 411/–

Per capita ($US):
1995: –4
(OECD average 1995: 65)

Energy consumption

	1973	1990	1996	(OECD average 1996)
Total (million toe)	36.0	..	101.6	(120.0)
Per capita (toe)	..	..	..	(3.19)
Per GDP (toe/$US000)	..	..	..	(0.17)

Central government expenditure on education, defence, and health

	Percentage of total central government expenditure		Percentage of GDP	
	1987	1996	1987	1996
Education	8.5	24.5	2.4	3.8
Military/defence	1.8	3.7	0.5	0.6
Health	1.2	3.3	0.3	0.5

Specific Environment Indicators

Atmosphere

SO_x EMISSIONS
Total emissions (000 tonnes):
1980: ..
1985: ..
1995: 1,600

Per unit of GDP (kg/$US000):
1995: 3.1
(OECD average: 2.4)

Per capita (kg/capita):
1995: 17.5
(OECD average: 40.1)

Change from 1980 (%): ..

National emissions reduction target:
(*a*) according to official statement:
No target.

(*b*) according to the 1985 Sulphur Protocol:
n.a.

(*c*) according to the 1994 Sulphur Protocol:
n.a.

NO$_X$ EMISSIONS
Total emissions (000 tonnes):
1980: ..
1987: ..
1995: 1,400

Per unit of GDP (kg/$US000):
1995: 2.8
(OECD average: 2.4)

Per capita (kg/capita):
1995: 14.8
(OECD average: 39.7)

Change from 1987 (%): ..

National emissions reduction target:
(a) according to official statement:
No target.

(b) according to the NO$_X$ Protocol:
n.a.

CO$_2$ EMISSIONS
Energy-related emissions (million tonnes):
1973: ..
1990: 308.2
1996: 348.9

Per unit of GDP (tonnes/$US000):
1996: 1.17
(OECD average: 0.63)

Per capita (tonnes/capita):
1996: 3.61
(OECD average: 11.1)

Change from 1990 (%): +13.2

National emissions reduction target according to the Kyoto Protocol:
n.a.

CH$_4$ EMISSIONS (METHANE)
Total emissions (000 tonnes):
1985: ..
1990: ..
1995: ..

Per unit of GDP (kg/$US000):
1995: ..

Per capita (kg/capita):
1995: ..

Change from 1990 (%): ..

National emissions reduction target according to the Kyoto Protocol:
n.a.

CFC CONSUMPTION
Total consumption (tonnes):
1986: 8,818
1996: 4,859

Per capita (kg/capita):
1996: 0.05

Change from 1986 (%): –45

National reduction target according to the Montreal Protocol, Copenhagen Amendment:
A freeze of 1995–7 average level by 1999, –50% by 2005, –85% by 2007, and complete elimination by 2010.

Hazardous substances
Consumption of pesticides per km² of arable land
(kg active ingredients per km²):
1980: ..
1985: ..
1995: 146
(OECD average 1995: 337)

Change from 1985 (%): ..
(OECD average: –15.8)

Hazardous waste
Production:
Total (000 tonnes): 8,000 (1995)

Per unit of GDP (kg/$US000): 11.5
(OECD average mid-1990s: 6.6)

Imports:
Total (000 tonnes): 159
% production: 2.0

Exports:
Total (000 tonnes): 6
% production: –

Amounts to be managed (000 tonnes): 8,153

Nuclear waste
Total (tonnes HM): 39 (1996)
Per unit of total primary energy supply (tonnes/Mtoe):
0.3

Marine living resources
Fish catches in marine and inland waters
Total catch (000 tonnes):
1980: 1,250
1990: 1,325
1995: 1,290

% of world catches:
1995: 1.4

Per capita (kg/person):
1995: 13.4

Nature conservation and terrestrial living resources
Wooded area
Area (000 km²):
1995: 568,740

Change in wooded area
Area (000 km²):
1990–95: +1,910

As percentage of total area:
1990–95: +0.3

Forest damage
Trees with greater than 25% defoliation (%):
1990: ..
1997: ..

Recycling of paper and cardboard
Recycling rate (%):
1985: ..
1990: 2
1995: 2
(OECD average 1995: 42)

Change from 1985 (%): ..

Protection (totally and partially) of natural areas
Area (000 ha): 4,553 (1997)
Percentage of land area: 2.4

World Heritage sites
Number: 2 (1997)
Area (000 ha): 898

Threatened species
Percentage of species known, mid-1990s:
Mammals: 33.5
Birds: 16.9
Fish: 5.7
Reptiles: 18.1
Amphibians: 17.0
Vascular plants: 2.5

Wetlands of international importance
Number: 6 (1997)
Area (000 ha): 701

Freshwater resources
Safe water
Percentage of the population having access: 83 (1995)

Annual internal renewable water resources
Total (km³): 357.40
Per capita (m³): 3,815 (1995)

Annual withdrawals
1970–98:
Total (km³): 77.62
Percentage of total water resources: 22
Per capita (m³): 899

Waste-water treatment
Percentage of population served by waste-water treatment
plants:
All treatments:
1985: ..
1995: 21.8

New Zealand

Area and population
Total area (km²): 271,000
Population (million): 3.6
Population density (inh/km²): 13.5
Life expectancy at birth (years): 78 (1998)
  (world average: 63)
Total fertility rate (children): 1.9 (1998)
  (world average: 2.9)

Economy
GNP per capita ($US000): 16.5 (1997)
  (world average: 5.1)

Growth rate
Average annual growth rate (%):
GNP per capita 1996–97: 1.0 (world average: 1.8)
GDP 1990–97: 3.2 (world average: 2.3)

Relations to Main International Agreements and Intergovernmental Organizations
Debt to the United Nations
Prior years: –
1998: $US110,127
Total: $US110,127

Compliance with reporting requirements

	Latest report submitted (latest year due to report)	Proportion of national reports submitted by all Parties (%)	Quality of data submitted
Transb. Air Pollution (LRTAP)	n.a.	..	n.a.
Climate Change (UNFCCC)	Late (1997)	100	..
Montreal Protocol	On time (1997)	60	Complete
Basel Convention	On time (1999)	31	..
London Convention 1972	On time (1998)	..	..
MARPOL 73/78	No report (1998)	15	n.a.
CITES	On time (1998)	49	Complete
Ramsar Convention	On time (1998)	97	Complete

Contributions to funds related to agreements and main IGOs with environmental activities

	Amount	Share of total budget (%)
Transb. Air Pollution (LRTAP): Programme for Monitoring and Evaluation of the Long-Range Transmission of Air Pollutants in Europe (EMEP) (1999)	n.a.	n.a
Ozone Layer Convention: Multilateral Fund for the Implementation of the Montreal Protocol (1997)	$US440,992	0.28
Global Environment Facility (GEF) (1994–7)	SDR4,000,000	0.28
International Maritime Organization (IMO) (1998)	$US32,318	0.11
United Nations Development Programme (UNDP) (1998)	$US2,570,000	0.34
United Nations Environment Programme (UNEP): Environment Fund (1998)	$US116,400	0.25
United Nations Population Fund (UNFPA) (1997)	$US821,640	0.29

General Environment and Development Performance Indicators

Official development aid (ODA)
Average annual ODA ($US million/% of GNP):
1993–95: 110/–

Per capita ($US):
1995: 35
(OECD average 1995: 65)

Energy consumption

	1973	1990	1996	(OECD average 1996)
Total (million toe)	6.1	9.5	10.6	(120.0)
Per capita (toe)	2.04	2.82	2.92	(3.19)
Per GDP (toe/$US000)	0.18	0.22	0.21	(0.17)

Central government expenditure on education, defence, and health

	Percentage of total central government expenditure		Percentage of GDP	
	1987	1996	1987	1996
Education	12.5	14.7	5.4	4.7
Military/defence	4.8	3.3	2.1	1.0
Health	12.7	15.3	5.4	4.9

Specific Environment Indicators

Atmosphere

SO$_x$ EMISSIONS
Total emissions (000 tonnes):
1980: ..
1985: ..
1995: 41

Per unit of GDP (kg/$US000):
1995: 0.8
(OECD average: 2.4)

Per capita (kg/capita):
1995: 11.5
(OECD average: 40.1)

Change from 1980 (%): ..

National emissions reduction target:
(*a*) according to official statement:
No specified target.

(*b*) according to the 1985 Sulphur Protocol:
n.a.

(*c*) according to the 1994 Sulphur Protocol:
n.a.

NO$_X$ EMISSIONS
Total emissions (000 tonnes):
1980: ..
1987: ..
1995: 206

Per unit of GDP (kg/$US000):
1995: 4.0
(OECD average: 2.4)

Per capita (kg/capita):
1995: 57.5
(OECD average: 39.7)

Change from 1987 (%): ..

National emissions reduction target:
(*a*) according to official statement:
No specified target.

(*b*) according to the NO$_X$ Protocol:
n.a.

CO$_2$ EMISSIONS
Energy-related emissions (million tonnes):
1973: 18.3
1990: 25.7
1996: 32.4

Per unit of GDP (tonnes/$US000):
1996: 0.64
(OECD average: 0.63)

Per capita (tonnes/capita):
1996: 8.9
(OECD average: 11.1)

Change from 1990 (%): +26.1

Emissions reduction target, covering CO$_2$ and five other greenhouse gases, according to the Kyoto Protocol:
0% increase by the period 2008–12, taking 1990 as base year.
Not ratified.

CH$_4$ EMISSIONS (METHANE)
Total emissions (000 tonnes):
1985: ..
1990: 1,706
1995: 1,635

Per unit of GDP (kg/$US000):
1995: 30.7

Per capita (kg/capita):
1995: 456.7

Change from 1990 (%): –4

Emissions reduction target, covering CH$_4$ and five other greenhouse gases, according to the Kyoto Protocol:
0% increase by the period 2008–12, taking 1990 as base year.
Not ratified.

CFC CONSUMPTION
Total consumption (tonnes):
1986: 2,088
1996: 2

Per capita (kg/capita):
1996: –

Change from 1986 (%): –99.9

National reduction target according to the Montreal Protocol, Copenhagen Amendment:
–75% by 1994, taking 1986 as base year. Complete elimination by 1996. Target not achieved.

Hazardous substances
Consumption of pesticides per km² of arable land
(kg active ingredients per km²):
1980: ..
1985: 625
1995: 851
(OECD average 1995: 337)

Change from 1985 (%): +36.3
(OECD average: –15.8)

Hazardous waste
Production:
Total (000 tonnes): 110 (1993)

Per unit of GDP (kg/$US000): 2.1
(OECD average mid-1990s: 6.6)

Imports:
Total (000 tonnes): –
% production: –

Exports:
Total (000 tonnes): 10
% production: 9.1

Amounts to be managed (000 tonnes): 100

Nuclear waste
Total (tonnes HM): – (1996)
Per unit of total primary energy supply (tonnes/Mtoe): –

Marine living resources
Fish catches in marine and inland waters
Total catch (000 tonnes):
1980: 156
1990: 344
1995: 544

% of world catches:
1995: 0.6

Per capita (kg/person):
1995: 149.5

Nature conservation and terrestrial living resources
Wooded area
Area (000 km²):
1995: 75,400

Change in wooded area
Area (000 km²):
1990–95: +1,900

As percentage of total area:
1990–95: +2.6

Forest damage
Trees with greater than 25% defoliation (%):
1990: ..
1997: ..

Recycling of paper and cardboard
Recycling rate (%):
1985: 19
1990: ..
1995: ..
(OECD average 1995: 42)

Change from 1985 (%): ..

Protection (totally and partially) of natural areas
Area (000 ha): 6,322 (1997)
Percentage of land area: 23.6

World Heritage sites
Number: 2 (1997)
Area (000 ha): 2,680

Threatened species
Percentage of species known, mid-1990s:
Mammals: 100
Birds: 29.5
Fish: 37.0
Reptiles: 48.9
Amphibians: 100
Vascular plants: 9.0–14.0

Wetlands of international importance
Number: 5 (1997)
Area (000 ha): 39

Freshwater resources
Safe water
Percentage of the population having access: .. (1995)

Annual internal renewable water resources
Total (km³): 327.00
Per capita (m³): 91,469 (1995)

Annual withdrawals
1970–98:
Total (km³): 2.00
Percentage of total water resources: 1
Per capita (m³): 589

Waste-water treatment
Percentage of population served by waste-water treatment plants:
All treatments:
1985: 88.0
1995: ..

Switzerland

Area and population
Total area (km²): 41,000
Population (million): 7.3
Population density (inh/km²): 175.8
Life expectancy at birth (years): 79 (1998)
  (world average: 63)
Total fertility rate (children): 1.5 (1998)
  (world average: 2.9)

Economy
GNP per capita ($US000): 44.3 (1997)
  (world average: 5.1)

Growth rate
Average annual growth rate (%):
GNP per capita 1996–97: .. (world average: 1.8)
GDP 1990–97: –0.1 (world average: 2.3)

Relations to Main International Agreements and Intergovernmental Organizations
Debt to the United Nations
Prior years: n.a.
1998: n.a.
Total: n.a.

Compliance with reporting requirements

	Latest report submitted (latest year due to report)	Proportion of national reports submitted by all Parties (%)	Quality of data submitted
Transb. Air Pollution (LRTAP)	1996 data reported	..	Complete
Climate Change (UNFCCC)	Late (1997)	100	..
Montreal Protocol	No report (1997)	60	n.a.
Basel Convention	No report (1999)	31	n.a.
London Convention 1972	On time (1998)	..	..
MARPOL 73/78	No report (1998)	15	n.a.
CITES	Late (1998)	49	Complete
Ramsar Convention	Late (1998)	97	Complete

Contributions to funds related to agreements and main IGOs with environmental activities

	Amount	Share of total budget (%)
Transb. Air Pollution (LRTAP): Programme for Monitoring and Evaluation of the Long-Range Transmission of Air Pollutants in Europe (EMEP) (1999)	$US57,929	2.84
Ozone Layer Convention: Multilateral Fund for the Implementation of the Montreal Protocol (1997)	$US2,223,335	1.41
Global Environment Facility (GEF) (1994–7)	SDR31,970,000	2.21
International Maritime Organization (IMO) (1998)	$US69,686	0.23
United Nations Development Programme (UNDP) (1998)	$US41,790,000	5.60
United Nations Environment Programme (UNEP): Environment Fund (1998)	$US2,518,098	5.39
United Nations Population Fund (UNFPA) (1997)	$US6,896,552	2.40

General Environment and Development Performance Indicators

Official development aid (ODA)
Average annual ODA ($US million/% of GNP):
1993–95: 953/–

Per capita ($US):
1995: 151
(OECD average 1995: 65)

Energy consumption

	1973	1990	1996	(OECD average 1996)
Total (million toe)	17.6	19.6	20.6	(120.0)
Per capita (toe)	2.73	2.88	2.90	(3.19)
Per GDP (toe/$US000)	0.10	0.09	0.09	(0.17)

Central government expenditure on education, defence, and health

	Percentage of total central government expenditure		Percentage of GDP	
	1987	1996	1987	1996
Education	..	2.6	..	0.7
Military/defence	..	5.8	..	1.5
Health	..	15.6	..	4.1

Specific Environment Indicators

Atmosphere

SO$_x$ EMISSIONS
Total emissions (000 tonnes):
1980: 116
1985: 76
1995: 34

Per unit of GDP (kg/$US000):
1995: 0.2
(OECD average: 2.4)

Per capita (kg/capita):
1995: 4.9
(OECD average: 40.1)

Change from 1980 (%): –70.7

National emissions reduction target:
(a) according to official statement:
–57% by 2010, taking 1980 as base year.

(b) according to the 1985 Sulphur Protocol:
–30% by 1993, taking 1980 as base year. Target achieved.

(c) according to the 1994 Sulphur Protocol:
–52% by 2000, taking 1980 as base year.

NO$_x$ EMISSIONS
Total emissions (000 tonnes):
1980: 170
1987: 174
1995: 136

Per unit of GDP (kg/$US000):
1995: 0.9
(OECD average: 2.4)

Per capita (kg/capita):
1995: 19.3
(OECD average: 39.7)

Change from 1987 (%): −21.8

National emissions reduction target:
(*a*) according to official statement:
To reduce emissions to 1960 levels, i.e. −69%, taking 1984 as base year.

(*b*) according to the NO$_x$ Protocol:
Stabilization by 1995, taking 1987 as base year.

CO$_2$ EMISSIONS
Energy-related emissions (million tonnes):
1973: 45.9
1990: 44.2
1996: 42.9

Per unit of GDP (tonnes/$US000):
1996: 0.19
(OECD average: 0.63)

Per capita (tonnes/capita):
1996: 6.0
(OECD average: 11.1)

Change from 1990 (%): −2.9

Emissions reduction target, covering CO$_2$ and five other greenhouse gases, according to the Kyoto Protocol:
−8% by the period 2008–12, taking 1990 as base year. Not ratified.

CH$_4$ EMISSIONS (METHANE)
Total emissions (000 tonnes):
1985: 239
1990: 244
1995: 235

Per unit of GDP (kg/$US000):
1995: 1.6

Per capita (kg/capita):
1995: 33.3

Change from 1990 (%): −3

Emissions reduction target, covering CO$_2$ and five other greenhouse gases, according to the Kyoto Protocol:
−8% by the period 2008–12, taking 1990 as base year. Not ratified.

CFC CONSUMPTION
Total consumption (tonnes):
1986: 7,960
1996: −43

Per capita (kg/capita):
1996: −

Change from 1986 (%): −100.5

National reduction target according to the Montreal Protocol, Copenhagen Amendment:
−75% by 1994, taking 1986 as base year. Complete elimination by 1996. Target achieved.

Hazardous substances
Consumption of pesticides per km² of arable land
(kg active ingredients per km²):
1980: 418
1985: 497
1995: 411
(OECD average 1995: 337)

Change from 1985 (%): −17.2
(OECD average: −15.8)

Hazardous waste
Production:
Total (000 tonnes): 854 (1994)

Per unit of GDP (kg/$US000): 5.0
(OECD average mid-1990s: 6.6)

Imports:
Total (000 tonnes): 17
% production: 2.0

Exports:
Total (000 tonnes): 117
% production: 13.7

Amounts to be managed (000 tonnes): 754

Nuclear waste
Total (tonnes HM): 64 (1996)
Per unit of total primary energy supply (tonnes/Mtoe): 2.5

Marine living resources
Fish catches in marine and inland waters
Total catch (000 tonnes):
1980: 4
1990: 3
1995: 2

% of world catches:
1995: –

Per capita (kg/person):
1995: 0.3

Nature conservation and terrestrial living resources
Wooded area
Area (000 km^2):
1995: 12,520

Change in wooded area
Area (000 km^2):
1990–95: –

As percentage of total area:
1990–95: –

Forest damage
Trees with greater than 25% defoliation (%):
1990: 15.5
1997: 16.9

Recycling of paper and cardboard
Recycling rate (%):
1985: 38
1990: 49
1995: 61
(OECD average 1995: 42)

Change from 1985 (%): +60.5

Protection (totally and partially) of natural areas
Area (000 ha): 713 (1997)
Percentage of land area: 18.0

World Heritage sites
Number: 0 (1997)
Area (000 ha): –

Threatened species
Percentage of species known, mid-1990s:
Mammals: 33.8
Birds: 44.2
Fish: 59.6
Reptiles: 78.6
Amphibians: 94.1
Vascular plants: 22.1

Wetlands of international importance
Number: 8 (1997)
Area (000 ha): 7

Freshwater resources
Safe water
Percentage of the population having access: 100 (1995)

Annual internal renewable water resources
Total (km^3): 42.50
Per capita (m^3): 5,802 (1998)

Annual withdrawals
1970–98:
Total (km^3): 1.19
Percentage of total water resources: 3
Per capita (m^3): 173

Waste-water treatment
Percentage of population served by waste-water treatment plants:
All treatments:
1985: 84.0
1995: 94.0

Turkey

Area and population
Total area (km²): 779,000
Population (million): 64.6
Population density (inh/km²): 82.7
Life expectancy at birth (years): 73 (1998)
  (world average: 63)
Total fertility rate (children): 2.5 (1998)
  (world average: 2.9)

Economy
GNP per capita ($US000): 3.1 (1997)
  (world average: 5.1)

Growth rate
Average annual growth rate (%):
GNP per capita 1996–97: 6.4 (world average: 1.8)
GDP 1990–97: 3.6 (world average: 2.3)

Relations to Main International Agreements and Intergovernmental Organizations
Debt to the United Nations
Prior years: $US1,067,089
1998: $US666,568
Total: $US733,657

Compliance with reporting requirements

	Latest report submitted (latest year due to report)	Proportion of national reports submitted by all Parties (%)	Quality of data submitted
Transb. Air Pollution (LRTAP)	1996 data reported	..	n.a.
Climate Change (UNFCCC)	n.a	100	n.a.
Montreal Protocol	On time (1997)	60	Complete
Basel Convention	On time (1999)	31	..
London Convention 1972	n.a.	..	n.a.
MARPOL 73/78	No report (1998)	15	n.a.
CITES	On time (1998)	49	Complete
Ramsar Convention	On time (1998)	97	Complete

Contributions to funds related to agreements and main IGOs with environmental activities

	Amount	Share of total budget (%)
Transb. Air Pollution (LRTAP): Programme for Monitoring and Evaluation of the Long-Range Transmission of Air Pollutants in Europe (EMEP) (1999)	$US20,978	1.03
Ozone Layer Convention: Multilateral Fund for the Implementation of the Montreal Protocol (1997)	–	–
Global Environment Facility (GEF) (1994–7)	SDR4,000,000	0.28
International Maritime Organization (IMO) (1998)	$US355,418	1.19
United Nations Development Programme (UNDP) (1998)	–	–
United Nations Environment Programme (UNEP): Environment Fund (1998)	$US100,000	0.21
United Nations Population Fund (UNFPA) (1997)	$US90,000	0.03

General Environment and Development Performance Indicators

Official development aid (ODA)
Average annual ODA ($US million/% of GNP):
1993–95: 292/–

Per capita ($US):
1995: –5
(OECD average 1995: 65)

Energy consumption

	1973	1990	1996	(OECD average 1996)
Total (million toe)	20.0	40.2	49.8	(120.0)
Per capita (toe)	0.52	0.72	0.79	(3.19)
Per GDP (toe/$US000)	0.28	0.27	0.26	(0.17)

Central government expenditure on education, defence, and health

	Percentage of total central government expenditure		Percentage of GDP	
	1987	1996	1987	1996
Education	6.6	11.2	2.1	3.0
Military/defence	5.4	8.4	1.7	2.3
Health	1.2	2.3	0.4	0.6

Specific Environment Indicators

Atmosphere

SO$_x$ EMISSIONS
Total emissions (000 tonnes):
1980: ..
1985: ..
1995: ..

Per unit of GDP (kg/$US000):
1995: ..
(OECD average: 2.4)

Per capita (kg/capita):
1995: ..
(OECD average: 40.1)

Change from 1980 (%): ..

National emissions reduction target:
(a) according to official statement:
No target.

(b) according to the 1985 Sulphur Protocol:
n.a.

(c) according to the 1994 Sulphur Protocol:
n.a.

NO$_x$ EMISSIONS
Total emissions (000 tonnes):
1980: 380
1987: ..
1995: 512

Per unit of GDP (kg/$US000):
1995: 2.1
(OECD average: 2.4)

Per capita (kg/capita):
1995: 9.3
(OECD average: 39.7)

Change from 1987 (%): ..

National emissions reduction target:
(*a*) according to official statement:
No target.

(*b*) according to the NO$_x$ Protocol:
n.a.

CO$_2$ EMISSIONS
Energy-related emissions (million tonnes):
1973: 56.9
1990: 138.4
1996: 168.5

Per unit of GDP (tonnes/$US000):
1996: 0.89
(OECD average: 0.63)

Per capita (tonnes/capita):
1996: 2.7
(OECD average: 11.1)

Change from 1990 (%): +21.7

National emissions reduction target according to the Kyoto Protocol:
n.a.

CH$_4$ EMISSIONS (METHANE)
Total emissions (000 tonnes):
1985: ..
1990: ..
1995: ..

Per unit of GDP (kg/$US000):
1995: ..

Per capita (kg/capita):
1995: ..

Change from 1990 (%): ..

National emissions reduction target according to the Kyoto Protocol:
n.a.

CFC CONSUMPTION
Total consumption (tonnes):
1986: 4,122
1996: 3,758

Per capita (kg/capita):
1996: 0.06

Change from 1986 (%): –9

National reduction target according to the Montreal Protocol, Copenhagen Amendment:
A freeze of 1995–7 average level by 1999, –50% by 2005, –85% by 2007, and complete elimination by 2010.

Hazardous substances
Consumption of pesticides per km² of arable land
(kg active ingredients per km²):
1980: 95
1985: 133
1995: 124
(OECD average 1995: 337)

Change from 1985 (%): –7.0
(OECD average: –15.8)

Hazardous waste
Production:
Total (000 tonnes): .. (1995)

Per unit of GDP (kg/$US000): ..
(OECD average mid-1990s: 6.6)

Imports:
Total (000 tonnes): ..
% production: ..

Exports:
Total (000 tonnes): ..
% production: ..

Amounts to be managed (000 tonnes): ..

Nuclear waste
Total (tonnes HM): – (1996)
Per unit of total primary energy supply (tonnes/Mtoe): –

Marine living resources
Fish catches in marine and inland waters
Total catch (000 tonnes):
1980: 427
1990: 379
1995: 631

% of world catches:
1995: 0.7

Per capita (kg/person):
1995: 10.1

Nature conservation and terrestrial living resources
Wooded area
Area (000 km²):
1995: 207,030

Change in wooded area
Area (000 km²):
1990–95: +5,040

As percentage of total area:
1990–95: +2.5

Forest damage
Trees with greater than 25% defoliation (%):
1990: ..
1997: ..

Recycling of paper and cardboard
Recycling rate (%):
1985: 30
1990: 27
1995: 34
(OECD average 1995: 42)

Change from 1985 (%): +13.3

Protection (totally and partially) of natural areas
Area (000 ha): 1,071 (1997)
Percentage of land area: 1.4

World Heritage sites
Number: 1 (1997)
Area (000 ha): 10

Threatened species
Percentage of species known, mid-1990s:
Mammals: 8.6
Birds: 13.9
Fish: 2.3
Reptiles: 4.7
Amphibians: 4.8
Vascular plants: 5.8

Wetlands of international importance
Number: 5 (1997)
Area (000 ha): 66

Freshwater resources
Safe water
Percentage of the population having access: 92 (1995)

Annual internal renewable water resources
Total (km³): 193.10
Per capita (m³): 3,117 (1995)

Annual withdrawals
1970–98:
Total (km³): 33.50
Percentage of total water resources: 17
Per capita (m³): 585

Waste-water treatment
Percentage of population served by waste-water treatment plants:
All treatments:
1985: 0.1
1995: 12.1

Technical Notes and References, OECD Countries

Data Reliability

Despite considerable effort to standardize the data, coverage, practices, and definitions differ among countries, and the usual warnings about using the figures carefully still apply. Moreover, cross-country and cross-time comparisons always involve complex technical problems which cannot be fully resolved. Although the data are drawn from authoritative sources, readers are urged to take these limitations into account in interpreting the indicators, particularly when making comparisons across countries. These limitations should also be taken into account when comparing country figures with world and OECD figures.

Area and population

These data are taken from the Central Intelligence Agency (1998), *World Factbook 1998* (Washington, DC: CIA). The data source for all figures is the CIA.

Population figures are estimated by the Bureau of the Census, based on statistics from population censuses, vital statistics registrations systems, or sample surveys pertaining to the recent past, and on assumptions about future trends. *Life expectancy at birth* indicates the number of years a newborn infant would live if prevailing patterns of mortality at the time of its birth were to stay the same throughout its life. World figures are weighted average. The *total fertility rate* represents the number of children that would be born to a woman if she were to live to the end of her child-bearing years and bear children at each age in accordance with prevailing age-specific fertility rates. World figures are weighted average. All figures are mid-1998 estimates.

Economy

The data are taken from The World Bank (1998), *World Development Report 1998/99* (New York: Oxford University Press) and World Resources Institute (1998), *World Resources 1998/99* (New York: World Resources Institute).

GNP per capita figures are calculated according to the *World Bank Atlas* method of converting data in national currency to US dollars. According to this method, the conversion factor for the latest indicated year is the average exchange rate for that year and the two preceding years, adjusted for differences in rates of inflation between the country concerned and the USA. This averaging smooths fluctuations in prices and exchange rates. To derive GNP per capita, GNP in US dollars is divided by the mid-year population for the latest of the three years. It is estimated by World Bank staff based on national accounts data collected by World Bank staff during economic missions or reported by national statistical offices such as the OECD. *GNP and GDP average annual growth rate* is calculated by the World Bank by using the least-squares regression method.

Mexico: Data on GDP growth rate 1990–97 cover a different time period, although the World Bank does not specify which.

Relations to Main International Agreements and Intergovernmental Organizations

Debt to the United Nations

These figures reflect outstanding contributions to the United Nations' regular budget, international tribunals, and peace-keeping operations as of 31 December 1998. The figures were provided by the United Nations Information Centre for the Nordic Countries.

Compliance with reporting requirements

The data included are compiled directly from the conventions secretariats in question, through a survey by *Yearbook of International Co-operation on Environment and Development*–Fridtjof Nansen Institute in April, May, and June 1999.

Compliance with reporting under the Convention on Long-Range Transboundary Air Pollution (LRTAP): Data correct as of June 1999. Emission data on SO_2, NO_2, and NMVOC are collected and analysed under the EMEP programme. There are no deadlines specified.

Compliance with reporting requirements under the United Nations Framework Convention on Climate Change (UNFCCC): Data correct as of June 1999. Only Annex I Parties were required to report 'second national communication' in 1997, with exception made for Parties with economies in transition (due date in 1998). Parties which are not Annex I Parties have in some cases reported voluntarily.

Czech Republic and *Hungary*: Both countries are defined as Annex I countries with economies in transition. Accordingly, their second national communications were due by 15 April 1998.

Compliance with reporting under the Montreal Protocol: Data correct as of 8 June 1999.

Compliance with reporting requirements under the Basel Convention: Data correct as of 31 May 1999. The formal deadline for reporting was 15 March 1999. The reports covered activities carried out in 1997.

Compliance with reporting requirements under the London Convention 1972: Data correct as of 24 May 1999. The deadline for reporting was 1 November 1998.

Compliance with reporting requirements under the MARPOL 73/78: The formal deadline for reporting was 31 September 1998. These data are correct as of that date. The data cover activities carried out in 1997.

Compliance with reporting requirements under CITES: Data correct as of June 1999. The deadline for submittance of the 1997 report was 31 October 1998. Data on submission was provided by the World Conservation Monitoring Centre (WCMC), United Kingdom.

Compliance with reporting requirements under the Ramsar Convention: Data correct as of 14 April 1999. The formal deadline for reporting was 1 September 1998.

Luxembourg: Luxembourg was a new party to the convention, and was not expected to report.

Contributions to funds related to agreements and intergovernmental organizations

The data included are compiled directly from the secretariats in question, through a survey by *Yearbook of International Co-operation on Environment and Development* –Fridtjof Nansen Institute in April, May, and June 1999.

Contributions to the LRTAP Convention: The figures are mandatory contributions to the *Protocol to the LRTAP Convention on Long-Term Financing of the Co-operative Programme for Monitoring and Evaluation of the Long-Range Transmission of Air Pollutants in Europe (EMEP)*.

Contributions to the Ozone Layer Convention: Multilateral Fund for the Implementation of the Montreal Protocol: Figures correct as of 25 May 1999.

Finland: $US93,490 were to be provided through bilateral assistance, rather than cash payments.

Switzerland: $US33,900 were bilateral assistance.

Contributions to the Global Environment facility (GEF): The figures show commitments received for the first replenishment of the GEF Trust Fund (GEF-1) in the period 1994–7 as of 15 April 1999. (The second replenishment (GEF-2) is a four-year capitalization for the period 1998–2002.) Special Drawing Rights (SDR) is a World Bank/GEF currency. SDR1 equals $US1,4010. The data are based on grant equivalence. Total pledges are SDR1,449.14 million. Total commitments received as of 15 April 1999 are SDR1,445.14. The commitment from Brazil for SDR4 million had not yet been received.

Contributions to the International Maritime Organization (IMO): Figures are national contributions by 31 December 1998.

Contributions to the United Nations Development Programme (UNDP) core budget: Figures are correct as of 1 July 1999. They are based on actual income received by UNDP in 1998, rather than pledged contributions.

Australia: The figure includes the payment of the 1996 and 1997 pledges, as they were both received by UNDP in 1998.

Contributions to the United Nations Environment Programme (UNEP) Environment Fund: The figures are based on actual payment, not pledges. The figures are correct as of 20 November 1998. At that date, total contributions of $US42,710,000 had been paid to the Environment Fund, while the outstanding pledges amounted to $US2,700,000. Further estimated contributions of $US1,310,000 were expected to be paid in respect of 1998, making a total of pledged/estimated contributions of $US46,720,000. The pledged/estimated contributions are $US115,030,000 for the biennium 1998–9.

Contributions to the United Nations Populations Fund (UNFPA): The figures are pledged contributions. As per 31 December 1997, the Czech Republic had yet to pay any of its pledged contribution. The contribution as a percentage of UNFPA's total budget has been calculated using the total government contributions as amount for total budget. In addition, UNFPA had income from interest and miscellaneous, amounting to $US2,900,000.

Finland: The amount includes $US1,700,000 for reproductive health programmes and $562,852 for Year 2000 Round of Population Censuses in Central Asian countries.

General Environment and Development Performance Indicators

Official development aid (ODA)

The figures on ODA are taken from World Resources Institute (1998), *World Resources 1998–99*. Data sources are OECD, the World Bank, and UN Population Division. A – (minus) in front of the figure means that the country receives aid.

Average annual official development assistance (in current US dollars) is the net amount of disbursed grants and concessional loans given by a country. Grants include gifts of money, goods, or services for which no repayment is required. A concessional loan has a grant element of 25 per cent or more. The GNP data used to calculate ODA as a percentage of GNP are *World Bank Atlas* GNP estimates (see Economy above).

The *ODA per capita* estimates are calculated using 1995 ODA estimates in current US dollars and UN Population Division data. The *OECD average ODA per capita* is calculated by *Yearbook of International Co-operation on Environment and Development*–Fridtjof Nansen Institute, based on the World Resources data. Luxembourg is not included.

Energy consumption

The data on energy consumption are from IEA/OECD (1998), *Energy Policies of IEA Countries: 1998 Review* (Paris: OECD).

The figures on *total consumption* relate to final consumption of energy by the different end-use sectors (i.e. industry, transport, agriculture, commerce, public services, and residential, as well as non-energy uses of gas, coal, oil, and oil products). They include consumption of solid fuels (mainly coal), oil, gas, electricity, and heat. Energy consumption *per capita* and *per GDP* are OECD/IEA calculations. Data sources are OECD and IEA.

Central government expenditure on education, defence, and health

Yearbook of International Co-operation on Environment and Development–Fridtjof Nansen Institute calculations, based on data on consolidated central government expenditure taken from International Monetary Fund (1990, 1995, 1998), *Government Finance Statistics Yearbook*, vols. xiv, xviv, and xxii (Washington: IMF), and data on GDP from OECD (1998), *National Accounts* (Paris: OECD). Data source: Data reported to the IMF by country correspondents. Some of the data are preliminary.

Australia, Republic of Korea, New Zealand, and *Turkey*: 1987 figures are 1988 data.

Denmark: 1996 and Ireland figures refer to 1995.

Greece: 1987 figures refer to 1991.

Hungary: 1987 figures refer to 1990.

Luxembourg: Data on military/defence refer to 1986 and 1993.

Specific Environment Indicators

Most of the data in this section are from country secretariats. It should therefore be kept in mind that definitions and estimation methods may vary among countries.

Atmosphere

SO$_x$ EMISSIONS

The figures for SO$_x$ emissions are from OECD (1995), *Environmental Data: Compendium 1995* (Paris: OECD) and OECD (1997), *Environmental Data: Compendium 1997* (Paris: OECD). Data source: OECD.

Australia: Rough Secretariat estimate based on a study by the Department of Primary Industries and Energy of Australia.

Czech Republic, Iceland, and *Republic of Korea*: Data are SO$_2$ only.

Greece: 1995 figure is from 1990 data.

Mexico: Provisional Secretariat estimates based on data from several sources.

New Zealand: Estimates based on a study by Auckland University.

The figures on change since 1980 are *Yearbook of International Co-operation on Environment and Development*–Fridtjof Nansen Institute calculations based on the data used.

NO$_x$ EMISSIONS

The figures for NO$_x$ emissions are from OECD (1995), *Environmental Data: Compendium 1995* (Paris: OECD) and OECD (1997), *Environmental Data: Compendium 1997* (Paris: OECD). Data source: OECD.

Australia: Rough Secretariat estimate based on a study by the Department of Primary Industries and Energy of Australia. 1987 figure refers to 1988.

Greece: 1995 figure is from 1990 data. 1987 figure is from 1985 data.

Luxembourg: 1987 figure is from 1985 data.

Mexico: Provisional Secretariat estimates based on data from several sources.

New Zealand: Estimates based on a study by Auckland University.

The figures for NO_x emissions per GDP and per capita are from OECD (1997), *Environmental Data*, and refer to the latest year available. The figures on change since 1980 are *Yearbook of International Co-operation on Environment and Development*–Fridtjof Nansen Institute calculations based on the data used.

CO_2 EMISSIONS

Energy-related CO_2 emissions are from IEA–OECD (1998), *Energy Policies of IEA Countries: 1998 Review* (Paris: IEA–OECD), IEA–OECD (1995), *Energy Policies of IEA Countries: 1994 Review* (Paris: IEA–OECD), IEA–OECD (1994), *Climate Change Policy Initiatives: 1994 Update*, i: *OECD Countries* (Paris: IEA–OECD), IEA–OECD (1992), *Climate Change Policy Initiatives* (Paris: IEA–OECD). Data source: IEA. The term 'energy-related CO_2 emissions' specifically means CO_2 from the combustion of coal and coal products, crude oil and derived products, natural gas, and peat.

CO_2 emission percentage *changes* are *Yearbook of International Co-operation on Environment and Development*–Fridtjof Nansen Institute calculations, based on the data already used.

CH_4 EMISSIONS (METHANE)

These data for *total emissions* and *change from 1990* are from the United Nations Framework Convention on Climate Change secretariat, available at <http://www.unfccc.de>. The data are anthropogenic emissions of methane. Data for 1995 refer to the latest year available. Data source: country reports.

Emissions per GDP and per capita are *Yearbook of International Co-operation on Environment and Development*–Fridtjof Nansen Institute calculations, based on the data used, and OECD/IEA data on population and GDP.

National emissions reduction *targets* are from IEA–OECD (1995), *Energy Policies of IEA Countries: 1994 Review* (Paris: IEA–OECD), IEA–OECD (1996), IEA–OECD (1994), *Climate Change Policy Initiatives: 1994 Update*, i: *OECD Countries* (Paris: IEA–OECD), *Global Environmental Change Report*, vol. viii, no. 21, 4, and Europe Environment, no. 514, 13 January 1998, 12. The reduction figure according to the Kyoto Protocol does not relate to CH_4 emissions alone. The countries shall ensure that their aggregate anthropogenic carbon dioxide equivalent of the Protocol's Annex A greenhouse gases (CO_2, CH_4, N_2O, HFC, PFC, and SF_6) does not exceed their assigned amounts in the commitment period 2008–12. The European Union signed the Kyoto Protocol as a unity. By the time the *Yearbook of International Co-operation on Environment and Development* went to press, the Union had not yet distributed the burdens among its member countries.

Australia, Denmark, and *Luxembourg*: 1995 figure refers to 1994.

CFC CONSUMPTION

Data from the United Nations Environment Programme secretariat. Data source: national secretariats. The consumption figures are multiplied by ozone-depleting potential.

CFC per capita figures are *Green Globe Yearbook*–Fridtjof Nansen Institute calculations based on the data used and population data.

Austria, Denmark, Finland, Greece, Ireland, and *Luxembourg*: The European Community (now European Union) reports CFC consumption on a total EC basis only. Consumption by country is thus not available. The included *per capita* and *change from 1986* figures are EC averages.

Switzerland: The figures representing negative totals are not explained in the UNEP Report.

Data on national reduction *target* according to the Copenhagen Amendment of the Montreal Protocol are from the UNEP Ozone Secretariat's Internet site at http://www.unep.org/unep/secretar/ozone/issues.htm.

For all time limits before total elimination is reached, another 10 per cent of base-level production is allowed to be produced additionally to meet the basic domestic needs of Parties operating under Article 5(1). Countries expected to have phased out CFC completely by 1996 are allowed 15 per cent of base-level production from then on to meet the needs of Article 5 Parties.

Hazardous substances

The data on consumption of pesticides are taken from OECD (1997), *Environmental Data: Compendium 1997* (Paris: OECD). All figures are *Yearbook of International Co-operation on Environment and Development*–Fridtjof Nansen Institute calculations based on the OECD data. 1995 data refer to the latest year available. Please note that the actual level of toxicity and persistence varies according to the type of pesticides used, and that definitions may vary among countries. Data source: OECD.

Greece and *Republic of Korea*: 1985 data refer to 1986.

Ireland: 1995 data refer to 1992. 1985 data refer to 1988.

Luxembourg: 1995 data refer to 1991.

Mexico and *New Zealand*: 1995 data refer to 1983.

Switzerland: 1995 data refer to 1994. 1985 data refer to 1988.

The figures on *OECD average* and *OECD change since 1985* are calculated by *Yearbook of International Co-operation on Environment and Development*–Fridtjof Nansen Institute, and based on the latest available year. On OECD average consumption in 1995, Australia and Iceland are excluded. The OECD average change since 1985 includes only the 24 countries with available data. Data source: OECD.

Data on *hazardous waste* are from OECD, *Environmental Data: Compendium 1997*. Definitions used refer to the waste streams to be controlled according to the Basel Convention on the Control of Transboundary Movements of Hazardous Wastes and their Disposal. Please bear in mind that the data do not necessarily represent all hazardous waste, nor its potential toxicity, and that definitions and methods of estimation vary from country to country. Figures on *imports* and *exports* should refer to actual amounts moved, but may in some cases refer to total authorizations granted. OECD average, waste as percentage of GDP, and import and export as percentage of production are calculated by *Yearbook of International Co-operation on Environment and Development*–Fridtjof Nansen Institute, on the basis of the data used, and national GDP statistics. In the OECD average, the Czech Republic, Hungary, Japan, and Turkey are not included. Data source: OECD.

Austria, Denmark, Finland, Hungary, Ireland, Luxembourg, and *Switzerland*: Figures are based on national definitions of hazardous waste, not the definitions according to the Basel Convention.

Greece, Republic of Korea, and *Mexico*: It is unclear which definitions have been used.

Greece: Exports: PCB waste only.

Hungary: According to the Basel definition, hazardous waste amounted to 2,306 kt in 1994.

Iceland: Excludes hazardous waste from households and small enterprises.
Mexico: 1995 production data refer to 1994.
New Zealand: Production: 1990 data. Exports: for recovery only.
Switzerland: Amount generated: all waste is defined as special waste in Swiss legislation. Amount generated according to Basel Convention: 504 kt in 1994.

Nuclear waste refers to spent fuel arisings expressed in tonnes of heavy metal. These data are from OECD, *Environmental Data: Compendium 1997*. Nuclear waste per unit of total primary energy supply (TPES) calculated by *Yearbook of International Co-operation on Environment and Development*–Fridtjof Nansen Institute, on the basis of the data used and TPES data from OECD. Data source: OECD.

Marine living resources

Data from OECD, *Environmental Data: Compendium 1997*. Data source: FAO. Data refer to fish catches in inland and marine waters, including freshwater fish, diadromous fish, marine fish, crustaceans, and molluscs. Figures for *catches per capita* and as *percentage of world catches* are *Yearbook of International Co-operation on Environment and Development*–Fridtjof Nansen Institute calculations based on the data used and OECD population data.

Denmark: Excludes Greenland and Faroe Islands.

Nature conservation and terrestrial living resources

Data for *wooded areas* are from OECD, *Environmental Data: Compendium 1997*. Sources: FAO, OECD, and national statistical yearbooks. Data include secretariat estimates. All figures are rounded to the nearest 10 km².

Austria: 1990–95 refer to 1986–90. Exploitable forests only.
Denmark: 1995 data refer to 1990.
Finland: 1995 figure is based on National Forest Inventory 1989–94. Includes all the wooded land where the annual potential wood production exceeds 0.1 m³/ha.
Iceland: Data refer to land outside agricultural areas.
Mexico: Excludes vegetation in arid areas, hydrophilic and halophilic vegetation, and affected forest areas included in Mexican forestry inventory.
New Zealand: 1995: 1992 data.

Data on *forest damage* are from UN/ECE and European Commission (1998), *Forest Condition in Europe: Results of the 1997 Survey* (Geneva: UN/ECE; Brussels: EC). Please note that the figures are based on national surveys and are not suitable for comparison between individual countries.

Czech Republic: Mainly trees older than 60 years assessed. 1990 figure is 1991 data.
Greece: Data exclude maquis.
Luxembourg: 1990 figure is 1991 data.

Data on *recycling* are from OECD, *Environmental Data: Compendium 1997*. Data source: OECD and Confederation of European Paper Industries (CEPI). Recycling is defined as reuse of material in a production process that diverts it from the waste stream, except for recycling within industrial plants and the reuse of material as fuel. The recycling rate is the ratio of the quantity recycled to the apparent consumption (domestic production + imports – exports). The *OECD average* is calculated by *Yearbook of International Co-operation on Environment and Development*–Fridtjof Nansen Institute, based on the data used. 1995 figures refer to the latest year available. The OECD average excludes the Czech Republic, Hungary, Iceland, Luxembourg, Mexico, New Zealand, and Poland.

Australia: 1995 figure refers to 1991. Data refer to newsprint, cardboard, and paper packagings: definitions of recycling vary according to the material collected (e.g. it may include amounts incinerated to divert them from landfill).
Czech Republic and *Ireland*: 1990 figure refers to 1987.
Denmark: 1995 figure refers to 1994.
Greece: Amounts recycled exclude imports and exports.
Iceland: 1995 figure refers to 1991.
Mexico: 1990 figure refers to 1991. Recycling rates are based on amounts of waste generated.
New Zealand: 1985 figure refers to 1983.
Turkey: 1985 figure refers to 1988.

Data for *protection of natural areas, World Heritage sites, and wetlands of international importance* are from World Resources Institute, *World Resources 1998–99*. Data source: World Conservation Monitoring Centre (WCMC). *Totally protected areas* are maintained in a natural state and are closed to extractive uses. *Partially protected areas* are areas that may be managed for specific uses, such as recreation or tourism, or areas that provide optimum conditions for certain species or communities of wildlife. Some extractive use within these areas is allowed.
World Heritage sites represent areas of 'outstanding universal value' for their natural features, their cultural value, or both their cultural and natural values. The data here include only natural and mixed natural and cultural sites. Any party to the Convention on Wetlands of International Importance Especially as Waterfowl Habitat (Ramsar, 1971) that agrees to respect the site's integrity and to establish wetland reserves can designate *wetlands of international importance*.

Data on *threatened species* are from OECD, *Environmental Data: Compendium 1997*. 'Threatened' refers to the sum of species in the 'endangered' and 'vulnerable' categories. Data source: OECD.

Austria: Threatened mammals: includes extinct and/or vanished species; birds: breeding species of national territory only; fish: freshwater only.
Czech Republic: Data refer to indigenous species.
Denmark: Fish: freshwater only.
Finland: Excludes extinct species. Mammals: indigenous species only; fish: excludes introduced species and occasionally present marine fish.
Greece: Fish: freshwater only; no marine species are threatened (1993 data).
Hungary: Threatened mammals, reptiles, and amphibians: protected and highly protected species; fish: freshwater species, includes indeterminate species.
Iceland: Birds: breeding species only; fish: freshwater species only.
Republic of Korea: Excludes extinct species. Fish: freshwater only.
Mexico: Excludes extinct species. Birds: resident and migratory species; fish: freshwater and marine species.
New Zealand: 'Threatened' refers to indigenous species only (many species have been introduced, most classed as noxious). Mammals: land-breeding mammals only; cetaceans are excluded; fish: freshwater fish only.
Switzerland: Mammals: indigenous species; birds: all breeding species on national territory; fish: indigenous species of Pisces and Cyclostomata.
Turkey: Birds: regularly breeding species.

Freshwater resources

Data for *safe water* is from World Bank, *World Development Report 1998/99*. Population with access to safe water is the percentage of the population with reasonable access to a safe water supply, including treated surface waters or untreated but uncontaminated water.
Annual internal renewable water resources and *annual withdrawals* data are from World Resources Institute, *World Resources 1996–97* and *1998–99*. Data compiled by WRI. *Annual internal renewable water resources* refers to the average annual flow of rivers and groundwater

from endogenous precipitation. Estimates of both runoff into rivers and recharge of groundwater should be used with caution when comparing different countries since they are based on differing sources and dates. These annual averages also disguise large seasonal, interannual, and long-term variations. *Per capita annual internal renewable water* data were calculated by using 1995 population estimates.

Data on *annual withdrawals* may refer to any year between 1980 and 1994. *Annual withdrawals as a percentage of water resources* refer to total water withdrawals, not counting evaporative losses from storage basins, as a percentage of internal renewable water resources and river flows from other countries.

Australia: data refer to 1985.
Austria, Czech Republic, Finland, Hungary, Iceland, Mexico, New Zealand, Switzerland, and *Turkey*: data refer to 1991.
Denmark: data refer to 1990.
Greece and *Ireland*: data refer to 1980.
Republic of Korea: data refer to 1992.

Data on *waste-water treatment* are taken from OECD, *Environmental Data: Compendium 1997,* and are defined as national population connected to public sewage treatment. Population connected to public sewage network without treatment is excluded. Data source: OECD. 1995 data refer to the latest available year; data prior to 1993 have not been considered.

Denmark: data refer to 1986 and 1994.
Finland, Hungary, and *Mexico*: 1995 figures refer to 1993.
Republic of Korea: 1995 figure refers to 1994.
Turkey: Data result from an inventory covering municipalities with an urban population of over 3,000, assuming that the sewerage system and treatment facilities serve the whole population of the municipalities.

Selected non-OECD Countries

Brazil

Area and population
Total area (km²): 8,511,965
Population (million): 169.8
Population density (inh/km²): 19.9
Life expectancy at birth (years): 64 (1998)
 (world average: 63)
Total fertility rate (children): 2.3 (1998)
 (world average: 2.9)

Economy
GNP per capita ($US000): 4.7 (1997)
 (world average: 5.1)

Growth rate
Average annual growth rate (%):
GNP per capita 1996–97: 1.1 (world average: 1.8)
GDP 1990–97: 3.1 (world average: 2.3)

Relations to Main International Agreements and Intergovernmental Organizations
Compliance with reporting requirements

	Latest report submitted (latest year due to report)	Proportion of national reports submitted by all Parties (%)	Quality of data submitted
Climate Change (UNFCCC)	Data not yet reported	100	n.a.
Montreal Protocol	Late (1997)	60	..
Basel Convention	On time (1999)	31	..
London Convention 1972	On time (1998)	..	..
MARPOL 73/78	On time (1998)	15	..
CITES	Late (1998)	49	Complete
Ramsar Convention	Late (1998)	97	..

Contributions to funds related to agreements and main IGOs with environmental activities

	Amount	Share of total budget (%)
Global Environment Facility (GEF) (1994–7)	SDR4,000,000	0.28
International Maritime Organization (IMO) (1998)	$US308,220	1.03
United Nations Environment Programme (UNEP): Environment Fund (1998)	$US113,364	0.24
United Nations Population Fund (UNFPA) (1997)	–	–

General Environment and Development Performance Indicators
Energy consumption

	1987	1990	1993	(OECD average 1993)	Change 1990–93 (%)
Total (million toe)	..	..	..	(124.5)	..
Per capita (toe)	..	..	..	(3.23)	..
Per GDP (toe/$US000)	..	..	..	(0.18)	..

Specific Environment Indicators

Atmosphere

CO₂ EMISSIONS
Total emissions from fuel combustion (million tonnes):
1990: 215.46
1996: 285.6

Per GDP (kg/$US)
1996: 0.51
(OECD average: 0.63)

Per capita (tonnes/capita):
1996: 1.8
(OECD average: 7.8)

Change from 1990 (%): +32.6

CFC CONSUMPTION
Total consumption (tonnes):
1986: 10,974
1996: 11,696

Per capita (kg/capita):
1996: 0.07

Change from 1986 (%): +7

National reduction target according to the Montreal Protocol, Copenhagen Amendment:
A freeze of 1995–7 average level by 1999, –50 per cent by 2005, –85 per cent by 2007, and complete elimination by 2010.

Nature conservation and terrestrial living resources
Forest area
Area (000 ha):
1995: 551,139

Average annual per cent change
1990–95: –0.5

Protection (totally and partially) of natural areas
Area (000 ha): 35,548 (1995)
Percentage of land area: 14.4

Freshwater resources
Safe water
Percentage of the population having access: 72 (1998)

Annual internal renewable water resources
Total (km³): 5,190.0 (1992)
Per capita (m³): 33,680

Annual withdrawals
1980–94
Total (km³): 36.47
Percentage of total water resources: 1
Per capita (m³): 245

Indonesia

Area and population
Total area (km²): 1,919,440
Population (million): 212.9
Population density (inh/km²): 110.9
Life expectancy at birth (years): 62 (1998)
    (world average: 63)
Total fertility rate (children): 2.6 (1998)
    (world average: 2.9)

Economy
GNP per capita ($US000): 1.1 (1997)
    (world average: 5.1)

Growth rate
Average annual growth rate (%):
GNP per capita 1996–97: 2.8 (world average: 1.8)
GDP 1990–97: 7.5 (world average: 2.3)

Relations to Main International Agreements and Intergovernmental Organizations
Compliance with reporting requirements

	Latest report submitted (latest year due to report)	Proportion of national reports submitted by all Parties (%)	Quality of data submitted
Climate Change (UNFCCC)	Data not yet reported	100	n.a.
Montreal Protocol	On time (1997)	60	Complete
Basel Convention	No report (1999)	31	n.a.
London Convention 1972	n.a.	..	n.a.
MARPOL 73/78	No report (1998)	15	n.a.
CITES	Late (1998)	49	Complete
Ramsar Convention	On time (1998)	97	..

Contributions to funds related to agreements and main IGOs with environmental activities

	Amount	Share of total budget (%)
Global Environment Facility (GEF) (1994–7)	–	–
International Maritime Organization (IMO) (1998)	$US167,857	0.56
United Nations Environment Programme (UNEP): Environment Fund (1998)	$US15,000	0.03
United Nations Population Fund (UNFPA) (1997)	$US174,148	0.06

General Environment and Development Performance Indicators
Energy consumption

	1987	1990	1993	(OECD average 1993)	Change 1990–93 (%)
Total (million toe)	24.45	52.36	69.06	(124.5)	+26.7
Per capita (toe)	0.14	0.19	0.24	(3.23)	+20.7
Per GDP (toe/$US000)	0.06	0.08	0.08	(0.18)	+4.9

Specific Environment Indicators

Atmosphere

CO_2 EMISSIONS

Total emissions from fuel combustion (million tonnes):
1990: 143.5
1996: 237.9

Per GDP (kg/$US)
1996: 1.33
(OECD average: 0.63)

Per capita (tonnes/capita):
1996: 1.2
(OECD average: 7.8)

Change from 1990 (%): +65.7

CFC CONSUMPTION

Total consumption (tonnes):
1986: 350
1996: 1,179

Per capita (kg/capita):
1996: –

Change from 1986 (%): +237

National reduction target according to the Montreal Protocol, Copenhagen Amendment:
A freeze of 1995–7 average level by 1999, –50 per cent by 2005, –85 per cent by 2007, and complete elimination by 2010.

Nature conservation and terrestrial living resources
Forest area
Area (000 ha):
1995: 109,791

Average annual per cent change
1990–95: –1.0

Protection (totally and partially) of natural areas
Area (000 ha): 17,509 (1995)
Percentage of land area: 9.7

Freshwater resources
Safe water
Percentage of the population having access: 62 (1995)

Annual internal renewable water resources
Total (km³): 2,530 (1992)
Per capita (m³): 13,230

Annual withdrawals
1980–94
Total (km³): 16.59
Percentage of total water resources: 1

Nigeria

Area and population
Total area (km²): 923,770
Population (million): 110.5
Population density (inh/km²): 119.7
Life expectancy at birth (years): 54 (1998)
  (world average: 63)
Total fertility rate (children): 6.3 (1998)
  (world average: 2.9)

Economy
GNP per capita ($US000): 0.3 (1997)
  (world average: 5.1)

Growth rate
Average annual growth rate (%):
GNP per capita 1996–97: 1.2 (world average: 1.8)
GDP 1990–97: 2.7 (world average: 2.3)

Relations to Main International Agreements and Intergovernmental Organizations
Compliance with reporting requirements

	Latest report submitted (latest year due to report)	Proportion of national reports submitted by all Parties (%)	Quality of data submitted
Climate Change (UNFCCC)	Data not yet reported	100	n.a.
Montreal Protocol	Late (1997)	60	Complete
Basel Convention	No report (1999)	31	n.a.
London Convention 1972	No report (1998)	..	n.a.
MARPOL 73/78	n.a.	15	n.a.
CITES	On time (1998)	49	Complete
Ramsar Convention	n.a.	97	n.a.

Contributions to funds related to agreements and main IGOs with environmental activities

	Amount	Share of total budget (%)
Global Environment Facility (GEF) (1994–7)	–	–
International Maritime Organization (IMO) (1998)	$US35,043	0.12
United Nations Environment Programme (UNEP): Environment Fund (1998)	–	–
United Nations Population Fund (UNFPA) (1997)	–	–

General Environment and Development Performance Indicators
Energy consumption

	1987	1990	1993	(OECD average 1993)	Change 1990–93 (%)
Total (million toe)	..	..	..	(124.5)	..
Per capita (toe)	..	..	..	(3.23)	..
Per GDP (toe/$US000)	..	..	..	(0.18)	..

Specific Environment Indicators

Atmosphere

CO$_2$ EMISSIONS
Total emissions from fuel combustion (million tonnes):
1990: 34.1
1996: 48.0

Per GDP (kg/$US)
1996: 1.42
(OECD average: 0.63)

Per capita (tonnes/capita):
1996: 0.4
(OECD average: 7.8)

Change from 1990 (%): +40.8

CFC CONSUMPTION
Total consumption (tonnes):
1986: 568
1996: 1,536

Per capita (kg/capita):
1996: 0.01

Change from 1986 (%): +170

National reduction target according to the Montreal Protocol, Copenhagen Amendment:
A freeze of 1995–7 average level by 1999, –50 per cent by 2005, –85 per cent by 2007, and complete elimination by 2010.

Nature conservation and terrestrial living resources
Forest area
Area (000 ha):
1995: 13,780

Average annual per cent change
1990–95: –0.9

Protection (totally and partially) of natural areas
Area (000 ha): 3,020 (1995)
Percentage of land area: 3.3

Freshwater resources
Safe water
Percentage of the population having access: 39 (1995)

Annual internal renewable water resources
Total (km^3): 221.0 (1998)
Per capita (m^3): 1,815

Annual withdrawals
1980–94
Total (km^3): 3.63
Percentage of total water resources: 2
Per capita (m^3): 41

South Africa

Area and population
Total area (km²): 1,219,912
Population (million): 42.8
Population density (inh/km²): 35.1
Life expectancy at birth (years): 56 (1998)
  (world average: 63)
Total fertility rate (children): 3.2 (1998)
  (world average: 2.9)

Economy
GNP per capita ($US000): 3.4 (1997)
  (world average: 5.1)

Growth rate
Average annual growth rate (%):
GNP per capita 1996–97: –0.5 (world average: 1.8)
GDP 1990–97: 1.5 (world average: 2.3)

Relations to Main International Agreements and Intergovernmental Organizations
Compliance with reporting requirements

	Latest report submitted (latest year due to report)	Proportion of national reports submitted by all Parties (%)	Quality of data submitted
Climate Change (UNFCCC)	Data not yet reported	100	n.a.
Montreal Protocol	No report (1997)	60	n.a.
Basel Convention	No report (1999)	31	n.a.
London Convention 1972	On time (1998)	..	..
MARPOL 73/78	No report	15	n.a.
CITES	Late (1998)	49	Complete
Ramsar Convention	Late (1998)	97	..

Contributions to funds related to agreements and main IGOs with environmental activities

	Amount	Share of total budget (%)
Global Environment Facility (GEF) (1994–7)	–	–
International Maritime Organization (IMO) (1998)	$US45,080	0.15
United Nations Environment Programme (UNEP): Environment Fund (1998)	$US22,000	0.05
United Nations Population Fund (UNFPA) (1997)	–	–

General Environment and Development Performance Indicators
Energy consumption

	1987	1990	1993	(OECD average 1993)	Change 1990–93 (%)
Total (million toe)	39.6	42.8	41.5	(124.5)	–2.9
Per capita (toe)	1.12	1.13	1.02	(3.23)	–9.4
Per GDP (toe/$US000)	0.26	0.27	0.26	(0.18)	–1.6

Specific Environment Indicators

Atmosphere

CO₂ EMISSIONS
Total emissions from fuel combustion (million tonnes):
1990: 231.5
1996: 317.3

Per GDP (kg/$US)
1996: 2.77
(OECD average: 0.63)

Per capita (tonnes/capita):
1996: 8.4
(OECD average: 7.8)

Change from 1990 (%): +37.1

CFC CONSUMPTION
Total consumption (tonnes):
1986: 12,499
1996: –

Per capita (kg/capita):
1996: –

Change from 1986 (%): –100

National reduction target according to the Montreal Protocol, Copenhagen Amendment:
–75 per cent by 1994, taking 1986 as base year. Complete elimination by 1996. Target achieved.

Nature conservation and terrestrial living resources
Forest area
Area (000 ha):
1995: 8,499

Average annual per cent change
1990–95: –0.2

Protection (totally and partially) of natural areas
Area (000 ha): 6,578 (1995)
Percentage of land area: 5.4

Freshwater resources
Safe water
Percentage of the population having access: 70 (1995)

Annual internal renewable water resources
Total (km³): 44.8 (1995)
Per capita (m³): 1,011

Annual withdrawals
1980–94
Total (km³): 13.31
Percentage of total water resources: 30
Per capita (m³): 359

Thailand

Area and population
Total area (km²): 514,000
Population (million): 60.0
Population density (inh/km²): 116.8
Life expectancy at birth (years): 69 (1998)
  (world average: 63)
Total fertility rate (children): 1.8 (1998)
  (world average: 2.9)

Economy
GNP per capita ($US000): 2.8 (1997)
  (world average: 5.1)

Growth rate
Average annual growth rate (%):
GNP per capita 1996–97: –1.3 (world average: 1.8)
GDP 1990–97: 7.5 (world average: 2.3)

Relations to Main International Agreements and Intergovernmental Organizations
Compliance with reporting requirements

	Latest report submitted (latest year due to report)	Proportion of national reports submitted by all Parties (%)	Quality of data submitted
Climate Change (UNFCCC)	Data not yet reported	100	n.a.
Montreal Protocol	On time (1997)	60	Complete
Basel Convention	On time (1999)	31	..
London Convention 1972	n.a.	..	n.a.
MARPOL 73/78	n.a.	15	n.a.
CITES	Late (1998)	49	Complete
Ramsar Convention	Late (1998)	97	..

Contributions to funds related to agreements and main IGOs with environmental activities

	Amount	Share of total budget (%)
Global Environment Facility (GEF) (1994–7)	–	–
International Maritime Organization (IMO) (1998)	$US121,130	0.40
United Nations Environment Programme (UNEP): Environment Fund (1998)	$US15,000	0.03
United Nations Population Fund (UNFPA) (1997)	$US96,009	0.03

General Environment and Development Performance Indicators
Energy consumption

	1987	1990	1993	(OECD average 1993)	Change 1990–93 (%)
Total (million toe)	..	..	..	(124.5)	..
Per capita (toe)	..	..	..	(3.23)	..
Per GDP (toe/$US000)	..	..	..	(0.18)	..

Specific Environment Indicators

Atmosphere

CO_2 EMISSIONS
Total emissions from fuel combustion (million tonnes):
1990: 88.0
1996: 175.2

Per GDP (kg/$US)
1996: 1.28
(OECD average: 0.63)

Per capita (tonnes/capita):
1996: 2.9
(OECD average: 7.8)

Change from 1990 (%): +99.2

CFC CONSUMPTION
Total consumption (tonnes):
1986: 2,300
1996: 5,550

Per capita (kg/capita):
1996: 0.05

Change from 1986 (%): +141

National reduction target according to the Montreal Protocol, Copenhagen Amendment:
A freeze of 1995–7 average level by 1999, –50 per cent by 2005, –85 per cent by 2007, and complete elimination by 2010.

Nature conservation and terrestrial living resources
Forest area
Area (000 ha):
1995: 11,630

Average annual per cent change
1990–95: –2.6

Protection (totally and partially) of natural areas
Area (000 ha): 6,688 (1995)
Percentage of land area: 13.1

Freshwater resources
Safe water
Percentage of the population having access: 81 (1995)

Annual internal renewable water resources
Total (km^3): 110.0 (1992)
Per capita (m^3): 3,190

Annual withdrawals
1980–94
Total (km^3): 23.75
Percentage of total water resources: 12
Per capita (m^3): 433

Technical Notes and References, non-OECD Countries

Data Reliability

Despite considerable effort to standardize the data, coverage, practices, and definitions differ among countries, and the usual warnings about using the figures carefully still apply. Moreover, cross-country and cross-time comparisons always involve complex technical problems which cannot be fully resolved. Although the data are drawn from authoritative sources, readers are urged to take these limitations into account in interpreting the indicators, particularly when making comparisons across countries. These limitations should also be taken into account when comparing country figures with world and OECD figures.

Area and population

These data are taken from the Central Intelligence Agency (1998), *World Factbook 1998* (Washington, DC: CIA). Data source for all figures are the CIA.

Population figures are estimated by the Bureau of the Census, based on statistics from population censuses, vital statistics registrations systems, or sample surveys pertaining to the recent past, and on assumptions about future trends. *Life expectancy at birth* indicates the number of years a newborn infant would live if prevailing patterns of mortality at the time of its birth were to stay the same throughout its life. World figures are weighted average. The *total fertility rate* represents the number of children that would be born to a woman if she were to live to the end of her child-bearing years and bear children at each age in accordance with prevailing age-specific fertility rates. World figures are weighted average. All figures are mid-1998 estimates.

South Africa: South Africa took a census on 10 October 1996, which showed a total of 37,859,000 (after a 6.8 per cent adjustment for underenumeration based on a post-enumeration survey); this figure is still about 10 per cent below projections from earlier censuses. Since the full results of the census have not been released for analysis, the numbers shown for South Africa do not take into consideration the results of this 1996 census.

Economy

The data are taken from the World Bank (1998), *World Development Report 1998/99* (New York: Oxford University Press).

GNP per capita figures are calculated according to the *World Bank Atlas* method of converting data in national currency to US dollars. According to this method, the conversion factor for the latest indicated year is the average exchange rate for that year and the two preceding years, adjusted for differences in rates of inflation between the country concerned and the USA. This averaging smooths fluctuations in prices and exchange rates. To derive GNP per capita, GNP in US dollars is divided by the mid-year population for the latest of the three years. It is estimated by World Bank staff based on national accounts data collected by World Bank staff during economic missions or reported by national statistical offices such as the OECD. *GNP and GDP average annual growth rate* is calculated by the World Bank by using the least-squares regression method.

Relations to Main International Agreements and Intergovernmental Organizations

Compliance with reporting requirements

The data included are compiled directly from the conventions secretariats in question, through a survey by *Yearbook of International Co-operation on Environment and Development*–Fridtjof Nansen Institute in April, May, and June 1999.

Compliance with reporting requirements under the United Nations Framework Convention on Climate Change (UNFCCC): Data correct as of June 1999. The first national communications from these Parties, not included in Annex I to the UNFCCC, have due dates in accordance with Article 12.5 of the Convention. These data are not comparable with the data on OECD countries.

Compliance with reporting under the Montreal Protocol: Data correct as of 28 February 1998.

Compliance with reporting requirements under the Basel Convention: Data correct as of 31 May 1999. The formal deadline for reporting was 15 March 1999. The reports covered activities carried out in 1997.

Compliance with reporting requirements under CITES: Data correct as of June 1999. The deadline for submission of the 1997 report was 31 October 1998. Data on submission was provided by the World Conservation Monitoring Centre (WCMC), United Kingdom.

Compliance with reporting requirements under the London Convention 1972: Data correct as of 24 May 1999. The deadline for reporting was 1 November 1998.

Compliance with reporting requirements under the MARPOL 73/78: The formal deadline for reporting was 31 September 1998. These data are correct as of that date. The data cover activities carried out in 1997.

Compliance with reporting requirements under the Ramsar Convention: Data correct as of 14 April 1999. The formal deadline for reporting was 1 September 1998.

Contributions to funds related to agreements and intergovernmental organizations

The data included are compiled directly from the secretariats in question, through a survey by *Yearbook of International Co-operation on Environment and Development*–Fridtjof Nansen Institute in April, May, and June 1999.

Contributions to the Global Environment facility (GEF): The figures show commitments received for the first replenishment of the GEF Trust Fund (GEF-1) in the period 1994–7 as of 15 April 1999. (The second replenishment (GEF-2) is a four-year capitalization for the period 1998–2002.) Special Drawing Rights (SDR) is a World Bank/GEF currency. SDR1 equals $US1,4010. The data are based on grant equivalence. Total pledges are SDR1,449.14 million. Total commitments received as of 15 April 1999 are SDR1,445.14. The commitment from Brazil for SDR4 million had not yet been received.

Contributions to the International Maritime Organization (IMO): Figures are national contributions by 31 December 1998.

Contributions to the United Nations Environment Programme (UNEP) Environment Fund: The figures are based on actual payment, not pledges. The figures are correct as of 20 November 1998. At that date, total contributions of $US42,710,000 had been paid to the Environment Fund, while the outstanding pledges amounted to $US2,700,000. Further estimated contributions of $US1,310,000 were expected to be paid in respect of 1998, making a total of pledged/

estimated contributions of $US46,720,000. The pledged/estimated contributions are $US115,030,000 for the biennium 1998–9.

Contributions to the United Nations Populations Fund (UNFPA): The figures are pledged contributions. The contribution as a percentage of UNFPA's total budget has been calculated using the total government contributions as an amount for the total budget. In addition, UNFPA had income from interest and miscellaneous sources, amounting to $US2,900,000.

Thailand: Part or whole of the payment was made in non-convertible currency.

General Environment and Development Performance Indicators
Energy consumption

The data on energy consumption are from IEA–OECD (1996), *Climate Change Policy Initiatives–1995/96 Update. Volume II: Selected Non-IEA Countries* (Paris: IEA–OECD). The data on OECD average are from IEA–OECD (1995), *Energy Policies of IEA Countries, 1994 Review* (Paris: OECD–IEA). Data source: IEA.

Total energy consumption covers the sum of consumption by the following sectors: industry, transport, agriculture, residential, commercial, public services, and non-specified.

Total final consumption per GDP is measured in metric tonnes of oil equivalent (toe) per $US000 (at 1990 prices and exchange rates) of GDP.

Figures on *average OECD energy consumption* are Yearbook of International Co-operation on Environment and Development–Fridtjof Nansen Institute calculations, based on the IEA data. The calculation basis for OECD average energy consumption per capita and per unit of GDP does not include Iceland. The average is unweighted.

Specific Environment Indicators

Most of the data in this section are from country secretariats. It should therefore be kept in mind that definitions and estimation methods may vary among countries, and there may be serious uncertainties about these data.

Atmosphere
CO₂ EMISSIONS

Data on CO_2 emissions are from IEA (1997), *Key World Energy Statistics* (Paris: IEA), and other IEA data received from the IEA Secretariat. Data source: IEA. The figures include emissions from coal, oil, and gas in the following sectors: public electricity and heat production, unallocated heat producers, other energy industries, manufacturing industries and construction, transport (including international aviation bunkers), 'other sectors' (including residential), and unallocated energy use. Although the OECD averages are included in this section, the OECD emissions are energy-related emissions (see Technical Notes and References, OECD section, for a complete definition); thus, owing to minor definition details, the figures are not completely comparable.

CFC CONSUMPTION

Data from the United Nations Environment Programme secretariat. Data source: national secretariats. The consumption figures are multiplied by ozone-depleting potential.

CFC per capita figures are Yearbook of International Co-operation on Environment and Development–Fridtjof Nansen Institute calculations based on the data used and population data.

Nigeria: 1986 figure refers to 1989, 1996 figure refers to 1995..

Data on national reduction *target* according to the Copenhagen Amendment of the Montreal Protocol are from the UNEP Ozone Secretariat's Internet site at http://www.unep.org/unep/secretar/ozone/issues.htm.

For all time limits before total elimination is reached, another 10 per cent of base-level production is allowed to be produced additionally to meet the basic domestic needs of Parties operating under Article 5(1). Countries expected to have phased out CFC completely by 1996 are allowed 15 per cent of base-level production from then on to meet the needs of Article 5 Parties.

Nature conservation and terrestrial living resources

Data on *forest area, average annual per cent change*, and *protection of natural areas* are from World Resources Institute (1998), *World Resources 1998/99* (New York: World Resources Institute). Forest area consists of all forest area for temperate developed countries, and the sum of natural forest and plantation area categories. Change of forest area, deforestation, is defined as the clearing of forest lands for all forms of agricultural uses (shifting cultivation, permanent agriculture, and ranching) and for other land uses such as settlements, other infrastructure, and mining. In tropical countries this entails clearing that reduces tree crown cover to less than 10 per cent. It should be noted that deforestation, as defined here, does not reflect changes within the forest stand or site, such as selective logging (unless the forest cover is permanently reduced to less than 10 per cent). *Totally protected areas* are maintained in a natural state and are closed to extractive uses. *Partially protected areas* are areas that may be managed for specific uses, such as recreation or tourism, or areas that provide optimum conditions for certain species or communities of wildlife. Some extractive use within these areas is allowed. Data sources: Food and Agricultural Organization (FAO) and World Conservation Monitoring Centre (WCMC).

Freshwater resources

Data for *safe water* is from World Bank, *World Development Report 1998/99*. Population with access to safe water is the percentage of the population with reasonable access to a safe water supply, including treated surface waters or untreated but uncontaminated water.

Annual internal renewable water resources and *annual withdrawals* data are from World Resources Institute, *World Resources 1996–97* and *1998–99*. Data compiled by WRI. *Annual internal renewable water resources* refers to the average annual flow of rivers and groundwater from endogenous precipitation. Estimates of both runoff into rivers and recharge of groundwater should be used with caution when comparing different countries since they are based on differing sources and dates. These annual averages also disguise large seasonal, interannual, and long-term variations. *Per capita annual internal renewable water* data were calculated by using 1995 population estimates.

Data on *annual withdrawals* may refer to any year between 1980 and 1994. *Annual withdrawals as a percentage of water resources* refer to total water withdrawals, not counting evaporative losses from storage basins, as a percentage of internal renewable water resources and river flows from other countries.

Brazil and *South Africa*: data refer to 1990.
Indonesia and *Nigeria*: data refer to 1987.
Thailand: data refer to 1989.

Index

Entries in the reference sections are denoted in italics

CCD, *see* Convention to Combat Desertification
CDM, *see* UN Framework Convention on Climate Change: Clean Development Mechanism
Center for Russian Environmental Policy, 49
Central America, 23
Central Europe, 20, 71
CEO, *see* chief executive officer
Ceres Initiative, 66
Certificates of Financial Responsibility (COFRs), 35
CFCs, *see* chlorofluorocarbons
CGIAR, *see* Consultative Group on International Agricultural Research
CH2M Hill, 67
CH$_4$, *see* methane
Changing Course: A Global Business Perspective on Development and the Environment, 66, 70
Chaytor, Beatrice, 55–64
chemical hazards, *see* hazardous substances
Chemical Works Sokolov, 67
Chernobyl, 49–50, 52
Chicago Convention on International Civil Aviation, *see* Annex 16, vol. II (Environmental Protection: Aircraft Engine Emissions) to the 1944 Chicago Convention on International Civil Aviation
chief executive officer (CEO), 67, 69
China, People's Republic of, 24, 49, 67:
  climate policy of, 24;
  nuclear reactors of, 49
China Petro-Chemical, 67
Chlorine Chemistry Council (CCC), 68
chlorofluorocarbons (CFCs), 57
CI, *see* Consumers International
CII, *see* Confederation of Indian Industry
CITES, *see* Convention on International Trade in Endangered Species of Wild Fauna and Flora
civil liability, 52
CLC, *see* Convention on Civil Liability for Oil Pollution 1969
Clean Development Mechanism (CDM), *see* UN Framework Convention on Climate Change
clean technology, 70
Climate Action Network (CAN), 20, *260*, *277–84*
climate change, *see* global climate
climate convention, *see* Framework Convention on Climate Change
Clinton, Bill, President of the United States of America, 24
CMS, *see* Convention on the Conservation of Migratory Species of Wild Animals
CO$_2$, *see* carbon dioxide
coastal states, 31–6
COFRs, *see* Certificates of Financial Responsibility
Commission on Sustainable Development (CSD), *see* UN Commission on Sustainable Development
commodities, 36
common heritage of mankind, 41
compensation, 31–7, 40, 45, 52
compensation system, 31–7
compliance, 23–4, 35–6, 39–45, 57
Confederation of Indian Industry (CII), 71
conference of the parties (CoP), 19–21, 23–4, 44
conservation, 39–43, 45–56, 59–60
Consultative Group on International Agricultural Research (CGIAR), 44
Consumers International (CI), 72, *261*, *277–84*
consumption, 19, 56, 71
continental shelf, 34
contingent valuation methodology (CVM), *see* United States of America: Oil Pollution Act

Convention(s):
  Concerning the Protection of the World Cultural and Natural Heritage (World Heritage Convention), *166–7*, *196–211*;
  for Co-operation in the Protection and Development of the Marine and Coastal Environment of the West and Central African Region, *155*, *196–211*;
  for the Conservation of Atlantic Tunas (ICCAT), *158–9*, *196–211*;
  for the Conservation of the Red Sea and Gulf of Aden Environment, *see* Regional Convention for the Conservation of the Red Sea and Gulf of Aden Environment;
  for the Prevention of Pollution from Ships, 1973, as modified by the Protocol of 1978 relating thereto (MARPOL 1973/78), *124–6*, *196–211*;
  for the Protection and Development of the Marine Environment of the Wider Caribbean Region (Cartagena Convention), *148*, *196–211*;
  for the Protection, Management, and Development of the Marine and Coastal Environment of the Eastern African Region, *149*, *196–211*;
  for the Protection of the Marine Environment and Coastal Area of the South-East Pacific, *154*, *196–211*;
  for the Protection of the Marine Environment of the North-East Atlantic (OSPAR Convention), *140–1*, *196–211*;
  for the Protection of the Marine Environment and the Coastal Region of the Mediterranean (Barcelona Convention), *151*, *196–211*;
  for the Protection of the Mediterranean Sea against Pollution (Barcelona Convention), *see* Convention for the Protection of the Marine Environment and the Coastal Region of the Mediterranean;
  for the Protection of the Natural Resources and Environment of the South Pacific Region (SPREP Convention), *153*, *196–211*;
  for the Protection of the Ozone Layer, including the 1987 Montreal Protocol on Substances that Deplete the Ozone Layer, *96–101*, *196–211*;
  for the Regulation of Whaling (ICRW), *160–2*, *196–211*;
  on Access to Information, Public Participation in Decision-Making and Access to Justice in Environmental Matters (Århus Convention), *78–9*, *196–211*;
  on Assistance in the Case of a Nuclear Accident or Radiological Emergency (Assistance Convention), 50–1, *186–7*, *196–211*;
  on atmospheric pollution, 19–29, *82–101*, *196–211*;
  on the Ban of the Import into Africa and the Control of Transboundary Movements and Management of Hazardous Wastes within Africa (Bamako Convention), *102–3*, *196–211*;
  on Biological Diversity (CBD), *39–47*, *168–71*, *196–211*:
    Conference of the Parties (COP), 44;
    declaration on intellectual property rights, 44;
    Executive Secretary of, 44;
  on Civil Liability for Damage Caused during Carriage of Dangerous Goods by Road, Rail, and Inland Navigation Vessels (CRTD), *104–5*, *196–211*;
  on Civil Liability for Nuclear Damage, *see* Vienna Convention on Civil Liability for Nuclear Damage;
  on Civil Liability for Oil Pollution Damage 1969 (1969 CLC), 33–5, *126–9*, *196–211*;
  on climate change, *see* UN Framework Convention on Climate Change;
  on the Conservation of Antarctic Marine Living Resources (CCAMLR), *156–7*, *196–211*;
  on the Conservation of Migratory Species of Wild Animals (CMS), *172–3*, *196–211*;
  on the Control of Transboundary Movements of Hazardous Waste and their Disposal (Basel Convention), 60, *106–9*, *196–211*;
  on Early Notification of a Nuclear Accident (Notification Convention), 50–1, *188–9*, *196–211*;
  on Environmental Impact Assessment in a Transboundary Context, *80–81*, *196–211*;

on the Establishment of an International Fund for Compensation for Oil Pollution Damage 1971 (1971 Fund Convention), 33–5, *128–9*, *196–211*;
on freshwater resources, *194–211*;
on general environmental concerns, 78–81, *196–211*;
on hazardous substances, *102–120*, *196–211*;
on International Trade in Endangered Species of Wild Fauna and Flora (CITES), *174–5*, *196–211*;
on the Law of the Sea, *see* UN Convention on the Law of the Sea (UNCLOS);
on liability, 52, *104–5*, *126–7*, *130–1*, *192–3*, *196–211*;
on Liability and Compensation for Damage in Connection with the Carriage of Hazardous and Noxious Substances by Sea (HNS), 35, *130–1*, *196–211*;
on Long-Range Transboundary Air Pollution (LRTAP), *84–9*, *196–211*;
on marine environment, 31–5, *121–55*, *196–211*;
on marine living resources, *156–62*, *196–211*;
on marine pollution, 31–5, *121–55*, *196–211*;
on nature conservation and terrestrial living resources, 39–47, *163–85*, *196–211*;
on nuclear safety, 49–53, *186–93*, *196–211*;
on Nuclear Safety, 51–2, *190–1*, *196–211*;
on Oil Pollution Preparedness, Response, and Co-operation (OPRC), *132–3*, *196–211*;
on the Physical Protection of Nuclear Material, 51–2;
on the Prevention of Marine Pollution by Dumping of Wastes and Other Matter (London Convention 1972), *121–3*, *196–211*;
on the Prior Informed Consent Procedure for Certain Hazardous Chemicals and Pesticides in International Trade (PIC Convention), *110–12*, *196–211*;
on the Protection and Use of Transboundary Watercourses and International Lakes (ECE Water Convention), *194–211*;
on the Protection of the Black Sea against Pollution, *147*, *196–211*;
on the Protection of the Marine Environment of the Baltic Sea Area (1974 Helsinki Convention), *142–3*, *196–211*;
on the Protection of the Marine Environment of the Baltic Sea Area (1992 Helsinki Convention), *144–5*, *196–211*;
on Salvage, 31;
on Standards of Training, Certification and Watchkeeping (STCW), 31, 36;
on Substances that Deplete the Ozone Layer, *see* Convention for the Protection of the Ozone Layer;
on Supplementary Compensation for Nuclear Damage, 52;
on Third Party Liability in the Field of Nuclear Energy, 52;
on the Transboundary Effects of Industrial Accidents, *113–14*, *196–211*;
on Wetlands of International Importance, especially as Waterfowl Habitat (Ramsar Convention), *176–7*, *196–211*;
Relating to Intervention on the High Seas in Cases of Oil Pollution Casualties (Intervention Convention), *134*, *196–211*;
to Ban the Importation into Forum Island Countries of Hazardous and Radioactive Wastes and to Control the Transboundary Movement and Management of Hazardous Wastes within the South Pacific Region (Waigani Convention), *115–16*, *196–211*;
to Combat Desertification (CCD), *178–9*, *196–211*;
within the UNEP Regional Seas Programme, *see* UN Environment Programme
Cooper, Richard N., 25
CoP, *see* conference of the parties
Corporate Planet, 72
Corporate Watch, 72–3
cost-effectiveness, 20–1
country profiles, *285–363*
CRTD, *see* Convention on Civil Liability for Damage Caused during Carriage of Dangerous Goods by Road, Rail, and Inland Navigation Vessels

CSD, *see* UN Commission on Sustainable Development
CTE, *see* World Trade Organization: Committee on Trade and Environment
CVM, *see* United States of America: Oil Pollution Act: contingent valuation methodology
Czech Republic, 67, *294–7*, *346–50*
dangerous substances, *see* hazardous substances
Denmark, 50, *298–301*, *346–50*
DeSimone, Livio, former Chairman of the World Business Council for Sustainable Development and Chief Executive Officer of the 3M Company, 65
development aid, *see* aid
development assistance, *see* aid
discharges at sea, 31–7
Dispute Settlement Body (DSB), *see* World Trade Organization
Dispute Settlement Understanding (DSU), *see* World Trade Organization
dispute settlement system, 55, 58–9, 62
disputes, 55, 58–60, 62
donors, *see* financial assistance
Dow Chemicals, 67
DSB, *see* World Trade Organization: Dispute Settlement Body
DSU, *see* World Trade Organization: Dispute Settlement Understanding
Du Pont, 66–7
Earth Council, *261*
Earth Summit, *see* UN Conference on Environment and Development
Earthwatch Institute, *262*, *277–84*
East Germany, 22
Eastern Europe, 20, 22, 71
Eastman Kodak, 67
EC, *see* European Union
ECE Water Convention, *see* Convention on the Protection and Use of Transboundary Watercourses and International Lakes
ECJ, *see* European Court of Justice
ECO, 20
eco-efficiency, 65–6, 69–71, 73
Eco-Efficiency, 66
ecology, 71–1, 72
economic growth, 19
economic sanctions, 41
economies in transition, *see* transitional economies
ecosystem, 19, 23
EEB, *see* European Environmental Bureau
EEC, *see* European Union
El Salvador, 24
ELCI, *see* Environmental Liaison Centre International
emission credits, 20, 23, 25
emission quotas, 20, 25
emission trading, 20–1, 23, 25, 69
emission trading schemes, 20
endangered species, 43, 57, 59
energy consumption, 71
enforcement, 24, 36, 43, 45, 57–8, 60
environmental groups, *see* non-governmental organizations
Environmental Liaison Centre International (ELCI), *262*, *277–84*
environmental organizations, *see* NGOs
Environmental Performance and Shareholder Value, 66
EPA, *see* United States of America: Environmental Protection Agency
EPOC, *see* Organization for Economic Co-operation and Development, Environment Policy Committee
equitable sharing, 39–41, 43, 45
Eurogas, *see* European Gas Industry
Europe, 20–2, 23–6, 41, 43, 59–60, 62, 71
European Agreement Concerning the International Carriage of Dangerous Goods by Road (ADR), *117–18*, *196–211*
European Business Council for a Sustainable Energy Future, E5, 23

European Commission, *see* European Union (EU)
European Community, *see* European Union (EU)
European Court of Justice (ECJ), 60–2:
  Belgian waste case, 60;
  Cassis de Dijon case, 60;
  waste oils case, 60
European Environmental Bureau (EEB), *263, 277–84*
European Economic Community (EEC), *see* European Union (EU)
European Gas Industry (Eurogas), 23
European Parliament, *see* European Union
European Patent Convention, 41
European Union (EU), 20–2, 24–6, 41, 43, 59–60, 62, *216*:
  climate policy of, 21, 24, 26;
  Council Directive 75/439 of, 60;
  directive on biotechnology patents, 43;
  EC Treaty, 59;
  European Commission of, 43, 60;
  European Parliament, 25, 43;
  global climate emissions of, 20–2
exclusive economic zones, 34
Exxon Valdez, 31–2, 34–6
FAO, *see* Food and Agriculture Organization
farmers' cultivars, 40–1
FBSD, *see* Foundation for Business and Sustainable Development
FCCC, *see* UN Framework Convention on Climate Change
Federal Water Pollution Control Act (FWPCA), *see* United States of America
Fiat Auto, 67
Fiji, 24
financial assistance, 20, 23, 25, 40, 42
financial markets, 69, 71
Financing Change, 66
Finland, 50, *302–5, 346–50*
fishery zone, 34
Fissile Material Cut-off Treaty, 53
FoEI, *see* Friends of the Earth International
food, 19, 40, 42
Food and Agriculture Organization (FAO), 42, 44, *119–20, 180–2, 196–211, 219*:
  International Undertaking on Plant Genetic Resources, *180–2, 196–211*;
  International Code of Conduct on the Distribution and Use of Pesticides, *119–20, 196–211*
food security, 40–1
Forest Stewardship Council (FSC), *264, 277–84*
forestry, 22–4
forests, 69
Foundation for Business and Sustainable Development (FBSD), 66, 70, 74
Framework Convention on Climate Change, *see* UN Framework Convention on Climate Change
France, 49, 67:
  nuclear reactors of, 49
freshwater resources, 69
Friends of the Earth International (FoEI), *264, 277–84*
From Ideas to Action, 66
FSC, *see* Forest Stewardship Council
Fund Convention, *see* Convention on the Establishment of an International Fund for Compensation for Oil 1971
funds, *see* financial assistance
FWCPA, *see* United States of America: Federal Water Pollution Control Act
G-7, *see* Group of Seven
GATT, *see* World Trade Organization: General Agreement on Tariffs and Trade
GCC, *see* Global Climate Coalition
GEF, *see* Global Environment Facility

gene banks, 41, 44
General Agreement on Tariffs and Trade (GATT), *see* World Trade Organization
General Motors, 26, 67
genetic piracy, 43
genetic resources, 39–45
Geneva, 53, 58, 67
Geneva Conference on Disarmament, 53
Germany, 22, 67:
  global climate emissions of, 22
Glaxo Wellcome, 67
global climate, 19–27, 57, 69
Global Climate Coalition (GCC), 26
global climate emissions, 19–27, 62
Global Environment Facility (GEF), 20, 22, *220*
Global Legislators for a Balanced Environment (GLOBE), 26, *275*
global market liberalization, 72
Global Sustainable Development Facility—2B2M: 2 Billion People to Market by 2020, 65
global warming, *see* global climate
globalization, 72
GLOBE, *see* Global Legislators for a Balanced Environment
Gold, Edgar, 31–7
Great Britain, *see* United Kingdom
Greece, *306–9, 346–50*
Green or Greenwash? A Greenpeace Direction Kit, 72
greenhouse, *see* global climate
Greenpeace (International), 23, 65, 72–3, *265, 277–84*
greenwash, 65, 72–3
Group of Seven (G-7), 24
Grupo Vitro, 67
Gupta, Joyeeta, 19–29
Hare, Bill, 23
hazardous substances, 32, 57, 70–1
hazardous wastes, 57
Heineken, 67
Helsinki Convention(s), *see* Convention on the Protection of the Marine Environment of the Baltic Sea Area
High Level Symposium on Trade and Environment, *see* World Trade Organization
high-yielding varieties, 40
Hitachi, 67
HNS, *see* on Liability and Compensation for Damage in Connection with the Carriage of Hazardous and Noxious Substances by Sea
Hoechst, 67
hot air, 23, 25
Hungary, *310–13, 346–50*
hunger, 23
Hurtado, Maria Elena, 72
hydrocarbons, 35
hydrofluorocarbons, 20
IAEA, *see* International Atomic Energy Agency
IBAPCC, *see* International Business Action Plan on Climate Change
ICAO, *see* Annex 16, International Civil Aviation Organization Convention
ICBG, *see* International Co-operation Biodiversity Group
ICC, *see* International Chamber of Commerce
ICCAT, *see* International Convention for the Conservation of Atlantic Tunas
Iceland, 20, *314–17, 346–50*:
  global climate emissions of, 20
ICES, *see* International Council for the Exploration of the Sea
ICFTU, *see* International Confederation of Free Trade Unions
ICI (Imperial Chemicals Industries), 67
ICRISAT, *see* International Crops Research Institute for the Semi-Arid Tropics
ICRW, *see* International Convention for the Regulation of Whaling

IFAD, *see* International Fund for Agricultural Development

IGOs, *see* intergovernmental organizations

IIED, *see* International Institute for Environment and Development

IISD, *see* International Institute for Sustainable Development

ILO, *see* International Labour Organization

IMF, *see* International Monetary Fund

IMO, *see* International Maritime Organization

Imperial Chemicals Industries, *see* ICI

India, 24, 41, 44, 49, 59:
  climate policy of, 24;
  nuclear reactors of, 49

indigenous communities, 40, 42–3

Indonesia, 67, *354–5, 362–3*

industry, 19, 21, 23–4, 26, 31–2, 34–6, 52, 65–74

INES, *see* International Atomic Energy Agency: International Nuclear Event Scale

insurance industry, 32–4

intellectual Property rights (IPR), 39–45

Interfax News Agency, 50

intergovernmental organizations (IGOs), 31, 49, 58, 65–6, 71, *213–58*

Intergovernmental Panel on Climate Change (IPCC), 19, 21–3

international agreement(s), *see* convention(s)

International Association of Independent Tanker Owners (INTERTANKO), 35

International Atomic Energy Agency (IAEA), 49–53, *221*:
  Health and Safety Measures, 50
  Assessment of Safety Significant Events Teams (ASSETs), 50;
  Basic Safety Standards for Radioactive Protection, 50;
  Board of Governors, 50;
  International Nuclear Event Scale, 50:
  Nuclear Safety Standards (NUSS), 50;
  Operational Safety Review Teams (OSARTs), 50;
  Radiation Protection Advisory Teams (RARATs), 50;
  Safety Standards Series, 50;

International Chamber of Commerce (ICC), 66, 69, *266, 277–84*:
  Environmental Bureau of, 66;
  Working Party for Sustainable Development, 66

International Civil Aviation Organization (ICAO) Convention, *see* Annex 16, vol. II (Environmental Protection: Aircraft Engine Emissions) to the 1944 Chicago Convention on International Civil Aviation

International Business Action Plan on Climate Change (IBAPCC), 66, 69

International Co-operation Biodiversity Group (ICBG), 44

International Code of Conduct on the Distribution and Use of Pesticides, *see* Food and Agriculture Organization

International Confederation of Free Trade Unions (ICFTU), *267, 277–84*

international convention(s), *see* convention(s)

International Council for the Exploration of the Sea (ICES), *225, 277–84*

International Crops Research Institute for the Semi-Arid Tropics (ICRISAT), 44

International Fund for Agricultural Development (IFAD), *226*

International Group of P & I Clubs, 33

International Institute for Environment and Development (IIED), 65, 69

International Institute for Sustainable Development (IISD), 71

International Labour Organization (ILO), 50, *228*

International Maritime Organization (IMO), 31–6, *230*:
  conventions of, 31–6;
  Diplomatic Conference of, 34;
  Srivastava, C. P., former Secretary-General of, 31, 36

International Monetary Fund (IMF), *232*

International Oil Pollution Compensation Funds (IOPC Funds), 33–5, *234*

International Paper, 67

International Solar Energy Society (ISES), *267, 277–84*

International Tropical Timber Agreement, 1994 (ITTA, 1994), *183–5, 196–211*

International Undertaking on Plant Genetic Resources, *see* Food and Agriculture Organization

International Union for Conservation of Nature and Natural Resources, *see* IUCN – The World Conservation Union

International Union for the Protection of Nature, *see* IUCN – The World Conservation Union

International Whaling Convention, *see* Convention for the Regulation of Whaling

Internet, 69–70

Intervention Convention, *see* Convention Relating to Intervention on the High Seas in Cases of Oil Pollution Casualties

Inti Karya Persada Tehnik, 67

investment projects, *see* financial assistance

Ioirysh, Abram, 49–53

IOPC Funds, *see* International Oil Pollution Compensation Funds

IPCC, *see* Intergovernmental Panel on Climate Change

IPCC/SBSTA Joint Working Group, 21

IPR, *see* intellectual property rights

Ireland, *318–21, 346–50*

Iron Baron, 31–2

irradiated fuel, 52

ISES, *see* International Solar Energy Society

Italy, 67

ITTA, *see* International Tropical Timber Agreement, 1994

IUCN – The World Conservation Union, 65, 69, *267, 277–84*

Jacobson, Harold K., 24

Japan, 20–2, 24, 26, 41, 67, 71:
  climate policy of, 22, 24, 26;
  global climate emissions of, 20

Johnson & Johnson, 67

Joint Convention on the Safety of Spent Fuel Management and on the Safety of Radioactive Waste Management, 51

joint implementation, 20, 23, 25, 69

Jordan, 22

Karliner, Joshua, 72

Kazakhstan, 24:
  climate policy of, 24

Kempton, Willet, 26

Keohane, Robert O., 24

Kew, 43

Kharg V, 31–2

Kirki, 31–2

Korea, Republic of, 22, 24, 49, 67, *322–5, 346–50*:
  nuclear reactors of, 49

KPFCCC, *see* UN Framework Convention on Climate Change: Kyoto Protocol to the Framework Convention on Climate Change

Kuwait Regional Convention for Co-operation on the Protection of the Marine Environment from Pollution, *150, 196–211*

Kyoto, 19–27, 62, 69

Kyoto Protocol to the Framework Convention on Climate Change (KPFCCC), *see* UN Framework Convention on Climate Change

labour rights, 61

Lanchbery, John, 23

Lashoff, Daniel, 26

Latin America, 71

Law of the Sea, *see* UN Convention on the Law of the Sea

LDC, *see* least developed countries

least developed countries, 41

LG (formerly Lucky Goldstar) Group, 67

liability, 31–7

liability system, 31–7

Lithuania, 49:
  nuclear reactors of, 49

London Convention 1972, *see* Convention on the Prevention of Marine

Pollution by Dumping of Wastes and Other Matter
London Dumping Convention, *see* Convention on the Prevention of Marine Pollution by Dumping of Wastes and Other Matter
Louis Harris and Associates, 26
Luxembourg, *326–9*, *346–50*
Maersk Navigator, 31–2
Malacca Straits, 31
Malaysia, 59
Maldives, 24
marine environment, 31–7
marine pollution, 31–7
maritime industry, 31–2, 34–6
maritime law, 31–7, (*see also* Convention(s))
MARPOL 1973/78, *see* Convention for the Prevention of Pollution from Ships, 1973, as modified by the Protocol of 1978 relating thereto
Marvin, Michael, 25
Massachusetts Institute of Technology (MIT), 65
medicinals, 40
Mellman Group, 26
methane (CH$_4$), 19–20
Mexico, 22, 55, 60, 67, *330–3*, *346–50*
MFN, *see* World Trade Organization: Most Favoured Nation
Michigan, 61
Micronesia, 22
minerals, 41
MIT, *see* Massachusetts Institute of Technology
Mitsubishi, 67
monitoring, 25, 43, 51–2
Monsanto, 67
Montreal Protocol on Substances that Deplete the Ozone Layer, 26, 57, *96–101*, *196–211* (*see also* Convention for the Protection of the Ozone Layer)
Moscow, 49
Most Favoured Nation, *see* World Trade Organization
multilateral corporations, *see* transnational corporations
multilateral environmental agreements (MEAs), 56–8, 60, 62 (*see also* Convention(s))
multilateral trading system, 55, 58–9, 61–2
NAFTA, *see* North American Free Trade Agreement
Nagasaki Spirit, 31–2
Najam, Adil, 65–75
Narain, Sanita, 25
national communications, *see* UN Framework Convention on Climate Change
National Treatment, *see* World Trade Organization
Natural Resources Defence Council, 26, 49
negotiations, 19–22, 24–7, 32, 36, 39, 41–3, 45, 52–3, 62, 69
Nestlé, 67
Netherlands, the, 67
New Zealand, 22, *334–7*:
   climate policy of, 22;
   global climate emissions of, 22
newly industrialized countries (NICs), 44
NGOs, *see* non-governmental organizations
NICs, *see* newly industrialized countries
Nigeria, *356–7*, *362–3*
Nissan Motors, 67
nitrous oxide, 20
non-governmental organizations (NGOs), 19–21, 23, 26, 34, 49, 55, 58–9, 62, 65–74, *259–84*
Norsk Hydro, 67
North Africa, 31
North America, 59–60, 71
North American Free Trade Agreement (NAFTA), 59–60
Norway, 49, 66–7
Norwegian School of Management, 66
notification, 50

Notification Convention, *see* Convention on Early Notification of a Nuclear Accident
noxious substances, *see* hazardous substances
NT, *see* World Trade Organization: National Treatment
nuclear accident, 50
nuclear energy, 49–53
Nuclear Energy Agency, 50
nuclear reactors, 49–53
nuclear safety, 49–53
Nuclear Safety and Security Summit, 49:
   Declaration of, 49
Nuclear Safety Standards (NUSS), *see* International Atomic Energy Agency
nuclear substances, 49–53
nuclear wastes, 50–1
NUSS, *see* International Atomic Energy Agency: Nuclear Safety Standards
ocean pollution, *see* marine pollution
ODA, *see* official development assistance
ODS, *see* ozone-depleting substances
OECD, *see* Organisation for Economic Co-operation and Development
Official Development Assistance (ODA), 42
Ohio State University, 26
oil, 31–6, 41
oil companies, 36
oil pollution, 31–7
oil trade, 32
Ontario Hydro, 67
OPA '90, *see* United States of America: Oil Pollution Act of 1990
Operational Safety Review Teams (OSARTs), *see* International Atomic Energy Agency
OPRC, *see* Convention on Oil Pollution Preparedness, Response and Co-operation
Organization for Economic Co-operation and Development (OECD), 22, 42, 52, 57, 69, *235*, *277–84*:
   Advisory Board of, 69;
   Environment Policy Committee (EPOC), *235*, *277–84*
OSARTs, *see* International Atomic Energy Agency: Operational Safety Review Teams
OSPAR Convention, *see* Convention for the Protection of the Marine Environment of the North East Atlantic
ozone, 58
ozone-depleting substances (ODS), 57
ozone depletion, 57
P & I Clubs, *see* protection and indemnity insurers
Pakistan, 59
PAN, *see* Pesticide Action Network
Panama, 24
Paris, 52
patent law, 39–41, 43–5
patent legislation, 39–41, 43–5
patent system, 40–1, 43–5
patents, 39–45
perfluorocarbons, 20
Pesticide Action Network (PAN), *269*, *277–84*
pharmaceutical products, 41, 43
Philadelphia v. New Jersey case, 61
Philips Electronics, 67
PIC, *see* prior informed consent
PIC Convention, *see* Convention on the Prior Informed Consent Procedure for Certain Hazardous Chemicals and Pesticides in International Trade
Pike test, 61
plant breeders, 40
plant genetic resources, 41
plant varieties, 40–1
plutonium, 52

polluters pays principle, 36
pollution, *see* air- *or* marine pollution
population, 61
port states, 36
Portugal, 22:
  global climate emissions of, 22
poverty, 72
PPMs, *see* process and production methods
precautionary principle, 66
Preparatory Meeting in Advance of the Nuclear Safety Summit, 49
prior informed consent (PIC), 41–3
private sector, 45
privatization, 41
process and production methods (PPMs), 62
Proctor & Gamble, 67
property rights, 39–47
protection and indemnity insurers (P & I Clubs), 33–5
protectionism, 42, 61
quota, 20, 25, 56
Radiation Protection Advisory Teams (RARATs), *see* International Atomic Energy Agency
radioactive wastes, *see* nuclear wastes
radiological emergency, 50–1
RAED, *see* Arab Network for Environment and Development
Ramsar Convention, *see* Convention on Wetlands of International Importance, especially as Waterfowl Habitat
RARATs, *see* International Atomic Energy Agency: Radiation Protection Advisory Teams
REC, *see* Regional Environmental Center for Central and Eastern Europe
recycling, 57, 70–1
Regional Convention for the Conservation of the Red Sea and Gulf of Aden Environment, *152, 196–211*
Regional Environmental Center for Central and Eastern Europe (REC), *276*
Regional Seas Programme, *see* UN Environment Programme
renewable energy, 22–3
renewable resources, 70
Report on Eco-Efficiency Metrics and Reporting, 71
Rhône-Poulenc, 67
Rio de Janeiro, 22, 31, 39, 65
Rio Earth Summit, *see* UN Conference on Environment and Development
Rio Forum, 69
Rio+5, 65–6, 69
Rosendal, G. Kristin, 39–47
Rosenergoatom, 50
Ross Stevens III, W., 66
Rotterdam, 66
Rotterdam Convention, *see* Convention on the Prior Informed Consent Procedure for Certain Hazardous Chemicals and Pesticides in International Trade (PIC Convention)
Royal Botanical Gardens, 43
royalties, 40, 44–5
Russian Federation, 26, 49–53:
  nuclear reactors of, 49–50;
  State Duma of, 52
Samsung, 67
sanctions, 41–2, 44
Sand, Peter H., 24
SBI, *see* UN Framework Convention on Climate Change: Subsidiary Body for Implementation
SBSTA, *see* UN Framework Convention on Climate Change: Subsidiary Body for Scientific and Technical Advice
Schelling, Thomas C., 25
Schmidheiny, Stephan, 65–6, 73
Schupolme, Peter, 66

scientific knowledge, 19, 21
SDRs, *see* Special Drawing Rights
Sea Empress, 31–2
sea level, 23
Second World Industry Conference on Environmental Management, 66
seeds, 41, 44–5
SEI, *see* Stockholm Environment Institute
Seiko, 67
Senegal, 22
SGS, *see* Société Générale de Surveillance
Shaman Pharmaceuticals, 43
Shell International, 23, 67
Shell Renewables, 23
ship discharges, *see* discharges at sea
ship-source marine pollution, 31–7
shipping, 31–7
shipping industry, 32, 34, 36
SID, *see* Society for International Development
Sierra Club, *270, 277–84*
Signals of Change, 66
Singapore, 57
sinks, 19, 23–4
Slovakia, 49:
  nuclear reactors of, 49
small island states, 26
SO₂, *see* sulphur dioxide
Société Générale de Surveillance, 67
Society for International Development (SID), *270, 277–84*
Sony, 67
South Africa, *358–9, 362–3*
South America, 23
Special Drawing Rights (SDRs), 33, 35
species, 39–40, 43
species extinction, *see* endangered species
Spencer, Tom, 25
SPREP Convention, *see* Convention for the Protection of the Natural Resources and Environment of the South Pacific Region
Srivastava, C. P., former Secretary-General of IMO, 31, 36
standards, 58
Standards for Reformulated and Conventional Gasoline, 58
STCW, *see* Convention on Standards of Training, Certification and Watchkeeping
Stockholm, 71
Stockholm Environment Institute (SEI), 71
Strong, Maurice, former Secretary-General of the UN Conference on Environment and Development, 65
Subak, Susan, 22
Subsidiary Body for Implementation (SBI), *see* UN Framework Convention on Climate Change
Subsidiary Body for Scientific and Technical Advice (SBSTA), *see* UN Framework Convention on Climate Change
sui generis, 41, 43
sulphur dioxide (SO₂), 19
sulphur hexafluoride, 20
Summit of the Americas, 24
Survey on Corporate Environmental Reports, 66
Sustainable Business Challenge, The, 66, 69–70
Sustainable Business Challenge: A Briefing for Tomorrow's Business Leaders, 70
Sweden, 49–50:
  nuclear reactors of, 49
Switzerland, 22, 49, 65, 67, *338–41, 346–50*:
  global climate emissions of, 22;
  nuclear reactors of, 49
3M Company, 65, 67
Tanio case, 33

tanker industry, 32, 34, 36
tariffs, 56
technology, 20–6, 39–45, 70
technology transfer, 20, 22–3, 40–2, 44
Texaco, 26
Thailand, 59, *360–3*
Third World Network (TWN), *271, 277–84*
Three Mile Island, 49
Timerbaev, Roland, 49–53
Tokyo, 67
Tokyo Electric, 67
Torrey Canyon, 31
toxic chemicals, *see* hazardous substances
toxic substances, *see* hazardous substances
toxic waste, *see* hazardous wastes
Toyota, 26, 67
trade, 20–1, 23, 25, 32, 34–6, 39–47, 55–64, 69
trade agreements, 55–62
trade and environment, 55–64, 69
trade discrimination, 56, 58–62
trade liberalization, 39–40
trade measures, 55–62
Trade-Related Aspects of Intellectual Property Rights (TRIPs), *see*
    World Trade Organization
trade restrictions, 42, 44, 56, 58–62
trade sanctions, 41–2, 44
trading system, 55, 58–9, 61–2
transitional economies, 20, 22–5
transnational corporations, 42, 67, 72
transparency, 53
transport, 31–6, 50–2
treaty, *see* convention
Trinidad and Tobago, 24
TRIPs, *see* World Trade Organization: Trade-Related Aspects of
    Intellectual Property Rights
tropical countries, 40
Turkey, *342–50*
Tuvalu, 24
TWN, *see* Third World Network
UK, *see* United Kingdom
Ukraine, 49:
    nuclear reactors of, 49
UN, *see* United Nations
UNCED, *see* UN Conference on Environment and Development
UNCLOS, *see* UN Convention on the Law of the Sea
UNDP, *see* UN Development Programme
UNEP, *see* UN Environment Programme
UNESCO, *see* UN Educational, Scientific and Cultural Organisation
UNFCCC, *see* UN Framework Convention on Climate Change
UNFPA, *see* UN Population Fund
UNGASS, *see* UN General Assembly: Special Session
UNICEF, *see* UN Children's Fund
UNIDO, *see* UN Industrial Development Organization
Union for the Protection of New Varieties of Plants (UPOV), 41
UN-NGLS, *see* UN Non-Governmental Liaison Service
United Kingdom (UK), 31, 36, 43–4, 67:
    marine pollution policy of, 31, 36
United Nations (UN), 65, 69:
    Annan, Kofi, Secretary-General of, 65;
    Secretary-General of, 65
UN Children's Fund (UNICEF), *238*
UN Commission on Sustainable Development (CSD), 58, 69, *214*
UN Conference on Environment and Development (UNCED), 25, 31,
    42–3, 65–6, 68–9, 72:
    Agenda 21, 25;
    Earth Summit, 43, 65–6, 69, 72;
    Strong, Maurice, former Secretary-General of, 65–6

UN Convention on the Law of the Sea (UNCLOS), 33, *135–9*, *196–211*
UN Development Programme (UNDP), 65–6, 69, 71, *240*
UN Educational, Scientific, and Cultural Organisation (UNESCO),
    242
UN Environment Programme (UNEP), 42, 58, 66, 69–71, *243*:
    Cleaner Production Programme of, 71;
    Regional Seas Programmes, *146–55*, *196–211*
UN Framework Convention on Climate Change (UNFCCC), 19–29,
    72, *90–5*, *196–211*:
    Activities Implemented Jointly, 20, 23, 25;
    Berlin Mandate, 21–2;
    Buenos Aires Plan of Action, 23;
    Clean Development Mechanism (CDM), 20–1, 25;
    Conference of the Parties, 19–21, 23–4;
    flexibility mechanisms, 21;
    Kyoto Protocol to the Framework Convention on Climate Change
        (KPFCCC), 19–27, 62;
    national communications to, 20–2;
    Secretariat of, 20;
    Subsidiary Body for Implementation, 20, 22;
    Subsidiary Body for Scientific and Technical Advice (SBSTA), 20, 21
UN General Assembly, 65:
    President of, 65
    Special Session (UNGASS), 69
UN Industrial Development Organization (UNIDO), *246*
UN Non-Governmental Liaison Service (UN-NGLS), *276*
UN Population Fund (UNFPA), *248*
United States of America (USA), 20–7, 32–6, 41–2, 44, 49, 52–3, 55,
    58–61, 65, 67:
    Administration of, 32, 34–5;
    Clean Air Act of, 58;
    climate policy of, 21–2, 24, 26;
    Clinton Administration, 21;
    Clinton, Bill, President of, 24;
    Coast Guard of, 32, 34;
    Commerce Clause of the US Constitution of, 60;
    Congress of, 33, 60;
    Constitution of, 60:
        Commerce Clause of, 60;
    Continental Shelf of, 34;
    Endangered Species Act of, 59;
    Environmental Protection Agency (EPA) of, 58;
    Federal Water Pollution Control Act (FWPCA), 34–5;
    fishery zone of, 34;
    global climate emissions of, 20–2, 24–6;
    marine pollution policy of, 32–6;
    National Institutes of Health (NIH), 44;
    National Science Foundation of, 44;
    Oil Pollution Act of (OPA '90), 32–5:
        contingent valuation methodology (CVM), 35;
    Secretary of State, 22;
    State Department of, 32;
    state governments of, 35;
    Supreme Court of, 60–1
United States Business Council for Sustainable Energy, 25
United States Maritime Law Association, 32
Unilever, 67
Union for the Protection of New Varieties of Plants (UPOV), 41
Units of Account (UOA), 35
University of Cambridge, 65–6, 70
UOA, *see* Units of Account
UPOV, *see* Union for the Protection of New Varieties of Plants
uranium, 52
Uruguay, 22
Uruguay Round, *see* World Trade Organization
Venezuela, 58
verification, 23, 25, 53

'very large crude carrier' (VLCC), 36
vessels, 32–6
Vienna, 51–2
Vienna Convention for the Protection of the Ozone Layer, *see* Convention for the Protection of the Ozone Layer
Vienna Convention on Civil Liability for Nuclear Damage, 52, *192–3, 196–211*:
  Protocol to Amend the Vienna Convention on Civil Liability for Nuclear Damage, 52
VLCC, *see* 'very large crude carrier'
Waigani Convention, *see* Convention to Ban the Importation into Forum Island Countries of Hazardous and Radioactive Wastes and to Control the Transboundary Movement and Management of Hazardous Wastes within the South Pacific Region
Wallonia region, 60
Washington, 35
waste oils, 60
wastes, 56–7, 60–1, 71
water, 19
water resources, *see* freshwater resources
Water Environment Federation (WEF), *271, 277–84*
WBCSD, *see* World Business Council for Sustainable Development
WEDO, *see* Women's Environment and Development Organization
WEF, *see* Water Environment Federation
Weiss, Edith B., 24
WFM, *see* World Federalist Movement
WFP, *see* World Food Programme
WHO, *see* World Health Organization
WICE, *see* World Industry Council for the Environment
WMO, *see* World Meteorological Organization
Women's Environment and Development Organization (WEDO), 272
World Bank, 33, 35, *249*
World Business Council for Sustainable Development (WBCSD), 65–75, *272, 277–84*:
  Annual Review of, 71;
  Business Councils for Sustainable Development, 71;
  Button, Ted, Director for External Co-operation, 72;
  DeSimone, Livio, former Chairman of, 65;
  Eco-Efficiency Kit, 70;
  Executive Committee of, 67, 69;
  Global Scenarios Project, 66;
  Global Sustainable Development Dictionary, 70;
  President of, 67–9;
  Secretariat of, 67–8;
  Stakeholder Dialogues on Sustainable Consumption, Corporate Social Responsibility, and Sustainable Business, 66;
  Stigson, Björn, President of, 68;
  Sustainable Business Challenge, 66;
  Virtual University, 66, 70, 74

World Climate Conference, 19
World Commission on Environment and Development (WCED), 70
World Conservation Union, *see* IUCN – The World Conservation Union
World Economic Forum, 65
World Federalist Movement (WFM), *273, 277–84*
World Food Programme (WFP), *251*
World Health Organization (WHO), 50, *253*
World Heritage Convention, *see* Convention Concerning the Protection of the World Cultural and Natural Heritage
World Industry Conference on Environmental Management, 66
World Industry Council for the Environment (WICE), 65–7, 74
World Meteorological Organization (WMO), *255*
World Resources Institute (WRI), 65
World Trade Organization (WTO), 39–47, 55–64, *257*:
  Appellate Body of, 55, 58–9, 61;
  Committee on Trade and Environment (CTE) of, 44, 55, 57–9, 62;
  Dispute Settlement Body (DSB) of, 55, 58;
  Dispute Settlement Panels of, 55, 58–9
  dispute settlement system, 55, 58–9, 62;
  Dispute Settlement Understanding (DSU), 58;
  Expert Review of, 55;
  GATT Article XX, 56, 58–9, 62;
  GATT Secretariat, 57;
  General Agreement on Tariffs and Trade (GATT), 40–1, 43, 55–9, 61–2;
  High Level Symposium on Trade and Environment, 58;
  Ministerial Conference of, 55, 57–8;
  Most Favoured Nation (MFN), 56;
  National Treatment (NT), 56;
  reformulated gasoline case, 58;
  Secretariat of, 44, 58;
  shrimp/turtle case, 59;
  Trade-Related Aspects of Intellectual Property Rights (TRIPs), 39–47:
    Council, 44;
    tuna/dolphin case, 55–6;
    Uruguay Round, 40–1
World Wide Fund For Nature (WWF), 69, *273, 277–84*
World Wildlife Fund, *see* World Wide Fund For Nature
WRI, *see* World Resources Institute
WTO, *see* World Trade Organization
WWF, *see* World Wide Fund For Nature
Xerox, 67
Yearbook of International Co-operation on Environment and Development, 68
Zimbabwe, 22
Århus Convention, *see* Convention on Access to Information, Public Participation in Decision-Making and Access to Justice in Environmental Matters

List of Articles in 1992–1999/2000 Volumes

Please note that the title of the 1992–7 volumes was Green Globe Yearbook (published by Oxford University Press)

AGREEMENTS ON ENVIRONMENT AND DEVELOPMENT

General

International Environmental Treaty Secretariats: Stage-Hands or Actors?, Rosemary Sandford (1994)
Russia and International Environmental Co-operation, Vladimir Kotov and Elena Nikitina (1995)
Twenty Years On and Five Years In, Richard Sandbrook (1998/9)

Atmosphere

A Global Climate Regime: Mission Impossible?, Helge Ole Bergesen (1995)
European Climate Change Policy in a Global Context, Michael Grubb (1995)
Evaluation of the Climate Change Regime and Related Developments, Joyeeta Gupta (1999/2000)
International Co-operation to Combat Acid Rain, Marc A. Levy (1995)
International Protection of the Ozone Layer, Edward A. Parson (1996)
Protection of the Global Climate: Ecological Utopia or Just a Long Way to Go?, Helge Ole Bergesen and Anne Kristin Sydnes (1992)
The Role of Science in the Global Climate Negotiations, John Lanchbery and David Victor (1995)
Stratospheric Ozone Depletion: Can we Save the Sky?, Alan Miller and Irving Mintzer (1992)

Hazardous substances

Dumping on Our World Neighbours: The International Trade in Hazardous Wastes, and the Case for an Immediate Ban on All Hazardous Waste Exports from Industrialized to Less-Industrialized Countries, Jim Puckett (1992)
The Success of a Voluntary Code in Reducing Pesticide Hazards in Developing Countries, Barbara Dinham (1996)

Marine environment

Beyond Dumping? The Effectiveness of the London Convention, Olav Schram Stokke (1998/9)
Deep Seabed Mining and the Environment: Consequences, Perceptions, and Regulations, Jan Magne Markussen (1994)
The International Convention for the Regulation of Whaling: From Over-Exploitation to Total Prohibition, Sebastian Oberthür (1998/9)
International Co-operation to Prevent Oil Spills at Sea: Not Quite the Success it should Be, Gerard Peet (1994)
International Efforts to Combat Marine Pollution: Achievements of North Sea Co-operation and Challenges Ahead, Steinar Andresen, Jon Birger Skjærseth, and Jørgen Wettestad (1993)
Liability and Compensation for Ship-Source Marine Pollution: The International System, Edgar Gold (1999/2000)
Protecting the Marine Environment of the Wider Caribbean Region: The Challenge of Institution-Building, Marian A. L. Miller (1996)
The 20th Anniversary of the Mediterranean Action Plan: Reason to Celebrate?, Jon Birger Skjærseth (1996)

Nature conservation and terrestrial living resources

Biodiversity: Between Diverse International Arenas, G. Kristin Rosendal (1999/2000)
Biological Diversity in a North–South Context, Cary Fowler (1993)
Combating Desertification: Encouraging Local Action within a Global Framework, Camilla Toulmin (1994)
Combating the Illegal Timber Trade: Is there a Role for ITTO?, Clare Barden (1994)
Commodity or Taboo? International Regulation of Trade in Endangered Species, Peter H. Sand (1997)
The Convention on Biological Diversity: A Viable Instrument for Conservation and Sustainable Use?, G. Kristin Rosendal (1995)
International Controversy over Sustainable Forestry, Vandana Shiva (1993)
The Problem of Migratory Species in International Law, Cyrille de Klemm (1994)
Protecting the Frozen South, Olav Schram Stokke (1992)
Trade with Endangered Species, Joanna Boddens Hosang (1992)

Nuclear safety

International Co-operation in Nuclear Safety, Roland Timerbaev and Abram Iorysh (1999/2000)
International Co-operation to Promote Nuclear Reactor Safety in the Former USSR and Eastern Europe, Michael Herttrich, Rolf Janke, and Peter Kelm (1994)

INTERGOVERNMENTAL ORGANIZATIONS (IGOs)

Can GATT Survive the Environmental Challenge?, David Pearce (1993)
The Commission on Sustainable Development: Paper Tiger or Agency to Save the Earth?, Martin Khor (1994)
The CSD Reporting Process: A Quiet Step Forward for Sustainable Development, Farhana Yamin (1998/9)
From 'Lead Agency' to 'Integrated Programming': The Global Response to AIDS in the Third World, Christer Jönsson (1996)
The Global Challenges of Aids, Christer Jönsson (1992)
The Global Environment Facility: International Waters Coming into its Own, Lisa Jorgenson (1997)
Has the World Bank Greened?, Amulya K. N. Reddy (1993)
The Treatment of Environmental Considerations in the World Trade Organization, Beatrice Chaytor and James Cameron (1999/2000)
UNDP and Global Environmental Problems: The Need for Capacity Development at Country Level, Poul Engberg-Pedersen and Claus Hvashøj Jørgensen (1997)
Why UNEP Matters, Konrad von Moltke (1996)

NON-GOVERNMENTAL ORGANIZATIONS (NGOs) AND CIVIL SOCIETY

Building an Environmental Protection Framework for North America: The Role of the Non-governmental Community, Betty Ferber, Lynn Fischer, and Janine Ferretti (1995)

Democracy, Development, and Environmental Sustainability, Jeanette Hartmann (1992)

The Forest Stewardship Council: Using the Market to Promote Responsible Forestry, Eleonore Schmidt (1998/9)

Greenpeace: Storm-Tossed on the High Seas, Fred Pearce (1996)

Indigenous People's Role in Achieving Sustainability, Russel Barsh (1992)

The Inside Out, the Outside In, Pros and Cons of Foreign Influence on Brazilian Environmentalism, Ricardo Arnt (1992)

International Attitudes towards Environment and Development, Riley E. Dunlap (1994)

IUCN: A Bridge-Builder for Nature Conservation, Leif E. Christoffersen (1997)

Non-governmental Organizations at UNCED: Another Successful Failure?, Elin Enge and Runar I. Malkenes (1993)

Non-governmental Organizations: The Third Force in the Third World, Bill Hinchberger (1993)

The World Wide Fund for Nature: Financing a New Noah's Ark, Jacob Park (1997)

ENVIRONMENT AND SUSTAINABLE DEVELOPMENT

An Overview of Follow-up of Agenda 21 at the National Level, Alicia Bárcena (1994)

Development Assistance and the Integration of Environmental Concerns: Current Status and Future Challenges, Torunn Laugen and Leiv Lunde (1996)

Energy for Sustainable Development in the Third World, Amulya K. N. Reddy (1992)

Promoting International Transfer of Environmentally Sound Technologies: The Case for National Incentive Schemes, Calestous Juma (1994)

INTERNATIONAL BUSINESS AND INDUSTRY

International Business and Sustainable Development, Alex Trisoglio (1993)

Transnational Corporations' Strategic Responses to 'Sustainable Development', Harris Gleckman (1995)

World Business Council for Sustainable Development: The Greening of Business or a Greenwash?, Adil Najam (1999/2000)

www.ingramcontent.com/pod-product-compliance
Ingram Content Group UK Ltd.
Pitfield, Milton Keynes, MK11 3LW, UK
UKHW020401010325
455677UK00021B/577